Lecture Notes in Computer Science

Lecture Notes in Computer Science

Edited by G. Goos and J. Hartmanis

415

C. Choffrut   T. Lengauer   (Eds.)

STACS 90

7th Annual Symposium on Theoretical Aspects
of Computer Science
Rouen, France, February 22–24, 1990
Proceedings

Springer-Verlag

Berlin Heidelberg New York London Paris Tokyo Hong Kong

Editors

Christian Choffrut
Université de Rouen, Faculté des Sciences
Laboratoire d'Informatique Rouen
B. P. 118 – Place Emile Blondel, F-76134 Mont-Saint-Aignan Cedex, France

Thomas Lengauer
Universität-GH Paderborn, FB 17
Postfach 16 21, D-4790 Paderborn, FRG

CR Subject Classification (1987): F, G.2, I.1, I.3.5

ISBN 3-540-52282-4 Springer-Verlag Berlin Heidelberg New York
ISBN 0-387-52282-4 Springer-Verlag New York Berlin Heidelberg

Printing and binding: Druckhaus Beltz, Hemsbach/Bergstr.
2145/3140-543210 – Printed on acid-free paper

Foreword

The Symposium on Theoretical Aspects of Computer Science is organized jointly by the Special Interest Group for Applied Mathematics of AFCET (Association Française de Cybernétique Economique et Technique) and the Special Interest Group for Theoretical Computer Sciences of GI (Gesellschaft für Informatik). It is held alternately in France and in Germany (Paderborn in 1989, Bordeaux in 1988, Passau in 1987, Orsay in 1986, Saarbrücken in 1985 and Paris in 1984).

STACS 1990 was held in Rouen, February 22-24, 1990. Three invited talks were given : K. Indermark (Aachen, GFR) : Computational Aspects of Structural Recursion, G. Viennot (Bordeaux, France): Combinatorial Methods in Computer Science, M. Yannakakis (Murray Hill, USA): The Analysis of Local Search Problems and Their Heuristics. Also, 24 other communications were chosen from 76 papers of very good quality. As in the earlier years, some software systems were presented showing the possibilities of applying theoretical research to the realization of software tools.

The program committee of STACS 1990 consisted of

J. Beauquier(Orsay)   E.W. Mayr (Frankfurt)
C. Choffrut (Rouen,   F. Orejas (Barcelona)
Chairman)   M.H. Overmars (Utrecht)
P. Darondeau (Rennes)   A. Restivo (Palermo)
H. Ehrig (W. Berlin)   P. Schupp (Urbana)
H. Jung (E. Berlin)   J.M Steyaert (Palaiseau)
T. Lengauer (Paderborn,   K.W. Wagner (Würzburg).
Chairman)

Many other referees helped the program committee in evaluating papers and the committee meeting on October 13, 1989 was very fruitful.

The support of

C.N.R.S.
University of Rouen
Conseil Régional de Haute-Normandie
is gratefully acknowledged.

Rouen, Paderborn
February 1990   C. Choffrut, T. Lengauer

Acknowledgement

Every paper was carefully reviewed by (at least) three referees. Their assistance is gratefully acknowledged.

Arnold A.	Kowaluk M.
Artalejo M. .R.	Krause M.
Autebert J.-M.	Lang B.
Badouel E.	Latteux M.
Bauernoppel F.	Le Ny L. M.
Berghammer R.	Lenz K.
Berry G.	Lowe M.
Berstel J.	Mahr B.
Besnard P.	Mauri G.-C.
Boasson L.	Meinel Ch.
Bodlaender H.	Mignosi F.
Boehm P.	Muller R.
Boissonnat J.-D.	Nivela Alos M. P.
Boudol G.	Padawitz P.
Bouge L.	Pecuchet J.-P.
Buntrock G.	Pelz E.
Caucal D.	Pepper P.
Classen I.	Perrin D.
Condon A.	Petit A.
Coquand T.	Petra R.
Courcelle B.	Pin J.-E.
Crochemore M.	Poigné A.
Damm C.	Quinton P.
De Berg M.	Raoult J.-C.
De Frutos D.	Rehrmann R.
Diaz J.	Reisig W.
Dietzfelbinger M.	Rohmert H.
Dimitrovici C.	Rouaix A.
Doenhardt J.	Rozoy B.
Dosch W.	Saltor F.
Duval J.-P.	Santha M.
Etiemble D.	Saquet J.
Gabarro J.	Senizergues G.
Gamatie B.	Sericola B.
Gardy D.	Siefkes D.
Gaudel M.-C.	Speckenmeyer E.
Giancarlo R.	Straubing H.
Girault C.	Thomas W.
Goltz U.	Torenvliet L.
Grigorieff S.	Torras C.
Grosse-Rhode M.	Unger W.
Guessarian I.	Valk R.
Haddad S.	Van Kreveld M.
Hanatani Y.	Van Leeuwen J.
Hanus M.	Veldhorst M.
Hertrampf U.	Vollmer H.
Hoofman R.	Wagener H.
Hummert U.	Wanke E.
Josko B.	Wechler W.
Jouannaud J.-P.	Weese H.
Kirchner H.	Wieners-Lummer C.
Knynenburg P.	Zeugmann T.

Contents

A Note on the Almost-Everywhere Hierarchy for Nondeterministic Time

Eric Allender*
Department of Computer Science, Rutgers University
New Brunswick, NJ, USA 08903

Richard Beigel[†]
Department of Computer Science, Yale University
New Haven, CT, USA 06520

Ulrich Hertrampf
Institut für Informatik, Universität Würzburg
D-8700 Würzburg, Federal Republic of Germany

Steven Homer[‡]
Department of Computer Science, Boston University
Boston, MA, USA 02215

SUMMARY *We present an a.e. complexity hierarchy for nondeterministic time, and show that it is essentially the best result which can be proved using relativizable proof techniques.*

1 Introduction

The hierarchy theorems for time and space are among the oldest and most basic results in complexity theory. One of the very first papers in the field of complexity theory was [HS-65], in which it was shown that if $t(n)^2 = o(T(n))$, then DTIME($T(n)$) properly contains DTIME($t(n)$), for any time-constructible functions t and T. This result was later improved by Hennie and Stearns [HS-66], who proved a similar result, with "$t(n)^2$"

*Supported in part by National Science Foundation Research Initiation Grant number CCR-8810467. Some of this research was performed while the author was a visiting professor at Institut für Informatik, Universität Würzburg. D-8700 Würzburg, Federal Republic of Germany.

[†]Supported in part by the National Science Foundation under grants CCR-8808949 and CCR-8958528. Work done in part while at the Johns Hopkins University.

[‡]Supported in part by National Science Foundation grants number MIP-8608137 and CCR-8814339, National Security Agency grant number MDA904-87-H, and a Fulbright-Hays research fellowship. Some of this research was performed while the author was a Guest Professor at Mathematisches Institut, Universität Heidelberg.

replaced by "$t(n) \log t(n)$". Still later, Cook and Reckhow [CR-73] and Fürer [Fü-84] proved stronger results for RAM's and Turing machines with a fixed number of tapes, respectively.

The time hierarchy theorems proved in this series of papers may be described as "infinitely often" (or "i.o.") time hierarchies, because they assert the existence of a set $L \in \mathrm{DTIME}(T(n))$ which requires more than time $t(n)$ for infinitely many inputs. Note, however, that it may be the case that for all n, membership in L for ninety-nine percent of the inputs of length n can be decided in linear time. That is, the i.o. time hierarchy theorems assert the existence of sets which are hard infinitely often, although it is possible that the "hard inputs" for these sets form an extremely sparse set.

However it turns out that much stronger time hierarchy theorems can be proved. One can show the existence of sets L in $\mathrm{DTIME}(T(n))$ which require more than time $t(n)$ for *all* large inputs. This notion is called "almost everywhere" (or a.e.) complexity, and has been investigated in [GHS-87, GHS-89]. The following definitions make this precise.

Definitions:

- For any Turing machine M, the function $T_M : \Sigma^* \to \mathbf{N} \cup \{\uparrow\}$ is the *time function of M*. $T_M(x)$ is the number of steps which M uses on input x, or is $\uparrow$ when M on input x does not halt.

- For functions f and g, we say that $f = \omega(g)$ iff, for all $r > 0$ and for all but finitely many x, $f(x) > rg(x)$.

- We say that L is a.e. complex for $\mathrm{DTIME}(t)$ iff for all deterministic Turing machines M, $L(M) = L \Longrightarrow T_M(x) = \omega(t(|x|))$.

One of the a.e. time hierarchy theorems of [GHS-89] can now be stated:

Theorem 1 [GHS-89] If T is a time-constructible function and $t(n) \log t(n) = o(T(n))$, then there is a set in $\mathrm{DTIME}(T(n))$ which is a.e. complex for $\mathrm{DTIME}(t(n))$.

Thus for deterministic time complexity classes, the a.e. hierarchy is just as tight as the i.o. hierarchy. However much less is known about hierarchies for probabilistic and nondeterministic time.

The best (i.o.) time hierarchy theorem for probabilistic time which has appeared in the literature is due to Karpinski and Verbeek [KV-88]; however they are only able to show that $\mathrm{BPTIME}(t(n))$ is properly contained in $\mathrm{BPTIME}(T(n))$ when $T(n)$ grows very much more quickly than $t(n)$. On the other hand, a recent oracle result of Fortnow and Sipser [FS-89] shows that it is not possible to prove a very tight time hierarchy theorem for probabilistic time using relativizable techniques; they present an oracle according to which $\mathrm{BPP} = \mathrm{BPTIME}(O(n))$. Clearly the [FS-89] result also shows that there is no tight a.e. time hierarchy for probabilistic time which holds for all oracles.

An early i.o. hierarchy theorem for nondeterministic time was given by Cook [Co-73]. The strongest such theorem which is currently known is due to [Zá-83]. It is shown there that if t and T are time-constructible functions such that $t(n+1) = o(T(n))$, then there is a set L in $\mathrm{NTIME}(T(n)) - \mathrm{NTIME}(t(n))$ (and L can even be chosen to be a subset of 0^*). When t and T are bounded by polynomials, this result is even tighter than the best known results for deterministic time. However, when T and t are very large, the gap between

$t(n)$ and $t(n+1)$ is also quite large, and thus the nondeterministic time hierarchy seems not to be very tight. On the other hand, Rackoff and Seiferas show in [RS-81] that the i.o. time hierarchy theorem for nondeterministic time cannot be improved significantly using relativizable techniques. For example, they present an oracle relative to which NTIME(2^{2^n}) = NTIME$(2^{2^{n+1}}/\log^* n)$. (Note on the other hand that DTIME$^A(2^{2^n}) \neq$ DTIME$^A(2^{2^{n+1}}/\log^* n)$ for *all* oracles A.)

Surprisingly, it seems that no results concerning an a.e. hierarchy for nondeterministic time have appeared. Geske, Huynh, and Seiferas explicitly raise the question of an a.e. hierarchy for nondeterministic time as an open problem in [GHS-89].

This paper essentially settles this question. We present an a.e. hierarchy theorem for nondeterministic time, and we present an oracle relative to which the given theorem cannot be significantly improved.

The organization of the paper is as follows. In Section 2 we define precisely what we mean by almost everywhere complexity for nondeterministic time. In this section we also relate almost everywhere complexity to the concept of immunity. In Section 3 we present our main results. In section 4 we turn to the questions of bi-immunity and co-immunity, which also are relevant to almost everywhere complexity. The results we prove concerning co-immunity and bi-immunity are close to the best which can be proved using relativizable proof techniques.

2 A. E. Complexity and Immunity

In order to talk about an a.e. complexity hierarchy for nondeterministic time, we must first agree on the notion of running time for nondeterministic Turing machines. For deterministic Turing machines, it is clear how to define the running time. However there are at least two definitions which are commonly used in defining the running time of a nondeterministic Turing machine:

- NTM M runs in time t on input x if *every* computation path of M on input x has length $\leq t$.

- NTM M runs in time t on input x if [M accepts x implies there is an accepting computation path of length at most t].

Note that for time-constructible T, the class NTIME$(T(n))$ is the same, no matter which choice is made in defining the running time of an NTM. That is, when one is concerned mainly with placing an *upper* bound on the running time of an NTM, it makes little difference how one defines the running time.

However, in defining an a.e. complexity hierarchy for nondeterministic time, it is necessary to talk about *lower* bounds on the running time of an NTM. We feel that an a.e. complexity hierarchy defined in terms of the first notion would be unsatisfactory, since using that definition, the running time of M can be large, even when there is a very short accepting computation of M on input x. If there is a short computation of M accepting x, then our intuition tells us that x is an easy input for M to accept. Therefore we define our a.e. complexity hierarchy using the second notion of running time.

Definition:

- Let M be a NTM. Then the (partial) function T_M from Σ^* into $\mathbb{N}$ is defined by,
  $$T_M(x) = \min\{t : \text{there is an accepting path of } M \text{ on } x \text{ of length } t\}$$

- L is a.e. complex for NTIME(t) iff for all M, $[L(M) = L$ implies for all x in L, $T_M(x) = \omega(t(|x|))]$.

A concept which is closely related to a.e. complexity is *immunity*. Let L be a language and let C be a class of languages. Then L is *immune to* C if L is infinite and L has no infinite subset in C. L is *co-immune to* C if $\overline{L}$ is immune to C. L is *bi-immune to* C if L is both immune and co-immune to C.

In [BS-85], Balcázar and Schöning noted the following relationship between almost-everywhere complexity and immunity for deterministic classes.

Theorem 2 [BS-85] Let t be a time-constructible function. Then L is a.e. complex for DTIME($t(n)$) iff L is bi-immune to DTIME($t(n)$).

The forward implication in this theorem is in fact true for *all* functions t. However we note that time-constructibility is necessary for the reverse implication.

Theorem 3 There is a (non-time-constructible) function t and a set L which is bi-immune to DTIME($t(n)$) and not a.e. complex for DTIME($t(n)$).

Proof: (Sketch) Using diagonalization, one can construct a function t which oscillates back and forth between $t(n) = n^2$ and $t(n) = n^4$, such that every Turing machine which runs in time $t(n)$ actually runs in time n^2. Now using the a.e. complexity hierarchy for deterministic time, let L be a set in DTIME(n^4) which is a.e. complex for DTIME(n^2). It follows that L is bi-immune to DTIME($t(n)$), although L can be recognized in time n^4 which is less than or equal to $t(n)$ for infinitely many n. ∎

Although a.e. complexity for deterministic time is related to bi-immunity, we show below that a.e. complexity for nondeterministic time is related to immunity. This difference is due to the fact that the runtime for nondeterministic Turing machines is asymmetric, depending only on the length of accepting computations. (In section 4 we return to this point again, and discuss bi-immunity in more depth.) The next proposition is immediate from the above definitions.

Proposition 4 Let t be a time-constructible function, and let L be a language. Then L is a.e. complex for NTIME($t(n)$) iff L is immune to NTIME($t(n)$).

3 Main Results

In this section we prove some results concerning immunity among nondeterministic time classes. Because of the results of the preceding section, these results may be interpreted in terms of a.e. complexity.

We will need the following notational convention. For any function T and any natural number k, let $T^{(k)}$ denote T composed with itself k times.

First we prove an a.e. complexity hierarchy theorem for nondeterministic time. In this theorem, the conditions on the runtime functions are somewhat technical. In particular, we have tried, without success, to eliminate the condition that $t(T(n)) \leq T(t(n))$. Intuitively, the theorem applies to any function T one of whose iterates, $T^{(k)}$, grows exponentially faster than the corresponding iterate, $t^{(k)}$, of a function t. For example, it holds for $T(n) = 2^{\sqrt{n}}$ and $t(n) = n^{log^2 n}$. Although this result is proved using known translational methods, it appears to be a new result. Later on in the paper, we show that this hierarchy theorem cannot be improved substantially using relativizable techniques.

Theorem 5 Let T and t be monotone nondecreasing time-constructible functions such that, for some k, $T^{(k)}(n) = \omega(2^{t^{(k)}(n)})$, and such that, for all large n, $t(T(n)) \leq T(t(n))$. Then there is a set in NTIME$(T(n))$ which is immune to NTIME$(t(n))$.

Proof: Using the techniques used to prove the a.e. hierarchy theorem for deterministic time, we know that there is a set in DTIME$(T^{(k)}(n))$ (and hence in NTIME$(T^{(k)}(n))$) which is bi-immune (and thus immune) to NTIME$(t^{(k)}(n))$).

The proof proceeds by establishing the following claim.

Claim: If every set in NTIME$(T(n))$ has an infinite subset in NTIME$(t(n))$, then for all i, every set in NTIME$(T^{(i)}(n))$ has an infinite subset in NTIME$(t^{(i)}(n))$.

Thus if every set in NTIME$(T(n))$ has an infinite subset in NTIME$(t(n))$, then every set in NTIME$(T^{(k)}(n))$ has an infinite subset in NTIME$(t^{(k)}(n))$, in contradiction to the first paragraph.

Proof of Claim: The proof of this claim proceeds by induction on i. For $i = 1$ it is trivially true. Assume therefore that every infinite set in NTIME$(T^{(i)}(n))$ has an infinite subset in NTIME$(t^{(i)}(n))$, and let L be an infinite set in NTIME$(T^{(i+1)}(n))$.

Define A to be $\{x10^j : |x10^j| = T(|x|) \wedge x \in L\}$. A is also infinite, and A is in NTIME$(T^{(i)}(n))$. By assumption, A has an infinite subset B in NTIME$(t^{(i)}(n))$. Let $C = \{x : x10^{T(|x|)-|x|-1} \in B\}$. Then C is an infinite subset of L, and C is in NTIME$(t^{(i)}(T(n)))$. But from the monotonicity of t and from the assumption $t(T(n)) \leq T(t(n))$ we conclude $t^{(i)}(T(n)) \leq T(t^{(i)}(n))$ and so C is in NTIME$(T(t^{(i)}(n)))$ too.

Now let $D = \{x10^j : |x10^j| = t^{(i)}(|x|) \wedge x \in C\}$. Then D is also infinite, and D is in NTIME$(T(n))$.

By assumption, there is an infinite set E in NTIME$(t(n))$ which is a subset of D. Let $F = \{x : x10^{t^{(i)}(|x|)-|x|-1} \in E\}$. Then $F \in$ NTIME$(t^{(i+1)}(n))$, and F is an infinite subset of C (and thus of L). ∎

Corollary 6 Let T and t be time-constructible functions such that, for some k and almost all n, $T^{(k)}(n) \geq 2^n$. Then there is a set in NTIME$(T(n))$ which is a.e. complex for NTIME(n).

The following result shows that this almost-everywhere complexity hierarchy theorem cannot be improved by any relativizable proof technique. (For simplicity, we state and prove this result only for the NTIME$(T(n))$ vs NTIME$(t(n))$ where $t(n)$ is the identity function. The full paper will consider more general functions $t(n)$.)

Theorem 7 Let $T(n)$ be a monotone nondecreasing time-constructible function such that for all k and for all large n, $T^{(k)}(n) < 2^n$. Then there is an oracle A relative to which every set in NTIME$(T(n))$ has an infinite subset in NTIME$(O(n))$.

Proof: Let $\{M_1, M_2, ...\}$ be an indexing of nondeterministic oracle Turing machines which run in time $T(n)$ for all oracles. Because of the time-constructibility of T, any language in $\text{NTIME}^A(T(n))$ is accepted by one of the machines M_i with oracle A.

We will build A so that, for every machine M_i, if M_i^A accepts infinitely many strings, then there are infinitely many strings of the form $\langle i, x, y \rangle$ in A with $|x| = |y|$. Furthermore, we guarantee that, for all i, x, and y, if $\langle i, x, y \rangle \in A$, then $|x| = |y|$ and M_i accepts x with oracle A. Define $L_i = \{x : \exists y(|y| = |x| \text{ and } \langle i, x, y \rangle \in A)\}$. If A satisfies the properties above and $L(M_i^A)$ is infinite then L_i will be an infinite nondeterministic linear time subset of $L(M_i^A)$.

The oracle A is constructed by an initial segment argument. During stage $s + 1$ we attempt to add one element to each of $L_1, L_2, ..., L_s$. When an element is added to L_j by adding a string of the form $\langle j, x, y \rangle$ to A, this change in the oracle set may make it possible to add an element to some other L_k. In order to add elements to as many different L_i as possible at stage $s + 1$, we repeat our attempts s times during that stage.

Our assumption about T implies that for every k, there exists a number $N[k]$ such that, for all $n \geq N[k]$, $(k + 1)T^{(k+1)}(n) < 2^n$. The construction defines an increasing sequence of integers n_s with the property that all elements of A of length $\leq n_s$ are determined by the end of stage s. A set S is used to keep track of which L_i have been augmented in the current stage. k will denote the cardinality of S. A is a global variable in the following construction.

Stage 0: Set $n_0 = 0$ and set A to $\emptyset$.

Stage $s + 1$: Set $S = \emptyset$, $k = 0$, and $d_0 = 1 + \max(T^{(s)}(N[s]), T^{(s+1)}(n_s))$.

LOOP

Among all $i \leq s$ satisfying,

(1) i is not in S and,

(2) M_i^A accepts some string u with $T^{(k)}(|u|) \geq d_k$,

choose i such that $i + |L_i|$ is minimized. (If no such i exists then exit the LOOP.) If more than one such i exists then it does not matter which one we choose, so choose the least such i. Then choose the lexicographically least u satisfying line (2) of the LOOP and select an accepting path of $M_i^A(u)$. Reserve for $\overline{A}$ all strings queried negatively in this path. Choose v, $|v| = |u|$ such that $\langle i, u, v \rangle$ is not reserved for $\overline{A}$ and add $\langle i, u, v \rangle$ to A. (We will shortly prove that such a v exists.) Add i to S, set $d_{k+1} = \max(|u|, d_k)$ and set k to $k + 1$.

END OF LOOP

Set $n_{s+1} =$ the length of the longest string so far put into A or reserved for $\overline{A}$.

End of construction.

We first prove that, in the loop of the construction, when a new element of M_i^A is found, it is possible to find a triple $\langle i, u, v \rangle$ to add to A. This follows from the following claim.

Claim 1: When u is found as in part (2) of the LOOP during stage $s + 1$, the number of strings of length greater than n_s reserved for $\overline{A}$ is $< 2^{|u|}$.

Proof: Assume $u, |u| = m$, is found as in part (2) of stage $s + 1$ of the construction during the rth time through the LOOP. Now, prior to this point in the construction, $r - 1 \leq s - 1$ strings are added to A. During stage $s + 1$ the value of the d_k are nondecreasing and d_r is at least as large as the length of any of the previous strings found in part (2) at this stage. Hence the number of strings of length $> n_s$ reserved for $\overline{A}$ through the part of stage $s+1$ where u is found and acted upon is $\leq (s-1)T(d_r)+T(m) \leq (s-1)T(T^{(r)}(m)) + T(m) \leq (s+1)T^{(s+1)}(m) < 2^m$.

To verify this last inequality note that $d_r > T^{(s)}(N[s])$ and $T^{(s)}(m) \geq d_r$, hence $T^{(s)}(m) > T^{(s)}(N[s])$ which implies $m > N[s]$ and so $(s+1)T^{(s+1)}(m) < 2^m$. ∎

It is clear from the construction that for all i, x, and y, if $\langle i, x, y \rangle \in A$, then M_i accepts x with oracle A. It remains only to show that if M_i^A accepts infinitely many strings, then L_i is infinite.

Assume not and let i be the least such that M_i^A accepts infinitely many strings, but L_i is finite. Let t be a stage by which, for every $j \leq i + |L_i|$ with L_j finite, every string of the form $\langle j, x, y \rangle$ in A is in A by stage t, and for every $j \leq i + |L_i|$ with L_j infinite, either $j = i$ or there are more than $i - j = |L_i|$ elements in L_j by stage t. Note in particular that no element is added to L_i after stage t.

Let x be the lexicographically least string of length $> d_0$ accepted by M_i^B, where d_0 has the value defined at the beginning of stage $t+1$, and B denotes the contents of A at the end of stage t. Now if $M_i^B(x)$ does not query any string in A of length $> n_t$ then we add an element to L_i the first time through the loop on stage $t+1$, contrary to our definition of t.

So we conclude that $M_i^B(x)$ queries some string of length $> n_t$ along some (actually every) accepting path. Choose such a path and let z be the last string on this path which is added to A.

Let s be the stage in which z is put into A. In stage s we start with B_0, that part of A constructed so far. We then build a sequence of partial oracles $B_1, B_2, \ldots$, where for all $a = 1, 2, \ldots$ there exists a string $\langle j_a, u_a, v_a \rangle$, such that $B_a = B_{a-1} \cup \{\langle j_a, u_a, v_a \rangle\}$. (Note that $z = \langle j_a, u_a, v_a \rangle$ for some a.) Below we prove that for all a where u_a is defined, $T^{(a-1)}(|u_a|) \geq d_a$ (recall that d_a is defined inside the construction). For now, assume that this fact has already been proved.

As we have noted, there is some a such that $B_{a-1} \cup \{z\} = B_a$. Since M_i, on input x, queries z, it is clear that $T(|x|) > |z|$. By the claim proved below, $T^{(a-1)}(|z|) \geq d_a$. But now it follows that $M_i^{B_a}$ accepts the string x with $T^{(a)}(|x|) \geq d_a$, and thus the next time through the loop in stage s we add x to L_i, in contradiction to our assumption that L_i has reached its final value.

All that remains now is to prove the following

Claim 2: In stage s, $T^{(a-1)}(|u_a|) \geq d_a$ for all a.

Proof: The proof is by induction on a.

Base case: $a = 1$. Here, by choice of u_1, we have that $|u_1| = d_1$, so the claim trivially holds.

Induction step: Assume the claim holds for a and consider $a+1$. If u_{a+1} is defined, then there is some triple such that $\{\langle j_{a+1}, u_{a+1}, v_{a+1} \rangle\} = B_{a+1} - B_a$. In this case u_{a+1} was found in part (2) of the LOOP and $T^{(a)}(|u_{a+1}|) \geq d_a$. Now either $d_{a+1} = d_a$ or $d_{a+1} = |u_{a+1}|$. In either case $T^{(a)}(|u_{a+1}|) \geq d_{a+1}$ as needed. ∎

The argument given in the last proof is nonconstructive. It is possible to construct a recursive oracle A with the desired properties, but that construction is more complicated.

It should also be mentioned that there are oracles relative to which NTIME($O(t)$) = DTIME($O(t)$) for all time-constructible t, and thus relative to these oracles, the a.e. hierarchy theorem for deterministic time also carries over to nondeterministic time.

4   Consistent Nondeterministic Turing Machines

Although we showed above that immunity is the natural notion to consider when defining an almost-everywhere complexity notion for nondeterministic time complexity, it must be admitted that there is something unsatisfying about our definition of a.e. NTIME complexity. For example, Theorem 5 shows the existence of a set in $NTIME(2^{\sqrt{n}})$ which has no infinite subset in $NTIME(n)$. This set is a subset of $Z = \{x10^j : |x10^j| = 2^{\sqrt{|x|}}\}$. Thus every input which is *not* in Z can be rejected immediately. It would be more satisfactory if our notion of almost-everywhere complexity precluded the possibility that infinitely many inputs could be *rejected* easily. This section introduces consistent nondeterministic Turing machines, in order to form a more acceptable notion of a.e. complexity for nondeterministic time.

Consistent NTMs were considered by Buntrock [Bu-89]. We are unaware of any earlier mention of this notion in the literature. Consistent Turing machines are very similar in some respects to the strong nondeterministic Turing machines which were defined by Long [Lo-82]. Among other uses, strong nondeterministic Turing machines provide a nice characterization of NP ∩ coNP.

Definition: A nondeterministic Turing machine M is *consistent* if, on every input x, either all halting computation paths are accepting or all halting computation paths are rejecting.

(Note – Long's *strong* nondeterministic Turing machines [Lo-82] are simply consistent Turing machines which always halt.)

Given a consistent nondeterministic Turing machine M, we define the "consistent" running time of M on input x as follows: $CT_M(x) = \min\{t : $ there is a halting path of M on input x of length $t\}$.

We say that L is a.e. complex for consistent $NTIME(T(n))$ iff $[L(M) = L$ and M a consistent NTM implies $CT_M(x) = \omega(T(|x|))]$. The next theorem follows immediately from these definitions.

Theorem 8 Let T be a time constructible function. Then L has consistent a.e. NTIME complexity T iff L is bi-immune with respect to $NTIME(T(n))$.

Proposition 9 If $T(n) = \omega(2^{t(n)})$, then there is a set in $NTIME(T(n))$ which is bi-immune to $NTIME(t(n))$.

Proof: This follows immediately, using the standard techniques used to prove the a.e. hierarchy theorem for deterministic time. ∎

The following theorem shows that this bi-immunity result cannot be improved using relativizable proof techniques.

Theorem 10 Let T and t be time-constructible functions such that for all large n, $T(n) < 2^{t(n)}$. Then there is an oracle A relative to which no set in $NTIME(T(n))$ is bi-immune to $NTIME(t(n))$.

Proof: In fact, we prove the stronger result that there is an oracle relative to which, for every infinite set L in $NTIME(T(n))$, either L has an infinite subset in $NTIME(t(n))$, or $\overline{L}$ has an infinite subset in $DTIME(n)$.

Stage $\langle i, l \rangle$. Let A be the finite oracle constructed so far, and let n be the length of the longest string in A. If there exists any string x of length longer than n so that M_i rejects x with oracle $A \cup \{\langle i, x \rangle\}$, then let A be extended to $A \cup \{\langle i, x \rangle\}$, and reserve all strings shorter than $\langle i, x \rangle$ for $\overline{A}$.

Else, if no such string x exists, then for all large strings x, there is an accepting computation of M_i on x with oracle $A \cup \{\langle i, x \rangle\}$. "Reserve" one such accepting computation. Note that along this path, at most $T(|x|) < 2^{t(|x|)}$ strings are queried. Let y be a string of length $t(|x|)$ such that $\langle i, x, y \rangle$ is not queried along this path, and extend A to the new oracle $A \cup \{\langle i, x \rangle, \langle i, x, y \rangle\}$.

That completes the construction.

Let L be an infinite set in $\mathrm{NTIME}^A(T(n))$, where L is accepted by M_i with oracle A. If for all large l, case 1 is used in stage $\langle i, l \rangle$, then the following algorithm accepts an infinite set which contains only finitely many elements of L: On input x, accept iff $\langle i, x \rangle \in A$.

If this is not the case, then for infinitely many l, case 2 is used in stage $\langle i, l \rangle$. In this case, the following algorithm accepts infinitely many elements of L: on input x, accept iff $\langle i, x \rangle \in A$ and there exists a string y of length $t(|x|)$ such that $\langle i, x, y \rangle \in A$. ∎

Having settled the questions of immunity and bi-immunity, it now remains only to consider co-immunity.

Theorem 11 Let T and t be time-constructible functions with T monotone and $t(n) = o(T(n))$. Then there is a set in $\mathrm{NTIME}(T(n))$ which is co-immune with respect to $\mathrm{NTIME}(t(n))$

Proof: What is needed is to construct a set $L \in \mathrm{NTIME}(T(n))$ which is co-infinite and intersects every infinite set in $\mathrm{NTIME}(t(n))$.

Choose r an unbounded nondecreasing function such that $r(n)$ is computable in time $T(n)$, and such that $r(n)^2 2^{T(\log r(n))} \leq T(n)$. (For example $r(n)$ can be defined to be the largest $i \leq \log n$ such that $2^{T(\log i)} \leq T(n)/\log^2 n$.)

Let $M_1, M_2 \ldots$ be an enumeration of nondeterministic Turing machines which run in time $t(n)$.

Consider the following program P, which has a variable parameter M:

On input z of length n PART 1: Run M on inputs $x \in \{1, \ldots, r(n)\}$, and let $\mathrm{OUT}(z)$ = the number of these inputs which M does not accept within $T(|x|)$ time.

Let $\mathrm{LIST} = \{1, 2, \ldots, \mathrm{OUT}(z)\}$

For all $i \in \mathrm{LIST}$ For all $y \in \{1, 2, \ldots r(n)\}$ Using exhaustive search of the computation trees, determine if $y \in L(M_i) \cap L(M)$. (Here, we consider y to be in $L(M)$ only if there is an accepting computation of M on y of length at most $T(|y|)$.) If so, remove i from LIST. Let $\mathrm{LIST}(z)$ denote the current contents of LIST.

PART 2: Nondeterministically guess $i \in \mathrm{LIST}(z)$. Use $T(n)$ time to simulate M_i on input z.

For any fixed Turing machine M, the running time of this (nondeterministic) program P is $(r(n)) 2^{T(\log r(n))} + (r(n))^2 2^{T(\log r(n))} + T(n) = O(T(n))$.

By the recursion theorem, there is a Turing machine $\mathcal{M}$ which executes P with parameter $\mathcal{M}$. By analyzing the proof of the recursion theorem, $\mathcal{M}$ can be seen to have time complexity $O(T(n))$. We claim that $L(\mathcal{M})$ is co-immune with respect to $\mathrm{NTIME}(t(n))$.

That is, we need to show that M rejects infinitely many strings, and that $L(M)$ intersects every set in NTIME$(t(n))$.

In order to do this, first we argue that OUT(z) is a monotone nondecreasing, unbounded function. It is obvious that OUT(z) is monotone nondecreasing. Assume for the sake of a contradiction that OUT$(z) < k$ for all z. Then for all z, LIST(z) is always a subset of $\{1, 2, \ldots, k\}$. Note also that $x > z \implies$ LIST$(x) \subseteq$ LIST(z). Thus there is some set $S \subseteq \{1, 2, \ldots, k\}$ such that for all large z, LIST$(z) = S$. Note that $i \in S \implies L(M_i)$ is finite, since if (1) $i \in$ LIST(z) and (2) M_i accepts z and (3) the computation of M_i on z can be simulated in $T(|z|)$ steps, then $z \in L(M)$. Thus on inputs of length n such that $\log \log n > |z|$, it will be discovered that $z \in L(M_i) \cap L(M)$, and thus i will be removed from S, contrary to our choice of S. Thus $i \in S \implies L(M_i)$ is finite. Thus for all large inputs z, none of the simulations carried out in PART 2 lead to acceptance, and thus $L(M)$ is finite. But then for all large z there are more than k strings of length $r(|z|)$ which are rejected by M, and thus OUT$(z) > k$ for all large z. Thus we have proved that OUT(z) is an unbounded function. (And thus M rejects infinitely many strings.)

Now let L be any infinite set in NTIME$(t(n))$. Then $L = L(M_i)$ for some i. Let z be a string in L such that OUT$(z) > i$ and such that a simulation of M_i on input z can be carried out in time $T(|z|)$. It is clear from the construction that either $z \in L(M)$, or there is some $x < z$ such that $x \in L(M_i) \cap L(M)$. The Theorem follows. ∎

5 Conclusions

Note that in our oracle constructions, we actually prove that there are oracles relative to which every infinite set in NTIME$(T(n))$ has an infinite subset in UTIME$(t(n))$, for appropriate T and t. Similarly, as Rutger Verbeek [Ve-89] has suggested, the same arguments could be used to produce an infinite subset in RTIME$(t(n))$.

We have considered the question of whether one can prove a tight a.e. hierarchy theorem for nondeterministic time. We have considered different ways in which one might define what is meant by a.e. complexity for nondeterministic Turing machines, and in all cases we have presented hierarchies which are close to the best which can be proved using relativizable proof techniques.

6 Acknowledgments

We thank the authors of [GHS-89] for sharing this paper with us, and John Geske, Joel Seiferas, Alan Selman and Jie Wang for helpful discussions.

References

[BS-85]   J. Balcázar and U. Schöning, *Bi-immune sets for complexity classes*, Mathematical Systems Theory 18, 1–10.

[Bu-89]   G. Buntrock, *Logarithmisch platzbeschränkte Simulationen*, Dissertation, Technische Universität Berlin.

[Co-73]   S. Cook, *A hierarchy for nondeterministic time complexity*, Journal of Computer and System Sciences 7, 343–353.

[CR-73]   S. Cook and R. Reckhow, *Time-bounded random access machines*, Journal of Computer and System Sciences 7, 354–375.

[FS-89]   L. Fortnow and M. Sipser, *Probabilistic computation and linear time*, Proc. 21st IEEE FOCS Conference, pp. 148–156.

[Fü-84]   M. Fürer, *Data structures for distributed counting*, Journal of Computer and System Sciences 28, 231–243.

[GHS-87]   J. Geske, D. Huynh, and A. Selman, *A hierarchy theorem for almost everywhere complex sets with application to polynomial complexity degrees*, Proc. 4th Symposium on Theoretical Aspects of Computer Science, Lecture Notes in Computer Science 247, Springer Verlag, Berlin, pp. 125–135.

[GHS-89]   J. Geske, D. Huynh, and J. Seiferas, *A note on almost-everywhere-complex sets and separating deterministic-time-complexity classes*, Technical Report, University of Rochester.

[HS-65]   J. Hartmanis and R. Stearns, *On the computational complexity of algorithms*, Transactions of the AMS 117, 285–306.

[HS-66]   F. Hennie and R. Stearns, *Two-tape simulation of multitape Turing machines*, J. ACM 13, 533–546.

[KV-88]   M. Karpinski and R. Verbeek, *Randomness, provability, and the separation of Monte Carlo time and space*, Lecture Notes in Computer Science 270, pp. 189–207.

[Lo-82]   T. Long, *Strong nondeterministic polynomial-time reductions*, Theoretical Computer Science 21, 1–25.

[RS-81]   C. Rackoff and J. Seiferas, *Limitations on separating nondeterministic complexity classes*, SIAM J. Comp. 10, 742–745.

[Ve-89]   R. Verbeek, personnal communication.

[Zá-83]   S. Zák, *A Turing machine hierarchy*, Theoretical Computer Science 26, 327–333.

The Ring of k-Regular Sequences

(Extended Abstract)

Jean-Paul Allouche *
C. N. R. S. (U. R. A. 226)
Mathématiques et Informatique
33405 Talence Cedex
FRANCE
allouche%frbdx11.bitnet

Jeffrey Shallit **
Mathematics and Computer Science
Dartmouth College
Hanover, NH 03755
USA
shallit@dartmouth.edu

Abstract

The *automatic sequence* is the central concept at the intersection of formal language theory and number theory. It was introduced by Cobham, and has been extensively studied by Christol, Kamae, Mendès France and Rauzy, and other writers. Since the range of an automatic sequence is finite, however, their descriptive power is severely limited.

In this paper, we generalize the concept of automatic sequence to the case where the sequence can take its values in a (possibly infinite) ring R; we call such sequences k-*regular*. (If R is finite, we obtain automatic sequences as a special case.) We argue that k-regular sequences provide a good framework for discussing many "naturally-occurring" sequences, and we support this contention by exhibiting many examples of k-regular sequences from numerical analysis, topology, number theory, combinatorics, analysis of algorithms, and the theory of fractals.

We investigate the closure properties of k-regular sequences. We prove that the set of k-regular sequences forms a ring under the operations of term-by-term addition and convolution. Hence the set of associated formal power series in $R[[X]]$ also forms a ring.

We show how k-regular sequences are related to $\mathbb{Z}$-rational formal series. We give a machine model for the k-regular sequences. We prove that all k-regular sequences can be computed quickly.

Let the *pattern sequence* $e_P(n)$ count the number of occurrences of the pattern P in the base-k expansion of n. Morton and Mourant showed that every sequence over $\mathbb{Z}$ has a unique expansion as sum of pattern sequences. We prove that this "Fourier" expansion maps k-regular sequences to k-regular sequences. In particular, the coefficients in the expansion of $e_P(an + b)$ form a k-automatic sequence.

I. Introduction

Let $\{S(n)\}_{n \geq 0}$ be a sequence with values chosen from a finite set Σ. Then $\{S(n)\}_{n \geq 0}$ is said to be k-automatic if, informally speaking, $S(n)$ is a finite-state function of the base-k expansion of n.

* Research supported in part by "PICS: Théorie des nombres et ordinateurs"
** Research supported in part by NSF Grant CCR-8817400, the Wisconsin Alumni Research Foundation, and a Walter Burke award.

Automatic sequences have been studied by Cobham [Cob], Christol, Kamae, Mendès France and Rauzy [CKMR], and others. (For example, see the survey paper of Allouche [A1].) There are many other ways to characterize automatic sequences. For example, consider the following

Definition 1.1.
   The *k-kernel* of a sequence is the set of all subsequences of the form $\{S(k^e n + a)\}_{n \geq 0}$, where $e \geq 0$ and $0 \leq a < k^e$.

   Cobham [Cob] proved the following

Theorem 1.2.
   A sequence is k-automatic if and only if its k-kernel is finite.

   Unfortunately, the range of an automatic sequence is necessarily finite, and this restricts their descriptive power.
   In this paper, we are concerned with a natural generalization of automaticity to the case where the sequence $\{S(n)\}_{n \geq 0}$ takes its values in a (possibly infinite) ring; we call such sequences *k-regular*. We use an analogue of Theorem 1.2 as our *definition*. We show that *k*-regular sequences provide an excellent framework for describing many "naturally occurring" sequences, such as the numerators of the left endpoints of the Cantor set, binary Gray code, numerators of entries of the Stern-Brocot tree, etc.

II. *k*-regular sequences: definition and properties
   Let R' be a commutative Noetherian ring, i. e. every ideal is finitely generated. (Examples of such rings include all finite rings, $\mathbb{Z}$, all fields K, and the polynomial rings $K[X]$.) Let R' be a subring of R.
   Let $S(R)$ denote the set of sequences with values in R. Let $\{S(n)\}_{n \geq 0}$ be a sequence with values in R, and let k be an integer ≥ 2.

Definition 2.1.
   We say $\{S(n)\}_{n \geq 0}$ is (R', k)-*regular* if there exist a finite number of sequences

$$S_1, S_2, \ldots, S_j$$

with values in R, such that each sequence in the *k*-kernel of $\{S(n)\}_{n \geq 0}$ is an R'-linear combination of the S_i.

   Let $\mathcal{K}$ denote the *k*-kernel of $\{S(n)\}_{n \geq 0}$. Then $\{S(n)\}_{n \geq 0}$ is (R', k)-regular means that

$$\langle \mathcal{K} \rangle \subseteq \langle S_1, S_2, \ldots S_n \rangle,$$

i. e. $\langle \mathcal{K} \rangle$ is a sub-module of a finitely generated R'-module. By a well-known theorem (see, e. g., [Lan, pp. 142-144]), it follows that $\langle \mathcal{K} \rangle$ itself is finitely generated.
   Thus Definition 2.1 can be restated as follows: a sequence $\{S(n)\}_{n \geq 0}$ with values in R is (R', k)-regular if the R'-module generated by its *k*-kernel is a *finitely generated* R'-submodule of $S(R)$.
   If the context is clear, we usually write just *k*-regular.

Note that if R' is a finite ring, then we recover the case of k-automatic sequences. For if every subsequence in the k-kernel can be written as an R'-linear combination of a finite set of sequences, then there are only a finite number of distinct elements of the k-kernel.

Our first theorem gives several alternative characterizations of k-regular sequences:

Theorem 2.2.

The following are equivalent:

(a) $\{S(n)\}_{n \geq 0}$ is (R', k)-regular;

(b) The R'-module generated by the k-kernel of $\{S(n)\}_{n \geq 0}$ is generated by a finite number of its subsequences of the form $S(k^{f_i} n + b_i)$ where $0 \leq b_i < k^{f_i}$;

(c) There exists an integer E such that for all $e_j > E$, each subsequence $S(k^{e_j} n + a_j)$ with $0 \leq a_j < k^{e_j}$ can be expressed as an R'-linear combination

$$S(k^{e_j} n + a_j) = \sum_i c_{ij} S(k^{f_{ij}} n + b_{ij}),$$

where $f_{ij} \leq E$ and $0 \leq b_{ij} < k^{f_{ij}}$;

(d) There exist an integer r and r sequences $S = S_1, S_2, \ldots, S_r$, such that for $1 \leq i \leq r$, the k sequences $\{S_i(kn + a)\}_{n \geq 0}$, $0 \leq a < k$, are R'-linear combinations of the S_i;

(e) There exist an integer r and r sequences $S = S_1, S_2, \ldots, S_r$ and k matrices

$$B_0, B_1, \ldots, B_{k-1}$$

in $M_{r,r}(R')$ such that if

$$V(n) = \begin{pmatrix} S_1(n) \\ \vdots \\ S_r(n) \end{pmatrix},$$

one has $V(kn + a) = B_a V(n)$ for $0 \leq a < k$.

Proof.

Omitted for space considerations. ∎

We introduce some notation. Let $k \geq 2$ be a fixed integer, and let $\Sigma = \{0, 1, \ldots, k - 1\}$. Then we can write every $n \geq 0$ uniquely as an integer in base k:

$$n = \sum_{0 \leq i < e} a_i k^i,$$

where $a_{e-1} \neq 0$. The string

$$a_{e-1} \cdots a_1 a_0$$

is called the *standard base-k representation* of n. The set of all standard representations is $\epsilon + (\Sigma - 0)\Sigma^*$.

Lemma 2.3.

Let $\{S(n)\}_{n \geq 0}$ be a sequence with entries in R. Then $\{S(n)\}_{n \geq 0}$ is (R', k)-regular if and only if there exist matrices $M_0, M_1, \ldots, M_{k-1}$ with entries in R' and vectors λ, κ with entries in R such that

$$S(n) = \lambda M_{a_0} M_{a_1} \ldots M_{a_{e-1}} \kappa,$$

where $a_{e-1} a_{e-2} \ldots a_1 a_0$ is the standard base-k representation of n.

Proof.

Use Theorem 2.2 (e). The details will appear in the full paper. ∎

An example.

We give an example of the theorems above. Let $k = 2$ and $\Sigma = \{0, 1\}$. Let $P \in \Sigma^+$. Then we define the *pattern sequence* $e_P(n)$ to be the number of occurrences of the string P in the standard base-k representation of n. Thus for $k = 2$, we have $e_{11}(29) = 2$.

Let us examine the properties of the sequence $S(n) = e_1(3n)$, which has been studied extensively by Newman, Slater, and Coquet ([N], [NS], [Coq]). Here are the first few values of $S(n)$:

$$n \ = \ 0\ 1\ 2\ 3\ 4\ 5\ 6\ 7\ 8\ 9\ 10\ 11\ 12\ \cdots$$
$$S(n) = 0\ 2\ 2\ 2\ 2\ 4\ 2\ 3\ 2\ 4\ \ 4\ \ \ 2\ \ \ 2\ \cdots$$

It has been observed that the first few values of $S(n)$ are almost all even–a phenomenon that we will explain below.

To analyze $S(n)$, we will *bisect* the sequence into $S(2n)$ and $S(2n + 1)$:

$$n \ = \ 0\ 1\ 2\ 3\ 4\ 5\ 6\ 7\ 8\ 9\ 10\ 11\ 12\ \cdots$$
$$S(2n) \ = \ 0\ 2\ 2\ 2\ 2\ 4\ 2\ 3\ 2\ 4\ \ 4\ \ \ 2\ \ \ 2\ \cdots$$
$$S(2n + 1) = 2\ 2\ 4\ 3\ 4\ 2\ 4\ 4\ 4\ 4\ \ 6\ \ \ 3\ \ \ 4\ \cdots$$

It appears that $S(2n) = S(n)$, and indeed this is easily verified. However, $S(2n + 1)$ does not seem to be simply related to $S(n)$, so we bisect the sequence $S(2n + 1)$:

$$n \ = \ 0\ 1\ 2\ 3\ 4\ 5\ 6\ 7\ 8\ 9\ 10\ 11\ 12\ \cdots$$
$$S(4n + 1) = 2\ 4\ 4\ 4\ 4\ 6\ 4\ 5\ 4\ 6\ \ 6\ \ \ 4\ \ \ 4\ \cdots$$
$$S(4n + 3) = 2\ 3\ 2\ 4\ 4\ 3\ 3\ 5\ 4\ 5\ \ 2\ \ \ 4\ \ \ 4\ \cdots$$

It appears that $S(4n + 1) = S(n) + 2$, and this can easily be verified as follows:

$$S(4n + 1) = e_1(12n + 3) = e_1(4(3n) + 3) = e_1(3n) + 2 = S(n) + 2.$$

However, $S(4n + 3)$ does not seem to be related to either $S(n)$ or $S(2n + 1)$, so we bisect $S(4n + 3)$:

$$n \ = \ 0\ 1\ 2\ 3\ 4\ 5\ 6\ 7\ 8\ 9\ 10\ 11\ 12\ \cdots$$
$$S(8n + 3) = 2\ 2\ 4\ 3\ 4\ 2\ 4\ 4\ 4\ 4\ \ 6\ \ \ 3\ \ \ 4\ \cdots$$
$$S(8n + 7) = 3\ 4\ 3\ 5\ 5\ 4\ 4\ 6\ 5\ 6\ \ 3\ \ \ 5\ \ \ 5\ \cdots$$

It appears that $S(8n+3) = S(2n+1)$ and $S(8n+7) = S(4n+3)+1$, and these identities can also be verified, as follows:

$$S(8n + 3) = e_1(24n + 9) = e_1(8(3n + 1) + 1) = e_1(8(3n + 1) + 4)$$

$$= e_1(24n + 12) = e_1(4(6n + 3)) = e_1(6n + 3) = S(2n + 1),$$

and

$$S(8n + 7) = e_1(24n + 21) = e_1(8(3n + 2) + 5) = e_1(8(3n + 2) + 2) + 1$$

$$= e_1(24n + 18) + 1 = e_1(2(12n + 9)) + 1 = e_1(12n + 9) + 1 = S(4n + 3) + 1.$$

To conclude, we see that *every subsequence* of the form $\{S(2^j n + a)\}_{n \geq 0}$ can be written as a *linear combination* of the sequences $\{S(n)\}_{n \geq 0}$, $\{S(2n + 1)\}_{n \geq 0}$, $\{S(4n + 3)\}_{n \geq 0}$, and the constant sequence 1. Hence the 2-kernel of $\{S(n)\}_{n \geq 0}$ is finitely generated, and $\{S(n)\}_{n \geq 0}$ is 2-regular.

We now give an example of Lemma 2.3. Set

$$M_0 = \begin{bmatrix} 1 & 0 & 0 & 0 \\ 1 & 0 & 0 & 2 \\ 0 & 1 & 0 & 0 \\ 0 & 0 & 0 & 1 \end{bmatrix}, \quad M_1 = \begin{bmatrix} 0 & 1 & 0 & 0 \\ 0 & 0 & 1 & 0 \\ 0 & 0 & 1 & 1 \\ 0 & 0 & 0 & 1 \end{bmatrix},$$

and $\lambda = [1 \ \ 0 \ \ 0 \ \ 0]$, $\kappa = [0 \ \ 2 \ \ 2 \ \ 1]^T$. Let

$$V(n) = \begin{bmatrix} S(n) \\ S(2n+1) \\ S(4n+3) \\ 1 \end{bmatrix}.$$

Then we see $V(2n) = M_0 V(n)$ and $V(2n+1) = M_1 V(n)$. Lemma 2.3 implies that $S(n) = \lambda M_{a_0} M_{a_1} \cdots M_{a_{e-1}} \kappa$, where $a_{e-1} \cdots a_1 a_0$ is the standard base-2 representation of n.

We now state some more results; proofs can be found in the final paper.

Theorem 2.4.

Let $\{S(n)\}_{n \geq 0}$ and $\{T(n)\}_{n \geq 0}$ be k-regular sequences. Then so are $S + T = \{S(n) + T(n)\}_{n \geq 0}$, $-S = \{-S(n)\}_{n \geq 0}$, and $ST = \{S(n)T(n)\}_{n \geq 0}$.

Theorem 2.5.

Let $\{S(n)\}_{n \geq 0}$ be a k-regular sequence. Then for $a \geq 1, b \geq 0$, the sequence $\{S(an+b)\}_{n \geq 0}$ is k-regular.

Theorem 2.6.

Let $\{S(n)\}_{n \geq 0}$ be a sequence such that there exists an $a \geq 2$ such that $\{S(an+i)\}_{n \geq 0}$ is k-regular for $0 \leq i < a$. Then $\{S(n)\}_{n \geq 0}$ is k-regular.

Theorem 2.7.

Let f be an integer ≥ 1. Then $\{S(n)\}_{n \geq 0}$ is k^f-regular if and only if $\{S(n)\}_{n \geq 0}$ is k-regular.

Theorem 2.8.

Let $\{S(n)\}_{n \geq 0}$ be a k-regular sequence. Then there exists a constant c such that $S(n) = O(n^c)$.

Theorem 2.9.

Let $\zeta \neq 0$ be a complex number. Then the sequence of powers $\{\zeta^n\}_{n \geq 0}$ is $(\mathbb{C}, k)$-regular if and only if ζ is a root of unity.

III. The ring of k-regular sequences

Associated to every k-regular sequence $\{S(n)\}_{n \geq 0}$ is the formal power series in $\mathbb{Z}[[X]]$ defined by

$$\sum_{n \geq 0} S(n) X^n,$$

where X is an indeterminate. We call such a power series k-regular. In this section we show that the set of all k-regular power series forms a ring (but not a field). Proofs of the results can be found in the final paper.

Theorem 3.1.
    The set of k-regular sequences is closed under convolution.

Since the convolution of sequences is equivalent to (ordinary) multiplication of the associated power series, we have:

Corollary 3.2.
    The set of k-regular power series forms a ring.

Remark.
    The set of k-regular power series does not form a field. This follows from the identity

$$\frac{1}{1-2X} = 1 + 2X + 4X^2 + 8X^3 + \cdots$$

and the fact that $\{2^n\}_{n \geq 0}$ is not k-regular (Theorem 2.10).

Theorem 3.3.
    Let $f(X) = \sum_{n \geq 0} S(n)X^n$ be a formal power series with complex coefficients. Assume that $f(X)$ represents a rational function of X; i. e. there exist polynomials $p(X)$, $q(X)$ such that $f(X) = p(X)/q(X)$. Then $\{S(n)\}_{n \geq 0}$ is k-regular if and only if the poles of f are roots of unity.

IV. Rational series and k-regular sequences

At first glance, it might seem that there is no relationship between k-regular power series and the theory of $\mathbb{Z}$-rational formal series, as described in [SS] and [BR]. For $\sum_{n \geq 0} 2^n X^n$ is $\mathbb{Z}$-rational, but is not k-regular. Similarly, $\sum_{n \geq 0} e_1(n)X^n$ is k-regular, but is not $\mathbb{Z}$-rational.

Nevertheless, there *is* a relationship which can be roughly described as follows: 2-regular power series are the "binary" analogue of $\mathbb{Z}$-rational formal series in one variable. Alternatively, $\mathbb{Z}$-rational series in one variable are the "unary" analogue of k-regular power series.

In this section, we develop this relationship between k-regular sequences and $\mathbb{Z}$-rational formal series. From this, we get a machine model for the k-regular sequences. This model plays the same role as the ordinary finite automaton does for k-automatic sequences. We also prove that all k-regular sequences can be computed quickly.

We now show how k-regular sequences are related to $\mathbb{Z}$-rational formal series. Let $x_0, x_1, \ldots, x_{k-1}$ be non-commuting variables. If $w = w_1 \cdots w_r \in \Sigma^*$, then define $x_w = x_{w_1} \cdots x_{w_r}$. Let τ be the map that sends n to $x_{a_0} x_{a_1} \ldots x_{a_{e-1}}$, where the standard base-k representation of x is the string $a_{e-1} \cdots a_1 a_0$.

Theorem 4.1.
    $\{S(n)\}_{n \geq 0}$ is k-regular if and only if the formal series

$$\sum_{n \geq 0} S(n)\tau(n)$$

is $\mathbb{Z}$-rational.

Theorem 4.1 allows us to use the well-developed theory of $\mathbb{Z}$-rational series to discuss the properties of k-regular sequences, at least in some cases. Now we sketch a description of our machine model.

This model is essentially the same as that first given by Schützenberger [Sch]. However, we repeat the description for completeness.

Let us define what we call a *matrix machine*. It is a finite-state machine with auxiliary storage in the form of a column vector $v \in R_{j1}$ for some $j > 0$. Here is how the machine operates: Suppose we are in state q. Upon reading a symbol a from the input, the machine first replaces v with Mv, where $M = M(q,a)$ is a $j \times j$ matrix. Then the machine moves to a new state $\delta(q,a)$. The output is determined as follows: when the last input symbol is read, we are in state q'. There is a row vector $\lambda(q')$, and the output is the scalar $\lambda(q')v$.

Now consider the case where the input is the base-k representation of an integer n, starting with the most significant digit, and the matrix machine computes $S(n)$. We claim this is precisely the class of k-regular sequences. By Lemma 2.3, this equivalence is easily seen in the case of 1-state machines. Thus to prove the equivalence it suffices to prove the following

Theorem 4.2 (Schützenberger).
A matrix machine with r states can be simulated by a matrix machine with 1 state.

Corollary 4.3.
The n-th term of a k-regular sequence can be computed using $O(\log n)$ operations, where an operation is an addition or multiplication of elements in the ring R.

Corollary 4.4.
The n-th term of a k-regular sequence over $\mathbb{Z}$ can be computed in time polynomial in $\log n$.

V. Some "Fourier" expansions
For simplicity, all results and proofs in this section assume $k = 2$.

We introduce some notation that will be used throughout this section. Let $n_{(2)}$ denote the string in $A = \epsilon + 1(0 + 1)^*$ that represents n in base 2. If s is a string in A, let $v(S)$ denote the integer represented by s. Let $|s|$ denote the length of the string s. Let $\lambda(n)$ be the integer obtained from n by deleting the most significant bit of its base-2 expansion. Let m and n be integers; we write m suff n for the relation: the string $m_{(2)}$ is a suffix of the string $n_{(2)}$. Define $E = 1(0 + 1)^*$. Let $P \in E$, and let $e_P(n)$ denote the number of (possibly overlapping) occurrences of P in the base-k expansion of n.

Morton and Mourant proved [MM] that any sequence $\{S(n)\}_{n \geq 0}$ taking values in $\mathbb{Z}$ has a unique expansion as an infinite sum, as follows:

$$S(n) = S(0) + \sum_{P \in E} \hat{S}(v(P))e_P(n).$$

Here the "Fourier" coefficients $\hat{S}(m)$ are integers. We define $\hat{S}(0) = S(0)$, and call the sequence $\{\hat{S}(n)\}_{n \geq 0}$ the *pattern transform* of $\{S(n)\}_{n \geq 0}$.

In this section, we give the main result of our paper: a sequence is 2-regular if and only if its pattern transform is 2-regular. Proofs can be found in the final paper.

Theorem 5.1.
The sequence $\{e_P(n)\}_{n \geq 0}$ is 2-regular for any pattern $P \in E$.

Corollary 5.2.
$\{e_P(an + b)\}_{n \geq 0}$ is 2-regular for all $a, b \geq 0$.

Lemma 5.3.

For all $n \geq 0$ we have

$$S(2n) = S(n) + \sum_{\substack{m \geq 1 \\ m \text{ suff } n}} \hat{S}(2m)$$

and

$$S(2n+1) = S(n) + \hat{S}(1) + \sum_{\substack{m \geq 1 \\ m \text{ suff } n}} \hat{S}(2m+1).$$

Lemma 5.4.

For all $n \geq 1$ we have

$$\hat{S}(2n) = S(2n) - S(n) - S(2\lambda(n)) + S(\lambda(n)).$$

For all $n \geq 1$ we have

$$\hat{S}(2n+1) = S(2n+1) - S(n) - S(2\lambda(n)+1) + S(\lambda(n)).$$

Theorem 5.5.

$\{S(n)\}_{n \geq 0}$ is 2-regular if and only if $\{\hat{S}(n)\}_{n \geq 0}$ is 2-regular.

It is possible to view Theorem 5.5 as a generalization of results of Choffrut and Schützenberger [CS]. They discussed counting functions similar to our sum

$$\sum_{P \in E} \hat{S}(v(P)) e_P(n).$$

However, because they restricted their attention to finite automata with counters, they were forced to put restrictions on the set E.

Theorem 5.5 is also a generalization of previous results of Allouche, Morton, and Shallit [AMS].

Our last result concerns the pattern transform of $\{e_P(an+b)\}_{n \geq 0}$. We prove that, in this case, the coefficients $\hat{S}(m)$ are bounded and in fact, are k-automatic.

Theorem 5.6.

Let

$$e_P(an+b) = \hat{S}(0) + \sum_{P \in E} \hat{S}(v(P)) e_P(n).$$

Then $\hat{S}(m)$ is a 2-automatic sequence.

An example.

Continuing the example of section II, we see

$$e_1(3n) = 2e_1(n) - 2e_{11}(n) + e_{111}(n) - 2e_{1011}(n) + e_{11011}(n) - 2e_{101011}(n) + e_{1101011}(n) - \cdots$$

$$= 2e_1(n) - 2\sum_{i \geq 0} e_{(10)^i 11}(n) + \sum_{i \geq 0} e_{11(01)^i 1}(n).$$

This explains why the first few values of $e_1(3n)$ are even.

VI. Some examples

In all the examples that follow, we assume $k = 2$. Sequence numbers refer to Sloane's book [Sl].

Example 1.

Consider the sequence

$$\{c(n)\}_{n \geq 0} = 0, 2, 6, 8, 18, 20, 24, 26, 54, 56, \ldots,$$

which lists the numerators of the left endpoints of the Cantor set. (Alternatively, these are the integers whose base-3 representations contain no 1's; see [MFP].) Then it is easy to see that $c(2n) = 3c(n)$ and $c(2n+1) = 3c(n) + 2$. Hence it is 2-regular. (Note, however, that its characteristic sequence $101000101 \cdots$ is actually 3-automatic.)

Example 2.

Let j be an integer ≥ 0. The sequence $\{n^j\}_{n \geq 0}$ is 2-regular, as its 2-kernel is generated by the constant sequence 1 and the sequences $\{n\}_{n \geq 0}$, $\{n^2\}_{n \geq 0}$, $\ldots$, $\{n^j\}_{n \geq 0}$.

From Theorem 5.5, we know the corresponding pattern transforms are 2-regular. Using Lemma 5.4, we find:

$$n = e_1(n) + e_{10}(n) + e_{11}(n) + 2(e_{100}(n) + \cdots + e_{111}(n))$$
$$+ 4(e_{1000} + \cdots + e_{1111}(n)) + 8(e_{10000}(n) + \cdots + e_{11111}(n)) + \cdots$$

Example 3.

Let $d(0) = 0$, $d(1) = 1$, $d(2n) = d(n)$, and $d(2n+1) = d(n) + d(n+1)$. This sequence forms the numerators of the entries in the *Stern-Brocot tree* (see [St], [GKP]). It was also studied by de Rham [R] and is Sloane's sequence #56. The first few terms are

$$0, 1, 1, 2, 1, 3, 2, 3, 1, 4, 3, 5, 2, 5, 3, 4, \ldots.$$

It is easy to see that $d(4n+1) = d(n) + d(2n+1)$, and $d(4n+3) = 2d(2n+1) - d(n)$, and it follows that d is 2-regular.

A similar sequence is given by $a(0) = 0$, $a(1) = 1$, $a(2n) = a(n)$, and $a(2n+1) = a(n+1) - a(n)$. It satisfies $a(4n+1) = a(2n+1) - a(n)$ and $a(4n+3) = a(n)$ and hence is 2-regular. See [Rez1], [Rez2].

Example 4.

Let $\{C(n)\}_{n \geq 0}$ be the sequence of *Moser-de Bruijn* ([Mos], [B2]): $0, 1, 4, 5, 16, 17, 20, 21, \ldots$ It consists of integers that can be written as the sum of distinct powers of 4. This is Sloane's sequence #1315. Note that $C(2n) = 4C(n)$ and $C(2n+1) = 4C(n) + 1$; hence C is 2-regular. Also, see [BM] and [LMP].

Similarly, the sequence of *Loxton-van der Poorten* [LP1]

$$0, 1, 3, 4, 5, 11, 12, 13, 15, 16, 17, 19, 20, 21, 43, 44, \ldots$$

of integers that can be represented in base 4 using only the digits $-1, 0, 1$ is 3-regular.

Example 5.

Let $G(n) = 2^{e_1(n)}$. This is *Gould's sequence* [G], and Sloane's sequence #109. It satisfies $G(2n) = G(n)$; $G(2n+1) = 2G(n)$ and hence is 2-regular.

Glaisher [Gl] showed that $G(n)$ counts the number of odd binomial coefficients in row n of Pascal's triangle. See also [Fi].

Example 6.

Let $\{b(n)\}_{n\geq 0}$ be the sequence of numbers represented by binary Gray code [Gi]:

$$0, 1, 3, 2, 6, 7, 5, 4, 12, 13, 15, 14, 10, 11, 9, 8, \cdots$$

Then it is easy to see that $b(4n) = 2b(2n)$, $b(4n + 1) = 2b(2n) + 1$, $b(4n + 2) = 2b(2n + 1) + 1$, and $b(4n + 3) = 2b(2n + 1)$. Hence $\{b(n)\}_{n\geq 0}$ is 2-regular.

Similarly, if $\gamma(n)$ denotes the sum of the bits in the Gray code representation of n, then we find $\gamma(2n + 1) = 2\gamma(n) - \gamma(2n) + 1$; $\gamma(4n) = \gamma(2n)$; and $\gamma(4n + 2) = \gamma(2n + 1) + 1$. Hence $\{\gamma(n)\}_{n\geq 0}$ is 2-regular. See [FR].

Example 7.

Consider the sequence of lattice points $(x(n), y(n))$ traced out by paperfolding curves with an ultimately periodic sequence of unfolding instructions [DMFP, MFS]. Then $\{x(n)\}_{n\geq 0}$ and $\{y(n)\}_{n\geq 0}$ are 2-regular.

For example, consider the sequence of lattice points $(x(n), y(n))$ traced out by the space-filling curve with unfolding instructions RLRLRL$\cdots$.

$$
\begin{array}{llllllllllllllllll}
n & = & 0 & 1 & 2 & 3 & 4 & 5 & 6 & 7 & 8 & 9 & 10 & 11 & 12 & 13 & 14 & 15 & \cdots \\
x(n) & = & 0 & 0 & 1 & 1 & 0 & 0 & 1 & 1 & 2 & 2 & 3 & 3 & 2 & 2 & 1 & 1 & \cdots \\
y(n) & = & 0 & 1 & 1 & 2 & 2 & 3 & 3 & 2 & 2 & 3 & 3 & 4 & 4 & 3 & 3 & 4 & \cdots
\end{array}
$$

Then the sequences satisfy the identities $x(0) = 0$, $x(2) = 1$, $x(2n + 1) = x(2n)$, $x(4n) = 2x(n)$, $x(8n + 2) = -2x(n) + 2x(2n) + x(4n + 2)$, $x(16n + 6) = 2x(n) + x(4n + 2)$, $x(16n + 14) = 2x(2n) + 2x(4n + 2) - x(8n + 6)$, and $y(0) = 0$, $y(1) = 1$, $y(4n) = 2y(n)$, $y(4n + 1) = y(4n + 2) = 2y(n) - y(2n) + y(2n + 1)$, $y(8n + 3) = y(8n + 7) = 2y(2n + 1)$.

Example 8.

Van der Corput's sequence $\varphi_2(n)$ is defined as follows [Cor]: if

$$n = \sum_{i\geq 0} b_i(n)2^i,$$

where $b_i \in \{0, 1\}$, then

$$\varphi_2(n) = \sum_{i\geq 0} b_i(n)2^{-i-1}.$$

We see that $\varphi_2(0) = 0$, $\varphi_2(2n) = \frac{1}{2}\varphi_2(n)$, and $\varphi_2(2n + 1) = \frac{1}{2} + \frac{1}{2}\varphi_2(n)$. Hence the sequence of rational numbers $\varphi_2(n)$ is $(\mathbb{Q}, 2)$-regular.

Halton [Hal] generalized van der Corput's sequence to bases $b \geq 2$.

Example 9.

Let $w = w_0 w_1 w_2 \cdots$ be an infinite word over a finite alphabet, and define $s_w(n)$ to be the number of distinct subwords (European terminology: factors) of length n in w. Then $s_w(n) - s_w(n - 1)$ is frequently k-automatic, and hence in these cases, $s_w(n)$ is k-regular. For example, this is true when w is the fixed point of the Toeplitz substitution given by $0 \rightarrow 0010$ and $1 \rightarrow 1010$ [Rau]; when w is the infinite word of Thue-Morse, the fixed point of the substitution given by $0 \to 01$ and $1 \to 10$ [Brl] [LV]; and in a more general class of infinite words given by iterated homomorphisms discussed by Tapsoba [Tap].

Example 10.

An *addition chain to* n is a sequence of pairs of positive integers

$$(a_1, b_1), (a_2, b_2), \ldots, (a_r, b_r)$$

where (i) $a_r + b_r = n$ and (ii) for all s, either $a_s = 1$, or $a_s = a_i + b_i$ for some $i < s$, and the same holds for b_s. The cost of the addition chain is $\sum_{1 \leq i \leq r} a_i b_i$. Denote the cost of the minimum cost addition chain to n as $c(n)$. Then it can be shown [GYY] that $c(1) = 0$, and $c(2n) = c(n) + n^2$, $c(2n+1) = c(n) + n^2 + 2n$ for $n \geq 1$. Hence $c(n)$ is 2-regular.

VI. Acknowledgments

We are grateful to O. Salon for suggesting the term k-kernel [Sa].

Part of this work was done while the first author was visiting Dartmouth College.

Part of this work was done while the second author was a visiting scientist at the University of Waterloo and a visiting professor at the University of Wisconsin, Madison.

The second author acknowledges with thanks conversations with E. Bach, C. Choffrut, L. Dickey, J. Driscoll, G. Frandsen, D. Joseph, S. Kurtz, R. Lipton, A. Lubiw, and D. Passman.

References

[A1] J.-P. Allouche, Automates finis en théorie des nombres, *Expo. Math.* **5** (1987), 239-266.

[AMS] J.-P. Allouche, P. Morton, and J. Shallit, Pattern spectra, substring enumeration, and automatic sequences, preprint.

[B2] N. G. de Bruijn, Some direct decompositions of the set of integers, *Math. Tables Aids Comput.* **18** (1964), 537-546.

[BM] A. Blanchard and M. Mendès France, Symétrie et transcendance, *Bull. Sci. Math.* **106** (1982), 325-335.

[BR] J. Berstel and C. Reutenauer, Rational series and their languages, Springer-Verlag, 1988.

[Brl] S. Brlek, Enumeration of factors in the Thue-Morse word, *Disc. Appl. Math.* **24** (1989), 83-96.

[CKMR] G. Christol, T. Kamae, M. Mendès France and G. Rauzy, Suites algébriques, automates et substitutions, *Bull. Soc. Math. France* **108** (1980), 401-419.

[Cob] A. Cobham, Uniform tag sequences, *Math. Systems Theory* **6** (1972), 164-192.

[Coq] J. Coquet, A summation formula related to the binary digits, *Invent. Math.* **73** (1983), 107-115.

[Cor] J. C. van der Corput, Verteilungsfunktionen, *Proc. Ned. Akad. v. Wet.* **38** (1935), 813-821.

[CS] C. Choffrut and M. P. Schützenberger, Counting with rational functions, *Theor. Comput. Sci.* **58** (1988), 81-101.

[DMFP] M. Dekking, M. Mendès France, and A. van der Poorten, FOLDS!, *Math. Intell.* **4** (1982), 130-138; 173-195.

[Fi] N. J. Fine, Binomial coefficients modulo a prime, *Amer. Math. Monthly* **54** (1947), 589-592.

[FR] P. Flajolet and L. Ramshaw, A note on Gray code and odd-even merge, *SIAM J. Comput.* **9** (1980), 142-158.

[G] H. W. Gould, Exponential binomial coefficient series, Technical Report 4, Department of Mathematics, W. Virginia Univ., September 1961.

[Gi] E. Gilbert, Gray codes and paths on the n-cube, *Bell Sys. Tech. J.* **37** (1958), 815-826.

[GKP] R. Graham, D. Knuth, and O. Patashnik, *Concrete Mathematics*, Addison-Wesley, 1989.

[Gl] J. W. L. Glaisher, On the residue of a binomial-theorem coefficient with respect to a prime modulus, *Quart. J. Pure Appl. Math.* **30** (1899), 150-156.

[GYY] R. Graham, A. Yao, and F. Yao, Addition chains with multiplicative cost, *Disc. Math.* **23** (1978), 115-119.

[Hal] J. H. Halton, On the efficiency of certain quasi-random sequences of points in evaluating multi-dimensional integrals, *Numer. Math.* **2** (1960), 84-90.

[Lan] S. Lang, Algebra, Addison-Wesley, 1971.

[LMP] D. H. Lehmer, K. Mahler, and A. J. van der Poorten, Integers with digits 0 or 1, *Math. Comp.* **46** (1986) 683-689.

[LP1] J. H. Loxton and A. J. van der Poorten, An awful problem about integers in base four, *Acta Arithmetica* **49** (1987), 193-203.

[LV] A. de Luca and S. Varricchio, Some combinatorial properties of the Thue-Morse sequence and a problem in semigroups, *Theor. Comput. Sci.* **63** (1989), 333-348.

[MFP] M. Mendès France and A. J. van der Poorten, From geometry to Euler identities, *Theor. Comput. Sci.* **65** (1989), 213-220.

[MFS] M. Mendès France and J. Shallit, Wire bending, *J. Combinatorial Theory, A* **50** (1989), 1-23.

[MM] P. Morton and W. Mourant, Paper folding, digit patterns, and groups of arithmetic fractals, *Proc. Lond. Math. Soc.* **59** (1989), 253-293.

[Mos] L. Moser, An application of generating series, *Math. Mag.* **35** (1962), 37-38.

[N] D. J. Newman, On the number of binary digits in a multiple of three, *Proc. Amer. Math. Soc.* **21** (1969), 719-721.

[NS] D. J. Newman and M. Slater, Binary digit distribution over naturally defined sequences, *Trans. Amer. Math. Soc.* **213** (1975), 71-78.

[R] G. de Rham, Un peu de mathématiques à propos d'une courbe plane, *Elem. Math.* **2** (1947), 73-77; 89-97.

[Rau] G. Rauzy, Suites à termes dans un alphabet fini, *Sém. Théorie des Nombres de Bordeaux*, 1982-3, 25.01-25.16.

[Rez1] B. Reznick, A new sequence with many properties, *Abs. Amer. Math. Soc.* **5** (1984), 16.

[Rez2] B. Reznick, Some extremal problems for continued fractions, *Ill. J. Math.* **29** (1985), 261-279.

[Sa] O. Salon, Quelles tuiles! (Pavages apériodiques du plan et automates bidimensionnels), Séminaire de Théorie des Nombres de Bordeaux, (2ème Série) **1** (1989), 1-25.

[Sch] M. P. Schützenberger, On the definition of a family of automata, *Information and Control* **4** (1961), 245-270.

[Sl] N. J. A. Sloane, A handbook of integer sequences, Academic Press, 1973.

[SS] A. Salomaa and M. Soittola, Automata-theoretic aspects of formal power series, Springer-Verlag, 1978.

[St] M. A. Stern, Über eine zahlentheoretische Funktion, *J. reine angew. Math.* **55** (1858), 193-220.

[Tap] T. Tapsoba, Thèse de troisième cycle, Université d'Aix-Marseille II, 1987.

Minimal Pairs and Complete Problems[1]
(Extended Abstract)

Klaus Ambos-Spies
Universität Heidelberg
Mathematisches Institut
D-6900 Heidelberg

Steven Homer[2]
Department of Computer Science
Boston University
Boston, Mass. 02215

Robert I. Soare[3]
Department of Mathematics
University of Chicago
Chicago, Illinois 60637

Introduction

Two sets are said to form a minimal pair for polynomial many-one reductions if neither set is in P and the only sets which are polynomially reducible (via polynomial many-one reductions) to both sets are in P. The existence of minimal pairs was among the initial questions considered concerning polynomial reducibilities. It was addressed in the paper of Richard Ladner [9] which first studied the structure of polynomial reducibilities. There Ladner showed that there exist two recursive sets which form a minimal pair. While the sets constructed are recursive, no bound is given on their complexity.

Machtey [11] was able to improve Ladner's result by constructing the minimal pair more effectively. He proved the existence of a minimal pair of sets both of which are in exponential time. The work of Landweber, Lipton and Robertson [10] provided a more general construction of minimal pairs. They proved that there is a minimal pair below any non-polynomial degree. Hence minimal pairs exist whose complexity is arbitrarily close to P. Schöning [13] gave a similar, but still more general minimal pair construction in which the halves of the

---

[1] This research was done while the second and the third authors were guest professors at the Mathematics Institute of the University of Heidelberg.

[2] Supported in part by National Science Foundation Grant CCR-8814339, National Security Agency Grant MDA904-87-H, and a Fulbright-Hays Research Fellowship.

[3] Supported in part by National Science Foundation Grants DMS-8807389 and INT-8722296 and a grant of the Deutsche Forschungsgemeinschaft.

minimal pairs are individually bounded. Ambos-Spies [1] addressed the question of which degrees can be half of a minimal pair and proved that any nonpolynomial recursive set is such. That is, given a recursive set $A \notin P$, there exists a recursive B such that A and B form a minimal pair. Book (see [1]) has observed that such halves of minimal pairs may be extremely complex. He showed that for any EXPTIME-hard set A and any recursive set B, if A and B form a minimal pair then B is not elementary recursive.

A related and slightly more refined question is which degrees can be the top (that is the supremum) of a minimal pair. This question has implications for the structure of the sets in a complexity class. To make this relationship precise, we say that a set $A \notin P$ has a strict p-splitting if there is a polynomial time computable set D such that $A \cap D$ and $A \cap \overline{D}$ form a minimal pair. Clearly, if A has a strict p-splitting then A is the top of the minimal pair formed by $A \cap D$ and $A \cap \overline{D}$. The converse of this statement is also true. That is, Ambos-Spies [3] proved that if A is the top of a minimal pair then A has a strict p-splitting. Hence being the top of a minimal pair says something about the structure of a set A and of its easily definable subsets and splittings.

The results concerning the existence of minimal pairs imply some properties of the suprema of minimal pairs with respect to many-one polynomial reducibility as well. In particular, as there exist minimal pairs below any non-polynomial set, there are sups of minimal pairs below any non-polynomial degree as well. On the other hand, as every recursive set forms half of a minimal pair, above any recursive polynomial many-one degree there is a degree which is top of a minimal pair. All of this suggests that any recursive degree above P is the top of a minimal pair. However, this is not true. In [3] Ambos-Spies constructed a recursive set which has no strict p-splitting and hence is not the top of a minimal pair.

One weakness of the previous results is that they give no information about natural sets and degrees. For example we are most interested in the properties of complete sets and degrees. Since some degrees are the tops of minimal pairs and others are not, which of these properties is true about complete degrees?

We answer this question here for most complexity classes. Our main result is that any elementary recursive set which is hard for deterministic exponential time cannot be the sup of a minimal pair. Hence in particular any complete set for an elementary recursive class containing exponential time cannot be such a supremum.

For NP-complete sets the problem remains open. However, we show here that it is oracle dependent. That is, there is a recursive oracle A relative to which P ≠ NP and the NP complete sets are the sup of a minimal pair. And there is a recursive oracle B relative to which P ≠ NP and the NP complete sets are not the sup of a minimal pair. This is the first example of an oracle dependent property which is completely degree theoretic. The question of the existence of such a property for NP sets was raised in the paper of Homer and Maass [8]. Many questions about the structure of NP sets have been shown to be oracle dependent. Properties such as P-immunity and P-simplicity of NP sets have this characteristic. However, here we have an oracle dependent property which concerns only the polynomial many-one degrees of NP sets. Moreover, it is a property of the most interesting NP-sets, the complete sets.

Preliminaries

Our notation is standard. Σ denotes the binary alphabet $\{0,1\}$. We consider only sets A of binary strings, i.e., $A \subseteq \Sigma^*$. The disjoint union $A \oplus B$ of two sets A and B is defined by $A \oplus B = \{0x : x \in A\} \cup \{1x : x \in B\}$. Recall that a set A is p-many-one reducible to a set B ($A \leq_m^p B$) if there is a polynomial time computable function f $: \Sigma^* \to \Sigma^*$ such that $x \in A$ iff $f(x) \in B$. We write $A =_m^p B$ if $A \leq_m^p B$ and $B \leq_m^p A$. Note that for any sets A and B, $A \oplus B$ is the supremum of A and B with respect to $\leq_m^p$. Two recursive sets A and B form a *minimal pair* (for $\leq_m^p$) if $A \notin P$, $B \notin P$ but, for any set C, $C \leq_m^p A$ and $C \leq_m^p B$ imply that $C \in P$. We say that sets B and C *p-split* a set A if $B = A \cap D$ and $C = A \cap \overline{D}$ for some set $D \in P$. The splitting is *strict* if B and C form a minimal pair. In the following we will use the following straightforward propositions (proofs can be found in Ambos-Spies [2,3]).

Proposition 1. Let A, B, C be (recursive) sets.
  (a)   If B and C p-split A then $A =_m^p B \oplus C$.
  (b)   If $A \leq_m^p B \oplus C$ then there is a p-splitting of A into sets A_B and A_C such that $A_B \leq_m^p B$ and $A_C \leq_m^p C$.

Proposition 2. For any recursive set A the following are equivalent.
  (i)   A is the top of a minimal pair, i.e., there is a $\leq_m^p$-minimal pair B, C such that $A =_m^p B \oplus C$.
  (ii)   A has a strict p-splitting.

Complete sets without strict p-splittings

In this section we show that complete sets for the natural complexity classes extending exponential time do not have strict p-splittings. The key to this observation is the following technical result.

Theorem 1. Let **C** and **D** be recursively presentable classes which are closed under finite variants, and let F and G be sets such that $F \notin \mathbf{C}$, $G \notin \mathbf{D}$, and F and G are both in $DTIME(2^{O(n)})$. Then there is a set A such that
  (1) $A \in DTIME(2^{poly(n)})$
  (2) $A \notin \mathbf{C}$ and $A \notin \mathbf{D}$
  (3)   A has no strict p-splitting.

Before sketching the proof of the theorem, we state the corollaries we are interested in.

Corollary 1. Let E be $\leq_m^p$-complete for $DTIME(2^{O(n)})$. Then E is not the top of a minimal pair.

Proof. For a contradiction assume that E is the top of a minimal pair. Then, by Proposition 2, there is a strict p-splitting of E into sets F and G. Then F and G are p-m-incomparable. Hence for the classes

$$\mathbf{C} = \{ X : X \leq_m^p G\} \text{ and } \mathbf{D} = \{ X : X \leq_m^p F\},$$

$F \notin \mathbf{C}$ and $G \notin \mathbf{D}$. Moreover, the classes $\mathbf{C}$ and $\mathbf{D}$ are recursively presentable and closed under finite variants (see e.g. [3]). It follows, by Theorem 1, that there is a set A satisfying conditions (1) - (3). Now, since any set which is hard for $DTIME(2^{O(n)})$ is also hard for $DTIME(2^{poly(n)})$, condition (1) and Proposition 1(a) imply

$$A \leq_m^p E =_m^p F{\oplus}G,$$

whence, by Proposition 1 (b), there is a p-splitting of A into sets A_F and A_G such that

$$A_F \leq_m^p F \text{ and } A_G \leq_m^p G.$$

Since, by (2), $A \nleq_m^p F$ and $A \nleq_m^p G$, it follows that A_F and A_G are p-m-incomparable. Moreover, since F and G form a minimal pair it follows that A_F and A_G form a minimal pair too. Hence the p-splitting of A into A_F and A_G is strict contrary to (3). ◆

Corollary 1 can be extended to the common complexity classes extending $DTIME(2^{O(n)})$. First, using the observation of Book (see Ambos-Spies [1], Proposition 4) that, for any minimal pair E, F such E is $DTIME(2^{O(n)})$-complete, F is not elementarily recursive, we can show the following:

Corollary 2. Let D be any elementarily recursive set which is $\leq_m^p$-hard for $DTIME(2^{O(n)})$. Then D has no strict p-splitting.

Proof. For a contradiction assume that there is a strict p-splitting of D into sets F and G. By hardness of D, $E \leq_m^p D$ for some $DTIME(2^{O(n)})$-complete set E. Hence, by Proposition 1, there is a p-splitting of E into sets $E_F \leq_m^p F$ and $E_G \leq_m^p G$. Since, by Corollary 1, the splitting of E into E_F and E_G is not strict, the choice of F and G implies that either E_F or E_G is in P. By symmetry assume $E_F \in P$. Then $E =_m^p E_G \leq_m^p G$, whence E and the elementarily recursive set F form a minimal pair contrary to the observation of Book stated above. ◆

Corollary 2 shows that complete sets for the standard deterministic or nondeterministic exponential time or exponential space classes do not possess strict p-splittings. In Corollary 2 the assumption that D is elementarily recursive cannot be dropped: Ambos-Spies [1] has shown that every recursive set which is not polynomial time computable is half of a minimal pair. In particular, for any DTIME($2^{O(n)}$)-complete set E we can find a recursive (but not elementarily recursive) set F such that E and F form a minimal pair. So, E⊕F is DTIME($2^{O(n)}$)-hard and yet has the strict p-splitting into the sets 0E = {0x : x∈ E} and 1F = {1x : x∈ F}. By a slight modification of Theorem 1, we can show however, that for any DTIME($2^{O(n)}$)-hard set D satisfying

$$\forall X\,(\, X \leq_T^p D \Rightarrow X \leq_m^p D)$$

(where $\leq_T^p$ denotes polynomial time Turing reducibility), D has no strict p-splitting. Hence, for any complexity class **C** extending DTIME($2^{O(n)}$) and downward closed under p-Turing reducibility, no **C**-complete set has a strict p-splitting.

In the remainder of this section we sketch the *Proof of Theorem 1:* The required set A is enumerated in stages. Before stating the construction of A, we describe our strategies for satisfying (2) and (3) separately.

Condition (2) is enforced by a standard delayed diagonalization argument. We use the "structural" variant of this diagonalization introduced by Landweber, Lipton and Robertson [10], which has later been simplified and extended by Chew and Machtey [5], Schöning [12], Ambos-Spies [2] and others. Here we directly apply a diagonalization lemma of [2] and refer the reader for details to this paper. For stating the diagonalization lemma we need some notation.

For any numbers n < m we let

$$[[n,m)) = \{\, x\in \Sigma^* : n \leq |x| < m\}.$$

For a function g : N → N, we let $g^n(m)$ denote the n-th iteration of g on input m, i.e. $g^0(m)=m$ and $g^{n+1}(m)=g(g^n(m))$. The n-th *g-interval* on Σ^* is defined by

$$I_{g,n} = [[\, g^n(0),g^{n+1}(0)\,)).$$

Note that, for g satisfying g(n) > n, the collection $I_{g,n}$ (n≥0) of g-intervals gives a partition of the class Σ^* of all strings. Moreover, if the function g is polynomially honest (i.e. fully time constructible modulo a polynomial), then the function ind mapping a string x to the number n such that x∈ $I_{g,n}$ is polynomial time computable, whence, for any polynomial time computable set M of numbers,

$$I_{g,M} = \bigcup\nolimits_{n\in M} I_{g,n} \in P$$

(see [2]).

Lemma 1 (Ambos-Spies [2]). For **C**, **D**, F, G as in Theorem 1, there is a polynomially honest function g: N → N, g(n)>n, such that for any set X the following holds

(i) If there are infinitely many n such that $I_{g,n} \cap X = I_{g,n} \cap F$ then X∉ **C**.

(ii) If there are infinitely many n such that $I_{g,n} \cap X = I_{g,n} \cap G$ then $X \notin D$.

By Lemma 1, condition (2) will hold if we construct A so that

(4)   There are infinitely many numbers n such that $I_{g,2n} \cap A = I_{g,2n} \cap F$.

(5)   There are infinitely many numbers n such that $I_{g,2n+1} \cap A = I_{g,2n+1} \cap G$.

The strategy for satisfying condition (3) is more involved. We first describe the basic idea.

Let $\{P_e : e \in N\}$ be a standard enumeration of all polynomial time computable sets and let p_e be a polynomial bound for P_e. For each e we have to ensure that $A \cap P_e$ and $A \cap \overline{P_e}$ is not a strict p-splitting of A. If P_e or $\overline{P_e}$ is finite, then $A \cap P_e$ or $A \cap \overline{P_e}$ is finite too and hence in P, whence trivially the splitting is not strict. So without loss of generality we may assume

(6) $|P_e| = |\overline{P_e}| = \infty$.

Then we will build a set B_e such that

(7) $B_e \leq^p_m A \cap P_e$, $B_e \leq^p_m A \cap \overline{P_e}$, and $B_e \notin P$.

The basic observation used for constructing such a set B_e is that (6) implies that there are infinitely many *e-switching points*, i.e. infinitely many strings x such that $x \in P_e$ and $x+1 \notin P_e$ (where x+1 denotes the successor of the string x under the canonical ordering) and that (for fixed e) the set of e-switching points is polynomial time computable:

$$S_e = \{x : x \in P_e \text{ and } x+1 \notin P_e\} \in P.$$

Hence for a single set P_e satisfying (6) we can get a set B_e satisfying (7) by requiring

(8)   For all $x \in S_e$, $x \in B_e$ iff $x \in A$ iff $x+1 \in A$

and by letting

(9) $[A(x_i) =] B_e(x_i) = 1 - P_i(x_i)$,

where x_i is the i-th element of S_e. (Note that for e-switching x, x+1 is not e-switching. Hence there is no conflict between (8) and (9).) Then obviously (8) implies

(10) $B_e \leq^p_m A \cap P_e$ via f_0, where $f_0(x) = x$ for $x \in S_e$ and $f_0(x)$ is some fixed string $z_0 \notin P_e$ otherwise

and

(11) $B_e \leq^p_m A \cap \overline{P_e}$ via f_1, where $f_1(x) = x+1$ for $x \in S_e$ and $f_1(x)$ is some fixed string $z_1 \in P_e$ otherwise,

while (9) guarantees that B_e is not in P.

This basic strategy has to be refined when considering two or more sets P_e. For instance take P_e and $P_{e'}$ to be the sets

$$P_e = \{z_{2n} : n>0\} \text{ and } P_{e'} = \overline{P_e} = \{z_{2n+1} : n>0\},$$

where z_n is the n-th string in order. Then (8) for S_e and $S_{e'}$ requires

$$z_0 \in A \quad \text{iff} \quad z_1\,(= z_0+1) \in A \quad \text{(since } z_0 \in S_{e'})$$
$$\text{iff} \quad z_2\,(= z_1+1) \in A \quad \text{(since } z_1 \in S_e)$$
$$\text{iff} \quad z_3\,(= z_2+1) \in A \quad \text{(since } z_2 \in S_{e'})$$
$$\text{iff} \quad ...,$$

i.e. $A(x) = A(z_0)$ for all strings x, thereby leaving no room for the diagonalization required by (9). We overcome this difficulty by refining an argument of Ambos-Spies [3] where the above ideas have been used to build a (tally) set $A \notin P$ without strict p-splittings. There the above conflict is solved by assigning to each P_e a subset T_e of S_e such that for infinite S_e the subset T_e remains infinite and, for $e \neq e'$, T_e and $T_{e'}$ are *strongly disjoint*, i.e., for any $x \in T_e$ neither $x \in T_{e'}$ nor $x+1 \in T_{e'}$. Therefore any conflicts among the different P_e's are eliminated, and the i-th element of T_e can be used again to ensure $B_e \neq P_i$.

The sets T_e, however, cannot be chosen to be polynomial time computable anymore, whence the set B_e has to be replaced by a shifted version $B'_e = \{1^{f(|x|)}0x : x \in B_e\}$ of it (where f is some appropriate time constructible function) to ensure (7). Furthermore, the reductions of B'_e to $A \cap P_e$ and to $A \cap \overline{P_e}$ have to been replaced by appropriate nonhonest ones.

Here we refine this approach, thereby insuring that the sets T_e are uniformly decidable in exponential time. In the following we denote the sets T_e by Fol_e and call their elements *e-followers*. A further restriction on the definition of Fol_e is imposed by the conditions (4) and (5) which ensure that (2) holds. In the following definition this is ensured by comparing the function $\mathrm{fol}_e(x)$ with the functions $\mathrm{even}(x)$ and $\mathrm{odd}(x)$. These functions approximate the number of e-followers less than x and the number of even respectively odd g-intervals less than x which do not contain any followers nor (direct) successors of followers. In the following definition <-,-> is a polynomial pairing function on the natural numbers.

Definition. We say that a string x is an *e-candidate* if the following conditions hold

(C1) $\quad p_e(|x|) < 2^{|x|}$

(C2) $\quad 2^e < |x|$ and $e < n$, where $x \in I_{g,n}$

(C3) $\quad$ x is e-switching.

The notion *e-follower* and subsidiary functions fol_e, even, and odd are defined by a simultaneous induction on x: Given x, fix the unique number n such that $x \in I_{g,n}$.

(a) For $e < n$ and $2^e < |x|$ let

$\mathrm{fol}_e(x) = $ the number of e-followers $y < x$ that can be found

by simulating the definition for $|x|$ steps
(Otherwise, $fol_e(x)=0$)

(b) Let

even(x) [odd(x)] = the number of even [odd] g-intervals $I_{g,2m[+1]}$ $(2m+1<n)$ containing neither an e-follower (for any $e \leq m$) nor the successor of such a follower, that can be found by simulating the definition for $|x|$ steps

(c) The string x becomes an *e-follower* if x is an e-candidate and the following conditions hold:

(C4) For any $e' \neq e$ $(e' < n+1)$: If x-1 or x or x+1 is an e'-candidate, then $<e,fol_e(x)> < <e',fol_{e'}(x)>$

(C5) even(x) $> <e,fol_e(x)>$ and odd(x) $> <e,fol_e(x)>$

Condition (C4) ensures that for each x there is at most one e such that x becomes an e-follower. Moreover the condition ensures that the assignments are fair, i.e., that if there are infinitely many e-switching strings then there are infinitely many e-followers. Similarly, (C5) ensures that there are infinitely many even and odd g-intervals free of followers and successors of followers.

The desired properties of the just defined notions are summarized in the following lemma.

Lemma 2. (a) The functions $fol_e(x)$, even(x) and odd(x) are nondecreasing and linear time computable.

(b) The function fol_e is unbounded iff there are infinitely many e-followers.

(c) The function even [odd] is unbounded iff there are infinitely many even [odd] g-intervals without followers and successors of followers.

(d) If P_e is infinite and coinfinite then there are infinitely many e-switching strings.

(e) There are infinitely many even [odd] g-intervals without followers and successors of followers.

(f) The functions even and odd are unbounded.

(g) If x is an e-follower than x is an e-switching string. If x is an e-switching string, then x+1 is not e-switching.

(h) If there are infinitely many e-switching strings, then the set Fol_e of e-followers is infinite.

(i) For $e \neq e'$ the sets Fol_e and $Fol_{e'}$ are strongly disjoint.

(j) For Fol = $\{<e,x> : x \in Fol_e\}$, Fol $\in$ DTIME($2^{O(n^2)}$).

Proof (sketch). **(a)**, **(b)**, **(c)** and **(d)** are straightforward by definition. **(e)** For a contradiction assume that there are only finitely many even g-intervals free of followers and their successors. Then, by (c), even is bounded. Hence, by condition (C5) and part (b) of the lemma, only finitely many followers will be appointed. A contradiction. **(f)** directly follows from (c) and (e). **(g)** is immediate by definitions.

(h) For a contradiction assume that there are infinitely many e-switching strings but the number of e-followers is finite, say y is the greatest e-follower. Then we can fix numbers $|y| < k_0 < k_1 < k_2 < k_3 < k_4$ such that

(i)   for any string x of length $\geq k_0$, (C1) and (C2) hold

(ii) $fol_e(y) < k_1$ for all y.

(iii)   for any $e' < <e,k_1>$, for which $fol_{e'}$ is bounded, there is no e'-follower y with $|y| \geq k_2$

(iv)   for any $e'< <e,k_1>$ for which $fol_{e'}$ is unbounded and for any string y of length $\geq k_3$, $fol_{e'}(y) > <e,k_1>$

(v)   for any string y of length $\geq k_4$, even (y) $> <e, k_1>$ and odd(y) $> <e,k_1>$

Note that k_1 exists by assumption and (b); k_2 by (b); k_3 by (a) and (b); and k_4 by (a),(c) and (e). Now, for any e-switching string x with $|x| > k_4$, conditions (C1)-(C5) of the above definition are satisfied, whence x becomes an e-follower. This contradicts maximality of y.

(i) follows from condition (C4) in the definition of e-followers.

(j) We first observe that for given e,x we can decide in $O(2^{|x|})$ steps whether x is an e-candidate. Hence, in $O(|x|2^{|x|})$ steps we can generate the list $e_0 < e_1 < ... < e_n$ of all numbers e' such that x-1, x or x+1 is an e'-candidate (note that $n < e_n < |x|$). Moreover, for each e_i we can compute $<e_i,fol_{e_i}(x)>$ and then find the j for which this coded pair becomes maximal (O(|x|) steps). Obviously, x is e-follower if $e=e_j$.

This completes the proof of Lemma 2. ◆

The next lemma formally describes the way we will reduce the set B_e to $A \cap P_e$ and $A \cap \overline{P_e}$.

Lemma 3. Fix P_e satisfying (6). Let X be any recursive set such that, for any e-follower x, X(x)=X(x+1) and let

$$B_{X,e} = \{1^m 0x : x \in Fol_e \text{ and } x \in X \text{ and } m=2^{(|x|^2)}\}.$$

Then $B_{X,e} \leq^p_m X \cap P_e$ and $B_{X,e} \leq^p_m X \cap \overline{P_e}$.

Proof. By Lemma 2 (j), the set

$$C_{X,e} = \{1^m 0x : x \in Fol_e \text{ and } m=2^{(|x|^2)}\}$$

is polynomial time computable. Hence $B_{X,e} \leq^p_m X \cap P_e$ via f_0 where $f_0(y) = x$ if $y = 1^m 0x \in C_{X,e}$ and $f_0(y) =$ some fixed string $z_0 \notin P_e$ otherwise; and $B_{X,e} \leq^p_m X \cap \overline{P_e}$ via f_1 where $f_1(y) = x+1$ if $y = 1^m 0x \in C_{X,e}$ and $f_1(y) =$ some fixed string $z_1 \in P_e$ otherwise. ◆

We are now ready to state the *construction* of A:

Input x

Fix n, $i \leq 1$ such that $x \in I_{g,2n+i}$.

Case 1: x is an e-follower for some e.

Then by an $|x|$-bounded search look for numbers k which have been e-certified (see below) before. Let k_0 be the greatest such number k (found in $|x|$ steps) which satisfies

$p_{k+1}(2^{(|x|^2)}) \leq 2^{(|x|^3)}$. (If there is no such k let k_0 = -1.) Let

$A(x) = 1 - P_{k_0+1}(1^m 0x)$ where $m = 2^{(|x|^2)}$.

Moreover say that k_0+1 has been *e-certified at x*.

Case 2: x-1 is an e-follower for some e.
Then let $A(x) = A(x-1)$.

Case 3: Otherwise.
Then let $A(x)=F(x)$ if $i=0$ and $A(x)=G(x)$ if $i=1$.

This completes the construction. Note that, by Lemma 2(i) and (g), for each x there is exactly one case which applies to x, and, in Cases 1 and 2, the number e is uniquely determined. Hence A is well defined. Obviously $A \in$ DTIME($2^{O(n^3)}$). Moreover, by Lemma 2(e) and by Case 3 of the construction, (4) and (5) are satisfied, whence, by Lemma 1, $A \notin C$ and $A \notin D$. It remains to show that A has no strict p-splitting. So fix P_e satisfying (6) and define $B_{A,e}$ as in Lemma 3. Since $A(x)=A(x+1)$ for any e-follower x, Lemma 3 implies that $B_{A,e} \leq_m^p A \cap P_e$ and $B_{A,e} \leq_m^p A \cap \overline{P_e}$. So it suffices to show that $B_{A,e} \notin P$, i.e., $B_{A,e} \neq P_k$ for all numbers k. Fix k. Note that if k is e-certified at x then

$$B_{A,e}(1^m 0x) = A(x) \neq P_k(1^m 0x) \quad (m=2^{(|x|^2)}),$$

whence it is sufficient that k becomes e-certified. Since there are infinitely many e-followers (Lemma 2 (d) and (h)) and since

$$p_k(2^{(|x|^2)}) \leq 2^{(|x|^3)}$$

for all sufficiently large x, this follows by a straightforward induction on k. ♦

NP-complete sets and strict p-splittings.

We shall show now that in contrast to the preceding results an answer to the question whether or not the NP-complete sets possess strict p-splittings is oracle dependent, even if we require P$\neq$NP. Since Proposition 2 relativizes this will show that any solution to the question whether the NP-complete p-m-degree is the top of a minimal pair does not relativize. The corresponding result for PSPACE-complete sets can also be obtained along the lines described below.

Theorem 2. There are recursive sets A and B such that

(i) $NP^A \neq P^A$ and no NP^A-complete set possesses a strict p^A-splitting.

(ii) $NP^B \neq P^B$ and every NP^B-complete set possesses a strict p^B-splitting.

Proof (sketch). Part (i) directly follows from the relativization of Corollary 2, since Heller [7] has constructed an oracle A such that $NP^A = DTIME^A(2^{POLY})$.
In case of part (ii), we only outline the ideas underlying the proof. Let

$$K^B = \{<e,x,0^n> : N_e(B) \text{ accepts } x \text{ in less than } n \text{ steps}\},$$

where $N_e(B)$, $e>0$, is a standard enumeration of all nondeterministic oracle Turing machines (with oracle set B). Then K^B is NP^B-complete for any oracle B (see Baker et al. [4]). We will construct B recursive such that K^B has a strict p^B-splitting. To be more specific, we will construct a partition of Σ^* into three polynomial time computable sets C_0, C_1, C_2 such that

(12) $K^B \cap C_i \notin P^B$ for i=0,2

(13) $K^B \cap C_1 \in P^B$

(14) If $D \leq^{p^B}_m K^B \cap C_0$ and $D \leq^{p^B}_m K^B \cap C_2$ then $D \in P^B$

Then, obviously $K^B \cap (C_0 \cup C_2)$ will be NP^B-complete (by (13)), and $K^B \cap C_0$ and $K^B \cap C_2$ will strictly p^B-split $K^B \cap (C_0 \cup C_2)$ (by (12) and (14)). By p-m-invariance of p-splitability (Proposition 2), it follows that every NP^B-complete set has a strict p^B-splitting. (Moreover, this obviously implies that $P^B \neq NP^B$.)

The construction of the set B combines Baker, Gill and Solovay's techniques in [4] to build oracles separating P from NP and collapsing NP to P (the latter by making $K^X = X$ for the oracle X) with the minimal pair technique in the style of Ladner [9].

For some p-honest function g: N $\rightarrow$ N defined in the course of the construction of B, we will have

$C_i = \bigcup_{n \in N} I_{g,4n+1+i}$ (i=0,2)

$C_1 = \bigcup_{n \in N} I_{g,2n}$

(for notation see the proof of Theorem 1). Since our construction uses the basic idea of Ladner's minimal pair construction, we shortly summarize the basic features of this construction and say what changes will become necessary.

In Ladner's construction, a top A of a minimal pair is built by constructing an appropriate function g, and, for C_i as above, it is insured that $A \cap C_1$ is empty while $A \cap C_0$ and $A \cap C_2$ form a minimal pair. Note that any two g-intervals contained in C_0 and C_2, respectively, are separated by a g-interval in C_1 (a "gap"). By making the gaps longer than a time bound for A, Ladner guaranteed that in a simultaneous reduction of a set D to $A \cap C_0$ and $A \cap C_2$ the oracle query y about A in the C_0 part or C_1 part has to be so short that, relative to the length of the input x of the reduction, A(y) can be computed in $O(|x|)$ steps, thereby ensuring that always one of the two sides of the reduction will be trivial, whence $D \in P$. On the other hand, by a straightforward diagonalization, Ladner made $A \cap C_i \neq P_e$ on some string of the e-th g-interval in C_i, thereby achieving $A \cap C_i \notin P$ (i=0,2).

In our proof, where, roughly speaking, A has to be replaced by K^B (and were it suffices to work relative to B), Ladner's construction is modified as follows: To ensure (12), we use a diagonalization argument related to Baker, Gill and Solovay's construction of an oracle separating P = NP. Again the idea is to define B on the e-th g-interval of C_i so that $K^B \cap C_i \neq P^B_e$ (i=0,2). On the other hand, to make K^B B-easy on C_1, we here use Baker, Gill and Solovay's strategy to make $K^B = B$. (Note that we cannot let B look like the empty set on C_1 because then K^B looks like the NP-complete set K on C_1, whence the construction will fail if $P \neq NP$.) Hence on consecutive g-intervals we alternately play the $P \neq NP$ and the $P = NP$ strategies. ◆

Open Problems

Our proofs heavily depend on the distributivity property of $\leq^p_m$ stated in Proposition 1 (b). Since this property fails for p-Turing reducibility (see [2]), the corresponding questions for this reducibility remain open. Recently Downey [6] has announced that there is a recursive set $A \notin P$ which is not the top of a minimal pair for $\leq^p_T$. His proof uses a variant of the technique of [1], however, which does not yield elementary recursive sets.

References

[1] K. Ambos-Spies, Minimal pairs for polynomial time reducibilities, in Computation Theory and Logic, E. Börger ed. , Lecture Notes in Computer Science, 270, (1987), 1-14.

[2] K. Ambos-Spies, Polynomial time degrees of NP sets, in Current Trends in Theoretical Computer Science, E. Börger ed. , Computer Science Press, 1987.

[3]   K. Ambos-Spies, An inhomogeneity in the polynomial time degrees, SIAM J. Comput. 15 (1986) 958-963.

[4]   T. Baker, J. Gill and R. Solovay, Relativizations of the P=?NP questions, SIAM J. Comput. 4 (1975), 431-442.

[5]   P. Chew and M. Machtey, A note on structure and looking back applied to the relative complexity of computable functions, J. Computer System Sci. 22 (1981), 53-59.

[6]   R. Downey, Nondiamond theorems for polynomial time reducibility (to appear).

[7]   H. Heller, Relativized polynomial hierarchy extending two levels, Thesis, Technische Universität Munich, (1980).

[8]   S. Homer and W. Maass, Oracle dependent properties of the lattice of NP sets, Theor. Comp. Science 24 (1983), 279-289.

[9]   R. E. Ladner, On the structure of polynomial time reducibility, JACM 22 (1975), 155-171.

[10] L. H. Landweber, R. J. Lipton and E.L. Robertson, On the structure of sets in NP and other complexity classes, Theor. Comp. Sci. 15 (1981), 103-123.

[11] M.Machtey, Minimal pairs of polynomial degrees with subexponential complexity, Theor. Comp. Sci. 2 (1976), 73-76.

[12] U. Schöning, A uniform approach to obtain diagonal sets in complexity classes, Theor. Comp. Sci. 18 (1982), 95-103.

[13] U. Schöning, Minimal pairs for P, Theor. Comp. Sci. 31 (1984), 41-48.

Hiding Instances in Multioracle Queries
(Extended Abstract)

Donald Beaver   and   Joan Feigenbaum

Aiken Computation Laboratory   AT&T Bell Labs, Rm 2C473

Harvard University   600 Mountain Avenue

Cambridge, MA 02138 USA   Murray Hill, NJ 07974 USA

beaver@harvard.harvard.edu   jf@research.att.com

Abstract

Abadi, Feigenbaum, and Kilian have considered *instance-hiding schemes* [1]. Let f be a function for which no randomized polynomial-time algorithm is known; randomized polynomial-time machine A wants to query an oracle B for f to obtain $f(x)$, without telling B exactly what x is. It is shown in [1] that, if f is an NP-hard function, A cannot query a single oracle B while hiding all but the size of the instance, assuming that the polynomial hierarchy does not collapse. This negative result holds for *all* oracles B, including those that are non-r.e.

In this paper, we generalize the definition of instance-hiding schemes to allow A to query several oracles $B_1, \ldots, B_m$ that are not allowed to communicate. We show that *every* function f *does* have a multioracle instance-hiding scheme, thus settling a question of Rivest.

1   Introduction

The following question is a special case of the one addressed by Abadi, Feigenbaum, and Kilian in [1]. Processor A needs the value $f(x)$ for some x but lacks the power to compute it. Processor B has the power to compute f and is willing to send $f(y)$ to A, for any $y \in Dom(f)$. Can A map the *cleartext instance* x to an *encrypted instance* y in such a way that A can infer $f(x)$ from $f(y)$, but B can infer only $|x|$ from y? If so, then the protocol that A and B use to accomplish this is called a *1-oracle instance-hiding scheme for f*.

Abadi, Feigenbaum, and Kilian developed a formal model in which to prove that an instance-hiding scheme leaks at most some function L of the instance or that it hides at least some function H. The practical motivation for their work was the possibility that a weak, private computing device, such as a smart card or terminal, could take advantage of a powerful, shared computing device while keeping private some important aspects of its user's data. The theoretical motivation was the question of whether several well-studied number-theoretic functions, such as discrete logarithm and quadratic residuosity, which *do* have 1-oracle schemes that hide some significant information about the cleartext instance, are examples of a more general phenomenon; that is, do they share this property with other seemingly intractable problems, such as SAT?

The main result in [1] is negative: no NP-hard function has a 1-oracle instance-hiding scheme that leaks at most $|x|$, unless the polynomial hierarchy collapses. The proof draws on a connection between 1-oracle instance-hiding schemes and the nonuniform complexity classes NP/poly and CoNP/poly, and it is related to other complexity-theoretic notions, such as random-self-reducibility. This negative result holds even if B is modeled as an oracle Turing Machine and is given access to an arbitrary (non-r.e.) oracle set. Full details can be found in [1].

The following question, originally posed by Rivest [16], was left open in [1]: suppose that the weak processor A is allowed to query multiple powerful processors, say B_1 through B_m, where m is polynomial in $|x|$, and the B_i's are kept physically separate? In other words, if allowed to communicate, some subset of the "oracles" B_1 through B_m may be able to determine x, but, in isolation, no B_i can deduce more than $|x|$ from the "encrypted query" y_i that it receives from A. Do NP-hard functions have such m-oracle instance-hiding schemes?

In this paper, we provide positive answers to Rivest's question. We model m-oracle instance-hiding schemes in two ways:

- Oracles B_1 through B_m may collude before the start of the protocol with A, but they are kept physically separate during the protocol. In this model, $m = |x|$ oracles suffice for any function f.

- Oracles B_1 through B_m may not collude at all, either before or during the protocol. In this model, $m = 2$ oracles suffice for any function f. Conversely, there are boolean functions f for which two oracles are necessary.

In the first model, our proof of sufficiency demonstrates an unintuitive connection between instance-hiding schemes and secure multiparty protocols [7, 8]. The connection is unintuitive for many reasons, the most obvious of which is that, in the first problem, we require explicitly that the oracles not communicate at all and, in the second problem, we require that they communicate extensively. More fundamentally, the two problems seem at first to exemplify two incompatible views of distributed computations with secret data. The instance-hiding problem first defined in [1] and generalized in Section 2 below formalizes the following view. Weak processor A requires interaction with powerful processors B_1 through B_m, *because A does not have enough computational resources to compute f*; A does not want to reveal more than necessary about its private input x because the B_i's are public resources. The secure-multiparty-protocol problem defined with complexity-theoretic assumptions in [18] and with non-complexity-theoretic assumptions in [7, 8] formalizes an alternative view: mutually untrusting, *equally powerful* processors B_1 through B_m must interact in a computation *because each of them has a private input x_i without which the computation cannot proceed.*

Preliminary versions of our results first appeared in two technical reports [3, 4]. In what follows, proofs are often sketched or omitted because of space limitations; full proofs of all claims will appear in the final paper.

2 Preliminaries

Following Abadi, Feigenbaum, and Kilian, we take A to be a randomized polynomial-time Turing Machine transducer [1]. Player A wishes to compute $f(x)$, where f is a boolean function of $\{0,1\}^*$ for which no randomized polynomial-time algorithm is known. A does this by communicating with players B_1, ..., B_m, where m is (necessarily) bounded by a polynomial in $|x|$. We model the B_i's as oracle Turing Machine transducers that can use an unbounded amount of time and space. It is convenient to think of the oracle tape of B_i as a random variable O_i; so B_i is completely specified by its finite control and the value of O_i.

An *m-oracle instance-hiding scheme* for f is a ρ-round, synchronous protocol executed by players A, B_1, ..., B_m; the round-complexity ρ is also bounded by a polynomial in $|x|$. In one round, A can do a randomized polynomial-time local computation, send a message to each B_i, and receive a message from each B_i. Also in one round, B_i can receive a message from A, do an unbounded amount of local computation, and send a message to A. Let τ_r denote the sequence of messages sent and received by A in rounds 1 through r, and let R_A denote the random tape of A. In the last round, A uses x, τ_ρ, and R_A to compute $f(x)$.

The input x is drawn from a distribution X. For $1 \leq i \leq m$, the message $y_{r+1,i}$ that A sends to B_i in round $r + 1$ is determined by x, τ_r, R_A, and A's finite control, which we denote by C_A. Let Y_i be the induced distribution on the sequence $\langle y_{1,i}, \ldots, y_{\rho,i} \rangle$.

We wish to make precise the statements that an instance-hiding scheme "leaks at most" some function $L(x)$ to player B_i or that it "hides at least" some function $H(x)$ from player B_i. Note that $L(X)$ and $H(X)$ are also induced random variables.

We consider two generalizations of the definitions in [1]. In both models, all players "know" the plaintext distribution X and the contents of the finite controls C_A, C_{B_1}, ..., C_{B_m}. Furthermore, in both models, each player B_i "does not know" the content of the random tape R_A, and, for $i \neq j$, player B_i "does not see" the messages $y_{r,j}$ that A sends to B_j or the responses that B_j sends back. The difference between the two models lies in whether or not B_i "knows" the content of oracle tape O_j.

Model 1:
(a *type1* m-oracle instance-hiding scheme)

- An instance-hiding scheme *leaks at most* L to oracle B_i if, for all plaintext distributions X, for all $u \in Range(L)$, the random variables X and $\langle Y_i, O_1, \ldots, O_m \rangle$ are independent given $L(X) = u$.

- An instance-hiding scheme *hides at least* H from oracle B_i if, for all plaintext distributions X, the random variables $H(X)$ and $\langle Y_i, O_1, \ldots, O_m \rangle$ are independent.

Thus, in Model 1, B_i "knows" O_j. Informally, this corresponds to the case in which the powerful players can collude before, but not during, the execution of the protocol.

Model 2:
(a *type2* m-oracle instance-hiding scheme)

- An instance-hiding scheme *leaks at most* L to oracle B_i if, for all plaintext distributions X, for all $u \in Range(L)$, the random variables X and $\langle Y_i, O_i \rangle$ are independent given $L(X) = u$.

- An instance-hiding scheme *hides at least* H from oracle B_i if, for all plaintext distributions X, the random variables $H(X)$ and $\langle Y_i, O_i \rangle$ are independent.

Thus, in Model 2, B_i "does not know" O_j. Informally, this corresponds to the case in which the powerful players cannot collude at all, before or during the execution of the protocol.

In either model, we say that the scheme "leaks L" if it leaks at most L to each B_i, and we say that it "hides H" if it hides at least H from each oracle B_i. Throughout this paper, we are primarily concerned with schemes that leak $|x|$. In either model, if we say that "f has an m-oracle instance-hiding scheme" or that "m oracles suffice for f," we mean that f has an m-oracle instance-hiding scheme that leaks $|x|$. As in [1], we must define leaking and hiding in terms of independence of random variables. Complexity-based cryptography is irrelevant, because A is time-bounded and the B_i's are time-unbounded.

Proposition 2.1: Models 1 and 2 are equivalent if $m = 1$.

The main theorem of [1] is that NP-hard functions have no 1-oracle instance-hiding schemes that leak $|x|$, unless the polynomial hierarchy collapses at the third level. This is a conditional negative result. No unconditional negative results about instance-hiding schemes that leak $|x|$ are provided in [1]. We give one here.

Lemma 2.1 *Random boolean functions do not have 1-oracle instance-hiding schemes that leak at most $|x|$.*

Proof (sketch): A "random boolean function" f is constructed by tossing a fair coin to determine $f(x)$ for each $x \in \{0,1\}^*$. Let S be the set of all x for which $f(x) = 1$. Consider the infinite sequence cv_0, cv_1, cv_2, ..., where cv_n is the characteristic vector of $S \cap \{0,1\}^n$ (e.g., cv_2 is the concatentation of $f(00)$, $f(01)$, $f(10)$, and $f(11)$). Because f is truly random, cv_n is a string whose Kolmogorov complexity is approximately 2^n. Suppose that f had a 1-oracle instance-hiding scheme that leaked $|x|$. Then the proof of the main theorem in [1] shows that S would be in NP/*poly*. This in turn would imply the existence of a polynomial p such that the Kolmogorov complexity of cv_n is bounded by $p(n)$, yielding a contradiction. ∎

We end this section with a lemma that shows that, if the querier A is limited in space, but not in time or in number of rounds of interaction with the B_i's, then the instance-hiding problem is trivial.

Lemma 2.2 *Every function has a 1-oracle instance-hiding scheme that leaks at most $|x|$ in which the querier A is limited to constant space. Moreover, a deterministic constant-space querier suffices.*

Refer to, e.g., [9, 10, 11, 14] for a discussion of the related topic of (zero-knowledge) interactive proof systems with space-bounded verifiers.

3   Model 1: $|x|$ Oracles Suffice

Our main result on type1 instance-hiding schemes uses Shamir's *secret sharing* protocol [17], which we now review. Let P_0, ..., P_{m-1} be a collection of players, and let E be a finite field of at least m elements. Assign to each P_i, $1 \leq i \leq m - 1$, a distinct $\alpha_i \in E$. Player P_0 *t-secretly shares* an element $s \in E$ with P_1, ..., P_{m-1} as follows. Choose a_1, ..., a_t uniformly at random from E, set $p(x) = s + a_1 x + \cdots + a_t x^t$, and (privately) give $p(\alpha_i)$ to P_i, $1 \leq i \leq m - 1$. We call $p(\alpha_i)$ a *t-share* of s. This scheme has the property that no coalition of up to t players can infer anything about s from its t-shares.

Let C_n be an n-input, 1-output boolean circuit composed of AND gates, OR gates, and NOT gates, and let E be a finite field. Recall that C_n can be simulated by an n-input, 1-output arithmetic circuit over E composed of MULTIPLY gates, ADD gates, and MULTIPLY-BY-CONSTANT gates as follows. Boolean 0's and 1's correspond to the 0 and 1 elements of E. AND gates with fan-in k correspond to k-ary MULTIPLY gates. An OR gate with inputs b_1 and b_2 corresponds to a circuit that implements $b_1 + b_2 + (-1) \times b_1 \times b_2$; this can be generalized in the obvious way to accommodate OR gates with fan-in $k > 2$. For our purposes, it suffices to note that an OR gate with fan-in k can be simulated directly by a k-ary ADD gate if it is known that at most one of its inputs is 1. A NOT gate with input b corresponds to a circuit that implements $1 + (-1) \times b$.

If elements γ_1, ..., γ_k of E are t-shares of secrets s_1, ..., s_k, respectively, then $\gamma_1 + \cdots + \gamma_k$ is a t-share of $s_1 + \cdots + s_k$; $\beta \times \gamma_i$ is a t-share of $\beta \times s_i$, for any $1 \leq i \leq k$ and any CONSTANT-MULTIPLIER β; and $\gamma_1 \times \cdots \times \gamma_k$ is a kt-share of $s_1 \times \cdots \times s_k$. Note that the degree of the polynomial one must interpolate in order to reconstruct a secret product is the sum of the degrees of the interpolation polynomials for the secret factors.

Theorem 3.1 *Every function has a type1 $|x|$-oracle instance-hiding scheme that leaks at most $|x|$.*

Proof (sketch):

Assume WLOG that f is boolean. The result for general functions then follows by regarding each output bit as a boolean function of the input. We first sketch a proof that $|x| + 1$ oracles suffice and then show how this construction can be improved. Let $\{C_n\}_{n=1}^{\infty}$ be a DNF circuit family for f. An n-bit input x is denoted $x_1 x_2 \cdots x_n$. For each n, let E_n be a finite field of size greater than n, and let $\alpha_{1,n}, \ldots, \alpha_{n+1,n}$ be $n + 1$ distinct elements of E_n. Player B_i, $1 \leq i \leq n + 1$, is given C_n, E_n, and $\alpha_{i,n}$.

Recall that, throughout the execution of the protocol, B_i can use its unbounded resources to try to recover x, but it cannot communicate with any B_j, $j \neq i$. In secret-sharing terms, this means that the only coalitions that are physically possible are trivial coalitions of size 1.

We can now describe the basic protocol. On input $x = x_1 x_2 \cdots x_n$, A first sends n to each B_i, and B_i sends back $\alpha_{i,n}$. A then 1-secretly shares each bit x_j with $B_1, \ldots, B_{n+1}$. Each B_i simulates C_n (with an arithmetic circuit over E_n) on its 1-shares of the inputs and sends its n-share of the output to A. Finally, A interpolates the $n + 1$ shares of the output; the constant term of the interpolation polynomial is $f(x)$.[1]

Note that this protocol satisfies the definition of a type1 instance-hiding scheme: B_i gains no information from the contents of the oracle tape of B_j provided that the communication between A and B_j is private. Indeed, the $n + 1$ oracle tapes can be made identical.

To reduce the number of B_i's queried in the protocol from $n + 1$ to n, we can "instantiate" the input bit x_1 and treat f as though it were a function of $n - 1$ inputs. A first executes the basic protocol on input $0x_2 \cdots x_n$, then executes it on input $1x_2 \cdots x_n$, and interpolates whichever result corresponds to the original input $x_1 x_2 \cdots x_n$. By instantiating $O(\log n)$ input bits, the number of B_i's queried can be reduced to $n - O(\log n)$.

∎

Beaver, Feigenbaum, Kilian, and Rogaway [5] recently improved the upper bound of Theorem 3.1 from $|x|$ to $|x|/\log|x|$.

---

[1] Note that the degree of the arithmetic circuit is in fact n, because C_n is DNF: each of the 2^n monomials has degree n and the disjunction can be implemented by 2^n-ary addition (which preserves degree), because at most one of its inputs is 1.

The techniques of secret sharing and arithmetic circuit simulation were first used in [7, 8] to construct privacy-preserving protocols for distributed computations by many equally-powerful players.

4   Model 2: Two Oracles Suffice

In this section, it is convenient to regard a boolean function f as the characteristic function χ_S of a set $S \subseteq \{0,1\}^*$. By *a random set S*, we mean one in which $\chi_S(x)$ is the outcome of a fair coin toss, for each $x \in \{0,1\}^*$. The expression $S_1 \triangle S_2$ denotes the symmetric difference of sets S_1 and S_2; that is,

$$\chi_{S_1 \triangle S_2}(x) \equiv \chi_{S_1}(x) \oplus \chi_{S_2}(x).$$

If s_1 and s_2 are both n-bit strings, then $s_1 \oplus s_2$ is the n-bit string whose i^{th} bit is the exclusive-or of the ith bits of s_1 and s_2.

We also use the following nonstandard terminology and notation. A *singleton sequence* is a subset of $\{0,1\}^*$ that contains exactly one string of each length. A *random singleton sequence* is one in which the length-n string is chosen u.a.r. from $\{0,1\}^n$. If S is an arbitrary set and $V = \{v_1, v_2, \ldots\}$ is an arbitrary singleton sequence, then $S \circ V$ denotes the set with characteristic function

$$\chi_{S \circ V}(x) \equiv \chi_S(x \oplus v_{|x|}).$$

Note that each v_n in V effects a permutation of the characteristic vector of $S \cap \{0,1\}^n$.

Theorem 4.1 *Every function has a type2 2-oracle instance-hiding scheme that leaks at most $|x|$. Conversely, there are boolean functions for which 2 oracles are necessary.*

Proof (sketch): Necessity follows from Proposition 2.1 and Lemma 2.1. We show sufficiency by demonstrating the existence of a type2 2-oracle instance-hiding scheme for an arbitrary function χ_S that leaks at most $|x|$. As in Theorem 3.1, we assume WLOG that f is boolean.

The basic idea of the proof is evident in the following simpler argument. Assume first that the conditional plaintext distribution $P(X \mid |X|)$ is uniform. Under this simplifying assumption, it is clear that the characteristic function of a random set S has a type2

2-oracle instance-hiding scheme that, with probability 1, leaks at most $|x|$ to B_1 and at most $\chi_S(x)$ to B_2: Let $V = \{v_n\}_{n=1}^{\infty}$ be a random singleton sequence, give V to B_1, and give $S \circ V$ to B_2. On cleartext input x, A first sends $|x|$ to B_1, who sends back $v_{|x|}$. A then sends $x \oplus v_{|x|}$ to B_2, who sends back $\chi_{S \circ V}(x \oplus v_{|x|}) = \chi_S(x)$. Obviously, B_1 learns only $|x|$. Intuitively, B_2 learns only $\chi_S(x)$ because, for random S and V, $S \circ V$ is also random, and the encrypted inputs $x \oplus v_{|x|}$ are uniformly distributed n-bit strings. To make this idea work for the theorem as stated, we must make an arbitary S "look random," and we must show how to avoid leaking $\chi_S(x)$ to B_2. We accomplish this by using the symmetric difference of S with a random set and by "splitting" the singleton sequence V into two halves, one of which is given to each of B_1 and B_2.

Suppose that χ_S is the (arbitrary) boolean function for which we seek an instance-hiding scheme. Let R be a random set, $V = \{v_n\}_{n=1}^{\infty}$ and $U = \{b_{1n}\}_{n=1}^{\infty}$ be random singleton sequences, and let $T = \{b_{2n}\}_{n=1}^{\infty}$ be such that $b_{2n} = v_n \oplus b_{1n}$. B_1 is given $R \circ V$ and U, and B_2 is given $(S \triangle R) \circ V$ and T. The instance-hiding scheme is as follows.

A: $n \leftarrow |x|$.
A $\rightarrow$ B_1, B_2: n.
$B_1 \rightarrow$ A: b_{1n}.
$B_2 \rightarrow$ A: b_{2n}.
A: $y \leftarrow x \oplus b_{1n} \oplus b_{2n}$.
A $\rightarrow$ B_1, B_2: y.
$B_1 \rightarrow$ A: $\chi_{R \circ V}(y)$.
$B_2 \rightarrow$ A: $\chi_{(S \triangle R) \circ V}(y)$.
A: $\chi_S(x) \leftarrow \chi_{R \circ V}(y) \oplus \chi_{(S \triangle R) \circ V}(y)$.

Here, as in the proof of Theorem 3.1, a complete proof (given in the full paper) entails detailed specifications of B_1 and B_2 as oracle Turing Machines. It also entails showing how to remove the assumption that $P(X \mid |X|)$ is uniform. Essentially, this is done by splitting S into many pairs $(R_i \circ V_i, U_i), ((S \triangle R_i) \circ V_i, T_i)$, instead of one pair, and giving half of each pair to B_1 and B_2. ∎

5   Random-Self-Reducing Circuits

Intuitively, a random-self-reduction of a set S is an expected-polynomial-time, randomized algorithm that maps S to S, maps $\overline{S}$ to $\overline{S}$, and, on each input x in S, outputs, with equal probability, each y in $S \cap \{0, 1\}^{|x|}$. Abadi, Feigenbaum, and Kilian defined random-self-reducing algorithms rigorously and related them to 1-oracle instance-hiding schemes [1]. In this section, we consider random-self-reducing *circuits* in the same context.

A *randomized* PSIZE *circuit family* is a set $\{C_n\}_{n=1}^{\infty}$ of circuits in which the number of gates in C_n is at most $p(n)$, for some polynomial p, an input string x to C_n has length n, and the number of random bits that C_n uses is $q(n)$, for some polynomial q. The family $\{C_n\}$ can be viewed as an ordinary polynomial-size circuit family in which C_n takes n user-supplied input bits x_1 through x_n and $q(n)$ random input bits r_1 through $r_{q(n)}$ and gives as output a sample point of a distribution $D_n(x)$. For certain choices of $r = r_1 \cdots r_{q(n)}$, the circuit C_n may fail to produce a value in $D_n(x)$, in which case it outputs some distinguished string $\Lambda \notin D_n(x)$ to indicate failure. The *expected running time* $\mu_x(C_{|x|})$ of $C_{|x|}$ on input x is the expected number of random vectors r that must be chosen u.a.r. from $\{0,1\}^{q(n)}$ before $C_{|x|}$, on input x, r, produces an element of $D_n(x)$. We say that the circuit family $\{C_n\}_{n=1}^{\infty}$ *runs in expected polynomial time* if there is a polynomial t such that, for all x, $\mu_x(C_{|x|}) \leq t(|x|)$.

Definition 5.1 *A set S has* random-self-reducing circuits *if there is a randomized* PSIZE *circuit family $\{C_n\}_{n=1}^{\infty}$ that runs in expected polynomial time such that, for all $x \in S$, $D_n(x)$ is the uniform distribution on $S \cap \{0,1\}^n$, and, for all $x \in \overline{S}$, $D_n(x)$ is some distribution on $\overline{S} \cap \{0,1\}^n$. The family $\{C_n\}$ is called a* random-self-reducing circuit *family for S.*

Definition 5.2 *A set S has* two-sided random-self-reducing circuits *if there is a randomized* PSIZE *circuit family $\{C_n\}_{n=1}^{\infty}$ that runs in expected polynomial time such that, for all $x \in S$, $D_n(x)$ is the uniform distribution on $S \cap \{0,1\}^n$, and, for all $x \in \overline{S}$, $D_n(x)$ is the uniform distribution on $\overline{S} \cap \{0,1\}^n$. The family $\{C_n\}$ is called a* two-sided random-self-reducing circuit *family for S.*

Lemma 5.1 *If S has two-sided random-self-reducing circuits, then χ_S has a type1 1-oracle instance-hiding scheme that leaks at most $|x|$ and $\chi_S(x)$.*

Abadi, Feigenbaum, and Kilian showed that certain well-known number-theoretic functions, such as discrete logarithm and quadratic residuosity, have one-oracle instance-hiding schemes that hide some significant information about the input [1]. However, those schemes *do* leak more than the size of the input x, and [1] provides no nontrivial examples of functions with instance-hiding schemes that leak at most $|x|$.[2] We show in the full paper that the standard examples discussed in [1] can be modified straightforwardly to yield instance-hiding schemes that leak at most $|x|$. The modified schemes use random-self-reducing circuits for sets that are not believed to have random-self-reducing algorithms.

Lemma 5.1 provides a way of showing that certain boolean functions have type1 instance-hiding schemes that use many fewer oracles than the schemes given by Theorem 3.1. Unfortunately, as Lemmas 5.2 and 5.3 indicate, neither SAT nor $\overline{\text{SAT}}$ is likely to have random-self-reducing circuits. (It is even less likely that SAT has two-sided random-self-reducing circuits, as it would have to be for Lemma 5.1 to apply.)

Lemma 5.2 *If $\overline{\text{SAT}}$ has random-self-reducing circuits, then the polynomial hierarchy collapses at the third level.*

Lemma 5.3 *If SAT has random-self-reducing circuits, then the polynomial hierarchy collapses at the third level.*

Proof (sketch): We use a proof of Nisan [15] that, if SAT had a random-self-reducing algorithm, then $\overline{\text{SAT}}$ would be in IP[2]. Then, we use the facts that IP[2] $\subseteq$ AM[4] $\subseteq$ AM[2] $\subseteq$ NP/*poly* (see [2, 12, 13]) and that $\overline{\text{SAT}} \subseteq$ NP/*poly* $\Rightarrow$ PH $\subseteq \Sigma_3^p$ (see [19]). All that remains for us to show is that these results extend *mutatis mutandis* to the case of random-self-reducing circuits for SAT and proof-systems with circuit-verifiers. ∎

References

[1] M. Abadi, J. Feigenbaum, and J. Kilian. On Hiding Information from an Oracle, *J. Comput. System Sci.* **39** (1989), 21–50.

[2] L. Babai and S. Moran. Arthur-Merlin Games: A Randomized Proof System, and a Hierarchy of Complexity Classes, *J. Comput. System Sci.* **36** (1988), 254–276.

[3] D. Beaver and J. Feigenbaum. Hiding Information from Several Oracles, Harvard University TR-10-89, May 1, 1989.

---

[2]Examples of trivial instance-hiding schemes that leak at most $|x|$ are the obvious schemes for χ_S, where S is a set in P/*poly*.

[4] D. Beaver and J. Feigenbaum. Encrypted Queries to Multiple Oracles, AT&T Bell Laboratories Technical Memorandum, August 14, 1989.

[5] D. Beaver, J. Feigenbaum, J. Kilian, and P. Rogaway. Cryptographic Applications of Locally Random Reductions, AT&T Bell Laboratories Technical Memorandum, November 15, 1989.

[6] M. Ben-Or, S. Goldwasser, J. Kilian, and A. Wigderson. Multi-Prover Interactive Proofs: How to Remove Intractability, Proc. of STOC88.

[7] M. Ben-Or, S. Goldwasser, and A. Wigderson. Completeness Theorems for Non-Cryptographic Fault-Tolerant Distributed Computation, Proc. of STOC88.

[8] D. Chaum, C. Crépeau, and I. Damgård. Multiparty Unconditionally Secure Protocols, Proc. of STOC88.

[9] A. Condon. Space-Bounded Probabilistic Game Automata, Proc. of STRUC-TURES88.

[10] A. Condon and R. J. Lipton. On the Complexity of Space-Bounded Interactive Proofs, Proc. of FOCS89.

[11] C. Dwork and L. Stockmeyer. Interactive Proof Systems with Finite State Verifiers, IBM Research Report RJ 6262 (61659), May 26, 1988. Extended Abstract in Proc. of CRYPTO88.

[12] S. Goldwasser, S. Micali, and C. Rackoff. The Knowledge Complexity of Interactive Proof Systems, *SIAM J. Comput.* **18** (1989), 186–208.

[13] S. Goldwasser and M. Sipser. Public Coins vs. Private Coins in Interactive Proof Systems, Proc. of STOC86.

[14] J. Kilian. Zero-Knowledge with Log-Space Verifiers, Proc. of FOCS88.

[15] N. Nisan. Private communication, 1988.

[16] R. Rivest. Workshop on Communication and Computing, MIT, October, 1986.

[17] A. Shamir. How to Share a Secret, *Commun. Assoc. Comput. Machinery* **22** (1979), 612-613.

[18] A. C. Yao. Protocols for Secure Computations, Proc. of FOCS82.

[19] C. Yap. Some Consequences of Nonuniform Conditions on Uniform Classes, *Theor. Comput. Sci.* **26** (1983), 287–300.

Counting Classes: Thresholds, Parity, Mods, and Fewness

Richard Beigel*   John Gill†   Ulrich Hertrampf‡

Abstract

Counting classes are classes of languages defined in terms of the number of accepting computations of non-deterministic polynomial-time Turing machines. Well known examples of counting classes are NP, co-NP, ⊕P, and PP. Every counting class consists of languages in $P^{\#P[1]}$, the class of languages computable in polynomial time using a single call to an oracle capable of determining the number of accepting paths of an NP machine.

We perform an in-depth investigation of counting classes defined in terms of thresholds and moduli. We show that the computational power of a threshold machine is a monotone function of the threshold. Then we show that the class $MODZ_kP$ is at least as large as FewP. Finally, we improve a result of Cai and Hemachandra by showing that recognizing languages in the class Few is as easy as distinguishing uniquely satisfiable formulas from unsatisfiable formulas (or detecting unique solutions, as in [21]).

1. Introduction

Valiant [20] defined the class #P of functions whose values equal the number of accepting paths of polynomial-time bounded nondeterministic Turing machines. Many interesting classes, such as PP [7, 14] and ⊕P [11, 8], are subclasses of $P^{\#P[1]}$, the class of languages computable in polynomial-time with one query to a function in #P.

Since a PP machine accepts when more than half of its paths accept, PP can be considered equivalent to

computing the high-order bit of a #P function. Since a ⊕P machine accepts when an odd number of its paths accept, ⊕P can be considered equivalent to computing the low-order bit of a #P function.

It is natural to consider the relative difficulty of computing different bits of information about a #P function. In this paper, we look at subclasses of $P^{\#P[1]}$ that are defined in terms of thresholds and in terms of moduli. We obtain several relationships among these classes. (Some separations relative to an oracle appear in [4].) Next, we show that the class FewP is a subset of $MODZ_kP$. Finally we show that every language in the class Few is as easy as distinguishing uniquely satisfiable formulas from unsatisfiable formulas; along with our closure properties, this yields a simple proof of Cai and Hemachandra's theorem that the class Few is a subset of MOD_kP.

Notation 1

- PF denotes the class of polynomial-time computable functions.

- NPM denotes the class of all nondeterministic polynomial-time bounded Turing machines.

- N denotes an element of NPM.

- x denotes an input string.

- n or $|x|$ denote the length of the input x.

- PATHS(N, x) denotes the set of computation paths of N on x.

- ACCEPT(N, x) denotes the set of accepting paths in PATHS(N, x).

- ρ denotes a computation path.

- $|S|$ denotes the cardinality of the set S.

- $\langle \cdot, \cdot \rangle$ denotes a pairing function that is computable and invertible in polynomial time.

*Dept. of Computer Science, 51 Prospect Street, P.O. Box 2158, Yale Station, New Haven, CT 06520-2158. Research performed at the Johns Hopkins University. Supported in part by the National Science Foundation under grants CCR-8808949 and CCR-8958528.

†Dept. of Electrical Engineering, Stanford University, Stanford, CA 94305-4055.

‡Institut für Informatik, Universität Würzburg, Am Hubland, D-8700 Würzburg.

Note that for fixed N, the predicates

$$\rho \in \text{PATHS}(N, x) \quad \text{and} \quad \rho \in \text{ACCEPT}(N, x)$$

are polynomial-time computable.

2. Closure properties of #P

The class #P was defined by Valiant [20].

Definition 2 [Valiant] A function f belongs to #P if there is a nondeterministic polynomial-time machine N such that $f(x)$ is the number of accepting computations of N with input x.

Because we will be defining new classes in terms of #P, it is valuable to obtain some closure properties of #P.

Property 3

(i) #P *is closed under addition.*

(ii) #P *is closed under multiplication.*

Proof: Let f_1 and f_2 be functions in #P via N_1 and N_2, respectively.

(i) Define N to behave as follows on input x:

Step 1: Guess $c \in \{1, 2\}$;

Step 2: If $c = 1$ then guess a path $\rho \in \text{PATHS}(N_1, x)$;

Step 3: If $c = 2$ then guess a path $\rho \in \text{PATHS}(N_2, x)$;

Step 4: Accept if ρ is an accepting path.

Then $f_1 + f_2$ is in #P via N.

(ii) Define N to behave as follows on input x:

Step 1: Guess $(\rho_1, \rho_2) \in \text{PATHS}(N_1, x) \times \text{PATHS}(N_2, x)$;

Step 2: Accept if both ρ_1 and ρ_2 are accepting paths.

Then $f_1 \cdot f_2$ is in #P via N.

∎

We will see below that this property is true of more general sums and products.

Valiant [19] defined the class UP of languages accepted by NP machines that have exactly one accepting path on strings in the language (and of course no accepting paths on strings not in the language). Machines with at most one accepting path are called *categorical*. By definition, UP ⊆ NP.

Definition 4 [Valiant] UP consists of those languages L for which there exists a nondeterministic polynomial-time machine N such that for all x

$$|\text{ACCEPT}(N, x)| = \begin{cases} 1 & \text{if } x \in L \\ 0 & \text{if } x \notin L. \end{cases}$$

The class UPF is defined by analogy with the class UP. UPF is the class of functions computed by an NP machine with exactly one accepting computation.

Definition 5 A function f belongs to UPF if there exists an NPM N such that for all x, $|\text{ACCEPT}(N, x)| = 1$ and $f(x)$ is equal to the output produced on the unique path in $\text{ACCEPT}(N, x)$.

The following result generalizes the closure of #P under addition and multiplication.

Property 6 Let f be a function in #P.

(i) For any $L \in$ UP *and any integer k, the following function of x belongs to #P:*

$$\sum_{|y| = |x|^k, \ (x,y) \in L} f(\langle x, y \rangle).$$

(ii) Let q be a function in UPF bounded by a polynomial in $|x|$. Then the following function of x belongs to #P:

$$\prod_{1 \leq y \leq q(x)} f(\langle x, y \rangle).$$

Proof: Similar to the proof of Property 3. ∎

Definition 7 Binomial and multinomial coefficients are defined as follows.

(i) $\binom{n}{k}$ is the coefficient of x^k in the expansion of $(x + 1)^n$.

(ii) $\binom{n}{k_1, \ldots, k_m}$ is the coefficient of $x_1^{k_1} \cdots x_m^{k_m}$ in the expansion of $(x_1 + \cdots + x_m)^n$.

In parts (ii) and (iii) of the next result we obtain closure properties of #P that do not follow from closure under addition and multiplication. We will see later, in Theorems 30 and 39, that these closure properties have surprising consequences.

Property 8 If f belongs to #P and if $g, g_1, \ldots, g_k$ are functions in UPF bounded by a polynomial in $|x|$, then the following functions of x are in #P:

(i) $f(x)^{g(x)}$

(ii) $\begin{pmatrix} f(x) \\ g(x) \end{pmatrix}$.

(iii) $\begin{pmatrix} f(x) \\ g_1(x), \ldots, g_k(x), f(x) - \sum_{1 \le i \le k} g_i(x) \end{pmatrix}$.

Proof: Let $f \in \#P$ via N. We show that the functions of each part of this result are in $\#P$ via the following nondeterministic machines:

(i) Define N' to behave as follows on input x:

Step 1: Categorically compute $g(x)$;

Step 2: Guess an ordered $g(x)$-tuple (allowing duplicates) of paths in $\text{PATHS}(N, x)$;

Step 3: Accept if all $g(x)$ paths accept.

(This also follows from Property 6(ii).)

(ii) Define N' to behave as follows on input x:

Step 1: Categorically compute $g(x)$;

Step 2: Guess a set containing $g(x)$ (distinct) paths in $\text{PATHS}(N, x)$;

Step 3: Accept if all $g(x)$ paths accept.

(iii) Similar to (ii).

∎

Property 9 *Let f be a function in $\#P$ bounded by a polynomial in $|x|$.*

(i) *The function $2^{f(x)} - 1$ belongs to $\#P$.*

(ii) *More generally, for every integer $k \ge 2$ the function $k^{f(x)} - 1$ belongs to $\#P$.*

Proof: Let $f \in \#P$ via N and let q be a polynomial such that $f(x) \le q(|x|)$ for all x.

(ii) A *multiset* is a "set" that may contain duplicates; that is, a multiset is a function from a universe to the nonnegative integers. Let N' behave as follows on input x:

Step 1: Guess a nonempty multiset S of paths belonging to $\text{PATHS}(N, x)$ such that $|S| \le (k-1)q(|x|)$ and such that no element appears in S more than $k - 1$ times.

Step 2: Accept if every element of S belongs to $\text{ACCEPT}(N, x)$.

(This also follows from Property 8(iii) and Property 6(i) by the multinomial theorem.)

∎

3. Threshold Classes

Many well known complexity classes can be defined in terms of nondeterministic polynomial-time machines by appropriate interpretation of the results of all possible computation paths. NP, PP, US [5], and members of the polynomial-time hierarchy [10, 16] are examples of such complexity classes. Counting classes consist of languages in which acceptance is determined by the *number* of accepting computations.

Definition 10 For a relation $R(x, \alpha, \pi)$ we define $\text{CP}_{R(x,\alpha,\pi)}$ to be the class of languages L for which

$$(\exists N)(\forall x)[x \in L \iff R(x, |\text{ACCEPT}(N, x)|, |\text{PATHS}(N, x)|)].$$

For example, NP is the counting class defined by $R(x, \alpha, \pi) \equiv \alpha > 0$, and PP is the counting class defined by $R(x, \alpha, \pi) \equiv \alpha > \frac{1}{2}\pi$.

Some researchers have considered machines that are defined to accept when exactly $t(x)$ paths accept; others have considered machines that accept when at least $t(x)$ paths accept. Still others take $t(x)$ to be a fraction of all paths, rather than an absolute number. Classes that arise from such considerations include US [5] and PP [7, 14]. The following definition introduces notation for some of these counting classes.

Definition 11

- $\text{CP}_{=f(x)} = \text{CP}_{\alpha=f(x)}$.

- $\text{CP}_{=f(x,\pi)} = \text{CP}_{\alpha=f(x,\pi)}$.

- $\text{CP}_{\ge f(x)} = \text{CP}_{\alpha \ge f(x)}$.

- $\text{CP}_{\ge f(x,\pi)} = \text{CP}_{\alpha \ge f(x,\pi)}$.

- $\text{CP}_= = \bigcup_{f \in PF} \text{CP}_{=f(x)}$.

- $\text{CP}_\ge = \bigcup_{f \in PF} \text{CP}_{\ge f(x)}$.

The classes $\text{CP}_=$ and $\text{CP}_\ge$ were defined by Wagner in [22]. They have also been studied by Toran in [17, 18].

In the notation of the above definition, NP is $\text{CP}_{\ge 1}$, co-NP is $\text{CP}_{=\pi}$, US is $\text{CP}_{=1}$, and PP is $\text{CP}_{\ge \lfloor \pi/2 \rfloor + 1}$.

4. Thresholds

In this section, we consider machines whose acceptance is based on the number of accepting paths reaching some threshold. Thresholds were studied in [14]. We show that in many cases computational power is a monotone function of the threshold.

Theorem 12 *If f and g are polynomial-time functions such that $f(x) \le g(x)$ for every x, then*

(i) $CP_{=f(x)} \subseteq CP_{=g(x)}$.

(ii) $CP_{\geq f(x)} \subseteq CP_{\geq g(x)}$.

In the remainder of this section, we consider machines that are defined to accept when the number of accepting paths exceeds some function of the total number of paths. A standard convention in this situation is to require that all paths make the same number of nondeterministic choices, for example, $p(|x|)$ for some polynomial that depends on the machine. We therefore consider only nondeterministic machines N such that the function $|\text{PATHS}(N, x)|$ is polynomial-time computable. In this framework, we also find that computational power is a monotone function of the threshold.

Theorem 13 *If f, g, and h are polynomial-time functions such that $f(x, \pi) \leq g(x, \pi + h(x, \pi)) \leq f(x, \pi) + h(x, \pi)$ for all x and π, then*

(i) $CP_{=f(x,\pi)} \subseteq CP_{=g(x,\pi)}$.

(ii) $CP_{\geq f(x,\pi)} \subseteq CP_{\geq g(x,\pi)}$.

Corollary 14 *Let r and s be polynomial-time computable, rational-valued functions such that $r(x) \leq s(x) \leq 1/2$. Then*

(i) $CP_{=\lceil r(x)\pi \rceil} \subseteq CP_{=\lceil s(x)\pi \rceil}$.

(ii) $CP_{\geq r(x)\pi} \subseteq CP_{\geq s(x)\pi}$.

The reader might wonder whether the inclusions above are proper. If r and s are polynomially related then the answer is no, because we can pad. Any separation would imply that $P \neq PP$, and hence will be difficult to establish. Moreover, when r and s are not polynomially related, standard techniques (see [3]) produce an oracle relative to which the separation is proper.

5. Number Theory

In studying $\oplus P$ and other subclasses of $P^{\#P[1]}$ defined in terms of moduli, we will need to use some facts from number theory.

Theorem 15 (Fermat) *Let p be prime. Then*

$$a^{p-1} \equiv \begin{cases} 0 \pmod{p} & \text{if } a \equiv 0 \pmod{p} \\ 1 \pmod{p} & \text{otherwise.} \end{cases}$$

We obtain a useful corollary about square-free integers.

Definition 16 *An integer is square-free if it is not divisible by the square of any positive integer larger than one.*

We write $p \mid k$ to denote that p is a divisor of k.

Corollary 17 *Let k be odd and square-free. Let*

$$\lambda = \prod_{p \mid k, \ p \text{ prime}} (p - 1).$$

Then $u^\lambda + v^\lambda \equiv 0 \pmod{k}$ if and only if $u \equiv v \equiv 0 \pmod{k}$.

Theorem 18 (Kummer) *Let p be prime, and let $n = a + b$. Then*

$$\binom{n}{a} \equiv 0 \pmod{p^c}$$

if and only if the number of carries when adding a to b in base p is at least c.

We will need only the following corollary of Kummer's theorem.

Corollary 19 *Let p be prime. Then*

$$\binom{n}{p^k} \equiv 0 \pmod{p}$$

if and only if the coefficient of p^k in the base-p expansion of n is zero.

6. MOD Classes

In this section, we define $\oplus P$ and the related classes $MOD_k P$ for $k > 2$. We prove closure properties and relations among these classes. (Similar results for circuit complexity were stated without proof in [15].) In Section 9., these closure properties will permit a simple proof that Cai and Hemachandra's class Few is a subset of $MOD_k P$.

The class $\oplus P$ was defined by Papadimitriou and Zachos [11]. $\oplus P$ can be expressed in the notation of this paper as follows:

Definition 20 $\oplus P = CP_{\alpha \equiv 1 \pmod{2}}$.

We will consider the analogous classes defined in terms of arbitrary moduli.

Definition 21 *For every positive integer k,*

$$MOD_k P = CP_{\alpha \not\equiv 0 \pmod{k}}.$$

That is, a language L belongs to $MOD_k P$ if there exists N such that

$$x \in L \iff |\text{ACCEPT}(N, x)| \not\equiv 0 \pmod{k}.$$

According to the above definition, if L belongs to MOD_kP via N, then $x \notin L$ when N has zero accepting paths (by analogy to NP). Because others have defined MOD_kP slightly differently, we show below that there is nothing special about the residue 0 (mod k); any other residue gives rise to the same class MOD_kP.

Theorem 22 *For every integer j,*

$$\text{MOD}_k\text{P} = \text{CP}_{\alpha \not\equiv j \,(\text{mod } k)}.$$

Proof: Without loss of generality, assume $0 \le j < k$. Let

$$\mathcal{C} = \text{CP}_{\alpha \not\equiv j \,(\text{mod } k)}.$$

Let $L \in \text{MOD}_k\text{P}$ via N. Since $\#\text{P}$ is closed under addition, there is a machine $N' \in \text{NPM}$ such that for all x

$$|\text{ACCEPT}(N', x)| = |\text{ACCEPT}(N, x)| + j,$$

so $|\text{ACCEPT}(N', x)| \not\equiv j \,(\text{mod } k)$ if and only if $|\text{ACCEPT}(N, x)| \not\equiv 0 \,(\text{mod } k)$. Therefore $\text{MOD}_k\text{P} \subseteq \mathcal{C}$. The converse is similar. ∎

When k is prime, we have the following normal form for languages in MOD_kP:

Theorem 23 *Let k be prime.*

(i) *A language L is in MOD_kP iff there there exists N such that for every x*

$$|\text{ACCEPT}(N, x)| \equiv \begin{cases} 1 \,(\text{mod } k) & \text{if } x \in L \\ 0 \,(\text{mod } k) & \text{if } x \notin L. \end{cases}$$

(ii) *More generally, if $i \not\equiv j \,(\text{mod } k)$, then $L \in \text{MOD}_k\text{P}$ iff there there exists N such that for every x*

$$|\text{ACCEPT}(N, x)| \equiv \begin{cases} i \,(\text{mod } k) & \text{if } x \in L \\ j \,(\text{mod } k) & \text{if } x \notin L. \end{cases}$$

Proof:

(i) If such a machine N exists then $L \in \text{MOD}_k\text{P}$ by definition. Conversely, assume that $L \in \text{MOD}_k\text{P}$ via a machine N. By Property 8(i), there is a machine N' such that for all x

$$|\text{ACCEPT}(N', x)|$$
$$= |\text{ACCEPT}(N, x)|^{k-1}$$
$$\equiv \begin{cases} 1 \,(\text{mod } k) & \text{if } |\text{ACCEPT}(N, x)| \not\equiv 0 \,(\text{mod } k) \\ 0 \,(\text{mod } k) & \text{if } |\text{ACCEPT}(N, x)| \equiv 0 \,(\text{mod } k), \end{cases}$$

by Fermat's theorem.

(ii) If such a machine N exists then we can add $(k - j) \bmod k$ to the number of accepting paths to obtain $L \in \text{MOD}_k\text{P}$. Conversely, assume that $L \in \text{MOD}_k\text{P}$ via the machine N' constructed in part (i). Since $\#\text{P}$ is closed under addition and multiplication, there is a machine N'' such that for all x

$$|\text{ACCEPT}(N'', x)|$$
$$= (i - j) \cdot |\text{ACCEPT}(N', x)| + j$$
$$\equiv \begin{cases} i \,(\text{mod } k) & \text{if } |\text{ACCEPT}(N', x)| \equiv 1 \,(\text{mod } k) \\ j \,(\text{mod } k) & \text{if } |\text{ACCEPT}(N', x)| \equiv 0 \,(\text{mod } k). \end{cases}$$

∎

In [11], Papadimitriou and Zachos proved that the class $\oplus\text{P}$ is equal to $\oplus\text{P}^{\oplus\text{P}}$. We will prove the same for MOD_kP whenever k is prime. First, it will be helpful to define a generalization of nondeterministic many-one reducibility.

Definition 24 Let Q be any predicate. $A \le_m^{\text{CP}_{Q(\alpha)}} B$ if there exists $f \in \text{PF}$ and a constant k such that

$$x \in A \iff Q(|\{y : |y| = |x|^k \text{ and } f(x, y) \in B\}|).$$

For the sake of intuition, consider a machine $N \in \text{NPM}^B$ that guesses a string y of length $|x|^k$ and accepts if $f(x, y) \in B$. The machine $N \le_m^{\text{CP}_{Q(\alpha)}}$-reduces A to B if $x \in A$ whenever the number of accepting paths of N on input x satisfies Q.

Proposition 25 *If $\mathcal{C}$ is closed under complement, join, polynomial-time conjunctive reducibility, and $\le_m^{\text{CP}_{Q(\alpha)}}$- reducibility, then $\mathcal{C} = \text{CP}_{Q(\alpha)}^{\mathcal{C}}$.*

Proof: Let $B \in \mathcal{C}$ and let $A \in \text{CP}_{Q(\alpha)}^B$ via N. Consider the following algorithm: On input x, (1) guess a computation ρ (including oracle answers) of $N^B(x)$; (2) verify that ρ accepts; (3) verify that all oracle answers in ρ are correct (the same as those given by oracle B).

Since $\mathcal{C}$ is closed under complement, join, and polynomial-time conjunctive reducibility, step (3) can be accomplished via a single query to a set B' in $\mathcal{C}$. Furthermore, the number of accepting paths for this algorithm is equal to the number of accepting computations of N. Let $f(x, \rho)$ produce the query from (3). Then $A \le_m^{\text{CP}_{Q(\alpha)}} B'$ via f, so $A \in \mathcal{C}$. ∎

Lemma 26 *Let k be prime.*

(i) MOD_kP *is closed under intersection.*

(ii) MOD_kP *is closed under polynomial-time conjunctive reducibility.*

(iii) $\mathrm{MOD}_k\mathrm{P}$ *is closed under complement.*

(iv) $\mathrm{MOD}_k\mathrm{P}$ *is closed under union.*

(v) $\mathrm{MOD}_k\mathrm{P}$ *is closed under polynomial-time disjunctive reducibility.*

(vi) $\mathrm{MOD}_k\mathrm{P}$ *is closed under join.*

(vii) $\mathrm{MOD}_k\mathrm{P}$ *is closed under* $\leq_{\mathrm{m}}^{\mathrm{MOD}_k\mathrm{P}}$*-reducibility.*

Proof:

(i) Let L_1 and L_2 be languages in $\mathrm{MOD}_k\mathrm{P}$ via machines N_1 and N_2, respectively. Since #P is closed under multiplication, there is a machine N_3 such that for every x

$$|\mathrm{ACCEPT}(N_3, x)| = |\mathrm{ACCEPT}(N_1, x)| \cdot |\mathrm{ACCEPT}(N_2, x)|.$$

Since k is prime, $|\mathrm{ACCEPT}(N_3, x)| \not\equiv 0 \pmod{k}$ if and only if $|\mathrm{ACCEPT}(N_1, x)| \not\equiv 0 \pmod{k}$ and $|\mathrm{ACCEPT}(N_2, x)| \not\equiv 0 \pmod{k}$. Therefore $L_1 \cap L_2 \in \mathrm{MOD}_k\mathrm{P}$.

(ii) This is similar to (i).

(iii) Let $L \in \mathrm{MOD}_k\mathrm{P}$ via N. For any integer j let

$$L_j = \{x : |\mathrm{ACCEPT}(N, x)| \not\equiv j \pmod{k}\}.$$

Then

$$\overline{L} = \bigcap_{1 \leq j < k} L_j.$$

Since each L_j belongs to $\mathrm{MOD}_k\mathrm{P}$ and $\mathrm{MOD}_k\mathrm{P}$ is closed under intersection, $\overline{L} \in \mathrm{MOD}_k\mathrm{P}$. (This property also follows from Theorem 23(ii).)

(iv) This follows from (i) and (iii) by DeMorgan's laws.

(v) This follows from (ii) and (iii) by DeMorgan's laws.

(vi) Obvious.

(vii) Let $A \leq_{\mathrm{m}}^{\mathrm{MOD}_k\mathrm{P}} B$ via f where $B \in \mathrm{MOD}_k\mathrm{P}$. By Theorem 23(i) there exists an NPM M_B such that for every x

$$|\mathrm{ACCEPT}(M_B, x)| \equiv \begin{cases} 1 \pmod{k} & \text{if } x \in B \\ 0 \pmod{k} & \text{if } x \notin B. \end{cases}$$

Construct a machine M that behaves as follows on input x:

Step 1: Guess y such that $|y| = |x|^k$;

Step 2: Nondeterministically simulate M_B on input $f(x, y)$.

First suppose that $x \notin A$. Then the number of y's such that $f(x, y) \in B$ is congruent to $0 \pmod{k}$. For each such y, $|\mathrm{ACCEPT}(M_B, f(x, y))| \equiv 1 \pmod{k}$. For the other y's, $|\mathrm{ACCEPT}(M_B, f(x, y))| \equiv 0 \pmod{k}$. Therefore $|\mathrm{ACCEPT}(M, x)|$ is congruent to $0 \cdot 1 + 0 \equiv 0 \pmod{k}$.

Now suppose that $x \in A$. Then the number of y's such that $f(x, y) \in B$ is congruent to $1 \pmod{k}$. Therefore $|\mathrm{ACCEPT}(M, x)|$ is congruent to $1 \cdot 1 + 0 \equiv 1 \pmod{k}$. Thus $A \in \mathrm{MOD}_k\mathrm{P}$ via M. ∎

By combining the preceding results we have the following theorem and corollary.

Theorem 27 *If k is prime then $\mathrm{MOD}_k\mathrm{P} = \mathrm{MOD}_k\mathrm{P}^{\mathrm{MOD}_k\mathrm{P}}$.*

Corollary 28 *If k is prime, then $\mathrm{MOD}_k\mathrm{P}$ is closed under polynomial-time Turing reductions.*

7. A Normal Form and Closure Under Union

In this section, we obtain a normal form for $\mathrm{MOD}_k\mathrm{P}$ which will enable us to prove closure under union. We begin with an easy proposition.

Proposition 29 *If $j \mid k$ then $\mathrm{MOD}_j\mathrm{P} \subseteq \mathrm{MOD}_k\mathrm{P}$.*

Theorem 30 *If k is prime then $\mathrm{MOD}_{k^i}\mathrm{P} = \mathrm{MOD}_k\mathrm{P}$ for every $i \geq 1$.*

Proof: By Proposition 29, $\mathrm{MOD}_k\mathrm{P} \subseteq \mathrm{MOD}_{k^i}\mathrm{P}$. We prove the reverse inclusion by induction on i. Assume that the theorem is true for some $i \geq 1$. Let $L \in \mathrm{MOD}_{k^{i+1}}\mathrm{P}$ via N. A number m is divisible by k^{i+1} if and only if

(1) m is divisible by k^i, and

(2) the coefficient of k^i in the base-k expansion of m is 0.

Condition (2) is equivalent to $\binom{m}{k^i} \equiv 0 \pmod{k}$ by Corollary 19. Therefore $|\mathrm{ACCEPT}(N, x)| \not\equiv 0 \pmod{k^{i+1}}$ if and only if $|\mathrm{ACCEPT}(N, x)| \not\equiv 0 \pmod{k^i}$ or $\binom{|\mathrm{ACCEPT}(N, x)|}{k^i} \not\equiv 0 \pmod{k}$. Let

$$L_1 = \{x : |\mathrm{ACCEPT}(N, x)| \not\equiv 0 \pmod{k^i}\},$$

and

$$L_2 = \left\{x : \binom{|\mathrm{ACCEPT}(N, x)|}{k^i} \not\equiv 0 \pmod{k}\right\}.$$

Then $L = L_1 \cup L_2$. By the induction hypothesis, L_1 is in MOD_kP. By Property 8(ii), there is a machine N_2 such that for all x

$$|\text{ACCEPT}(N_2, x)| = \binom{|\text{ACCEPT}(N, x)|}{k^i}.$$

Therefore $L_2 \in \text{MOD}_k\text{P}$ via N_2. Since MOD_kP is closed under union, $L \in \text{MOD}_k\text{P}$. $\blacksquare$

Because we expect PP to be incomparable to $\oplus\text{P}$, we expect that computing the highest order bit of $\#\text{P}$ functions is incomparable in difficulty to computing the lowest order bit of $\#\text{P}$ functions. However, the proof technique used above allows us to show that computing the $f(n)$-th low-order bit of a $\#\text{P}$ function (for small f) is exactly as difficult as computing the lowest-order bit of a $\#\text{P}$ function.

Theorem 31 *Let* $\text{bit}(i, b)$ *denote the b-th low-order bit of i (more precisely, $\lfloor i/2^b \rfloor \bmod 2$). Let b be a function in UPF such that $b(n) = O(\log n)$. Then*

$$\text{CP}_{\text{bit}(\alpha, b(n)) = 1} = \oplus\text{P}.$$

Proof: Computing the $b(n)$-th low-order bit of a $\#\text{P}$ function is the same as checking condition (2) in the preceding proof with $i = b(n)$ and $k = 2$. Since 2^i is bounded by a polynomial, that check is in MOD_2P by Property 8(ii). For the converse, we can use Property 3 to multiply the number of accepting paths by $2^{b(n)}$. $\blacksquare$

The next theorem brings us closer to our normal form.

Theorem 32 *Let j and k be relatively prime. Then $L \in \text{MOD}_{jk}\text{P}$ if and only if there exist $L_j \in \text{MOD}_j\text{P}$ and $L_k \in \text{MOD}_k\text{P}$ such that $L = L_j \cup L_k$.*

Proof: Assume that L belongs to MOD_{jk}P via N. Then let $L_i = \{x : |\text{ACCEPT}(N, x)| \not\equiv 0 \pmod i\}$, for $i = j, k$. Clearly $L = L_j \cup L_k$.

Conversely, let $L_i \in \text{MOD}_i\text{P}$ via N_i for $i = j, k$. Since $\#\text{P}$ is closed under addition and multiplication, there is a machine N such that

$$|\text{ACCEPT}(N, x)| = k \cdot |\text{ACCEPT}(N_j, x)| + j \cdot |\text{ACCEPT}(N_k, x)|.$$

Now, $L_j \cup L_k \in \text{MOD}_{jk}\text{P}$ via N. $\blacksquare$

Corollary 33 (Normal Form) *Let the prime factorization of k be $p_1^{e_1} \cdots p_m^{e_m}$. Then $L \in \text{MOD}_k\text{P}$ if and only if there exist $L_1 \in \text{MOD}_{p_1}\text{P}, \ldots L_m \in \text{MOD}_{p_m}\text{P}$ such that $L = L_1 \cup \cdots \cup L_m$.*

Proof: By Theorem 30, $\text{MOD}_{p_i^{e_i}}\text{P} = \text{MOD}_{p_i}\text{P}$. Now the corollary follows from the preceding theorem by induction. $\blacksquare$

Corollary 34 *Let the prime factorization of k be $p_1^{e_1} \cdots p_m^{e_m}$. Then $\text{MOD}_k\text{P} = \text{MOD}_{p_1 \cdots p_m}\text{P}$.*

Corollary 35 *For every k, MOD_kP is closed under union.*

Proof: Recall that MOD_pP is closed under union for each prime p, and apply Corollary 33. $\blacksquare$

8. Subclasses of NP

We can define "counting subclasses" of NP by placing a restriction on the number of accepting paths for strings in the language. Classes defined in this way include R [1, 12], UP, and the class FewP [2] defined by analogy to UP.

Definition 36 A language L is in FewP if there exist N and a polynomial q such that L is accepted by N and has at most $q(|x|)$ accepting paths for every x.

We define the class MODZ_kP, which is a subclass of NP corresponding to MOD_kP.

Definition 37 MODZ_kP consists of those languages L for which there exists a nondeterministic polynomial-time machine N such that for all x

$$\begin{aligned} |\text{ACCEPT}(N, x)| &\not\equiv 0 \pmod k && \text{if } x \in L \\ |\text{ACCEPT}(N, x)| &= 0 && \text{if } x \notin L. \end{aligned}$$

Note that $\text{MODZ}_k\text{P} \subseteq \text{MOD}_k\text{P} \cap \text{NP}$. We do not know whether the inclusion is proper. However, we have constructed oracles relative to which this is the case [4]. Most of the closure properties we obtained for MOD_kP go through for MODZ_kP with essentially the same proof. The only major difference is in proving closure under union; here we use Fermat's theorem in a novel way.

Theorem 38

(i) *If k is prime then MODZ_kP is closed under intersection.*

(ii) *If k is prime then MODZ_kP is closed under polynomial-time conjunctive reducibility.*

(iii) *If k is prime and $i \not\equiv 0 \pmod k$, then $L \in \text{MODZ}_k\text{P}$ iff there there exists N such that for every x*

$$\begin{aligned} |\text{ACCEPT}(N, x)| &\equiv i \pmod k && \text{if } x \in L \\ |\text{ACCEPT}(N, x)| &= 0 && \text{if } x \notin L. \end{aligned}$$

56

(iv) *If k is odd and square-free, then* MODZ_kP *is closed under union.*

(v) *If* $j \mid k$ *then* $\text{MODZ}_j\text{P} \subseteq \text{MODZ}_k\text{P}$.

(vi) *If k is an odd prime then* $\text{MODZ}_{k^i}\text{P} = \text{MODZ}_k\text{P}$ *for every* $i \geq 1$.

Proof:

(i) Same as the proof of Lemma 26(i).

(ii) Same as the proof of Lemma 26(ii).

(iii) Same as the proof of Theorem 23 with $j = 0$.

(iv) Let
$$\lambda = \prod_{p \mid k, \ p \text{ prime}} (p-1).$$

Let L_1 and L_2 be in MOD_kP via N_1 and N_2, respectively. Because #P is closed under multiplication and addition, there is a machine N_3 such that

$$|\text{ACCEPT}(N_3, x)| = |\text{ACCEPT}(N_1, x)|^\lambda + |\text{ACCEPT}(N_2, x)|^\lambda.$$

By Corollary 17, the only solution of $u^\lambda + v^\lambda \equiv 0 \pmod{k}$ is $u \equiv v \equiv 0 \pmod{k}$. Therefore, $|\text{ACCEPT}(N_3, x)| \not\equiv 0 \pmod{k}$ iff $x \in L_1 \cup L_2$.

(v) Same as the proof of Proposition 29.

(vi) We use (iv) to obtain closure under union. The remainder of the proof is the same as the proof of Theorem 30.

∎

9. Fewness

In [6] Cai and Hemachandra proved a surprising result: the class Few (defined below) is a subset of MOD_kP for every $k \geq 2$ (that result has been generalized by Köbler, Schöning, Toda, and Torán [9]). In this section, we prove a similar result via simpler techniques: $\text{FewP} \subseteq \text{MODZ}_k\text{P}$ for every $k \geq 2$. We also show that every language in the class Few is easy as distinguishing categorical acceptance from nonacceptance. This yields a simple proof of Cai and Hemachandra's result.

Theorem 39 *If* $k \geq 2$ *then* $\text{FewP} \subseteq \text{MODZ}_k\text{P}$.

Proof: Let $L \in \text{FewP}$ via a machine N. By Property 9(ii), there is a machine N' such that for every x

$$|\text{ACCEPT}(N', x)| = k^{|\text{ACCEPT}(N,x)|} - 1$$
$$\begin{cases} \not\equiv 0 \pmod{k} & \text{if } |\text{ACCEPT}(N, x)| \geq 1 \\ = 0 & \text{if } |\text{ACCEPT}(N, x)| = 0. \end{cases}$$

∎

In [13], Schöning applied similar techniques in the case $k = 2$.

The class Few is defined in [6] as follows.

Definition 40 A language L belongs to the class Few if there exist a nondeterministic polynomial-time machine N, a polynomial q such that $|\text{ACCEPT}(N, x)| \leq q(|x|)$, and a polynomial-time computable predicate R such that $x \in L$ iff $R(x, |\text{ACCEPT}(N, x)|)$.

Equivalently, a language L belongs to Few if $L \in P^{\#P[1]}$ via a #P oracle whose output *value* is bounded by a polynomial in the input length. Now we show that every language in Few is as easy as distinguishing categorical acceptance from nonacceptance.

Theorem 41 *Let* Q *be any predicate such that* $Q(1) = 1$ *and* $Q(0) = 0$. *Then*
$$\text{Few} \subseteq \text{P}^{\text{CP}_{Q(\infty)}}.$$

Proof: Let $L \in \text{Few}$ via machine N and polynomial-time computable predicate R. Let
$$L' = \left\{ \langle 0^i, x \rangle : Q\left(\binom{|\text{ACCEPT}(N,x)|}{i} \right) \right\}.$$

Then $L' \in \text{CP}_{Q(\alpha)}$ by Property 8(ii). Note that
$$\binom{|\text{ACCEPT}(N,x)|}{i} = \begin{cases} 1 & \text{if } i = |\text{ACCEPT}(N, x)| \\ 0 & \text{if } i > |\text{ACCEPT}(N, x)|. \end{cases}$$

Therefore,
$$|\text{ACCEPT}(N, x)| = \max\{i : \langle 0^i, x \rangle \in L'\}.$$

Consequently, $L(x) = R(x, \max\{i : \langle 0^i, x \rangle \in L'\}) =$
$$\bigvee_{0 \leq i \leq q(|x|)} \left(R(x, i) \wedge L'(\langle 0^i, x \rangle) \wedge \left(\bigwedge_{i < j \leq q(|x|)} \neg L'(\langle 0^j, x \rangle) \right) \right),$$
so, in fact, L is polynomial-time reducible to L' via a Boolean formula with depth 2. ∎

Valiant and Vazirani have shown that if it is possible to distinguish uniquely satisfiable formulas from unsatisfiable formulas in polynomial time, then R = NP. The preceding theorem implies an additional collapse:

Corollary 42 *If it is possible to distinguish uniquely satisfiable formulas from unsatisfiable formulas in polynomial time, then* P = Few.

The following result was proved previously via different techniques by Cai and Hemachandra [6].

Corollary 43 *If* $k \geq 2$ *then* $\text{Few} \subseteq \text{MOD}_k\text{P}$.

Proof: By Proposition 29, it suffices to prove this result for prime k. By the preceding theorem, Few $\subseteq$ $\text{P}^{\text{MOD}_k\text{P}}$, which is equal to MOD_kP by Corollary 28. ∎

10. Acknowledgments

The first author is grateful to Bob Floyd for his hospitality while the first author was visiting Stanford University.

References

[1] L. Adleman and K. Manders. Reducibility, randomness, and intractibility. In *Proceedings of the 9th Annual ACM Symposium on Theory of Computing*, pages 151–153, 1977.

[2] E. W. Allender. The complexity of sparse sets in P. In *Structure in Complexity Theory*, pages 1–11. Springer-Verlag, June 1986. Volume 223 of *Lecture Notes in Computer Science*.

[3] T. Baker, J. Gill, and R. Solovay. Relativizations of the $P =?$ NP question. *SIAM J. Comput.*, 4:431–442, 1975.

[4] R. Beigel. Relativized counting classes: Relations among thresholds, parity, and mods. *J. Comput. Syst. Sci.* To appear.

[5] A. Blass and Y. Gurevich. On the unique satisfiability problem. *Information and Control*, 55:80–88, 1982.

[6] J. Cai and L. A. Hemachandra. On the power of parity. In *Proceedings of the 6th Annual Symposium on Theoretical Aspects of Computer Science*, pages 229–240. Springer-Verlag, 1989. Lecture Notes in Computer Science.

[7] J. Gill. Computational complexity of probabilistic Turing machines. *SIAM J. Comput.*, 6:675–695, 1977.

[8] L. M. Goldschlager and I. Parberry. On the construction of parallel computers from various bases of Boolean functions. *Theoretical Comput. Sci.*, 43:43–58, 1986.

[9] J. Köbler, U. Schöning, S. Toda, and J. Torán. Turing machines with few accepting computations and low sets for PP. In *Proceedings of the 4th Annual Conference on Structure in Complexity Theory*, pages 208–215. IEEE Computer Society Press, June 1989.

[10] A. Meyer and L. J. Stockmeyer. The equivalence problem for regular expressions with squaring requires exponential space. In *Proceedings of the 13th Annual IEEE Symposium on Switching and Automata Theory*, pages 125–129, 1972.

[11] C. H. Papadimitriou and S. K. Zachos. Two remarks on the complexity of counting. In *Proceedings of the 6th GI Conference of Theoretical Computer Science*, pages 269–276. Springer-Verlag, 1983. Volume 145 of *Lecture Notes in Computer Science*.

[12] C. Rackoff. Relativized questions involving probabilistic algorithms. *Journal of the Association for Computing Machinery*, 29(1):261–268, Jan. 1982.

[13] U. Schöning. The power of counting. In *Proceedings of the 3rd Annual Conference on Structure in Complexity Theory*, pages 2–18. IEEE Computer Society Press, June 1988.

[14] J. Simon. *On Some Central Problems In Computational Complexity*. PhD thesis, Cornell University, Ithaca, New York, 1975. Dept. of Computer Science, TR 75-224.

[15] R. Smolensky. Algebraic methods in the theory of lower bounds for Boolean circuit complexity. In *Proceedings of the 19th Annual ACM Symposium on Theory of Computing*, pages 77–82, 1987.

[16] L. J. Stockmeyer. The polynomial-time hierarchy. *Theoretical Comput. Sci.*, 3:1–22, 1977.

[17] J. Torán. An oracle characterization of the counting hierarchy. In *Proceedings of the 3rd Annual Conference on Structure in Complexity Theory*, pages 213–223. IEEE Computer Society Press, June 1988.

[18] J. Torán. *Structural Properties of The Counting Hierarchies*. PhD thesis, Facultat d'Informàtica de Barcelona, 1988.

[19] L. G. Valiant. The relative complexity of checking and evaluating. *Inf. Process. Lett.*, 5:20–23, 1976.

[20] L. G. Valiant. The complexity of computing the permanent. *Theoretical Comput. Sci.*, 8:189–201, 1979.

[21] L. G. Valiant and V. V. Vazirani. NP is as easy as detecting unique solutions. In *Proceedings of the 17th Annual ACM Symposium on Theory of Computing*, 1985.

[22] K. W. Wagner. The complexity of combinatorial problems with succinct input representation. *Acta Inf.*, 23:325–356, 1986.

Playing Games of Incomplete Information

Jin-yi Cai[*]
Department of Computer Science
Princeton University
Princeton, New Jersey 08544

Anne Condon [†]
Computer Science Department
University of Wisconsin-Madison

Richard J. Lipton[‡]
Department of Computer Science
Princeton University
Princeton, New Jersey 08544

1   Introduction

We study two-person games of cooperation and multi-prover interactive proof systems. We first consider a two person game G, which we call a *free game*, defined as follows. A Boolean function ϕ_G is given. Player I and II each pick a random number i and j in private, where $1 \leq i, j \leq s$, and then each chooses a private number $f(i)$ and $g(j)$, $1 \leq f(i), g(j) \leq s$. If $\phi_G(i, j, f(i), g(j)) = 1$, then both players win, otherwise they lose. The objective of both players is to win collectively. We ask whether, if such a game is played n times in parallel, the probability of winning *all* the games decays exponentially in n. This question was posed in a more general context by Fortnow [4], which we discuss soon.

Formally we define the nth product game G^n as the following two person game. Player I and II each pick a vector of independent random numbers $\bar{i} = (i_1, \ldots, i_n)$ and $\bar{j} = (j_1, \ldots, j_n)$ in private, $1 \leq i_k, j_k \leq s$, and then each chooses a private sequence of numbers $f_1(\bar{i}), \ldots, f_n(\bar{i}), g_1(\bar{j}), \ldots, g_n(\bar{j})$.

[*]Research supported by NSF grant CCR-8709818.
[†]Work supported by NSF grant number DCR-8402565
[‡]Research supported by DARPA and ONR contracts N00014-85-C-0456 and N00014-85-K-0465

The goal for both players is to ensure $\bigwedge_{k=1}^{n} \phi_G(i_k, j_k, f_k(\bar{i}), g_k(\bar{j})) = 1$. We define the *winning probability* of the game G to be $\max_{f,g} \Pr[\phi_G(i, j, f(i), g(j)) = 1]$, where the probability is taken over all randomly and uniformly chosen i, j in the range $1, \ldots, s$, and we denote it by $w(G)$. The game G is called nontrivial if its winning probability is neither 0 nor 1. We shall only consider nontrivial free games. Similarly, the winning probability $w(G^n)$ of the product game G^n is defined to be $\max_{f_1, \ldots, f_n, g_1, \ldots, g_n} \Pr[\bigwedge_{k=1}^{n} \phi_G(i_k, j_k, f_k(\bar{i}), g_k(\bar{j})) = 1]$.

Intuitively, we might first expect that $w(G^n)$ is $w(G)^n$; since all n instances of game G are drawn independently, and if the players play all instances independently, the winning probability of the n-product game is $w(G)^n$. However, Fortnow [4] showed that the answer is not so simple; he gave an example of a free game G for which $w(G^2) > (w(G))^2$. He thus demonstrated that by using strategies that depend on *all* the instances of the game G, the players can increase their chance of winning the product game G^n.

Before this work, it was unknown even if $w(G^n) \to 0$ as $n \to \infty$. The first result of this paper is that the winning probability of the product game G^n converges to 0 exponentially fast as $n \to \infty$.

Theorem (2.1) *If G is a non-trivial free game, then there exists a $q < 1 - e^{-3s}/2$ and a universal constant c_0, such that the winning probability of G^n is at most $c_0 q^n$.*

We can generalize this result to another class of games, defined as follows. Let ϕ_G be a Boolean function as before, and let L be a nonempty subset of $\{1, \ldots, s\} \times \{1, \ldots, s\}$. L is the set of *legal* instances of the game. A pair (i, j) is chosen randomly and uniformly from L; i is given to player I and j is given to player II. As before, the players choose numbers $f(i)$ and $g(j)$; and the players win if $\phi_G(i, j, f(i), g(j)) = 1$. We similarly define the winning probability of the game $w(G)$, and call a game nontrivial if $0 < w(G) < 1$. Note that free games are a special case of these games, where there is no dependency between i and j. We refer to these games simply as *games* in this paper. Then

Theorem (2.2) *If G is a non-trivial game, then there exists a $q < 1 - e^{-3s}/2$ and a universal constant c_0, such that the winning probability of G^n is at most $c_0 q^n$.*

Our study of games was motivated by recent work on multi-prover interactive proof systems (MIP's), introduced by Ben-Or et al. [2]. These are generalizations of the interactive proof systems (IPS's) of Goldwasser, Micali and Rackoff [6] and Babai [1]. Roughly, an interactive proof system for a language L is a protocol between a prover P and a verifier V. The pair shares an input; the prover must be able to convince the verifier to accept an input if and only if it is in L. We only consider interactive proofs where the verifier is probabilistic and is polynomially time bounded. In a multi-prover system (MIP), the verifier interacts with many provers; the provers cannot communicate with each other during the proof. The protocol between the verifier and the provers consists of a number of *rounds*; in each round the verifier sends a message to each prover in turn and receives a response. Because the provers cannot communicate with each other, the response of any prover can only depend on the messages it has received from the verifier so far, and not on the messages sent to other provers.

We restrict our attention in this paper to the case that the verifier interacts with two provers, P_1 and P_2. A language L is accepted by a MIP (P_1, P_2, V) with error probability $\epsilon(n)$ if

1. for all $x \in L$, $|x| = n$, (P_1, P_2, V) accepts x with probability at least $1 - \epsilon(n)$; and

2. for all $x \notin L, |x| = n$, and any provers P_1^*, P_2^*, (P_1^*, P_2^*, V) accepts x with probability at most $\epsilon(n)$.

Fortnow, Rompel and Sipser [5] considered the question: are two provers more powerful than one? To address this question, they considered the number of rounds of a protocol and asked whether any language accepted by an unbounded round IPS has a constant round MIP. Since an IPS can run for polynomial time, the number of rounds, or interactions between the verifier and prover can be polynomial in the input size. Results of Babai [1] and Goldwasser and Sipser [7] show that if the number of rounds of a protocol is bounded by a constant independent of the input size, the number of rounds can be collapsed to two. However, it is an open problem whether unbounded round IPS's are equivalent to constant round IPS's. Therefore, a proof that any language accepted by an unbounded round IPS has a constant round MIP would be of interest.

Fortnow et al. showed how to simulate any IPS by a 1-round MIP with the following property.

1. if x is accepted by the IPS, $|x| = n$, then the probability x is accepted by the MIP is $\geq 1 - 1/2^n$; and

2. if x is rejected by the IPS, $|x| = n$, then the probability x is accepted by the MIP is $\leq 1 - 1/p(n)$, for some polynomial p.

We call a 1-round MIP protocol that simulates an IPS using the method of Fortnow at al. an *IPS-simulation* protocol.

Fortnow et al. claimed that an IPS-simulation protocol could be run in parallel a polynomial number of times in the length of the input, to obtain a 1-round MIP accepting L with error probability ϵ, for any constant ϵ. Intuitively this seems reasonable, since each of the games played in parallel is chosen independently. However, Fortnow [4] later showed that although the verifier chooses each game independently, it cannot be assumed that the provers play the games independently.

The protocol of Fortnow et al. on a fixed input is exactly a game of the type described above. Hence, the question of whether any IPS can be simulated by a constant round, 2-prover MIP can be reduced to the following problem: Is there some polynomial p' and a constant λ, $0 < \lambda < 1$, such that for any nontrivial game G the winning probability of G^n is at most λ, for $n = p'(\frac{1}{1-w(G)})$. Unfortunately, although Theorem 2.2 implies that the winning probability of G decays exponentially as $n \to \infty$, it is not strong enough to resolve this problem.

Our next result exploits a special property of IPS-simulation protocols to solve this problem in the case of free games. In the framework of the games described above, the property is roughly as follows. Once i and j are fixed and the response of one player is fixed, there is a limit on the number of possible responses of the other player that satisfy ϕ_G. More precisely, we say G is (l, l')-*limited* if

1. given any i, j, k, $|\{k' \mid \phi_G(i, j, k, k') = 1\}| \leq l$; and

2. given any i, j, k', $|\{k \mid \phi_G(i, j, k, k') = 1\}| \leq l'$.

Then the IPS-simulation protocols of Fortnow et al. [5] are $(1, 2)$-limited. We will first develop the idea in the special case of $(1, 1)$-limited free games, and then consider the more general $(1, 2)$-limited free games. Our result for $(1, 2)$-limited free games is the following:

Theorem (4.1) *Let G be a non-trivial, (1,2)-limited free game. Let $w(G) = 1 - \epsilon$. Then if $n = \lceil 1/\epsilon \rceil$, $w(G^n) \leq 11/12$.*

We conjecture that this theorem can be generalized to non-free games. Finally, we note that if this conjecture is true, then it follows that given any constant ϵ, any language accepted by an (unbounded round) IPS has a constant round 2-prover MIP that has error probability ϵ. This is because the IPS-simulation protocol can be run a polynomial number of times in parallel to reduce the error probability to $11/12$. Then for any constant k, this parallel protocol can be repeated sequentially a k times to reduce the error probability to $(11/12)^k$.

2 Results on the Convergence of Free and General Games

In this section we prove Theorem 2.1 and related results.

We begin by giving precise definitions of a game. We say $G = \langle \phi, L \subseteq X \times Y, S, T \rangle$ is a *game* if each set X, Y, S, T is finite, $L \neq \emptyset$, and

$$\phi : L \times S \times T \to \{0, 1\}.$$

Without loss of generality, we assume that X, Y, S, T all equal $\{1, \ldots, s\}$. We say G is a *free game* if $L = X \times Y$. We define the winning probability of G to be $\max_{f,g} \Pr[\phi(x, y, f(x), g(y)) = 1]$, where the probability is taken over all randomly and uniformly chosen pairs $(x, y) \in L$. We call f and g the strategies of Player I and II respectively. G is *non-trivial* if $w(G)$ is neither 0 nor 1. This implies $s > 1$.

We define the *product game* G^n of G to be the game $\langle \phi^n, L^n, S^n, T^n \rangle$, where

$$\phi^n(\bar{x}, \bar{y}, f(\bar{x}), g(\bar{y})) = \bigwedge_{i=1}^{n} \phi(x_i, y_i, f_i(\bar{x}), g_i(\bar{y})).$$

Here $\bar{v}$ is the n-vector $(v_1, \ldots, v_n)$ and $f(\bar{x}), g(\bar{y})$ are the n-vectors $(f_1(\bar{x}), \ldots, f_n(\bar{x}))$ and $(g_1(\bar{y}), \ldots, g_n(\bar{y}))$ respectively.

The probability that the players win all copies of the n-product game of G is at least $w(G)^n$. This is because if f, g are optimal strategies of players I and II of G respectively, that is, $\phi(x, y, f(x), g(y)) = w(G)$, then when the players use strategies f and g in parallel on each copy, the probability of winning is $\prod_{i=1}^{n} \phi(x_i, y_i, f(x_i), g(y_i)) = w(G)^n$, since the x_i and y_i are all chosen independently and randomly. Thus for any game G, $w(G^n) \geq w(G)^n$; a natural question is whether $w(G^n) = w(G)^n$. Fortnow [4] showed that the answer to this question is no, by constructing the following free game

G for which $w(G) = 1/2$ but $w(G^2) = 3/8 > (1/2)^2$. Fortnow's game G is defined by setting $X = Y = S = T = \{0, 1\}$ and defining ϕ by

$$\phi(x, y, f(x), g(y)) = [(x \vee f(x)) \neq (y \vee g(y))].$$

The winning probability of this game is $1/2$; an example of a pair of optimal strategies of the players is $f(x) = x$, $g(y) = y$. On these strategies, the players win when one receives a 0 and the other receives a 1, which occurs with probability $1/2$. Next consider the product game G^2. In this game, player I receives bits x_1 and x_2, player II receives bits y_1 and y_2; and the goal of the players is to ensure that

$$((x_1 \vee f_1(x_1, x_2)) \neq (y_1 \vee g_1(y_1, y_2))) \wedge ((x_2 \vee f_2(x_1, x_2)) \neq (y_2 \vee g_2(y_1, y_2))).$$

Suppose the players use the following strategy: $f(x_1, x_2) = (0, 0)$ if $x_1 = x_2 = 0$; otherwise $f(x_1, x_2) = (1, 1)$. Symmetrically, $g(y_1, y_2) = f(y_1, y_2)$. This pair of strategies guarantees that the players win with probability $3/8$: when $x_1 = x_2 = 0$, the players win when y_1 and y_2 are not both 0; and by symmetry when $y_1 = y_2 = 0$, the players win when x_1 and x_2 are not both 0. Hence the players win on 6 of the 16 possible random choices for $x_1, x_2; y_1, y_2$.

Fortnow also observed that the winning probability of the product game G^n is at most $(3/4)^n$, since the players can never win if $x_i = y_i = 1$ for some i. In general though, such an argument is not sufficient to show that $w(G^n) \to 0$ as $n \to \infty$, since there may not be an instance of the game on which the players *always* lose. For example, by modifying Fortnow's game so that the players automatically win when $x = y = 1$, that is, letting $\phi(x, y, f(x), g(y)) = ((x \vee f(x)) \neq (y \vee g(y))) \vee (x \wedge y)$, we obtain a non-trivial game for which this argument fails. Our first theorem uses a result of Zarankiewicz [3] to show that if a free game G is non-trivial, then the winning probability of the n-product game converges to 0 exponentially fast as $n \to \infty$.

Theorem 2.1 *If G is a non-trivial free game, then there exists a $q < 1 - e^{-3s}/2$, and a universal constant c_0, such that $w(G^n) < c_0 q^n$.*

Proof: Suppose a pair of strategies f, g for the two players are given. Let $N = s^n$, the size of the sample space in the product game. Define a bipartite graph (X, Y, E), where X and Y consist of all inputs to each player, thus $|X| = |Y| = N$. An edge $e(x, y)$ exists between x and y iff $\bigwedge_{k=1}^{n} \phi_G(x_k, y_k, f_k(x_1, \ldots, x_n), g_k(y_1, \ldots, y_n))$, where $x = (x_1, \ldots, x_n)$ and $y = (y_1, \ldots, y_n)$. We show that $|E| = O(N^{2-\lambda(s)})$, for some $\lambda(s) > 0$. This clearly implies a bound on the probability of winning the product game.

Consider the set of all pairs of (ordered) s-tuples from X and Y, $S = \{((x^1, \ldots x^s), (y^1, \ldots, y^s)) | x^i \in X, y^i \in Y\}$. Given any such pair $((x^1, \ldots x^s), (y^1, \ldots, y^s)) \in S$ and any k, $1 \leq k \leq n$, consider the pair of s-tuples formed by "the kth coordinates", $((x_k^1, \ldots x_k^s), (y_k^1, \ldots, y_k^s))$. The number of such pairs where both entries are permutations of 1 to s is $s!^2$. Thus the number of such pairs where at least one entry is not a permutation of 1 to s is $s^{2s} - s!^2$. Now consider the set of the pairs $((x^1, \ldots x^s), (y^1, \ldots, y^s)) \in S$ so that for all $k, 1 \leq k \leq n$, at least one of $(x_k^1, \ldots x_k^s)$ or $(y_k^1, \ldots, y_k^s)$ is not a permutation of 1 to s. This set has cardinality $(s^{2s} - s!^2)^n$. Hence, the set of the pairs

$((x^1, \ldots . x^s), (y^1, \ldots, y^s)) \in S$ such that there exists $k, 1 \le k \le n$, both $(x_k^1, \ldots . x_k^s)$ and $(y_k^1, \ldots, y_k^s)$ are permutations of 1 to s has cardinality $N^{2s} - (s^{2s} - s!^2)^n$. Each of these has been counted exactly $s!^2$ times in the totality of all (ordered) pairs of (unordered) set of s distinct elements from X and Y, thus the number of (ordered) pairs of (unordered) set of s distinct elements from X and Y, where, for all k "the kth coordinate tuple" $((x_k^1, \ldots . x_k^s), (y_k^1, \ldots, y_k^s))$ do not both form permutations, is

$$\binom{N}{s}^2 - \frac{N^{2s} - (s^{2s} - s!^2)^n}{s!^2}$$

$$\le \frac{(s^{2s} - s!^2)^n}{s!^2}$$

$$\le \frac{1}{s!^2}(s^{2s}(1 - \frac{1}{e^{2s}}))^n$$

$$= \frac{N^{2s + \log_s(1 - \frac{1}{e^{2s}})}}{s!^2}$$

$$\le \frac{N^{2s - \frac{1}{\log s \cdot e^{2s}}}}{s!^2}.$$

Let's consider the following sum

$$\sum_{A \subset X, B \subset Y, |A| = |B| = m} e(A, B) = |E| \binom{N}{m-1}^2,$$

where $e(A, B)$ denotes the number of edges between A and B, and $s \le m \le N$.

Let

$$\mathcal{M} = \{ (A, B) \mid |A| = |B| = m \ \& \ e(A, B) \ge \frac{|E|}{2} \frac{\binom{N}{m-1}^2}{\binom{N}{m}^2} \}.$$

The size of $\mathcal{M}$ can be estimated as follows:

$$|E| \binom{N}{m-1}^2 \le |\mathcal{M}| m^2 + \frac{|E|}{2} \binom{N}{m-1}^2,$$

$$|\mathcal{M}| m^2 \ge \frac{|E|}{2} \binom{N}{m-1}^2.$$

Applying Zarankiewicz's Theorem [3] to the bipartite graph induced on $A \times B$ for each $(A, B) \in \mathcal{M}$, we get a complete subgraph $K_{s,s}$, provided the number of edges is at least $(s-1)^{1/s} m^{2-1/s} + \frac{s-1}{2} m$. An easy consequence is that if the number of edges $e(A, B) > 2m^{2-1/s}$, then there is a subgraph $K_{s,s}$.

Now let $\lambda = \frac{1}{\log s(1 + 2s^2)e^{2s}}$, and suppose $|E| \ge 2eN^{2-\lambda}$. Let $n \ge 1/\lambda s = \log s \cdot (1 + 2s^2) \cdot e^{2s}/s$ and $m = \lceil N^{\lambda s} \rceil$. As $N = s^n$, clearly $m \ge s$. Moreover for $(A, B) \in \mathcal{M}$, $e(A, B) \ge eN^{2-\lambda}(\frac{m}{N-m+1})^2 > 2m^{2-1/s}$. Therefore we have at least one $K_{s,s}$ for each $(A, B) \in \mathcal{M}$. Each such $K_{s,s}$ can appear in at most $\binom{N}{m-s}^2$ many pairs, thus there are at least $\frac{|\mathcal{M}|}{\binom{N}{m-s}^2}$ many $K_{s,s}$.

We have

$$
\frac{|\mathcal{M}|}{\binom{N}{m-s}^2} \geq \frac{|E|}{2m^2} \frac{\binom{N}{m-1}^2}{\binom{N}{m-s}^2}
$$

$$
\geq eN^{2-\lambda} \frac{(N-m+1)^{2(s-1)}}{m^{2s}}
$$

$$
= \frac{eN^{2s-\lambda}}{m^{2s}} \left(1 - \frac{m-1}{N}\right)^{2(s-1)}.
$$

Since $m < N^{\lambda s} + 1$,

$$
\frac{1}{m^{2s}} > \frac{1}{(N^{\lambda s}+1)^{2s}} \geq \frac{1}{e^2 N^{\lambda 2s^2}},
$$

as $N^{\lambda s} \geq s$.

Also, $m - 1 < N^{\lambda s}$, thus,

$$
\left(1 - \frac{m-1}{N}\right)^{2(s-1)} > \left(1 - \frac{1}{N^{1-\lambda s}}\right)^{2(s-1)} = \left(1 - \frac{1}{s^{(1-\lambda s)n}}\right)^{2(s-1)}.
$$

Since $(1 - \lambda s)n \geq \frac{1}{\lambda s} - 1 = \frac{\log s(1+2s^2)e^{2s}-s}{s} \geq 2\log s \cdot s \cdot e^{2s}$,

$$
\left(1 - \frac{m-1}{N}\right)^{2(s-1)} > \left(1 - \frac{1}{s^{2\log s \cdot s \cdot e^{2s}}}\right)^{2(s-1)}
$$

$$
> \frac{e}{s!^2}.
$$

Hence

$$
\frac{|\mathcal{M}|}{\binom{N}{m-s}^2} > \frac{eN^{2s-\lambda(1+2s^2)}}{e^2} \frac{e}{s!^2}
$$

$$
= \frac{N^{2s-\frac{1}{\log s \cdot e^{2s}}}}{s!^2}.
$$

It follows that there are $K_{s,s}$ on some pair of (unordered) s-sets, such that, for some k, $1 \leq k \leq n$, "the kth coordinates" $((x_k^1, \ldots . x_k^s), (y_k^1, \ldots, y_k^s))$ both form permutations of 1 to s. Therefore the original game G has a perfect strategy, and is thus trivial.

Therefore, the winning probability of the product game for a nontrivial game is bounded by $2eq^n$, for $n \geq \log s(1 + 2s^2)e^{2s}/s$, where $q = e^{-1/(1+2s^2)e^{2s}} = 1 - \frac{1}{(1+2s^2)e^{2s}} + \cdots$, which is less than, say, $1 - e^{-3s}/2$, for all s. Note that for $n < \log s(1 + 2s^2)e^{2s}/s$, q^n is bounded below by $1 - \log 2/2 > 1/2$, so that the bound $w(G^n) \leq 2eq^n$ holds for all n and s. $\square$

For a nontrivial game G that is not free, one can easily extend ϕ to $\hat{\phi} = \phi \vee [(x,y) \notin L]$, so that the extended game $\hat{G}$ is free, and since $w(G) \leq w(\hat{G})$, and $1 - w(\hat{G}) \geq \frac{|L|}{s^2}(1 - w(G)) > 0$, $\hat{G}$ is nontrivial. Applying Theorem 2.1, we have

Theorem 2.2 *If G is a non-trivial game, then there exists a $q < 1 - e^{-3s}/2$ and a universal constant c_0, such that the winning probability of G^n is at most $c_0 q^n$.*

3 Games with the Uniqueness Property

In this section we consider games that satisfy the uniqueness property, that is, games such that for all x, y, x' there is at most one y' such that $\phi(x, y, x', y') = 1$ and for all x, y, y' there is at most one x' such that $\phi(x, y, x', y') = 1$. We need the following technical lemma.

Lemma 3.1 *Suppose $p_1, \ldots, p_s$ and $q_1, \ldots, q_s$ are nonnegative real numbers such that $\sum p_i \leq 1$ and $\sum q_i \leq 1$. Let $1/2 \leq \alpha \leq 1$. If $\sum p_i q_i > \alpha$, then for some k, $p_k > \alpha$ and $q_k > \alpha$.*

Proof: Without loss of generality suppose that $p_1 \geq p_2 \geq \ldots \geq p_s$. First note that $p_1 > \alpha$. Otherwise for all i, $p_i \leq \alpha$. Then $\sum p_i q_i \leq \alpha \sum q_i = \alpha$, contradicting the fact that $\sum p_i q_i > \alpha$.

Therefore we must show that $q_1 > \alpha$. We first argue that $\sum_{i=2}^{s} p_i q_i \leq (1 - p_1)(1 - q_1)$. This is because

$$\sum_{i=2}^{s} p_i q_i \leq p_2 \sum_{i=2}^{s} q_i \leq (1 - p_1)(1 - q_1).$$

Now, suppose to the contrary that $q_1 \leq \alpha$. Then since $p_1 > 1 - p_1$,

$$\sum p_i q_i \leq p_1 q_1 + (1 - p_1)(1 - q_1) \leq \alpha p_1 + (1 - \alpha)(1 - p_1) \leq \alpha p_1 + \alpha(1 - p_1) = \alpha.$$

This contradicts the fact that $\sum p_i q_i > \alpha$. □

Theorem 3.1 *Let G be a non-trivial free game that satisfies the uniqueness property. Let $w(G) = 1 - \epsilon$. Then if $n = \lceil 1/\epsilon \rceil$, $w(G^n) \leq 7/8$.*

Proof: Let G be the game $\langle \phi, X \times Y, S, T \rangle$ and assume that $|X| = |Y| = |S| = |T| = s$. To prove the theorem, we show by induction on n that if $n \leq \lceil 1/\epsilon \rceil$, then $w(G^n) \leq (1 - (1/4)\epsilon)^n$. From this the theorem follows easily, since when $n = \lceil 1/\epsilon \rceil$, $(1 - (1/4)\epsilon)^n \leq 7/8$.

The basis case, when $n = 1$, is trivial, since $w(G) = 1 - \epsilon \leq 1 - (1/4)\epsilon$. Let $n > 1$. Fix strategies f and g of the players in game G^n that maximize $w(G^n)$. With respect to these strategies, define $w(G^n | x_1 = a, y_1 = b)$ to be the probability that the players win the game G^n, given that $x_1 = a$ and $y_1 = b$. Note that for any pair (a, b), this probability is at most $w(G^{n-1})$. Also, let H be the set of pairs (a, b) in $X \times Y$ for which $w(G^n | x_1 = a, y_1 = b) \geq (3/4)(1 - (1/4)\epsilon)^{n-1}$.

$$
\begin{aligned}
w(G^n) &= 1/s^2 \sum_{(a,b) \in X \times Y} w(G^n | x_1 = a, y_1 = b) \\
&\leq 1/s^2 [\sum_{(a,b) \in H} w(G^{n-1}) + \sum_{(a,b) \in (X \times Y) - H} (3/4)(1 - (1/4)\epsilon)^{n-1}] \\
&\leq \frac{(1 - (1/4)\epsilon)^{n-1}}{s^2} [\sum_{(a,b) \in H} 1 + \sum_{(a,b) \in (X \times Y) - H} (3/4)].
\end{aligned}
$$

We claim that $|H| \le (1 - \epsilon)s^2$. From this the lemma follows easily, since then

$$w(G^n) \le (1 - (1/4)\epsilon)^{n-1}[(1 - \epsilon) + (3/4)\epsilon] = (1 - (1/4)\epsilon)^n.$$

It remains to prove the claim. For each $a \in X$, $k \in S$, let a_k be the probability that $f_1(a, x_2, \ldots x_n) = k$, where $x_2, \ldots x_n$ are chosen randomly and uniformly from X. Similarly, for each $b \in Y$ and $k' \in T$, let $b_{k'}$ be the probability that $g_1(b, y_2, \ldots y_n) = k'$, where $y_2, \ldots y_n$ are chosen randomly and uniformly from Y.

We define the set $U(a, b)$ to be $\{(k, k') | \phi(a, b, k, k') = 1\}$. By the uniqueness property, each k occurs in at most one pair and each k' occurs in at most one pair. Hence $\sum_{(k,k') \in U(a,b)} a_k \le 1$ and $\sum_{(k,k') \in U(a,b)} b_{k'} \le 1$.

Then $w(G^n | x_1 = a, y_1 = b) \le \sum_{(k,k') \in U(a,b)} a_k b_{k'}$. To see this, note that if $\bar{x} = (a, x_2, \ldots, x_n)$ and $\bar{y} = (b, y_2, \ldots, y_n)$, the players win only if for some pair $(k, k') \in U(a, b)$, $f_1(\bar{x}) = k$ and $g_1(\bar{y}) = k'$. The probability of this is $a_k b_{k'}$ for each pair (k, k'), since the x_i's and the y_i's are chosen independently.

Hence if $(a, b) \in H$, $\sum_{(k,k') \in U(a,b)} a_k b_{k'} \ge (3/4)(1 - (1/4)\epsilon)^{n-1}$. Since $n \le \lceil 1/\epsilon \rceil$, $(1 - (1/4)\epsilon)^{n-1} \ge 3/4$, and so $\sum a_k b_{k'} \ge (3/4)^2 > 1/2$. By Lemma 3.1, if $(a, b) \in H$ then for some pair $(k, k') \in U(a, b)$, $a_k > 1/2$ and $b_{k'} > 1/2$.

We now define strategies f' and g' for players I and II of G and show that if the players use these strategies, the probability of winning the game G is at least $|H|/s^2$. From this it follows that $|H| \le (1 - \epsilon)s^2$, since $w(G) = 1 - \epsilon$. For any $a \in X$, let $f'(a) = i$ where i is an arbitrary element of S such that $a_i = \max_k a_k$. Similarly, for any $b \in Y$, let $g'(b) = j$, where j is an arbitrary element of T such that $b_j = \max_k b_k$.

Finally, we show that on these strategies, the players win on all pairs $(a, b) \in H$. This is because if $(a, b) \in H$ and $f'(a) = i$, $g'(b) = j$, then $a_i > 1/2$ and $b_j > 1/2$. We already showed that if $(a, b) \in H$ then for some pair (k, k'), $a_k > 1/2$ and $b_{k'} > 1/2$. Also, since $\sum a_k \le 1$ and $\sum b_{k'} \le 1$, there must be a unique i, j for which $a_i > 1/2$ and $b_j > 1/2$. From this it follows that $(i, j) \in U(a, b)$. Hence, $\phi(a, b, i, j) = 1 \Rightarrow \phi(a, b, f'(a), g'(b)) = 1$. This completes the proof that $|H| \le (1 - \epsilon)s^2$. $\square$

4 Results on $(1, 2)$-limited Free Games

In this section we extend Theorem 3.1 to free games that are $(1, 2)$-limited. A game is $(1, 2)$-limited if for all x, y, x' there is at most one y' such that $\phi(x, y, x', y') = 1$ and for all x, y, y' there are at most two x' such that $\phi(x, y, x', y') = 1$.

Theorem 4.1 *Let G be a non-trivial, $(1,2)$-limited free game. Let $w(G) = 1 - \epsilon$. Then if $n = \lceil 1/\epsilon \rceil$, $w(G^n) \le 11/12$.*

Proof: Let G be the game $\langle \phi, X \times Y, S, T \rangle$ and assume that $|X| = |Y| = |S| = |T| = s$. Just as in Theorem 3.1, we show by induction on n that if $n \leq \lceil 1/\epsilon \rceil$, then $w(G^n) \leq (1 - (1/6)\epsilon)^n$. From this the theorem follows easily, since when $n = \lceil 1/\epsilon \rceil$, $(1 - (1/6)\epsilon)^n \leq 11/12$.

The basis case, when $n = 1$, is trivial, since $w(G) = 1 - \epsilon \leq 1 - (1/6)\epsilon$. Let $n > 1$. Fix strategies f and g of the players in game G^n that maximize $w(G^n)$. With respect to these strategies, define $w(G^n | x_1 = a, y_1 = b)$ to be the probability that the players win the game G^n, given that $x_1 = a$ and $y_1 = b$. Note that for any pair (a, b), this probability is at most $w(G^{n-1})$. Also, let H be the set of pairs (a, b) in $X \times Y$ for which $w(G^n | x_1 = a, y_1 = b) \geq (5/6)(1 - (1/6)\epsilon)^{n-1}$.

$$
\begin{aligned}
w(G^n) &= 1/s^2 \sum_{(a,b) \in X \times Y} w(G^n | x_1 = a, y_1 = b) \\
&\leq 1/s^2 \Big[\sum_{(a,b) \in H} w(G^{n-1}) + \sum_{(a,b) \in (X \times Y) - H} (5/6)(1 - (1/6)\epsilon)^{n-1} \Big] \\
&\leq \frac{(1 - (1/6)\epsilon)^{n-1}}{s^2} \Big[\sum_{(a,b) \in H} 1 + \sum_{(a,b) \in (X \times Y) - H} (5/6) \Big].
\end{aligned}
$$

We claim that $|H| \leq (1 - \epsilon)s^2$. From this the lemma follows easily, since then

$$
w(G^n) \leq (1 - (1/6)\epsilon)^{n-1} [(1 - \epsilon) + (5/6)\epsilon] = (1 - (1/6)\epsilon)^n.
$$

It remains to prove the claim. For each $b \in Y$, $k \in T$, let b_k be the probability that $g_1(b, y_2, \ldots y_n) = k$, where $y_2, \ldots y_n$ are chosen randomly and uniformly from Y. Clearly $\sum_k b_k = 1$.

Let $S(a, b, k)$ be the subset of S such that $k' \in S(a, b, k)$ if and only if $\phi(a, b, k', k) = 1$. Since G is $(1, 2)$-limited, $|S(a, b, k)| \leq 2$ for all a, b, k. Also, if $k_1 \neq k_2$ then $S(a, b, k_1) \cap S(a, b, k_2)$ is empty. This is because if $k' \in S(a, b, k_1) \cap S(a, b, k_2)$, then $\phi(a, b, k', k_1) = \phi(a, b, k', k_2) = 1$. Since G is $(1, 2)$-limited, there is at most one k for which $\phi(a, b, k', k) = 1$; hence $k_1 = k_2$. Let $a_{b,k}$ be the probability that $f_1(a, x_2, \ldots, x_n) \in S(a, b, k)$, where $x_2, \ldots x_n$ are chosen randomly and uniformly from X. Since the sets $S(a, b, k)$ are disjoint for fixed (a, b), $\sum_k a_{b,k} \leq 1$. Then

$$
\begin{aligned}
w(G^n | x_1 = a, y_1 = b) &\leq \Pr[(f_1(a, x_2, \ldots, x_n) \in S_k) \text{ and } (g_1(b, y_2, \ldots y_n) = k)] \\
&= \Pr[f_1(a, x_2, \ldots, x_n) \in S_k] \Pr[g_1(b, y_2, \ldots y_n) = k] \\
&\quad \text{(since the } x_i \text{ and } y_i \text{ are independent)} \\
&= \sum_k a_{b,k} b_k.
\end{aligned}
$$

Hence if $(a, b) \in H$, $\sum_k a_{b,k} b_k \geq (5/6)(1 - (1/6)\epsilon)^{n-1}$. Since $n \leq \lceil 1/\epsilon \rceil$, $(1 - (1/6)\epsilon)^{n-1} \geq 5/6$, and so $\sum a_{b,k} b_k \geq (5/6)^2 > 2/3$. By Lemma 3.1, if $(a, b) \in H$ then for some k, $a_{b,k} > 2/3$ and $b_k > 2/3$.

We now define strategies f' and g' for players I and II of G and show that if the players use these strategies, the probability of winning the game G is at least $|H|/s^2$. From this it follows that $|H| \leq (1 - \epsilon)s^2$, since $w(G) = 1 - \epsilon$. For any $b \in Y$, let $g'(b) = j$, where j is the first element of T such that $b_j = \max_k b_k$. Note that for any a and any b such that $(a, b) \in H$, $\Pr[f(a, x_2, \ldots, x_n) \in S(a, b, g'(b))] > 2/3$, since this probability is $a_{b,g'(b)}$.

For any $a \in X$, if $(a, b) \notin H$ for some b, define $f'(a)$ arbitrarily. Otherwise, let $f'(a)$ be the first element of

$$\cap_{\{b|(a,b)\in H\}} S(a, b, g'(b)).$$

The fact that f' is well-defined follows easily from the next claim.

Claim: Fix a, and suppose that $(a, b) \in H$ for some b. Then $\cap_{\{b|(a,b)\in H\}} S(a, b, g'(b))$ is not empty.

To prove the claim, fix some b such that $(a, b) \in H$. Then since $\Pr[f(a, x_2, \ldots, x_n) \in S(a, b, g'(b))] > 2/3$ and $|S(a, b, g'(b))| \leq 2$, there must exist $k' \in S(a, b, g'(b))$ such that $\Pr[f(a, x_2, \ldots, x_n) = k'] > 1/3$. Hence for all b' such that $(a, b') \in H$, $k' \in S(a, b', g'(b'))$: otherwise, $\Pr[f(a, x_2, \ldots, x_n) \in S(a, b', g'(b'))] \leq 1 - 1/3 < 2/3$. Hence $k' \in \cap_{\{b|(a,b)\in H\}} S(a, b, g'(b))$, completing the proof of the claim.

Finally, we show that on these strategies, the players win on all pairs $(a, b) \in H$. This is because if $(a, b) \in H$, $f'(a) \in S(a, b, g'(b))$, by the above claim. Then by the definition of $S(a, b, g'(b))$, $\phi(a, b, f'(a), g'(b)) = 1$. This completes the proof that $|H| \leq (1 - \epsilon)s^2$. $\square$

Theorem 4.1 can easily be extended to $(1, l)$-limited games, by replacing $11/12$ in the statement of the above theorem by $\frac{4(l+1)-1}{4(l+1)}$.

5 Conclusions and Open Problems

Theorem 2.1 shows that the winning probability of the product G^n of a free game G converges to 0 exponentially fast as $n \to \infty$; the rate of convergence is $O(q^n)$, where $q < 1 - e^{-3s}/2$. This theorem can be improved by decreasing the number q. Ideally, we would like to show that the winning probability of G^n is $O(w(G)^n)$; that is, the winning probability converges to 0 at the same rate as $w(G^n)$. However, we do not know how to prove this.

Another problem that remains unsolved is to generalize this result to other types of two-person games. In particular, the computation of a general class of 1-round, 2-prover interactive proof systems on a fixed input can be modeled by the following type of game: $\langle \phi, E \subseteq X \times Y, S, T \rangle$, where ϕ is a *probabilistic* function, $\phi : E \times S \times T \to [0, 1]$. Can Theorem 2.2 be extended to this class of games?

References

[1] L. Babai, Trading Group Theory for Randomness, Proceedings of 17th STOC, 1985, pp 421-429.

[2] M. Ben-Or, S. Goldwasser, J. Killian and A. Wigderson, Multi-Prover Interactive Proofs: How to Remove Intractability, Proceedings of the 20th STOC, May, 1988.

[3] B. Bollobás, *Extremal Gaph Theory*, Academic Press, 1978.

[4] L. Fortnow, Complexity-Theoretic Aspects of Interactive Proof Systems, Ph. D. Thesis, Tech Report #MIT/LCS/TR-447, MIT.

[5] L. Fortnow, J. Rompel and M. Sipser, On the Power of Multi-Prover Interactive Protocols, Proceedings of the conference on Structure in Complexity Theory, 1988, pp 156-161.

[6] S. Goldwasser, S. Micali and C. Rackoff, The knowledge complexity of interactive protocols, Proceedings of 17th STOC, 1985, pp 291-304.

[7] S. Goldwasser and M. Sipser, Private Coins versus Public Coins in Interactive Proof Systems, Proceedings of 18th STOC, 1986, pp 59-68.

CATERPILLARS
AND
CONTEXT-FREE LANGUAGES

Michal P. Chytil*
Charles University
Malostranske nam. 25
CS-11800 Praha 1

Burkhard Monien
Math. and Computer Science
University of Paderborn
D-4790 Paderborn

Abstract

We use the concept of a caterpillar tree to study the properties of context-free languages, in particular new results about the index of context-free languages and the recognition of context-free languages are obtained this way. The first group of results points to differences between ambiguous and unambiguous languages. For unambiguous languages we prove the existence of a gap between finite index and $O(\log n)$ index. For ambiguous languages there is no such a gap: we prove the existence of grammars with infinite but arbitrarily slowly growing index. We show that bounded languages are of finite index and give a deterministic log space algorithm for the recognition of deterministic finite index languages. We also describe a parallel algorithm recognizing deterministic context-free languages on a CREW-PRAM with $O(n^2)$ processors in time $O(\log^2 n)$.

1 Introduction

In this paper we use the concept of caterpillars, inviting to a simple structural induction on trees, to investigate derivation trees. We shall show that this graph theoretic approach leads to a very simple presentation of some previously known results about context-free languages and prove new results concerning the notion of the index of languages, the importance of which was recognized already in the late sixties [Ynt], [Bra], [GiSp].

We prove that unambiguous grammars are either of finite or $O(\log n)$ index. On the other hand, no such a gap effect appears at general context-free languages: for any arbitrarily slowly growing recursive function f there is an (ambiguous) context-free grammar of infinite, but $f(n)$-bounded index. Furthermore, we show that the finite index property is decidable for unambiguous grammars, in contrast with the old undecidable result [Gru] for general context-free grammars. The structural induction on trees is also used to show that all bounded context-free languages are of finite index. Finally we prove that deterministic finite index languages are deterministically recognizable in $O(\log n)$ space.

Now, we come to the main notion used throughout the paper. A <u>caterpillar</u> is an ordered tree in which all vertices of outdegree greater than one occur on a single path from the root to a leaf. Such a path is the <u>backbone</u> of the caterpillar (cf. fig. 1). Note that in general several different paths can be chosen as the backbone of the caterpillar. Once the backbone is fixed we refer to any path branching from the backbone to a leaf as to a <u>hair</u>.

The notion of caterpillar can be generalized in a natural way to the notion of k-caterpillar for any positive integer k. 1-caterpillar is simply a caterpillar and for $k > 1$ a k-caterpillar is a tree obtained from a caterpillar by replacing each hair by a tree which is at most $(k-1)$-caterpillar.

---

*The work of this author was partly done during his stay at the University of Paderborn and was supported by the German Research Association (DFG)

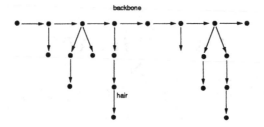

Figure 1: A caterpillar

Note that at any node in a k-caterpillar tree ($k > 1$), at most one edge leaving the node leads to a k-caterpillar tree. All other edges lead to subtrees which are at most $(k-1)$-caterpillars.

It is also easy to see that any tree is a k-caterpillar for some $k \leq \log n$, where n is the number of its leaves. Indeed, at most one edge leaving the root of a tree with n leaves leads to a subtree with more than $n/2$ leaves. This observation suggests a straightforward inductive proof of the assertion.

It is useful to mention the relation to the concept of the search number of a tree (cf. [MHGJP] and compare the notion of a backbone with that of an avenue). If a group of $k + 1$ searchers traverse a k-caterpillar in a pursuit of a fugitive, a successful strategy is to descend along the backbone. One searcher is left at the currently reached node v of the backbone and the remaining k searchers traverse the l-caterpillars ($l \leq k$) attached to v. Then all the group moves down to the next vertex of the backbone.

If applied to derivation trees, the above sketched searching strategy leads to a space efficient nondeterministic algorithm for the recognition of context-free languages as the following lemma shows.

Lemma 1. Let G be a context-free grammar. Then there exists a nondeterministic Turing machine M recognizing the language $L(G)$ and a constant $c > O$ such that any $w \in L(G)$ with a k-caterpillar derivation tree ($k \geq 1$) is accepted by M with a computation using not more than $c \cdot k \cdot \log |w|$ workspace.
Moreover, the machine M is such that any computation of M on any input string w makes at most $d|w|^2$ steps for a fixed constant d.

Proof. Assume for simplicity that the given context-free grammar G is in Chomsky normal form. We shall describe a nondeterministic off-line Turing machine M with one worktape. Let $w = a_1 \ldots a_n$ be an arbitrary input string. At any moment of its computation the machine M stores a sequence of triples on its worktape. Each triple is of the form (A, i, j), where A is a nonterminal symbol of the grammar G and $1 \leq i \leq j \leq n$. If such a triple appears on the worktape, the machine M will try to verify that

(1) $A \Rightarrow_G^* a_i \ldots a_j$.

If M fails to verify (1) then the computation is aborted, otherwise the triple (A, i, j) and all triples from it are eventually erased from the worktape. The work tape is operated as a pushdown store, the machine M always accesses only the rightmost triple. It performs the following types of operations.

1. At the beginning of the computation, the machine M places the triple $(S, 1, n)$ on its worktape. (S being the initial nonterminal of the grammar G.)

2. If a triple (A, i, j), where $1 \leq i < j \leq n$, is on the top of the pushdown then it is nondeterministically replaced by any of the following pairs of triples:
   (B, i, k), $(C, k + 1, j)$ or $(C, k + 1, j)$, (B, i, k), for any k such that $i \leq k < j$, provided that $A \rightarrow BC$ is a production of the grammar G.

3. If a triple (A, i, i) is on the top of the pushdown then M moves its input head to the i-th symbol of the input string. If $A \rightarrow a_i$ is a production of the grammar, then M pops the triple from the pushdown, otherwise it aborts the computation.

The input word is accepted if the worktape is completely emptied.

It is easy to see that the machine M accepts the string w iff it belongs to $L(G)$. An accepting computation completely traverses a derivation tree for w. The triples on the worktape can be interpreted as positions of searchers in the tree. In a space optimal computation the search follows the k-caterpillar structure of the derivation tree. (To facilitate it, both orderings of the pushed pair are allowed in steps of the type 2.) Therefore the optimal computation never stores more than $k + 1$ triples if the derivation tree is a k-caterpillar. This establishes the space bound.

To evaluate the time complexity, note that not more than n steps of the type 2 and not more than n steps of the type 3 are performed during any computation on any input of length n. Steps of type 2 and 3 can be done in time $O(\log n)$ and $O(n)$, respectively. From this follows the $O(n^2)$ time bound. ∎

The following corollary is a minor sharpening of a result by Ruzzo [Ruz], instead of polynomial time we have a quadratic time bound. The result is a nondeterministic counterpart of the result by von Braunmühl, Cook, Mehlhorn, und Verbeek [BCMV].

Corollary 2. Context-free languages are recognizable on nondeterministic Turing machines simultaneously in $O(\log^2 n)$ space and $O(n^2)$ time.

The notion of a k-caterpillar is closely related to the notion of the index of context-free languages [Ynt], [Bra], [GiSp]. Recall that the _index of a derivation_ $d : X \Rightarrow_G^* w$ in a context-free grammar G is the maximal number of nonterminals occurring simultaneously at an intermediate step of the derivation. We shall denote it by $Ind_G(d)$. Then define

$$Ind_G(X, w) = min\{Ind_G(d); d : X \Rightarrow_G^* w\} \text{ and}$$
$$Ind_G(w) = Ind_G(S, w),$$

where w, X, S stand for a terminal string, a nonterminal symbol and the initial nonterminal of the grammar G, respectively. For more details, see e.g. [Sal2]. The relation between k-caterpillar derivation trees and the index of derivations they describe is expressed by the following two lemmata (the proofs are omitted here).

Lemma 3. Let d be an arbitrary derivation in a context-free grammar and $Ind(d) = k$. Then the derivation tree for d is at most k-caterpillar.

If a context-free grammar G is such that for all $w \in L(G)$ is $Ind_g(w) \leq k$ for some fixed constant k, then the grammar is of _finite index_, otherwise it is of _infinite index_. A context-free language is of finite index if it can be generated by a context-free grammar of finite index. It is of infinite index otherwise. Lemma 1 and Lemma 3 immediately give complexity bounds for nondeterministic recognition of finite index context-free languages. It is again a minor sharpening of a result proved in [JoSk].

Corollary 4. Context-free languages of finite index are recognizable on nondeterministic Turing machines simultaneously in logarithmic space and quadratic time.

To get the exact converse of Lemma 3 we restrict in an unessential way the form of the context-free grammar.

Lemma 5. Let G be a context-free grammar without chain rules (i. e. rules of the form $X \to Y$, where X and Y are nonterminals) and such that the right hand side of any of its productions contains at most two symbols and let $k \geq 1$. Then to every k-caterpillar derivation tree of a terminal string w from a nonterminal symbol X there exists a derivation $d : X \Rightarrow^* w$ such that $Ind(d) \leq k$.

Observe how the formulation of Lemma 5 would change without the restrictions imposed on the form of the grammar. If the right-hand sides of the productions are of length at most l for some $l \geq 2$, then a k-caterpillar derivation tree leads to a derivation of index at most $k + l - 1$. Chain productions can create hairs longer than 1 in the derivation tree. Then a 1-caterpillar derivation tree of degree r can require derivations of index r.

From Lemma 5 and the fact that each tree with n leaves is at most $(\log n)$-caterpillar it follows that each terminal string generated by a context-free grammar G can be derived so that in any sentential form in its derivation there are at most $c \cdot \log |w|$ nonterminals, where c is a constant depending on G only. It is natural to ask whether there are grammars of infinite index for which the minimal number of nonterminals necessary to derive a string can be bounded by a function of order smaller than $\log n$. In the next section we shall show that the answer to this question distinguishes unambiguous from ambiguous languages.

The results in the following three sections are based on similar (though more sophisticated) reasoning about the caterpillar structure of derivation trees as was illustrated in this introduction. Because of lack of space we cannot present all proofs here and refer the reader to [ChMo].

2 Index and ambiguity

First of all we prove a "gap theorem" for unambiguous context-free grammars.

Theorem 6. Every unambiguous context-free grammar of index bounded by a function $f \in o(\log)$ is of finite index.

The theorem is a consequence of the following lemma.

Lemma 7. Let G be an arbitrary context-free grammar, r the number of its nonterminals and d the maximal length of the right-hand side of its productions. Then for every k-caterpillar derivation tree $T(k \geq 1)$ describing a derivation $X \Rightarrow^* w$, where X is a nonterminal and w a terminal string, there exist a k-caterpillar derivation tree T' describing a derivation $X \Rightarrow^* w'$ of some terminal string w' such that

$$|w'| \leq [r(d-1) + 1]^k.$$

Proof. Let us denote $l(k) = [r(d-1)+1]^k$. We prove the lemma by induction on k.

1) Consider the case $k = 1$. The derivation tree T is a caterpillar. If its backbone is longer than r then two nodes on it are labeled by an identical nonterminal. Let us choose two such maximally distant nodes u_1, u_2, u_1 being the node closer to the root of the tree T.

   Replacement of the subtree with the root u_1 by the subtree with the root u_2 yields a caterpillar derivation tree T' with the backbone not longer than r. It is easy to see that the number of its leaves is bounded by $r(d-1) + 1 = l(1)$.

2) Now assume that the lemma holds for derivation trees which are at most k-caterpillars and consider an arbitrary $(k+1)$-caterpillar derivation tree T. It is easy to see that the backbone of T contains a node v such that at least two successors of v are roots of k-caterpillar trees (cf. Fig. 2). This node is the node most remote from the root, which still induces a $k + 1$-caterpillar. If the path from the root to the node v is longer than r then similarly as in the preceding case, two nodes u_1, u_2 labeled by an identical nonterminal can be chosen so that omitting the intervall between u_1 and u_2 (the hatched area in Fig. 2) yields a tree T'' in which the distance between the root and the node v is at most r. As the subtree induced by v is still a subtree of T'', T'' is again a $(k+1)$-caterpillar.

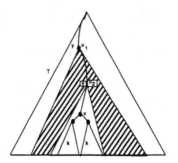

Figure 2: The existence of the tree T''

There are at most $r(d-1)+1$ nodes hanging on the path form the root of T'' to the vertex v and not belonging to the path. Each of them is the root of a subtree which is at most k-caterpillar.

By induction hypothesis every such an m-caterpillar ($m \leq k$) can be substituted by an m-caterpillar with at most $l(k)$ leaves. Let us denote T' the tree which results from all the substitutions. It is again a $k + 1$-caterpillar with at most

$$[r(d-1) + 1] \cdot l(k) = l(k+1)$$

leaves.

This completes the proof of the lemma. ∎

Proof of Theorem 6. Let G be an unambiguous context-free grammar of index bounded by a function f such that $f \in o(\log)$. Let r and d denote the same parameters as in the lemma 7.

From the assumption $f \in o(\log)$ it follows that $[r(d-1)+1]^{f(n)} < n$ for all n starting from some integer $m \geq 1$. In other words,

(*) $n \leq [r(d-1)+1]^{f(n)}$ implies that $n < m$.

Let us choose an arbitrary $w \in L(G)$ and let T be its derivation tree. T is a k-caterpillar for some $k \leq f(|w|)$. By Lemma 7, there exists a string $w' \in L(G)$ such that its unique (by unambiguity of G) derivation tree is also a k-caterpillar (hence $k \leq f(|w'|)$) and

$$|w'| \leq [r(d-1) + 1]^k \leq [r(d-1) + 1]^{f(|w'|)}.$$

By (*), w' is shorter than m.

We proved for w arbitrary that $Ind(w) = Ind(w')$ for some w' shorter than m. Therefore G is of finite index. ∎

It is quite clear that the proof of Theorem 6 will not go through for ambiguous grammars. However, it is surprising that at ambiguous grammars the index can be kept arbitrarily slowly growing but still infinite.

Theorem 8. For any arbitrary slowly growing unbounded recursive function f there exists a context-free grammar of infinite $f(n)$-bounded index.

Proof. We can assume that the function f is nondecreasing, otherwise it can be replaced by a nondecreasing unbounded recursive function majorized by f.

Let M be a Turing machine computing the function f in unary, i. e. if it starts with the input word 1^n scanning its leftmost symbol in its initial state, it terminates with the tape containing the string $1^{f(n)}$ and its head positioned on its first symbol.

Consider computations of the machine M. We shall represent them in the form

(*) $\qquad \#c_0\#c_1\#\ldots\#c_m$

where c_0 and c_m are initial and final configurations, respectively, and c_{i+1} is always the immediate successor of the configuration c_i. Each configuration is represented as a string $u(q,x)v$, where uxv is the content of the tape, q the state of the machine and the head is scanning the symbol x. Note that for any computation

$$w = \#c_0\#c_1\#\ldots\#c_m$$

of the machine M the condition $|c_m| \leq f(|w|)$ holds. It immediately follows from the fact that $|c_m| = f(|c_0|)$ and the monotonicity of f. Let Σ be the alphabet in which configurations are written, $\# \notin \Sigma$. Define the language

$$L_1 = \{\#c_0\#c_1\#\ldots\#x_1\ldots x_k\#y_1\ldots y_j \; ; \; x_1,\ldots,x_k \in \Sigma, \#c_0\#\ldots\#x_1\ldots x_k \text{ is a (full) computation of } M,$$
$$y_1,\ldots y_j \in \{0,1\}, \text{ and } j \leq k\}$$

It is not difficult to see that the complement L_2 of the language L_1 is a linear language.

It follows from the well-known fact that for any Turing machine, the language of all its computations written in the form (*) is the complement of a linear language and the complement of the language $\{a^k b^j ; 1 \leq k\}$ is also linear.

Let G_2 be a linear grammar generating L_2. Denote by D the Dyck language over the alphabet $\{0,1\}$ and define the language

$$L_3 = \{u\#x_1\ldots x_n\#y_1\ldots y_m; u \in (\Sigma \cup \{\#\})^*, x_1,\ldots x_n \in \Sigma, y_1,\ldots y_m \in \{0,1\}, y_1\ldots y_m \in D\}$$

Let us construct a context-free grammar G_3 generating L_3. The grammar has the rules

$$S \rightarrow AB$$
$$B \rightarrow aA|e, \text{ for each } a \in \Sigma \cup \{\#\}$$
$$B \rightarrow BB|0B1|e$$

where e stands for the empty word.

The context-free grammar G generating the language $L = L_2 \cup L_3$
can be constructed in the standard way as the disjoint union of the grammars G_2 und G_3. It is of infinite index. This fact immediately follows from the following observations:

- the grammar $S \rightarrow SS|0S1|e$ generating D is of infinite index, as was shown by Salomaa [Sal1];

- the language $L_3 - L_2$ is infinite;

- the left quotient $(\Sigma \cup \{\#\}) \setminus (L_3 - L_2)$ equals D.

It remains to prove that the grammar G is of $f(n)$-bounded index. Consider an arbitrary $w \in L(G)$. There are two cases to distinguish.

- If $w \in L_2$ then it can be generated following a derivation in G_2 of index 1.

- If $w \in L_3 - L_2$ then the word belongs to the language $L_3 \cap L_1$ and is of the form $w = u\#y_1\ldots y_n$, where $n \leq f(|w|)$. Then the string is generated following a derivation in G_3 and the derivation has index at most n. Hence $Ind_G(w) \leq (|w|)$.

Note the crucial role of ambiguity in this argument. The strings belonging to $L_2 \cap L_3$ can have derivations following G_3 which have very high index. Every such a string, however, has also a derivation of index 1, following the grammar G_2. ∎

In the balance of the section we point still to·one more difference between unambiguous and ambiguous context-free grammars.

Proposition 9. [Gru] The problem whether a context-free grammar is of finite index is undecidable.

A closer examination of the proof in [Gru] shows that it depends on ambiguity of grammars. The following result shows that it is an essential point.

Theorem 10. The problem whether an unambiguous context-free grammar is of finite index is decidable.

Sketch of the proof. We use the fact that a reduced unambiguous grammar G is of infinite index iff for at least one of its nonterminals there is a derivation $X \Rightarrow_G^* \alpha_1 X \alpha_2 X \alpha_3$ for some strings $\alpha_1, \alpha_2 \alpha_3$. This result, proved in general form in [GiSp] is very easy to see in the case of unambiguous grammars.
Now by the same technique of cutting out subparts of derivation trees as was used in the proof of Lemma 7 we can show that if $X \Rightarrow_G^* \alpha_1 X \alpha_2 X \alpha_3$ for some $\alpha_1, \alpha_3, \alpha_3$, then $X \Rightarrow_G^* \beta_1 X \beta_2 X \beta_3$ for some $\beta_1, \beta_2, \beta_3$ such that $|\beta_1 X \beta_2 X \beta_3| \leq k$, where k is a constant depending only on G.

Therefore to decide whether G is of infinite index, it is sufficient to check all derivations of strings bounded by k. ∎

3 Languages of finite index

From the early days of the theory of context-free languages, the class of bounded languages was recognized as an important subclass for which many of questions, undecidable in the general case, were algorithmically treatable. A context-free language L is called <u>k-bounded</u> if there exist words $w_1, \ldots, w_k$ such that $L \subset w_1^* w_2^* \ldots w_k^*$. It is called bounded if it is k-bounded for some k. The class of bounded languages appeared in new light after it was shown [LaTh] that bounded context-free languages are exactly sparse context-free languages. We shall show that all bounded languages are of finite index.

Theorem 11. Every k-bounded context-free language is of index at most $\lceil \log k \rceil$.

Proof. First we prove the theorem for the special case of strictly bounded languages. A language L is called strictly k-bounded if $L \subset a_1^* a_2^* \ldots a_k^*$, when $a_1, a_2, \ldots a_k$ are different letters. The proof is by induction on k.

It is not difficult to prove that every 2-bounded context-free language is a linear language (see [ChMo]).

Assume that the theorem holds for all strictly k-bounded languages for a $k \geq 2$. Let $L \subseteq a_1^* a_2^* \ldots a_{k+1}^*$ be an arbitrary context-free language derived by a context-free grammar G. Denote $i = \lfloor (k+1)/2 \rfloor$. The nonterminals of G can be divided into three categories:

1) the nonterminals deriving a subset of $a_1^* a_2^* \ldots a_i^*$
2) the nonterminals deriving a subset of $a_{i+1}^* \ldots a_{k+1}^*$
3) the remaining nonterminals.

Then in any rule of the form $X \rightarrow YZ$, where X is of the category 3, at most one of the nonterminals Y, Z is of the third category. Otherwise the derivation of a string not belonging to $a_1^* a_2^* \ldots a_{k+1}^*$ would be possible.

Hence in any sentential form there occurs at most one nonterminal of category 3 and in any derivation tree for a string $w \in a_1^* \ldots a_{k+1}^* \in L$ the occurences of nonterminals belonging to the third category are bound to the path splitting the string w into the $a_1^* \ldots a_i^*$-part and the $a_{i+1}^* \ldots a_{k+1}^*$-part (cf. fig. 3).

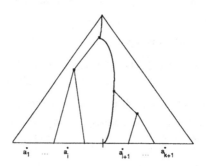

Figure 3: The path splitting the string w

Denote $r = (k + 1)/2$. By induction hypothesis, all languages generated from the nonterminals of the first category are of index at most $\lceil \log\lfloor r \rfloor \rceil$ and all languages generated from the nonterminals of the second category are of index at most $\lceil \log\lceil r \rceil \rceil$. As $\lceil \log\lfloor r \rfloor \rceil \leq \lceil \log\lceil r \rceil \rceil \leq \lceil \log(k + 1) \rceil - 1$, a grammar of index at most $\lceil \log(k + 1) \rceil$ generating L can be constructed.

This completes the proof for strictly bounded languages.

It remains to consider the general case, when $L \subset w_1^* w_2^* \dots w_k^*$ for some strings $w_1, \dots, w_k$. But then $L = h(L')$, where $L \subseteq a_1^* \dots a_k^*$ is a strictly bounded language and h is the homomorphism which maps each a_i on w_i. Hence $Ind(L) \leq Ind(L') \leq \log k$. ∎

Now we turn to the problem of context-free language recognition. Using similar tools as in preceding paragraphs, we shall describe a space efficient recognition algorithm for a natural subclass of deterministic context-free languages. We shall represent the languages by deterministic pushdown automata and make use of a tree structure underlying their computations. The tree structure is specified along the same lines as Wechsung [Wec] introduced the notion of "oscillation complexity".

We shall describe changes of the pushdown height during a computation of a pushdown automaton by a <u>surface curve</u> (cf. fig. 4).

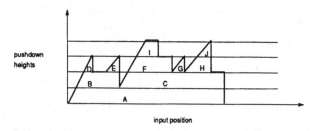

Figure 4: A surface curve

Note that the surface curve never reaches the x-axis before its endpoint, but even the endpoint can have positive height, because the deterministic pushdown automaton can have nonempty pushdown when accepting an input word by a final state.

If the area under the surface curve is cut by horizontal lines in positive integer heights and areas with a common segment border are called neighbour areas, then the areas with the neighbourhood relation form a tree (cf. fig. 4 and 5)

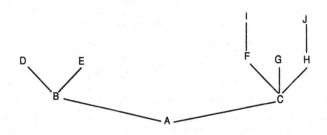

Figure 5: The tree underlying the surface curve

called <u>the tree underlying the surface curve</u>. The term <u>k-curve</u> will be used for any surface curve with the underlying k-caterpillar. The simplest case (corresponding to one-turn pushdown automata) is when the underlying tree is only a path, i. e. a caterpillar without hairs. Then the surface curve will be called a <u>0-curve</u>.

We shall say that a language L is of <u>deterministic index k</u> ($k \geq 0$) if the language is recognized by a deterministic pushdown automaton M such that surface curves of all accepting computations are at most k-curves.

Theorem 12. Any language of deterministic index k($k \geq 0$ can be recognized by a deterministic $3k + 2$ head finite automaton.

4 Parallel Recognition of deterministic context-free languages

We assume that the reader is familiar with the notions of parallel random access machines and refer for a detailed description to [GiRy]. We will use here the notions CREW-PRAM (concurrent read, exlusive write) and CRCW-PRAM (concurrent read, concurrent write). We will show:

Theorem 13: Any deterministic context-free language can be recognized by a CREW-PRAM with $O(n^2)$ processors within time $O(\log^2 n)$.

This is the smallest number of processors known for recognizing deterministic context-free languages on a parallel random access machine within polylogarithmic time. Let us recall previous results about the parallel recognition of context-free languages.

class of languages	processors	time, machine model	reference
general CFL	n^6	$\log n$, CRCW	[GiRy]
	n^6	$\log^2 n$, CREW	[GiRy]
unambiguous CFL	n^7	$\log n$, CREW	[Ryt]
	n^3	$\log^2 n$ CREW	[CCMR]
deterministic CFL	n^3	$\log n$, CREW	[KlRe]
	$n^2 \log n$	$\log n$, CREW	[KlRe]

Our algorithm uses the caterpillar structure defined by the computation of the deterministic pushdown automaton as it is described in the previous section. It is conceptually not difficult (compared for example with the algorithm presented in [KlRe]) and a complete ParPASCAL - like description of the algorithm is given in figure 10. It can be transformed easily to an algorithm running on a CREW-PRAM in time $O(\log n)$ with $O(n^3)$ processors.

Let P be a deterministic pushdown automaton. Let us denote its sets of states, input symbols and pushdown symbols by S, X and Γ, respectively. In the usual way let $(s, w, i, \gamma), s \in S, w \in X^n, i \in \{1, ..., n\}, \gamma \in \Gamma^*$ be a configuration of P and let $\longmapsto$ be the mapping on the set of configurations defined by the transition function δ. Since w is fixed during a computation we denote a configuration also by (s, i, γ). We can restrict P such that in every step P either pops or writes two pushdown symbols, i.e. δ is a mapping $\delta : S \times (X \cup \{\epsilon\}) \times \Gamma \to S \times \{0, +1\} \times (\{\epsilon\} \cup \Gamma^2)$. We also allow ϵ-moves (though the algorithm described below does not take this into account) and therefore we can assume that an accepting computation ends in a final state and with empty pushdown store.

Our algorithm uses four arrays $R[A]$ of $B, C[A]$ of $A, F[A]$ of A and $G[A, B]$ of B, where $A = S \times \Gamma \times \{1, ..., n\}$ and $B = S \times \{1, ..., n\}$. We want to describe the values which these arrays hold during the computation. A point of time during the run of our algorithm is given by three parameters $(v, t, \mu), 0 \leq v, t \leq \lceil \log n \rceil, \mu \in \{0, 1\}$. v and t denote the corresponding runs of the v-loop and of one of the t-loops, respectively. For $v > 0$ the value $\mu = 0$ denotes the positions within the blocks 3 and 4, $\mu = 1$ denotes the positions within the blocks 5 and 6. With $R(a, v, t, \mu)$ we denote the value stored by $R[a]$ at time point (v, t, μ). Similiar notations are used for C, F and G.

Our algorithm finds successively all computations of P on input w starting with one symbol on the pushdown tape and ending with empty tape. Let us call such a computation a "popping computation".

In the first $(v - 1)$ runs all "popping computations" of caterpillar type $< v$ have been computed. They are encoded by array R, i.e. $R(a, v, 0, 0) = b \Longleftrightarrow a \stackrel{*}{\longmapsto} (b, \epsilon)$ is a computation of caterpillar type $< v$. Above we identified an element $a = (s, \gamma, i) \in S \times \Gamma \times \{1, ..., n\}$ with the configuration (s, i, γ) and we will do this throughout this section.

Now in the v-th run all "popping computations" of type v are computed. Note that a computation of type v has the following properties. If all surfaces belonging to a computation of type $< v$ are cut by horizontal lines, then the curve generated this way is a simple "hill", i.e. a path climbing monotonically up to some height and then descending down monotonically (see figure 6). The height of this hill will be called the height of the computation.

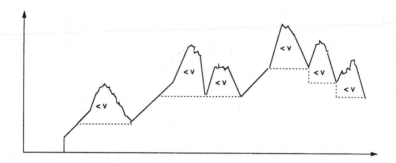

Figure 6: Computation of type v

When we start the v-th round all popping computations of type $< v$ have been simulated already. In the v-th round we use this information, and cut all these computations by a horizontal line. The resulting computation is simply a hill and this is the reason that $O(n^2)$ processors turn out to be sufficient.

In blocks 3,4 all computations of type v and height 1 are simulated.

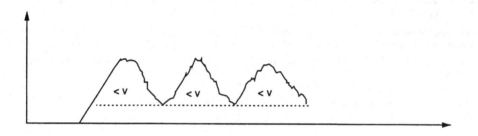

Figure 7: A computation of type v and height 1

Such a computation is shown in figure 7. It consists of a sequence of elementary computations, each of which consists of a pushing operations followed directly by a popping computation of type $< v$. We call this computation a chain, the length of a chain is its number of elementary computations. Chains are stored by the array C and the following will hold during the computation:

$C(a, v, t, 0) = a'$
$\Leftrightarrow a \xmapsto{\ *\ } a'$ is a computation of type v and height 1
    and either the chain has length 2^t or it is a maximal chain of length $\le 2^t$

A chain is called maximal if it can't be extended (i.e. the pushdown store is growing). A chain may be closed with a popping computation.

Block 3 computes chains of length 1 and by applying (in block 4) successively the operations
$\qquad C[a] := C[C[a]], \quad R[a] := R[C[a]]$
we finally get all maximal chains of type v and all popping computations of type v and height 1,
i.e. $\quad C(a, v, 0, 1) = a'$
$\qquad \Leftrightarrow a \xmapsto{\ *\ } a'$ is a maximal chain of type v
$\qquad R(a, v, 0, 1) = b$
$\qquad \Leftrightarrow a \xmapsto{\ *\ } (b, \epsilon)$ is a popping computation of type $< v$ or of type v and height 1.

In the remaining part of the v-loop we simulate every popping computation of type v. A computation is split into two subcomputations each of half the height of the original computation, see Figure 8.

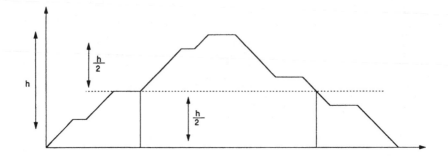

Figure 8: Splitting a popping computation

One of these computations is again a popping computation, the other one consists of two subcomputations which are connected by the pushdown tape. We will call this computation a volcano. A volcano is given by the parameters $a = (s_1, \gamma_1, i) \in A, b = (s_3, p) \in B, a' = (s_2, \gamma_2, j) \in A$ and $b' = (s_4, q) \in B$. It fullfills:

(1) $a \overset{*}{\longmapsto} (s_2, j, \zeta\gamma_2)$ for some $\zeta \in \Gamma^*$ is a height increasing computation of type v

(2) $(s_3, p, \zeta) \overset{*}{\longmapsto} (s_4, q, \epsilon)$ is a height decreasing computation of type v.

Such a volcano will be denoted by $V(a, b, a', b')$, its height is given by the length of ζ. Note that b' is uniquely determined by a, b and a'.

We will compute maximal volcanos of height 1 in block 5 and in the t-loop, block 6, maximal volcanos of height 2^t are computed. Note that if $V(a, b, a', b')$ is a maximal volcano of some fixed height, then a' is uniquely determined by a.

Therefore we can store $V(a, b, a', b')$ by the two arrays $F[a] = a', G[a, b] = b'$, i.e. the following will hold for all t :
$$F(a, v, t, 1) = a' \text{ and } G(a, b, v, t, 1) = b'$$
$$\Leftrightarrow V(a, b, a', b') \text{ is a maximal volcano of type } v \text{ and height } 2^t.$$

A volcano of height 2^t is combined from two volcanos of height 2^{t-1} as it is described in Figure 9.

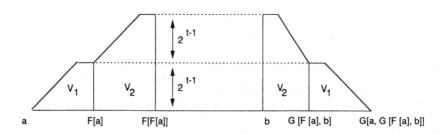

Figure 9: Generating a volcano of height 2^t

For every $a \in A, b \in B$ the two volcanos of height 2^{t-1}
$V_1 = V(a, G[F[a], b], F[a], G[a, G[F[a], b]])$,
$V_2 = V(F[a], b, F[F[a]], G[F[a], b])$
generate (if they exist) the new volcano V of height 2^t $V = V(a, b, F[F[a]], G[a, G[F[a], b]])$. Therefore in block 6 all volcanos of height 2^t are computed.

In block 6 also volcanos of height 2^{t-1} are combined with popping computations of height $\leq 2^{t-1}$ to form popping computations of height $\leq 2^t$, i.e.
$$R(a, v, t, 1) = b$$
$$\Leftrightarrow a \overset{*}{\longmapsto} (b, \epsilon) \text{ is a computation of type } < v \text{ or of type } v \text{ and height } \leq 2^t.$$

Since the height is always bounded by n, all popping computations of type v are computed by performing $\lceil \log n \rceil$ runs through the t-loop.

P is a deterministic pushdown and therefore every popping computation, every chain and every volcano is simulated by our algorithm exactly once. This implies that no write conflicts occur and completes the proof of theorem 13.

---

for all $\alpha \in S \times \Gamma$; $s \in S$; $i \in \{1, ..., n\}$ do parallel   (* block 1 *)
    if $\delta(\alpha, a_i) = (s, \eta, \epsilon)$ for some $s \in S$; $\eta \in \{0, 1\}$
    then $R[\alpha, i] := (s, i + \eta)$;

for $v := 1$ to $\lceil log_2 n \rceil$ do begin

    for all $a \in A$; $b \in B$ do begin   (* block 2 *)
       $H[a, b] := \emptyset$; $C[a] := \emptyset$ end;

    for all $\alpha \in S \times \Gamma$; $s \in S$; i, $p \in \{1, ..., n\}$ do parallel   (* block 3 *)
      if $\delta(\alpha, a_i) = (s, \eta, \gamma_1 \gamma_2)$ for some $s \in S$; $\eta \in \{0, 1\}$; $\gamma_1, \gamma_2 \in \Gamma$
       and $R[s, \gamma_2, i + \eta] = (s', j)$ for some $s' \in S$; $j \in \{1, ..., n\}$
      then $C[\alpha, i] := (s', \gamma_1, j)$
      else $C[\alpha, i] := (\alpha, i)$;

    for $t := 1$ to $\lceil log_2 n \rceil$ do begin   (* block 4 *)
      for all $a \in A$ do parallel $R[a] := R[C[a]]$;
      for all $a \in A$ do parallel $C[a] := C[C[a]]$;
    end;

    for all $a \in A$; $b \in B$ do parallel   (* block 5 *)
      if $C[a] = (\beta, j)$ for some $\beta \in S \times \Gamma$; $j \in \{1, ..., n\}$
       and $\delta(\beta, a_j) = (s', \eta, \gamma_1 \gamma_2)$ for some $s' \in S$; $\gamma_1, \gamma_2 \in \Gamma$
      then begin $F[a] := (s', \gamma_2, j + \eta)$; $G[a, b] := R[b, \gamma_1]$ end;

    for $t := 1$ to $\lceil log_2 n \rceil$ do begin   (* block 6 *)
      for all $a \in A$ do parallel $R[a] := G[a, R[F[a]]]$;
      for all $a \in A$; $b \in B$ do parallel begin
         $F[a] := F[F[a]]$; $G[a, b] = G[a, G[F[a], b]]$ end;
    end

end

Figure 10: The algorithm

Conclusion

We feel that considering the "caterpillar structure" of derivation trees is a fruitful tool in language theory. The results on index and ambiguity and on the complexity of recognition proved in this paper show that some properties of context-free languages are reflected already on the level of graph theoretic characteristics of the underlying sets of derivation trees. Similar conclusion for ETOL languages was derived in [ERV]

References

[Alt]   Alt, H., Lower bounds on space complexity of context-free recognition, AI 12 (1979), 33-61,

[Bra]   Brainerd, B., An analog of a theorem about context-free languages, Information and Control 11 (1968), 561-567,

[BCMV]   von Braunmuehl, B., Cook, S., Mehlhorn, K., Verbeek, R., The recognition of deterministic CFLs in small time and space, Information and Control 56 (1983), 34-51,

[CCMR]   Chytil, M., Crochemore, M., Monien, B., Rytter, W., On the parallel recognition of unambiguous context-free languages, submitted for publication

[ChJa]   Chytil, M., Jakl, V., Serial composition of 2-way finite state transducers and simple programs on strings, Proc. of ICALP'77, LNCS 52, Springer-Verlag 1977, 135-147,

[ChMo]   Chytil, M., Monien, B., Caterpillars and Context-free languages, technical report no. 56, University of Paderborn, October 1988

[DyRu]   Dymond, P.W., Ruzzo, W.L., Parallel RAMs with owned global memory and deterministic context-free language recognition, Proc. ICALP'86, Lecture Notes in Computer Science 226 (1986), 95-104,

[ERV]   Ehrenfeucht, A., Rozenberg, G., Vermeir, D., On ETOL systems with finite tree rank, SIAM J. Comput. 10 (1981), 40-58,

[GiRy]   Gibbons, A., Rytter, W., Efficient Parallel Algorithms, Cambridge University Press, 1988,

[GiSp]   Ginsburg, S., Spanier, E., Derivation - bounded languages, JCSS 2 (1968), 228-250,

[Gru]   Gruska, J., A few remarks on the index of context-free grammars and languages, Information and Control 19 (1971), 216-223,

[HoUl]   Hopcroft, J.E., Ullman, J.D., Formal languages and their relation to automata, Addison-Wesley, Reading, Mass. 1969,

[JoSk]   Jones, N.D., Skyum, S., Recognition of deterministic ETOL languages in logarithmic space, Information and Control 35 (1977), 177-181,

[KlRe]   Klein, P.N., Reif, J., Parallel time $O(\log n)$ acceptance of deterministic CFLs on an exclusive-write P-RAM, SIAM J. Computing 17 (1988, 463-485

[LaTh]   Latteaux, M., Thierrin, G., On bounded cf-languages, EIK 20 (1984),

[MHGJP]   Meggido, N., Hakimi S.L., Garey, M.R., Johnson, D.S., Papadimitriou, C.H., The complexity of searching a graph, Proc. FOCS'81, 376-385,

[Ruz]   Ruzzo, W.L., Tree-size bounded alternation, JCSS 21 (1980), 218-235,

[Ryt]   Rytter, W., Parallel time $O(\log n)$ recognition of unambiguous CFL's, Proc. FCT'85, Lecture Notes in Computer Science 199 (1985), 380-389,

[Sal1]   Salomaa, A., On the index of a context-free grammar and language, Information and Control 14 (1969), 474-477,

[Sal2]   Salomaa, A., Formal language theory, Academic Press 1973,

[Wec]   Wechsung, G., The oscillation complexity and a hierarchy of context-free languages, Proceedings of FCT'79, L. Budach (ed.), Akad. Verlag Berlin 1979, 508-515,

[Ynt]   Yntema, M., Inclusion relations among families of context-free languages, Information and Control 10 (1967), 572-597.

SEMI-COMMUTATIONS AND ALGEBRAIC LANGUAGES

Mireille CLERBOUT and Yves ROOS
L.I.F.L., CNRS UA 369,
Université des Sciences et Techniques de Lille, Flandres et Artois,
59655 Villeneuve d'Ascq, France

1.INTRODUCTION

The study of free partially commutative monoïds has been initiated by Cartier and Foata to solve combinatory problems ([1]) and Mazurkiewicz proposed traces languages as a tool for describing the behaviour of concurrent program schemes.

A free partially commutative monoïd can be described as a rewriting system $S = <X, P>$ where X is a finite alphabet and S is a set a symetrical productions of the form $xy \leftrightarrow yx$, where x and y are two letters of the alphabet x. These systems are also called "**partial commutation system**", and the operation which links to a word w of X^* the set of words which can be derived from w in the system S is called a "**partial commutation function**". The properties of these functions and of languages closed under these functions led to numerous works.

More recently, we introduced a non-symetrical version of partial commutation system, which are naturally associated with "**semi-commutation function**". (see [2], [3]). Since then, a lot of papers have been dealing with there properties: [6], [11], [13], [15]. In [4], [10] and [11], we can find results about sufficient conditions which ensure that the image by a semi-commutation function of a regular language remains regular or becomes algebraic. These conditions are about properties of the commutation graph or the non-commutation graph associated to the function. If $S = <X; P>$ is a semi-commutation system, we can define its semi-commutation graph as the directed graph whose vertices are letters of X and edges are the couples (x, y) where $xy \rightarrow yx \in P$. Symmetrically, the non-commutation graph of S is the directed graph whose vertices are letters of X and edges are the couples (x, y) where $x \neq y$ and $xy \rightarrow yx \notin P$.

Here we present two results about semi-commutation functions which transform rational languages into algebraic languages. The first one gives a characterization of semi-commutation functions which transform any rational language into algebraic language. We shall call these functions "**algebrico-rational functions**": A semi-commutation function f is algebrico-rational if and only if the semi-commutation graph of f neither contains a partial subgraph of the type $\odot \longrightarrow \odot \longleftarrow \odot \longrightarrow \odot$ nor $\odot \longrightarrow \odot \longleftarrow \odot$, where $\odot$ are different nodes of the graph.

In the second result, we characterize the words $u \in X^*$ such that for a given semi-commutation function f, $f(u^*)$ is algebraic: $f(u^*)$ is algebraic if and only if the restriction of the non-commutation graph of f to the alphabet of u has at most two strongly connected components.

2.DEFINITIONS AND NOTATIONS

We denote the set of natural numbers by $\mathbb{N}$ and the set of positive numbers by $\mathbb{N}^+$. If p and q are two elements of $\mathbb{N}$, $[p,q]$ will be the interval of integers defined by: if $p > q$ then $[p,q] = \emptyset$, else $[p,q] = \{p, p+1, ..., q\}$.

Let X be a finite alphabet, w a word of X^*, x a letter of X, and Y a subset of X. We then write $|\mathbf{w}|$ the length of w, $|\mathbf{w}|_{\mathbf{x}}$ the number of occurences of x in w, and $|\mathbf{w}|_{\mathbf{Y}}$ the number of occurences of the letters of Y in w. $\mathbf{alph(w)} = \{x \in X \; s.t \; |w|_x \neq 0\}$ is the set of letters which occure in w, $\mathbf{com(w)} = \{u \in X^* \; s.t \; \forall x \in X, |u|_x = |w|_x\}$ is the commutative closure of w, and if $L \subseteq X^*$,

$$com(L) = \bigcup_{w \in L} com(w)$$

$\mathbf{F(w)}$ is the set of factors of w, that is $F(w) = \{u \in X^*, \; \exists v, v' \in X^*, \; w = vuv'\}$ and if $L \subseteq X^*$, we extend the definition by

$$F(L) = \bigcup_{w \in L} F(w)$$

$\mathbf{LF(w)}$ is the set of left factors of w, that is $LF(w) = \{u \in X^*, \; \exists v \in X^*, \; w = uv\}$ and if $L \subseteq X^*$, we extend the definition by

$$LF(L) = \bigcup_{w \in L} LF(w)$$

Π_Y^X is the projection of X on the subset Y of X, that is the morphism defined on X by $\Pi_Y^X(x) = x$ if $x \in Y$, $\Pi_Y^X(x) = \varepsilon$ else. When there is no ambiguity on the alphabet X, we will note Π_Y the projection of X on Y.

Given two words w and w' of X^*, we write $\mathbf{w}\sqcup\mathbf{w'}$ the shuffle of w and w', that is $w\sqcup w' = \{u_1v_1u_2v_2...u_nv_n, u_i \in X^*, v_i \in X^*, w = u_1u_2...u_n, w' = v_1v_2...v_n\}$, and $\mathbf{w}\sqcap\mathbf{w'}$ ([5]), the synchronized shuffle, that is
$w\sqcap w' = \{u \in (alph(w) \cup alph(w'))^*, \Pi_{alph(w)}(u) = w \ and \ \Pi_{alph(w')}(u) = w'\}$

A semi-commutation relation defined on the alphabet X is a subset of

$$(X \times X) \setminus \{(x,x), \ x \in X\}$$

To a semi-commutation relation C defined on X, we associate **a semi-commutation system** $S = <X, P>$ where $P = \{xy \rightarrow yx, (x,y) \in C\}$ and **a semi-commutation function** f defined on X^* by

$$\forall w \in X^*, \ f(w) = \{u \in X^*, \ w \overset{*}{\Longrightarrow} u\}$$

and the image of a language $L \subseteq X^*$ is defined by

$$f(L) = \bigcup_{w \in L} f(w)$$

The semi-commutation graph associated to a semi-commutation f (and thus, to the corresponding semi-commutation relation C and system $S = <X, P>$) is the directed graph defined by the set of its vertices: X, and its edges: (x,y) is an edge if $xy \rightarrow yx \in P$. **The non commutation graph** associated to a semi-commutation f (and thus, to the corresponding semi-commutation relation C and system $S = <X, P>$) is the directed graph defined by the set of its vertices: X, and its edges: (x,y) is an edge if $x \neq y$ and $xy \rightarrow yx \notin P$. If G is a directed graph whose the set of vertices is X, we may define an equivalence relation γ on X by $\forall(x,y) \in X \times X$, $(x,y) \in \gamma$ if and only if there are a path from x to y and a path from y to x. A strongly connected component of the graph G is a subgraph whose vertices are each element of one equivalence class of γ. In the following, we will denote in the same way a strongly connected component and the set of its vertices.

We will note $D_1^*(x,y)$ the Dyck language on the alphabet $\{x,y\}$, that is

$$D_1^*(x,y) = \{w \in \{x,y\}^*, \ |w|_x = |w|_y\}$$

and $D_1'^*(x,y)$ the semi-Dyck language on $\{x,y\}$, that is

$$D_1'^*(x,y) = \{w \in \{x,y\}^*, \ |w|_x = |w|_y \ and \ \forall u \in LF(w), \ |u|_x \geq |u|_y\}$$
$$= \{w \in D_1^*(x,y), \ \forall u \in LF(w), \ |u|_x \geq |u|_y\}$$

It's clear that if f is a semi-commutation function defined on $\{x,y\}^*$ by the rules $xy \leftrightarrow yx$ and if f' is defined on the same alphabet by the rule $yx \rightarrow xy$, we get $f((xy)^*) = D_1^*(x,y)$ and $f'((xy)^*) = D_1'^*(x,y)$

At last, **RAT** will denotes the family of rational languages, **ALG** the family of algebraic languages and **OCL** the smallest set of languages which contains $D_1'^*(x,y)$ and closed under rational transductions, product, union and star. This family is also named the one-counter languages family.

3. ALGEBRICO RATIONAL FUNCTIONS

Definition 1: *A semi-commutation function f defined on an alphabet X is algebrico-rational if and only if for any rational language R included in X^*, the language $f(R)$ is algebraic.*

The main result of this section is the following characterization of algebrico-rational functions: A semi-commutation function f defined on an alphabet X is algebrico-rational if and only if the semi-commutation graph of f neither contains a partial subgraph of the type $\odot \rightarrow\!\!\!-\odot-\!\!\!\leftarrow \odot \rightarrow\!\!\!-\odot$ nor $\odot\rightarrow\!\!\!-\odot-\!\!\!\leftarrow \odot$, where $\odot$ are different nodes of the graph. The proof of this result is based on an induction on the cardinality of the alphabet X. Clearly, when X contains only one letter, the semi-commutation graph of any semi-commutation function f defined on X cannot contain a partial subgraph of the type $\odot \rightarrow\!\!\!-\odot -\!\!\!\leftarrow \odot \rightarrow\!\!\!-\odot$ or $\odot\rightarrow\!\!\!-\odot-\!\!\!\leftarrow\odot$, and it is easy to verify that f is algebrico-rational. To give an idea of what happens in the general case, we will also examine the case of a two letters alphabet. Let $X = \{a, b\}$. As in the case of a one letter alphabet, we have to verify that each semi-commutation function defined on X is algebrico-rational. We can define 4 functions on X: $f_1 = Id$, (no letter commute by this function), f_2 associated to the rule $ab \rightarrow ba$, f_3 associated to the rule $ba \rightarrow ab$, and f_4 associated to the rules $ab \leftrightarrow ba$.

At first, we give a necessary and sufficient condition for a word w' to be in the image of a word w of X^* by f_2 (the proof of this result is in [2]):

Lemma 1: *Let w and w' be two words of X^*. $w' \in f_2(w)$ if and only if $w' \in com(w)$ and $\forall(u, v) \in LF(w) \times LF(w')$, $|u| = |v| \Longrightarrow |u|_b \leq |v|_b$.*

Then we can state:

Proposition 1: *Any semi-commutation function defined on $X = \{a, b\}$ is algebrico-rational.*

Proof

If $f = f_1$, the result is obvious: $f(R) = R \in RAT \subset ALG$. If $f = f_4$, M.Latteux [7] proved that: $\forall R \in RAT, f_4(R) = com(R) \in OCL$.

So we have to establish that $f_2(R)$ is context-free, for each rational language R. The proof is symmetric for f_3.

Let h be the morphism defined on $\{a, b, \bar{b}\}$ by $h(a) = a$, $h(b) = b$, $h(\bar{b}) = \varepsilon$ and let g be the morphism defined on the same alphabet by $g(a) = a$, $g(b) = \varepsilon$, $g(\bar{b}) = b$. We have: $\forall u \in X^*$, $f(u) = g(h^{-1}(u) \cap (D_1'^*(\bar{b}, b) \sqcup a^*))$. Indeed, set $u' \in f(u)$ and let us denote by $\bar{u}'$ the word u' where each occurrence of the letter b has been marked. $(\bar{u}' = m(u')$ with $m : \{a, b\} \longmapsto \{a, \bar{b}\}$, $m(a) = a$, $m(b) = \bar{b})$. Set $v = u \sqcap \bar{u}' \cap (\bar{b}^* b^* a)^*$. With the lemma 1, it's clear that $\Pi_{\{b, \bar{b}\}}(v) \in D_1'^*(\bar{b}, b)$ so $v \in h^{-1}(u) \cap D_1'^*(\bar{b}, b) \sqcup a^*$ and $u' = g(v)$. On the other hand, if $u' \in h^{-1}(u) \cap (D_1'^*(\bar{b}, b) \sqcup a^*)$, each left factor α of $LF(u')$ satisfies: $|\alpha|_{\bar{b}} \geq |\alpha|_b$. So $g(u') \in f(\Pi_{\{a, b\}}(u')) = f(u)$. As $D_1'^*(\bar{b}, b) \in OCL$ which is a family closed under rational transduction, each rational language has its image by f in OCL, so f is algebrico-rational.

$\square$

Remark

If L is an algebraic language, $f_1(L) = L \in ALG$, and there is a rational language R such that $f_4(L) = f_4(R)$ so $f_4(L) \in ALG$. However, $f_2(L)$ is not always context-free: Set $L = \{(ba)^n b^n, n \geq 0\}$. $L \in ALG$, but $f_2(L) \cap b^* a^* b^* = \{b^{n+k} a^n b^{n-k}, n \geq k \geq 0\} = L_1$. And $LF(b^* L_1) = \{b^n a^p b^q, n \geq p \geq q \geq 0\} \notin ALG$.

Let us now suppose that the cardinality of the alphabet X is greater than 2.

Definition 2: *Let f be a semi-commutation function defined on the alphabet X. We say that f **satisfies the (C) condition** if the semi-commutation graph of f doesn't contain any partial subgraph as $\odot \!\!-\!\!\twoheadrightarrow\!\! \odot \!\!\twoheadleftarrow\!\!-\!\! \odot \!\!-\!\!\twoheadrightarrow\!\! \odot$ or $\odot \!\!-\!\!\twoheadrightarrow\!\! \odot \!\!\twoheadleftarrow\!\!-\!\! \odot$, each node of these subgraphs being different from each other.*

We may express this condition in the following way: *A semi-commutation function f on X associated to the semi-commutation relation C_0 verifies the (C) condition if and only if :*

$$(y, z) \in C_0 \implies ((y, x_1) \in C_0 \text{ and } (x_2, z) \in C_0 \Rightarrow x_1 = z \text{ or } x_2 = y)$$

Proposition 2: *If a semi-commutation function is algebrico-rational, then it satisfies the (C) condition .*

Proof:
Let f be a semi-commutation function defined on $X = \{a, b, c\}$ by the following commutation graph:

$$a \!\!-\!\!\twoheadrightarrow\!\! c \!\!\twoheadleftarrow\!\!-\!\! b$$

Set $R = (abc)^*$. Then

$$f(R) \cap c^* b^* a^* = \{c^n b^n a^n, n \in \mathbb{N}\} \notin ALG$$

Let g be the function defined on $\{a, b, c, d\}$ by the following semi-commutation graph:

$$a \rightarrowtail b \leftarrowtail c \rightarrowtail d$$

Set $R' = (cd)^*(ab)^*$. Then

$$g(R') \bigcap d^* b^* c^* a^* = \{d^n b^p c^n a^p,\ n, p \in \mathbb{N}\} \notin ALG$$

A function which doesn't't satisfy the (C) condition would never be algebrico-rational.

$\square$

The end of the first part of this paper deals with the proof of the converse of this proposition. We will consider two cases:

Definition 3: *We say that a semi-commutation function f defined on X satisfies* **(P)** **property** *if and only if there exists a letter $x \in X$ such that for each letter $y \in X$, $yx \in f(xy)$ or such that for each letter $y \in X$, $xy \in f(yx)$.*

So, let f be a semi-commutation function defined on X which satisfies both (C) condition and (P) property , that is there exists a letter x in X such that:

$$\forall y \in X,\ yx \in f(xy)$$

The other case $(xy \in f(yx))$ would be study in the same way. Let us explain what "make" the function f:

$$\forall y_1, y_2 \in X \setminus \{x\},\ y_1 y_2 \notin f(y_2 y_1)$$

Because the commutation graph of f already contains $y_1 \leftarrowtail x \rightarrowtail y_2$ it's impossible to add an arrow between y_1 and y_2, since f satisfies the (C) condition . However, we may have commutations of the kind $yx \rightarrow xy$, $y \in X \setminus \{x\}$. Thus the alphabet X may be partitionned into three disjoint subsets :
$X = X_1 \cup X_2 \cup \{x\}$, with $X_1 = \{y \in X \setminus \{x\},\ xy \in f(yx)\}$, $X_2 = \{y \in X,\ xy \notin f(yx)\}$.
It means that, in a word $w \in X^*$, the occurrences of the letter x are going to move on left or right, in each factor of w which is in X_1^*, but an occurrence of x may move over a letter of X_2 only from left to right. When adding in w the new positions of marked occurrences of the letter x ($\bar{x}$ instead of x) from a word w' in $f(w)$, we get words of $D_1^*(x, \bar{x}) \sqcup X_1^*$ and words of $D_1'^*(x, \bar{x}) \sqcup (X_1 \cup X_2)^*$. It's what is formalized in the following lemma.

Notation: If w is a word of X^*, $\bar{w}$ denotes the image of w by the morphism which marks the letter x: $m : X \longmapsto X \cup \{\bar{x}\}$, $m(x) = \bar{x}$, and $\forall y \in X \setminus \{x\}$, $m(y) = y$.

Lemma 2: *Let f be a semi-commutation function defined on X, which satisfies the (C) condition and for which there exists a letter x such that $\forall y \in X$, $yx \in f(xy)$. Let $u \in X^*$, and $u' \in f(u)$. Then we can find a word v in $u \shuffle \bar{u}'$ such that*

$$v \in ((D_1^*(x,\bar{x}) \shuffle X_1^*)(D_1'^*(x,\bar{x}) \shuffle (X_1 \cup X_2)^*))^*$$

where $X_1 = \{y \in X \setminus \{x\},\ xy \in f(yx)\}$, and $X_2 = \{y \in X,\ xy \notin f(yx)\}$.

The proof is based on an induction on the length of the word u. We don't detailed it. In this light, we can state

Proposition 3: *Let f be a semi-commutation function defined on the alphabet X, which satisfies the (C) condition and for which there exists a letter x such that $\forall y \in X$, $yx \in f(xy)$. Then, we can find morphisms h and g and two subsets of X, X_1 and X_2 such that*

$$\forall u \in X^*,\ f(u) = g(h^{-1}(u) \cap ((D_1^*(x,\bar{x}) \shuffle X_1^*)(D_1'^*(x,\bar{x}) \shuffle (X_1 \cup X_2)^*))^*)$$

So f is algebrico-rational.

Proof

Set $X_1 = \{y \in X \setminus \{x\},\ xy \in f(yx)\}$ and $X_2 = X \setminus (X_1 \cup \{x\})$. Let h and g be the morphisms defined on $X \cup \{\bar{x}\}$ by $\forall y \in X_1 \cup X_2$, $h(y) = y$, $g(y) = y$; $h(x) = x$, $g(x) = \varepsilon$; $h(\bar{x}) = \varepsilon$, $g(\bar{x}) = x$. Set $L = ((D_1^*(x,\bar{x}) \shuffle X_1^*)(D_1'^*(x,\bar{x}) \shuffle (X_1 \cup X_2)^*))$. We prove that:

$$\forall u \in X^*,\ f(u) = g(h^{-1}(u) \cap L^*).$$

Let $u' \in f(u)$. It's clear that $u \shuffle \bar{u}' \subseteq h^{-1}(u)$ and according to lemma 2, we can find a word $v \in u \shuffle \bar{u}' \cap L^*$; on the other hand, $g(v) = u'$. Consequently

$$u' \in g(h^{-1}(u) \cap ((D_1^*(x,\bar{x}) \shuffle X_1^*)(D_1'^*(x,\bar{x}) \shuffle (X_1 \cup X_2)^*))^*).$$

Conversely, let $u' \in h^{-1}(u) \cap L^*$. We can find a number p such that $u' \in h^{-1}(u) \cap L^p$. We proceed by induction on p:
If $p = 0$, $u' = \varepsilon$ so $u = \varepsilon$ and $g(u') \in f(u)$. If $p \geq 1$, $u' \in h^{-1}(u) \cap LL^{p-1}$. Thus $u' = u_1' u_2' v'$ where $u_1' \in D_1^*(x,\bar{x}) \shuffle X_1^*$, $u_2' \in D_1'^*(x,\bar{x}) \shuffle (X_1 \cup X_2)^*$ and $v' \in L^{p-1}$. So we can write $u = u_1 u_2 v$ where $u_1 = \Pi_X(u_1')$, $u_2 = \Pi_X(u_2')$, and $v = \Pi_X(v')$. Moreover, $g(u_1') \in f(u_1)$ (only with commutations $xy \leftrightarrow yx$, $y \in X_1$) since $\Pi_{X_1}(u_1') = \Pi_{X_1}(u_1)$ and $|u_1'|_x = |u_1|_x = |u_1'|_{\bar{x}}$. In the same way, $g(u_2') \in f(u_2)$: it's clear that $com(g(u_2')) = com(f(u_2))$ and $\forall 0 < t < |g(u_2')|$, $|g(u_2')(t)|_x \geq |g(u_2)(t)|_x$. And by induction hypothesis, $g(v') \in f(v)$ ($v' \in h^{-1}(u) \cap L^{p-1}$). Thus

$$g(u') = g(u_1')g(u_2')g(v') \in f(u_1)f(u_2)f(v) \subseteq f(u_1 u_2 v) = f(u).$$

$\square$

For a given semi-commutation function f, if no letter may commute with each of the others, shuffles will be local. So, to get the image of a word by f, it's sufficient to make shuffles on factors wich are defined on a smaller alphabet. This motivates the following lemma:

Lemma 3: *Let f be a semi-commutation function defined on X, which satisfies (C) condition but not (P) property. Then, for any word u of X^*, for any word v of $f(u)$, we can find decompositions $u = u_1 u_2$ and $v = v_1 v_2$ with $u_1 \neq \varepsilon$, $alph(u_1) \subsetneq X$ and $v_1 \in f(u_1)$.*

The proof is technical, and is not detailed here.

We are now able to state the main result of the first part:

Proposition 4: *Let f be a semi-commutation function defined on the alphabet X, and satisfying (C) condition. Then f is algebrico-rational.*

Proof

We proceed by induction on the cardinality of the alphabet X, denoted by $card(X)$. If $card(X) = 2$, the result is true: see Proposition 1. If $card(X) > 2$: If f satisfies (P) property, the result is true because of Proposition 3. If not, we are going to show that for each rational language R, $f(R) \in ALG$.

Let $R \in RAT$. We can define a deterministic automaton $M = (X, Q, q_0, *, F)$ which accepts R. If $q, q' \in Q$, we set $R_{q,q'} = \{w \in X^*, q * w = q'\}$. Let s be the substitution defined on $Q \times Q$ by

$$\forall (q, q') \in Q \times Q, \ s((q, q')) = \bigcup_{x \in X} f(R_{q,q'} \cap (X \setminus \{x\})^*)$$

By induction hypothesis, s is an algebraic substitution . Let K be the rational language defined on $Q \times Q$ by

$$K = \{(q_0, q_1)(q_1, q_2)....(q_{p-1}, q_p), \ p \geq 1, \ \forall i \in \{1, ..., p\}, \ q_i \in Q, \ q_p \in F\}$$

We can easily show that $f(R) = s(K)$, the proof is complete since the image of a rational language by an algebraic substitution is an algebraic language.

$\square$

In fact, propositions 2 and 4 permit us to state that the image of a rational language by a semi-commutation function is always in OCL. So we proclaim:

Proposition 5: *Let f be a semi-commutation function defined on X. The following assertions are equivalent:*

   1) f is algebrico-rational

   2) The semi-commutation graph of f doesn't contain any subgraph of the kind
$$\odot \twoheadrightarrow \odot \twoheadleftarrow \odot \twoheadrightarrow \odot \quad or \quad \odot \underset{\longrightarrow}{\twoheadrightarrow} \odot \twoheadleftarrow \odot$$

   3) For each rational language R, $f(R) \in OCL$

   4) For each rational bounded language R, $f(R) \in ALG$

   Proof

$1 \Longrightarrow 2$ by proposition 2.

$2 \Longrightarrow 3$ because constructions which give us the image by f of a rational language use $D_1'^*$ and D_1^* which are in OCL and operations under which OCL is closed.

$3 \Longrightarrow 4$ is obvious.

$4 \Longrightarrow 1$ when looking at the proof of proposition 2.□

In the particular case of partial commutation (associated to irreflexive and symmetrical relations), the results of propositions 2 et 4 become:

Proposition 6: *A partial commutation function is algebrico-rational if and only if its commutation graph doesn't contain path whose length is 3.*

4. AN OTHER RESULT ABOUT SEMI-COMMUTATIONS AND ALGEBRAIC LANGUAGES

The second part of this paper deals with the same kind of problem, since we are going to establish a property which links a semi-commutation function f and a word u so that $f(u^*)$ is algebraic. This property is the following: $f(u^*)$ is algebraic if and only if the restriction of the non-commutation graph of f to the alphabet of u has at most two strongly connected components.

For a given semi-commutation function f, and for a word u, if the restriction of the non-commutation graph of f to $alph(u)$ has strictly more than 2 strongly connected components, the result is easy to prove:

Proposition 7: *Let f be a semi-commutation function defined on the alphabet X, and let u be a word of X^* such that $alph(u) = X$. If the number of strongly connected components of the non-commutation graph of f is strictly greater than 2, then the language $L = f(u^*)$ is not algebraic.*

Proof

Let $\{X_1, X_2, ..., X_n\}$ be the set of strongly connected components of the non-commutation graph of f. If n is greater than 2, it's easy to verify that $\exists\, i \neq j \in [1, n]$ such that:
$$\forall x \in X_i,\ \forall y \in X - X_i,\ xy \in f(yx)$$
$$\forall x \in X_j,\ \forall y \in X - X_j,\ yx \in f(xy)$$
Set $u_1 = \Pi_{X_i}(u)$, $u_3 = \Pi_{X_j}(u)$, $u_2 = \Pi_{X-(X_i \cup X_j)}(u)$. As $n \geq 3$, u_2 is not the empty word and:
$$\forall i \in [1,3],\ \forall j \neq i \in [1,3],\ alph(u_i) \cap alph(u_j) = \emptyset$$

So we deduce that

$$f(u^*) \cap u_1^* u_2^* u_3^* = \{u_1^n u_2^n u_3^n,\ n \geq 0\} \notin ALG$$

$\square$

When the non-commutation graph of a function f reduced to the alphabet of a word u has only one strongly connected component, the following result has been prooved in [4]:

Proposition 8 *Let f be a semi-commutation function defined on X and let u be a word of X^*. If the restriction of the non-commutation graph of f to $alph(u)$ is strongly connected, then the language $L = f(u^*)$ is rational.*

So we have now to study the case in which the non-commutation graph of the function has exactly two strongly connected components. Let f be a semi-commutation function defined on X, let u be a word of X^*. Without loss of generality, we may assume that $X = alph(u)$ and $\forall x \in X$, $|u|_x = 1$. Let $\{X_1, X_2\}$ be the set of the two strongly connected components of the non-commutation graph of f. In the following, we denote $\Pi_{X_1}(u)$ by u_1 and $\Pi_{X_2}(u)$ by u_2. Just as in the Proposition 1, it's clear that:
$$\forall x \in X_1,\ \forall y \in X_2,\ xy \in f(yx) \text{ or}$$
$$\forall x \in X_1,\ \forall y \in X_2,\ yx \in f(xy)$$
If these two properties are simultaneously satisfied, it's easy to verify that:

$$f(u^*) = h^{-1}(D_1^*(x_1, x_2)) \cap (f(u_1)^* \shuffle f(u_2)^*))$$

where x_1 (resp. x_2) is the first letter of u_1 (resp. u_2) and h is a morphism from X^* onto $\{x_1, x_2\}^*$ defined by
$$\forall x \in \{x_1, x_2\},\ h(x) = x,$$
$$\forall x \in X - \{x_1, x_2\},\ h(x) = \varepsilon$$
Because of proposition 7, we get $f(u_1^*) \in RAT$, $f(u_2^*) \in RAT$ and so $f(u^*) \in ALG$.

In the other case, the proof is more technical and to simplify notations, let us give the following definition:

Definition 4: *We say that a semi-commutation function f defined on X and a word $u \in X^*$ satisfy the **H** hypothesis if: $\forall x \in X, |u|_x = 1$; the non-commutation graph of f has 2 strongly connected components: X_1 and X_2; $\forall x \in X_1, \forall y \in X_2, xy \in f(yx)$; $\exists x \in X_1, \exists y \in X_2$ such that $yx \notin f(xy)$.*

Remark: the case when $\forall x \in X_1, \forall y \in X_2, yx \in f(xy)$ and $\exists x \in X_1, \exists y \in X_2$ such that $xy \notin f(yx)$ would be examined in the same way.

For a given X, f, and u satisfying the **H** hypothesis, let us define a one counter automaton which accepts $f(u^*)$. Let $M = \{X, P, S, s_0, z_0, \delta, F\}$ be the automaton defined by:

$P = \{z_0, a\}$ is the pushdown alphabet

$S = \{w \in LF(f(u^{8|X|^2}))\}$ is the set of states,

$s_0 = \varepsilon$ is the initial state,

$F = \{s_0\}$ is the set of terminal states,

δ, the transition function, is defined by the four following rules:

$$\forall w \in S, \forall x \in X, \forall n \in \mathbb{N}, (w, x, z_0 a^n) \vdash_{1} (wx, \varepsilon, z_0 a^n), \; if \; wx \in S$$

$$\forall n \in \mathbb{N}, \forall w \in S \; such \; that \; \forall x \in X, |w|_x \geq 1, (w, \varepsilon, z_0 a^n) \vdash_{2} (w', \varepsilon, z_0 a^n), \; where$$
w' is obtained from w by erasing the first occurrence of each letter of X.

$$\forall n \in \mathbb{N}, \forall w \in S \; such \; that \; q = inf\{|w|_x, x \in X_1\} \geq 1,$$
$(w, \varepsilon, z_0 a^n) \vdash_{3} (w', \varepsilon, z_0 a^{n+1})$, if the word w' which is w where the qth occurence of each letter of X_1 has been erased, is an element of S.

$$\forall w \in S, \forall n \in \mathbb{N}^+,$$
$(w, \varepsilon, z_0 a^n) \vdash_{4} (u_1 w, \varepsilon, z_0 a^{n-1})$, if $u_1 w \in S$. $(u_1 = \Pi_{X_1}(u))$.

Let $T(M) = \{w \in X^*, (\varepsilon, w, z_0) \overset{*}{\vdash} (\varepsilon, \varepsilon, z_0)\}$ be the language accepted by the automaton. In order to prove the equality $T(M) = f(u^*)$, we need the two following lemmas:

Lemma 4: $\forall w \in X^*, \forall v \in S, \forall n \in \mathbb{N},$

$(\varepsilon, w, z_0) \overset{*}{\vdash} (v, \varepsilon, z_0 a^n) \Rightarrow w \in L = LF(f(u^*))$ and $\exists p \in \mathbb{N}$ s.t $w \in com(u^p u_1^n v)$.

Lemma 5: $\forall w \in L = LF(f(u^*)), \exists v \in S, \exists n \in \mathbb{N}$, such that $(\varepsilon, w, z_0) \overset{*}{\vdash} (v, \varepsilon, z_0 a^n)$.

The proofs of these two lemmas use a lot of results and are rather technicals, so we don't detail its here.

Finally we come to the proof of the equality: $T(M) = f(u^*)$: Let $w \in T(M)$. We have $(\varepsilon, w, z_0) \overset{*}{\vdash} (\varepsilon, \varepsilon, z_0)$ and with lemma 4, $w \in LF(f(u^*))$ and $w \in com(u^p)$. So, $w \in f(u^*)$. Conversely, let w be a word of $f(u^*)$. According to lemma 5, $\exists v \in S$, $\exists n \in \mathbb{N}$ such that

$$(\varepsilon, w, z_0) \overset{*}{\vdash} (v, \varepsilon, z_0 a^n).$$

Moreover, according to lemma 4, $\exists p \in \mathbb{N}$ such that $w \in com(u^p u_1^n v)$. As $w \in f(u^*)$, $\exists q \in \mathbb{N}$ such that $w \in f(u^q)$. So $v \in com(u_1^{q-(n+p)} u_2^{q-p})$ where $u_2 = \Pi_{X_2}(u)$ and $8|X|^2 \geq q - p$. We may then apply n times the rule 4 and we get:

$$(v, \varepsilon, z0a^n) \overset{*}{\vdash} (u_1^n v, \varepsilon, z_0) \text{ with } u_1^n v \in com(u_1^{q-p} u_2^{q-p}).$$

At last, when applying $(q - p)$ times the rule 2, we get:

$$(u_1^n v, \varepsilon, z_0) \overset{*}{\vdash} (\varepsilon, \varepsilon, z_0).$$

$\square$

So we may state

Proposition 9: *Let X be an alphabet, u a word of X^* and f a semi-commutation function defined on X. $L = f(u^*)$ is an algebraic language if and only if the restriction of the non-commutation graph of f to $alph(u)$ has at most two strongly connected components.*

We close by making the following remark: If this condition seems to be simple, it is not the same if we consider the problem for a language, even finite and "small" as in the following example:

Let $X = \{a, b, c\}$ and f be the semi-commutation function defined by the rules: $ba \longrightarrow ab$, $ac \longrightarrow ca$, and $bc \longrightarrow cb$. If $F = \{ab, ca\}$, it is easy to verify that the restrictions of the non-commutation graph of f to $alph(ab)$ and $alph(ca)$ have only two strongly connected components, but

$$f(F^*) \bigcap a^*c^*b^*a^* = f((ab)^*(ca)^*) \bigcap a^*c^*b^*a^* = \{a^p c^q b^p a^q, \; p, q \in \mathbb{N}\}$$

which is not algebraic.

REFERENCES

[1] P.Cartier and D.Foata, "Problèmes combinatoires de commutations et réarrangements", Lecture Notes in Mathematics 85, Springer-Verlag, Berlin.

[2] M.Clerbout, "Commutations partielles et familles de langages", thesis 1984, University of Lille I.

[3] M.Clerbout and M.Latteux, "On a generalization of partial commutation", in M.Arato, I.Katai, L.Varga, eds, Proc.Fourth Hungarian Computer Science Conference, 1985, pp 15-24.

[4] M.Clerbout and M.Latteux, "Semi-commutations", Information and Computation, 73 (1987), pp 59-74.

[5] R.De Simone, "Langages infinitaires et produit de mixage", Theoretical Computer Science 31 (1984), pp 83-100.

[6] G.Lampérth, "Reducedness of formal languages", IMYCS conference, Smolenice 1986, pp 215-219.

[7] M.Latteux, "Cônes rationnels commutatifs", JCSS 18 (1979), pp 307-333.

[8] A.Mazurkiewicz, "Concurrent Program Schemes and their interpretations", Daimi, pb 78, Aarhus University, 1977.

[9] Y.Métivier, "Semi-commutations dans le monoïde libre", Tech. Rep. University of Bordeaux1.

[10] Y.Métivier, "Contribution à l'étude des monoïdes de commutations", thesis 1987, University of Bordeaux I.

[11] Y.Métivier and E.Ochmanski, "On lexicographic semi-commutations", Tech. Rep., University of Bordeaux I, 1986.

[12] Y.Métivier and Sijelmassi, "Communications de processus et semi-commutations; algébricité de la clôture d'une classe de rationnels", Tech.Rep., University of Bordeaux I, 1987.

[13] H.Mountassir and R.Sijelmassi, "Formulation syntaxique de la communication de processus asynchrones à travers des canaux fifo", Tech. Rep., University of Bordeaux I, 1987.

[14] M.Szijarto, "The closure of languages on a binary relation", IMYCS Conference, Smolenice 1982.

[15] M.Szijarto and Dang Van Hung, "Synchronized parallel composition of languages", Proceedings of the conference 'On Automata, Languages and Programming Systems', Salgotarjan 1986, pp 281-288.

Towards a process semantics
in the logic programming style

Andrea Corradini   *Ugo Montanari*[1]

Università di Pisa
Dipartimento di Informatica
Corso Italia 40
I - 56125, Pisa, Italy

Abstract

We propose a new, more informative semantics for HCL: the meaning of a program is a set of observations over successful computations (refutations), which is parametric with respect to the observation function. The semantics is given in a logic programming style, i.e. with three different although equivalent characterizations (operational, model-theoretic and fixpoint). This semantics should fill the gap between the classic HCL semantics (not informative enough to be generalized to concurrent logic languages), and the process semantics used for imperative languages. Consistency of our approach with the classic semantics of HCL is checked by considering the *minimal* observation function, which observes just the initial and final state of a computation.

Actually, the semantic definitions are given at the very basic level of transition systems, and it is shown how to represent a logic program with such a system. Therefore, the same constructions can be applied to every formalism representable as a transition system.

1 Introduction

One of the most attractive aspects of the logic programming paradigm based on Horn Clause Logic resides undoubtedly in the ability of interpreting a logic program in many distinct, although consistent ways [Ll87]. In fact, the classic operational, model-theoretic and fixpoint semantics for HCL naturally correspond to three different readings of logic programs, and the equivalence proof of these semantics states the mutual consistency of these readings.

In the last years, a number of extensions to the logic programming paradigm have been proposed in the literature, including features like concurrency and synchronization [CG86, Mo86, Sh86, Ue85], constraint solving [JL87], functional aspects [BL86], or term inheritance [AN86]. Some attempts (not always fruitful) have been made in order to equip each of the above mentioned extensions with a logic programming style semantics.

In particular, in the case of *concurrent logic languages* (i.e. those with "don't care" nondeterminism plus some synchronization mechanisms on the variables [CG86, Sh86, Ue85]), the state of the art is still unsatisfactory. Those languages are fairly well understood from the operational point of view [Sa87], but still lack a declarative semantics in the logic programming style. More precisely, although some declarative descriptions have been proposed (for example in [LP87, Ma87] partial aspects of those languages are addressed), most of these semantics are essentially based on techniques used for the semantic description of concurrent *imperative* languages [GCLS88, Ko88, Mo86, Mu88]. This approach, from one side implies that it is hard to compare the operational intuition of concurrent logic languages with their declarative semantics, but from the other side, borrowing techniques developed for imperative languages, suggests

---

[1] Research performed while visiting ESLAI (Escuela Superior Latino-Americana de Informática, R. Argentina) with the support of the Italian Foreign Ministry, Programma di Cooperazione e Sviluppo.

which kind of properties a declarative semantics for concurrent logic languages must have: namely, it should be *compositional* [GS89] with respect to some operators over programs and/or goals (e.g. parallel composition), and should describe not only the final result of a computation, but also information about the actual computation performed; in short, it must be a *process* semantics.

These requirements explain why the classic semantics of logic programs cannot be generalized to concurrent logic languages: the classic semantics is neither compositional, nor observes anything of a computation, but the final (ground) substitution computed. In fact, since the semantics of a logic program is defined as a subset of the Herbrand base (i.e. a set of ground atomic formulas), there is no chance to distinguish between two different computations refusing the same goal.

Compositionality and informative power of the semantics are not independent requirements, however. The observation of certain aspects of the computation is a necessary (although not sufficient) condition for a semantics to be compositional with respect to the typical operations over concurrent agents (like parallel or interleaved composition). This fact is well understood since a long time in the studies on the semantics of process description languages (CCS [Mi84], CSP [Ho83], etc.).

Although the weaknesses of the classic semantics for HCL were pointed out while studying the *concurrent* logic languages, for which a concurrent semantics is obviously required, they also apply to *pure* HCL; therefore, we front this problem in that more basic context, without committing ourselves to a specific concurrent logic model. The main goal of our work is, indeed, to develop a formal framework in which a new *concurrent* semantics for logic programming can be defined. Four are the requirements we want to satisfy:

1) The semantics must be presented in a logic programming style, i.e. in three different but equivalent ways (operational, model-theoretic, and fixpoint).

2) The semantics must be informative, allowing to observe significant facts over computations, and not only the final result.

3) The semantics must be compositional with respect to significant operations on programs.

4) Last but not least, the semantics must be consistent with the classic semantics of Horn Clause Logic.

In this paper, we mainly address points 1), 2), and 4). For the second requirement, since we cannot determine *a priori* which are the relevant aspects of a computation, the semantics will be parametrized with respect to an *observation function*. Our semantic domains will be sets of *observations* over computations, or, equivalently, sets of *abstract* computations[2]. The final result of the paper shows that we can recover the classic HCL semantics by choosing as parameter for our semantics a *minimal* observation function, which just observes the initial and final states of a computation. This clarifies in which sense the classic HCL semantics can be considered as an input/output or initial/final state semantics, and therefore why our semantics is a true extension of the classic one: richer observation functions can be defined which consider, for example, the interactions of a computation with the outside world.

1.1 The technical approach

While studying the extension of the classic semantics of logic programming in order to consider observation functions over computations, we realized that the definitions of the operational, model-theoretic, and fixpoint semantics, and the proofs of their equivalence were expressible without making

---

[2] Using a *set* of abstract computations to specify a concurrent system is a common but simplistic view. To fully specify what a concurrent system both *may* and *must* do, it is usually necessary to consider tree-like structures, like synchronization trees or event structures. In this paper we will not be concerned with this aspect of the problem, but our approach generalizes straightforwardly to deal with those more complex structures [Co90].

reference to the peculiar features of logic programming, directly at the level of *transition systems*. Indeed, a transition system is the simplest engine for which a notion of *computation* can be defined.

Defining our semantics at this level has two main consequences. First, we equip transition systems, which are usually seen in a very operational way, with a logic programming style semantics, and therefore with a more declarative description of their behavior. Second, since transition systems are widely used to describe different kinds of computational models, this can be a starting point for the application of a logic programming-like semantics to other systems, too.

To be sound, after the definition of the transition system semantics (presented in Section 3), we have to show *how* a logic program can be represented by such a system. We introduce this construction in two steps.

First, we model a logic program as a structured graph. The leading idea is simple: a logic program is a graph where each program clause is an arc, and the nodes are tuples of atomic formulas. The source of a clause is its body, while the target is its head. For example, the clause $C = A$:- $B_1, ..., B_n$ is represented as an arc $C : <B_1, ..., B_n> \rightarrow <A>$. The nodes of such a graph form the set of arrows of a *cartesian category*, where arrow composition naturally models the application of a term substitution to a formula, and the categorical product allows to define tupling of formulas and corresponding projections (see [AM89, Go88, RB85] for similar approaches).

The second step consists of enriching the structure of the graph just introduced, in order to get a transition system which faithfully mimics the behavior of a logic program, in the following sense: a goal g is refutable with an answer substitution θ iff there is a computation in the corresponding transition system from the empty goal to (a suitable representation of) the goal $\theta(g)$. We claim that this can be achieved by adding to the arcs of the graph the same algebraic structure as that of nodes. The following example will clarify this point.

Let P be the logic program defined as follows (clauses are numbered for our convenience):

$P = \{ \quad c_1: q(x,y)$:- $p(x), r(y).$

$\qquad c_2: p(a).$

$\qquad c_3: r(b).\}$

Representing P as a graph, we get something like $P_T = \{c_1:<p(x), r(y)> \rightarrow <q(x,y)>, c_2:<> \rightarrow <p(a)>, c_3:<> \rightarrow <r(b)>\}$, where '<>' is the empty tuple (representing the empty goal). Now, suppose we want to mimic the refutation of the goal $g_1 = <q(a,b)>$ with a transition system computation.[3] Since in a transition system two transitions $t: u \rightarrow v$ and $t': w \rightarrow z$ can be (sequentially) composed iff v and w are identical, we cannot apply transition c_1 as it is to state g_1, because the target of c_1 is not *identical* to g_1. We must use instead an *instantiation* of the original clause, that is $c_1[x/a, y/b]: <p(a), r(b)> \rightarrow <q(a,b)>$; applying it to g_1 we get the next goal $g_2 = <p(a), r(b)>$. For the same reason, we cannot apply either c_2 or c_3 to g_2; however, we can apply them in parallel, using the tupled clause $(<c_2, c_3> : <> \rightarrow <p(a), r(b)>)$, or we can apply the parallel composition of, for example, c_2 and the *idle* transition $<r(b)>:<r(b)> \rightarrow <r(b)>$, that is $c_2 \times <r(b)>:<r(b)> \rightarrow <p(a), r(b)>$, and then reduce the resulting goal with c_3.

Summarizing, we get a transition system which faithfully mimics a logic program by closing the arcs of the corresponding graph under substitution application and tupling, and by adding all identity clauses (needed to model the fact that an atomic formula can remain idle during a resolution step). In short, we *lift* the structure of cartesian category from nodes to transitions, too.

Once the transition system which models the behavior of a logic program has been defined, we can

---

[3] To be consistent with the usual definition of refutation, we build our computations starting from the final state.

apply our definition of semantics to it. This automatically characterizes the meaning of a program as a set of abstract successful computations (i.e. refutations) with respect to a parametric observation function. We are then ready to compare the classic semantics of a logic program with its semantics as a transition system, when the minimal observation function is considered.

It should be stressed that the transition system which models a program P is obtained through a *free* enrichment, where the arcs of the graph act as *schemata* or *generators*. This kind of construction can be characterized in an algebraic context as a free adjoint functor between a category of graphs and a category of transition systems with the desired structure (see [CM89] for a complete treatment of this topic). However, such a construction goes beyond the scope of this paper.

The paper is organized in the following way. In Section 2 and 3 we introduce some basic notions about transition systems, and our definition of semantics of a transition system, respectively. Section 4 is devoted to the study of the transition system semantics of Horn Clause Logic. Most of the proofs omitted here because of space limitation can be found in the related reports [CM88] (for Sections 2 and 3) and [CM89] (for Section 4).

2 Transition Systems

In this section we introduce some basic notions about transition systems. A transition system is just a graph with an initial state. A computation is a sequence (path) of transitions starting from the initial state. A partial operation $\_;\_$ of concatenation (with identities) is defined over computations, and an observation function over computations is required to be consistent with $\_;\_$.

Definition 1 *(transition system)*

A *transition system* $G = \langle \partial_0, \partial_1 : T \to V, v_0 \rangle$ is a graph with a distinguished node, where T is a set of *transitions* (arcs), V is a set of *states* (nodes), ∂_0 and ∂_1 are the *source* and *target* functions, respectively, and $v_0 \in V$ is the *initial state*. Following the usual notation, we write $t:u \to v$ to denote $\partial_0(t)=u$, $\partial_1(t)=v$, for $t \in T$. ♦

A *computation* of a transition system G is a finite or infinite path of transitions, starting from v_0. In this paper, we consider just *finite* computations. Let us denote by G* the *free category* generated by G. Arrows of G* faithfully represent finite *generalized* computations, that is computations whose source is not necessarily v_0.

Definition 2 *(the category of computations)*

Given a transition system $G = \langle \partial_0, \partial_1 : T \to V, v_0 \rangle$, let $G^* = \langle \partial_0^*, \partial_1^* : T^* \to V, id, \_;\_, v_0 \rangle$ be the free category (with distinguished state v_0) generated by G. Arrows in T* are either identities (e.g. $id(u):u \to u$), or sequences of composable transitions in T (e.g. $t_1; \ldots; t_n$, where $\partial_1(t_i) = \partial_0(t_{i+1})$ for each i). ∂_0^* and ∂_1^* are the natural extensions of ∂_0 and ∂_1 to paths of transitions, while ';' denotes the sequential composition of computations, where s; s' is defined iff $\partial_1^*(s) = \partial_0^*(s')$. ♦

Usually, when observing the behavior of a transition system, one is interested in abstracting out from a given computation just the relevant informations. Therefore, we introduce the notion of *observation function* over computations.

Definition 3 *(observation function)*

Let $G = \langle \partial_0, \partial_1 : T \to V, v_0 \rangle$ be a transition system. A function $o: T^* \to D_o$ is an *observation function* over generalized computations of G iff o satisfies the following properties (D_o is a suitable domain of *observations*):

i)   There exist two partial functions from D_o to V, so_o (source) and tg_o (target), defined over the range of o, such that $so_o(o(s)) = \partial_0^*(s)$ and $tg_o(o(s)) = \partial_1^*(s)$.

ii) $o(s) = o(s')$ and $o(r) = o(r')$ implies $o(s; r) = o(s'; r')$, if the compositions are defined. ♦

Condition i) states that the initial and final states of a computation are always retrievable from its observation. This implies that two computations with identical observations must have the same initial and final states.

Every observation function o induces an equivalence relation $\approx_o$ over generalized computations in G, where $s \approx_o s'$ iff $o(s) = o(s')$. Actually, by condition ii), for each observation function o relation $\approx_o$ is a congruence with respect to $\_;\_$. Since congruences form a complete lattice under set inclusion, there exists a minimal congruence (the one induced by the identity observation function $I_{T^*}: T^* \to T^*$), and a maximal one, determined by the following

Proposition 4 *(the minimal observation function)*
Given a transition system G, let $\varphi: T^* \to V \times V$ be defined as $\varphi(s) = <\partial_0^*(s), \partial_1^*(s)>$, for $s \in T^*$. Then φ is an observation function, and $\approx_\varphi$ is the maximal congruence with respect to $\_;\_$ over T^*. ♦

3 Semantics of Transition Systems

In this section we define the semantics of a transition system G with respect to a set of final states Z and an observation function o over computations, as the set of all observations over successful computations w.r.t. Z, i.e. computations ending in a final state $z \in Z$. This semantics will be characterized in three different ways, and the equivalence of the approaches will be stated. More precisely, we introduce an *operational* semantics, defined as a set of observations over computations; a *model-theoretic* semantics, based on a notion of minimal model; and a *fixpoint* semantics, characterized as the least fixpoint of a continuous transformation. In what follows, let $G = <\partial_0, \partial_1: T \to V, v_0>$ be a fixed transition system.

3.1 Operational semantics

Definition 5 *(operational semantics)*
The operational semantics of a transition system G w.r.t. a set of final states $Z \subseteq V$ and an observation function $o:T^* \to D_o$, is the set of all observations over successful computations of G w.r.t. Z, that is:

$$[G, Z, o]_{op} = \{d \mid so_o(d) = v_0, tg_o(d) \in Z\}$$ ♦

Note that, although our transition systems are equipped with an initial state, the notion of successful computation is not committed to a particular computation rule. In fact, the basic operation of computation concatenation $\_;\_$ is associative, and the associativity axiom $(t_1 ; t_2) ; t_3 = t_1 ; (t_2 ; t_3)$ exactly means that one can read a given successful computation from either sides.

3.2 Model-theoretic semantics

The model-theoretic semantics is based on a notion of interpretation and model. An *interpretation* is a set of abstract computations which includes the observation over the empty computation (i.e. the identity arrow of the initial state, $id(v_0)$). A *model* M is an interpretation such that if an abstract computation s ending in a state u is in M, and there exists a transition t from u to v, then also s;o(t) is in M. With this definition there exists a minimal model (corresponding to all the observations of computations in the connected component of the graph starting from the initial state v_0), and the model-theoretic semantics is the set of all abstract computation in the minimal model ending in a final state.

In what follows, let $o: T^* \to D_o$ be a fixed observation function.

Definition 6 *(interpretations and models)*
Let I_o be the singleton $\{o(id(v_0))\}$, i.e. the observation of the empty computation. An *interpretation* of G w.r.t. o is any subset I of D_o, such that $I_o \subseteq I$. I_G^o is the set of all interpretations of G w.r.t. o.

A *model* of G w.r.t. o is an interpretation M of G such that whenever $d \in M$, then also $d;o(t) \in M$.[4] More informally, models are interpretations which are closed under forward concatenation with observations of simple transitions. M_G^o is the set of all models of G w.r.t. o. ◆

Proposition 7 *(I_G^o and M_G^o are complete lattices under set inclusion)*

I_G^o and M_G^o are closed under arbitrary union and intersection. Therefore, they are complete lattices under set inclusion. The minimal interpretation is I_o, and D_o is both the maximal interpretation and the maximal model. The minimal model is $\cap M_G^o$. ◆

Definition 8 *(model-theoretic semantics)*

The model-theoretic semantics of a transition system G w.r.t. a set of final states $Z \subseteq V$ and an observation function o: $T^* \rightarrow D_o$, is the subset of the minimal model $\cap M_G^o$ containing all observations of computations whose target is a final state, that is

$$[G, Z, o]_{mod} = \{d \in \cap M_G^o \mid tg_o(d) \in Z\} \qquad ◆$$

3.3 Fixpoint semantics

The fixpoint semantics of a transition system is defined as (a subset of) the least fixpoint of a continuous transformation over the lattice of interpretations.

Definition 9 *(the transformation associated with a transition system)*

Given a transition system G and an observation function o, let T_G^o be the transformation defined as follows:

$$T_G^o(X) = I_o \cup \{d;o(t) \mid d \in X\} \qquad ◆$$

Proposition 10 *(T_G^o is monotonic and continuous)*

T_G^o is monotonic and continuous as a transformation from sets to sets, ordered by set inclusion. Moreover, if X is an interpretation, then $T_G^o(X)$ is an interpretation, too. ◆

Since T_G^o is a monotonic and continuous transformation over the complete lattice $<I_G^o, \subseteq>$, by the Knaster-Tarski fixpoint theorem, there exists a least fixpoint, namely $\cup_n\{(T_G^o)^n (I_o)\}$, where I_o is the minimal interpretation of G (w.r.t. o). We use it to define the fixpoint semantics of a transition system.

Definition 11 *(fixpoint semantics)*

The fixpoint semantics of a transition system G w.r.t. a set of final states $Z \subseteq V$ and an observation function o: $T^* \rightarrow D_o$, is the subset of the least fixpoint of T_G^o including all observations of computations the target of which is a final state, that is

$$[G, Z, o]_{fix} = \{d \in \cup_n\{(T_G^o)^n (I_o)\} \mid tg_o(d) \in Z\} \qquad ◆$$

We can now present the fundamental result relating the three semantics introduced above.

Theorem 12 *(equivalence of all transition system semantics)*

The operational, model-theoretic, and fixpoint semantics of a transition system G with respect to a set of final states Z and an observation function o:$T^* \rightarrow D_o$ are equivalent, that is:

$$[G, Z, o]_{op} = [G, Z, o]_{mod} = [G, Z, o]_{fix}$$

Sketch of the proof. Models of G w.r.t. o are exactly the pre-fixpoints of T_G^o, i.e. $T_G^o(M) \subseteq M$. Since the least fixpoint of a continuous transformation over a complete lattice is also the least pre-fixpoint, the minimal model and the least fixpoint are identical. Moreover, the operational semantics can be defined incrementally, as the union of $\{R_n\}_{n<\omega}$, where R_n is the set of observations of computations of length at most n. Equivalence of the operational and the fixpoint semantics follows from the fact that $R_n = (T_G^o)^n (I_o)$. ◆

Thanks to this result, we can identify the three semantics, denoting them simply by $[G, Z, o]$.

---

[4] Obviously, d;o(t) is defined iff $tg_o(d) = u$, $t \in T$ and $\partial_0(t) = u$.

3.4 Final set semantics of a transition system

In some situations, the only relevant information about a computation is the final state reached. This is the case, for example, when defining the operational semantics of a sequential program through a transition system, if just an input-output relation is considered. A similar thing happens in the case of Horn Clause Logic, discussed in Section 4. Looking at a logic program as a transition system, it turns out that the classic HCL semantics only observes the final result of a computation, i.e. a substitution for the variables appearing in the goal, without worrying about *how* this substitution was generated.

We characterize this particular semantics of a transition system in the following way.

Definition 13 *(final set semantics of a transition system)*
The *final set semantics* of a transition system G with respect to a set of final states Z, is the second projection of the semantics of G w.r.t. Z and the minimal observation function φ, that is

$$[G, Z]_{FS} = \{z \mid <v_0, z> \in [G, Z, \varphi]\}$$ ♦

It is easy to verify, by the definition of φ, that $[G, Z]_{FS}$ is exactly the subset of all the states of Z which can be reached by a computation starting from v_0.

4 Transition system semantics of Horn Clause Logic

In order to apply our definition of transition system semantics to a logic program P, we represent it as a transition system via a two steps construction. First we define a structured graph, P_T, where the arcs correspond to the clauses of P. The nodes of P_T are tuples of atomic formulas, represented as arrows of a cartesian category. Then we enrich graph P_T, adding idle transitions to the arcs, and making them a cartesian category, too. This way we get the transition system of P, called P_T^*. In Section 4.1 we introduce and motivate the representation of formulas as arrows of a cartesian category. In Section 4.2 both P_T and P_T^* are defined, and in Sections 4.3 and 4.4 the transition system semantics of a logic program is defined and compared with other semantics. Let us start with some basic definitions.

Definition 14 *(terms, formulas and substitutions)*
Let Σ be a fixed set of (ranked) function symbols, Π be a fixed set of (ranked) predicate symbols, and $X = <x_1, ..., x_n>$ be a tuple of distinct variables. A *term (over X)* is an element of $T_\Sigma(X)$, that is an element of the free Σ-algebra generated by X. $p(t_1, ..., t_n)$ is an *atomic formula over X*, iff p is a predicate symbol, $p \in \Pi_n$, and $t_1, ..., t_n$ are terms over X. A (conjunctive) *formula* is a tuple of atomic formulas. If X and Y are tuples of variables, a *substitution from Y to X* is a function $\sigma: X \rightarrow T_\Sigma(Y)$, also represented as $<x_1/\sigma(x_1), ..., x_n/\sigma(x_n)>$. ♦

Definition 15 *(logic programs)*
A *(Horn) logic program* is a finite set $P = \{C_i\}_{i \leq n}$ of *definite clauses*, that is of expressions of the form:

$C_i : A_i :- B_{i1}, ..., B_{in_i}$ where A_i, B_{ij} are atomic formulas. ♦

In this paper we consider just programs over the fixed signature $<\Sigma, \Pi>$. The classic operational, model-theoretic, and fixpoint semantics for logic programs, together with the relative equivalence results, are presented for example in [Ll87].

A logic program can be regarded in a natural way as a graph, where the arcs represent the program clauses, and the nodes are tuples of atomic formulas. The nodes of a graph of this kind have a quite rich structure. We can imagine some very natural operations over tuples of formulas, like *projections*, to select an atomic formula out of a tuple, or *tupling*, or the application of a term substitution to a formula, or the unification of two formulas. These operations can be put in correspondence with the basic constituents of a *cartesian category* in a surprisingly natural way. We recall some definitions of category theory (for the missing definitions we refer to [ML71]).

Definition 16 *(product)*
Let C be a category, and a, b ∈ Obj(C). The (categorical) *product* of a, b is an object a×b ∈ Obj(C) with two arrows *(projections)*, $fst_{a,b}$: a×b → a and $snd_{a,b}$: a×b → b, such that for every pair of arrows f:c → a, g: c → b, there exists a unique arrow <f, g>: c → a×b such that the following diagram commutes:

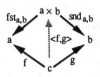

Definition 17 *(strict cartesian categories)*
A *cartesian category* C is a category with:
1)   A terminal object **1** ∈ Obj(C).
2)   All binary products, that is a product diagram for every pair of objects a, b ∈ Obj(C).

In a cartesian category C, it can be shown that product is associative up to isomorphisms, and that 1×a ≅ a ≅ a×1, for each a ∈ Obj(C). A *strict* cartesian category is a cartesian category where these isomorphisms are identities, i.e. such that
3)   (a × b) × c = a × (b × c)   for a, b, c ∈ Obj(C)
4)   **1** × a = a and a × **1** = a   for a, **1** ∈ Obj(C), **1** terminal object
The objects of a strict cartesian category form therefore a monoid with monoidal operation '×' and unit **1**. ◆

4.1 The category of formulas and substitutions of a logic program

In this section we introduce the category of formulas and substitutions for a fixed signature <Σ, Π>, SCC(Σ,Π). We first give a quite informal definition; then we characterize SCC(Σ,Π) as the free strict cartesian category generated by signature <Σ, Π>, and finally some results giving a formal correspondence between the two definitions are presented.

Definition 18 *(the category of formulas and substitutions)*
Category **SCC(Σ,Π)**, the *category of formulas and substitutions of signature <Σ, Π>*, includes, as objects, the free monoid generated by the two element set {T,P} (T for *terms*, P for *predicates*). In what follows, let T^n = T·...·T, n times, and T^0 = 0, the unit of the monoid {T,P}*. An element T^n of {T,P}* represents a (canonical) n-tuple of distinct variables $<x_1, ..., x_n>$.

Arrows of SCC(Σ,Π) include terms, formulas, substitutions, and projections, and are closed under composition and tupling. More precisely, arrows from T^n to T are terms over $<x_1, ..., x_n>$ (Definition 14); arrows from T^n to P are atomic formulas over $<x_1, ..., x_n>$; and if f: X → Y and g: X → Z are arrows, then <f, g>: X → Y·Z is an arrow, too. Therefore also substitutions (tuples of terms) and formulas (tuples of atomic formulas) are represented as arrows. **SCC(Σ,Π)** includes also projections, i.e. arrows $fst_{X,Y}$: X·Y → X and $snd_{X,Y}$: X·Y → Y for every pair of objects X, Y. Finally, if σ: T^n → T^m and σ': T^m → T^i are substitutions, and φ: T^m → P^j is a formula, then their composite arrows σ'∘σ: T^n → T^i and φ∘σ: T^n → P^j are, respectively, the composition of σ and σ' (as substitutions), and the application of σ to φ. The application of a substitution to a formula and the composition of substitutions are defined for example in [Ll87].[5]   ◆

Category SCC(Σ,Π) can also be characterized as the *free strict cartesian category* generated by the two-sorted signature <Σ,Π>, regarded as a graph. This fact allows to point out a deep analogy between the

---

[5] In the present categorical framework, substitution composition and application have to be intended as partial functions. For example, σ'∘σ is defined iff σ is from X to Y, σ' is from W to Z, and Y ≡ W.

following free construction defining $SCC(\Sigma,\Pi)$, and the free construction of the transition system from the graph representing a logic program, presented in the next section. Details of this correspondence can be found in [CM89].

Definition 19 *(the category of formulas and substitutions as a free strict cartesian category)*
Let $SCC(\Sigma,\Pi)$ be defined as follows. Objects of $SCC(\Sigma,\Pi)$ form the monoid $\{T,P\}^*$, exactly as in Definition 18. As arrows, $SCC(\Sigma,\Pi)$ includes all arrows needed to make it a strict cartesian category, with function and predicate symbols as generators. That is:

1)   if f is an n-adic function symbol in Σ, then f: $T^n \to T$ is an arrow.

2)   if p is an n-adic predicate symbol in Π, then p: $T^n \to P$ is an arrow.

Since $SCC(\Sigma,\Pi)$ must be a category, arrows must include identities and must be closed under composition (satisfying the usual axioms for identity and associativity); i.e., for X, Y, and Z objects in $SSC(\Sigma,\Pi)$:

3) $id_X: X \to X$,   if t: $X \to Y$ and t': $Y \to Z$, then $t' \circ t: X \to Z$

4) $id_Y \circ t = t$ $t \circ id_X = t$ $((t \circ t') \circ t'') = (t \circ (t' \circ t''))$

Since $SCC(\Sigma,\Pi)$ must also be strict cartesian, 0 (the unit of $\{T,P\}^*$) must to be the terminal object, and for each pair of objects $<X,Y>$, there must exists a product diagram $<X \cdot Y, fst_{X,Y}, snd_{X,Y}>$ satisfying the usual axioms:

5) $!X: X \to 0$, $fst_{X,Y}: X \cdot Y \to X$, $snd_{X,Y}: X \cdot Y \to Y$

6)   if t: $X \to Y$ and t': $X \to Z$, then $<t,t'>: X \to Y \cdot Z$

7) $!Y \circ t = !X$, $fst_{X,Y} \circ <t,t'> = t$, $snd_{X,Y} \circ <t,t'> = t'$, $<fst_{X,Y} \circ t, snd_{X,Y} \circ t> = t$

Arrows of $SCC(\Sigma,\Pi)$ are the equivalence classes determined by the above rules and equations, and will be (improperly) denoted by a representative.   ◆

The construction of category $SCC(\Sigma,\Pi)$ is inspired by, but slightly different from, that of [AM89]. It is worth noticing that an element T^n of the monoid of objects $\{T,P\}^*$ faithfully represents a (canonical) n-tuple of variables $<x_1, ..., x_n>$. From this point of view, a function symbol f: $T^n \to T$ can be regarded as represented by an 'abstract' term in n variables $f(x_1, ..., x_n)$, and a predicate symbol p: $T^n \to P$ by a formula $p(x_1, ..., x_n)$.

The following propositions state the equivalence of the two definitions given for $SCC(\Sigma,\Pi)$. Below, $SCC(\Sigma,\Pi)$ has to be indented as in Definition 19. Proofs are omitted, since they are straightforward generalizations of those in [AM89].

Proposition 20 *(formulas and substitutions are arrows in $SCC(\Sigma,\Pi)$)*

1)   Let $X = <x_1, ..., x_n>$ be a canonical tuple of distinct variables. Then there exists an isomorphism $For_{X,m}$ between the set of m-tuples of atomic formulas over X, and the arrows in $SCC(\Sigma,\Pi)$ with source T^n and target P^m.

2)   Let $X = <x_1, ..., x_n>$ and $Y = <y_1, ..., y_m>$ be two canonical tuples of variables, and let $Subs_{Y,X}$ be the set of substitutions from Y to X, i.e.

    $Subs_{Y,X} = \{\sigma = <x_1/t_1, ..., x_n/t_n> \mid t_i$ is a term with variables in Y$\}$.

Then there is an isomorphism $\mathbf{Sub}_{Y,X}$ between $Subs_{Y,X}$ and the arrows in $SCC(\Sigma,\Pi)$ with source T^m and target T^n. In particular, variables are represented by suitable compositions of projections. Indeed,

    $\mathbf{Sub}_{X,<y>}(x_i) = snd_{T^{i-1},T} \circ fst_{T^i,T} \circ ... \circ fst_{T^{n-1},T}: T^n \to T$.   ◆

Point 1) implies that every m-tuple of atomic formulas ϕ with n distinct variables has a different representation $\phi_p: T^p \to P^m$, for each $p \geq n$. For example, the empty formula (the tuple of length 0) is represented as $\varnothing: 0 \to 0$, but also as $\varnothing_n: T^n \to 0$ (the empty formula 'with n variables'). Moreover, the set of arrows from 0 to T in $SCC(\Sigma,\Pi)$ is isomorphic to the *word algebra* or *Herbrand Universe* of terms built from Σ, while $\{\phi \mid \phi: 0 \to P\}$ is isomorphic to the *Herbrand base* [Ll87].

Proposition 21 *(arrow composition in SCC(Σ,Π) models substitution composition and application)*
Let X, Y, and Z be three tuples of canonical variables, ϕ be a formula containing at most the variables in X, $\sigma \in Subs_{Y,X}$, and $\sigma' \in Subs_{Z,Y}$. Then

   i) $For_{X,n}(\phi) \circ Sub_{Y,X}(\sigma) = For_{Y,n}(\sigma(\phi))$

   ii) $Sub_{Y,X}(\sigma) \circ Sub_{Z,Y}(\sigma') = Sub_{Z,X}(\sigma'(\sigma))$.   ♦

Example The following diagram shows the representation in SCC(Σ,Π) of the atomic formula *member(x_1,cons(x_2,x_3))* as an arrow from T^3 to P, obtained by the composition of *member*: $T^2 \to P$ and the substitution $<y_1/x_1,y_2/cons(x_2,x_3)>$: $T^3 \to T^2$.

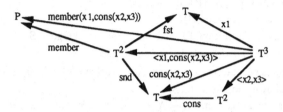

                                                              ♦

Another interesting correspondence between the components of category SCC(Σ,Π) and the world of formulas and substitutions on $<\Sigma,\Pi>$, is that the most general unifier of two formulas ϕ and ϕ', is their *equalizer* (if they share variables) or their *pullback* (if they do not) in SCC(Σ,Π) (see [AM89, Go88]).

    Since SCC(Σ,Π) is cartesian, it is well known that the product $X \times Y = X \cdot Y$ of objects can be extended to a functor. For f: $X \to X'$ and g: $Y \to Y'$, define f×g: $X \cdot Y \to X' \cdot Y'$ as $<f \circ fst_{X,Y}, g \circ snd_{X,Y}>$. The product of two formulas (or substitutions) models their parallel independent composition. The functoriality of × implies, for examples, that $(\sigma \circ \sigma') \times (\sigma_1 \circ \sigma_1') = (\sigma \times \sigma_1) \circ (\sigma' \times \sigma_1')$, whenever the compositions are defined. This captures the fact that the parallel composition of two independent sequences of substitutions can be broken into a sequence of parallel compositions of their elementary steps.

4.2 The transition system associated with a logic program

In this section we define the graph and the transition system associated with a logic program P. Both will have category SCC(Σ,Π) as states, and a categorical structure over arcs (transitions), too. The first one, denoted as P_T, includes as transitions just a suitable representation of the clauses of P. The second one, P_T^*, is obtained from P_T by lifting the cartesian structure from the nodes to the transitions, and by adding *idle transitions*, as motivated in Section 1.1.

Definition 22 *(the graph representing a logic program)*
Given a logic program P= $\{C_i : A_i :- B_{i1}, ..., B_{in_i}\}_{i \leq n}$, the graph associated to it, P_T, is defined as

    $P_T = \partial_0, \partial_1: C_P \to SCC(\Sigma,\Pi)$

where SCC(Σ,Π) is the category of formula and substitutions of Section 4.1, and category C_P (the *category of clauses* of P) and functors ∂_0, ∂_1 are defined as follows.

    Objects of C_P are elements of the free monoid $(\{C_i\}_{i \leq n} \cup \{P,T\})^*$ (i.e., there are generators P and T, like in SCC(Σ,Π), and one new generator for each clause). Functors ∂_0 and ∂_1 are monoid morphisms over objects, such that $\partial_0(T) = \partial_1(T) = T$, $\partial_0(P) = \partial_1(P) = P$, and if $[C_i : A_i :- B_{i1}, ..., B_{im}]$ is a clause, then $\partial_1(C_i) = P$, and $\partial_0(C_i) = P^m$ (m is the number of atomic formulas in the body of C_i).

    Arrows in C_P are clauses of P. For each clause $[C_i : A_i :- B_{i1}, ..., B_{im}]$ there is an arrow c_i: $T^n \to C_i$, where n is the number of distinct variables appearing in C_i. ∂_0 and ∂_1 map c_i to (the representation of) its body $For_{T^n,m}(<B_{i1}, ..., B_{im}>)$, and to its head $For_{T^n,1}(<A_i>)$, respectively (see Proposition 20).   ♦

    It must be stressed that the clauses of P are represented, in category C_P, exactly in the same way function and predicate symbols are represented in $SCC(\Sigma,\Pi)$, i.e. as arrows $T^n \to X$ for suitable n and X. Indeed, C_P can be regarded as a many-sorted signature including one operator for each clause.

The transition system P_T^* is obtained by enriching category C_P with a cartesian structure and with idle transitions, and by extending consistently functors ∂_0 and ∂_1. Actually, the category of transitions of P_T^* is the free strict cartesian category generated by the union of signature C_P and signature $<\Sigma,\Pi>$, in the same way $SCC(\Sigma,\Pi)$ was generated by signature $<\Sigma,\Pi>$. Transitions generated by $<\Sigma,\Pi>$ act the rôle of idle transitions. We discuss later the choice of the initial state for P_T^*.

Definition 23 *(the transition system representing a logic program)*
The transition system of a logic program P is defined as

$$P_T^* = \partial'_0,\partial'_1: SCC(C_P) \to SCC(\Sigma,\Pi),$$

where $SCC(\Sigma,\Pi)$ is as in Definition 19, and the cartesian category $SCC(C_P)$ (a shorthand for $SCC(<C_P,\Sigma,\Pi>)$) and functors ∂'_0, ∂'_1 are defined as follows.

$SCC(C_P)$ has the same objects of C_P, and ∂'_0, ∂'_1 behave like ∂_0, ∂_1 over objects. Arrows of $SCC(C_P)$ are determined by the following rules:

0)   if $c:X \to Y$ is an arrow in C_p, then $c:X \to Y$ is an arrow in $SCC(C_P)$, and $\partial'_i(c) = \partial_i(c)$, $i \in \{0,1\}$.

1-2) Exactly as in Definition 19. These add to $SCC(C_P)$ arrows representing function and predicate symbols in $<\Sigma,\Pi>$. If $t: T^n \to X$ is one of these arrows, $\partial'_0(t) = \partial'_1(t) = t$.

3-7) As in Definition 19. These rules create the free strict cartesian structure generated by arrows of points 0) to 2). Functors ∂'_0 and ∂'_1 are extended in the unique way that makes them cartesian functors.   ◆

Therefore, transitions of P_T^* includes, among others, the original clauses of P, all their possible instantiations (e.g. arrow $c \circ \sigma: T^m \to C$, where $c: T^n \to C$ is a clause with n variables, and $\sigma: T^m \to T^n$ is a substitution), and their 'parallel composition' given by the product functor, e.g. if $c_i: T^n \to C_i$ and $c_j: T^m \to C_j$, then $c_i \times c_j: T^{n+m} \to C_i \cdot C_j$.

We still have to choose an initial state for P_T^*. Since 'successful computations' of a logic program are *refutations*, i.e. sequences of resolution steps ending in the empty goal, quite obviously the initial state should be a representation of the empty formula $\varnothing$ (for what concerns the apparent incongruity of taking as initial state the *last* goal of a refutation, see the observation after Definition 5). However, it must be stressed that the source and target of a transition in P_T^* are always formulas with *the same number of variables*. In fact, both functors ∂'_0 and ∂'_1 are identities on objects like T^n (Definition 21), which represent tuples of variables. This implies that if we choose as initial state of P_T^* a *single* representation of the empty formula, say $\varnothing_n: T^n \to 0$, every formula reachable by a computation will have *at most* n variables (see Proposition 20). Indeed, if we are just interested in *ground* computations, we can safely choose $\varnothing: 0 \to 0$ as the initial state. But if we want to consider computations involving an unpredictable number of variables, we are forced to consider *a set* of initial states, namely $\{\varnothing_n\}_{n<\omega}$, i.e. all the representations of the empty formula. It is possible to show that all the definitions of semantics of transition systems easily generalize to the case of multiple initial states.

Thus, we will consider two versions of the transition system P_T^*, namely $<P_T^*,\varnothing>$, with $\varnothing: 0 \to 0$ as initial state, and $<P_T^*,\{\varnothing_n\}>$, with set $\{\varnothing_n\}_{n<\omega}$ as initial states.

4.3 The transition system semantics of a logic program

The transition systems just introduced faithfully mimic the operational behavior of a logic program, in the sense of Section 1.1. We can now apply our definition of semantics to the transition systems representing a logic program. As anticipated in the Introduction, we stick to the minimal observation function in order to compare our semantics with the classic one. Nevertheless, we can choose among different sets of final states, obtaining different semantics which have interesting relationships with some HCL semantics proposed in the literature. For example, we can choose as final states either atomic or non atomic formulas, and independently, either ground or also non ground formulas. This selection can be applied either to the whole set of formulas, obtaining a sort of *success set* of the program, or just to the instantiations of a specific goal, yielding a set of *answer substitutions*.

In the following definition, we denote by F the set of all formulas (i.e. all arrows in $SCC(\Sigma,\Pi)$ from T^m to P^n, for some m, n); F_{at} denotes *atomic* formulas (i.e. $F_{at} = \{\phi \mid \exists n.\phi: T^n \to P\}$); F_{gr} denotes *ground* formulas (arrows from 0 to P^n, n arbitrary); and, for a formula $\phi: T^m \to P^n$, Z_ϕ denotes the set of all the instantiations of ϕ, that is the set of all arrows of the form $\sigma{\circ}\phi: T^{m'} \to P^n$.

Definition 24 *(the transition system semantics of a logic program)*
The *transition system semantics of P* is the final set semantics of the transition system representing P (with $\{\varnothing_n\}_{n<\omega}$ as initial states), with respect to the set of all formulas as final states:

$$[P]_{TS} = [<P_T^*,\{\varnothing_n\}>, F]_{FS}$$

The *atomic, ground,* and *ground-atomic* TS-semantics of P are defined, respectively, as

$$[P]_{TS,at} = [<P_T^*,\{\varnothing_n\}>, F_{at}]_{FS}, \qquad\qquad [P]_{TS,gr} = [<P_T^*,\{\varnothing_n\}>, F_{gr}]_{FS},$$

$$[P]_{TS,gr,at} = [<P_T^*,\{\varnothing_n\}>, F_{gr} \cap F_{at}]_{FS}.$$

Moreover, the *transition system semantics of P with respect to a goal g* is the final set semantics of that transition system with respect to the set of all the instantiations of g, that is

$$[P, g]_{TS} = [<P_T^*,\{\varnothing_n\}>, Z_g]_{FS} \qquad\qquad\qquad\blacklozenge$$

Fact 25 The ground and ground-atomic TS-semantics of P can be equivalently defined considering just $\varnothing: 0 \to 0$ as initial state, that is, $[P]_{TS,gr} = [<P_T^*,\varnothing> F_{gr}]_{FS}$ and $[P]_{TS,gr,at} = [<P_T^*,\varnothing>, F_{gr} \cap F_{at}]_{FS}$. This is obvious, since $[P]_{TS,gr}$ and $[P]_{TS,gr,at}$ include just ground formulas, which are reachable through ground computations. $\qquad\qquad\blacklozenge$

4.4 Relations between classic and transition system semantics

There are strong relationships between the classic semantics for HCL and our transition system semantics, although there are some fundamental differences in the structure of models and interpretations. In fact, in our semantics, a (final set) interpretation is a set of arrows like $\phi: T^n \to P^m$, for some n and m, in category $SCC(\Sigma,\Pi)$, i.e. a set of tuples of atomic formulas, possibly containing variables. On the contrary, classic Herbrand interpretations include just *ground atomic* formulas. Nevertheless, we can compare directly our semantics to the classic one choosing a suitable set of final states, as shown in the theorem below.

In [FLMP88] the classic semantics of HCL is enriched considering Herbrand interpretations containing non-ground atoms (modulo variance). Two approaches are presented there: the C-approach, in which models of a program must be upward closed (i.e. if an atom belongs to M, all its instantiations must belong to M, too), and the S-approach, where this constraint is removed thanks to a different notion of truth. Both approaches are shown to be more informative than the classic semantics (more programs can be distinguished), but just the S-approach is shown to capture the operational notion of *computed* answer substitution (instead of the *correct* answer substitutions). In our case, we are similar to the C-approach: in fact it can be shown that our models are upward closed. However, our domains are strictly richer because of the presence of tuples instead of just atomic formulas.

For what concerns the last point, i.e. the existence of tuples of atoms, we have to compare our semantics with that of [FLP84]. In [FLP84] clauses with multiple heads are allowed in programs, and models are collections of multisets of ground atoms. We can allow clauses with multiple heads in a program, too, without even changing our definitions.

In summary, giving all formal definitions the following can be proved:

Theorem 26 *(relations between classic and (final set) transition system semantics of HCL)*

Let P be a logic program. Then

1) $[\![P]\!]_{TS,gr,at}$ is exactly the classic minimal model of P [Ll87].

2) $[\![P]\!]_{TS,at}$ is the minimal C-model of P as defined in [FLMP88], up to the naming of variables.

3) $[\![P]\!]_{TS,gr}$ is isomorphic to the free (not commutative) monoid generated by the classic minimal model of P (while the minimal model of [FLP84] is (up to a closure) the corresponding free *commutative* monoid).

4) $[\![P, g]\!]_{TS}$, is isomorphic to the set of all *correct* answer substitutions of g in the classic sense.

Sketch of the proof

0)   Since final set semantics consists of all final states reachable from the initial state(s) (Definition 13), it must be proved that reachable formulas are all and only the conjunctive formulas provable from clauses in P. It can be shown, by structural induction, that all transitions "of sort P" are logically sound, and are also complete if P includes just definite clauses (by completeness of resolution for HCL).

Statements 1) to 4) follows from 0) and from the following observations:

1) $F_{at} \cap F_{gr}$ is the Herbrand base (Proposition 20).

2)   Models are upward closed, and formulas differing just for the name of variables are not identified in $SCC(\Sigma,\Pi)$.

3)   The monoidal operator is tupling, which is not commutative. The analogy with [FLMP88] also holds if non-definite clauses are allowed in P. In this case tupling does not correspond to logical conjunction.

4)   Since models are upward closed, it is not possible to get just *computed* answer substitutions.   ♦

5 Conclusions

We proposed a new semantics for HCL, parametric with respect to an observation function over computations: the meaning of a program is a set of observations over successful computations (refutations). The semantics has been given in a logic programming style, i.e. with three different although equivalent characterizations (operational, model-theoretic and fixpoint). This semantics should fill the gap between the classic HCL semantics, concerned just with the final result of a refutation (i.e. answer substitutions), and the process semantics used for imperative languages, more informative but less elegant. Actually, in order to define a true process semantics, our approach should be generalized to deal also with *infinite* computations

Consistency with the classic semantics has been checked by considering the *minimal* observation function, which observes just the initial and final state of a computation. Also in this case our semantics is more informative than the classic one, and captures some extensions proposed in the literature. Our methodology should be generalizable to concurrent logic languages, as a basis for a true compositional process semantics, in the logic programming style.

Actually, the framework we depicted is not bound to logic programming. The definition of semantics has been given at the very basic level of transition systems, thus isolating the issues of control from the structure of the data. Then we showed how a logic program can be represented as a structured transition system. This means that our framework can be applied to every system that can be represented as a transition system, providing it with a logic programming-like semantics.

6 References

[AM89]   Asperti, A., Martini, S., *Projections instead of variables, A category theoretic interpretation of logic programs*, Proc. 6th Int. Conf. on Logic Programming, Lisboa, Portugal, 1989.

[AN86]   Aït-kaci, H., Nasr, R., *LOGIN: a logic programming language with built-in inheritance*, Journal of Logic Programming 3, pp. 185-215, 1986.

[BL86]   Bellia, M., Levi, G., *The relation between logic and functional languages: A survey*, Journal of Logic Programming 3, pp. 217-236, 1986.

[CG86]   Clark, K.L., Gregory, S., *PARLOG: Parallel Programming in Logic*, ACM TOPLAS 8(1),pp. 1-49, 1986.

[CM88]   Corradini, A., Montanari, U., *(Concurrent) Logic Programming as Transition Systems and viceversa*, Internal Report TP 13, Escuela Superior Latino-Americana de Informática (ESLAI), Buenos Aires, R. Argentina, December 1988.

[CM89]   Corradini, A., Montanari, U., *An Algebraic Representation of Logic Program Computations*, Technical Report TR-36/89, Dipartimento di Informatica, Università di Pisa, December 1989.

[Co90]   Corradini, A., *Ph.D. Thesis*, Dipartimento di Informatica, Università di Pisa, forthcoming.

[FLMP88] Falaschi, M., Levi, G., Martelli, M., Palamidessi, C., *Declarative Modeling of the Operational Behaviour of Logic Languages*, Technical Report TR-10/88, Dipartimento di Informatica, Univ. di Pisa, 1988; a preliminary version also appeared as: *A new declarative semantics for logic languages*, in Proc. 5th Int. Conf. Symp. on Logic Programming, Seattle, MIT Press, pp. 993-1005, 1988.

[FLP84]   Falaschi, M., Levi, G., Palamidessi, C., *A Synchronization Logic: Axiomatics and Formal Semantics of Generalized Horn Clauses*, in Information and Control, 60(1-3), Academic Press, 1984.

[GS89]   Gaifman, H., Shapiro, E., *Fully Abstract Compositional semantics for Logic Programs*, Proc. of the 1989 ACM Conf. on Principles of Logic Programming, 1989.

[GCLS88] Gerth, R., Codish, M., Lichtenstein, Y., Shapiro, E., *Fully Abstract Denotational Semantics for Flat Concurrent Prolog*, Proc. 3th Annual Symposium on Logic In Computer Science, Edinburgh, UK, 1988.

[Go88]   Goguen, J.A., *What is Unification? A Categorical View of Substitution, Equation and Solution*, Research Report SRI-CSL-88-2R2, SRI International, Menlo Park, California, 1988.

[Ho83]   Hoare, C.A.R., Communicating Sequential Processes, Prentice-Hall, 1983.

[JL87]   Jaffar, J., Lassez, J.-L., *Constraint Logic Programming*, Proc. 12th ACM Symp. on Principles of Programming Languages, pp. 111-119, 1987.

[Ko88]   Kok, J.N., *A Compositional Semantics for Concurrent Prolog*, in Proc. of the Symposium on Theoretical Aspects of Computer Science (STACS), Bordeaux, 1988.

[LP87]   Levi, G., Palamidessi, C., *An approach to the declarative semantics of synchronization in logic languages*, Proc. 4th Int. Conf. on Logic Programming, MIT Press Series in Logic Programming, pp. 877-893, 1987.

[Ll87]   Lloyd, J.W., *Foundations of Logic Programming*, Springer Verlag, 1984, (2nd Edition 1987).

[ML71]   Mac Lane, S., *Categories for the Working Mathematician*, Springer Verlag, New York, 1971.

[Ma87]   Maher, M.J., *Logic semantics for a class of committed-choice programs*, Proc. 4th Int. Conf. on Logic Programming, MIT Press Series in Logic Programming, pp. 858-876, 1987.

[Mi84]   Milner, R., *Notes on a Calculus for Communicating Systems*, in Control Flow and Data Flow: Concepts of Distributed Programming, (M. Broy, ed.), NATO ASI Series F: Vol. 14, Springer-Verlag, pp. 205-228, 1984.

[Mo86]   Monteiro, L., *Distributed Logic: A Theory of Distributed Programming in Logic*, Internal Report, Universidade Nova de Lisboa, Portugal, April 1986.

[Mu88]   Murakami, M., *A Declarative Semantics of Parallel Logic Programs with Perpetual Processes*, Proc. FGCS '88, 1988.

[RB85]   Rydeheard, D.E., Burstall, R.M., *The Unification of Terms: A Category-Theoretic Algorithm*, Internal Report UMCS-85-8-1, Dept. Comp. Sci., University of Manchester, August 1985.

[Sa87]   Saraswat, V.A., *The concurrent logic programming language CP: definition and operational semantics*, Proc. of the SIGACT-SIGPLAN Symposium on Principle of Programming Languages, ACM, Jan. 1987.

[Sh86]   Shapiro, E., *Concurrent Prolog: A Progress Report*, in Fundamentals of Artificial Intelligence, (W. Bibel e Ph. Jorrand eds.), LNCS 232, Springer Verlag, pp. 277-313, 1986.

[Ue85]   Ueda, K., *Guarded Horn Clauses*, ICOT TR-103, June 1985.

Parallel computations on strings and arrays[1]

Maxime Crochemore[2] and **Wojciech Rytter**[3]

Abstract

We present several new parallel algorithms in the field of string and array processing. We give almost optimal algorithms for pattern matching in arrays and for related problem : longest common subarray, longest repeated subarray and longest symmetric subarray. We also give almost optimal algorithms for problems on strings : finding squares, testing even palstars, computing Lyndon factorizations and building pattern matching automata. In the PRAM model without concurrent writes, the parallel time is $\log(n)^2$ with n processors and, in the PRAM model with concurrent writes, the time, for most of the problems, is $\log(n)$ with n processors. All the algorithms have in common the use of a parallel version of the Karp, Miller and Rosenberg's algorithm.

Introduction

In the domain of parallel computation, it is often the case that the most simpler sequential algorithms contain ideas for designing efficient parallel algorithm. The results presented in this paper provide a further confirmation of this fact.

The Karp, Miller and Rosenberg's algorithm [KMR 72] was one of the first efficient (almost linear) sequential algorithms for finding repeated patterns and for matching strings. In this latter area, it has been superseded by more efficient and more sophisticated sequential algorithms (see for instance [KMP 77], [BM 77], [GS 83], [CP 89]). But we show that the Karp, Miller and Rosenberg's algorithm (KMR) must be considered as a basic technique in parallel computations. For many problems, variations of KMR give the most (known) efficient parallel algorithms.

The basic point used by KMR is to consider, in increasing order, substructures which sizes are powers of two. These substructures are called here *basic substructures*. The representation of set of basic factors (subarrays) of a string (array) produced by the algorithm KMR is an extremely useful data structure in

---

[1] This work has been realized at the University of Paris-Nord.

[2] LITP, Université de Paris 7, 2, place Jussieu, 75251 Paris Cedex 05, France.

[3] Institute of Informatics, Warsaw University, PKiN 8p., 00901 Warsaw, Poland.

parallel algorithms on strings and arrays. This consideration also gives a general unifying framework for a large variety of problems.

We show that the following problems for strings and arrays can be solved by almost optimal parallel algorithms: pattern-matching, longest repeated factor (subarray), longest common factor (subarray), maximal symmetric factor (subarray). For strings only, we also show that the following problems can be solved within the same complexity bounds: finding squares, testing even palstars (and compositions of k palindromes for k=2,3,4), computing Lyndon factorizations and building minimal pattern-matching automata. In the PRAM model without concurrent writes (CREW PRAM) the parallel time is $\log(n)^2$ (with n processors) and, in the PRAM model with concurrent writes (CRCW PRAM) the time, for most of the problems, is $\log(n)$ (with n processors).

For two problems related to the one-dimensional case (longest repeated factor and longest common factor) previous parallel algorithms have been designed. These algorithms are based on a parallel construction of suffix-trees [AILSV 88]. However, our data structure is more simpler and, furthermore, works for the two-dimensional case contrary to the use of suffix-trees.

The complexity of our algorithms does not depend on the size of the alphabet except for the computation of pattern-matching automata. As a consequence, if the size of the alphabet is fixed, each of the presented algorithms which work in $\log(n)$ time with n processors on a concurrent-write PRAM, can be transformed into a strictly optimal parallel algorithm by using the "four Russians" trick (see, for instance, [AHU 74]). This gives, in the case of small alphabets, optimal parallel algorithms ($\log(n)$ time - $n/\log(n)$ processors on a concurrent-write PRAM) for two-dimensional string matching, for computing maximal symmetric subarrays, for testing even palstars, and for building minimal pattern-matching automata.

1. Basic techniques

The Karp, Miller, Rosenberg's algorithm deals with identification of well structured objects: this means that the identifier of an object of size 2n can be easily computable from identifiers of few subobjects of size n. Examples of well structured objects are strings, arrays and trees. The algorithm is applied to find repeated objects: multiple occurrences of a same suboject. This is equivalent to finding two objects with the same identifier. Hence the identification procedure is the crucial idea of the algorithm. The computations are well structured due to the fact that the data are well structured. The identifiers of objects of size 1 are computed, then are those of sizes 2, 4, 8, etc. The identifiers of objects whose size is not a power of two can be computed by decomposing these objects into objects whose sizes are powers of two. We have a recursion of depth $\log(n)$ with independent recursive calls. Such a type of sequential computations is ideally suited to efficient parallel computations.

In the case of strings the subobjects are factors (or substrings). The KMR algorithm creates names for all factors whose size is a power of two; we call the created data structure the *dictionary of basic factors*. This dictionary can be computed by an efficient parallel algorithm: a parallel version of the KMR algorithm. This gives, as an application, a series of efficient parallel algorithms for strings and arrays.

By an efficient parallel algorithm we mean an algorithm working in polylogarithmic time with polynomial number of processors. In this class of algorithms, especially efficient are optimal and almost optimal parallel algorithms. An algorithm (working in polylogarithmic parallel time) is *optimal* iff its total number of elementary operations is linear, while *almost optimal algorithm* is an algorithm that is optimal within a polylogarithmic factor (polylogarithmic time - linear number of processors). From the point of view of any application, optimal or almost optimal do not make very big difference.

Our basic model of parallel computations is a *parallel random access machine* (PRAM) without write conflicts (CREW PRAM). However a model with write conflicts (concurrent writes) will be also discussed (CRCW PRAM).

The parallelism will be expressed by the following type of parallel statement:

for all x in X **in parallel do** action(x).

The execution of this statement consists of:

a) assigning a processor to each element of X;

b) executing in parallel by the assigned processors all those operations specified by action(x).

We are interested in parallel time T(n) as well as the number of processors employed by the parallel algorithm. The product T(n)P(n) gives the total number of operations.

The PRAM model is best suited to work with tree-structured objects or recursive computations. We start with such type of computations. One of the basic parallel technique is the *prefix computation*. Given a vector x of n values, we want to compute all prefix products: $y[1]=x[1]$, $y[2]=x[1]\otimes x[2]$; $y[3]=x[1]\otimes x[2]\otimes x[3]$;... The prefix computation means computing the values $y[1]$, $y[2]$, $y[3]$,.... The operation $\otimes$ is assumed to be associative and computable in $O(1)$ time. We use frequently the following fact (see for instance [GR 88]).

Lemma 1.1

Prefix computation applied to a vector x of size n can be done in $\log(n)$ time with $n/\log(n)$ processors.

Another basic parallel methods to construct efficient algorithms is the *doubling technique*. Roughly speaking it consists in computing each time object of the size twice bigger as before, knowing the previously computed objects. The word 'doubling' is often misleading because in many algorithms of such type the size of objects grows with a ratio c>1; not necessarily with c=2. The typical use of this technique is in the proof of the following lemma (see [GR 88]). Suppose we have a vector of size n with some of the positions marked, denote by Minright[i] and Maxleft[i] the nearest marked position to the right (to the left) of position i.

Lemma 1.2

If we have a vector of size n with some of the nodes marked then we can compute vectors Minright, Maxleft in $\log(n)$ time with $n/\log(n)$ processors.

The doubling technique is also the crucial feature of the KMR algorithm in a parallel setting. In one stage the algorithm computes the names (identifiers) for all words of size k. In the next stage using these names it computes names of words of the size twice bigger.

To make a parallel version of KMR algorithm, it is sufficient to design an efficient parallel version of one stage. This essentially reduces to the parallel computation of the procedure RENUMBER(x) which aim is to assign names to objects. If this procedure is implemented in T(n) parallel time with n processors, then we have a parallel version of the algorithm KMR working in T(n)log(n) time with the same number n of processors. This is due to the doubling technique and the fact that there are only log(n) stages. Essentially the same problems as those computed by the sequential algorithm can be computed by its parallel version in T(n)log(n) time.

The complexity of computing RENUMBER(x) heavily depends on the model of parallel computations used. It can be computed in time log(n) without concurrent writes and in constant time with concurrent writes. In the latter case, one needs a memory bigger than the total number of operations (auxiliary table with n^2 entries; or -by making some arithmetic tricks- with $n^{1+\varepsilon}$ entries). This looks slightly artificial, though entries of auxiliary memory have not to be initialized. The details related to the distribution of processors are also very technical in the case of concurrent write model. Therefore we present our algorithms using a model without concurrent writes. This increases the time by a logarithmic factor. This logarithmic factor gives also a big margin of time for technical problems related to the assignment of processors. We indicate shortly how to remove this logarithmic factor when concurrent writes are used. The main difference is the implementation of the procedure RENUMBER and the computation of classes of objects having the same name.

2. KMR algorithm and the dictionary of basic substructures

Given a string t we say that two positions are k-equivalent iff the factors of length k starting at these positions are equal. Such an equivalence is best represented by assigning to each position a name to the factor of length k starting at this position. We shall compute names of all factors of a given length k for k=1, 2, 4,.... We consider only factors of length which is a power of two: such factors are called *basic factors*. The name of a factor is its rank in the lexicographic ordering of factors of a given length. We also call these names k-letters. For each k-letter r we also require (for further applications) a link pos[r,k] to a position at which an occurrence of the k-letter r starts.

We consider only factors starting at positions [1..n-1]. The n-th position contains the special endmarker #. The endmarker has highest rank in the alphabet. We can generally assume w.l.o.g. that n-1 is a power of two.

The tables name and pos are called together the *dictionary of basic factors*.. This dictionary is our basic data structure.

Example: let t be abaabbaa# (seven additional #'s are appended to guarantee that each factor x of length 8 starting in [1..8] is well defined). Figure 2.1 shows tables 'name' and 'pos'.

```
i   =  1  2  3  4  5  6  7  8
t   =  a  b  a  a  b  b  a  a  ########
```

k=1 name[i,k]=	1	2	1	1	2	2	1	1
k=2 name[i,k]=	2	4	1	2	5	4	1	3
k=4 name[i,k]=	3	6	1	4	8	7	2	5

```
r  =  1  2  3  4  5  6  7  8
```

k=1 pos[r,k]=	1	2	undefined					
k=2 pos[r,k]=	3	1	8	2	5	undefined		
k=4 pos[r,k]=	3	7	1	4	8	2	6	5

Fig 2.1. The dictionary of basic factors.

In the case of arrays, basic factors are replaced by k*k subarrays, where k is a power of two. In this case name[(i,j),k] is the name of an k*k subarray t' of a given array t with upper-left corner at position (i,j). We will discuss mostly the construction of dictionaries of basic factors for strings; the construction in the two-dimensional case is an easy extension of that for one-dimensional data.

Let x be a vector (an array) of total size n containing elements of some linearly ordered set. The procedure RENUMBER assigns new values to the entries of x. Let val(x) be the set of values of all entries of x. Let x' be the value of x after performing RENUMBER(x). We require:

(a) if x[i]=x[j] then x'[i]=x'[j], and

(b) val(x') is a subset of [1..n].

There are two variations of the procedure depending on whether the following condition is also satisfied or not:

(c) x'[i] is the rank of x[i] in the set val(x).

We require also that the procedure computes, as a side effect, the vector POS defined by: if q is in val(x'), then POS[q] is any position i such that x'[i]=q.

Lemma 2.1

(1) The procedure RENUMBER satisfying (a), (b) and (c) can be implemented in log(n) time with n processors on an exclusive-write PRAM;

(2) Assume that val(x) consists of integers (or pairs of integers) in the range [1..n]. Then the procedure RENUMBER satisfying (a) and (b) can be computed in O(1) time with n processors on a concurrent-write PRAM. In this case the size of auxiliary memory is bigger than the total number of operations: it is $O(n^{1+\epsilon})$. However auxiliary tables have not to be initialized.

Idea of the proof.

(1) The main part of the procedure is a parallel sort for which the algorithm of Cole can be applied (log(n) time - n processors). The renumbering can be done in O(1) parallel time once we know to which group each element belongs. Doing so, the whole procedure RENUMBER has the same complexity as sorting n elements.

(2) The trick is to use a bulletin board as in [Ga 85b] or [AILSV 88]. ◊

Algorithm KMR   /* computation of the dictionary of basic factors of t */
/* the last symbol of t is #, |t|=n, n-1 is a power of two */
x:=t; RENUMBER(x); k:=1;
for i:=1..n **do in parallel** { name[i,1]:=x[i]; pos[1,i]:=POS[i]; };
  while k<n-1 **do**
  { **for** i:=1..n-2k+1 **do in parallel** x[i]:=(x[i],x[i+k]);
    delete the last 2k-1 entries of x;
    RENUMBER(x);
    for i:=1..n-2k+1 **do in parallel** { name[i,2k]:=x[i]; pos[2k,i]:=POS[i]; }
    k:=2k; }
end.

Figure 2.2. Parallel version of the Karp, Miller and Rosenberg's algorithm.

Theorem 2.2

The dictionary of basic factors (basic subarrays) of a given string (array) can be computed with n processors in $\log(n)^2$ time on an exclusive-write PRAM, and in $\log(n)$ time on a concurrent-write PRAM (in the latter case an auxiliary space of size $O(n^{1+\varepsilon})$ is used).

Proof.

The crucial fact is the simple observation, intensively used by the algorithm of Figure 2.2:

(*) name[i,2k] =name[j,2k] iff (name[i,k]=name[j,k]) and (name[i+k,k]=name[j+k,k]),

from which the correctness of the algorithm follows. The number of iterations is logarithmic and the dominating operation is the procedure RENUMBER. The thesis follows from Lemma 2.1.

In the case of arrays, let name[(i,j),p] be the name of an p*p subarray of a given array t with upper-left corner at position (i,j). Then (see Figure 2.3):

(**) name[(i,j),2p]=name[(k,l),2p] <=>
        (name[(i,j),p]=name[(k,l),p] and name[(i+p,j),p]=name[(k+p,l),p] and
name[(i+p,j+p),p]=name[(k+p,l+p),p] and name[(i,j+p),p]=name[(k,l+p),p]).

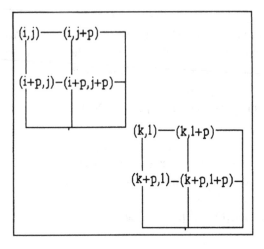

Fig 2.3. A subarray of size 2p*2p repeats (the subarrays can overlap).

Using fact (**) the algorithm KMR (Figure 2.2) can be easily modified to compute the dictionary of basic subarrays. ◊

3. Almost optimal parallel algorithms for strings

We first present a simple application to make some acquaintance with dictionaries of basic factors. The table PREF is a close "relative" of the failure table P commonly used in efficient string-matching sequential algorithms. The name 'failure' comes from the way the table is used: it helps in situations when a failure (mismatch) occurs. For a string p of length n, we define

PREF[i]=max{j/ i+j≤n and p[i+1..i+j] is a prefix of p} and

P[i] = max {0≤j<i: p[1..j] is a suffix of p[1..i] }, for 1≤i≤n.

The table PREF and its symmetric table SUF are crucial tables in the Main-Lorentz square-finding algorithm, which we later parallelize.

Theorem 3.1

The table PREF can be computed in log(n) time with n processors without using concurrent writes, if the dictionary of basic factors is already computed.

Proof.

Assign one processor to each position i and computes PREF[i] using a kind of binary search. ◊

3.1 Finding squares in strings

We start the applications of the previous algorithms with the problem of searching squares in strings. It is a non-trivial problem to find a square factor within a word in sequential linear time. A simple application of failure functions gives a quadratic sequential algorithm and also a parallel NC-algorithm. To do so, we can compute a failure function P_i for each suffix $x[i..n]$ of the word x. Then, there is a square in x, prefix of the suffix $x[i..n]$, iff $P_i[j] \geq (j-i+1)/2$ for some $j > i$. Computing a linear number of failure functions leads to a quadratic sequential algorithm and to a parallel NC-algorithm. However, with such an approach, the parallel computation requires a quadratic number of processors. We show how the divide-and-conquer method used in the sequential case saves time and space in parallel computation.

The main part of one of the known most efficient sequential algorithms for finding a square in a word is an operation called *test*. This operation applies to squarefree words u and v and tests whether the word uv contains a square (the square must begin in u and end in v). This operation is a composition of two smaller ones *righttest* and *lefttest*. The first (resp. second) operation tests whether uv contains a square which center is in v (resp. u).

The operation test may be implemented by using two auxiliary tables related to string-matching technique. For a given word $v = v[1]..v[m]$ and position k ($1 \leq k \leq m$) recall that PREF[k] is the length of the longest prefix of v which occurs at k in v (i.e. which is a prefix of $v[k+1]..[m]$). Let also $SUF_u[k]$ be the length of longest suffix of $v[1..k]$ which is also a suffix of u. This table SUF_u can be computed in the same way as PREF, by computing PREF for $u^R \& v^R$ for instance.

Lemma 3.2

Tables PREF and SUF_u being computed, functions righttest(u,v), lefttest(u,v) and test(u,v) can be computed in $O(\log(n))$ time with $n/\log(n)$ processors (in constant time with n processors in the concurrent-write model).

Proof. The existence of a square reduces to the comparisons of k and $PREF[k] + SUF_u[k]$, for all positions k. ◊

A recursive algorithm for testing occurrences of squares can be easily constructed with the help of the function test (Figure 3.1).

Algorithm SQUARE

```
/* checks if word x[1...n] contains a square. It is assumed w.l.o.g. that n is a power of two */
  if n>1 then
  { for i ∈ {1,n/2+1} do in parallel
        check recursively whether x[i..i+n/2-1] contains a square;
        /* if the algorithm has not already stopped then */
        if ( test( x[1..n/2], x]n/2..n] ) then return true; }
    return false; /*if the value true has not been already returned */
  end.
```

Figure 3.1. Searching for a square in a string x.

Theorem 3.3

The algorithm SQUARE tests squarefreeness of a word $x[1]..x[n]$ in $O(\log(n)^2)$ parallel time using $O(n)$ processors in model without concurrent writes.

Proof.

The complexity of the algorithm SQUARE essentially comes from the computation of basic factors (Theorem 2.2). Each recursive step during the execution of the algorithm takes $O(\log(n))$ time with n processors as shown by Theorem 3.1 and Lemma 3.2. The number of steps is $\log(n)$. This gives the result. $\Diamond$

3.2 Failure functions, periods and pattern-matching automata

We start this section with a parallel computation of failure tables defined at the beginning of Section 3.

Lemma 3.4

The failure table P can be computed in $\log(n)^2$ time with n processors without using concurrent writes (in $\log(n)$ time if the dictionary of basic factors is already computed).

Proof.

We can assume that the table PREF is already computed. Let us consider pairs $(i+1, i+PREF[i])$. These pairs correspond to intervals $[i+1..j]$. The first step is to compute all such intervals which are maximal in the sense of set inclusion order. It can be done with the use of parallel prefix computation (see Section 1). For each position k $(1 \leq k \leq n)$ compute

$$maxval(k)=max(PREF[1], PREF[2], PREF[3],...., PREF[k-1]).$$

Then we "turn off" all positions k such that $maxval(k) \geq PREF[k]$. We are left with maximal subintervals $(i+1, i+PREF[i])$. Let us (in one parallel step) mark all right ends of these intervals and compute for all right ends j of these intervals the table $PREF^{-1}[j]$ defined as $i+1$ such that $i+PREF[i]=j$. For the other values j, $PREF^{-1}[j]$ is undefined.

Again, using a prefix computation, for each position k, we can compute minright[k] to be the minimum marked position to the right of k. Then, in one parallel step, we set $P[k]:=0$ if minright[k] is undefined, and $P[k]:=max(0,k-PREF^{-1}[minright[k]])$ otherwise (see Figure 3.2). This completes the proof. $\Diamond$

structure of maximal intervals $(i+1, i+PREF[i])$

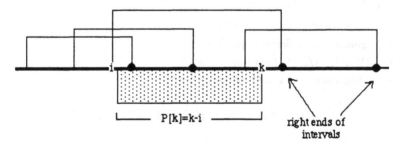

Fig 3.2. Computation of P[k] in case $i=PREF^{-1}[minright[k]] \leq k$.

One may observe that if the table PREF is given then even n/log(n) processors are sufficient to compute table P, because our main operations are prefix computations.

Corollary 3.5

The periods of all the prefixes of a word can be computed in $\log(n)^2$ time with n processors without using concurrent writes (in log(n) time if the dictionary of basic factors is already computed).

Proof. The period of prefix $x[1..i]$ is $i-P[i]$. $\lozenge$

We now give another consequence of Lemma 3.4 connected to the previous result. Given a word x the minimal pattern-matching automaton for x is the minimal deterministic automaton which recognizes the language A*x. The construction of such automata is a basic technique in string-matching problems. Its sequential construction is straightforward, but it is usually related in literature to the failure function P. We can use this fact to develop a parallel algorithm.

Theorem 3.6

Assume that the basic dictionary is computed and the alphabet has O(1) size. Then, we can compute the minimal pattern-matching automata for a string of length n, or for a finite set of strings of total length n, in log(n) time with n processors on an exclusive-write PRAM.

3.3 Testing even Palstar

The next application of algorithms of Section 2 is to algorithmic questions related to palindromes. We consider in the paper only even length palindromes: let PAL denote the set of such nonempty even palindromes (words of the form ww^R). Inside a given string p, Rad[i] is the radius of the palindrome centered at position i:

$$Rad[i] = \max \{ \ k : p[i-k+1..i] = (p[i+1..i+k])^R \},$$

where R is the operation of reversing a string.

If k is the maximal integer satisfying $p[i-k+1..i] = (p[i+1..i+k])^R$ then we say that i is the center of the maximal palindrome $p[i-k+1..i+k]$. In many cases we will identify palindromes with their corresponding subintervals of $[1..n]$.

Lemma 3.7

Assume that the dictionaries of basic factors for the word and its reverse are computed. Then the table Rad of maximal radii of palindromes can be computed in log(n) time with n processors.

Proof.

The proof is essentially the same as the one for the computation of table PREF: a variant of parallel binary search is used. $\lozenge$

Denote by Firstcenter[i] (resp. Lastcenter[i]) the tables of first (resp. last) centers to the right of i (including position i) of palindromes containing position i.

Lemma 3.8

If the table Rad is computed then the table Firstcenter and can be computed in log(n) time with n processors on the exclusive-write model.

Theorem 3.9

Even palstars can be tested in log(n) time with n processors on the exclusive-write model, if the dictionary of basic factors is already computed.

Proof.

Let first[i] be a table whose value is the first position j in t such that t[i..j] is an even nonempty palindrome; it is zero if there is no such prefix even palindrome. Define first[n]=n. This table can be easily computed using the values of Firstcenter[i]. Then the sequential algorithm in the following natural way tests even palstars: it finds the first prefix even palindrome and cuts it; then such a process is repeated as long as possible; if we are done with an empty string then we return 'true': the initial word is an even palstar. The correctness of the algorithm is proved in [GS 78]. We make a parallel version of the algorithm.

Compute table $first^*[i]=first^k[i]$, where $first^k[i]=first^{k+1}[i]$ using a doubling technique.

Now the text is an even palstar iff $first^*[1]=n$. This can be tested in one step.

This completes the proof. ◊

Unfortunately the natural sequential algorithm described above for even palstars is incorrect for arbitrary palstars. However, in this more general case, the similar table first can be defined and computed in essentially the same way as for even palindromes. Then the palstar recognition can be easily reduced to the following reachability problem: is there a path from the position 1 to n. The positions are nodes of a directed graph whose maximal outdegree is three, see [GS 78]. It is easy to solve such a reachability problem in linear sequential time, however we do not know how to solve it by an almost optimal parallel algorithm.

In fact, the case of even palstars could be also viewed as a reachability problem: its simplicity is related to the fact that in this case the outdegree is one.

Lemma 3.10

The table Lastcenter can be computed in log(n) time on the exclusive-write model.

Proof.

We compute the maximal (with respect to inclusion) half-palindromes. We mark their leftmost positions and then compute the table Lastcenter. The position k has to find only the first (to the left, including k) marked position. This completes the proof. ◊

Theorem 3.11

Compositions of k palindromes, k=2,3,4, can be tested in log(n) time with n/log(n) processors on the exclusive-write model, if the dictionary of basic factors is computed.

Proof.

The parallel algorithm is an easy parallel version of the sequential algorithm in [GS 78] which applies to k=2,3,4. The key point is that if a text t is a composition uv of even palindromes then there is a composition u'v' such that u' is a maximal prefix palindrome or v' is a maximal suffix palindrome of t. The maximal prefix (suffix) palindrome for each position of the text can be computed efficiently using the table Lastcenter (in the case of suffix palindromes the table is computed for the reverse of the string).

Given the tables Rad and Lastcenter (also the reversed string) the question: is the text t[1..i] a composition of two palindromes can be answered in constant time using one processor. The computation of logical 'or' of questions of this type can be done by a parallel prefix computation. The time is log(n) and n/log(n) processors suffice, see Lemma 1.1. This completes the proof.◊

3.4 Lyndon factorization of strings

Several combinatorial algorithms on graphs and strings consider strings on an ordered alphabet. A basic algorithm often used in this context is the computation of maximal suffixes, or of the minimal non-empty suffixes, according to the alphabetic ordering. These algorithms are strongly related to the computation of the Lyndon word factorization of a word, that is recalled now. A Lyndon word is a non-empty word which is minimal among its non-empty suffixes. Chen, Fox and Lyndon (see [Lo 83]) proved that any word x can be uniquely factorized as $l_1 l_2..l_h$ such that h≥0, the l_i's are Lyndon words and $l_1 \geq l_2 \geq ..\geq l_h$. It is known that l_h is the minimal non-empty suffix of x.

In the next parallel algorithm, we will use the following characterization of the Lyndon word factorization of x.

Lemma 3.12

The sequence of non-empty words $(l_1, l_2,..., l_h)$ is the Lyndon factorization of the word x iff $x = l_1 l_2..l_h$ and the sequence $(l_1 l_2..l_h, l_2 l_3..l_h, ..., l_h)$ is the longest sequence of suffixes of x in decreasing alphabetical order.

Theorem 3.13

The maximal suffix of a text of length n, and its Lyndon factorization can be computed in $\log(n)^2$ time with n processors on an exclusive-write PRAM.

Proof.

We first apply the KMR algorithm of Section 2 using the exclusive-write model to the word x#..#. We assume (contrary to the previous sections) that the special character # is the minimal symbol. We then get the ordered sequence of basic factors of x given by tables pos. After padding enough dummy symbols to the right, each suffix of x becomes also a basic factor. Hence for each position i, we can easily get Rank[i] : the rank of the i-th suffix x[i]..x[n] in the sequence of all suffixes. One may note that the padded character # has no effect on the alphabetical ordering since # is less than any other character.

Let us define L[i] to be that position j such that j≤i and Rank[j]=min{Rank[j']; 1≤j'≤i}. By the above characterization of the Lyndon word factorization of x, L[i] gives the starting position of the Lyndon factor containing i. L[i] can be computed by prefix computation..

Define an auxiliary table $G[i]=L[i]-1$. Now it is enough to compute the sequence $G[n]$, $G^2[n]$, $G^3[n]$,..., $G^h[n]=0$. In fact table G gives the list starting in position n. It is easy to mark all positions of $[0..n]$ contained on this list in $\log(n)^2$ parallel time (see, for instance, [GR 88]). These positions decompose the word into the Lyndon factorization. This completes the proof. ◊

4. Almost optimal parallel algorithms for strings and arrays

We consider three problems whose algorithmic solution for one-dimensional and two-dimensional cases are essentially the same. These problems consist in finding a longest factor (largest subarray) which:

(1) repeats (occurs at least twice);

(2) is a common factor (subarray) of given two texts (arrays);

(3) is symmetric.

Denote by Cand1(s), Cand2(s), Cand3(s) a function whose value is any factor (subarray) of size s which satisfies respectively condition (1), (2) or (3). If there is no such factor (subarray) then the value of the function is *nil.*. The values of the function are *candidates of size s*. The problem is thus to find a non-nil candidate with maximum size s.

Assume, more generally, that we have a function Cand(s) satisfying the following monotonicity property:

$\text{Cand}(s+1) \neq \text{nil} \Rightarrow \text{Cand}(s) \neq \text{nil}$.

Consider

Maxcand = { Cand(s) : s is maximum such that Cand(s)≠nil }.

Assume also that Cand(0) is some special value.

Lemma 4.1

Assume that the function Cand(s) can be computed with P(n) processors in T(n) parallel time. Then the value of Maxcand can be computed with the same number of processors in $\log(n)T(n)$ time.

Proof. Apply a variant of binary search. ◊

Assume that the dictionary of basic factors is computed. We can easily test equality of two factors whose size is a power of two. However, what about factors whose size is not a power of two? It happens that we can test equality of such factors also in constant time. We define identifiers for factors (subarrays) whose size s is not a power of two. In the case of strings let identifier of the factor of length s starting at i be Ident(i,s) = (name(i,k),name(i+s-k,k)) where k is the highest power of 2 less than s. In the case of arrays the identifier of the s*s subarray with left upper corner positioned at v1 is Ident(v1,s) = (name(v1,k), name(v2,k), name(v3,k), name(v4,k)), as can be seen on figure below.

For each i and s we can compute Ident(i,s) in constant time, if the dictionary of basic factors is computed. The equality of two factors (subarrays) can be checked in constant time. The key point is that identifiers are of constant size.

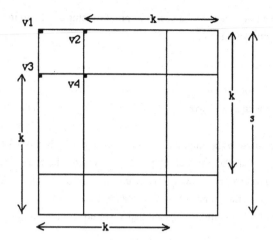

Fig 3.7. Ident(v1,s) = (name(v1,k),name(v2,k),name(v3,k),name(v4,k))
where k is the highest power of 2 less than s.

The identifiers can be used to look for factors (subarrays) whose sizes are not powers of two. A typical example is the pattern-matching problem.

Theorem 4.2

The pattern-matching problem for strings (arrays) can be solved with n processors in $\log(n)^2$ time in the exclusive-write model, and in $\log(n)$ time in the concurrent-write model.

Proof.

If p is a pattern and t is a text then we create the dictionary of basic factors common to p and t. The identifier ID of the pattern is computed. Then we look, in parallel, for a factor p' of t (of size |p|) whose identifier equals ID. This completes the proof. $\Diamond$

Observe that none of the linear time sequential algorithm for two-dimensional pattern-matching is well parallelizable (see [Ba 78], [Bi 77]).

Next we apply Lemma 4.1 to Cand1, Cand2 and Cand3.

Theorem 4.3

The longest repeated factor (largest repeated subarray) can be computed with n processors in $\log(n)^2$ time in the exclusive-write model, and in $\log(n)$ time in the concurrent-write model.

Proof.

It is enough to compute Cand1(s) with n processors in $\log(n)$ time in an exclusive-write model and in $O(1)$ time in a concurrent-write model.

Given identifiers of all factors (subarrays) for each position of the text (array) it is an easy matter to compute in $\log(n)$ time two positions with the same identifier. We can sort pairs (Ident(i,s),i) lexicographically. Any two such consecutive pairs with the same identifier part in the sorted sequence will give required positions. The model is the exclusive-write PRAM. With concurrent writes we can use an bulletin board and proceed in a way similar to that of proof of lemma 1.1. No initialization of the bulletin board is required. This completes the proof. ◊

Theorem 4.4

The longest common factor of two strings (largest common subarray of two arrays) can be computed with n processors in $\log(n)^2$ time in a exclusive-write model and in $\log(n)$ time in the concurrent-write model.

Proof.

In this case we compute, at the beginning, the common dictionary for both texts (arrays) X,Y.The further proof is essentially the same as the proof of the previous theorem. There are small technical differences. We sort pairs (Ident(i,s),i) lexicographically. Now i's are positions in X and Y. We can partition the sorted sequence into segments consisting of pairs having the same first component (identifier). In these segments it is now easy to look for two positions i, j such that i is a position in X and j is a position in Y. This completes the proof. ◊

An array is called symmetric if it is symmetric according to its center.

Theorem 4.5

The longest symmetric factor (largest symmetric subarray) can be computed with n processors in $\log(n)^2$ time in the exclusive-write model and in $\log(n)$ time in the concurrent-write model.

Proof.

In the case of strings the algorithm can be designed using the table Rad of radii of maximal palindromes. Hence we have only to prove the two-dimensional case. Let X be an n*n array of symbols or elements of any linearly ordered set (with constant time comparison of elements).

It is enough to compute Cand3(s) with n processors in $\log(n)$ time in the exclusive-write model and in $O(1)$ time in the concurrent-write model.

Let us compute the array Y which results by reflecting each entry of X with respect to the center. Denote by reflect(i,j,s) the left upper corner in Y of s*s subarray B which results from the subarray A by reflection with respect to the center, see the figure below. Now we can compute the common dictionary of basic subarrays of arrays X and Y. The subarray A is symmetric iff A=B, which can be checked in constant time using s-identifiers of position (i,j) in X and position reflect(i,j,k) in Y. The function reflect is easily computable in constant time. Once we know which s*s subarrays A are symmetric we can easily choose one of them (if there is any) as a value of Cand3(s). Hence Cand(s) can be computed within required bounds of the complexity. This completes the proof. ◊

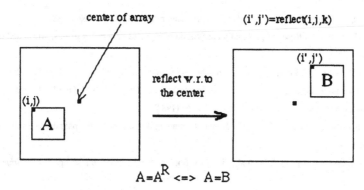

Fig 12. The k*k subarray A is symmetric iff Ident((i,j),k)=Ident((i',j'),k).

Concluding remark

If the size of the alphabet is fixed then each of the presented algorithms which works in log(n) time with n processors on a concurrent-write PRAM can be transformed to a strictly optimal algorithm (log(n) time - n/log(n) processors) by using the "four Russians" trick, see [AHU 74].

References

[AC 75] A. Aho, M. Corasick, Efficient string-matching: an aid to bibliographic search, *CACM* 18 (1975) 333-340.

[AHU 74] A. Aho, J. Hopcroft, J. Ullman, *The design and analysis of computer algorithms*, Addison-Wesley (1974).

[AILSV 88] A. Apostolico, C. Iliopoulos, G. Landau, B. Schieber, U. Vishkin, Parallel construction of a suffix tree with applications, *Algorithmica*, 3, 3 (1988) 347-365.

[Ba 78] T. Baker, A technique for extending rapid exact string matching to arrays of more than one dimension, *SIAM J.Comp.* 7 (1978) 533-541.

[Bi 77] R.S. Bird, Two-dimensional pattern-matching, *IPL* 6 (1977) 168-170.

[BM 77] R. Boyer, J. Moore, A fast string searching algorithm, *CACM* 20 (1977)

[Co 87] R. Cole, Parallel merge sort, *FOCS* (1987).

[Cr 87] M. Crochemore, Longest common factor of two words, CAAP'87, 23-36.

[Cr 89] M. Crochemore, String matching and periods, to appear in *Bullet. EATCS* (1989).

[CP 89] M. Crochemore, D.Perrin, Two way string matching, 1989, submitted to *JACM*.

[CR 89] M. Crochemore, W. Rytter, Usefulness of the Karp-Miller-Rosenberg algorithm in parallel computations on strings and arrays, 1989, to appear in *TCS*.

[Du 83] J-P. Duval, Factorizing words over an ordered alphabet, *J.Algorithms* 4 (1983) 363-381.

[Ga 85a] Z. Galil, Open problems in stringology, in: (*Combinatorial algorithms on words*, A. Apostolico, Z. Galil eds, Springer-Verlag, 1985) 1-12.

[Ga 85b] Z. Galil, Optimal parallel algorithm for string matching, *Information and Control* 67,(1985) 144-157.

[GS 83] Z. Galil, J. Seiferas, Time space optimal string matching, *JCSS* 26 (1983) 280-294.

[GS 78] Z.Galil, J.Seiferas, A linear time on line recognition algorithm for palstars, *J.ACM* 25 (1978) 102-11.

[GR 88]   A. Gibbons, W. Rytter, *Efficient parallel algorithms*, Cambridge University Press (1988).

[KMR 72] R. Karp, R. Miller, A. Rosenberg, Rapid identification of repeated patterns in strings, arrays and trees, STOC 4 (1972) 125-136.

[KMP 77] D. Knuth, J. Morris, V. Pratt, Fast pattern matching in strings, *SIAM J.Comp.* 6 (1977) 322-350.

[LSV 87] G. Landau, B. Schieber, U. Vishkin, Parallel construction of a suffix tree, ICALP (1987) 314-325.

[Lo 83]   M. Lothaire, *Combinatorics on words*, Addison Wesley (1983).

[Ma 75]   G. Manacher, A new linear time on-line algorithm for finding the smallest initial palindrome of the string, *J. ACM* 22 (1975) 345-351.

[ML 84]   M. Main, R. Lorentz, An O(n log(n)) algorithm for finding all repetitions in a string. *J. Algorithms* (1984) 422-432.

[ML 85]   M. Main, R. Lorentz, Linear time recognition of square-free strings, in: (*Combinatorial algorithms on words*, A. Apostolico, Z. Galil eds, Springer-Verlag, 1985) 271-278.

[Ry 89]   W. Rytter, On the parallel transformations of regular expressions to nondeterministic finite automata, *Inf.Proc.Letters* 31 (1989) 103-109.

[Vi 85]   U. Vishkin, Optimal parallel pattern matching in strings, *Information and Control* 67 (1985) 91-113.

MINIMUM VERTEX HULLS FOR POLYHEDRAL DOMAINS [1]
(Conference abstract)

GAUTAM DAS – University of Wisconsin

DEBORAH JOSEPH – University of Wisconsin

1. INTRODUCTION

In this paper we investigate several variations of the following problem:

> Given a collection of pairwise disjoint polygons and their spatial positions in
> the plane, cover each with a polygonal hull such that
> (i) the hulls are pairwise disjoint, and
> (ii) the total number of vertices of the hulls is minimized.

This problem can be readily extended to three dimensions, where polyhedrons replace
polygons, or it can be restricted to special types of polygons such as rectilinear polygons
or convex polygons. If the objects are sufficiently far apart, each object can be enclosed
in a triangle (or tetrahedron); however, if the objects are placed closer together, then
because we require that the hulls are disjoint the problem is nontrivial.

Our problem belongs to the important area of object approximations, where the
goal is to approximate complex objects by simpler shapes [A, AB, CY, KL]. The situation we consider typically arises in circuit design where rectilinear polygons represent
circuit components, or in robot motion planning where polyhedrons represent obstacles
inside a workspace. Our goal of obtaining minimum vertex hulls, if efficiently accomplished, may speed up subsequent processing because of the reduced input size. For
example, an algorithm for constructing a communication network between the objects
based on the *link metric* may be sped up because this preprocessing straightens out
"bends" in the objects.

Our results are the following.

Result 1: The two dimensional minimum vertex hulls problem is NP-hard. The
proof follows from a reduction from the Planar-3SAT problem, [L]. The problem is
NP-hard even when restricted to convex polygons, or rectilinear convex polygons.

Result 2: For the restricted case of rectilinear polygons there is an efficient approximation algorithm which constructs hulls that achieve more than half the maximum
possible reduction in vertices. If n is the input size and k is the number of polygons,
this algorithm runs in $O(n\log k + n\log\log n)$, and uses the algorithm in [TV] as a
subroutine. As an application this algorithm, along with ideas from [CKV], led to an
algorithm for computing shortest rectilinear paths amidst rectilinear polygonal obstacles in $O(k(\log k)^2 + n\log k + n\log\log n)$ time. Other applications of the algorithm

[1] This work was supported in part by the National Science Foundation under NSF PYI grant
DCR-8402375. Authors' address: Computer Sciences Department, University of Wisconsin,
1210 West Dayton St., Madison, WI 53706, USA.

include algorithms for computing rectilinear minimum spanning trees and rectilinear *Steiner trees* [GJ] between the polygons.

Result 3: There is an algorithm for constructing rectilinear minimum vertex hulls in two dimensions which is based on dynamic programming, whose running time is exponential in the *number of polygons* rather than the input size. Thus, the difficulty of the problem is related more to the number of polygons than to their shapes and positions. As we shall note later, this is *not true* for the three dimensional case. This algorithm may be useful in practice, when the number of objects is small.

Result 4: In three dimensions the minimum vertex hull problem is also NP-hard. Again, this result holds for convex polyhedrons and for rectilinear convex polyhedrons. In addition, the following more interesting result holds for three dimensions. The problem is NP-hard *even for only two nonconvex polyhedrons.* This is also true for rectilinear polyhedrons. Thus, unlike the two dimensional case, here the difficulty lies in the complex shapes that three dimensional objects can have. The assumption we make here is that the polyhedrons are of *genus* 0; that is they are topologically homeomorphic to the sphere.

Result 5: Klee [O] posed the following related problem: given two concentric convex polytopes in arbitrary dimensions, fit a minimum vertex convex polytope between them. A generalization is to allow nonconvexity in the problem. While the two dimensional problems have been solved, [AB], the higher dimensional versions remain open. As an important corollary of Result 4, we show that Klee's problem generalized for nonconvex polyhedrons is NP-hard. (Again, the assumption is that the polyhedrons are of genus 0, and the result is seen to hold even for rectilinear polyhedrons).

Our research differs from most previous research on object approximations in two important ways. First, the measures of simplicity previously studied have usually been continuous (for instance, *area* [KL], or *symmetric differences* [A]), while ours is combinatorial, as in [AB]. Second, complex objects have usually been considered in isolation, while we have a more restrictive environment where a number of neighboring objects can hinder the simplification process.

Section 2 defines some terms and notations. Section 3 provides some details of the NP-hardness proof of our two dimensional problem (part of Result 1). Section 4 describes the approximation algorithm for obtaining rectilinear hulls (part of Result 2). Section 5 describes the exact algorithm for the special case of rectilinear polygons (Result 3). Section 6 provides some details of the NP-hardness proof of our three dimensional problem (part of Result 4). Due to space limitations we omit details of the other results, which may be found in [DJ]. We conclude with a list of open problems.

2. DEFINITIONS AND NOTATIONS

A *simple polygon* is a piecewise linear, nonintersecting closed curve on the plane. A *rectilinear polygon* is one where each piece (or *edge*) is parallel to either the x or the y axis. Adjacent edges meet at *vertices*. A *convex polygon* is one where the line segment joining any pair of interior points lies wholly inside the polygon. A *rectilinear convex* polygon is one where the above is true for all pairs of interior points that have the same x co-ordinate or the same y co-ordinate. A *polygon set* is a collection of pairwise disjoint polygons on the plane. Given a polygon set, a *hull set* is another collection of pairwise disjoint polygons (or *hulls*), such that each hull encloses exactly one polygon from the polygon set. If P is a polygon set, $\#(P)$ denotes the number of vertices in P.

In three dimensions the definitions are similar. A *simple polyhedron* is a closed region in space with a piecewise planar surface. Each planar piece is known as a *facet*. Facets are adjacent at *edges*, and edges are adjacent at *vertices*. A polyhedron is of *genus g* if it is topologically homeomorphic to a sphere with g handles. Throughout we restrict the polyhedrons to be of genus 0. One reason for having this assumption is because the graphs defined by the vertices and edges of genus 0 polyhedrons are planar. So, the overall size of the input description is linearly related to the number of vertices, and thus reducing vertices reduces the input. The remaining definitions are similar to their two dimensional counterparts.

The next section describes some details of the two dimensional NP-hardness proof.

3. NP-HARDNESS IN TWO DIMENSIONS

In this section we outline a proof which shows that constructing minimum vertex hulls for a convex polygonal set (with integer co-ordinates) is NP-hard.

We shall prove NP-completeness for the decision version of our problem, which is: Given a convex polygon set P, with all vertices having integer co-ordinates, and an integer K, is there a set of hulls H, such that $\#(P) - \#(H) \geq K$? Clearly, the problem is in NP because a nondeterministically constructed H can be verified in polynomial time. For proving NP-completeness, the reduction will be from Planar-3SAT, [L], which is defined as follows. A *variable-clause* graph of a 3SAT instance (with n variables and m clauses) is a graph where (i) vertices are variables and clauses, and (ii) edges are between variable vertices and clause vertices, with the rule that if a clause C has a literal of a variable V, then $[C, V]$ is an edge. Also, an edge is marked "$+$" or "$-$", depending on which literal is in the clause. Planar-3SAT may now be formally stated as: Given a planar variable-clause graph for a 3SAT formula, is there a satisfying truth assignment?

In our reduction, we design components for variables, clauses, and edges of a given planar variable-clause graph. Each component will be a collection of convex polygons. All components will be "superimposed" on the planar graph, so that we have a global collection of convex polygons. The planarity of the drawing will ensure that these polygons remain pairwise disjoint. In this outline, we omit details on how to lay out the polygons on integer co-ordinates. The following definitions will be useful in describing the remaining steps.

Consider the two groups of polygons in Figure 1. The central quadrilateral of each group defines an empty triangular region called a *block*, which would be filled if the quadrilateral was extended into a triangle. Thus a minimum vertex hull for the quadrilateral either *selects* the block, or excludes it. Two blocks belonging to different groups can intersect as the figure shows. If the minimum vertex hulls of one group selects its block, clearly the hulls of the other group will have to exclude the intersecting block. Throughout our construction we only place such groups on the plane so that appropriate blocks intersect. To construct minimum vertex hulls it is to our advantage to select as many such blocks as possible.

Variable Component: There is one variable component per variable, and the design of each component is dependent upon the total number of clauses, m. In particular, each component consists of $2m$ polygon groups (as defined above), with the blocks intersecting in a cycle, as in Figure 2. Let one set of m alternating blocks in the cycle be called *positive* blocks, while the other set be called *negative* blocks. Clearly, a set of minimum vertex hulls for the component will select either the positive blocks only, or the negative blocks only. In the former case, the variable is set *FALSE*, and in the latter case it is set *TRUE*. Finally, we superimpose each variable component as a "macro vertex" in the variable-clause graph.

Clause Component: Since a clause has three literals, its component will consist of three polygon groups whose blocks intersect in a cycle, in a manner similar to above. Thus, a set of minimum vertex hulls for the component can select only one of the blocks. As before, we superimpose each clause component as a macro vertex in the variable-clause graph.

Edge Component: Edge components provide a means of linking up the configuration. We shall illustrate this by an example. Consider a "−" edge of the variable clause graph. The component is realized in Figure 3, and should altogether have an even number of blocks intersecting in a chain. We superimpose the chain on the edge in the graph, such that one end block intersects a negative block in the variable component, and the other intersects a literal block in the clause component. (The actual number of blocks in the chain can be shown to be polynomial). Since there are enough blocks in each variable component to acommodate all clauses, all edge components may be laid out without encountering polygon crossovers. Since an edge component has an even number of blocks, its best hull set has to select at least one of the end blocks. In that case, the block that intersects it (which may belong to either the variable or the clause component) will not be selected.

Clearly, the reduction requires only polynomial time. Let P be the set of polygons of all components and let the total number of blocks of all edge components be $2r$. Let $K = nm + m + r$. Note that the first term corresponds to the reduction in vertices if all variable components had their best hulls. Similarly, the second and third terms correspond to clause and edge components respectively. We pose the problem: Is there a set of hulls H such that $\#(P) - \#(H) \geq K$? From the reduction, we can conclude that this is true if and only if the instance of Planar-3SAT is satisfiable. Thus constructing minimum vertex hulls for a set of convex polygons is NP-hard.

The proof for the case of rectilinear convex polygons is more involved, and the reader may find it in [DJ]. The next section describes an approximation algorithm for the rectilinear problem.

4. AN APPROXIMATION ALGORITHM FOR RECTILINEAR HULLS

In this section we shall only be concerned with rectilinear polygons. We describe a polynomial time algorithm which constructs valid hulls that closely approximate minimum vertex hulls, in a sense described below.

Let P be a rectilinear polygon set. It is not hard to see that there exists a set of minimum vertex hulls which is *tight*, that is, each hull edge touches some polygon edge. This is easily proven, because any set of minimum vertex hulls can be tightened by pushing each hull edge towards the enclosed polygon in a direction perpendicular to the edge, until it hits the polygon. We may lengthen / shorten adjacent hull edges, but no new vertices will be added. For notational convenience, henceforth $MinHull(P)$ will denote a set of tight minimum vertex hulls of P. The algorithm outputs a hull set H such that $\#(P) - \#(H) \geq \frac{1}{2}[\#(P) - \#(MinHull(P))]$. The output H may not be tight; the concept of tightness is primarily used in analyzing the algorithm.

The algorithm is essentially greedy in nature; it iteratively performs local modifications to the shapes of the polygons, such that each iteration reduces the number of vertices. There are two such local operations, and both are the major iterative steps of the algorithm.

Fill-Well(P): Consider any polygon of P. Suppose its boundary has a shape similar to Figure 4, or symmetric to it. The polygonal region enclosed by its boundary between a and b, and the straight line $[a, b]$, is called a *well*. Note that a and b need not be vertices. $Fill - Well$ identifies a well that does not intersect with any polygon, and *fills* it by replacing the segment of the polygon's boundary between a and b by the straight line $[a, b]$. Clearly if a well does get filled, then $\#(Fill - Well(P)) \leq \#(P)$.

Fill-Corner(P): Consider any polygon of P. Suppose its boundary has a shape similar to Figure 5, or symmetric to it. The polygonal region enclosed by its boundary between a and b, and the straight lines $[a, d]$ and $[b, d]$, is called a *corner*. Unlike wells, note that a and b are vertices. $Fill - Corner$ identifies a corner that does not intersect with any polygon, and fills it, by replacing the segment of the polygon's boundary between a and b by the two lines $[a, d]$ and $[b, d]$. Clearly if a corner does get filled, then $\#(Fill - Corner(P)) < \#(P)$.

It is easy to see that a set of minimum vertex hulls can be constructed by applying a particular sequence of these operations. Unfortunately, it is unlikely that the exact sequence can be determined in polynomial time. However, we now outline our polynomial time algorithm which applies these operations in a sequence that guarantees the error bound claimed above in the approximate solution. The algorithm has two major steps. In the first step wells are filled, and in the second step corners are filled.

Step 1: In this step, $Fill - Well$ operations are applied exhaustively on P, converting it to P_1. At any stage, the selection of the well to be filled is arbitrary. Thus P_1 should have no further wells that can be filled. It is not hard to see that $Fill - Well$ operations are "harmless", that is $\#(MinHull(P)) = \#(MinHull(P_1))$.

Step 2: In this step, $Fill - Corner$ operations are applied exhaustively on P_1, converting it to H, the final output. It is easy to see that H should have neither wells nor corners that can be filled. Unlike Step 1 however, at any stage the selection of the corner to be filled is *not* arbitrary. The selection procedure is the key idea of the algorithm, and we describe it after the following definitions and facts.

After Step 1, the boundary of each resulting polygon is a cycle of alternating fragments that are exposed to the exterior (called *open fragments*), and fragments that are adjacent to a neighboring polygon (called *closed fragments*), as in Figure 6. It is easy to see that *all* closed fragments belong to any final set of minimum vertex hulls. Thus the algorithm has to only examine and modify open fragments. The open fragments can be further divided into *staircases*. Observe that the open edge between any two staircases also belongs to any final set of tight minimum vertex hulls. Staircases themselves are sequences of *steps*. Suppose a polygon has a corner that can be filled. Then the common boundary between the corner and the polygon has to be a sequence of adjacent steps of some staircase. Define the *size* of a staircase as the number of steps it contains. Also, a step at either end of a staircase is called a *head*.

The selection procedure in Step 2 can now be described. A head of any staircase is examined to determine if the corner that it defines can be filled. Two cases arise:

(1) *The corner cannot be filled:* Then the head is clearly a part of a final hull, and is thus removed from the staircase. (Figure 7).

(2) *The corner can be filled:* Then the corner is filled, and the updates made to the staircase are indicated in Figure 8.

We observe that in either case, the size of a staircase is decreased, thus the iteration of the selection procedure will terminate. The result of the iteration, H, is the final output. Clearly the whole process is polynomial. The following lemma proves that H indeed satisfies the claimed error bound.

Lemma: $\#(P) - \#(H) \geq \frac{1}{2}[\#(P) - \#(MinHull(P))]$.

Proof: From Step 1, we know that,

(1) $\#(P) \geq \#(P_1)$, and

(2) $\#(MinHull(P)) = \#(MinHull(P_1))$.

Since H does not have any wells and corners to be filled,

(3) $\#(H) = \#(MinHull(H))$.

Now let the total number of $Fill - Corner$ operations be c. Let the sequence of polygon sets produced during Step 2 be $P_1 = R^0, R^1, R^2, .. , R^c = H$. Consider $MinHull(R^i)$ of a set of polygons R^i. Since it is tight, in the worst case it is conceivable that it intersects the next corner to be filled as shown in Figure 9. However, we can construct a valid new hull set for R^{i+1} which has at most 2 more vertices than $MinHull(R^i)$, by "bending" the intersecting portions of $MinHull(R^i)$ outwards to avoid the corner, as shown in Figure 9. But after filling the corner, the new set of polygons R^{i+1} has at least 2 vertices less than R^i. We thus get two more conditions,

(4) $\#(MinHull(H)) \leq \#(MinHull(P_1)) + 2c$.

(5) $\#(H) \leq \#(P_1) - 2c$.

In the 5 conditions above, there are 7 quantities, 3 of which appear in the statement of the lemma. If we eliminate the other 4 quantities, the lemma follows. ∎

The algorithm can be implemented using elementary data structures and a bounded number of plane sweeps to run in $O(nlogn)$ time. A more careful implementation, using the algorithm in [TV], runs in $O(nlogk + nloglogn)$ time. Details of this and various applications of the algorithm may be found in [DJ].

The next section describes an exact algorithm for the above problem.

5. AN EXACT ALGORITHM FOR RECTILINEAR HULLS

Given a rectilinear polygon set with k polygons and a total of n vertices, we have designed an algorithm that computes their minimum vertex hulls in $P(n^k)$ time, where P is a polynomial. The algorithm works even for nonconvex rectilinear polygons. This result shows that the difficulty of the problem is related to the *number of polygons* more than their shapes and spatial positions. As we shall note later, this is *not true* for the three dimensional case. We shall only outline the algorithm, and details may be found in [DJ].

Suppose we *grid* the area exterior to the polygons by extending vertical and horizontal lines through each vertex in both directions until they either extend to infinity, or terminate at some polygon's boundary. It is not hard to see that there exists a set of minimum vertex hulls whose edges lie along the grid. If we perform a brute force search on this grid, the time will be exponential in n. To achieve the claimed time bound, we need to do better. Our algorithm is based on dynamic programming. We will assume the usual nondegeneracies in the input data such as, no two horizontal (vertical) edges share the same y co-ordinate (x co-ordinate) etc, as is usual with geometric algorithms.

We first fill all wells in the input, exactly as the algorithm in the previous section does. After that, there is a difference in how open fragments are modified by this algorithm. The process of filling wells may result in *trapped* regions between pairs of polygons, such that the region's boundary is two open fragments. Within such a region, the boundary of a minimum vertex hull for one polygon is also the boundary of a minimum vertex hull for the other polygon. This boundary fragment can be easily computed by a shortest path search along the grid within the region (where path length is measured by number of bends). For each trapped region, this computation is carried out, the new fragment is added to the set of closed fragments, and the two open fragments are removed from their set. Conceptually, the polygons grow and the trapped regions shrink.

We next break up the remaining area exterior to the polygons into $O(k)$ regions, such that each region is adjacent to at most two polygons. This is done as follows. From planar graph theory it can be shown that the remaining number of open fragments is $O(k)$. Let a *monotone* curve be a curve on the plane whose y co-ordinate monotonically increases, (or monotonically decreases). We split each remaining open fragment into a minimum number of monotone open fragments. We can show that the total number of such fragments is still $O(k)$. We now extend horizontal lines through the end vertices of each monotone open fragment in both directions until they hit other edges, or extend to infinity (Figure 10). Clearly this will break up the exterior area into $O(k)$ regions, and each region will resemble a "generalized" square, such that each vertical side is a monotone portion of some polygon's boundary. Note that each region will contain two fragments of the final hulls, a *left* fragment covering the left vertical side, and a *right* fragment covering the right vertical side.

Consider such a region $ABCD$, as in Figure 10. In the most general case, the grid divides the horizontal edges AB and CD into $O(n)$ points each. Let the sequence of points from left to right be $A = u_0, u_1, ..., u_p = B$ ($C = l_0, l_1, ..., l_q = D$). The left fragment may enter AB through any u_i, and the right fragment through any $u_j, j \geq i$. Similarly, the left fragment may exit CD through any l_r, and the right fragment through any $u_s, s \geq r$. If these entry and exit points are known, we claim (to be proven shortly) that the fragments with minimum number of vertices can be computed in polynomial time. We associate with each region a $O(n^4)$ sized table, where each entry, indexed by the quadruple (i, j, r, s), contains the two fragments with minimum vertices. By the above claim, these tables can be computed in polynomial time. Now a combination of one entry from each table (properly connected using a minimum number of additional vertices), defines a valid set of hulls. The algorithm steps through all the combinations and outputs the one with minimum vertices. Clearly this takes $P(n^k)$ time, where P is a polynomial.

Finally, we show that the tables can be computed in polynomial time. Consider the region $ABCD$. The horizontal lines of the grid break its interior into rectangles. Let the sequence of rectangles be R_0, R_1, ..., R_m, ordered from top to bottom. We shall build the table inductively. Assume the table for the subregion $R_0 \cup R_1 \ldots \cup R_i$ has been constructed. It is not hard to see that the table for the region $R_0 \cup R_1 \ldots \cup R_{i+1}$ can be constructed in polynomial time.

The next section describes some details of the three dimensional NP-hardness proof.

6. NP-HARDNESS IN THREE DIMENSIONS

In three dimensions the problem is to construct a minimum vertex hull set for a given polyhedron set. Recall that we require all polyhedrons to be of genus 0. The problem is NP-hard even for convex / rectilinear convex polyhedrons, by a trivial generalization of the proofs of Result 1. However, for simple polyhedrons, we show the problem to be NP-hard even if *only two polyhedrons are present*. This result indicates that in three dimensions, shapes and spatial positions do matter, and two objects could be interwined in a very complex manner which prevents easy computation of their minimum vertex hulls. We outline the proof below.

The decision problem is: Given two polyhedrons with all vertices having integer co-ordinates, and an integer K, is there a pair of hulls which have at least K fewer vertices? Clearly the problem is in NP. For proving NP-completeness, the reduction shall be from 3SAT, and some ideas will be borrowed from the two dimensional construction. As before, we will ignore the details involving integer co-ordinates. Our basic component will be a *prism*, which is a 6-vertex polyhedron, as in Figure 11. The empty tetrahedral region adjacent to the smaller triangular facet is called a *block*, which would be filled if the prism was extended into a tetrahedron. Our construction will consist of (among other things) such prisms with blocks intersecting appropriately. We will also position obstacles alongside all but the smaller triangular facet of each prism, so that the prism can only grow by filling its block. (Henceforth, the construction of a hull will sometimes be regarded as the "growth" of a polyhedron until it becomes the hull).

Given a (not necessarily planar) variable-clause graph of a 3SAT instance, we construct variable, clause, and edge components as in Section 3, except that we replace polygon groups by prisms. Since this is a construction in three dimensions, there is no planarity requirement. Next, we connect all prisms into a single polyhedron (called A) by attaching their larger triangular facets to a common *rail*, which is itself a long polyhedral structure (Figure 12). Clearly A is of genus 0.

Suppose we had obstacles alongside all facets of A except the smaller triangular facet of each prism. Then A can only grow by filling adjacent blocks. But intersecting blocks cannot be simultaneously filled, otherwise A will grow to have a handle, and hence have genus $\geq$ 1. Thus the next major step of the reduction is to construct a single polyhedron (called B), which will act as an obstacle along all appropriate facets of A. Let C be an artificial polyhedron composed of the union of A and all adjacent blocks. Clearly C may have a large genus. Let B be a large tetrahedral object which completely contains C in its interior. It has two connected surfaces, one exterior, and one interior, with the latter adjacent to C. To force it to have a single connected surface, we drill a hole (with a suitably small triangular cross section) from the exterior surface to the interior surface, such that the interior opening is adjacent to some facet of A's rail. Now B is a polyhedron with a single connected surface, though with a possibly large genus.

At this stage, the problem of finding a minimum vertex hull for only A, in the presence of B, is at least as hard as finding a satisfying assignment for the 3SAT instance. This is because the hull for A can only select nonintersecting blocks, and clearly cannot grow through the hole in B. To complete the construction, we have to satisfy two more requirements. First, we have to convert B to a genus 0 object, and second, pose the problem as finding hulls for both objects simultaneously.

To satisfy the first, we break internal handles of B by cutting portions of suitably small width (Figure 13), until the genus becomes 0. However, one complication arises. It may now be possible for A to grow by selecting intersecting blocks, and yet avoid its resulting handle by also growing through a created gap in a former handle of B. To make it expensive for A to grow through these gaps, we let each cut portion have a shape roughly like a cup with at least as many vertices as A currently has.

The reduction is now complete. The second requirement is automatically satisfied because of the following. Suppose we find a minimum vertex hull for A alone. Then we can create a minimum vertex hull for B by growing B until it is everywhere adjacent to A's hull, except at the interior opening of the hole. We omit further details and claim that this reduction is sufficient to prove that computing minimum vertex hulls for simple polyhedrons of genus 0 is NP-hard.

A similar result can be established for a pair of rectilinear polyhedrons. As a corollary, the generalized Klee's problem can also be shown to be NP-hard, even for rectilinear polyhedrons. Details may be found in [DJ].

7. OPEN PROBLEMS

In three dimensions the main open problem is whether it is hard to construct hulls for convex polyhedron sets with a *bounded* number of polyhedrons. We do not think the problem is NP-hard. Results on this problem may shed some light on Klee's original problem. It would also be interesting if some results on polyhedrons with higher genus could be established.

In neither two nor three dimensions have we designed approximation algorithms for the simple polygons (polyhedrons) problem. Good approximation algorithms, or even heuristics, would be interesting because they have practical applicability.

It seems to be necessary to define a good *general measure of simplicity*, rather than special ones such as minimum vertices, area, etc. Such a measure should be investigated from a computational complexity point of view.

8. REFERENCES

[A] H. Alt, "Approximation of Convex Polygons by Rectangles and Circles", Manuscript, (1989).

[AB] A. Aggarwal, H. Booth J. O'Rourke, S. Suri, C.K. Yap, "Finding Minimal Convex Nested Polygons", Proc. 1st Annual Symp. on Comp. Geometry (1985), pp 296-303.

[CKV] K. Clarkson, S. Kapoor, P. Vaidya, "Rectilinear Shortest Paths through Polygonal Obstacles in $O(n(logn)^2)$ Time", Proc. 3rd Annual Symp. on Comp. Geometry (1987), pp 251-257.

[CY] J.S. Chang, C.Y. Yap, "A Polynomial Solution for Potato Peeling and Other Polygon Inclusion and Enclosure Problems", IEEE Symp. on Foundations of Computer Sciences, (1984), pp 408-417.

[DJ] G. Das, D. Joseph, "Minimum Vertex Hulls for Polyhedral Domains", Technical Report, (Nov 1989), University of Wisconsin-Madison.

[GJ] M. Garey, D. Johnson, "Computers and Intractability", Published by W. H. Freeman and Co. (1979).

[KL] V. Klee, M.C. Laskowski, "Finding the Smallest Triangle Containing a Given Convex Polygon", Journal of Algorithms, (1985).

[L] D. Lichtenstein, "Planar Formulae and their Uses", SIAM Journal Comp., (1982), pp 329-343.

[O] J. O'Rourke, "Computational Geometry Column", SIGACT News, (1988).

[TV] R. Tarjan, C. Van Wyk, "An $O(nloglogn)$-Time Algorithm for Triangulating a Simple Polygon", SIAM Journal Comp. (1988), pp 143-178.

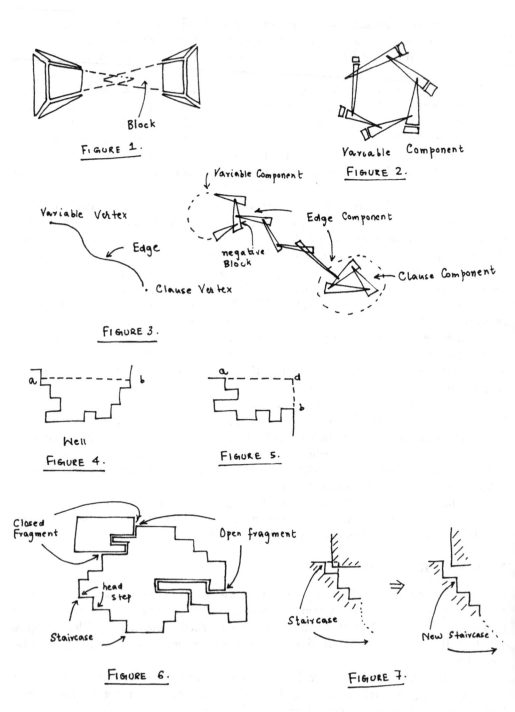

Block

FIGURE 1.

Variable Component

FIGURE 2.

Variable Component

Variable Vertex

Edge Component

Edge

negative Block

Clause Component

Clause Vertex

FIGURE 3.

a ----------- b

a ----- d

b

Well

FIGURE 4.

FIGURE 5.

Closed Fragment

Open fragment

head step

Staircase

FIGURE 6.

Staircase

New Staircase

FIGURE 7.

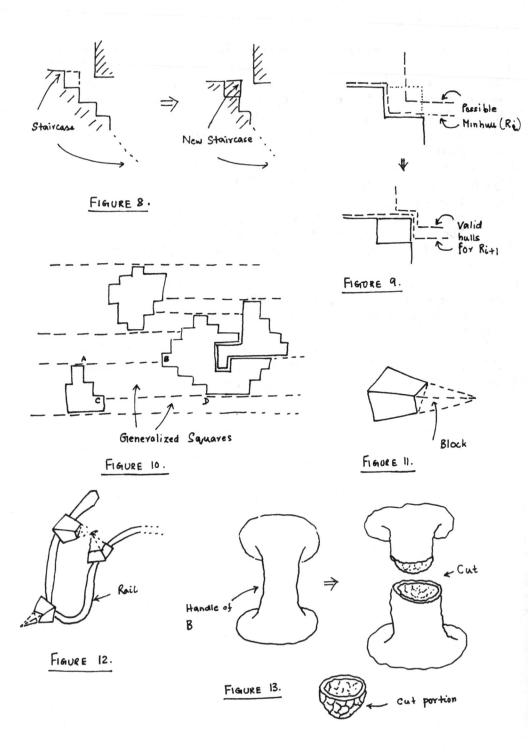

FIGURE 8.

FIGURE 9.

Staircase

New Staircase

Possible Minhull (R_i)

Valid hulls for R_{i+1}

Generalized Squares

FIGURE 10.

Block

FIGURE 11.

Rail

FIGURE 12.

Handle of B

Cut

Cut portion

FIGURE 13.

COMBINATORIAL REWRITING ON TRACES

Volker Diekert
Institut für Informatik
Technische Universität München
Arcisstr. 21, D-8000 München 2

Abstract

There are two main problems in working with replacement systems over free partially commutative monoids: For finite noetherian systems confluence is undecidable, in general, and the known algorithm to compute irreducible normal forms need time square in the derivation length instead of linear. We first give a decidable and sufficient condition for finite noetherian systems such that confluence becomes decidable. This condition is weaker than the known ones before. Then we give a decidable and sufficient condition such that irreducible normal forms are computable in time linear to the derivation length. Furthermore, we prove that the first condition is implied by the second. We also present a new uniform algorithm for computing normal forms using Zielonka's theory of asynchronous automata.

1 Introduction

Free partially commutative monoids have been recognized in computer science as an algebraic model for concurrent processes. This is mainly due to the work of A. Mazurkiewicz [Maz77] who called the elements of these monoids traces, a notion which is now standard. Since then an intensive study of traces under various aspects has begun, let us mention [Maz87], [AR88] and [Per89] for recent overviews.

In the present paper we continue to consider rewriting on traces. In [Die87] we introduced trace replacement systems in order to have an abstract calculus for transformations of concurrent processes. Trace replacement system generalize (and unify) the notion of semi-Thue systems and vector replacement systems. They could also be viewed as semi-Thue systems together with specified set of symmetric rules, this is the approach, for example, in [BL87], [NO88], [Wra88], or as term rewriting system modulo an equivalence relation [Ott89].

A basic question with respect to trace replacement systems is how to decide their word problem. This leads to the investigation of noetherian and confluent systems. The noetherian property can always be achieved by directing the rules of the systems appropriately. But unfortunately, even for finite length reducing systems, deciding confluence is recursively unsolvable. Therefore we need (good) sufficient and computable conditions for deciding confluence.

Another important question is how fast we can decide the word problem by means of a finite noetherian and confluent system. This is essentially the same question as to ask how fast irreducible descendants are computable. Now, if the number of possible derivation steps is polynomial in the length of input traces, then it is trivial to see that the problem of computing irreducible normal forms rests tractable. But this is a very weak assertion. In order to allow efficient calculations it is desirable (and may be necessary) that we can compute irreducible normal forms of traces for a given finite noetherian system in time linear to the number of derivation steps. (Let us abbreviate this by *relatively linear time complexity*). However, the known algorithms achieve time square in that number only. In [Die89] we gave a sufficient condition on the set of left-hand sides such that the relatively linear time complexity can be obtained. But we left open the question whether confluence is decidable if this condition holds. In the present paper we give a slightly weaker condition which is still decidable and sufficient to ensure the relatively linear time complexity and we also prove that confluence is decidable if this weaker condition holds. This result is shown in the second section and based on the first section where we analyse the structure of the set of traces which are critical for confluence. Our result roughly says that we can decide the confluence of a noetherian system by inspecting the set of traces which are generated by two left-hand sides and where no third rule appears. This is an analogue of the critical pair criterion of Winkler-Buchberger for term rewriting systems. (It is not exactly a special case of this criterion since trace replacement systems are term rewriting systems modulo an equivalence relation.) Our main contribution is to show that this critical set of traces is effectively recognizable. Therefore we have an effective procedure to decide whether this set is finite and if it is finite then we can test confluence on this finite set. This set is, of course, finite for semi-Thue systems or vector replacement systems. It is also finite for systems which are called coherent and convergent in [Ott89]. Thus, the decidability result of [Ott89] can be viewed as a special case of our situation. It is also possible to combine our result with the condition A2) of [Die87] to obtain a even smaller set of critical traces. In the third section we present a new algorithm for computing irreducible normal forms. This algorithm terminates in all cases in time square to the number of derivation steps and its worst-case behaviour is of that complexity for certain systems. However, the interesting point is that whenever the system satisfies the condition of section two, then the same algorithm realizes the relatively linear time complexity. The existence of such a uniform algorithm was not known before and its implementation depends essentially on the Zielonka's theory of asynchronous automata. This gives further evidence for the importance of the notion of asynchronous automata.

2 Preliminaries

Throughout this paper X means a fixed finite alphabet with independence relation $I \subseteq X \times X$ which for technical reasons is assumed to be reflexive and symmetric. The complement of I is denoted by $D = X \times X \setminus I$ and called the dependence relation. We use M to denote the associated free partially commutative monoid $M = X^* / \{ab = ba \mid (a, b) \in I\}$, the elements of M are called *traces*. Each trace $t \in M$ is identified with a labelled partially ordered set as usual: the empty trace $t = 1$ is identified with the empty set, if $t \in M$ is a trace and $a \in X$ is a letter then ta is the disjoint union of t and a new point labelled with a. The partial order $\leq$ of ta is induced by t and the requirement that the new point is behind every point of t which has a label depending on a. If $t \in M$ is a trace and $a \in X$ is a letter then, by abuse of language, we shall write $a \in t$ if we mean a fixed point of t with label a. Similary we proceed with subsets of t. Note that every subset $l \subseteq t$ defines a unique trace $l \in M$. A subset $l \subseteq t$ of a trace $t \in M$ is called a *subtrace* if for all $x, y, z \in t$ with $x \leq y \leq z$ and $x, z \in l$ we have $y \in l$. If $l \subseteq t$ is a subtrace then we can write $t = ulv$ for some $u, v \in M$ and vice versa: if we have any factorization $t = ulv$ then the factor l defines a unique subtrace $l \subseteq t$. For any subset $l \subseteq t$ we define the *generated subtrace* of l in t by the smallest subtrace of t containing l. We denote this subtrace by $\langle l \rangle$. We can also define the generated subtrace by $\langle l \rangle = \{y \in t \mid \exists x, z \in l : x \leq y \leq z\}$. With a subtrace $l \subseteq t$ we associate the following subtraces:

$$
\begin{aligned}
\mathrm{pre}(l) &= \{x \in t\backslash l \mid x \leq y \text{ for some } y \in l\} \text{ of elements before } l, \\
\mathrm{suf}(l) &= \{z \in t\backslash l \mid y \leq z \text{ for some } y \in l\} \text{ of elements behind } l, \text{ and} \\
\mathrm{ind}(l) &= t\backslash(l \cup \mathrm{pre}(l) \cup \mathrm{suf}(l)) \text{ of elements which are independent of } l.
\end{aligned}
$$

The following simple observation is important: let $l \subseteq t$ be a subtrace then a factorization $t = ulv$ defines this subtrace $l \subseteq t$ if and only if we have equations $u = \mathrm{pre}(l)u_1$, $v = v_1 \mathrm{suf}(l)$ for some $u_1 v_1 = \mathrm{ind}(l)$.

Two subtraces $l_1 \subseteq t$, $l_2 \subseteq t$ are called *strictly separated* if $l_i \subseteq (\mathrm{pre}(l_j) \cup \mathrm{ind}(l_j))$ for some $\{i, j\} = \{1, 2\}$. Thus, $l_1 \subseteq t$, $l_2 \subseteq t$ are strictly separated if and only if we can write $t = ul_i v l_j w$ for some $u, v, w \in M$ and $\{i, j\} = \{1, 2\}$. (In previous papers we said that $l_1 \subseteq t$, $l_2 \subseteq t$ are not in mixed order.)

For a trace $t \in M$ its length is denoted by $|t|$ and its alphabet by $\mathrm{alph}(t)$. The independence relation I is extended to $I \subseteq M \times M$ by setting $(t, t') \in I$ if $\mathrm{alph}(t) \times \mathrm{alph}(t') \subseteq I \subseteq X \times X$. For a trace $t \in M$ the trace $\min(t)$ ($\max(t)$ respectively) is defined by the set of minimal (maximal respectively) elements of the labelled partial order t.

A trace replacement system is a subset $S \subseteq M \times M$. Rules $(l, r) \in S$ are also written in the form $l \Rightarrow r$. A system $S \subseteq M \times M$ defines a reduction relation $\underset{S}{\Longrightarrow}$ on traces by $t \underset{S}{\Longrightarrow} t'$ if $t = ulv$, $t' = urv$ for some $u, v \in M$, $(l, r) \in S$. By $\underset{S}{\overset{*}{\Longrightarrow}}$ ($\underset{S}{\overset{*}{\Longleftrightarrow}}$ respectively) we mean the reflexive, transitive (, and symmetric respectively) closure of the relation $\underset{S}{\Longrightarrow}$. By $\mathrm{Irr}(S)$ we denote the set of irreducible traces. The word problem of S is to decide on input traces $t, t' \in M$ whether or not $t \underset{S}{\overset{*}{\Longleftrightarrow}} t'$ holds. For time complexities we view the replacement system S as fixed, i.e., we measure the non-uniform word problem where the input size is given by the length of the traces t and t'.

A trace replacement system $S \subseteq M \times M$ is called noetherian if there are no infinite derivation chains $t_0 \underset{S}{\Longrightarrow} t_1 \underset{S}{\Longrightarrow} \ldots$, and confluent if for all $t_1 \underset{S}{\overset{*}{\Longleftarrow}} t \underset{S}{\overset{*}{\Longrightarrow}} t_2$ there exists a trace $\hat{t}$ such that $t_1 \underset{S}{\overset{*}{\Longrightarrow}} \hat{t} \underset{S}{\overset{*}{\Longleftarrow}} t_2$. If a finite system $S \subseteq M \times M$ is noetherian and confluent then the word problem of S is decidable. But, of course, without further restrictions the time complexity may become arbitrary high. (This follows since the computation of a deterministic always halting Turing machine can be simulated by a noetherian and confluent semi-Thue system.)

3 A sufficient decidable condition for testing confluence

For deciding the word problem of a given trace replacement system it is no restriction to assume that the system is noetherian. We simply direct the rules such that the system becomes noetherian. This is possible since every free partially commutative monoid has a so-called admissible well-ordering, see [Die87, Prop. 1.1]. However, one of the main problems is dealing with trace replacement systems is that the confluence may be undecidable even for finite length-reducing systems, see [NO88]. The general attempt to overcome this difficulty is to find decidable sufficient conditions which guarantee that the confluence of the system can be tested on an effectively calculable finite subset of the monoid. We give such a condition below which is weaker than the ones known before, [Die87], [BL87], [Ott89].

Before we state this condition let us recall another problem which one meets in the replacement of traces. (This problem is not present in the semi-Thue or vectorreplacement case.) Let $(l, r) \in S$ be the rule and $t \underset{(l,r)}{\Longrightarrow} t'$ be a reduction step. Then the result t' is not uniquely by the subtrace $l \subseteq t$ which is replaced and by the rule (l, r). It may depend on the explicit factorization $t = ulv$. Indeed, let $a \in X$ be a letter which is independent of l, then there is a unique subtrace $l \subseteq t$ in the trace $t = al = la$ but we have $ar \underset{(l,r)}{\Longleftarrow} t \underset{(l,r)}{\Longrightarrow} ra$. This observation led us in previous papers [Die87], [Die89] to the assumption, called A1), that a and r should commute in all these cases. However, for deciding confluence this assumption is not really necessary. It is enough if the system is confluent on all these pairs (ar, ra). The first lemma is obvious and simply states that the confluence of these pairs is decidable.

Lemma 3.1 *Let $S \subseteq M \times M$ be a finite noetherian trace replacement system, $(l, r) \in S$ be a rule, and $a \in X$ be a letter such that $(a, l) \in I$. Then it is decidable whether the pair (ar, ra) is confluent.* □

The following considerations are based on a certain partial ordering $\prec$ of M which is canonically associated with any noetherian trace replacement system $S \subseteq M \times M$. For $x, y \in M$ we put $x \preceq y$ if $y \overset{*}{\underset{S}{\Longrightarrow}} uxv$ for some $u, v \in M$, i.e., x is "smaller" than y if and only if x is a subtrace of some descendant of y. As usual $x \prec y$ means $x \preceq y$ and $x \neq y$. It is an easy exercise to see that, since S is noetherian, this defines a well-founded ordering of M. This means that every non-empty subset of M has minimal elements with respect to $\prec$. The reason that we do not need the assumption A1) here results from the next lemma.

Lemma 3.2 *Let $S \subseteq M \times M$ be a noetherian trace replacement system, $t \in M$ be a trace, $l \subseteq t$ be a subtrace and $(l, r) \in S$ be rule. Let $u_1 v_1 = u_2 v_2$ be two factorizations of $\mathrm{ind}(l)$ and $t_i = \mathrm{pre}(l)u_i r v_i \mathrm{suf}(l)$ for $i = 1, 2$, i.e., $t_1 \underset{(l,r)}{\Longleftarrow} t \underset{(l,r)}{\Longrightarrow} t_2$. Then the following implication holds. If the pair (ar, ra) is confluent for all $a \in X$ such that $(a, l) \in I$ and if the system S is confluent on all traces $t' \in M$ such that $t' \prec t$ then the pair (t_1, t_2) is confluent, too.*

Proof: For simplification of notation it is convenient to observe first that we may assume $pre(l) = suf(l) = 1$. Thus, we have $t = ind(l)l$ and $t_i = u_i r v_i$ for $i = 1, 2$. If we have $|u_1 u_2| = 0$ then $t_1 = t_2$ and the claim follows. If $|u_1 u_2| > 0$ then we may assume $u_1 = ua$ for some $u \in M, a \in X$ with $(a, l) \in I$. Since (ar, ra) is confluent, the pair $(t_1, urav_1)$ is confluent, too. The pair $(urav_1, t_2)$ is confluent by induction since $|uu_2| < |u_1 u_2|$. The lemma follows since $urav_1 \prec t$. $\square$

For a noetherian trace replacement system $S \subseteq M \times M$ and rules $(l_1, r_1), (l_2, r_2) \in S$ let us define the *set of critical traces* $CT(l_1, l_2, S)$ by the set of traces $t \in M$ satisfying the following two conditions:

1) The left-hand sides l_1, l_2 are subtraces $l_1 \subseteq t, l_2 \subseteq t$ such that $\langle l_1 \cup l_2 \rangle = t$ and $l_1 \subseteq t, l_2 \subseteq t$ are not strictly separated.

2) For all subtraces $l \subseteq t$ such that $(l, r) \in S$ for some $r \in M$ we have for $i = 1$ or for $i = 2$ that $\langle l_i \cup l \rangle = t$ and $l_i \subseteq t, l \subseteq t$ are not strictly separated.

To illustrate the notion of $CT(l_1, l_2, S)$ consider the semi-Thue case $S \subseteq X^* \times X^*$, where for further simplification S is assumed to be normalized, thus every left-hand side of S is irreducible with respect to all other rules. Then a word $w \in X^*$ belongs to $CT(l_1, l_2, S)$ if and only if $w = l_1 v = u l_2, l_1, l_2$ have over-lapping, and there is no third left-hand-side occuring in w. It is the last property which will become important.

The following theorem shows that the decidability of confluence can be based on these sets $CT(l_1, l_2, S)$. It can be viewed as an analogue to the Winkler-Buchberger criterion for term rewriting systems [WB83], see also [KMN88, section 4,(C1)] and [BD88] for a rather general treatment of critical pair criteria.

Theorem 3.3 *Let $S \subseteq M \times M$ be a noetherian trace replacement system. Then the system S is confluent if and only if the following two assertions hold:*

i) The pair (ar, ra) is confluent for all $(l, r) \in S, a \in X$ such that $(a, l) \in I$

ii) For all $(l_1, r_1), (l_2, r_2) \in S$ the system S is confluent on the set $CT(l_1, l_2, S)$ of critical traces defined above.

Remark 3.4 Before we prove the theorem observe that, in general ii) does not imply i), unless M is free or commutative (in which case it does for trivial reasons). Indeed if M is neither free nor commutative then there are three different letters $a, b, c \in X$ such that $(a, c) \in I$ and $(b, c) \in D$. Consider the one-rule system $S = \{a \Longrightarrow b^2\}$. Then $CT(a, a, S) = \{a\}$ and the system is confluent on $\{a\}$ although $(b^2 c, cb^2)$ is not confluent.

Proof of Theorem 3.3: Since the only-if-part is trivial, it is enough to show that if i) and ii) hold then S is confluent. Let $(l_1, r_1), (l_2, r_2) \in S$ be rules, $t \in M$ be a trace with subtraces $l_1 \subseteq t, l_2 \subseteq t$, and $t_1 \xLeftarrow{(l_1, r_1)} t \xRightarrow{(l_2, r_2)} t_2$. We shall prove that (t_1, t_2) is confluent. By noetherian induction we may assume that S is confluent on all traces $t' \in M$ such that $t' \prec t$. Clearly, we may also assume that t does not belong to $CT(l_1, l_2, S)$. Hence, for some rule $(l, r) \in S$ we find a subtrace $l \subseteq t$ such that for $i = 1$ and $i = 2$ we have that $\langle l_i \cup l \rangle \neq t$ or $l_i \subseteq t, l \subseteq t$ are strictly separated. For $i = 1, 2$ we choose any $t_i' \xleftarrow[(l_i, r_i)]{} t \xrightarrow[(l, r)]{} t_i''$ such that (t_i', t_i'') is confluent. This is possible: if $l_i \subseteq t, l \subseteq t$ are strictly separated then we may write $t = ul_ivlw$ ($t = ulvl_iw$ respectively) and the pair (ur_ivlw, ul_ivrw) ($(urvl_iw, ulvr_iw)$ respectively) will do, if $\langle l_i \cup l \rangle \neq t$ there exists such a pair since $\langle l_i \cup l \rangle \prec t$. By standard techniques we are reduced to show the confluence of the following pairs $(t_1, t_1'), (t_1', t_1''), (t_1'', t_2''), (t_2'', t_2'), (t_2', t_2)$. The confluence of (t_1', t_1'') and (t_2', t_2'') is known by construction. The confluence of the other three pairs follows by Lemma 3.2. □

The key to our decidability result below is the fact that the sets $CT(l_1, l_2, S)$ are effectively calculable recognizable trace languages. To see this we introduce sets $B(p, q, Y)$ which roughly stands for the set of possible traces between p and q with alphabet Y. Formally $B(p, q, Y)$ is defined for traces $p, q \in M$ and subsets $Y \subseteq X$ by

$$B(p, q, Y) = \{y \in M \mid \text{alph}(y) = Y \text{ and with respect to}$$
$$\text{the trace } pyq \text{ it holds}$$
$$\text{suf}(p) = yq \text{ and } \text{pre}(q) = py\}$$

Note that in the free commutative case $M = \mathbf{N}^X$ the set $B(p, q, Y)$ will be empty unless $Y \subseteq \text{alph}(p) = \text{alph}(q)$. More generally, $B(p, q, Y)$ is empty unless for each maximal element $a \in p$ there exists some $b \in Y \cup \text{alph}(q)$ with $(a, b) \in D$ and for each minimal element $c \in q$ there exists $b \in Y \cup \text{alph}(p)$ with $(b, c) \in D$. If $B(p, q, Y)$ is non-empty then it contains those $y \in M$ with $\text{alph}(y) = Y$ such that every minimal letter of y depends on some letter in p and every maximal letter of y depends on some letter in q. Thus, in all cases $B(p, q, Y)$ is recognizable.

Theorem 3.5 *Let $S \subseteq M \times M$ be a noetherian trace replacement system such that the set of left hand sides is recognizable. Then for each $(l_1, r_1), (l_2, r_2) \in S$ the set $CT(l_1, l_2, S)$ is an effectively calculable recognizable subset.*

Proof: Let $t \in M$ such that $t \in CT(l_1, l_2, S)$. Then $l_1 \subseteq t$, $l_2 \subseteq t$ are non-strictly separated subtraces and we have $t = \langle l_1 \cup l_2 \rangle$. Define the following nine subtraces of t:

$$
\begin{aligned}
p_i &= l_i \cap \text{pre}(l_j) &&, \{i, j\} = \{1, 2\}, \\
s_i &= l_i \cap \text{ind}(l_j) &&, \{i, j\} = \{1, 2\}, \\
q_i &= l_i \cap \text{suf}(l_j) &&, \{i, j\} = \{1, 2\}, \\
s &= l_1 \cap l_2, \\
y_1 &= \text{suf}(l_1) \cap \text{pre}(l_2) \\
y_2 &= \text{suf}(l_2) \cap \text{pre}(l_1)
\end{aligned}
$$

We have a picture as in Figure 1.
The following formulae hold:

1) $p_i s_i s q_i = l_i$ for $i = 1, 2$,

2) $(s_i, l_j) \in I$ for $\{i, j\} = \{1, 2\}$

3) $(p_1, p_2) \in I$, $(q_1, q_2) \in I$,

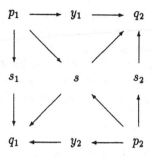

Figure 1: A trace $t = \langle l_1 \cup l_2 \rangle$ devided into nine subtraces.

4) $y_i \in B(p_i, q_j, Y_i)$ for some $Y_i \subseteq \{a \in X \mid (a, p_j s_1 s s_2 q_i) \in I\}$, $\{i, j\} = \{1, 2\}$, $Y_1 \times Y_2 \subseteq I$

5) $s \neq 1$ or $p_1, p_2, q_1, q_2 \neq 1$.

Vice versa, if the formulae 1) - 5) hold for some p_i, s_i, s, q_i, y_i and $i = 1, 2$ then $t = p_1 p_2 y_1 s_1 s s_2 y_2 q_1 q_2$ yields a trace with non-strictly separated subtraces $l_1 \subseteq t, l_2 \subseteq t$ such that $\langle l_1 \cup l_2 \rangle = t$. Thus, the set $CT(l_1, l_2, S)$ is a subset of a finite union of recognizable sets of the form

$$p_1 p_2 B(p_1, q_2, Y_1) s_1 s s_2 B(p_2, q_1, Y_2) q_1 q_2.$$

In the following we may think that the data $p_1, p_2, s_1, s, s_2, q_1, q_2 \in M$ and $Y_1, Y_2 \subseteq X$ are fixed. There are only finitely many traces where $p_1 s_1 q_1 = 1$ or $p_2 s_2 q_2 = 1$, thus we assume $p_1 s_1 q_1 \neq 1 \neq p_2 s_2 q_2$. In the next step one replaces $B(p_i, q_j, Y_i)$ by $B_i = \{y \in B(p_i, q_i, Y_i) \mid p_i s_i y, y s_j q_j \in \mathrm{Irr}(S)\}$ for $\{i, j\} = \{1, 2\}$. This is possible without loosing anything from $CT(l_1, l_2, S)$. In fact, say $p_1 s_1 y_1$ is reducible by some rule $(l, r) \in S$. Then the subtrace $l \subseteq p_1 s_1 y_1 \subset t$ is strictly separated from $l_2 \subseteq t$ and $\langle l_1 \cup l \rangle \neq t$ since $p_2 s_2 q_2 \neq 1$. Note that $B = p_1 p_2 B_1 s_1 s s_2 B_2 q_1 q_2$ is recognizable. But it is still too large. It may contain traces t such that $l \subseteq t$ is a subtrace for some left-hand side where $\langle l_1 \cup l_2 \rangle \neq t \neq \langle l_2 \cup l \rangle$. It is not very difficult to exclude these traces, too, by distinguishing several cases. This is left to the reader, since in our application of the next section the set B is already finite. $\square$

We now state the main result of this section which follows directly from the theorem above together with Lemma 3.1.

Corollary 3.6 *Let S be a finite noetherian trace replacement system. Then it is decidable whether the set $CT(S) = \bigcup \{CT(l_1, l_2, S) \mid (l_i, r_i) \in S, i = 1, 2\}$ is finite. If the set $CT(S)$ is finite then it is decidable whether the system S is confluent.* $\square$

Remark 3.7 i) The exact calculation of the set $CT(S)$ above seems to be very difficult in general. However, in order to prove that $CT(S)$ is finite it is enough to prove an upper bound on this set. For example we might prove that the length of traces in $CT(S)$ cannot exceed a certain length. Then we can test confluence on all traces up to this length without knowing the explicit description of $CT(S)$.

ii) The reader might convince himself that it is possible to combine the corollary above with [Die87, Thm. 3.1]. Then we obtain an even weaker condition for the decidability of confluence. Since this is rather technical but not very difficult we have not shown it here.
□

4 The condition G_k for $k \geq 0$

We are going to measure the time complexity to compute irreducible forms for finite noetherian systems $S \subseteq M \times M$ in terms of the following function

$$d_S : \mathbf{N} \to \mathbf{N}, \quad d_S(n) = \max\{m \in \mathbf{N} \mid t \overset{m}{\underset{S}{\Longrightarrow}} \hat{t},\ |t| = n\}$$

This means $d_S(n)$ is the maximal number of possible reduction steps starting on a trace of length n. For applications, one is mainly interested in cases where d_S grows slowly. This is for example the case when $S \subseteq M \times M$ is weight-reducing, then d_S is a linear function. It is easy to see that irreducible normal forms can be computed (on some multi-tape Turing machine) in time $O(d_S^2)$. But we have no idea whether this bound is optimal, and for semi-Thue systems we can achieve a time bound $O(d_S)$, see [Boo82]. In [Die89] we exhibited a sufficient decidable condition for trace replacement systems $S \subseteq M \times M$ such that irreducible normal forms can be computed by a very simple algorithm in time $O(d_S)$. The condition of [Die89] is equivalent to condition $G_0(S)$ below. We left open the question whether confluence is decidable when $G_0(S)$ holds. We will see here that the question has a positive answer. We present in fact a slightly weaker condition.

The informal reason why, so far, we can not prove a better time bound than $O(d_S^2)$ is that for some $c > 0$ there might be irreducible traces $t \in \mathrm{Irr}(S)$ such that if we multiply t by a letter $a \in X$ from the left (or right) then at (or ta) becomes reducible by some rule $(l, r) \in S$, but for all factorizations $at = ulv$, we have $|u| \geq c|t|$ and $|v| \geq c|t|$. Even if there would be, at this stage, a fast way (constant time) to compute the reduction step $at = ulv \underset{S}{\Longrightarrow} urv$, we see no fast way to test whether urv is irreducible, it will take time linear to the length of $|t|$. Of course, all these problems vanish if we could bound the length of $|u|$ in the situation above by some constant $k \geq 0$ depending on S only. This is exactly what the following condition says.

Definition: Let $k \geq 0$, $X^{(k)} = \{t \in M \mid |t| \leq k\}$, and $S \subseteq M \times M$ be a noetherian trace replacement system with set of left-hand sides $L = \{l \in M \mid (l, r) \in S \text{ for some } r \in M\}$. We say that the condition $G_k(S)$ holds if we have

$$X \, \mathrm{Irr}(S) \subseteq \mathrm{Irr}(S) \cup X^{(k)} LM.$$

Theorem 4.1 Let $k \geq 0$ and $S \subseteq M \times M$ be a finite noetherian trace replacement system and L be the set of left-hand sides. Then we have the following assertions.

i) It is decidable whether $G_k(S)$ holds.

ii) If $G_k(S)$ holds then we can decide whether S is confluent.

iii) If $G_k(S)$ holds and if S is confluent then we can decide the word problem of S in time $O(d_S)$.

Proof: i) trivial since all sets involved for deciding $G_k(S)$ are recognizable.

iii) Follows easily by an obvious modification, which depends on k, of the very simple algorithm right-reduce presented in [Die89]. Details are omitted since the new (but more complicated) algorithm of the next section yields the same time bound up to constants.

ii) We show that the set $CT(l_1, l_2, S)$ introduced in the previous section is finite for all $l_1, l_2 \in L$. The result then follows by Corollary 3.6.

Let $l_1, l_2 \in L$ and $t \in M$ be a trace with subtraces $l_1 \subseteq t$, $l_2 \subseteq t$ such that $\langle l_1 \cup l_2 \rangle = t$ and $l_1 \subseteq t$, $l_2 \subseteq t$ are not strictly separated. As in the proof of Theorem 3.5 we devide t into nine subtraces:

$$
\begin{aligned}
p_i &= l_i \cap \mathrm{pre}(l_j) &,&\quad \{i,j\} = \{1,2\}, \\
s_i &= l_i \cap \mathrm{ind}(l_j) &,&\quad \{i,j\} = \{1,2\}, \\
q_i &= l_i \cap \mathrm{suf}(l_j) &,&\quad \{i,j\} = \{1,2\}, \\
s &= l_1 \cap l_2, \\
y_i &= \mathrm{suf}(l_i) \cap \mathrm{pre}(l_j) &,&\quad \{i,j\} = \{1,2\}.
\end{aligned}
$$

Then we have $t = p_1 p_2 y_1 s_1 s s_2 q_1 q_2$.

By symmetry we may assume that $|y_1| \geq |y_2|$ and it will be enough to show that if $t \in CT(l_1, l_2, S)$ then the length of y_1 is bounded by some constant not depending on t. Let $m = \max\{|l| \mid l \in L\}$ and assume that $|y_1| \geq |p_2 s| + k + m$. (Note that $|p_2 s|$ is bounded by $|l_2|$ and this bound is independent of $|t|$).

Now, if the subtrace $y_1 s_2 q_2 \subseteq t$ is reducible by some rule $(l, r) \in S$ then t contains a subtrace $l \subseteq t$ such that $l_1 \subseteq t$, $l \subseteq t$ are strictly separated and $\langle l_2 \cup l \rangle \neq t$. (Note that $p_1 \neq 1$ since $|y_1| \geq 1$). Hence, we have $t \notin CT(l_1, l_2, S)$ in this case. Therefore we may assume that $y_1 s_2 q_2 \in \mathrm{Irr}(S)$. On the other hand, $p_2 s y_1 s_2 q_2 = y_1 l_2$ is reducible since $l_2 \in L$. Now, it follows from $G_k(S)$ that $p_2 s y_1 s_2 q_2 = u l v$ for some $(l, r) \in S$, $u, v \in M$ with $|u| \leq |p_2 s| + k - 1$. Since $p_2 s y_1 s_2 q_2 = y_1 l_2$ is a subtrace of t, we may identify u, l, v with subtraces of t, too. Since $|y_1| \geq |p_2 s| + k + m$, at least one letter of the subtrace $y_1 \subseteq t$ belongs to $v \subseteq t$, hence $\langle l_1 \cup l \rangle \neq t$. Since $p_1 \neq 1$ we also have $\langle l_2 \cup l \rangle \neq t$, thus we have $t \notin CT(l_1, l_2, S)$. The theorem follows. $\square$

Open problem Is it decidable whether for given finite $S \subseteq M \times M$ there exists $k \geq 0$ such that $G_k(S)$ holds? This question would have an affirmative answer if we could decide for given recognizable trace languages $A, B \subseteq M$ with $A \subseteq MB$ whether there exists a finite set $F \subseteq M$ such that $A \subseteq FB$. This seems to be an interesting question for recognizable trace languages independent of trace rewriting. It can be solved for regular word languages.

The reason to consider the condition $G_k(S)$ for different $k \geq 0$ follows from the next proposition:

Proposition 4.2 *Let $k \geq 0$ and M be neither free nor commutative then there exists a length-reducing trace replacement system $S \subseteq M \times M$ of at most two rules such that $G_{k+1}(S)$ holds but not $G_k(S)$.*

Proof: Since M is neither free nor commutative we find three different letters $a, b, c \in X$ such that $(a, b) \in D$ and $(a, c) \in I$. Consider the system $S = \{cb \Longrightarrow 1, a^{k+2} \Longrightarrow 1\}$. Then $t = ca^{k+1}b \in X\,\mathrm{Irr}(S)$ but neither $t = a^{k+1}cb \in \mathrm{Irr}(S)$ nor $a^{k+1}cb \in X^{(k)}\{cb, a^{k+2}\}$. Hence $G_k(S)$ does not hold whereas it is easy to see that $G_{k+1}(S)$ is true. $\square$

Remark 4.3 i) If M is free or commutative then $G_0(S)$ holds for every system $S \subseteq M \times M$. For one-rule systems $G_k(S)$ implies $G_0(S)$ for any $k \geq 0$. Therefore, the proposition above is tight. In the terminology of [Die89], the property $G_0(S)$ for a one-rule system $S = \{(l, r)\}$ is equivalent with the property that l is a cone or a block.

ii) In [Ott89] another decidable and sufficient condition is given such that the confluence of finite noetherian trace replacement systems becomes decidable. The approach of Otto is based on the notion of convergence and coherence for term rewriting systems which was developed by Jouannaud [Jou83]. Inspecting Otto's condition it turns out to be equivalent with confluence in our sense and $G_0(S)$. Since $G_0(S)$ implies $G_k(S)$ for all $k \geq 0$ and any $G_k(S)$ implies the condition given in Corollary 3.6, but non of these implications is reversible, our condition is clearly weaker. Furthermore our approach has the advantage of staying entirely in the theory of traces.

5 An efficient algorithm for computing irreducible normal forms

In this section we present an algorithm which computes always irreducible normal forms in time $O(d_S^2)$ but which has the property that whenever the system satisfies $G_k(S)$ for some $k \geq 0$ then it works in time $O(d_S)$. From this viewpoint it is the best known algorithm in this area. The implementation of the algorithm depends essentially on the existence of finite asynchronous automata which were introduced in [Zie87]. The proof that every recognizable trace language is accepted by such automaton seems to be one of the most difficult in the field of trace theory. Unfortunately, the constants which are obtained constructing these automata are extremely high. So, in practice it might be necessary to work with "less optimal" algorithms. But may be a better understanding of asynchronous automata will change the situation.

The algorithm we are going to construct is based on a notion of protocols which is available for asynchronous automata, but not for usual finite M-automata. In fact, we shall use a minor modification of asynchronous automata which we will call asynchronous cellular [1]. This modification is not important, it is done here to have smaller state sets.

A finite M-automaton $U = (Z, \delta, q_0, F)$ (where Z denotes the finite state set, $\delta : Z \times M \to Z$ is the (partially defined) transition mapping, $q_0 \in Z$ is the initial state,

---

[1] In a previous version of this paper these automata were called "uniform". The new notation is due to W. Zielonka who introduced this modification independently

and $F \subseteq Z$ is the set of final states) is called *asynchronous cellular* if the following two conditions hold:

1) The state set Z is a cartesian product $Z = \prod_{x \in X} Z_x$

2) The partially defined transition mapping δ is given by a collection of partial mappings

$$\{\delta_a : (\prod_{b \in D(a)} Z_b) \to Z_a \mid a \in X\}$$

where $D(a) = \{b \in X \mid (a, b) \in D\}$ for $a \in X$.

3) For all traces $t \in M$ the state $\delta(q_0, t)$ is defined.

Condition 2) means that for $a \in X$, $(z_x)_{x \in X} \in \prod_{x \in X} Z_x$ the state $\delta((z_x)_{x \in X}, a)$ is defined if and only if $\delta_a((z_b)_{b \in D(a)})$ is defined. In this case we have $\delta((z_x)_{x \in X}, a)_y = z_y$ for $y \neq a$ and $\delta((z_x)_{x \in X}, a)_a = \delta_a((z_b)_{b \in D(a)})$.

Condition 3) is included for technical reasons only.

The deep theorem of Zielonka [Zie87] can be read as follows: For every recognizable trace language $L \subseteq M$ there exists effectively a finite asynchronous cellular automaton which recognizes L. In fact, in the known proofs of Zielonka's theorem [Zie87], or [CM87], (implicitly) a asynchronous cellular automaton is constructed first and the asynchronous automaton in the sense of [Zie87] is obtained simply by blowing-up the state space. We avoid this (unnecessary) blow-up. (The reader can also translate the following construction to the "usual" asynchronous automata).

Let $U = (\prod_{a \in X} Z_a, \delta, q_0, F)$ be a asynchronous cellular automaton. Protocols of U are elements of the product space $\prod_{a \in X}(Z_a^+)$ which are inductively defined as follows:

The element $q_0 \in \prod_{x \in X} Z_x \subseteq \prod_{x \in X}(Z_x^+)$ is a protocol. If $p \in \prod_{x \in X}(Z_x^+)$ is a protocol and $a \in X$ is a letter then the protocol ap is defined as follows: Take $q \in \prod_{x \in X} Z_x$ such that $p = qp'$ for some $p' \in \prod_{x \in X} Z_x^*$. Then compute $\delta(q, a)_a \in Z_a$ and multiply this state from the left to the a-component of p, the other components are unchanged. The reason that we build up protocols from right-to-left is that we view protocols contained in a stack and we follow the convention that the top of a stack is on the left-hand side. It follows from the definition that if $t \in M$ is a trace then $p = tq_0$ denotes a well-defined protocol with $p \in \prod_{x \in X} Z_x^+$. The crucial point is that if $p = tq_0$ is a protocol and $t = at'$ for some $t' \in M$, $a \in X$ then the protocol $t'q_0$ can be computed from tq_0 in constant time by erasing the left most state in the a-component of the protocol tq_0. More generally, if $p = tq_0$ and $t = uv$ then we may compute the protocol vq_0 starting from p in $|u|$-steps. We also shall write $u^{-1}p$ to denote the protocol vq_0 if $p = uvq_0$. This will also be done for traces: if $t = uv$ then $u^{-1}t$ denotes the trace v.

If $U = (\prod_{x \in X} Z_x, \delta, q_0, F)$ is a finite asynchronous cellular automata then a protocol $p \in \prod_{x \in X} Z_x^+$ is called *final* if $p = zp'$ for some $z \in \prod_{x \in X} Z_x$, $p' \in \prod_{x \in X} Z_x^*$ with $z \in F$. (We could also view $\prod_{x \in X} Z_x^+$ as a state set of an infinite asynchronous cellular automata where M operates on the left). We are now ready to prove the following result.

Theorem 5.1 *There is a construction giving on input a finite noetherian trace replacement system $S \subseteq M \times M$ an algorithm right_reduce$_\infty$ which satisfies the following assertions:*

i) It holds right_reduce$_\infty(s) \in$ Irr(S) *for all* $s \in M$ *and* right_reduce$_\infty$ *terminates in time* $O(d_S^2)$.

ii) *For some systems* $S \subseteq M \times M$ *the worst-case behaviour of* right_reduce$_\infty$ *is* $\Theta(d_S^2)$.

iii) *Whenever* $S \subseteq M \times M$ *satisfies* $G_k(S)$ *for some* $k \geq 0$ *then* right_reduce$_\infty$ *terminates in time* $O(d_S)$.

Proof: For $S \subseteq M \times M$ let $U = (\prod_{x \in X} Z_x, \delta, q_0, F)$ be a finite asynchronous cellular automaton which recognizes the set of reducible traces if they are read from right-to-left. A protocol means an element $p \in \prod_{x \in X} Z_x^+$ as defined above. Define the algorithm right_reduce$_\infty$ as follows

function right_reduce$_\infty$ (s:trace):trace
var t:trace:=1;
var p:protocol:=q$_0$;
while s $\neq$ 1 **do**
choose some $a \in X$ which is maximal in s;
$s := sa^{-1}$; $t := at$; $p := ap$;
("time: $O(1)$")
if p is a final protocol ("recall that p is final if and only if t is reducible; time: $O(1)$")
then compute some $u \in M$ of minimal length such that
$t = ulv$ for some $(l, r) \in S$, $v \in M$;
("It is crucial that $|u|$ is minimal and to note that this can be done in time $O(|u|)$. Note also that we must have $l \in aM$, hence $v = (ul)^{-1}t \in$ Irr(S) ")
$s := sur$; $t := (ul)^{-1}t$; $p := (ul)^{-1}p$; ("time: $O(|u|)$")
endif
endwhile
return t
endfunction.

It is easy to verify the correctness of the algorithm, i.e., right_reduce$_\infty(s) \in$ Irr(S) for all $s \in M$, by the following invariants: st is a descendant of the input trace, t is irreducible and p is the protocol tq_0. For the time complexity see the comments above. Two points are important: First, the "if-test" can be performed in constant time. This means we try to find a left-hand side inside (the stack) t only if we know that such a left-hand side exists. This was the only reason to work with asynchronous or asynchronous cellular automata. Second, the factorization $t = ulv$ for some $u, v \in M$, $(l, r) \in M$ with $|u|$ minimal can be performed in $O(|u|)$ steps. This can be seen, for example, from the representation of a trace as a tuple of words. Now, if the system S satisfies $G_k(S)$ for some $k \geq 0$ then we will have $O(|u|) = O(1)$. This proves iii). Assertion i) is obvious since we do not enter the then-part of the while-loop if t is an irreducible trace. Assertion ii) is shown in the following example. $\square$

Example: Let (X, D) be given by the graph $a - b - c - d$. Consider the following special trace replacement system $S = \{bc \Longrightarrow 1,\ ad \Longrightarrow 1\}$. This system is confluent and the function d_S is linear. Independently of implementation details the worst-case behaviour of the algorithm right-reduce$_\infty$ above will be $\Theta(n^2)$.

Indeed, consider an input trace of the form $s = (ab)^n c^n d^n$. Of course, s reduces to the empty trace. But the algorithm right-reduce$_\infty$ will perform $\Theta(n^2)$ times the while-loop. Thus, the time complexity of the algorithm can not be better than $\Theta(n^2)$ even if the whole while-loop could always be performed in constant time. $\square$

Acknowledgement I would like to thank Friedrich Otto and the anonymous referees of STACS for valuable comments. Special thanks are due to Harald Hadwiger for excellent cooperation.

References

[AR88]   I.J. Aalbersberg and G. Rozenberg. Theory of traces. *Theoret. Comput. Sci.*, 60:1–82, 1988.

[BD88]   L. Bachmair and N. Dershowitz. Critical pair criteria for completion. *J. Symbolic Computation*, 6:1–18, 1988.

[BL87]   R. Book and H.-N. Liu. Rewriting systems and word problems in a free partially commutative monoid. *Inform. Proc. Letters*, 26:29–32, 1987.

[Boo82] R. Book. Confluent and other types of Thue systems. *J. Assoc. for Comp. Mach.*, 29:171–182, 1982.

[CM87]   R. Cori and Y. Métivier. Approximation d' une trace, automates asynchrones et ordre des evenement dans les systemes repartis. Technical Report 1-8708, UER de Mathematiques et d' Informatique, Université de Bordeaux I, 1987.

[Die87] V. Diekert. On the Knuth-Bendix completion for concurrent processes. In Th. Ottmann, editor, *Proc. of the 14th International Colloquium on Automata Languages and Programming, Karlsruhe 1987, (ICALP'87)*, number 267 in Lect. Notes in Comp. Sci., pages 42–53. Springer, 1987. Appeared also in a revised version in Theoret. Comp. Science 66:117-136, 1989.

[Die89] V. Diekert. Word problems over traces which are solvable in linear time. In B. Monien et al., editors, *Proceedings of the 6th Annual Symposium on Theoretical Aspects of Computer Science (STACS'89), Paderborn 1989*, number 349 in Lect. Notes in Comp. Sci., pages 168–180. Springer, 1989. To appear in revised version in Theoret. Comp. Science.

[Jou83] J.P. Jouannaud. Confluent and coherent equational term rewriting systems applications to proofs in abstract data types. In Ausiello G. et al., editors, *Proceeding of the conference of Trees in Algebra and Programming (CAAP'83)*, number 159 in Lect. Notes in Comp. Sci., pages 269–283. Springer, 1983.

[KMN88] D. Kapur, D. Musser, and P. Narendran. Only prime superposition need be considered in the Knuth-Bendix completion procedure. *J. Symbolic Computation*, 6:19–36, 1988.

[Maz77] A. Mazurkiewicz. Concurrent program schemes and their interpretations. DAIMI Rep. PB 78, Aarhus University, Aarhus, 1977.

[Maz87] A. Mazurkiewicz. Trace theory. In W. Brauer et al., editors, *Petri Nets, Applications and Relationship to other Models of Concurrency*, number 255 in Lect. Notes in Comp. Sci., pages 279–324. Springer, 1987.

[NO88] P. Narendran and F. Otto. Preperfectness is undecidable for Thue systems containing only length-reducing rules and a single commutation rule. *Information Proc. Letters*, 29:125–130, 1988.

[Ott89] F. Otto. On deciding confluence of finite string rewriting systems modulo partial commutativity. *Theoret. Comput. Sci.*, 67:19–36, 1989.

[Per89] D. Perrin. Partial commutations. In *Proc. of the 16th International Colloquium on Automata, Languages and Programming (ICALP '89), Stresa 1989, Italy*, number 372 in Lect. Notes in Comp. Sci., pages 637–651. Springer, 1989.

[WB83] F. Winkler and B. Buchberger. A criterion for eleminating unnecessary reductions in the Knuth-Bendix algorithm. In *Proc. Coll. on Algebra, Combinatorics and Logic in Computer Science, Györ, Hungary*, 1983.

[Wra88] C. Wrathall. The word problem for free partially commutative groups. *J. Symbolic Computation*, 6:99–104, 1988.

[Zie87] W. Zielonka. Notes on finite asynchronous automata. *R.A.I.R.O.-Informatique théorique et Application*, 21:99–135, 1987.

KOLMOGOROV COMPLEXITY, RESTRICTED NONDETERMINISM

AND

GENERALIZED SPECTRA

DEBORAH JOSEPH[1]
University of Wisconsin - Madison

MEERA SITHARAM
University of Wisconsin - Madison

Abstract. This paper uses the technique of generalized spectra and expressibility of complexity classes in logic, developed by Fagin and Immerman, to give alternate characterizations of specific subclasses of NP. These characterizations serve to unify concepts that appear in seemingly different areas of complexity theory; namely, the restricted nondeterminism of Kintala and Fischer and the time bounded Kolmogorov complexity of Daley and Ko. As consequences of these characterizations we show that relatively easy subsets of $NP - P$ can not be pseudorandomly generated, unless $UTIME[t(n)] = DTIME[t(n)]$ for certain exponential functions t. Secondly, we show that no easy subset of the set of all satisfying assignments of satisfiable $g(n)$-easy formulas contains an assignment for each of these formulas, unless $NEXPTIME = EXPTIME$. The latter partially answers a question raised by Hartmanis.

1. INTRODUCTION

In this paper we use the technique of generalized spectra and expressibility of complexity classes in logic, developed by Fagin and Immerman ([Fa 74] and [Im 82,87]), to give alternate characterizations of subclasses of NP. Our characterizations serve to unify concepts that appear in seemingly different areas of complexity theory, namely restricted nondeterminism of Kintala and Fischer ([KiFi 80], [ADT 89]), and time bounded Kolmogorov complexity of Daley and Ko ([Da 77], [Ko 83]).

In addition, we can use these characterizations to draw conclusions about the Kolmogorov complexity of certain sets. More specifically, our results show that even highly restricted sets in NP do not consist entirely of Kolmogorov-easy strings unless higher complexity classes collapse. This relates to a result of Hartmanis ([HaYe 83]) that sets in P cannot separate SAT from the set of Kolmogorov-easy strings in SAT unless higher complexity classes collapse. Furthermore, since the outputs of pseudorandom generators are Kolmogorov-easy, our results establish the exact complexity of pseudorandomly generated sets. This relates to recent work in [Ya 82], [Al 88], and [NiWi 88] that can

---

[1]   This work was supported in part by a National Science Foundation Presidential Young Investigator Award.

Authors' address: Computer Sciences Department, University of Wisconsin, 1210 West Dayton St., Madison, WI 53706, USA.

be viewed as a study of the approximability of pseudorandomly generated sets. On a different level, our results provide a comparison between the power of existential second order explicit definitions and implicit definitions, and thus contribute to the study of expressibility in logic.

Our primary results are the following.

Result 1: We give a logical characterization of Kintala and Fischer's restricted nondeterministic classes, $P_{g(n)}$.

> The class $P_{g(n)}$ consists of sets accepted by NP machines that make at most $g(n)$ nondeterministic moves, where n is the length of the input and $g(n)$ is a sublinear function of n. We use the notion of generalized spectra to give an alternate characterization of the classes $P_{g(n)}$. Just as Fagin ([Fa 74]) showed that the sets in NP are exactly the generalized spectra (or, the set of finite models) that satisfy a second order existential ($2^{nd}O\exists_{g(n)}$) sentence, we show that that by restricting the second order quantifier in $2^{nd}O\exists$ sentences we can obtain a class $2^{nd}O\exists_{g(n)}$ that characterizes $P_{g(n)}$.

> Kintala and Fischer ([KiFi 80]) introduced these subclasses of NP as a way to study the fine structure of $NP - P$. They constructed oracles that separate the classes $P_{g(n)}$ for functions g that have different growth rates, and argued that the number of nondeterministic guesses is a resource that is independent of the number of steps of an NP computation. Renewed interest in these classes came when Stearns and Hunt ([StHu 86]) related them to the classification of sets in NP based on the (sub) exponential complexities of their deterministic algorithms. More recently, Álvarez, Díaz, and Torán ([ADT 89]) exhibited natural self-reducible complete problems for the classes $P_{log^j(n)}$ for fixed $j > 1$. In addition, they showed that the classes $P_{log^j(n)}$ have many structural properties similar to those of NP.

Result 2: We give a logical characterization of the uniform subsets of the time bounded Kolmogorov complexity classes, $KT[g(n), n^k]$.

> The time bounded Kolmogorov complexity classes, $KT[g(n), n^k]$, were introduced by Daley and Ko ([Da 77], [Ko 83]). Intuitively, the class $KT[g(n), n^k]$ consists of "$g(n)$-easy" strings, i.e, the information content of the string is efficiently retrievable from a compressed string of length $g(n)$, where $g(n)$ is sublinear. We characterize the complexity of uniform subsets of $KT[g(n), n^k]$, by restricting the deterministic checking part of NP computations. In particular, we additionally restrict the first order formulas in $2^{nd}O\exists_{g(n)}$ sentences to be explicit definitions and denote the class of these restricted sentences as $2^{nd}O\exists^E_{g(n)}$.

The above results can be viewed as characterizations of subclasses of NP, obtained by restricting the second order existential quantifier and the first order formula in $2^{nd}O\exists$ sentences. It is worth noting that classes obtained by restricting the second order quantifier have been studied earlier by Fagin ([Fa 74,75]) and Lynch ([Ly 82]). Fagin showed that $2^{nd}O\exists$ sentences, in which the arity of the second order relational variable is bounded by $2k$, characterize sets in $NTIME[n^k]$. Lynch showed that the same restriction on $2^{nd}O\exists$ sentences, in the language of $+$, characterizes $NTIME[n^{2k}]$. Subclasses of NP

obtained by restricting the first order formula in $2^{nd}O\exists$ sentences have also been studied earlier. Papadimitriou and Yannakakis ([PaYa 88]) considered the subclass, SNP, of NP, obtained by restricting the first order formula to be universal, i.e. in the prefix class $\forall$. They showed that a corresponding optimization class $MAXSNP$ is easily approximable. However, none of these restrictions differentiate between the number of nondeterministic moves, and the number of steps in an NP computation.

Our next result relates a question in second order logic to a problem in complexity theory.

Result 3: We show that existential second order implicit definitions have more power than explicit definitions, unless higher complexity classes collapse.

Here we compare $2^{nd}O\exists^{E}_{g(n)}$ with another subclass of NP, the class $2^{nd}O\exists^{Implicit}_{g(n)}$, or $2^{nd}O\exists^{I}_{g(n)}$. This class is obtained by restricting the first order formulas in $2^{nd}O\exists_{g(n)}$ sentences to implicit rather than explicit definitions. Intuitively, a set L in $2^{nd}O\exists^{I}_{g(n)}$ has the property that any string w can witness at most one string x in L. If we additionally require x to be polynomially computable from w, then L is in $2^{nd}O\exists^{E}_{g(n)}$. We give evidence that the strings in L may not be polynomially computable from their short witnesses, and thus they may not be $g(n)$-easy. In particular, we show that every set, in $2^{nd}O\exists^{I}_{g(n)}$ is "strongly equivalent" to a set in $2^{nd}O\exists^{E}_{g(n)}$, i.e, the two sets are equal *and* their witness sets are identical, if and only if, certain higher deterministic complexity classes are equal, to their corresponding unambiguous nondeterministic ($UTIME$) classes.

The question of implicit versus expicit definability over finite structures has been studied earlier by Gurevich ([Gu 84]). He showed that implicit definability in fixpoint logic (first order logic with the fixpoint operator) has more power than explicit definability unless $P = UP \cap co\,UP$. More recently, Kolaitis [Kol 89] strengthened Gurevich's result by showing that formulas that are implicitly definable in fixpoint logic are in fact implicitly definable by a *pair* of formulas in first order logic.

We note that Grollmann and Selman ([GrSe 84]) have shown that if one-way functions exist, then $P \neq UP$. To explain the similarity between the consequence in Grollmann and Selman's result, and those mentioned in the previous paragraphs, we recall some details of Grollmann and Selman's result. Their proof proceeds by showing that if there are functions that are not polynomially computable, but whose graphs are in P, then $P \neq UP$. We will see that this latter assumption is intuitively similar to assumptions about the equivalence of implicit and explicit definabilities.

From the above results we can draw two interesting conclusions. The first shows that the relationship between implicit and explicit definitions is not merely a question of interest to logicians: it can be used to define the exact complexity of the ranges of pseudorandomly generated sets.

Conclusion 1: Relatively easy sets in $NP - P$ can not be pseudorandomly generated, unless certain deterministic and nondeterministic complexity classes collapse.

To explain further, we will see that the sets in $2^{nd}O\exists^I_{g(n)}$ are highly restricted, and are hence relatively easy sets in $NP - P$, and that sets in $2^{nd}O\exists^E_{g(n)}$ are exactly the ranges of pseudorandom generators. Hence, the assumption that relatively easy sets in $NP - P$ can be pseudorandomly generated is equivalent to the hypothesis of Result 1, and yields the same consequence.

This relates to recent work by Allender in [Al 88] and Nisan and Widgerson in [NiWi 88] on the consequences of the existence of pseudorandom generators. In contrast, their results can be viewed as defining the complexity of sets that can approximate the ranges of pseudorandom generators.

Our second conclusion gives a partial answer to a question posed by Hartmanis in [Ha 83]: Do all $log(n)$-easy satisfiable formulas have at least one $log(n)$-easy satisfying assignment?

Conclusion 2: No easy subset of the set of all satisfying assignments of $g(n)$-easy formulas contains an assignment for each $g(n)$-easy satisfiable formula, unless certain deterministic and nondeterministic complexity classes collapse.

In the next sections we discuss our results in more detail and relate them to other work on the restricted nondeterministic classes, time bounded Kolmogorov complexity, pseudorandom generators and generalized spectra. In a concluding section we present some interesting open problems related to this work.

2. CHARACTERIZING THE CLASSES $P_{g(n)}$

To give a logical characterization of the classes $P_{g(n)}$ we first require some background and definitions concerning these classes and the use of expressibility in logic as a complexity measure.

In the study of nondeterministic computations one commonly equates the number of nondeterministic moves with the number of steps of the computation. However, Kintala and Fischer ([KiFi 80]) began work aimed at classifying NP machines based on the number of "strict" c-ary nondeterministic moves; i.e., moves for which there are at least $c \geq 2$ choices for the next instantaneous description of the machine. They defined the classes $P_{g(n)}$ as follows.

Definition. [KiFi 80] *For any function $g(n)$, the class $P_{g(n)}$ consists of sets that are accepted by a polynomial time Turing machine that makes at most $g(n)$ c-ary nondeterministic moves on inputs of size n, for some constant c.*

Kintala and Fischer's motivation for introducing the classes $P_{g(n)}$ arose from the observation that most known NP-complete sets can be recognized by machines that make a linear number of nondeterministic moves. This led them to ask which languages can be recognized using sublinear functions, for example $g(n) = log^j n$ or $g(n) = n^{1/j}$, for fixed $j > 1$, and thereby investigate the fine structure of $NP - P$. A second motivation for studying these classes arises from later work of Stearns and Hunt ([StHu 86]) that classifies sets in NP based on the complexity of deterministic simulations of their NP algorithms. For sublinear functions g the sets in $P_{g(n)}$ have deterministic algorithms that run in subexponential time. A third motivation for studying these classes arises from a more recent work of Àlvarez, Díaz, and Torán. They showed that the structural properties of the classes $P_{log^j n}$ are similar to those of NP, for instance the existence of natural self-reducible complete sets.

Kintala and Fischer posed the questions: Is $P_{log^j n} = P_{log^{j+1} n}$, and is $P_{log^j n}$ closed under complement? They provided evidence that answering these questions will be difficult by proving relativized separation and equivalence results. From this they argued that the number of nondeterministic moves is a resource that is independent of the number of steps in an NP computation.

We will characterize the classes $P_{g(n)}$ by defining the logics that express them. For this we assume the readers' acquaintance with the basic notions of expressibility in first and second order logic, and use the notation of Immerman's survey paper [Im 87]. In our discussion, we deal with finite structures that represent Boolean strings. I.e, we consider structures $\langle A, B^1 \rangle$ where the universe, A, is linearly ordered, and B^1 is a one-place relation symbol. We refer to these as *input* structures of length n, where $|A| = n$. We consider *generalized spectra* (or, sets of input structures) that satisfy sentences in different logics. The *generalized spectrum* of a sentence ϕ is the set

$$\{\langle A, B^1 \rangle : \langle A, B^1 \rangle \models \phi\};$$

i.e., the set of input structures that satisfy ϕ, where the semantic notion of satisfaction is defined in the usual manner.

We deal with sentences in first order logic, *FO*, a logic with the *least fix point* operator applied to first order formulas, *FO + LFP*, and existential second order logic, $2^{nd}O\exists$. Sentences in the latter logic are of the form: $\exists W^k \phi(W^k)$, where ϕ is a first order formula and W^k is a relational variable of arity k. The following are some of the characterizations of complexity classes given by Immerman and Fagin.

Theorem. [Im 82], [Fa 74]
1. *P is the class of spectra of FO + LFP sentences.*
2. *NP is the class of spectra of $2^{nd}O\exists$ sentences.*

We are now ready to characterize the classes $P_{g(n)}$. Throughout this section, we will assume that $g(n)$ is either $log^j n$ or $n^{1/j}$ for some $j \geq 1$; however, our results extend to other nicely behaved sublinear functions. We begin by defining a restricted second order existential quantifier that will, intuitively, quantify over encodings of short sequences of nondeterministic moves. That is, the quantifiers "$\exists_{g(n)}$" semantically quantify over monadic relations (of arity one) that are defined on a fixed $g(n)$-sized subset of the input structures' universe.

Definition. Let $\langle A, B^1 \rangle$ be a structure such that $|A| = n$, let ϕ be any formula in $FO + LFP$, and let $g(n)$ be $log^j n$ or $n^{1/j}$, $j > 1$.

$$\langle A, B^1 \rangle \models \exists_{g(n)} W^1 \phi(W^1) \iff \exists W^1 [\forall x \ [x > g(n) \Rightarrow \neg W^1(x)] \ \wedge \ \phi(W^1)].$$

The class of sentences of the form $\exists_{g(n)} W^1 \phi(W^1)$, where ϕ is a formula in $FO + LFP$, is denoted as $2^{nd}O\exists_{g(n)}$.

We now have a characterization of $P_{g(n)}$.

Theorem 1. Let $g(n)$ be $log^j n$ or $n^{1/j}$, $j > 1$. Then, $P_{g(n)}$ is the class of languages that correspond to the generalized spectra of $2^{nd}O\exists_{g(n)}$ sentences.

Proof. The containment $2^{nd}O\exists_{g(n)} \subseteq P_{g(n)}$ is clear. To prove that $P_{g(n)} \subseteq 2^{nd}O\exists_{g(n)}$ we consider a set S in $P_{g(n)}$ and a nondeterministic polynomial time Turing machine, N, for S that consists of a deterministic machine, M, an input tape y of length n and a guess tape W of length $g(n)$. The machine M takes the tuple $\langle y, W \rangle$ as input, runs in time n^k for some k and N accepts y, if and only if, M accepts $\langle y, W \rangle$ for some W. Without loss of generality, the inputs y are structures of the form $\langle A, B^1 \rangle$, where $|A| = n$. The inputs to the machine M are structures, $\langle A, B^1, W^1 \rangle$, where W^1 is a monadic relation whose domain is restricted to the smallest $g(n)$ elements of A, and encodes the Boolean string on the guess tape W. Let ϕ be the $FO + LFP$ sentence whose generalized spectrum is the set of structures accepted by M. Thus, N accepts $\langle A, B^1 \rangle$, if and only if, for some relation W^1, $\langle A, B^1, W^1 \rangle \models \phi$. That is, the set of structures accepted by N is the generalized spectrum of the $2^{nd}O\exists_{g(n)}$ sentence $\exists_{g(n)} W^1 \phi(W^1)$. ∎

It is important to note that in the above proof we require ϕ to be a $FO + LFP$ sentence. In contrast, in his proof that NP is $2^{nd}O\exists$, Fagin ([Fa 74]) just required that ϕ be an FO sentence. To elaborate: although sentences of the form $\exists W^k \phi(W^k)$, where $\phi(W^k)$ is a formula in $FO + LFP$, are equivalent to sentences of the form $\exists V^j \psi(V^j)$, where $\psi(V^j)$ is a formula in FO, the arity of the second order variable increases in the rewriting, i.e., $j > k$. This is because the relational variable V^j ranges over the encodings of entire polynomial time computations that check the $FO + LFP$ formula $\phi(W^k)$. Thus, the arity j depends on the deterministic time complexity of the generalized spectrum of ϕ. When we restrict the arity and domain of the second order relational variable, W^1, as in $2^{nd}O\exists_{g(n)}$ sentences, it is not clear that a sentence, $\exists_{g(n)} W^1 \phi(W^1)$, where ϕ is in $FO + LFP$, is equivalent to a sentence $\exists_{g(n)} V^1 \psi(V^1)$, where ψ is in FO.

3. CHARACTERIZING THE CLASSES $KT[g(n), n^k]$

In this section we introduce the logic of *existential second order explicit definitions*, and use it to characterize the complexity of pseudorandomly generated sets and uniform subsets of the time bounded Kolmogorov complexity classes. We begin with a brief discussion of time bounded Kolmogorov complexity.

The time bounded Kolmogorov complexity classes, $KT[g(n), t(n)]$ were introduced by Daley ([Da 77]), and Ko ([Ko 83]).[2] Intuitively, a string y, of length n, is in the class $KT[g(n), t(n)]$ if it can be generated from a string of length $g(n)$ in $t(n)$ steps.[3] More formally,

Definition. *Let M_u be a universal Turing machine. The class $KT[g(n), t(n)] =_{def}$*

$$\{y : |y| = n \text{ and } \exists w \, [|w| \leq g(n) \text{ and } M_u(w) = y \text{ and } M_u \text{ halts in at most } t(n) \text{ steps}\}$$

The notion of time bounded Kolmogorov complexity has applications in the theory of pseudorandom number generators. Pseudorandom generators are polynomially computable functions that typically map short seeds, say of length $n^{1/j}$, to longer pseudorandom strings of length n. Hence, the range, or set of outputs, of a pseudorandom generator is a *uniformly generated* subset of $n^{1/j}$-easy strings.

We can use a version of second order logic, which we will denote $2^{nd}O\exists_{g(n)}^{Explicit}$, to characterize the exact complexity of recognizing pseudorandomly generated sets. $2^{nd}O\exists_{g(n)}^{Explicit}$ is obtained by restricting the syntactic complexity of the $FO+LFP$ formula, $\phi(W^1)$, in a $2^{nd}O\exists_{g(n)}$ sentence $\exists_{g(n)}W^1\phi(W^1)$ in the following manner. For any relation W^1 on a universe A we demand that $\phi(W^1)$ *explicitly* define a unique relation B^1 such that $\langle A, B^1, W^1 \rangle \models \phi$.

Definition. *A $FO+LFP$ formula $\phi(W^1)$ explicitly defines the relation symbol B^1 if $\phi(W^1)$ is of the form:*

$$\forall x[\sigma(W^1, x) \iff B^1(x)],$$

where $\sigma(W^1, x)$ is a $FO+LFP$ formula that does not contain the relational variable B^1. The logic $2^{nd}O\exists_{g(n)}^{Explicit}$, also denoted $2^{nd}O\exists_{g(n)}^E$, consists of sentences of the form $\exists_{g(n)}W^1\phi(W^1)$, where $\phi(W^1)$ explicitly defines the relational variable B^1 of the input structures $\langle A, B^1 \rangle$.

The next theorem shows that the logic $2^{nd}O\exists_{g(n)}^E$ characterizes uniformly generated subsets of $g(n)$-easy strings; i.e., it characterizes pseudorandomly generated sets.

Theorem 2.

1. *A set L is the spectrum of a $2^{nd}O\exists_{g(n)}^E$ sentence if and only if L is the set of outputs of a pseudorandom generator that generates strings of length n from random seeds of length $g(n)$, in time polynomial in n.*

2. *If a set L is the spectrum of a $2^{nd}O\exists_{g(n)}^E$ sentence, then $L \subseteq KT[g(n) + c, n^k]$, for some constant k.*

Proof. The proof of (2) follows immediately from (1).

---

[2] These citations refer to the first uses of resource bounded Kolmogorov complexity *within* complexity theory. However, we note that the first known result about time bounded Kolmogorov complexity was proved by Barzdin in [Ba 68].

[3] We will not use Levin's version of this notion, commonly referred to as time limited Kolmogorov complexity ([Le 64]). Interested readers are referred to surveys by Longpré ([Lo 86]), and Li and Vitanyí ([LiVi 88]), for definitions and applications of different variants of Kolmogorov complexity.

The forward direction of (1) will follow from the fact that any set, L, which is characterized by a $2^{nd}O\exists^E_{g(n)}$ formula, is an NP set with the following additional properties.

a. Each string $\langle A, B^1 \rangle$ of length n in L has a short witness string W^1 of length $g(n)$.
b. Any string W^1 witnesses at most one string in L.
c. Each string $\langle A, B^1 \rangle$ in L can be generated from its witness string W^1 in time polynomial n.

Suppose that L is the set of input structures, $\langle A, B^1 \rangle$, that satisfy a sentence, $\exists_{g(n)}W^1\phi(W^1)$, where $\phi(W^1)$ is of the form:

$$\forall x[\sigma(W^1, x) \iff B^1(x)]$$

for some $FO+LFP$ formula, $\sigma(W^1, x)$, that contains the only the relation symbol W^1. In addition assume that the generalized spectrum of ϕ is in $DTIME[n^k]$ and that Q is a program that checks ϕ given the input structure $\langle A, B^1, W^1 \rangle$, where $|A| = n$. Without loss of generality, Q consists of a program Q' of size c that, on input $\langle A, W^1 \rangle$ of size $g(n)$, generates a structure $\langle A, \sigma^1 \rangle$, followed by a program Q'' that checks if $\langle A, \sigma^1 \rangle = \langle A, B^1 \rangle$. Q' runs in at most n^k steps, and is the required pseudorandom generator.

To prove the reverse direction of (1), we adapt the proof of Theorem 1: we consider the nondeterministic Turing machine N that accepts L. The machine N consists of an input tape y of length n, a guess tape W of length $g(n)$, and the pseudorandom generator M of the hypothesis that takes W as input, and outputs the string σ of length n, in n^k steps. The machine N accepts y if and only if $\sigma = y$. As in Theorem 1, the inputs y are structures of the form $\langle A, B^1 \rangle$, the inputs to M are structures of the form $\langle A, W^1 \rangle$, and the outputs of M are structures of the form $\langle A, \sigma^1 \rangle$. Thus the set, L accepted by N is the generalized spectrum of a sentence,

$$\exists_{g(n)}W^1\forall x\ [\sigma(W^1, x) \iff B^1(x)],$$

and the set of structures, $\langle A, B^1, W^1 \rangle$, that satisfy the sentence $\forall x\ [\sigma(x) \iff B^1(x)]$ is in $DTIME[n^k]$, since given $\langle A, B^1 \rangle$ and $\langle A, \sigma^1 \rangle$, checking the sentence $\forall x\ [\sigma(x) \iff B^1(x)]$ can be done in n steps. ∎

4. THE CLASSES $2^{nd}O\exists^{Implicit}_{g(n)}$

Our third result requires that we distinguish between explicit and implicit definitions in existential second order logic. In the previous section, we saw that the spectra of $2^{nd}O\exists^E_{g(n)}$ sentences consist of elements that can be polynomially generated from their short witnesses. Here we will see that the spectra of $2^{nd}O\exists^{Implicit}_{g(n)}$ sentences, consist merely of elements with short "exclusive" witnesses, i.e., each string witnesses at most one element in such sets. In this sense, the spectra of $2^{nd}O\exists^I_{g(n)}$ sentences are highly restricted NP sets, and can be considered as relatively easy sets in $NP - P$. Below, we formally define the logic $2^{nd}O\exists^I_{g(n)}$.

Definition. *A FO+LFP formula, $\phi(W^1)$ implicitly defines the relational variable B^1 if for every relation W^1 and pair of structures $\langle A, B^1, W^1 \rangle$ and $\langle A, C^1, W^1 \rangle$ that satisfy ϕ, the relations B^1 and C^1 are equivalent. I.e., the structure $\langle A, B^1, C^1, W^1 \rangle \models \forall x[B^1(x) \iff C^1(x)]$. The logic $2^{nd} O \exists_{g(n)}^{Implicit}$, (also denoted $2^{nd} O \exists_{g(n)}^I$) consists of sentences of the form $\exists_{g(n)} W^1 \phi(W^1)$, where $\phi(W^1)$ implicitly defines the relational variable B^1 of the input structures $\langle A, B^1 \rangle$.*

Our third result will show that certain *UTIME* classes collapse to the corresponding *DTIME* classes under the assumption that the spectra of $2^{nd} O \exists_{g(n)}^I$ are equivalent to those of $2^{nd} O \exists_{g(n)}^E$ sentences. However, we need a strong notion of equivalence by which not only are two sets X and Y equivalent but in addition, there is some representation for each set such that the sets of witnesses for X and Y induced by these representations are equivalent. Below we formally define the notion of strong equivalence.

Definition. *Two sets X and Y in NP are strongly equivalent if*
1. *$X = Y$ and*
2. *there are NP machines N_X and N_Y for X and Y such that a string w represents an accepting computation of N_X on $y \in X$ if and only if w also represents an accepting computation of N_Y on y.*

We note that Grollmann and Selman ([GrSe 84]) have shown that if one-way functions exist, then $P \neq UP$. Their proof proceeds by considering the intermediate assumption that there are functions that are not polynomially computable, but whose graphs are in P. They show that under this latter assumption, $P \neq UP$. From the above definition of the logic $2^{nd} O \exists_{g(n)}^I$, it is intuitively clear that for spectra of $2^{nd} O \exists_{g(n)}^I$ sentences, the relation between the elements and witnesses is the graph of a function. For the spectra of $2^{nd} O \exists_{g(n)}^E$ sentences, we additionally know that this function is computable in polynomial time. Hence, it is not surprising that we obtain similar consequences starting from the assumption that $2^{nd} O \exists_{g(n)}^I$ sentences are are equivalent to $2^{nd} O \exists_{g(n)}^E$ sentences. In fact, as mentioned earlier, similar consequences were obtained by Gurevich ([Gu 84]) and Kolaitis ([Kol 89]) by assuming the equivalence of explicit and implicit definitions in other logics.

Theorem 3. *The following statements are equivalent.*
1. *The spectrum of each $2^{nd} O \exists_{g(n)}^I$ sentence is strongly equivalent to the spectrum of a $2^{nd} O \exists_{g(n)}^E$ sentence.*
2. *$UTIME[2^{O(n^{1/j})}] = DTIME[2^{O(n^{1/j})}]$, if $g(n) = log^j n$, and $UP = P$, if $g(n) = n^{1/j}$.*

Proof. We will use the intuitive notion of "witness sets." Given a set, L, in $P_{g(n)}$, the witness set of L consists of all strings of length $g(n)$ that witness strings of length at least n in L. We use the fact that the spectra of $2^{nd} O \exists_{g(n)}^I$ and $2^{nd} O \exists_{g(n)}^E$ sentences have witness sets in in the appropriate *UTIME* and *DTIME* classes. It then follows that the strong equivalence of the former two classes results in the equivalence of the later two classes, and vice versa. We prove the theorem for $g(n) = log^j n$. For $g(n) = n^{1/j}$, the proof is similar.

$(1 \Leftarrow 2)$ Let $L \in 2^{nd} O \exists_{g(n)}^I$, where L is the generalized spectrum of the sentence $\exists_{g(n)} W^1 \phi(W^1)$, and $\phi(W^1)$ can be checked in $DTIME[n^k]$. Let $\langle A_{g(n)}, W^1 \rangle$ be the substructure of $\langle A, W^1 \rangle$ induced by the smallest $g(n)$ elements of A, where $|A| = n$. Let U be a $UTIME[2^{O(n^{1/j})}]$-acceptor that, on input $\langle A_{g(n)}, W_1, b \rangle$, guesses a unique structure $\langle A, B^1 \rangle$ of size n, checks if $\langle A, B^1, W^1 \rangle \models \phi$ (in n^k steps), and verifies if $B^1(b)$. By hypothesis, there is a $DTIME[2^{O(n^{1/j})}]$-acceptor M that accepts the same set as U. Let $\sigma(W^1, x)$ be the formula that expresses "M accepts $\langle A, W^1, x \rangle$." Clearly, the set of structures $\langle A, B^1, W^1 \rangle$ that satisfy ϕ and those that satisfy $\psi = \forall x[\sigma(x) \iff B^1(x)]$ are identical, and thus L is strongly equivalent to the spectrum of the $2^{nd}O\exists_{g(n)}^E$ sentence: $\exists W^1 \forall x [\sigma(W^1, x) \iff B^1(x)]$.

$(1 \Rightarrow 2)$ Let U be a $UTIME[2^{O(n^{1/j})}]$-acceptor. Without loss of generality, on input $\langle A_{g(n)}, W^1 \rangle$, U first guesses a unique witness structure $\langle A, B^1 \rangle$, such that $|A| \leq n^k$ for some fixed k, and $\exists x \geq n [B^1(x)]$. Then, U checks if $\langle A, W^1, B^1 \rangle \models \phi$ where ϕ is a $FO + LFP$ sentence. Then the witness set of structures, $\langle A, B^1 \rangle$ is the spectrum of the $2^{nd}O\exists_{g(n)}^I$ sentence $\exists_{g(n)} W^1 \phi(W^1)$. By assumption, there is a formula $\psi(W^1) = \forall x[\sigma(W^1, x) \iff B^1(x)]$ such that the set of structures $\langle A, B^1, W^1 \rangle$ that satisfy ψ is identical to those that satisfy ϕ, and $\sigma(W^1, x)$ is a $FO + LFP$ formula. Let M be the deterministic machine that, on input $\langle A_{g(n)}, W^1 \rangle$, generates $\langle A, \sigma^1 \rangle$, and checks if $\exists x \geq n [\sigma^1(x)]$, in n^k steps. Clearly, M simulates U, and runs in $2^{O(n^{1/j})}$ steps. ∎

Since all sets in $2^{nd}O\exists_{g(n)}^E$ can be pseudorandomly generated, our result gives evidence that pseudorandom generators cannot generate even relatively easy sets in $NP-P$, namely the spectra of $2^{nd}O\exists_{g(n)}^I$ sentences. This is formalized in the following interesting corollary of Theorem 3.

Corollary 1. *The following statements are equivalent.*

1. *The spectrum of each $2^{nd}O\exists_{g(n)}^I$ sentence is strongly equivalent to the set of outputs of a pseudorandom generator that generates strings of length n from random seeds of length $g(n)$.*

2. *$UTIME[2^{O(n^{1/j})}] = DTIME[2^{O(n^{1/j})}]$, if $g(n) = log^j n$, and $UP = P$, if $g(n) = n^{1/j}$.*

This result relates to recent work by Yao ([Ya 82]), Allender ([Al 88]), and Nisan and Widgerson ([NiWi 88]), on the consequences of the existence of good pseudorandom generators. A pseudorandom generator is considered *good* if efficient algorithms cannot distinguish its outputs from a truly random set of strings. A consequence of the existence of a good pseudorandom generator is that probabilistic algorithms can be efficiently simulated deterministically, by using the range of the generators to mimic coin-tosses. The results in [Ya 82], [Al 88] and [NiWi 88] differ in their exact definition of a good pseudorandom generator. The notion of a statistical test to make the notion of a good pseudorandom generator precise. A *statistical test* for pseudorandom generators is typically a probabilistic polynomial time acceptor, or a (non-uniform) family of polynomial sized circuits, whose inputs are the outputs of the pseudorandom generators. A pseudorandom generator passes a statistical test if the set accepted by the statistical test and the range of the generator differ substantially and are uncorrelated; that is, the statistical test cannot distinguish between the range of the generator and a set of truly random strings. Thus, a pseudorandom generator is considered $\mathcal{C}$-*good,* if it passes all statistical tests of complexity $\mathcal{C}$. In other words, the assumption that $\mathcal{C}$-good pseudorandom generators exist is equivalent to the assumption that pseudorandomly generated sets cannot be *approximated* by sets of complexity C. Alternatively, uniformly generated subsets of $n^{1/j}$-easy strings cannot be approximated by sets of complexity C. In contrast, we have shown consequences of the assumption that a certain complexity class C, namely the class spectra of $2^{nd}O\exists^I_{g(n)}$ sentences, can be pseudorandomly generated.

As another corollary to Theorem 3, we obtain a comparison of the sets in $P_{g(n)}$ with the spectra of $2^{nd}O\exists^I_{g(n)}$ and $2^{nd}O\exists^E_{g(n)}$ sentences. Clearly, sets in $P_{g(n)}$ can contain arbitrarily Kolmogorov-hard strings, as the number of $g(n)$-easy strings of length n is at most $2^{g(n)}$, while a single witness string of length $g(n)$ may witness the membership of arbitrarily many elements (of length n) of some set in $P_{g(n)}$. However, the following question is more interesting: given a set L in $P_{g(n)}$ does every string w of length $g(n)$ that witnesses some element of L, also witness at least one $g(n)$-easy string of length n? By observing that the set, $SAT\text{-}ASSIGN_{g(n)}$, of satisfying assignments of $g(n)$-easy satisfiable formulas is in $P_{g(n)}$, (and is complete,) the above question can be rephrased as: Does every $g(n)$-easy satisfiable formula have at least one $g(n)$-easy satisfying assignment? Hartmanis ([Ha 83]) posed this question for the case when $g(n) = log(n)$. The following corollary gives a partial answer.

Corollary 2. *Let S be any subset of $SAT\text{-}ASSIGN_{g(n)}$ that contains at least one satisfying assignment of each $g(n)$-easy satisfiable formula. Furthermore, let S be the generalized spectrum of a sentence, $\exists_{g(n)}F^1$ ["F^1 is a $g(n)$-easy satisfiable formula and $\langle A, B^1 \rangle$ is a satisfying assignment of F^1" and $\phi(F^1)$]. If S is strongly equivalent to the spectrum of a $2^{nd}O\exists^I_{g(n)}$ sentence, then all sparse sets in $NP - P$ are in UP, and if S is strongly equivalent to the spectrum of a $2^{nd}O\exists^I_{g(n)}$ sentence, then $NEXPTIME = EXPTIME$.*

Proof. We use the following theorem of Hartmanis.

Theorem. [Ha 83] *For $g(n) \geq log(n)$,*
1. *$SAT \cap KT[g(n), n^2]$ is a hard set for all sparse sets in NP.*
2. *The following statements are equivalent.*
   a. *$SAT \cap KT[log(n), n^2] \in P$*
   b. *There are no sparse sets in $NP - P$*
   c. *$NEXPTIME = EXPTIME$.*

If S is strongly equivalent to the set of structures $\langle A, B^1 \rangle$ that satisfy the sentence $\exists_{g(n)}F^1\psi(F^1)$, where $\psi(F^1)$ is a $FO+LFP$ formula that implicitly defines B^1, then the witness set of S :

$$SAT_{g(n)} = \{ \langle A, F^1 \rangle : \langle A, F^1 \rangle \models \exists B^1 \psi(B^1) \}$$

is clearly in UP, and consists exactly of $g(n)$-easy satisfiable formulas. By the above theorem, the set of $g(n)$-easy satisfiable formulas, (for $g(n) \geq log\ n$) is hard for all sparse sets in $NP - P$. Hence, all sparse sets in $NP - P$ are in UP. If the formula $\psi(F^1)$ above explicitly defines B^1, then $SAT_{g(n)}$ is in P, and hence by the above theorem, $NEXPTIME = EXPTIME$. ∎

5. OPEN PROBLEMS

We have seen that interesting results emerge from a careful study of the relationships between sets in NP and their corresponding witness sets. In particular, we have seen that forcing certain relationships between sets in NP and their witness sets leads to robust complexity classes that have alternate characterizations. We gave evidence that if two such classes, $2^{nd}O\exists^I_{g(n)}$ and $2^{nd}O\exists^E_{g(n)}$ are strongly equivalent, then higher complexity classes collapse. An interesting question arises in this setting.

1. What are the consequences of an assumption that $2^{nd}O\exists^I_{g(n)}$ and $2^{nd}O\exists^E_{g(n)}$ are *equivalent*? In particular, does Theorem 3 hold if we weaken the assumption of strong equivalence to just equivalence?

An answer to this question would help to determine the exact complexity of $2^{nd}O\exists^E_{g(n)}$ more accurately. The question of determining the *approximate* complexity of $2^{nd}O\exists^E_{g(n)}$ is also interesting since this characterizes the complexity of statistical tests that pseudorandom generators can not pass. Hence, the following question arises.

2. Using one of the standard definitions of approximability (for example, that given in [NiWi 88]) can we provide an alternate characterization of the smallest complexity class, C, such that every set in $2^{nd}O\exists^E_{g(n)}$ can be approximated by a set in C?

A third question arises by observing that thus far we have only considered the complexity of uniformly generated subsets of the class $KT[g(n), n^k]$.

3. Can we characterize the complexity of other interesting subsets of $KT[g(n), n^k]$, for example, $NP \cap KT[g(n), n^k]$?

Even for $g(n) = log(n)$, an answer to this question would characterize the complexity of the set $SAT \cap KT[log(n), n^k]$, which has many interesting applications following the results of Hartmanis mentioned earlier ([Ha 83], [HaYe 83]).

6. BIBLIOGRAPHY

[Al 88] E.W. Allender, "Some consequences of the existence of pseudorandom generators," *to appear, JCSS*.

[ADT 89] C. Àlvarez, J. Díaz, J. Torán, "Complexity classes with complete problems between P and NP-C," *Fund. Comput. Theory conference, Lecture notes in computer science*, **380**, *Springer-Verlag*, pp. 13-24, 1989.

[Ba 68] Y.M. Barzdin, "Complexity of programs to determine whether natural numbers not greater than n belong to a recursively enumerable set," *Soviet Math. Dokl.* **9**, pp. 1251-1254, 1968.

[Da 77] R.P. Daley, "On the inference of optimal descriptions," *Theoretical Comp. Sci.* **4**, pp. 301-309, 1977.

[Fa 74] R. Fagin, "Generalized first order spectra and polynomial time recognizable sets," *Complexity of computation, AMS*, Providence, pp. 44-73, 1974.

[Fa 75] R. Fagin, "Monadic generalized spectra," *Z. Math. Logic Grundlagen Math.* **21**, pp. 89-96, 1975.

[Gu 84] Y. Gurevich, "Toward logic tailored for computational complexity," *Computation and Proof Theory, Lecture notes in mathematics* **1104**, *Springer-Verlag*, pp. 175-216, 1984.

[Ha 83] J. Hartmanis, "Generalized Kolmogorov complexity and the structure of feasible computations," *IEEE FOCS*, 1983.

[HaYe 83] J. Hartmanis, "Computation times of *NP* sets of different densities," *ICALP, Lecture notes in computer science* **154**, *Springer-Verlag* pp. 319-330, 1983.

[Im 82] N. Immerman, "Upper and lower bounds for first order expressibility," *J. of Computer and System Sciences* **22**, *no.3*, 1982.

[Im 87] N. Immerman, "Expressibility as a complexity measure: results and directions," *Structure in complexity theory conf.*, 1987.

[KiFi 80] C.M.R. Kintala, P. Fischer, "Refining nondeterminism in relativized polynomial time bounded computations," *SIAM J. Comput.* **9**, *no. 1*, 1980.

[Ko 83] K-I. Ko, "Resource bounded program size complexity and pseudorandom sequences," *Dept. of comp. sci., University of Houston*, 1983.

[Kol 89] P.G. Kolaitis, "Implicit definability on finite structures and unambiguous computations," *Manuscript*, 1989.

[Le 73] L.A. Levin, "Universal search problems," *Problems in Information Transmission* **9**, 1973.

[LiVi 88] M. Li, P.M.B. Vitanyi, "Two decades of applied Kolmogorov complexity," *Structure in complexity theory conf.*, 1973.

[Lo 86] L. Longpré, "Resource bounded Kolmogorov complexity, a link between complexity theory and information theory," *Ph.D. Thesis, Dept. of Computer Sciences, Cornell Univ.*, 1986.

[Ly 82] J.F. Lynch, "Complexity classes and theories of finite models," *Math. Systems Theory* **15**, pp.127-144, 1982.

[NiWi 88] N. Nisan, A. Widgerson, "Hardness vs. randomness," *IEEE FOCS*, pp.2-24, 1988.

[PaYa 88] C. Papadimitriou, M. Yannakakis, "Optimization, approximation, and complexity classes," *ACM STOC*, pp.229-234, 1988.

[StHu 86] R.E. Stearns, H.B. Hunt, "On the complexity of the satisfiability problem and the structure of NP," *TR 86-21, SUNY Albany*, 1986.

[Ya 82] A. Yao, "Theory and applications of trapdoor functions," *IEEE FOCS*, pp.80-91, 1982.

Relation-Sorted Algebraic Specifications with Built-in Coercers: Basic Notions and Results[1]

Hans-Jörg Kreowski, Zhenyu Qian

Department of Computer Science, University of Bremen,
D-2800 Bremen 33, Fed. Rep. Germany

Abstract: A relation-sorted algebraic specification SPEC with built-in coercers is, syntactically seen, quite similar to an order-sorted specification, i.e. SPEC consists of a signature, a set of equations and an arbitrary relation $\triangleright$ on the set of sorts. But our notion of SPEC-algebras is more general. In particular, if two sorts are in the sort relation $s \triangleright s'$, then we assume that, in each SPEC-algebra A, the corresponding carriers A_s and $A_{s'}$ are related by an operator $A_{s \triangleright s'}: A_s \rightarrow A_{s'}$, which is considered as a component of A, rather than by inclusion $A_s \subseteq A_{s'}$ as required in order-sorted algebras. This allows us to map a sort into a sort and simultaneously forget about some aspects as it occurs in object-oriented programming. Although our approach is more general than order-sorted specification, we get similar results, e.g. concerning the construction of initial algebras and a complete deduction system. Our approach may serve as a general framework for investigating subtypes as injective as well as non-injective conversion.

1. Introduction

The generalization of many-sorted algebra to order-sorted algebra by Goguen [78] makes it possible to consider subtype and inheritance in an algebraic framework. Gogolla [84] continued the work and solved some technical problems with this approach. Goguen and Meseguer [87] applied order-sorted algebra to provide elegant solutions to a lot of problems like the specifications of partial functions without error values, the specifications of constructors and selectors. A slightly different study has been made by Smolka, Nutt, Goguen and Meseguer [87], where a universe has been introduced to include all carriersets. An operational semantics of order-sorted algebra is given by Goguen, Jouannaud and Meseguer [85] by reducing order-sorted rewriting to many-sorted rewriting. A direct order-sorted operational semantics has been given by Kirchner's and Meseguer [87]. (For a comprehensive study, cf. Goguen and Meseguer [88] or Smolka, Nutt, Goguen and Meseguer [87].)

All the work above captures the set-theoretic subset relation in a very natural way, but not other kinds of subtype relations.

In general, however, there are at least the following kinds of subtypes occurring in computer programming:

(1) (Inclusion) The subtype is a set-theoretic subset of the supertype;

(2) (Injection) The supertype contains an isomorphic copy of the subtype, i.e. each element in the subtype corresponds to a unique element in the supertype;

(3) (Conversion Function) The elements of the subtype are classified by the elements of the supertype, i.e. each element in the subtype corresponds to an element in the supertype.

Obviously, point 2 is a generalization of point 1, and point 3 is the most general case. The study of the general form of subtypes has been started by Reynolds [80] in his category-sorted algebras. Subtypes, in

---

[1] The research of the second author has been partially supported by the Commission of the European Communities under the ESPRIT Programme in the PROSPECTRA Project, ref #390.

his view, correspond to conversion functions which forget information and may be therefore not injective. For example, we would like to regard a list as a set by forgetting the order of occurrences of elements and unnecessarily repetitive occurrences of elements. Here, the type List of lists may be regarded as a subtype of the type Set of sets with a non-injective conversion. In fact, this conversion can be viewed as a simple implementation of sets by lists.

Indeed, there are a lot of situations in existing programming languages, where the general form of subtypes is desirable. For example, additional to a type Real of real numbers many languages have a type Long-Real of real numbers with double precision. One might expect Real to be a subtype of Long-Real, but it is dangerous to use a number of Real in a context which requires a number of Long-Real: numbers in Real are not precise enough. It is numerically safe to consider a number with double precision to be a number with single precision, and thus Long-Real as a subtype of Real.

Bruce and Wegner [86] also examined the general form of subtype from a λ-calculus theoretic point of view. Neither Reynolds [80] nor Bruce and Wegner [86] gave any deduction mechanism.

In this paper, we introduce an arbitrary relation ▷, called a **sort relation**, on the sorts of a many-sorted specification to formulate the general notion of subtype. If s▷s', an operator $A_{s▷s'}:A_s \rightarrow A_{s'}$, called a **coercer**, is assumed to relate the corresponding carriers A_s and $A_{s'}$ in each algebra A. Different kinds of subtypes may be formulated within a specification in our framework. Furthermore, we present a complete deduction system for these specifications.

This paper is organized as follows: In Section 2, we give the basic notions of relation-sorted signatures and algebras with built-in coercers. In Section 3, we introduce equations. A complete deduction system is presented. And the existence of initial and free models is shown. The notion of consistent algebras and the meaning of inherited functions are discussed in Section 4. In Section 5, we discuss the simplification of the notation of terms. Conclusions and some further developments are given in Section 6. In the present version, proofs are omitted.

2. Relation-sorted Algebras with Built-in Coercers

In this section, we introduce the basic notions. The key concepts are, syntactically, relations on the set of sorts and, semantically, algebras with built-in coercers, which are functions between carriers of related sorts. We assume familiarity with the notions of many-sorted algebras (cf., e.g., Ehrig and Mahr [85]) such as signatures, algebras, terms, homomorphisms, specifications, etc.

Definition 2.1: A **relation-sorted signature** (short: RS-signature) is a triple (S, ▷, Σ), where
    (2.1.1) (S,Σ) is a many-sorted signature, and
    (2.1.2) ▷ ⊆ S×S is a relation on sorts.

Remarks:
(1) The symbols s, r possibly with subscripts, are used to denote sorts. We also write σ[w,s] or σ:w →s for σ∈$\Sigma_{w,s}$. σ∈$\Sigma_{\lambda,s}$ is called a **constant**. We denote the set of function symbols as |Σ| = $\cup_{w \in S^*, s \in S} \Sigma_{w,s}$. If σ∈$\Sigma_{w,s} \cap \Sigma_{w',s'}$ with w≠w' or s≠s', we say that σ is **multiply declared**.

(2) The smallest reflexive and transitive closure of $\rhd$ is a quasi-ordering on S, denoted as $\rhd^*$. $\rhd$ can be extended to strings of sorts of the same length by: $s1...sn \rhd s'1...s'n$ if $si \rhd s'i$, for $i=1,...,n$. We denote $s \lozenge s'$ if $s \rhd^* s'$ or $s' \rhd^* s$. For $s \lozenge s'$, we define $\min(s,s')=s$ if $s \rhd^* s'$, $\min(s,s')=s'$ if $s' \rhd^* s$.

(3) Consequently, $(S, \rhd^*, \Sigma)$ is also an RS-signature.

(4) For the RS-signature $SIG=(S,\rhd,\Sigma)$, the SIG-**induced signature** $SIG^{\rhd}=(S,\Sigma^{\rhd})$ is defined by

$\quad$ (a) $\Sigma^{\rhd}_{s,s'} := \Sigma_{s,s'} \cup \{ s \rhd s' \}$ for all $s, s' \in S$ if $s \rhd s'$, and

$\quad$ (b) $\Sigma^{\rhd}_{w,s} := \Sigma_{w,s}$ otherwise.

(5) $SIG^{\rhd}$ is a many-sorted signature. A many-sorted $(S,\Sigma^{\rhd})$-algebras is of the form $((A_s)_{s \in S}; A_{\Sigma^{\rhd}})$, where $A_{\Sigma^{\rhd}}$ $= A_{\Sigma} \cup A_{\rhd}$, with $A_{\Sigma} = (A_{\sigma[w,s]}: A_{s1} \times ... \times A_{sn} \to A_s \mid \sigma \in \Sigma_{w,s}$ $w=s1...sn \in S^*$, $s \in S)$ and $A_{\rhd} = (A_{s \rhd s'}: A_s \to A_{s'} \mid$ $s \rhd s' \in \Sigma^{\rhd}_{s,s'})$. We also write $A_{s1...sn}$ for $A_{s1} \times ... \times A_{sn}$. $\quad$ []

Definition 2.2: Let $SIG=(S,\rhd,\Sigma)$ be an RS-signature, and $SIG^{\rhd}$ the $(S,\rhd^*,\Sigma)$-induced signature.

(1) A **relation-sorted SIG-algebra** (short: SIG-algebra) is a many-sorted $SIG^{\rhd}$-algebra $((A_s)_{s \in S}; A_{\Sigma} \cup A_{\rhd^*})$ satisfying the following conditions:

$\quad$ (2.2.1) $A_{s \rhd^* s''}(a) = A_{s' \rhd^* s''}(A_{s \rhd^* s'}(a))$, for $s \rhd^* s' \rhd^* s''$ and for each $a \in A_s$;

$\quad$ (2.2.2) $A_{s \rhd^* s} = 1_{A_s}$ (where 1_{A_s} is the identity on A_s).

(2) Let A and B be two SIG-algebras. A **relation-sorted SIG-homomorphism** (short: SIG-homomorphism) h: A$\to$B is a many-sorted $SIG^{\rhd}$-homomorphism satisfying:

$\quad$ (2.2.3) $h_{s'}(A_{s \rhd s'}(a)) = B_{s \rhd s'}(h_s(a))$ for $s \rhd s'$ and any $a \in A_s$.

Remarks:

(1) If $s \rhd s'$, we call $A_{s \rhd s'}$ a **coercer**, A_s the **sub-** and $A_{s'}$ the **supercarrier**.

(2) Let $w=s1...sn$ and $w'=s'1...s'n$. We write $A_{w \rhd w'}(a)$ instead of $(A_{s1 \rhd s'1}(a1),..., A_{sn \rhd s'n}(an))$ with $a=(a1,...,an) \in A_w$.

(3) The condition (2.2.1) implies the uniqueness of the coercer between any two related sorts. Without this technical simplicity, we would not be able to have the coercers anonymous, since each time we have to decide which coercer to apply.

(4) The operators $A_{\sigma[w,s]}$ and $A_{\sigma[w',s']}$ are called **overloaded** if $w \neq w'$ or $s \neq s'$.

(5) By convention, we write $a \in A$ to denote $a \in A_s$ for some $s \in S$.

(6) All SIG-algebras with all SIG-homomorphisms comprise a category, denoted as Alg(SIG). $\quad$ []

Example 2.3: The following is a very simple RS-signature that illustrates how to construct a sort Nat of natural numbers from a sort Bin-String of strings of binary digits. The notations used below are those by Ehrig and Mahr [85] extended with a description of sort relation.

NAT-BIN-STRING

$\quad$ **sorts**: Bin-Digit, Bin-String, Nat

$\quad$ **sort-relation**: Bin-Digit $\rhd$ Bin-String, Bin-String $\rhd$ Nat

$\quad$ **opns**: $\quad$ 0,1: $\quad \to$ Bin-Digit

$\quad \quad \quad \quad$ cat: $\quad$ Bin-String$^2 \to$ Bin-String

$\quad$ A possible NAT-BIN-STRING-algebra is given by the tuple $(A_{Bin-Digit}, A_{Bin-String}, A_{Nat}; A_0, A_1, A_{cat}, A_{Bin-Digit \rhd Bin-String}, A_{Bin-String \rhd Nat})$, where $A_{Bin-Digit}$ is the set $\{0,1\}$ with $A_0=0$ and $A_1=1$, $A_{Bin-String}$ the strings of 0,1 and A_{Nat} the set of natural numbers, $A_{Bin\text{-}Digit \rhd Bin\text{-}String}$ converts the digits 0,1 into the strings 0,1, resp. $A_{Bin\text{-}String \rhd Nat}$ converts binary strings into the binary numbers they represent.

Note that the relation Bin-String $\rhd$ Nat is interpreted as a non-injective function $A_{Bin\text{-}String \rhd Nat}$, which forgets the heading 0's in the strings. []

Now, we are going to introduce the notions of terms, term algebras and assignments w.r.t. RS-signatures. We show that each assignment (of values in an algebra to variables) can be homomorphically and uniquely extended to the term algebra over the variables or, in other words, that the term algebra is free over the variables.

Definition 2.4: Let SIG=(S,$\rhd$,Σ) be an RS-signature. A **variable family** is a family of sets of symbols $X=(X_s)_{s \in S}$ disjoint with SIG. The family of sets of SIG(X)-**terms** $T_{SIG}(X) = \{T_{SIG}(X)_s | s \in S\}$ is constructed as follows (hereafter, we also write T(X) for $T_{SIG}(X)$, $T(X)_s$ for $T_{SIG}(X)_s$, if SIG is clear from the context):

    (2.4.1) $\sigma_s \in T(X)_s$ if $\sigma \in \Sigma_{\lambda,s}$;

    (2.4.2) $x_s \in T(X)_s$ if $x \in X_s$;

    (2.4.3) $\sigma_{w,s}(t1...tn) \in T(X)_s$ if $\sigma \in \Sigma_{w,s}$ and $ti \in T(X)_{si}$, $1 \le i \le n$, w= s1...sn;

    (2.4.4) $T(X)_s \subseteq T(X)_{s'}$ if s$\rhd$s'.

The SIG(X)-**term algebra** $T_{SIG}(X)$ is equipped with the following operators:

    (2.4.5) For each $\sigma \in \Sigma_{\lambda,s}$, $T(X)_{\sigma[\lambda,s]}: \rightarrow T(X)_s$ is defined by $T(X)_{\sigma[\lambda,s]}=\sigma_s$;

    (2.4.6) For each $\sigma \in \Sigma_{w,s}$ and w=s1...sn, $T(X)_{\sigma[w,s]}: T(X)_{s1} \times ... \times T(X)_{sn} \rightarrow T(X)_s$ is defined by $T(X)_{\sigma[w,s]}(t1,...,tn))=\sigma_{w,s}(t1...tn)$ for any $ti \in T(X)_{si}$;

    (2.4.7) The coercer $T(X)_{s \rhd s'}:T(X)_s \rightarrow T(X)_{s'}$ is defined for each s$\rhd$s' by $T(X)_{s \rhd s'}(t)=t$ for any $t \in T(X)_s$.

Remark: Like in the many-sorted case, overloaded function symbols are also distinguished by their arities. If a function symbol is not overloaded, its arity can be omitted. **Ground terms** are the terms without variables. We write T_{SIG} for $T_{SIG}(X)$ if X=$\varnothing$. []

Definition 2.5: Let SIG=(S,$\rhd$,Σ) be an RS-signature, X a variable family and A a SIG-algebra. A SIG-**assignment** $\theta:X \rightarrow A$ is an S-sorted set of functions $(\theta_s)_{s \in S}$ with $\theta_s:X_s \rightarrow A_s$.

Remark:

(1) The above SIG-assignment can be extended into an S-sorted set of functions $\theta^* = (\theta^*_s)_{s \in S} = (T(X)_s \rightarrow A_s)_{s \in S}$, called an **extended assignment**, in the following way:

    (a) $\theta^*_s(x) = \theta_s(x)$ for $x \in X_s$;

    (b) $\theta^*_s(\sigma_s) = A_{\sigma[\lambda,s]}$ for $\sigma \in \Sigma_{\lambda,s}$;

    (c) $\theta^*_s(\sigma_{w,s}(t1...tn)) = A_{\sigma[w,s]}(\theta^*_{s1}(t1),...,\theta^*_{sn}(tn))$ for $\sigma_{w,s}(t1...tn) \in T(X)_s$ and w=s1...sn;

    (d) $\theta^*_{s'}(t)= A_{s \rhd s'}(\theta^*_s(t))$ for $t \in T(X)_s$ and s$\rhd$s'.

For simplicity, we also write θ instead of θ^*.

(2) An assignment $\theta:T_{SIG}(X) \rightarrow T_{SIG}(Y)$ is called a **substitution**. []

Theorem 2.6: The term algebra $T_{SIG}(X)$ is free over X in Alg(SIG). []

Since relation-sorted algebras are certain many-sorted algebras, the notions for many-sorted algebras apply to relation-sorted algebras. Examples are the notions of subalgebras, congruences and quotients. We reformulate the notion of congruence as follows.

Definition 2.7: Let $SIG=(S,\triangleright,\Sigma)$ be an RS-signature and A a SIG-algebra. Then a SIG-**congruence** $\equiv$ is an S-sorted set of equivalence relations $(\equiv_s)_{s\in S}$ such that for $f:A_{s1}\times...\times A_{sn}\to A_s$ (being an operator in A_Σ or a coercer in $A_\triangleright$), if $a_i \equiv_{si} b_i$ in A_{si}, i=1,...,n, then $f(a_1, ..., a_n) \equiv_s f(b_1, ..., b_n)$. $\quad\Box$

3. Equations, Specifications and the Deduction System

In this section, we introduce equations. Because a term may represent different values in several sorts, an equation is associated with a set of sorts to restrict its valid scope. We are able to give a complete and sound deduction system.

Definition 3.1: Let $SIG=(S,\triangleright,\Sigma)$ be an RS-signature. Let A be a SIG-algebra, and T(X) the SIG(X)-term algebra. For $K \subseteq S$ and $s\in S$, we write $K\triangleright s$ if for each $r\in K$, $r\triangleright s$.

(1) An **unconditional** SIG-**equation** is a formula $\forall X\, t =_K t'$ with X being a variable family, $t,t'\in T(X)$ and $K \subseteq S$.

(2) $\forall X\, t =_K t'$ is **satisfied in A w.r.t. the assignment** $\theta:X\to A$ if $\theta_s(t)=\theta_s(t')$ for each sort s with $K\triangleright s$ and $t,t'\in T(X)_s$. It is **satisfied in** A if it is satisfied in A w.r.t. each possible assignment.

(3) A SIG-**equation** is a formula $\forall X\, C \Rightarrow t =_K t'$, where $\forall X\, t =_K t'$ is an unconditional equation, C a set of unconditional equations $\{\forall X\, t_i =_{K_i} t'_i \,|i=1,...,n\}$.

(4) The above equation is **satisfied** in A if, for each assignment $\theta:X\to A$, $\forall X\, t =_K t'$ is satisfied in A w.r.t. θ, provided that each $\forall X\, t_i =_{K_i} t'_i \in C$ is satisfied in A w.r.t. θ.

Remarks:

(1) Any unconditional SIG-equation is a SIG-equation with empty C.

(2) A set of equations is **satisfied** in A if each equation in the set is satisfied in A.

(3) We can drop the sort set K in $\forall X\, C \Rightarrow t =_K t'$ if K consists of the target sorts of the outermost functions of t and t', i.e., instead of $\forall X\, \sigma_{w,s}(t) =_{\{s,s'\}} \sigma_{w',s'}(t')$, we can write $\forall X\, \sigma_{w,s}(t) = \sigma_{w's'}(t')$.

(4) An equation $\forall X\, C \Rightarrow t =_K t'$ is called **trivial** if there is no $s\in S$ with $t,t'\in T(X)_s$ and $K\triangleright s$. This means that either there is no $s\in S$ with $K\triangleright s$, or $t\notin T(X)_s$ or $t'\notin T(X)_s$ for each $s\in S$ with $K\triangleright s$. Note that any trivial equation is trivially satisfied $\quad\Box$

Definition 3.2:

(1) A **relation-sorted specification** (short: RS-specification) is a pair SPEC = (SIG,E) consisting of an RS-signature SIG and a set E of SIG-equations.

(2) A SIG-algebra A is called a SPEC-**algebra** if all equations in E are satisfied in A.

Remark: We use Alg(SPEC) to denote the full subcategory of all SPEC-algebras in Alg(SIG). $\quad\Box$

Definition 3.3: Given an RS-specification SPEC = $(S, \triangleright, \Sigma, E)$, the following are the **inference rules** of the deduction |- for deriving unconditional equations.

(1) (Reflexivity) |- $\forall X\, t =_K t$, for each term t.

(2) (Symmetry) If |- $\forall X\, t =_K t'$, then |- $\forall X\, t' =_K t$.

(3) (Transitivity) If |- $\forall X\, t =_K t'$ and |- $\forall X\, t' =_{K'} t''$, then |- $\forall X\, t =_{K \cup K'} t''$.

(4) (Congruence) If |- $\forall X\, t_i =_{K_i} t'_i$ with $t_i, t'_i \in T(X)_{s_i}$ and $K_i \triangleright^* s_i$, $i=1,\ldots,n$,

   then |- $\forall X\, \sigma_{w,s}(t1, \ldots, tn) =_{\{s\}} \sigma_{w,s}(t'1, \ldots, t'n)$, for $\sigma \in \Sigma_{w,s}$, $w=s1\ldots sn$.

(5) (Substitutivity) If $\forall X\, C \Rightarrow t =_K t'$ is in E and $\theta:T(X) \to T(Y)$ is a substitution such that

   |- $\forall Y\, \theta(u) =_{K'} \theta(u')$ for each $\forall X\, u =_{K'} u' \in C$, then |- $\forall Y\, \theta(t) =_K \theta(t')$.

(6) (Sort-Introduction) If |- $\forall X\, t =_K t'$, then |- $\forall X\, t =_{K \cup \{s\}} t'$ for any $s \in S$.

(7) (Sort-Elimination) If |- $\forall X\, t =_{K \cup \{s,s'\}} t'$ with $s \triangleright^* s'$, then |- $\forall X\, t =_{K \cup \{s'\}} t'$. []

Theorem 3.4: For the above SPEC and X, let the S-sorted set of binary relations $\sim_{X,E} := (\sim_{X,E,s})_{s \in S}$ defined by $t \sim_{X,E,s} t'$ if |- $\forall X\, t =_{\{s\}} t'$ with $t, t' \in T(X)_s$. Then $\sim_{X,E}$ is a congruence relation on $T_{SIG}(X)$. []

Theorem 3.5: Let $T_{SPEC}(X)$ denote the quotient algebra of $T_{SIG}(X)$ through $\sim_{X,E}$. Then $T_{SPEC}(X)$ is free over X in Alg(SPEC).   []

Theorem 3.6 (Soundness and Completeness): For an RS-specification SPEC = (SIG,E) and a SIG-equation $\forall X\, t =_K t'$, the following statements are equivalent:

(1) $\forall X\, t =_K t'$ is satisfied in each SPEC-algebra.

(2) |- $\forall X\, t =_K t'$, provided it is not trivial.   []

Example 3.7: We continue the discussion of Example 2.3 by adding some equations to the signature NAT-BIN-STRING. In addition, we define a succ-operation on Nat. The NAT-BIN-STRING-algebra given in Example 2.3 is not initial in Alg(NAT-BIN-STRING), but initial in Alg(NAT-BIN-STRING°).

   NAT-BIN-STRING°
      sorts: Bin-Digit, Bin-String, Nat
      sort-relation: Bin-Digit $\triangleright$ Bin-String, Bin-String $\triangleright$ Nat
      opns: 0,1: $\to$ Bin-Digit
               cat: Bin-String$^2 \to$ Bin-String
               succ: Nat $\to$ Bin-String
      ***var** x,y,z:Bin-String*
      eqns: *cat(x,cat(y,z)) = cat(cat(x,y),z)*
               cat(0,x) =_{Nat} x   ....(*)
               succ(0) = 1
               succ(1) = cat(1,0)
               succ(cat(x,0)) = cat(x,1)
               succ(cat(x,1)) = cat(succ(x),0)

The equation (*) only says that cat(0,x) and x represents the same natural numbers in the sort Nat, although cat(0,x) and x are two different strings.

A lot of similar situations, where the subsort provides certain representations for the supersort, but not necessarily unique ones, can be specified in the similar way, e.g. defining sets based on lists. []

4. Overloaded Operators and Its Consistence under Coercion

In our approach, multiple declarations of an operator is not forbidden. In the general case, this is a mere coincidence of names, while the corresponding semantic operations have nothing to do with each other. Sometimes, however, one may like to express a relationship among operations by using the same function symbol for them. One may like to overload an operator purposefully such that the corresponding operations behave consistently in proper sense.

As an example, consider the set NAT of natural numbers and the set INT of integers with INT⊇NAT with the arithmetic plus: $+:NAT^2 \rightarrow NAT$ and $+:INT^2 \rightarrow INT$, denoted as $+_{Nat}$ and $+_{Int}$, resp. Since INT⊇NAT, the operator $+_{Int}$ is applicable to natural numbers. Obviously, the constraint of $+_{Int}$ to NAT should be equal to $+_{Nat}$. But this is not guaranteed by the use of RS-specification techniques automatically. To handle the consistence of overloaded operators, we introduce consistent algebras as possible semantics of signatures with multiply declared function symbols.

Definition 4.1: Let SIG = $(S,\triangleright,\Sigma)$ be an RS-signature, A a SIG-algebra. Let $\sigma \in \Sigma_{w,s} \cap \Sigma_{w',s'}$ with $w \diamondsuit^* w'$ and $s \triangleright^* s'$. A is said to be **consistent** w.r.t. (σ,w,s,w',s') if

(4.1.1) $A_{s \triangleright^* s'}(A_{\sigma[\lambda,s]}) = A_{\sigma[\lambda,s']}$ in the case $w=w'=\lambda$, and

(4.1.2) $A_{s \triangleright^* s'}(A_{\sigma[w,s]}(b)) = A_{\sigma[w',s']}(b')$, in the case $w=s1...sn$, $w'=s'1...s'n$, $n>0$,

where $b=(b1, ..., bn)$, $b'=(b'1, ..., b'n)$, for any $ai \in A_{min(si,s'i)}$, $i=1,...,n$, with

$$bi = \left[\begin{array}{ll} ai & \text{if } si \triangleright^* s'i \\ A_{s'i \triangleright^* si}(ai) & \text{if } s'i \triangleright^* si, \end{array} \right. \quad \text{for } i=1,...,n,$$

$$b'i = \left[\begin{array}{ll} ai & \text{if } s'i \triangleright^* si \\ A_{si \triangleright^* s'i}(ai) & \text{if } si \triangleright^* s'i, \end{array} \right. \quad \text{for } i=1,...,n.$$

Remarks:

(1) The above situation can be illustrated by the following diagram:

$$
\begin{array}{ccc}
s & \triangleright^* & s' \\
\uparrow\sigma & & \uparrow\sigma \\
w & \diamondsuit^* & w'
\end{array}
$$

Note that consistent algebras are not defined w.r.t. functions in $\Sigma_{w,s} \cap \Sigma_{w',s'}$ that do not satisfy $w \diamondsuit^* w'$ and $s \triangleright^* s'$.

(2) Smolka, Nutt, Goguen and Meseguer [87] assume consistence from the very beginning by requiring that all multiply declared functions are restrictions of the the same function on the universe.

(3) Goguen and Meseguer [87] discuss a special case of consistence that may be called covariance-consistence, which means that one operator can be seen as an extension of the other by extending its domain and value carriers to some supercarriers. More formally, Let A be consistent w.r.t. $\sigma \in \Sigma_{w,s} \cap \Sigma_{w',s'}$. A is said to be **covariance-consistent** w.r.t. (σ,w,s,w',s') if $w \triangleright^* w'$ and $s \triangleright^* s'$. []

Definition 4.2: Let S = { Nat, Int, PoRat} be a sort set with a sort relation ▷ = {Nat▷Int, Nat▷PoRat}. Assume +:Nat,Nat→Nat, +:Int,Int→Int,+:PoRat,PoRat→PoRat. A SIG-algebra A can be given as follows: The carriers A_{Nat}, A_{Int} and A_{PoRat} are the set of natural numbers, the set of integers and the set of positive rational numbers, resp. The relation ▷ corresponds to set inclusion. + corresponds to the normal arithmetic operator "plus". A is obviously covariance-consistent w.r.t. +.   ▯

Unfortunately, we cannot present a really natural and convincing example for our more general notion of consistence. Nevertheless, it works nicely as you can see below.

Definition 4.3: Let SIG = (S,▷,Σ) be an RS-signature. A set CB ⊆ |Σ|×S*×S×S*×S is called a **consistence base** if (σ,w,s,w',s')∈ CB implies σ∈$\Sigma_{w,s}$∩$\Sigma_{w',s'}$ with w◇*w' and s▷*s'.

Remarks:
(1) A SIG-algebra A is called CB-**consistent** if A is consistent w.r.t. each (σ,w,s,w',s')∈ CB. A can also be called **consistent** if CB consists of all (σ,w,s,w',s') with σ∈$\Sigma_{w,s}$∩$\Sigma_{w',s'}$, w◇*w' and s▷*s'.
(2) A consistency base CB is called **covariance-complete** if CB consists of all (σ,w,s,w',s') with (w,s)▷*(w',s').
(3) We use CAlg(SIG)$_{CB}$ to denote the full subcategory of Alg(SIG) containing all CB-consistent SIG-algebras, and use CAlg(SIG) to denote that containing all consistent SIG-algebras.   ▯

It turns out that CB-consistent SIG-algebras are just SIG-algebras satisfying some additional SIG-equations.

Lemma 4.4: Let SIG = (S,▷,Σ) be an RS-signature, A a SIG-algebra. Let CB be a consistency base. We define a set of SIG-equations as follows:
Π_{CB} :=
{∀X $\sigma_{w,s}(x_{r1}...x_{rm})=\sigma_{w',s'}(x_{r1}...x_{rm})$ | (σ,w,s,w',s')∈CB,w=s1...sn,w=s'1...s'n,X_{ri}={x},r_i=min(si,s'i), i=1,...,n}
∪{ ∀X $\sigma_s = \sigma_{s'}$ | (σ,λ,s,λ,s')∈CB, X=∅},
Then A is CB-consistent if and only if A satisfies Π_{CB}.   ▯

The above discussions apply to RS-specifications. Two immediate consequences are as follows:
Theorem 4.5: Let SPEC=(S,▷,Σ,E) be an RS-specification with the consistency base CB. Let CSPEC=(S,▷,Σ,E∪Π_{CB}). Then the following hold:
(1) CAlg(SPEC)$_{CB}$=Alg(CSPEC).
(2) There is an initial algebra in CAlg(SPEC)$_{CB}$.   ▯

We finish this section by mentioning the relationship of the relation-sorted algebras with the order-sorted algebras by Goguen and Meseguer [87].
An order-sorted signature (S,≤,Σ) is an RS-signature with ≤ being a partial ordering on S. An order-sorted (S,≤,Σ)-algebra is a many-sorted (S,Σ)-algebra A such that s≤s' implies A_s⊆$A_{s'}$ and σ∈$\Sigma_{w,s}$∩$\Sigma_{w',s'}$

with $(w,s)\leq(w',s')$ implies that $A_{\sigma(w,s)}{:}A_w{\to}A_s$ equals $A_{\sigma(w',s')}{:}A_{w'}{\to}A_{s'}$ on A_w. We use $OSA((S,\leq,\Sigma))$ to denote the category of all order-sorted $(S,\leq,\Sigma)$-algebras.

Each order-sorted $(S,\leq,\Sigma)$-algebra A is obviously a relation-sorted $(S,\leq,\Sigma)$-algebra, where the coercion corresponding to $\leq$ is the set inclusion. Let CB be a covariance-complete consistency base in $(S,\leq,\Sigma)$. Then A is a CB-consistent relation-sorted algebra. Conversely, a relation-sorted $(S,\leq,\Sigma)$-algebra B is isomorphic to an order-sorted $(S,\leq,\Sigma)$-algebra if B is CB-consistent and all coercers are injective operators. Note that the injectivity of coercion can be specified by the set of conditional equations:

$$\{\forall X.\ x =_{s'} y \Rightarrow x =_s y \mid \text{for each } s{\triangleright}s' \text{ in S with } X_s{=}\{x,y\}\}.$$

Theorem 4.6: Let CB be a covariance complete consistency base in $(S,\leq,\Sigma)$. Let C_{inj} be a full subcategory of $CAlg((S,\leq,\Sigma))_{CB}$ consisting of all algebras with injective coercers. Then for each algebra in C_{inj}, there is a relation-sortedly isomorphic algebra in $OSA((S,\leq,\Sigma))$, and vice versa. []

5. Bare Terms, Infimum- and Supremum-Regularity

It is inconvenient to write the sorts of function symbols explicitly in terms. But without them, the evaluation of function symbols in terms may be ambiguous. The evaluation of terms without sorts is unambiguous if the result algebra obtained from the term algebra by dropping sorts in each term is initial.

Definition 5.1: Let $SIG=(S,\triangleright,\Sigma)$ be an RS-signature, X a variable family. A **bare term** $|t|$ is obtained by dropping sort information in a term t. The **bare term algebra** $|T_{SIG}(X)|$ (short: $|T(X)|$) is defined as follows:
(1) For each $s\in S$, $|T(X)|_s = \{\ |t| \mid t\in T(X)_s\ \}$;
(2) For each $\sigma\in \Sigma_{w,s}$, $|T(X)|_{\sigma(w,s)}$ is defined by $|T(X)|_{\sigma(w,s)}(|t1|,...,|tn|) = |T(X)_{\sigma(w,s)}(t1,...,tn)|$ for any $ti\in T(X)_{si}$, $i=1,...,n$, $w=s1...sn$;
(3) For each $s{\triangleright}s'$, $|T(X)|_{s{\triangleright}s'}$ is defined by $|T(X)|_{s{\triangleright}s'}(|t|) = |T(X)_{s{\triangleright}s'}(t)|$ for any $t\in T(X)_s$.

Remarks: The operators $|T(X)|_{\sigma(w,s)}$ and $|T(X)|_{s{\triangleright}s'}$ are well-defined, since $|t|=|t'|$ implies $|T(X)_{\sigma(w,s)}(t)|=|T(X)_{\sigma(w,s)}(t')|$ and $|T(X)_{s{\triangleright}s'}(t)|=|T(X)_{s{\triangleright}s'}(t')|$. []

Unfortunately, for an arbitrary RS-signature SIG, $|T_{SIG}(X)|$ may be not initial in $Alg(SIG)$, even not in $CAlg(SIG)_{CB}$. Further restrictions on signatures have to be imposed. Here we refine the regularity condition introduced by Goguen and Meseguer [87].

Definition 5.2: Let $(S,\triangleright,\Sigma)$ be an RS-signature. A function symbol $\sigma\in |\Sigma|$ is said to be **infimum-regular** if for any $w0,w1\in S^*$ with $w0{\triangleright}^*w1$ and $\sigma\in \Sigma_{w1,s1}$, there is $(w,s)\in S^*{\times}S$ such that $w0{\triangleright}^*w$ and $(w,s){\triangleright}^*(w',s')$ for any $\sigma\in \Sigma_{w',s'}$ with $w0{\triangleright}^*w'$. []

In fact, the above (w,s) can be seen as the least sort string with $\sigma\in \Sigma_{w,s}$ and $w0{\triangleright}^*w$. We call the above $\sigma\in \Sigma_{w,s}$ **canonical over** w0.

If the sort set S is finite, then the infimum-regularity is equivalent to the following condition:
Whenever $\sigma\in \Sigma_{w1,s1}\cap\Sigma_{w2,s2}$ and there is some $w0{\triangleright}^*w1,w2$, then there is w,s such that $w0{\triangleright}^*w{\triangleright}^*w1,w2$ and $s{\triangleright}^*s1,s2$ with $\sigma\in \Sigma_{w,s}$. The condition is illustrated by the following diagram:

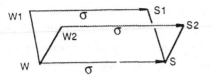

In Example 4.3, for any natural number n, not only $+_{Nat}$, but also $+_{Int}$ and $+_{PoRat}$ are also applicable on n. The coercers are the set inclusion. $+_{Nat}$ is canonical.

Let A be a consistent algebra of an infimum-regular signature and $a \in A_w$. Then among all overloaded operators with domains greater than w, there is always a canonical operator with the least domain and range. Up to coercion, the value of each of these overloaded operator on a is equal to the value of the canonical operator on a.

Infimum-regularity of each function symbol is not the unique condition to ensure the initiality of $|T_{SIG(X)}|$ in CAlg(SIG). Another kind of regularity may be introduced, which requires the existence of a canonical operator with the greatest domain and the least range among all overloaded operators considered.

Definition 5.3: Let $(S, \triangleright, \Sigma)$ be an RS-signature. A function symbol $\sigma \in |\Sigma|$ is said to be **supremum-regular** if for any w0,w1$\in S^*$ with w0$\triangleright$*w1 and $\sigma \in \Sigma_{w1,s1}$, there is $\sigma \in \Sigma_{w,s}$ such that w0$\triangleright$*w and w'$\triangleright$*w and s$\triangleright$*s' for any $\sigma \in \Sigma_{w',s'}$ with w0$\triangleright$*w'.   []

In fact, the   above w and s can be seen as the greatest sort string and the least sort, resp. such that $\sigma \in \Sigma_{w,s}$ with w0$\triangleright$*w. We also call the above $\sigma \in \Sigma_{w,s}$ **canonical over** w0.

If the sort set S is finite, then the supremum-regularity is equivalent to the following condition: Whenever $\sigma \in \Sigma_{w1,s1} \cap \Sigma_{w2,s2}$ and there is some w0$\triangleright$*w1,w2, there are w,s such that w1,w2$\triangleright$*w and s$\triangleright$*s1,s2 with $\sigma \in \Sigma_{w,s}$. The condition is illustrated by the following diagram:

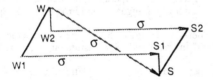

Note that neither of the above two regularities implies the other.

Definition 5.4: Let $(S, \triangleright, \Sigma)$ be an RS-signature. Let C and C' be two subsets of $|\Sigma|$. We say that SIG is (C,C')-**regular** (short: regular, when C,C' are clear) if each function symbol in C is infimum-regular and each function symbol in C' is supremum-regular.

Remark: In general, we do not require $C \cap C' = \emptyset$. This means that one function symbol $\sigma \in |\Sigma|$ can be both infimum- and supremum-regular.   []

Theorem 5.5: Let SIG=$(S, \triangleright, \Sigma)$ be an RS-signature. If SIG is (C,C')-regular with $C \cup C' = |\Sigma|$, then the bare term SIG-algebra $|T_{SIG(X)}|$ is initial in CAlg(SIG).

Idea of proof: For any $A \in CAlg(SIG)$, we define a homomorphism $|T_{SIG}(X)| \to A$ by induction of construction of bare terms in $|T_{SIG}(X)|$. At each depth, the construction of terms corresponds to an application of a function symbol σ. The homomorphism of all overloaded operators σ applicable at this place is uniquely determined by the homomorphism of a canonical operator. []

By the result in Goguen and Meseguer [87], we know that for the above SIG, each bare term has a least sort. The least sort determines all the sorts, to which the bare term belongs.

6. Conclusion

We have discussed a kind of algebraic models for a fairly general notion of subtype and shown similar results as in many-sorted algebra, e.g., concerning the construction of free algebras and a complete deduction system. Under a general syntactic condition, we can drop the sort information in terms.

The subtype relation is captured by built-in non-injective functions, which can be considered not only as conversion functions, but also as a general dependent relation of elements that are relevant in the areas such as object-oriented, higher-order and algebraic process specifications. However, the details of combining such specification techniques with our concept of sort relation have to be worked out in further investigations. Another interesting line is to consider the notion of parameterization and parameter passing in our framework (cf. Qian [89]).

References

Bruce,K.B. and Wegner,P. [86]: "An Algebraic Model for Subtypes in Object-Oriented Languages (Draft) In: SIGPLAN Vol.21, No.10. (1986) 163-172.

Ehrig,H., Mahr,B. [85]: "Fundamentals of Algebraic Specification 1- Equations and Initial Semantics" Springer-Verlag 1985.

Gogolla,M. [84]: "Partially Ordered Sorts in Algebraic Specifications." Proc. 9th CAAP, Cambrigde University Press, 139-153. (1984)

Goguen,J.A. [78]: "Order-Sorted Algebra. Semantics and Theory of Computation." Report No. 14, UCLA computer Science Dept. 1978.

Goguen,J.A., Jouannaud,J.-P. and Meseguer,J. [85]: "Operational Semantics of Order-sorted Algebra." In: Proc. International Conference on Automata, Languages and Programming, Springer-LNCS 194. (1985)

Goguen,J.A. and Meseguer,J. [87]: "Order-sorted Algebra Solves the Constructor-Selector, Multiple Representation and Coercion Problems" In: Proc. 1987 Symposium on Logic in Computer Science, Cornell. 1987. 18-29

Goguen,J.A. and Meseguer,J. [88]: "Order-Sorted Algebra I: Equational Deduction for Multiple Inheritance, Polymorphism, and Partial Operations." Tech. Report SRI (1988).

Kirchner, C., Kirchner,H. and Meseguer,J. [87]: Operational semantics of OBJ3. In: Proc. 15th ICALP (1988)

Qian, Zh. [89]:"Relation-Sorted Algebraic Specifications with Built-in Coercers: Parameterization and Parameter Passing." In: Proc. Categorical Methods in Computer Science with Aspects from Topology, LNCS 393, 244-260. (1989)

Reynolds, J. [80]: "Using category theory to design implicit conversions and generic operations." In: Semantics-Directed Compiler Generation, LNCS 94. (1980) 211-258

Smolka,G., Nutt,W., Goguen,J.A. and Meseguer,J. [87]: "Order-Sorted Equational Computation" SEKI Rep. SR-87-14. In: H.Ait-Kaci, M.Nivat.(eds.) Resolution of Equations in Algebraic Structures; Academic Press.

COMPUTATIONAL POWER OF ONE-WAY
MULTIHEAD FINITE AUTOMATA

Mirosław Kutyłowski

Institute of Computer Science, University of Wrocław,
ul. Przesmyckiego 20, 51-151 Wrocław, Poland [1]

In this paper we sketch our results concerning one-way multihead finite automata (1-MFA). The full version with complete proofs can be found in a series of papers ([3],[4],[5],[6]).

1-MFA belong to the weakest models of computational devices. Despite that, they recognize many interesting and important languages. They work in linear time, so the algorithms running on 1-MFA are in some sense practical. Unfortunately, many important questions concerning 1-MFA have turned out to be hard to answer, despite the simplicity of the computational model. We get the results which answer some of such open questions. Before we proceed, we recall shortly the definition of 1-MFA.

A 1-MFA consists of an input tape, some number of read-only heads and a control unit with finitely many internal states (see figure 1). Input words are placed on the input tape, each symbol occupying one cell. The heads are placed initially at the first from the left input symbol. During a computation the heads move independently on the tape (no moves to the left are allowed) and read different symbols of the input word.

The computation consists of several steps, during which the internal state can change and the heads can move to the right. These actions are determined at each step by:

- the internal state of the automaton,

- the symbols currently read by the heads.

To express it more precisely, we associate with each automaton M so called transition function δ_M. If at some moment of a computation automaton M is in state q, the heads $H_1, H_2, ..., H_k$ of M see symbols $a_1, a_2, ..., a_k$ on the tape and $\delta_M(q, a_1, ..., a_k) = (p, d_1, ..., d_k)$ then during this step:

---

[1]Most of this research have been made while the author visited Institut für Theoretische Informatik, Technische Hochschule Darmstadt, BRD, receiving support from the Alexander von Humboldt Foundation.

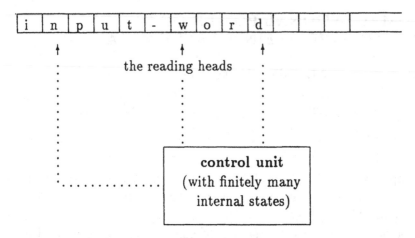

Figure 1: A 4-head one-way finite automaton.

- the internal state of M changes from q to p,

- for each $i \leq k$ head H_i moves d_i positions to the right ($d_i \in \{0, 1\}$).

Notice that the computation is deterministic and the heads do not see each other (the "non-sensing model"). A word x is accepted by a 1-MFA M if during the computation on x automaton M reaches an accepting state.

From the very beginning of the studies on 1-MFA the following problem has been investigated:

Problem. *Given a language L which can be recognized by some 1-MFA. Find the minimal number k such that L can be recognized by some k-head 1-MFA.*

We consider this problem trying to find how the number of heads influences the computational power of 1-MFA.

Most intensively studied was the behaviour of 1-MFA on so called bounded languages. We say that a language L is bounded if there is $m \in \mathbf{N}$ such that each word $x \in L$ has the form $x = 1^{a_1} * 1^{a_2} * \ldots * 1^{a_m}$ for some $a_1, \ldots, a_m \in \mathbf{N}$. In the above situation we say also that language L is m-bounded.

$$\cdots * w_{i-1} * w_i * w_{i+1} * \quad \cdots \quad * w_{i+1} * w_i * w_{i-1} * \cdots$$

↑the first head   ↑the second head

Figure 2: The checking that the corresponding subwords are equal for a word belonging to $\mathcal{L}_m$.

1. Rosenberg's languages

To prove the hierarchy theorem for 1-MFA with respect to the number of heads A.L. Rosenberg [7] introduced the languages P_m:

$$P_m = \{1^{a_1} * 1^{a_2} * \ldots * 1^{a_m} \# 1^{a_m} * 1^{a_{m-1}} * \ldots * 1^{a_1} : a_1, \ldots, a_m \in \mathbf{N}\}.$$

He conjectured that language P_m cannot be recognized by any k-head 1-MFA if $m > \frac{1}{2}k(k-1)$. Unfortunately, the proof was incorrect. Languages P_m have been modified by Yao and Rivest [8]. They considered languages $\mathcal{L}_m$ where

$$\mathcal{L}_m = \{w_1 * w_2 * \ldots * w_{2m} : \forall i \ w_i \in \{0,1\}^* \ \& \ w_i = w_{2m-i+1}\}.$$

Using information theoretic arguments they showed that $\mathcal{L}_m$ cannot be recognized by any k-head automaton if $m > \frac{1}{2}k(k-1)$ (it is easy to see that such an automaton exists if $m = \frac{1}{2}k(k-1)$). The basic idea is that there is only one method to check whether $w_i = w_{2m-i+1}$. Namely, we should take two heads and place one of them in front of w_i and the other one in front of w_{2m-i+1} (see figure 2). Then by moving them simultaneously through w_i and w_{2m-i+1} we check whether the corresponding symbols are equal.

After checking that $w_i = w_{2m-i+1}$ ($i \le m$) we cannot repeat the same procedure for a different pair of subwords using the same heads. This is because the first head has already read the subwords $w_1, w_2, \ldots, w_{i-1}$ (and cannot return to them) while the second head has on its right side only the subwords corresponding to $w_{i-1}, w_{i-2}, \ldots, w_1$. However, for languages P_m the presented procedure is not the only way to check the equality of the corresponding subwords, since only their length should be compared. But the length of a block can be stored by a position of a head in some other block and used afterwards in a convenient moment. We show how to store the length of block 1^{a_i} inside block 1^{a_j}, such that $a_j \ge a_i$. We need 3 heads. One of them, say H, reads word 1^{a_i}. Two other heads, say H_1 and H_2, stay inside word 1^{a_j}. Initially the heads stand in front of the subwords 1^{a_i} and

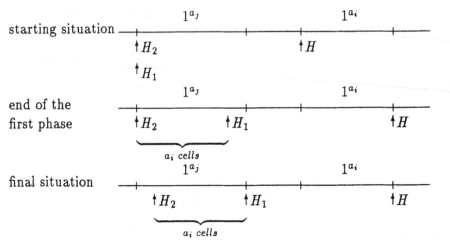

Figure 3: Storing information about the subword 1^{a_i} by head H_2 inside the subword 1^{a_i}.

1^{a_j} (see figure 3). Then H and H_1 move simultaneously through 1^{a_i} and 1^{a_j}. When H reaches the end of 1^{a_i} then H_1 stands at distance a_i from the beginning of the subword 1^{a_j}. From this moment heads H_1 and H_2 move simultaneously (preserving their distance) until H_1 reaches the end of subword 1^{a_j}. At this moment head H_2 stands at the distance a_i from the end of the subword 1^{a_j}. In that sense head H_2 stores the full information about subword 1^{a_i}.

Using this technique we show that the original idea of Rosenberg cannot be used alone to prove his conjecture.

Theorem 1. ([3]) *If we restrict ourselves to the inputs of the form $1^{a_1} *$ ... $* 1^{a_{2m}}$ such that $a_i \leq c \cdot a_j$ for each i and j (c is a fixed constant), then language P_m can be recognized by a k-head 1-MFA, where k is a number satisfying inequality $m \geq \frac{k^3}{24}$.*

Fortunately, we can get an upper bound, however higher than that claimed by Rosenberg.

Theorem 2. ([3]) *If language P_m is recognized by a k-head 1-MFA then $m \leq \frac{1}{2}k^3$.*

To get this and other results we had first to prove some fundamental technical facts. We restrict the inputs to be of the form $x = 1^{a_1} * 1^{a_2} * ... * 1^{a_n}$. The subwords $1^{a_1}, *1^{a_2}, ..., *1^{a_n}$ are called the blocks of x. So x consists of

n different blocks, each containing the symbol 1 repeated some number of times. It will be convenient to identify word $1^{a_1} * 1^{a_2} * ... * 1^{a_n}$ with the point $(a_1, a_2, ..., a_n) \in \mathbf{N}^n \subseteq \mathbf{Q}^n$. The whole computation on x can be divided into stages, a stage terminates when the symbol read by some head changes from 1 to $*$ (or to a blank if it is the end of the input word).

Theorem 3. ([3],[4]) *Suppose M is a 1-MFA with heads $H_1, ..., H_k$. There is a constant g having the following properties. Let $r_1, ..., r_n \in \mathbf{N}$, $r_1, ..., r_n < g$. Put $I = I(r_1, ..., r_n) = \{1^{a_1} * 1^{a_2} * ... * 1^{a_n} : \forall j \leq n \ a_j = r_j \bmod g\}$. Let $t \in \mathbf{N}$. With the beginning of stage t we can associate sets $A_1, ..., A_s \subseteq I$ such that:*

- *$A_1, ..., A_s$ are disjoint and $\bigcup A_j = I$,*

- *each A_j is defined by some number of linear equations and inequalities (with the variables standing for the lengths of the blocks of the inputs),*

- *with each A_j there are associated:*

  - *q_{A_j}, a state of M,*

  - *numbers $b_1, ..., b_k \leq n$,*

  - *linear functions $f_1, ..., f_k$.*

For each input $1^{a_1} * 1^{a_2} * ... * 1^{a_n} \in A_j$ at the beginning of stage t automaton M is in state q_{A_j}, head H_i stays in block b_i at the distance $f_i(a_1, ..., a_n)$ from the end of this block.

In a view of the above theorem during the computation of automaton M each set of inputs $I(r_1, ..., r_n)$ is divided into several sets defined by linear expressions. In that sense the languages recognized by 1-MFA are semi-linear.

Because of the space limitations we cannot present even a sketch of the deeply technical proof of Theorem 2. We only try to give the reader some flavour of it. We consider only inputs $1^{a_1} * 1^{a_2} * ... * 1^{a_n}$ such that $a_i = 0 \bmod g$ for each i. At the end of the last stage the set of inputs is divided into disjoint sets $A_1, ..., A_u$ defined by linear equations and inequalities. Each of them can be regarded as a subset of $\mathbf{Q}^{2m}$. Let $V = \{(a_1, ..., a_{2m}) : \forall i \leq m \ a_i = a_{2m-i+1}\}$. We find a large accepting set A_i. Namely, we find a set A_i such that $V \cap A_i$ is not a subset of any proper layer of V. Then we show that among the equations and inequalities defining A_i there are m linearly independent conditions of the form:

$$\sum_{i \leq m} c_i \cdot a_i - \sum_{i \leq m} c_i \cdot a_{2m-i+1} \quad \mathcal{R} \quad c \tag{1}$$

where $c_1, ..., c_m, c \in \mathbf{Q}$ and $\mathcal{R} \in \{=, <\}$. We call a pair of heads H_1, H_2 "dead" if there is $i \leq 2m$ such that H_1 stands on the right side of the ith block and H_2 stands on the right side of the block $2m - i + 1$ (compare the mentioned general idea used by Rosenberg, Yao and Rivest). During the computation on an input from A_i the automaton makes sure that each of m linearly independent conditions (1) holds. It has its price. We prove that while the automaton verifies k subsequent conditions (1) then at least one pair of heads which was "alive" becomes "dead". So m is not greater than k times the number of different pairs, $m \leq k \cdot \frac{1}{2}k^2 = \frac{1}{2}k^3$ (both elements of a pair are allowed to be the same).

2. Pattern recognition and sorting

Consider the following weak form of the pattern recognition problem: *given a word* $1^{a_1} * 1^{a_2} * ... * 1^{a_n}$. *Verify whether there are* $i \neq j$ *such that* $a_i = a_j$. Let

$$N_m = \{1^{a_1} * 1^{a_2} * ... * 1^{a_n} : \exists i, j \leq m \ \ i \neq j \ \& \ a_i = a_j\}.$$

Obviously, language N_m can be recognized by a m-head 1-MFA. Let $g(m)$ be the minimal number of heads required to recognize language N_m. We shall try to estimate $g(m)$. But first we notice something about function g. Put $B_m = \{1^{a_1} * 1^{a_2} * ... * 1^{a_n} : a_1, ..., a_m \in \mathbf{N}\}$. We say that a 1-MFA M sorts B_m if for each input $1^{a_1} * 1^{a_2} * ... * 1^{a_n} \in B_m$ automaton M ends its computation in a final state, which determines a permutation σ such that $a_{\sigma(1)} \leq a_{\sigma(2)} \leq ... \leq a_{\sigma(m)}$.

Theorem 4. ([5]) *The minimal number of heads required to sort* B_m *is equal to* $g(m)$.

The proof of this theorem is based on Theorem 3. First we can show that any automaton recognizing N_m can be slightly modified to sort B_m. This is because at the end of the last stage the set of inputs is partitioned into finitely many disjoint sets $A_1, ..., A_s$. If $A_i \subseteq \mathbf{Q}^m \backslash N_m$, i.e. A_i is a "rejecting" set, then A_i does not cross any hyperplane of the form $\{\vec{x} \in \mathbf{Q}^m : x_u = x_v\}$.

Hence for every point from A_i the relative order of the length of the blocks is the same. Showing that an automaton sorting B_m can be modified to recognize N_m is based on a similar, but more technical observation.

One may at first expect that $g(m) = m$. This is not true, since there is a simple algorithm using only $\frac{2}{3}m + 3$ heads.

Fact. ([5]) $g(m) \le \frac{2}{3}m + 3$.

On the other hand we prove that:

Theorem 5. ([5]) $g(m) > \frac{1}{8} \cdot \sqrt[3]{\frac{m}{4}}$.

The proof of Theorem 5 is based on the fact that to check if $x = 1^{a_1} * 1^{a_2} * \dots * 1^{a_n} \in P_m$, it suffices to "sort" a word $\bar{x}$, where word $\bar{x}$ is constructed by replacing each subword 1^{a_i} by $1^{2a_i-1} * 1^{2a_i}$. Indeed, if $a_i < a_j$ then $2a_i < 2a_j - 1$, if $a_i > a_j$ then $2a_j < 2a_i - 1$, but for $a_i = a_j$ we have $2a_i > 2a_j - 1$ and $2a_j > 2a_i - 1$. So if we get the blocks of $\bar{x}$ ordered by relation $\le$, then the relative position of blocks $1^{2a_i}, 1^{2a_j}, 1^{2a_i-1}, 1^{2a_j-1}$ show if $a_i = a_j$. With additional heads we can simulate sorting $\bar{x}$ while working on x. This together with the lower bound for P_m (Theorem 2) gives us the lower bound proposed by Theorem 5.

3. Hierarchy theorem for 2-bounded languages (constructively)

The hierarchy theorem for 1-MFA was one of the most popular problems in this area. First it was shown that 3-head 1-MFA are more powerful than 2-head 1-MFA (Ibarra, Kim [2]), then that $k + 1$-head 1-MFA are more powerful than k-head 1-MFA (Yao, Rivest [8]), but using languages which are not bounded. Finally, Chrobak [1] proved that the hierarchy theorem holds even when we restrict ourselves to 2-bounded languages. He considered languages

$$L_n = \{1^x * 1^{ix} : i, x \in \mathbf{N}, i \le n\}$$

and showed that for each k there is the maximal m such that L_m can be recognized by a k-head 1-MFA. Let $f(k)$ be this maximal number m. It is easy to notice that $L_{f(k)+1}$ can be recognized by a $k + 1$-head 1-MFA, but by the definition, it is impossible with only k heads. Hence the hierarchy theorem follows. The weak point of the proof from [1] is that it does not say anything about function f and in this sense the proof is not constructive.

Function f has values bigger than one may expect, for instance $f(3) \geq 17$ (communicated by B.Monien [1], we prove that $f(3) = 17$). This indicates that for certain tasks 1-MFA show much computational power. We present inductive formulas, which can be used to compute values of function f:

Theorem 6. ([4]) $f(k) = E(k,0)$ *where function* E *is defined as follows:*

$$E(0,q) = D(0,q),$$
$$E(p,q) = q + q \cdot D(p,q-1) + E(p-1,q+1),$$

where in turn function D *is defined by the expressions:*

$$D(0,0) = 0,$$
$$D(p,q) = (p+q-1) + p \cdot D(p-1,q+1) + q \cdot D(p,q-1).$$

The above rather complicated formulas can be approximated as follows:

Theorem 7. ([4]) $\dfrac{(2k-5)! \cdot (k-2) \cdot (k-1)}{2^{k-3}} \leq f(k) \leq \dfrac{(2k-5)! \cdot (k-2) \cdot (k-1) \cdot 3k^2}{2^{k-3}}$ *for* $k \geq 3$.

So by Theorem 6 we get: $f(3) = 17$, $f(4) = 209$, $f(5) = 4679$, ... Theorem 7 confirms that function f grows very rapidly. Hence using a small number of heads we can recognize languages L_n for very large n.

Now we would like to outline the proof of Theorem 6. A complete but rather very long and technical proof can be found in [4]. Let M be a 1-MFA recognizing L_n. From now on we consider only 2-bounded inputs. By Theorem 3 at the beginning of each stage of computation the inputs can be divided into finitely many sets. For inputs from one of such sets the heads stay in the same blocks and the distances to the ends of these blocks are described by the same linear functions. The set of inputs plus the functions describing the positions of the heads are forming a *configuration* of M. Such a configuration is called a (p,q)-configuration if p heads stand in the first and q heads stand in the second block. Let C be a configuration and A be the set of inputs leading to this configuration. We define

$$Proj(A) = \{c \in \mathbf{Q} : \exists^{\infty} x \ (x, cx) \in \mathbf{N} \cap A\}$$

(see figure 4). If C is an accepting configuration, then $Proj(A) \subseteq \{1, 2, ..., n\}$. If C is the initial configuration then $Proj(A) = \mathbf{Q}_+$. It can be proved that $Proj(A)$ is an interval (A is a set of grid points of a convex

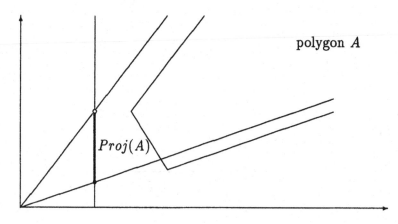

Figure 4: An example of set $Proj(A)$.

polygon), so if C is an accepting configuration, then $Proj(A)$ must contain at most a single point.

One can prove that if C is a (p, q)-configuration then the set $Proj(A) \cap \{1, 2, ..., n\}$ contains at most $D(p, q)$ elements. The proof is by induction on $2p + q$ and leads to the formula defining function D. On the other hand, if a (p, q)-configuration satisfies some condition ("stability") then there is an automaton starting in this configuration which accepts only words of the form $1^x * 1^{ix}$ for $i \in \{i_1, i_2, ..., i_{D(p,q)}\}$ (the numbers $i_1, i_2, ..., i_{D(p,q)}$ are arbitrarily chosen). The construction of such an automaton is based on the "divide and conquer" method. Since the initial configuration of the heads is not "stable", so we had to introduce function E which handles the situation until the configuration becomes "stable".

4. Sensitivity

In the definition of 1-MFA we have assumed that the heads do not see each other. Sometimes so called sensing automata are defined, which can detect coincidence of the heads. Already on one-symbol languages the difference between sensing and non-sensing 1-MFA is apparent. Sensing 1-MFA can recognize many not regular one-symbol languages, while non-sensing 1-MFA on one-symbol languages are limited to only regular languages. Surprisingly, the situation is similar for 2-bounded languages, despite the fact that the class of 2-bounded languages recognized by (non-sensing) 1-MFA is much richer than the class of 2-bounded regular languages.

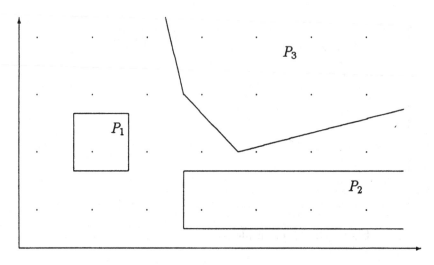

Figure 5: An example of the structure of the set $L(r_1, r_2)$.

Theorem 8. ([6]) *Each 2-bounded language which can be recognized by a non-sensing 1-MFA (with arbitrarily many heads) can be recognized by a sensing 4-head 1-MFA.*

The above theorem shows that sensitivity can provide enough computational power to override the lack of more than 4 heads. It is possible to generalize Theorem 8 for non-sensing one-way deterministic pushdown automata, since the stack adds not much power for bounded languages (see Chrobak [1]).

We simplify the characterization of 2-bounded languages recognized by 1-MFA (non-sensing) given by Chrobak [1]. For such a language L we prove that there is a constant g with the following properties. If $r_1, r_2 < g, r_1, r_2 \in$ **N** then the set $L(r_1, r_2) = L \cap \{1^{x_1} * 1^{x_2} : x_1 = r_1 \bmod g, x_2 = r_2 \bmod g\}$ can be regarded as a set of some grid points in $\mathbf{Q}^2$. We prove that

$$L(r_1, r_2) = \{(x_1, x_2) : x_1 = r_1 \bmod g, \ x_2 = r_2 \bmod g\} \cap \bigcup_{i \in F} P_i$$

where each P_i is a convex polygon (not necessarily bounded) and F is a finite set (see figure 5). For the inputs with both coordinates large enough the situation looks like on the figure 6.

The 4-head sensing 1-MFA M recognizing language L works as follows. One head computes to which of the sets $L(s_1, s_2)$ the current input belongs. Simultaneously, it can give the answer, if the input belongs to the "area of

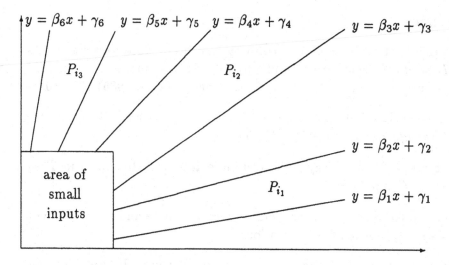

Figure 6: The polygons defining set $L(r_1, r_2)$ for inputs of large coordinates.

small inputs". If not then using the remaining 3 heads automaton M checks subsequently the inequalities:

$$y \geq \beta_1 x + \gamma_1, \ y \geq \beta_2 x + \gamma_2, \ y \geq \beta_3 x + \gamma_3, \ ...$$

(compare figure 6). In this process M uses the sensitivity of the heads and some techniques developed to prove Theorem 6. Thanks to this, the checking is possible without leaving the input word.

5. Final Remarks

While relatively many results about non-sensing 1-MFA have been proved, our knowledge on the sensing 1-MFA is still unsatisfactory. For instance it seems that the hierarchy theorem holds for sensing 1-MFA already for one-symbol languages, but there is still no proof for that. While considering non-sensing automata, the case of not bounded languages still deserves much attention. Technical tools developed for bounded languages can serve as some hint, but the complicated proofs for bounded languages indicate how complex this problem might be.

References

[1] Chrobak M., Hierarchies of one-way multihead automata languages, *Theoretical Comp. Sci.* 48 (1986) 153-181, also in *Proc. ICALP'85, Lecture Notes in Comp. Sci.* 194 (Springer, Berlin, 1985) 101-110.

[2] Ibarra O.H. and Kim C.E., On 3-head versus 2-head finite automata, *Acta Informatica* 4 (1975) 173-200.

[3] Kutyłowski M., One-way multihead finite automata, to appear in *Theoretical Comp. Sci.* .

[4] Kutyłowski M., One-way multihead finite automata and 2-bounded languages, submitted for publication.

[5] Kutyłowski M., Remarks on sorting and one-way multihead finite automata, to appear in *Mathematical Systems Science.*

[6] Kutyłowski M., Stack versus sensitivity for one-way automata, submitted for publication.

[7] Rosenberg A.L., On multihead finite automata, *IBM J. Res. Develop.* 10 (1966) 388-394.

[8] Yao A.C. and Rivest R.L., $K+1$ heads are better than K, *J. ACM* 25 (1978) 337-340.

Updating Almost Complete Trees

or

One Level Makes All the Difference

Tony W. Lai   Derick Wood

Data Structuring Group
Department of Computer Science
University of Waterloo
Waterloo, Ontario N2L 3G1
CANADA

Abstract

An almost complete (or 2-complete) tree is a binary search tree in which any two external nodes are no more than two levels apart. While complete binary search trees have an amortized update cost of $\Theta(n)$, we demonstrate that almost complete binary search trees have an amortized update cost of $O(\log^2 n)$. Thus, they are an attractive alternative for those situations that require fast retrieval, that is, $\log n + O(1)$ comparisons, and have few updates.

1   Introduction

Many kinds of binary search trees have been devised to guarantee that the worst-case search and update cost is $O(\log n)$; for example, red-black trees [5], height-balanced trees [1], and weight-balanced trees [7]. However, none of these data structures ensure that the worst-case search cost is $\log n + O(1)$. If searches are performed much more frequently than updates, it may be advantageous to employ a slower updating algorithm that ensures the search cost is $\log n + O(1)$.

Gerasch [4] devised an insertion algorithm for minimum internal path length binary search trees, or *1-complete trees*. The use of 1-complete trees ensures that searches require $\lceil \log(n+1) \rceil$ comparisons in the worst-case, but the worst-case and amortized cost of his insertion algorithm is $\Theta(n)$. A deletion algorithm analogous to Gerasch's algorithm for 1-complete trees can be devised, but the amortized cost of updating a 1-complete tree is still $\Theta(n)$.

We consider updating algorithms for binary search trees in which any two external nodes are no more that two levels apart; we refer to these trees as *2-complete*. Such trees have two advantages: their worst-case search cost is $1 + \lceil \log(n+1) \rceil$, and their amortized update cost is $O(\log^2 n)$. Hence one level does, indeed, make all the difference.

The scheme we propose is a type of dynamization [11]. In particular, it is a partial rebuilding scheme in the terminology of Overmars [8]: we have a balance criterion and we reconstruct subtrees that become unbalanced with respect to our criterion. Other partial rebuilding schemes have been devised by Overmars and van Leeuwen [9] using a weight balance criterion, and by Andersson [2] using a height balance criterion. However, both schemes ensure only that the height of a tree is $O(\log n)$ rather than $1 + \lceil \log(n+1) \rceil$.

We propose a simple, novel technique for updating 2-complete trees called *k-layering*. One interesting aspect of this scheme is that it requires no additional balance information and that it needs to compute only subtree sizes. We also discuss a variant of k-layering called *level-layering*.

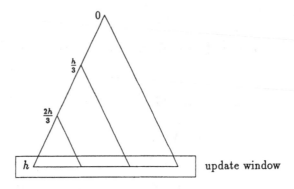

Figure 1: A schematic diagram of 3-layering.

2 Definitions and notation

We define the *depth* of a node x of a tree to be the number of edges in the root-to-x path; the depth of the root is 0. The *nodes on level l* of a tree are the set of nodes of depth l in the tree. The *height*, $h(T)$, of a tree T is the number of internal nodes in the longest root-to-leaf path in the tree, so that a tree of one external node has height 0.

A tree T is *perfectly balanced* if for each node p in T, the number of nodes in p's left and right subtrees differ by at most one. We use $|T|$ to denote the number of nodes in T and use $n(T, r)$ to denote the number of descendents of a node r in a tree T, including r itself.

3 2-complete trees and k-layering

3.1 An example: the 3-layering scheme

We propose a class of schemes for updating 2-complete trees called *k-layering* schemes. In the k-layering scheme, where k is some positive integer, we allow subtree reconstructions on only k distinct levels of the tree. As an example of k-layering, we discuss the 3-layering scheme.

To maintain a 2-complete tree, we maintain a two-level *update window* at the bottom of the tree and ensure that the tree is complete if the nodes in the window are excluded. Hence we guarantee that the tree is 2-complete by ensuring that all insertions and deletions take place inside the update window. Note that we assume that only leaves are deleted; to delete an internal node x, we find the successor or predecessor y of x, move y's contents into x, and delete y instead.

In the 3-layering scheme, we allow subtrees to be reconstructed only if they are rooted on levels 0, $h/3$, or $2h/3$, where h is the height of the tree. A schematic diagram is shown in Figure 1. Observe that a subtree rooted on level 0 is of size n, a subtree rooted on level $h/3$ is of size approximately $n^{2/3}$, and a subtree rooted on level $2h/3$ is of size approximately $n^{1/3}$.

We claim that updates in the 3-layering scheme have an amortized cost of $O(n^{1/3})$, assuming that we have an $O(n)$ worst-case time perfect rebalancing algorithm. To show this, we consider the amortized cost of reconstructions at levels $2h/3$, $h/3$, and 0. To simplify the analysis, we assume that the update window is positioned on levels $h-1$ and h, and that only insertions are performed.

To compute the amortized cost, we first count the minimum number, $m(T)$, of insertions we can perform in a subtree T before being forced to reconstruct a proper supertree of T. Observe that $m(T)$ is approximately the number of nodes of T that can lie in the update window. Because the update window is two-leveled, it contains some subset of the leaves of T and their parents, which implies that the number of nodes of T that can lie in the update window is $\Theta(|T|)$. Therefore, $m(T) = \Omega(|T|)$.

The amortized cost of reconstructing a subtree rooted on level $2h/3$ is $O(n^{1/3})$, since the size of the subtree is $O(n^{1/3})$, and we may have to perform a reconstruction after each update. The cost of reconstructing a subtree rooted on level $h/3$ is $O(n^{2/3})$, but this is necessary only when we cannot update a subtree rooted on level $2h/3$. Since a subtree on level $2h/3$ allows $\approx n^{1/3}$ insertions before it is too large or $\approx n^{1/3}$ deletions before it is too small, $\Omega(n^{1/3})$ updates must have occurred previously, so the amortized cost is again $O(n^{1/3})$. Finally, the cost of reconstructing a subtree rooted on level 0 is $O(n)$, but this is required only when we cannot update a subtree T rooted on level $h/3$. $\Omega(|T|) = \Omega(n^{2/3})$ updates must have occurred previously, which implies that the amortized cost of reconstructing the entire tree is $O(n^{1/3})$.

An update simultaneously affects subtrees rooted on levels $2h/3$, $h/3$, and 0, which implies that the total amortized cost is the sum of amortized costs at each level, which is $O(n^{1/3}) + O(n^{1/3}) + O(n^{1/3}) = O(n^{1/3})$. In general, for any positive integer k, the amortized cost of the k-layering scheme can be shown to be $O(kn^{1/k}) = O(n^{1/k})$.

From the above analysis, it appears that the cost of the k-layering scheme is $O(kn^{1/k})$, so that we have an amortized cost of $O(\log n)$ if we set $k = O(\log n)$. However, our time bound is actually a factor of k too low. The problem is that if we reconstruct a proper supertree of some subtree T only when forced to, then there are pathological update sequences of very high cost. To avoid this difficulty, we introduce a balance criterion to ensure that $\Omega(|T|/k)$ updates have occurred since the last time a proper supertree of T was reconstructed. In the next section, we discuss the k-layering scheme more formally to obtain an exact analysis.

3.2 The general scheme

In the previous section, we neglected the problem of choosing the location of the update window. For a binary tree of height h, we choose the levels of the window as follows. If level $h - 1$, that is, the lowest level, contains no less than $2^{h-1} - 1 + \frac{2}{9}(2^{h-1} + 2^h)$ nodes, then we position the window at levels $h - 1$ and h; otherwise, we position it at levels $h - 2$ and $h - 1$. Suppose that we have placed the window at levels l and $l + 1$. This way, we ensure that the number of nodes in the window is in the interval $[2^l - 1 + \lceil \frac{2}{9}(2^{l+2} - 2^l) \rceil, 2^{l+2} - 1 - \lceil \frac{2}{9}(2^{l+2} - 2^l) \rceil]$.

In the k-layering scheme, where k is some positive integer constant, we choose constants $\rho_1 = 0 < \rho_2 < \cdots < \rho_k = 2/9$ and functions $L_1, \ldots, L_k$ of positive integers such that $l > L_1(l) > L_2(l) > \cdots > L_k(l) = 0$. Note that we require $l \geq k$. The functions $L_1, L_2, \ldots, L_k$ determine the levels at which we may reconstruct subtrees, and the constant ρ_i determines the balance criterion applied to subtrees at level L_i, for $i = 1, 2, \ldots, k$.

We define the *update window density* $\rho(T, r', l)$ of a subtree T' of T rooted at node r' to be the proportion of T''s nodes in the update window to the maximum possible number of nodes; actually, if r' is on level l', then we define

$$\rho(T, r', l) = \frac{n(T, r') - (2^{l-l'} - 1)}{2^{l+2-l'} - 1 - (2^{l-l'} - 1)}.$$

Observe that we allow $\rho(T, r', l) < 0$ and $\rho(T, r', l) > 1$.

Our imbalance criterion is: for any subtree T' rooted on level $L_i(l)$, the update window density of T' is restricted to the interval $[\rho_i, 1 - \rho_i]$, for $i = 1, 2, \ldots, k$. This interval is smaller for subtrees rooted at higher levels, so that costly reconstruction high in the tree ensures that subsequent updates are inexpensive. More precisely, we reconstruct a subtree if it satisfies the following imbalance criterion.

1. Any update imbalances the subtree rooted at level $L_1(l)$ in which the update takes place.

2. A subtree rooted at node r on level $L_i(l)$, where $i > 1$, is imbalanced if there exists some imbalanced subtree rooted at a descendant r_{i-1} of r on level $L_{i-1}(l)$ such that $n(T, r_{i-1}) \notin [2^{l-L_{i-1}(l)} - 1 + \rho_{i-1} \cdot (2^{l-L_{i-1}(l)+2} - 2^{l-L_{i-1}(l)}), 2^{l-L_{i-1}(l)+2} - 1 - \rho_{i-1} \cdot (2^{l-L_{i-1}(l)+2} - 2^{l-L_{i-1}(l)})]$.

This imbalance criterion yields straightforward insertion and deletion algorithms. As an example, suppose we want to insert some key x into T. We first insert x naively. Let r_i be the ancestor of depth L_i of x. We determine the highest node r_i such that $\rho(T, r_i, l) \leq 1 - \rho_i$ and for all $j > i$, $\rho(T, r_j, l) > 1 - \rho_j$, and then reconstruct the subtree rooted at r_i. If we reconstruct the entire tree, then we reposition the update window.

The insertion and deletion algorithms are as follows. Recall that we assume that only leaves are deleted, since the deletion of an internal node can be transformed into a deletion of leaf. For brevity, in the following we refer to $L_i(l)$ as L_i, for $i = 1, 2, \ldots, k$.

insert(T, x)
 $i \leftarrow 1$
 insert x
 $r \leftarrow$ ancestor of x on level L_i in T
 while $i < k$ and $n(T, r) > 2^{l-L_i+2} - 1 - \rho_i \cdot (2^{l-L_i+2} - 2^{l-L_i})$
  $i \leftarrow i + 1$
  $r \leftarrow$ ancestor of r on level L_i
 end
 reconstruct subtree of T rooted at r
 if $i = k$, then reposition update window
end insert

delete(T, x)
 $i \leftarrow 1$
 $r \leftarrow$ ancestor of x on level L_i in T
 delete x
 while $i < k$ and $n(T, r) < 2^{l-L_i} - 1 + \rho_i \cdot (2^{l-L_i+2} - 2^{l-L_i})$
  $i \leftarrow i + 1$
  $r \leftarrow$ ancestor of r on level L_i
 end
 reconstruct subtree of T rooted at r
 if $i = k$, then reposition update window
end delete

To reconstruct a tree T, we use a perfect rebalancing algorithm, such as Stout and Warren's algorithm [10]. In the next two sections, we prove that the amortized update cost is $O(k^2 n^{1/k})$ in the k-layering scheme, for any positive integer k, if we choose $L_i = \lfloor (1 - i/k)l \rfloor$ and $\rho_i = \frac{2(i-1)}{9(k-1)}$, for $i = 1, 2, \ldots, k$; and the amortized update cost is $O(\log^2 n)$ in the l-layering scheme if we choose $L_i = l - i$ and $\rho_i = \frac{2(i-1)}{9(l-1)}$, for $i = 1, 2, \ldots, l$.

Observe that with the above choice of ρ_i and L_i, only the parameters k and l need be kept in the k-layering scheme, since ρ_i and L_i can be computed from i, k, and l in constant time. Similarly, only l need be kept in the l-layering scheme.

4 Analysis

Below we give an outline of the analysis; details are given in the full paper [6].

Theorem 4.1 *The amortized update cost of the k-layering scheme, for constant k, is $O(k^2 n^{1/k})$, for an appropriate choice of $\rho_1, \rho_2, \ldots, \rho_k, L_1, L_2, \ldots, L_k$.*

Proof: Suppose that we have a reconstruction algorithm that requires cn time in the worst case. We choose $\rho_i = \frac{2}{9} \cdot \frac{i-1}{k-1}$ and $L_i = \lfloor \frac{k-i}{k} \cdot l \rfloor$, for $i = 1, 2, \ldots, k$. Let A be the amortized update cost.

To perform an amortized analysis we first state a bound on the number of updates that must have occurred since the last reconstruction of a layered subtree.

Lemma 4.2 *If a subtree T_i of T rooted at node r_i at level L_i is reconstructed, where $i > 1$, then at least $(\rho_i - \rho_{i-1})(2^{l-L_{i-1}+2} - 2^{l-L_{i-1}}) - 1$ updates must have occurred since the last time a supertree of T_i was reconstructed.*

Observe that $\rho_i - \rho_{i-1} = \frac{2}{9(k-1)}$ and $|T_{i-1}| \leq 2^{l-L_{i-1}+2} - 1$, which implies the following.

Corollary 4.3 *If a subtree T_i of T rooted on level L_i is reconstructed, where $i > 1$, then $\Omega(|T_{i-1}|/k)$ updates must have occurred in some subtree T_{i-1} of T_i rooted on level L_{i-1} since the last time a supertree of T_i was reconstructed.*

The above lemma implies that the amortized update cost is

$$A < c \cdot 2^{l-L_1+2} + \sum_{i=2}^{k} \frac{c \cdot 2^{l-L_i+2}}{(\rho_{i-1} - \rho_i)(2^{l-L_{i-1}+2} - 2^{l-L_{i-1}}) - 1}$$

$$= c \cdot 2^{l-L_1+2} + \sum_{i=2}^{k} \frac{4c \cdot 2^{L_{i-1}-L_i}}{(\rho_{i-1} - \rho_i)(4-1) - 2^{L_{i-1}-l}}$$

$$= O\left(2^{l/k} + \sum_{i=2}^{k} \frac{2^{l/k}}{\frac{2}{3} \cdot \frac{1}{k-1} - 2^{-(i-1)l/k}} \right).$$

For sufficiently large l, we know that $2^{-(i-1)l/k} \ll \frac{2}{3} \cdot \frac{1}{k-1}$. Thus,

$$A = O\left(2^{l/k} + \sum_{i=2}^{k} (k-1) \cdot 2^{l/k} \right).$$

Since $l \leq \log n$,

$$A = O(n^{1/k} + (k-1)^2 n^{1/k}) = O(k(k-1)n^{1/k}) = O(k^2 n^{1/k}).$$

Observe that the amortized update cost increases by at most a constant factor if we determine $n(T, r)$ in time proportional to $n(T, r)$. $\quad\square$

This scheme is attractive because of its simplicity — it is simpler than Gerasch's scheme, yet it performs better. However, it still has super-polylogarithmic behavior. In the next section, we give a simple modification that achieves polylogarithmic behavior.

5 Level-layering

The update cost of our layering scheme can be greatly improved if we use all levels as layers; we refer to this as *l-layering* or *level-layering*. We choose the number of layers to be the number of levels l and, for $i = 1, 2, \ldots, l$, we choose $\rho_i = \frac{2}{9} \cdot \frac{i-1}{l-1}$ and $L_i = l - i$.

Theorem 5.1 *The amortized update cost of the level-layering scheme is $O(\log^2 n)$.*

Proof: Let A be the amortized update cost. To perform an amortized analysis, we claim that for all $i > \lceil \log l \rceil + 3$, at least two updates must occur between reconstructions of any subtree rooted at level L_i. That is, for all $i > \lceil \log l \rceil + 3$,

$$(\rho_i - \rho_{i-1})(2^{l-L_{i-1}+2} - 2^{l-L_{i-1}}) - 1 \geq 2.$$

This implies that for all $i > \lceil \log l \rceil + 3$,

$$(\rho_i - \rho_{i-1})(2^{l-L_{i-1}+2} - 2^{l-L_{i-1}}) - 1 \geq \frac{2}{3}(\rho_i - \rho_{i-1})(2^{l-L_{i-1}+2} - 2^{l-L_{i-1}}).$$

We note that any subtree rooted at level L_i can be reconstructed at most once per update, for $i \leq \lceil \log l \rceil + 3$.

Let $\mathcal{L} = \lceil \log l \rceil + 3$. Recall that $l \leq \log n$; hence:

$$
\begin{aligned}
A &< c \sum_{i=1}^{\mathcal{L}} 2^{l-L_i+2} + \sum_{i=\mathcal{L}+1}^{l} \frac{c \cdot 2^{l-L_i+2}}{(\rho_i - \rho_{i-1})(2^{l-L_{i-1}+2} - 2^{l-L_{i-1}}) - 1} \\
&\leq c \cdot 2^{l-L_{\mathcal{L}}+3} + \sum_{i=\mathcal{L}+1}^{l} \frac{c \cdot 2^{l-L_i+2}}{3(\rho_i - \rho_{i-1}) \cdot 2^{l-L_{i-1}} \cdot 2/3} \\
&\leq c \cdot 2^{l-L_{\mathcal{L}}+3} + \sum_{i=\mathcal{L}+1}^{l} \frac{2c \cdot 2^{L_{i-1}-L_i}}{\rho_i - \rho_{i-1}} \\
&= c \cdot 2^{l-(l-\lceil \log l \rceil - 3)+3} + \sum_{i=\mathcal{L}+1}^{l} \frac{2c \cdot 2}{2/9 \cdot \frac{1}{l-1}} \\
&< 128 c \log n + \sum_{i=\mathcal{L}+1}^{l} 18 c \log n \\
&= 128 c \log n + (l - \lceil \log l \rceil - 3) \cdot 18 c \log n \\
&= O(\log^2 n).
\end{aligned}
$$

$\square$

Therefore, the use of the $O(\log n)$-layering scheme leads to an amortized update cost of $O(\log^2 n)$ for 2-complete trees.

6 Concluding remarks

We have presented an algorithm to update 2-complete trees with an amortized cost of $O(\log^2 n)$, which leads to the question of whether binary search trees with a constant number of incomplete levels can be updated in $O(\log n)$ amortized time. Recently, Andersson and Lai [3] have answered this question affirmatively. By exploiting the $O(\log^2 n)$ amortized update cost of 2-complete trees, they achieve an amortized cost of $O(\log n)$ for updating 4-complete trees.

Acknowledgements

The work of the first author was supported under an NSERC Postgraduate Scholarship and that of the second under a Natural Sciences and Engineering Research Council of Canada Grant No. A-5692 and under an Information Technology Research Centre Grant.

References

[1] G. M. Adel'son-Vel'skii and E. M. Landis. An algorithm for the organization of information. *Sov. Math. Dokl.*, 3:1259–1262, 1962.

[2] A. Andersson. Improving partial rebuilding by using simple balance criteria. In *Proceedings of the 1989 Workshop on Algorithms and Data Structures*, pages 393–402. Springer-Verlag, 1989.

[3] A. Andersson and T. W. Lai. Efficient maintenance of almost perfectly balanced trees. In preparation.

[4] T. E. Gerasch. An insertion algorithm for a minimal internal path length binary search tree. *Communications of the ACM*, 31:579–585, 1988.

[5] L. J. Guibas and R. Sedgewick. A dichromatic framework for balanced trees. In *Proceedings of the 19th Annual IEEE Symposium on Foundations of Computer Science*, pages 8–21, 1978.

[6] T. W. Lai and D. Wood. Updating approximately complete trees. Technical Report CS-89-57, Univ. of Waterloo, 1989.

[7] J. Nievergelt and E. M. Reingold. Binary search trees of bounded balance. *SIAM Journal on Computing*, 2:33–43, 1973.

[8] M. H. Overmars. *The Design of Dynamic Data Structures*, volume 156 of *Lecture Notes in Computer Science*. Springer-Verlag, 1983.

[9] M. H. Overmars and J. van Leeuwen. Dynamic multi-dimensional data structures based on quad- and k-d trees. *Acta Informatica*, 17:267–285, 1982.

[10] Q. F. Stout and B. L. Warren. Tree rebalancing in optimal time and space. *Communications of the ACM*, 29:902–908, 1986.

[11] J. van Leeuwen and D. Wood. Dynamization of decomposable searching problems. *Information Processing Letters*, 10:51–56, 1980.

SORTING THE SUMS $(x_i + y_j)$ IN $O(n^2)$ COMPARISONS

Jean-Luc LAMBERT

Université de Paris-Nord
Avenue Jean-Baptiste Clément
93 430   Villetaneuse FRANCE

Université de Paris-Sud
Laboratoire de recherche en informatique
CNRS UA 410
91405 Orsay France

ABSTRACT Let $(x_i)_{1 \leq i \leq n}$ and $(y_j)_{1 \leq i \leq n}$ be two sequences of numbers. It was proved by M.L. Fredman in [1] that the n^2 sums $(x_i + y_j)_{1 \leq i, j \leq n}$ can be sorted in $O(n^2)$ comparisons, but until now, no explicit algorithm was known to do it. We present such an algorithm and generalize it to sort $(x_{i_1}^1 + ... + x_{i_k}^k)_{1 \leq i_1, ... i_k \leq n}$ in $O(n^k)$ comparisons.

Let $(x_i)_{1 \leq i \leq n}$ and $(y_j)_{1 \leq i \leq n}$ be two sequences of numbers. The problem of sorting the n^2 sums $(x_i + y_j)_{1 \leq i, j \leq n}$ in the smallest number of comparisons was posed by E. Berlekamp and first studied by Harper, Payne, Savage and Straus in [2] who proved that $n^2 \log_2(n)$ comparisons are sufficient and even necessary if we just sort $(x_i)_{1 \leq i \leq n}$ then $(y_j)_{1 \leq j \leq n}$ and use only the fact that $x_i \leq x_i', y_j \leq y_j' \Rightarrow x_i + y_j \leq x_i' + y_j'$.

In [1] M. Fredman proved a result that seems to contradict the previous one: there exists a decision tree for this problem whose depth is $O(n^2)$. This implies that $(x_i + y_j)_{1 \leq i, j \leq n}$ can be sorted in $O(n^2)$ comparisons. But his result is non-constructive and until now no explicit algorithm was known to generate the comparisons sequence corresponding to such decision tree.

We present such an algorithm. More precisely we exhibit an algorithm which given $2n$ numbers $(x_i)_{1 \leq i \leq n}$ and $(y_j)_{1 \leq j \leq n}$ sorts $(x_i + y_j)_{1 \leq i, j \leq n}$ in $O(n^2)$ <u>comparisons</u>. Unfortunately, the additional complexity due to the replacement of comparisons by other calculations makes this algorithm not efficient in practice.

The first section of this article is devoted to sorting sums of the form $\sum_{k=i}^{j} a_k$ where the a_i are n given numbers. This is our fundamental algorithm and further ones are deduced from it. It is at the end of this first section that we present an adaptation of this algorithm which sorts $(x_i + y_j)_{1 \leq i, j \leq n}$ in $O(n^2)$ comparisons. In the second section we generalize the algorithm to sort $(x_{i_1}^1 + ... + x_{i_k}^k)_{1 \leq i_1, ... i_k \leq n}$ in $O(n^k)$ comparisons.

1 Sorting sums of consecutive numbers

In this section we are going to describe an algorithm which sorts sums of the form $\sum_{k=i}^{j} a_k$ in $O(n^2)$ comparisons. Before entering the details we briefly explain the reason why we are interested in this problem.

We remark that $x_i + y_j \leq x_k + y_l$ is equivalent to $x_i - x_k \leq y_l - y_j$. Suppose that we have an algorithm which sorts $(x_i - x_k)_{1 \leq i \leq k \leq n}$ in $O(n^2)$ comparisons, then it is clear that by merging the sorted lists $(x_i - x_k)_{1 \leq i \leq k \leq n}$, $(x_i - x_k)_{1 \leq k \leq i \leq n}$, $(y_l - y_j)_{1 \leq l \leq j \leq n}$, $(y_l - y_j)_{1 \leq j \leq l \leq n}$ we finally sort $(x_i + y_j)_{1 \leq i, j \leq n}$ in $O(n^2)$ comparisons. If we define $a_1 = x_1 - x_2, a_2 = x_2 - x_3, ... a_{n-1} = x_{n-1} - x_n$, the set $(x_i - x_k)_{1 \leq i \leq k \leq n}$ is the set of $(\sum_{l=i}^{k-1} a_l)_{1 \leq i \leq k \leq n}$.

In paragraph 1-4-1 we will slightly modify this scheme, but the main idea is the same.

1-1 Some definitions

In this article, [x] denotes the floor of x and $\lceil x \rceil$ the ceiling of x.

We consider n numbers $a_1, \ldots a_n$ and define for $1 \leq i \leq j \leq n$:

$$\sigma(i, j) = \sum_{k=i}^{j} a_k$$

Our goal is to sort the $\frac{n(n+1)}{2}$ sums of consecutive numbers

$$A^+ = \{\sigma(i, j), 1 \leq i \leq j \leq n\}$$

in $O(n^2)$ comparisons.

The algorithm we are going to present may be seen through a particular representation of the set A^+. Namely we structure the set in a pyramid:

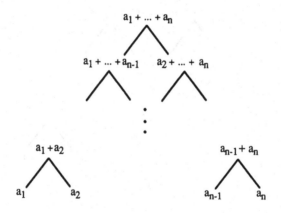

figure 1-1

The root of the pyramid is $a_1 + \ldots + a_n$ and for each vertex $\sigma(i, j) = a_i + \ldots + a_j$, its left son is $\sigma(i, j-1)$, its right son is $\sigma(i+1, j)$.

The algorithm is founded on the remark that if the hachured region of figure 1-2 is sorted then the triangles are sorted.

Now the principle is clear: at each step we sort the triangles, merge them and get a new sorted region of height h + 1. We merge the two regions of heights h and h + 1 and extend the sorted region to the height 2h + 1. And so on until the sorted region has height at least n.

For some technical reasons that will be clear in subsequent sections we will need to add to the initial set A^+ the numbers 0 and $-\sigma(i, j)$ for $1 \leq i \leq j \leq n$. We define

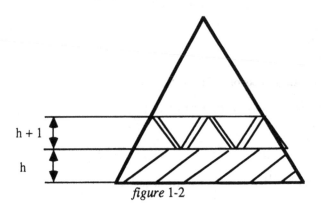

figure 1-2

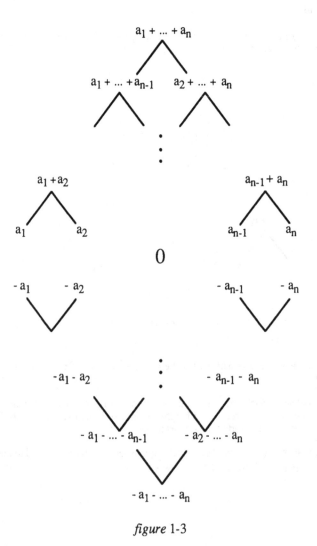

figure 1-3

$$\sigma_0 = 0$$
$$\sigma^-(i, j) = -\sigma(i, j)$$

We also define the length of $\sigma(i, j)$ by

$$\lg(\sigma(i, j)) = \lg(\sigma^-(i, j)) = j - i + 1 \text{ and}$$
$$\lg(\sigma_0) = 0$$

Our algorithm will sort the set $A = \{ \sigma(i\ j), \sigma^-(i, j) \text{ for } 1 \le i \le j \le n\} \cup \{\sigma_0\}$ that can be represented by the double pyramid of figure 1-3.

1-2 Breaking down the pyramid in subsets

For sorting the sums we will divide the pyramid into particular sets which will be easier to sort than the entire set. We first define the notion of a slice.

Definition *For $0 \le h < h'$ we define*

$$SLICE(h, h') = \{ \sigma(i, j), \sigma^-(i, j) / h \le \lg(\sigma(i, j)), \lg(\sigma^-(i, j)) < h'\}$$

This set is delimited by rectangles in figure 1-4

We also define triangles UP and DOWN, namely:

Definition *The triangles UP and DOWN are defined by*

$$DOWN (i, j, h) = \{\sigma(k, l) / i \le k, l \le j \lg(\sigma(k, l)) \ge j - i + 1 - (h - 1)\}$$
$$UP(i, j, h) = \{\sigma(k, l) / k \le i, j \le l, \lg(\sigma(k,l)) \le j - i + 1 + (h - 1)\}$$

By convention those triangles do not contain $\sigma_0 = 0$.

If we draw a figure it is easy to represent those triangles. Both have height h, $\sigma(i, j)$ is the top of DOWN(i, j, h) and the bottom of UP(i, j, h). This is represented in figure 1-5.

It must be noticed that those triangles may eventually not be complete and for DOWN triangles the top can be outside the pyramid (i.e. $j \ge n$ or $i \le 0$). (see figure 1-6)

Similarly we define the same triangles for the $\sigma^-(i, j)$:

Definition

$$DOWN^-(i, j, h) = \{\sigma^-(k, l) / i \le k, l \le j, \lg(\sigma^-(k, l)) \ge j - i + 1 - (h - 1)\}$$
$$UP^-(i, j, h) = \{\sigma^-(k, l) / k \le i, j \le l, \lg(\sigma^-(k, l)) \le j - i + 1 + (h - 1)\}$$

Now we are going to rely the triangles and the slices. It is not difficult to remark that $SLICE(2^h, 2^{h+1})$ can be divided into triangles as illustrated by figure 1-7.

If we look at this decomposition more precisely as done in figure 1-8 , we are leaded to state the following lemma

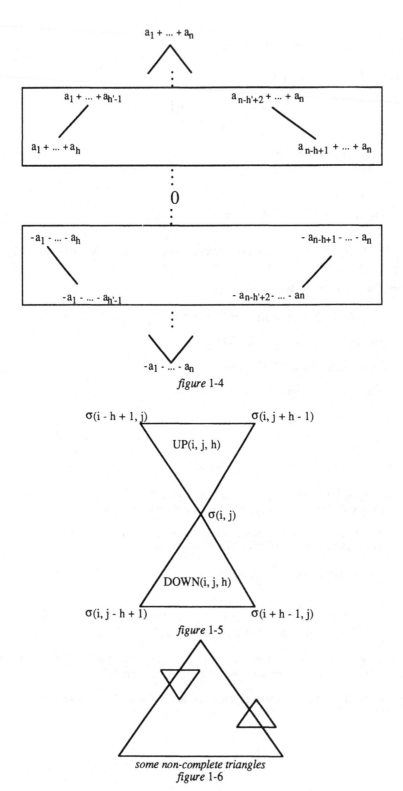

$a_1 + ... + a_n$

$a_1 + ... + a_{h'-1}$

$a_{n-h'+2} + ... + a_n$

$a_1 + ... + a_h$

$a_{n-h+1} + ... + a_n$

0

$-a_1 - ... - a_h$

$-a_{n-h+1} - ... - a_n$

$-a_1 - ... - a_{h'-1}$

$-a_{n-h'+2} - ... - a_n$

$-a_1 - ... - a_n$

figure 1-4

$\sigma(i - h + 1, j)$

$\sigma(i, j + h - 1)$

UP(i, j, h)

$\sigma(i, j)$

DOWN(i, j, h)

$\sigma(i, j - h + 1)$

$\sigma(i + h - 1, j)$

figure 1-5

some non-complete triangles
figure 1-6

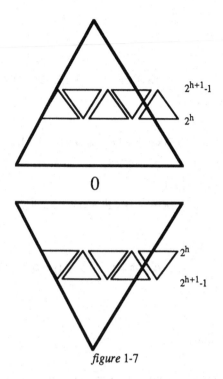

figure 1-7

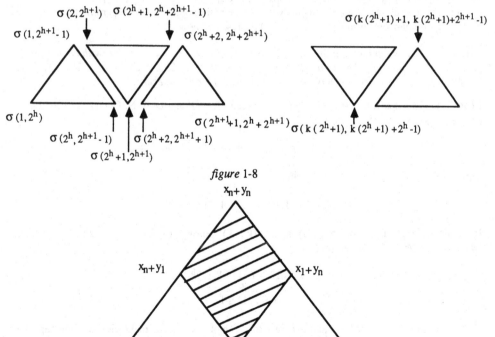

figure 1-8

figure 1-9

Lemma 1-1

$$\text{SLICE } (2^h, 2^{h+1}) = \bigcup_{k=0}^{\left\lceil \frac{n}{2^h+1} \right\rceil - 1} \text{DOWN}(k\,(2^h+1)+1, k\,(2^h+1)+2^{h+1}-1, 2^h)$$

$$\bigcup \quad \bigcup_{k=1}^{\left\lceil \frac{n}{2^h+1} \right\rceil} \text{UP}(k\,(2^h+1), k\,(2^h+1)+2^h-1, 2^h)$$

$$\bigcup \quad \bigcup_{k=0}^{\left\lceil \frac{n}{2^h+1} \right\rceil - 1} \text{DOWN}^-(k\,(2^h+1)+1, k\,(2^h+1)+2^{h+1}-1, 2^h)$$

$$\bigcup \quad \bigcup_{k=1}^{\left\lceil \frac{n}{2^h+1} \right\rceil} \text{UP}^-(k\,(2^h+1), k\,(2^h+1)+2^h-1, 2^h)$$

1-3 Sorting A in $O(n^2)$ comparisons

The idea to sort the all set A in $O(n^2)$ comparisons is at each step to sort SLICE(2^h, 2^{h+1}) then to extend the set of already sorted elements with it. The main argument which permits to reduce the number of comparisons to sort SLICE(2^h, 2^{h+1}) is presented now.

Lemma 1-2 *Let us suppose that* SLICE(0, 2^h) *is already sorted then we can sort with no additional comparison any of the triangles* UP(i, $i + 2^h - 1$, 2^h), UP$^-$(i, $i + 2^h - 1$, 2^h), DOWN(i, $i + 2^{h+1} - 2$, 2^h) *and* DOWN$^-$(i, $i + 2^{h+1} - 2$, 2^h) *for any integer i.*

Proof It is clear that it is sufficient to prove the result for UP and DOWN. One easily gets that if $\sigma(k, l) \in$ UP(i, $i + 2^h - 1$, 2^h) then

$$i - 2^h + 1 \le k \le i \text{ and } i + 2^h - 1 \le l \le i + 2^{h+1} - 2$$

and if $\sigma(k, l) \in$ DOWN(i, $i + 2^{h+1} - 2$, 2^h) then

$$i \le k \le i + 2^h - 1 \text{ and } i + 2^h - 1 \le l \le i + 2^{h+1} - 2$$

In consequence if both $\sigma(k, l)$ and $\sigma(k', l')$ belong to UP(i, $i + 2^h - 1$, 2^h) or DOWN(i, $i + 2^{h+1} - 2$, 2^h), one first has

$$| k - k'| \le 2^h - 1, \ |\, l - l'| \le 2^h - 1$$
$$\text{and}$$
$$k \le l', \, k' \le l$$

Now we suppose $k \ne k'$ or $l \ne l'$ and compare $\sigma(k, l)$ and $\sigma(k', l')$. To make clear we can suppose that $k < k'$ and since $k' \le l$, we get:

$$\sigma(k, l) - \sigma(k', l') = \begin{cases} \sigma(k, k'\text{-}1) - \sigma(l + 1, l') & \text{if } l < l' \\ \sigma(k, k'\text{-}1) - \sigma_0 & \text{if } l = l' \\ \sigma(k, k'\text{-}1) - \sigma^-(l' + 1, l) & \text{if } l > l' \end{cases}$$

But $\mid k - k' \mid \le 2^h - 1$ and $\mid l - l' \mid \le 2^h - 1$ which implies that $\lg(\sigma(k, k'\text{-}1))$, $\lg(\sigma(l + 1, l'))$ and $\lg(\sigma^-(l' + 1, l))$ are less than $2^h - 1$ and are in SLICE$(0, 2^h)$. The result of the comparison between $\sigma(k, l)$ and $\sigma(k', l')$ can be obtained with no comparison if SLICE$(0, 2^h)$ is sorted. $\Diamond$

The consequence of this result is that once SLICE$(0, 2^h)$ is sorted, we can sort SLICE$(2^h, 2^{h+1})$ by decomposing it in triangles according to lemma 1-1, sorting them without comparison and merging them. To compute the complexity of this algorithm we recall the well-known:

Lemma 1-3 *Let L be a list of n elements. Suppose that L is divided in k sorted lists* $L_1,... L_k$. *Then L may be sorted in at most* $n \lceil \log_2(k) \rceil$ *comparisons.*

We now prove our first result

Theorem 1 *Let* $a_1, ..., a_n$ *be n numbers. The set* $A^+ = \{\sigma(i, j) = \sum_{k=i}^{j} a_k, 1 \le i \le j \le n\}$ *may be sorted in* $O(n^2)$ *comparisons.*

Proof We complete A^+ into A by adding $\sigma_0 = 0$ and $\sigma^-(i, j) = - \sigma(i, j)$. The algorithm is the following:

```
h := 0
while 2^h ≤ n do
        SORT(SLICE(2^h, 2^{h+1}))
        MERGE(SLICE(2^h, 2^{h+1}), SLICE(0, 2^h))
        h := h + 1
```

It is clear by recursion that after step h, SLICE$(0, 2^{h+1})$ is sorted. When $2^{h+1} > n$, SLICE$(0, n)$ is sorted and this is just our set A. Thus our algorithm sorts A in $[\log_2(n)] + 1$ iterations.

To evaluate the complexity of this algorithm we notice that there are at most n numbers $\sigma(i, j)$ such that $\lg(\sigma(i, j)) = k$ (resp. $\lg(\sigma^-(i, j)) = k$). Consequently

$$\text{Card(SLICE}(2^h, 2^{h+1})) \le 2n \cdot 2^h$$

Moreover by lemmas 1-1 and 1-2, SLICE$(2^h, 2^{h+1})$ is divided in $4 \lceil \frac{n}{2^{h+1}} \rceil$ sorted lists and by lemma 1-3 it may be sorted in

$$\left\lceil \log_2\left(4 \left\lceil \tfrac{n}{2^{h+1}} \right\rceil\right) \right\rceil \cdot 2n \cdot 2^h$$

comparisons. On the other side, SLICE$(2^h, 2^{h+1})$ and SLICE$(0, 2^h)$ may be merged in

$$2n \cdot 2^h + 2n \cdot 2^h = 4n \cdot 2^h$$

comparisons. Let $K = [\log_2(n)]$. The total number of comparisons is bounded by

$$2n \sum_{h=0}^{K} 2^h \left(\left\lceil \log_2\left(4 \left\lceil \tfrac{n}{2^{h+1}} \right\rceil\right) \right\rceil + 2\right)$$

$$\leq 2n \sum_{h=0}^{K} 2^h \left(\left\lceil \log_2 (4 \cdot 2^{K+1-h}) \right\rceil + 2 \right)$$

$$= 2n \sum_{h=0}^{K} 2^h \left((K + 1 - h) + 4 \right)$$

$$= 2n \left(4 \sum_{h=0}^{K} 2^h + 2^{K+1} \sum_{i=1}^{K+1} \frac{i}{2^i} \right)$$

$$\leq 2n \cdot 2^{K+1} \cdot 6$$

$$\leq 24 \, n^2$$

which is $O(n^2)$.   ◊

1-4 Sorting $(x_i + y_j)_{1 \leq i, \, j \leq n}$ in $O(n^2)$ comparisons

It is easy to adapt the previous algorithm to sort $(x_i + y_j)_{1 \leq i, j \leq n}$ in $O(n^2)$ comparisons. We just consider the $2n - 1$ numbers

$$a_1 = y_n - y_{n-1}, \ldots a_{n-1} = y_2 - y_1, \, a_n = x_1 + y_1, \, a_{n+1} = x_2 - x_1, \ldots a_{2n-1} = x_n - x_{n-1}$$

It is clear that

$$x_i + y_j = \sum_{k=n+1-j}^{n-1+i} a_k = \sigma(n + 1 - j, n - 1 + i)$$

and with the previous algorithm we sort the set $\{\sigma(i, j), 1 \leq i \leq j \leq 2n - 1\}$. In particular the initial sequence $(x_i + y_j)_{1 \leq i, j \leq n}$ will be sorted as a subsequence of the new one. (see figure 1-9)

It is interesting to remark the strange fact that we add new elements to sort the set $(x_i + y_j)_{1 \leq i, j \leq n}$. The reason is that sorting some of those new elements gives some information that avoid sorting most of the initial elements.

2 Sorting $(x_{i_1}^1 + \ldots + x_{i_k}^k)_{1 \leq i_1, \ldots i_k \leq n}$ in $O(n^k)$ comparisons

2-1 Extending the pyramid to a prism

Let $a_1 \ldots a_n$ be n numbers, $b_1 \ldots b_m$ be m additional numbers. We are now interested in sorting the numbers

$$\sigma(i, j, r) = \sum_{l=i}^{j} a_l + b_r$$

for $1 \leq i \leq j \leq n$ and $1 \leq r \leq m$.

Let $B^+ = \{ \sigma(i, j, r), 1 \leq i \leq j \leq n, 1 \leq r \leq m \}$, we extend this set by adding

$$\sigma^-(i, j, r) = \sum_{l=i}^{j} - a_l + b_r$$

$$\sigma_0(r) = b_r$$

this new set is called B. This set can be represented as a double prism which is drawn in figure 2-1.

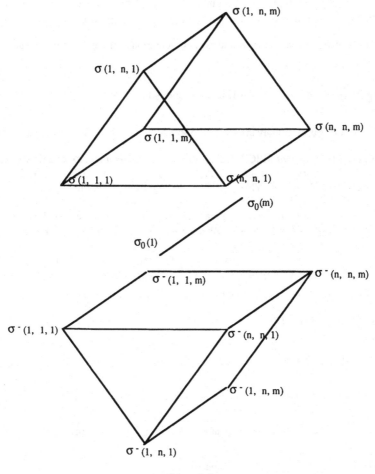

figure 2-1

Now the subsets we defined at section 1-2 can be directly generalised. We first define the length of an element of B.

Definition $\lg(\sigma(i, j, r)) = j - i + 1 = \lg(\sigma^-(i, j, r))$, $\lg(\sigma_0(r)) = 0$

Then the slice

Definition *For* $0 \leq h < h'$ *we define*

$$\text{SLICE}(h, h') = \{ \sigma(i, j), \sigma^-(i, j) / h \leq \lg(\sigma(i, j)), \lg(\sigma^-(i, j)) < h'\}$$

And the triangles UP and DOWN

Definition *The triangles* UP *and* DOWN *are defined by*

$$DOWN\ (i, j, h) = \{\sigma(k, l, r) / 1 \leq r \leq m, i \leq k, l \leq j, \lg(\sigma(k, l, r)) \geq j - i + 1 - (h - 1)\}$$
$$UP(i, j, h) = \{\sigma(k, l, r) / 1 \leq r \leq m, k \leq i, j \leq l, \lg(\sigma(k,l, r)) \leq j - i + 1 + (h - 1)\}$$

and

$$DOWN^-(i, j, h) = \{\sigma^-(k, l, r) / 1 \leq r \leq m, i \leq k, l \leq j, \lg(\sigma^-(k, l, r)) \geq j - i + 1 - (h - 1)\}$$
$$UP^-(i, j, h) = \{\sigma^-(k, l, r) / 1 \leq r \leq m, k \leq i, j \leq l, \lg(\sigma^-(k, l, r)) \leq j - i + 1 + (h - 1)\}$$

Now it is straightforward to check that with these new definitions, lemma 1-1 remains valid.

2-2 Sorting B in $O(Max(n^2, \log(m)).m)$ comparisons

The algorithm to sort B is essentially the same as to sort A. Lemma 1-2 is generalised as follows.

Lemma 2-1 *Let us suppose that SLICE(0, 2^h) is already sorted then we can sort with no additional comparison any of the triangles* UP(i, i + 2^h - 1, 2^h), UP$^-$(i, i + 2^h - 1, 2^h), DOWN(i, i + 2^{h+1} - 2, 2^h) *and* DOWN$^-$(i, i + 2^{h+1} - 2, 2^h) *for any integer i.*

Proof The proof is similar to the one of lemma 1-2 except at one point. Let $\sigma(k, l, r)$ and $\sigma(k', l', r')$ be in the same set UP(i, i + 2^h - 1, 2^h) or DOWN(i, i + 2^{h+1} - 2, 2^h) and suppose k < k', we get:

$$\sigma(k, l, r) - \sigma(k', l', r') = \begin{cases} \sigma(k, k'-1, r) - \sigma(l + 1, l', r') \text{ if } l < l' \\ \sigma(k, k'-1, r) - \sigma_0(r') \text{ if } l = l' \\ \sigma(k, k'-1, r) - \sigma^-(l' + 1, l, r') \text{ if } l > l' \end{cases}$$

And we conclude as in lemma 1-2.   ◊

We now prove our second result.

Theorem 2 *Let* $a_1,...a_n$ *be* n *numbers,* $b_1..;b_m$ *be* m *other numbers. The set*

$$B^+ = \{\sigma(i, j, r) = \sum_{l = i}^{j} a_l + b_r, 1 \leq i \leq j \leq n, 1 \leq r \leq m\}$$

may be sorted in $O(Max(n^2, \lg_2(m)) . m)$ *comparisons.*

Proof We complete B^+ in B as we explained previously. The algorithm is the following:

```
h := 0
SORT(SLICE(0, 1))
while 2^h ≤ n do
    SORT(SLICE(2^h, 2^h+1))
    MERGE(SLICE(2^h, 2^h+1), SLICE(0, 2^h))
    h := h + 1
```

The only difference with the algorithm of theorem 1 is that SLICE(0, 1) is no longer reduced to {0} and we must sort it in $O(m \lg_2(m))$ comparisons.

To evaluate the complexity of the **while** loop we just remark that now:

$$Card(SLICE(2^h, 2^{h+1})) \leq 2n . 2^h. m$$

and the same calculation than in theorem 1 proves that the number of comparisons required for this loop is bounded by ($K = [\log_2(n)]$):

$$2n \cdot m \sum_{h=0}^{K} 2^h \left(\left\lceil \log_2\left(4 \left\lceil \frac{n}{2^{h+1}} \right\rceil \right) \right\rceil + 2 \right)$$

$$\leq 24\, n^2\, m$$

The total number of comparisons is thus

$$O(\text{Max}(n^2\, m, m\, \lg_2(m))) = O(m \cdot \text{Max}(n^2, \lg_2(m)))$$

$\Diamond$

2-3 Sorting $(x_{i_1}^1 + \ldots + x_{i_k}^k)_{1 \leq i_1, \ldots i_k \leq n}$ in $O(n^k)$ comparisons

As in section 1 we define the $2n-1$ numbers

$$a_1 = x_n^2 - x_{n-1}^2, \ldots a_{n-1} = x_2^2 - x_1^2,\ a_n = x_1^2 + x_1^1,\ a_{n+1} = x_2^1 - x_1^1,\ \ldots a_{2n-1} = x_n^1 - x_{n-1}^1$$

and denote the n^{k-2} numbers $(x_{i_3}^3 + \ldots + x_{i_k}^k)_{1 \leq i_3, \ldots i_k \leq n}$ by $(z_r)_{1 \leq r \leq nk-2}$ we get if $z_r = x_{i_3}^3 + \ldots + x_{i_k}^k$:

$$x_{i_1}^1 + \ldots + x_{i_k}^k = \sigma(n + 1 - i_2, n - 1 + i_1, r)$$

By theorem 2 we can sort the set B^+ in

$$O(n^{k-2}\, \text{Max}(n^2, \lg_2(n^{k-2}))) = O(n^k)$$

comparisons.

$\Diamond$

Conclusion

We have presented an algorithm to sort $(x_i + y_j)_{1 \leq i, j \leq n}$ in $O(n^2)$ comparisons and generalized it to sorting sums of k numbers. This algorithm strongly uses comparisons between differences of numbers.

In any of those algorithms we need to compare elements which are not in the set we are sorting (i.e. these elements are not of the form $x_i + y_j$). This led us to conjecture that it is not possible to sort the set $(x_i + y_j)_{1 \leq i, j \leq n}$ in $O(n^2)$ comparisons and only use comparisons between elements of that set.

REFERENCES

[1] M.L. Fredman, How good is the information theory about sorting ?, Theoretical Computer Science 1 (1976) 355-361.
[2] L.H. Harper, T.H. Payne, J.E. Savage, E. Straus, Sorting X + Y, Comm. ACM, June 1975, Volume 18, Number 6, 347-349.
[3] N.Jacobson, "Basic algebra I", W.H.Freeman and company, 1974.

Efficient Checking of Computations

Richard J. Lipton*
Department of Computer Science
Princeton University

Abstract

We show how to efficiently check computations using only logspace even if they are only given *once*. This result implies that a polynomial-time verifier can also be restricted to be logspace with essentially no loss in performance. We also use this result to show that every set in NP is equal to $h(L)$ where h is a homomorphism and L is accepted by a one-way probabilistic logspace machine.

1   Introduction

In recent years there has been great interest in the verification or checking of computations. Interactive proofs introduced by Goldwasser, Micali and Rackoff [5] and Babi [1] can be viewed as a model of the verification process. In these systems a powerful "prover" attempts to convince a "verifier" of the correctness of some computation. Dwork and Stockmeyer [4] and Condon [3] have studied interactive proofs where the verifier is a space bounded computation instead of the original model where the verifer is a time bounded computation. More recently, Blum and Kannan [2] has studied another model where the goal is to check a computation based solely on the final answer.

A recurrent theme in all this research is to understand how weak a verifier can be and still be able to check the given computation. For example, Dwork and Stockmeyer show that a probabilistic polynomial-time verifer can also be restricted to use only logspace. Since polynomial-time is not known to be equal to logspace this uses in an essential way the ability of the prover to *repeat* the computation over and over. Roughly, the verifier guesses what part of the computation to check each time the prover repeats the computation. After a polynomial number of repetitions, there is a high probability that if the prover is cheating, the verifier will detect it.

Our results are a dramatic improvement. We show that a verifier can check a prover's computation using only logspace even if the prover only states the computation *once*. The method used to prove this has independent interest and is based on a technique from Lipton [10]. The same method can be used to show other results. We believe, however, that the most interesting is the following structure theorem:

Theorem 1.1 *For each S in NP, there is a homomorphism h and a language L accepted by a one-way probabilistic logspace machine such that $S = h(L)$.*

A one-way probabilistic logspace machine is a probabilistic machine that is restricted to only use logspace and can only read the input once left-to-right. The restriction to a one-way machine is critical: without

*Work supported by DARPA and ONR contracts N00014-85-C-0456 and N00014-85-K-0465, and by NSF Cooperative Agreement DCR-8420948

it the result is easy (see [4]). It is interesting to note that this theorem is similar in form to the Chomsky-Schutzenberger Theorem [6]. Here the role of the Dyck set is played by the one-way probabilistic language L.

Our main result can be described in a more "colorful" way. Consider a prover who is doing a large crossword puzzle: see figure 1. Assume that a verifier is listening to the prover as he solves the puzzle. The prover says, "16 down is 'hello', 19 across is 'goodbye'" and so on. We assume that the verifier checks each word as the prover states them. Thus, when the prover claims that 16 down is 'hello', the verifier can immediately check that 'hello' is a possible choice for 16 down. Here possible choice means that 'hello' has the right number of letters and is a possible match for the definition of 16 down. We, however, assume that the verifier cannot record the prover's statements, i.e. the verifier does not have a pencil and cannot write down the words as the prover does the crossword puzzle. The key difficulty for the verifier is *global consistency*, i.e. since 16 down and 19 across intersect in a letter, the verifier must check that they agree ('goodbye' and 'hello' do not). The prover is not allowed to choose the across and down words independently. Where they intersect they must agree; this is the whole point of a crossword puzzle. Surprisingly, we can show that a probabilistic verifier can check the prover even if the verifier has only a small amount of memory.

Figure 1: a simple crossword puzzle

The rest of the paper is organized as follows. In the next section we will define a class of directed graphs that are used to encode computations. We then show how to "fingerprint" multi-sets. Such fingerprints have many applications; see Lipton [10] for a number of examples. We then show how to use these fingerprints to check computations. We do this first for computation graphs and then for Turing Machine computations. The latter leads directly to our structure theorem for *NP*.

2   Computation Graphs

In this section we will define our notion of "computation graphs". Essentially, they are just "generalized" boolean circuits. However, it is important to have a precise definition, since our main theorem on checking requires a careful analysis of their structure.

Say that $< \Omega, f_1, \ldots, f_d >$ forms a *function basis* provided Ω is a finite set and for each k, f_k maps the set Ω^k to the set Ω. C is a *computation graph* over the function basis $< \Omega, f_1, \ldots, f_d >$ with inputs $x_1, \ldots, x_n$ provided the following is true: C consists of a finite sequence of *nodes*. These are either *inputs* and are associated with an input x_i. Or, they are *internal nodes*. In this case they are associated with a function f_k from the function basis and with a k-tuple of predecessors nodes, $< P_1, \ldots, P_k >$. We use $res(i)$ to denote the result computed at the node i. It is defined inductively. For an input node i, $res(i)$ is equal to the value of its associated input x_j. For an internal node i, $res(i)$ is equal to the value $f_k(res(P_1), \ldots, res(P_k))$ where i is associated with the function f_k and the k-tuple $< P_1, \ldots, P_k >$.

In a natural way each computation graph has an underlying acyclic directed graph: $< i, j >$ is an edge whenever node j uses i as one of its predecessors. See figure 2 for an example of a computation graph. The *fan-in* (resp. *fan-out*) of a node is just the fan-in (resp. fan-out) of the node in the underlying graph. It is convenient to have a technical restriction on our computation graphs: we will assume that they have no multiple edges. It is also convenient to extend $res()$ to edges: if $< i, j >$ is an edge, then define $res(< i, j >)$ to be equal to $res(i)$. Thus, we think of values as associated not only with a node, but also with its out edges.

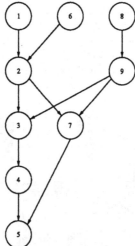

Figure 2: a computation graph

3 Fingerprinting Sets

We need a result from Lipton [10] concerning how to "fingerprint" multi-sets. It will be used to check computation graphs. We include the details here for completeness. Choose two random numbers, p a prime and $r \in \{0, 1, \ldots, p - 1\}$; we will discuss their size in a moment. Define the *fingerprint* of the multi-set $\{x_1, \ldots, x_k\}$ to be

$$\prod_{i=1}^{k}(x_i + r) \bmod p.$$

There are several key remarks we wish to make. First, this can clearly be computed in the space required to store p. Second, it is also clear that our fingerprint is *invariant* under permutations, i.e. $\{x_{\pi_1}, \ldots, x_{\pi_k}\}$ has the same fingerprint for all permutations π. Finally, we claim that the probability of two unequal sets getting the same fingerprint is very small. This is stated precisely in our next theorem:

Theorem 3.1 *The probability that* $\{x_1, x_2, \ldots, x_k\}$ *and* $\{y_1, y_2, \ldots, y_l\}$ *are unequal and get the same fingerprints is at most*

$$O\left(\frac{\log(n) + \log(m)}{nm} + \frac{1}{n^2 m}\right)$$

where all numbers are n bit numbers and $m = \max(k, l)$ provided the prime p is selected randomly from the interval

$$[(nm)^2, 2(nm)^2].$$

Thus, the prime p and hence the fingerprint has at most $O(\log(n) + \log(m))$ bits. This method of computing fingerprints has a number of advantages. First, it can be computed in at most the amount of space needed to store the fingerprints. Second, it can be computed in at most the time required to multiply numbers of this size. Just as important it can be computed "on-line", i.e. the fingerprint can be computed in a single pass over the multi-sets. This last property is critical for our applications. Finally, note, Wegman and Carter [12] also have a method for fingerprinting sets. It, however, cannot be used here. For one, it does not work with multi-sets; in addition, it uses space linear in the size of the sets.

Before we can prove this theorem we need one definition and a simple lemma. The *height* $H(\Phi)$ of a polynomial $\Phi(x) = \Phi_d x^d + \ldots + \Phi_0$ is the maximum of $|\Phi_d|, \ldots, |\Phi_0|$. Then,

Lemma 3.1 *(1) Let $\Phi_1(x)$ and $\Phi_2(x)$ be polynomials. Then, $H(\Phi) \leq H(\Phi_1) + H(\Phi_2)$. (2) Let $\Phi(x) = (x - a_1)\ldots(x - a_m)$. Then,*

$$H(\Phi) \leq (1 + |a_1|)\ldots(1 + |a_m|)$$

Proof: (1) is obvious. (2) follows by induction and the simple observation that

$$H(\Phi(x)(x - a)) \leq H(\Phi)(1 + |a|).$$

□

We now turn to the proof of the theorem.

Proof: Let $f(u) = (u - x_1)\ldots(u - x_k)$ and $g(u) = (u - y_1)\ldots(u - y_l)$ be polynomials in u. Also, let $\Phi(u) = f(u) - g(u)$. Since $x_1, \ldots, x_k$ and $y_1, \ldots, y_l$ are unequal as multisets, the polynomial $\Phi(u)$ is not identically zero. Clearly, its degree is at most m. By the lemma its height is at most,

$$\prod_{i=1}^{k}(1 + |x_i|) + \prod_{j=1}^{l}(1 + |y_j|).$$

Since each number is at most n bit it follows that $H(\Phi)$ is at most 2^{nm+1}. Now let $t = (nm)^2$ and let p be a random prime with $t \leq p \leq 2t$ and let r be a random residue modulo p.

We must now show that it is unlikely that $\Phi(r) \equiv 0 \bmod p$ since this implies that $x_1, \ldots, x_k$ and $y_1, \ldots, y_l$ have different fingerprints. Since Φ is not identically 0 it has at least one coefficient say c that is not 0. By the lemma, c is at most 2^{nm+1}. Therefore, c has at most $nm + 1$ prime factors. Thus, the probability that $c \equiv 0 \bmod p$ is at most

$$O\left(\frac{nm}{\frac{t}{\log(t)}}\right)$$

since there are approximately $\frac{t}{\log(t)}$ primes in the given interval. Since $t = (nm)^2$ it follows that this probability is

$$O\left(\frac{\log(n) + \log(m)}{nm}\right).$$

Next we need to compute the probability that $\Phi(r) \equiv 0 \bmod p$ given that $c \not\equiv 0 \bmod p$. Since Φ is not identically zero it follows that it has at most m roots. Thus, the probability that $\Phi(r) \equiv 0 \bmod p$

is at most m/p or $1/n^2m$. Therefore, the total probability the two sets have the same fingerprint is at most

$$O\left(\frac{\log(n) + \log(m)}{nm} + \frac{1}{n^2m}\right).$$

□

4 Checking Computation Graphs

In this section we will show how to check that a computation graph is correct. A prover who is trying to convince a verifier of the value of a computation will do so by presenting what we call a "valuation" sequence. Each step of the valuation sequence will consist of a small "local" part of the whole computation. The task of verifier will be to check that all these local pieces fit together correctly.

Let C be a computation graph over the function basis $< \Omega, f_1, \ldots, f_d >$. Then V is a *valuation sequence* for C provided it is a sequence of objects of the form $< (i, v), (P_1, u_1), \ldots, (P_k, u_k) >$ where i is an node from C with predecessors $P_1, \ldots, P_k$ and $v, u_1, \ldots, u_k$ are values from Ω with $f_k(u_1, \ldots, u_k) = v$. If P_j is an input node, then u_j is equal to its associated value x_l. If i is an input node, then the object is of the form $< (i, v) >$: in this case we insist that v be the value associated with the input i. Call this object a *step* for the node i. Intuitively, each step of a valuation sequence is "local"; it asserts that the node's value is v and that u_j is the value coming from node P_j.

Not all valuation sequences are "meaningful"; therefore, we must further restrict them. A valuation sequence is *complete* provided for each node i, there is exactly one step in the valuation sequence for the node.

Now suppose that V is a complete valuation sequence. Then we define a function $val()$ as follows. For any node i, let $< (i, v), (P_1, u_1), \ldots, (P_k, u_k) >$ be its unique step. Then, define $val(i)$ to be v. Also define $val(< P_j, i >) = u_j$. Note, since there are no multiple edges $val()$ is well defined. Now say that V is *globally consistent* provided for all edges $< i, j >$, $val(i)$ is equal to $val(< i, j >)$.

The point of these definitions is the following theorem:

Theorem 4.1 *(1) Any computation graph C has a complete and globally consistent valuation sequence V. (2) Suppose that V is a valuation sequence for C that is both complete and globally consistent. Then for any node i, $val(i)$ is equal to $res(i)$.*

Thus, if a valuation sequence has these two properties, then it correctly computes the values of the computation graph. Once we have proved this theorem we will use it to get our efficient checkers.

Proof: (1) Suppose that C is a computation graph. Let V be the following valuation sequence: for each node i include the step, $< (i, res(i)), (P_1, res(P_1)), \ldots, (P_k, res(P_k)) >$. Clearly, this is a valuation sequence. It is easily seen to be complete. Finally, for this sequence, for each node i, $val(i) = res(i)$ and for each edge $< i, j >$, $val(< i, j >) = res(i)$. Thus, it is globally consistent.

(2) Now suppose that V is a complete and globally consistent valuation sequence. We will prove the following by induction, for each node i, $val(i) = res(i)$. Once this is proved the theorem will follow.

Clearly, it is true for any input node i by definition. Suppose that i is an internal node, and that the inductive hypothesis is true for all predecessor nodes. Now let $< (i, v), (P_1, u_1), \ldots, (P_k, u_k) >$ be its unique step. By definition of a step, $v = f_k(u_1, \ldots, u_k)$. Now $val(i) = v$ also by definition. The inductive hypothesis shows that

$$val(P_1) = res(P_1), \ldots, val(P_k) = res(P_k).$$

The key is that V is globally consistent; hence,

$$val(< P_1, i >) = val(P_1), \ldots, val(< P_k, i >) = val(P_k).$$

By definition of $val()$ for edges,

$$val(< P_1, i >) = u_1, \ldots, val(< P_k, i >) = u_k.$$

Thus, putting these together shows that $val(i)$ is equal to $f_k(res(P_1), \ldots, res(P_k))$. However, this is just $res(i)$ and it follows that $val(i) = res(i)$. $\square$

Our next goal is to show how a logspace machine can check a computation graph; more precisely, how such a machine can check that a valuation sequence is complete and globally consistent. Let us, first, focus our attention on the latter issue. Global consistency appears to require that the checker remember the all the values of the function $val()$. However, the critical insight is that we can show that global consistency is equivalent to the *equality* of certain multi-sets. Then, the fingerprinting techniques of the last section will apply.

Let V be a valuation sequence for the computation graph C over the function basis $< \Omega, f_1, \ldots, f_d >$. We define a family of multi-sets E_k and U_k as follows. Let the following $< (i, v), (P_1, u_1), \ldots, (P_k, u_k) >$ be a step of the valuation sequence. Then place m copies of (i, v) in the multi-set E_m where m is the fan-out of i. Also if P_j is an internal node, add (P_j, u_j) to the multi-set U_l where l is equal to the fan-out of the node P_j. No other elements are put into these multi-sets. The following theorem is key:

Theorem 4.2 *Let the valuation V be complete. Then, it is globally consistent if and only if for each k, E_k is equal to U_k as multi-sets.*

Proof: First, we prove two facts about these multi-sets. Let i be an node with fan-out m. Then we claim that the following are true:

1. $val(i) = v$ if and only if (i, v) is put into E_m a total of m times.

2. $val(< i, j >) = u$ if and only if (i, u) is put into U_m.

In order to see (1) suppose that $val(i) = v$. Then, by the definition of $val()$ there is a step of the form $< (i, v), (P_1, u_1), \ldots, (P_k, u_k) >$. Thus, (i, v) is put into E_m a total of m times. On the other hand, suppose that (i, v) is placed into E_m. Then it follows that there is a step for i so that $val(i) = v$. This proves (1). In order to see (2) suppose that $val(< i, j >) = u$. Then, there must be a step for j of the form $< (j, v), (P_1, u_1), \ldots, (P_k, u_k) >$ with one of the P_l equal to i and u_l equal to u. Thus, $(P_l, u_l) = (i, u)$ is placed into the multi-set U_m. On the other hand, suppose that (i, u) is placed into the multi-set U_m. Then there must be a step for some node j of the form $< (j, v), (P_1, u_1), \ldots, (P_k, u_k) >$ with some P_l equal to i and u_l equal to u. Then by the definition of $val()$ for edges, it follows that $val(< i, j >) = u$. This proves (2).

Now suppose that V is globally consistent. We will show that E_m and U_m are equal. Let i be an node. Then global consistency implies that $val(i) = val(< i, j >)$ for any edge $< i, j >$. Thus, by (1) and (2) it follows that E_m and U_m are equal as multi-sets. On the other hand, suppose that E_m and U_m are equal. Then by (1) and (2) it clearly follows that V is globally consistent. $\square$

We will now describe how computations are checked. Suppose that our checker is given a valuation sequence. It has to check that it is a complete and globally consistent valuation sequence. In order to do this the checker must:

1. Check that each step $< (i, v), (P_1, u_1), \ldots, (P_k, u_k) >$ is a valuation step, i.e. that $P_1, \ldots, P_k$ are the correct predecessors of i and that $f_k(u_1, \ldots, u_k) = v$. It must also check that if P_j is an input node that u_j is equal to the correct value. Finally, it must check that if i is an input node that v is the value associated with this node.

2. Check that the valuation sequence is complete.

3. Check that the valuation sequence is globally consistent.

The key point is that (1) is often easy to check. If the computation graph is "uniform" then a logspace machine can easily check that $P_1, \ldots, P_k$ are the correct predecessors. Also if the functions f_k are simple checking $f_k(u_1, \ldots, u_k) = v$ is easy. Finally, there is the question of checking the correctness of the inputs. Usually, this is trivial to check. Often we can assume that the inputs are supplied to us as part of the valuation sequence; thus, no checking is required for inputs.

The remaining two properties (2) and (3) can be checked by using our fingerprinting method. We have already seen in Theorem 4.2 that (3) is equivalent to the equality of multi-sets. Indeed it is easy to reduce (3) to the equality of just two multi-sets. Let E be the marked union of the E_k, i.e. if (i, v) is placed into E_k, then put (k, i, v) into E. In the same way let U be the marked union of the U_k. Then, clearly, E is equal to U if and only if for each k, E_k is equal to U_k. Finally, a valuation sequence is complete provided each internal node i has exactly one step. In order to check this define a new multi-set N. For each step $< (i, v), (P_1, u_1), \ldots, (P_k, u_k) >$ of the valuation sequence place i into the multi-set N. Clearly, the valuation sequence is complete if and only if this is equal to the set of all internal nodes. In this way we reduce completeness to a test for the equality of multi-sets.

Consider a *family* of computation graphs. Say that the family is *locally computable in logspace* provided if C is a computation graph in the family over the function basis $< \Omega, f_1, \ldots, f_d >$, then (i) it has n inputs for some n; (ii) the nodes of C are labelled $1, \ldots, m$ for some $m = n^{O(1)}$; (iii) the elements of Ω all are encodable in at most $O(\log(n))$ space; (iv) for each function f_k, whether $f_k(u_1, \ldots, u_k) = v$ is checkable in $O(\log(n))$ space; (v) it is checkable whether or not $P_1, \ldots, P_k$ are the predecessors of node i in at most $O(\log(n))$ space. Note, each computation graph can use a different function basis.

We now can summarize our analysis in the following theorem:

Theorem 4.3 *If a family of computation graphs is locally computable in logspace, then any valuation sequence for them can be checked by a one-way probabilistic logspace machine.*

Note, a one-way probabilistic logspace is a logspace machine that can only read its input once left-to-right. Also, it has the ability to "flip" a fair coin and base its state transition on the value of the coin. It must accept or reject with bounded error, i.e. it must either accept or reject with probability uniformly bounded away from 1/2. One-way logspace machines without the ability to flip coins have been studied before in [7]. A final comment: the probabilistic machine constructed in Theorem 4.3 uses only $\log(n)$ coin flips.

Proof: The proof of the theorem follows directly from Theorem 3.1 and Theorem 4.2 and the above discussion. □

5 Applications

In this section we will use Theorem 4.3 to prove a number of results. All these results rely on the fact that many computations can be encoded as families of computation graphs that are locally computable in logspace.

Our first concerns the so called circuit value problem. Ladner [9] showed that evaluating a boolean circuit is logspace complete for P. More precisely Ladner considered the *boolean circuit value problem*: Given a boolean circuit as a linear sequence of gates. Find the values of the output of the circuit. He showed that any problem in P can be reduced by a logspace machine to this problem. Thus, if the value of a boolean circuit could be computed in logspace, then all of P would be equal to logspace. Since this is believed to be unlikely, Ladner's result is evidence that evaluating a boolean circuit requires more than logspace. Now consider a related problem: Given a boolean circuit with values associated with each gate. Determine whether or not the values are correctly assigned. Call this the *boolean circuit checking problem*. Then,

Theorem 5.1 *The boolean circuit checking problem can be solved by a one-way probabilistic logspace machine.*

Proof: Clearly, the class of boolean circuits with values associated with each node form a family of computation graphs that are locally computable in logspace. Then, they can be checked by a one-way probabilistic logspace machine by Theorem 4.3. □

We now turn to the proof of our structure theorem. Recall that the structure theorem states:

Theorem 5.2 *For each S in NP, there is a homomorphism h and a language L accepted by a one-way probabilistic logspace machine such that $S = h(L)$.*

Proof: Let S be a set in NP. Then it is well known that there is a deterministic Turing Machine M that accepts the set S' of elements $< x, y >$ such that y is a "proof" that x is in S. We can further assume that y is in a different alphabet from x so that there is a homomorphism h' so that $h'(S')$ is equal to S.

It is standard that we can further restrict M as follows: it has only one tape and it only sweeps its head across the tape in an alternating manner. First left to right, then right to left, and so on. (See figure 3 for a simple example of such a computation graph.) Thus, M is "oblivious", i.e. its head motion only depends on the length of the input. It therefore follows that there is a computation graph C of polynomial size such that x is in S' if and only if C with input x accepts.

Now define L to be the language that consists of the set of valuation sequences for such computation graphs. Clearly, we can by choosing the alphabet correctly arrange it so there is a homomorphism h so that $h(L)$ is equal to S'. Thus, by Theorem 4.3 it follows that L is accepted by a one-way probabilistic logspace machine. □

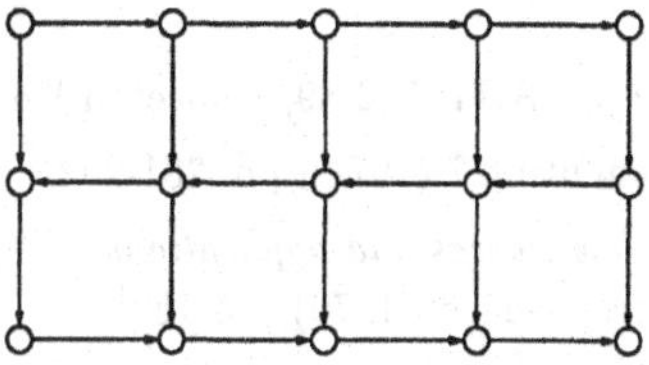

Figure 3: computation graph for M

We now consider how much time is lost, if any, by restricting the verifier to have only logspace. In the proof of the structure theorem we lost a great deal of time by forcing our Turing Machines to be in a simple normal form. We will now remove this restriction and show that almost no time is lost.

Theorem 5.3 *A prover can convince a verifier of the correctness of a computation with t steps in time $O(t\log(t)\log\log(t))$ provided the verifier has $O(\log(t))$ space.*

Proof: The key to this improvement of Theorem 5.2 is to avoid forcing the Turing Machine to be in a very simple normal form. Following [8] restrict the Turing Machine instead to be "block-respecting" with block size b equal to $t^{2/3}$. Then the verifier must check that a computation graph of size t/b is correct. Again by Theorem 4.3 this is possible with only logspace. The time required for the veifier is bounded by at most t/b times the cost of processing each step. The main cost is easily seen to be computing the required fingerprints. This can be done in the time it takes to multiply b bit numbers ([11]), i.e. $O(b\log(b)\log\log(b))$. Thus, the veifier takes a total time of t/b times $b\log(b)\log\log(b)$; this implies the claimed bound. □

Acknowledgements

I would like to thank Anne Condon for a number of helpful comments. I would also like to thank Bob Sedgewick for creating the crossword puzzle figure. I would also like to thank Steve North for creating the other figures.

References

[1] L. Babai, *Trading Group Theory for Randomness*, Proc. 17th STOC, 1985, pp. 421-429.

[2] M. Blum, S. Kannan, *Program Correctness Checking*, Tech. Report TR-88-103, International Computer Science Institute, 1988.

[3] A. Condon, *Computational Models of Games*, Ph.D. Thesis, Tech. Report 87-04-04, Computer Science Dept., University of Washington, Seattle, WA, 1987.

[4] C. Dwork, L. Stockmeyer, *Interactive Proof Systems with Finite State Verifiers*, Tech. Report RJ 6262, IBM Research Division, Almaden Research Center, San Jose, CA, 1988.

[5] S. Goldwasser, S. Micali, and C. Rackoff, *The Knowledge Complexity of Interactive Proofs*, Proc. of 17th STOC, 1985, ppp. 291-304.

[6] M. Harrison, *Introduction to Formal Language Theory*, Addison-Wesley Publishing Company, 1978.

[7] J. Hartmanis, N. Immerman, and S. Mahaney, *One-Way Log-Tape Reductions*, Proc. of 19th FOCS, 1978, pp. 65-72.

[8] J. E. Hopcroft, W. J. Paul, and L. G. Valiant, *On Time versus Space*, JACM, 14 (1977), pp. 332-337.

[9] R. E. Ladner, *The circuit value problem is logspace complete for P*, SIGACT News, 7 (1975), pp. 18-20.

[10] R. J. Lipton, *Fingerprinting Sets*, CS-TR-212-89, Princeton Univeristy, 1989.

[11] A. Schonhage, V. Strassen, Computing 7 (1971), pp. 281-292.

[12] M. N. Wegman, J. L. Carter, *New classes and applications of hash functions*, 20th Annual Symposium on Foundations of Computer Science, (1979) 175-182.

Hard Promise Problems and Nonuniform Complexity

Luc Longpré   and   Alan L. Selman *
College of Computer Science
Northeastern University
Boston, MA 02115

Abstract

For every recursive set A, let PP-A denote the following promise problem.

> **input** x and y
> **promise** $(x \in A) \oplus (y \in A)$
> **property** $x \in A$.

We show that if L is a solution of PP-A, then $A \in P^L/Poly$. From this result, it follows that if A is $\leq_T^P$-hard for NP, then all solutions of PP-A are hard for NP under a reduction that generalizes both $\leq_T^P$ and $\leq_T^{SN}$. Specifically, if A is NP-hard, then all solutions of PP-A are *generalized high$_2$*. [BBS86b]. The main theorem that leads to this result states that if B is a self- reducible set, $B \leq_T^P A$, and $A \in P^L/Poly$, then $\Sigma_2^{P,B} \subseteq \Sigma_2^{P,L}$. Several interesting connections between uniform and nonuniform complexity follow directly from this theorem.

1   Introduction

In [Sel88], the second author initiated a project to develop a theory of hard promise problems, somewhat akin to the theory that was developed over the years for NP- complete decision problems. A general framework was given. The methodology introduced was the same as the familiar one for decision problems — to show that a promise problem is hard, reduce a known hard promise problem to it. To this end, a particular class of promise problems was invented: for every set A, PP-A is the promise problem

> **input** x and y
> **promise** $(x \in A) \oplus (y \in A)$
> **property** $x \in A$.

The principal theorem proved in [Sel88] is that if A is $\leq_d^P$-equivalent to a disjunctive-self-reducible set in NP, then it is as hard to solve PP-A as it is to recognize A. In particular, for every $\leq_d^P$-complete set A, every solution of PP- A is NP-hard. Thus, these promise problems form a class of known hard promise problems. In order to prove

*Funding for this research was provided by the National Security Agency under grant MDA-87-H-2020

that some promise problem (Q, R) is NP-hard, it suffices to reduce one of these promise problems to (Q, R).

The techniques of [Sel88] apply only when $A \in$ NP and, at that, only when A is $\leq_d^P$-equivalent to a disjunctive-self-reducible set. In this paper we address the questions, what can be said of the solutions of PP-A when A is $\leq_T^P$-complete for NP, and what can be said when A is $\leq_T^P$- hard for NP (i.e. NP-hard). Our results will show that solutions are "hard" in both cases. Specifically, we show that if A is NP-hard, then all solutions of PP-A are *generalized high$_2$*. (I.e., $\Sigma_3^P \subseteq \Sigma_2^{P,A}$. Definitions will be given in the next section.)

This paper is about more than hard promise problems. It is also about connections between uniform and nonuniform complexity. The main theorem that leads to the result just cited is Theorem 4, which states that if B is a self-reducible set, $B \leq_T^P A$, and $A \in P^L/Poly$, then $\Sigma_2^{P,B} \subseteq \Sigma_2^{P,L}$. Observe that is A is taken to be any NP-hard set, and $A \in P^L/Poly$, then the hypothesis holds, where B can be any self-reducible NP-complete set. Thus, $\Sigma_2^{P,B} = \Sigma_3^P \subseteq \Sigma_2^{P,L}$, and so L is *generalized high$_2$*. As a corollary, if A is NP-hard, $A \in P^L/Poly$, and L is *generalized low$_2$*, then the polynomial hierarchy must collapse to Σ_2^P. This corollary (Corollary 11 below) strenthens a result of [AFK87]. The general paradigm illustrated here is to use Theorem 4 to show that certain sets are *generalized high*. It follows directly that such sets cannot be *generalized low* unless the polynomial hierarchy collapses.

2 Preliminaries

Promise problems are first described in [EY80] and, for an in-depth treatment, the reader is referred to [ESY84].

A promise problem is a formulation of a partial decision problem. Informally, a promise problem has the structure

> **input** x
> **promise** $Q(x)$
> **property** $R(x)$,

where Q and R are predicates. Formally, a recursive promise problem is a pair of recursive predicates (Q, R). A deterministic Turing machine M that halts on every input *solves* (Q, R) if

$$\forall x[Q(x) \rightarrow [M(x) = \text{"yes"} \leftrightarrow R(x)]].$$

If M solves (Q, R), then the language $L(M)$ accepted by M is a *solution* to (Q, R). Every recursive set of the form $(Q \cap R) \cup X$, where $X \cap Q = \emptyset$, is a solution to (Q, R). Thus, $Q \cap R$, R, and $\overline{Q - R} = (Q \cap R) \cup \overline{Q}$ are all solutions to (Q, R).

We will be interested in promise problems PP-A when some self- reducible set is reducible to A. Thus, we recall the definition of self-reducibility due to Meyer and Paterson [MP79].

Definition 1 *A polynomial time recognizable partial order $<$ on Σ^* is OK if and only if*

(i) *every strictly decreasing chain is finite, and there is a polynomial p such that every finite $<$-decreasing chain is shorter than p of the length of its maximum element, and*

(ii) $x < y$ implies $|x| \leq q(|y|)$, for some polynomial q, and all x and y in Σ^*.

Definition 2 *A set A is self-reducible if and only if there is an OK partial order and a query machine M such that M accepts A in polynomial time with oracle A and, moreover, on any input x in Σ^*, M asks its oracle only about words strictly less than x in the partial order.*

[MP79] does not require an OK ordering to be polynomial time recognizable, but this proviso suffices for all known examples and applications in the literature. We require this condition in the proof of Theorem 4.

2.1 Generalized lowness and generalized highness

In [BBS86b], the authors lifted Schöning's *low* and *high* hierarchy [Sch83] out of NP by defining *generalized low* and *generalized high* hierarchies. A set A is defined to be *generalized low$_n$* if $\Sigma_n^{P,A} \subseteq \Sigma_n^P$, and A is defined to be *generalized high$_n$* if $\Sigma_{n+1}^P \subseteq \Sigma_n^{P,A}$. It is useful for us to understand these hierarchies in terms of reducibilities. (The following observations derive from polynomial analogs of reducibilities defined in [Sel71] and are taken in current form nearly directly from an article by Schöning [Sch84].) For each $n \geq 0$, define the reducibility R_n^P, by

$$A R_n^P B \text{ if and only if } \Sigma_n^{P,A} \subseteq \Sigma_n^{P,B}.$$

R_0^P is the same as polynomial-time Turing reducibility, $\leq_T^P$. R_1^P is the same as polynomial-time strong nondeterministic reducibility, $\leq_T^{SN}$ [Lon82]. The relations R_n^P are reflexive and transitive and so $R_n^P \cap (R_n^P)^{-1}$ is an equivalence relation.

Observe that a set A is R_n^P-equivalent to $\emptyset$ if and only if $\Sigma_n^{P,A} \subseteq \Sigma_n^P$. Thus a set belongs to the zero degree of the R_n^P reducibility if and only if it is *generalized low$_n$*. Also observe that a set A is R_n^P-hard for NP if and only if $\Sigma_n^{P,SAT} = \Sigma_{n+1}^P \subseteq \Sigma_n^{P,A}$. Thus a set is R_n^P-hard for NP if and only if it is *generalized high$_n$*. It is straightforward to observe that a set cannot be both *generalized low$_n$* and *generalized high$_n$* unless the polynomial hierarchy collapses to Σ_n^P.

It follows from the observations of the previous paragraph that *generalized high* is a generalization to R_n^P of NP- hardness. Similarly, *generalized low* is an easyness notion.

A set is *high$_n$* in the sense of Schöning, [Sch83] if and only if it is *generalized high* and belongs to NP. Thus, *high$_n$* is a generalization to R_n^P of the NP-completeness notion. Similarly, a set is *low$_n$* if it is *generalized low$_n$* and belongs to NP.

It is easy to see that every *generalized low$_n$* set belongs to Σ_n^P. Thus, *generalized low$_1$* and *low$_1$* are identical. Namely, a set A is *generalized low$_1$* if $NP^A = NP$, that is, if and only if $A \in NP \cap coNP$.

Part of this work will involve an excursion into Karp-Lipton type results [KL80]. Here we note only the following: Let A and L be arbitrary sets. Standard techniques show that $A \in P^L/Poly$ if and only is there is a sparse set S such that $A \leq_T^P L \oplus S$ if and only if A has a family of polynomial size circuits, where the circuits contain nodes that are oracle calls to L.

The power of the *generalized high* and *generalized low* concepts are that they enable Karp-Lipton type results to be obtained without the technical difficulties apparent in the original proofs [KL80,AFK87]. This has been noted before by Ko and Schöning [KS85].

3 Results

Theorem 1 *If L is a solution of PP-A, then there is a sparse set $S \subseteq A$ such that $A \leq_T^P L \oplus prefix(S)$.*

Proof. Let L be a solution of PP-A. Let $L_1 = \{(x, y)|(x, y) \in L \wedge (y, x) \notin L\}$. Note that L_1 is the set L where we remove the pairs (x, y) such that both (x, y) and (y, x) are in L. Because the changes can occur only for pairs where the promise is false, L_1 is also a solution of PP-A.

We will construct a sparse set S such that

$$x \in A \leftrightarrow (\exists z \in S)[|z| = |x| \text{ and } (z, x) \notin L_1]$$

Since $L_1 \leq_T^P L$, we can conclude $A \leq_T^P L \oplus prefix(S)$.

The set S will be $\bigcup S_n$, where $S_n \subseteq \Sigma^n$. Each finite set S_n is constructed in stages, each stage putting one element into S_n.

For each integer n, build a graph whose nodes are the strings of size n and whose edges are defined by L_1. Then, split G into two subgraphs G_1 and G_2, where the nodes of G_1 are the elements of A and the nodes of G_2 are the elements of $\bar{A}$. Because L_1 is a solution, there is an edge from every node in G_1 to every node in G_2 and there is no edge from any node in G_2 to a node in G_1. Also, by the way L_1 was constructed, G_1 and G_2 are antisymmetric graphs.

Let $W_0 = G_1$. For stage i, choose the node y_i in W_{i-1} which has the fewest number of successors. Put y_i into S. Remove y_i and all the nodes that are not successor of y_i from W_{i-1}, together with all the edges incident to those nodes, to form W_i. Continue building S_n by stages until W_i is empty.

If the graph W_{i-1} has k nodes, it has at most $k(k-1)/2$ edges. Then, there must be a node with fewer than $k/2$ successors, so the number of nodes in W_i is at most half the number of nodes in W_{i-1}. Thus there are at most n stages and S_n contains at most n strings of length n. Hence, S is sparse.

Now, if $x \in A$, then there is an i such that $x \in W_{i-1}$ but $x \notin W_i$. Because x gets removed, we have that $(y_i, x) \notin L_1$. (Note that $(y_i, x) \notin L_1$ even if $y_i = x$.)

If $x \notin A$, then for any string $z \in S$, we have $z \in A$, so $(x \in A) \oplus (z \in A)$ is true. Since L_1 is a solution we must have $(z, x) \in L_1$. □

Corollary 1 *If L is a solution of PP-A, then $A \in P^L/Poly$.*

The following proposition was noted in [Sel88].

Proposition 1 *A set A is p-selective if and only if PP-A has a solution in P.*

Thus, Theorem 1 extends Ko's result [Ko83] that all p-selective sets are in $P/Poly$. The proof of Theorem 1 is actually less complicated than the proof in Ko.

Corollary 2 (Ko [Ko83]) *If A is a p-selective set, then $A \in P/Poly$.*

Theorem 2 *If A is in Σ_i^P and L is a solution of PP-A, then $A R_{i+1}^P L$ (ie. $\Sigma_{i+1}^{P,A} \subseteq \Sigma_{i+1}^{P,L}$).*

Proof. If $i = 0$, the theorem is trivial. Let $i \geq 1$. Let C be a set in $\Sigma_{i+1}^{P,A}$. Then, there is a relation $R \in P^A$ such that

$$x \in C \leftrightarrow \exists y_1 \forall y_2 ... Q y_{i+1} R(x, y_1, y_2, ..., y_{i+1}).$$

We have to find a new relation that uses L as oracle instead of A. Let M be a polynomial time oracle Turing machine such that

$$L^A(M) = \{< x, y_1, ..., y_{i+1} > | R(x, y_1, ..., y_{i+1})\}.$$

Let p be a polynomial such that M uses less than $p(|x|)$ time. Let S be the sparse set given by the previous theorem. Let M' be a polynomial time oracle Turing machine that accepts A using $L \oplus \text{prefix}(S)$ as oracle. We know M' exists by the previous theorem. Let q be a polynomial such that M' uses less than $q(n)$ time.

For any finite set A, we let $c(A)$ denote an encoding of A. It is assumed that for any string x and finite set A, deciding if $x \in A$ from $c(A)$ and x can be done in time polynomial in $|c(A)| + |x|$. For any set A and natural number n, let $A^{\leq n}$ denote set of all strings in A of length less than or equal to n. Then, $c(A^{\leq n})$ denotes the encoding of an initial segment of A.

We can create M'' such that if $l(x) = q(p(|x|))$, then

$$\langle x, y_1, ..., y_{i+1}, c(S^{\leq l(x)}) \rangle \in L^L(M'') \leftrightarrow R(x, y_1, ..., y_{i+1}).$$

M'' simply simulates M, and whenever M makes a query, M'' simulates M'. Queries of M' are of size $\leq q(p(|x|))$ and can be answered by either asking directly to L or by using $c(S^{\leq l(x)})$.

To show that $C \in \Sigma_{i+1}^{P,L}$, the idea is to guess $c(S^{\leq l(x)})$, verify that it's correct and verify that M''^L accepts. This is formally expressed by the following predicate:

$$x \in C \quad \leftrightarrow \quad \exists c(S^{\leq l(x)})[(c(S^{\leq l(x)}) \text{ is correct}) \text{ and}$$
$$\exists y_1 \forall y_2 ... y_{i+1}[M''^L \text{ accepts } \langle x, y_1, ..., y_{i+1}, c(S^{\leq l(x)}) \rangle]]].$$

The second part of the "and" is a $\Sigma_{i+1}^{P,L}$ predicate. It remains to show that "$c(S^{\leq l(x)})$ is correct" is a $\Sigma_{i+1}^{P,L}$ predicate. For "$c(S^{\leq l(x)})$ is correct", we use the test

$$S^{\leq l(x)} \subseteq A \text{ and } \forall v \in A \ (|v| \leq l(x) \rightarrow (\exists z \in S^{\leq l(x)})[(z, v) \notin L_1]).$$

where L_1 is as in the previous theorem: $(z, v) \in L_1 \leftrightarrow [(z, v) \in L \text{ and } (v, z) \notin L]$.

This test is a $\Sigma_{i+1}^{P,L}$ predicate, because $S^{\leq l(x)} \subseteq A$ is a Σ_i^P predicate, and the second implication can be replaced by

$$\forall v : |v| \leq l(x) \ [v \notin A \text{ or } (\bigvee_{z \in S^{\leq l(x)}} (z, v) \notin L_1)]$$

which is a $\Pi_1^{P,L}$ predicate.

The set S given by the previous theorem surely has this property. It remains to show that any set S having the property is a valid witness.

Suppose $S \subseteq A$. Then, because L_1 is a solution of A, we know that if $x \notin A$, then for any $z \in A$, $(z, x) \in L_1$, so queries to oracle A of strings not in A will always be answered correctly using $L \oplus \text{prefix}(S)$. Now, if $x \in A$, the second part of the implication in the test guaranties that the query to the oracle will also be answered correctly. This means that if S is correct according to the test above, then our simulation of queries to A using $L \oplus \text{prefix}(S)$ will be correct. $\qquad \square$

Corollary 3 (Ko-Schöning [KS85]) *If A is in NP and A is p-selective, then A is low$_2$.*

Corollary 4 *If $A \in \Sigma_i^P$ and A is generalized high$_{i+1}$, then every solution of PP-A is generalized high$_{i+1}$.*

Of course, the Corollary applies when A is a $\leq_T^P$-complete set in NP. Thus, we have a specific hardness result for solutions of PP-A, when A is $\leq_T^P$-Turing complete for NP.

Corollary 5 *If A is $\leq_T^P$-complete for NP, then every solution of PP-A is generalized high$_2$.*

Note that the following theorem has a weaker hypothesis and weaker conclusion than does Theorem 2.

Theorem 3 *If A is in Σ_i^P and $A \in P^L/Poly$, then $AR_{i+2}^P L$.*

The proof of this theorem is like the proof of Theorem 2, except that verifying correctness of advice ("$c(S^{\leq l(x)})$ is correct") is now a straightforward Π_{i+1}^P test using only the hypothesis that A is in Σ_i^P. The proof is not given, for it is similar to the proof of Theorem 2, as well as a straightforward generalization of the following known corollary.

Corollary 6 (Ko-Schöning [KS85]) *If A is in NP and $A \in P/Poly$, then A is low$_3$.*

What can be said about solutions L when A is $\leq_T^P$-hard for NP, but one does not assume that A belongs to NP? It turns out that the solutions are still *generalized high$_2$* as a corollary of the following theorem:

Theorem 4 *If $B \leq_T^P A$, B is self-reducible, and $A \in P^L/Poly$, then $BR_2^P L$.*

Proof. Let $C \in \Sigma_2^{P,B}$. Then there is a $R \in P^B$ such that

$$x \in C \leftrightarrow \exists y_1 \forall y_2 R(\langle x, y_1, y_2 \rangle)$$

The aim is to find a R' in P^L instead of P^B.

Since $A \in P^L/Poly$, let a_n be polynomial size advice for strings of length $\leq n$. Let A' be the set in P^L such that for $n \geq |x|$,

$$x \in A \leftrightarrow \langle x, a_n \rangle \in A'.$$

Let $M_{A'L}$ be an oracle Turing machine accepting A' using oracle L. This machine exists because $A \in P^L$.

Let M_{BA} be an oracle Turing machine accepting B using oracle A. This machine exists because by assumption $B \leq_T^P A$.

Let M_{RB} be an oracle Turing machine accepting R using oracle B. This machine exists because $R \in P^B$.

We design a machine M_{BaL} to accept B using advice a and oracle L. Define M_{BaL} as follows. On input $\langle z, a \rangle$, M_{BaL} simulates M_{BA} on z. Whenever M_{BA} makes a query y to its oracle, M_{BaL} simulates $M_{A'L}$ on $\langle y, a \rangle$ to answer it. M_{BaL} uses its own oracle to answer queries of $M_{A'L}$. Notice that if $a = a_n$, for n large enough to make $M_{A'L}$ answer correctly all the queries of M_{BA}, then

$$M_{BaL}^L \text{ accepts } \langle z, a \rangle \leftrightarrow z \in B.$$

Since the machines are polynomial time bounded, n needs only be polynomial in the size of z.

Now, define M_{RaL} as follows. On input $\langle x, y_1, y_2, a \rangle$, M_{RaL} simulates M_{RB} on $\langle x, y_1, y_2 \rangle$. Whenever M_{RB} makes a query z to its oracle, M_{RaL} simulates M_{BaL} on $\langle z, a \rangle$ to answer it. M_{RaL} uses its own oracle to answer queries of M_{BaL}.

Notice again that if $a = a_n$ for large enough n, say $n > p(|x|)$ for a polynomial p majorizing the time taken by M_{RaL}, then

$$M_{RaL}^L \text{ accepts } \langle x, y_1, y_2, a_n \rangle \leftrightarrow \langle x, y_1, y_2 \rangle \in R.$$

Now we have

$$x \in C \leftrightarrow \quad (\exists \langle n, w \rangle : n > p(|x|)) \quad [w = a_n \text{ and} \tag{1}$$
$$\exists y_1, y_2 (M_{RaL}^L \text{ accepts } \langle x, y_1, y_2, w \rangle)]$$

The second part of the "and" is a $\Sigma_2^{P,L}$ predicate. We cannot show that $w = a_n$ is also a $\Sigma_2^{P,L}$ predicate, but we will show that it can be replaced by such a predicate.

For checking that an advice w is suitable, we only need that it's good enough to make M_{BaL}^L simulate a B oracle correctly on all the queries of M_{RaL}^L on $\langle x, y_1, y_2, a_n \rangle$. We check this by checking that the answers of M_{BaL}^L conform to the self reducibility of B. To be more precise, let M_{sr} be an oracle Turing machine that implements the self reducibility, i.e. M_{sr}^B accepts B by making only smaller queries to its oracle. Let $\leq_o$ denote the OK partial order imposed by the self reducibility.

Let $B(w) = \{z | \langle z, w \rangle \text{ is accepted by } M_{BaL}^L\}$. We show below that the test $w = a_n$ in (1) can be replaced by the following test of validity:

$$\langle n, w \rangle \text{ is valid} \leftrightarrow (\forall z : |z| \leq n)(\forall z' \leq_o z)$$
$$[z' \in B(w) \leftrightarrow z' \text{ is accepted by } M_{sr}^{B(w)} \text{ and}$$
$$\text{all queries generated by } M_{sr}^{B(w)}$$
$$\text{on input } z' \text{ are } \leq_o z'].$$

This predicate is in $\Pi_1^{P,L} \subseteq \Sigma_2^{P,L}$.

We show first that for every n, valid advice exists. Then we show that M_{BaL}^L using valid advice simulates B correctly for the appropriate queries. This will complete the proof.

For every n, consider the pairs $\langle n, a_m \rangle$. Let z be a string of size $\leq n$. The strings $z' \leq_o z$ will have their size bounded by a polynomial. If m is large enough (but still polynomial in n), then $z' \in B \leftrightarrow z' \in B(a_m)$ for any of those strings z'. This means that $\langle n, a_m \rangle$ is valid.

Now, let x be a string, let $n \geq p(|x|)$ and let $\langle n, w \rangle$ be valid advice. The machine M_{RaL}^L on $\langle x, y_1, y_2, w \rangle$ simulates M_{BaL}^L on strings of size $\leq n$. M_{BaL}^L accepts $\langle z, w \rangle$ if and only if $z \in B(w)$, by definition of $B(w)$. We need $z \in B(w) \leftrightarrow z \in B$.

We show by induction on $\leq_o$ that for any string $z' \leq_o z$,

$$ z' \in B(w) \leftrightarrow z' \in B. $$

Suppose $\langle n, w \rangle$ is valid. If z' is a minimum string, then the self reduction will make no query to the oracle. Then,

$$
\begin{aligned}
z' \in B(w) \quad &\leftrightarrow \quad z' \text{ is accepted by } M_{sr}^{B(w)} \quad &&\text{(by the validity of } w\text{)}\\
&\leftrightarrow \quad z' \text{ is accepted by } M_{sr}^{B} \quad &&\text{(because no query to oracle)}\\
&\leftrightarrow \quad z' \in B \quad &&\text{(by self reducibility)}
\end{aligned}
$$

Now, assume that $z'' \in B \leftrightarrow z'' \in B(w)$ for strings $z'' \leq_o z'$. The self reduction will only make queries for strings smaller than z' to the oracle. Then again,

$$
\begin{aligned}
z' \in B(w) \quad &\leftrightarrow \quad z' \text{ is accepted by } M_{sr}^{B(w)} \quad &&\text{(by the validity of } w\text{)}\\
&\leftrightarrow \quad z' \text{ is accepted by } M_{sr}^{B} \quad &&\text{(because only smaller queries)}\\
&\leftrightarrow \quad z' \in B \quad &&\text{(by self reducibility)}
\end{aligned}
$$

□

It may be worth reexaming subtleties in the definition of self-reducibility in light of the proof of Theorem 4. We assume that all queries generated by the oracle Turing machine M_{sr} are smaller, in the OK ordering $\leq_o$, than the input string, when M_{sr} is executed with B as the oracle. This assumption leaves open the possibility that execution of M_{sr} with some other oracle does not preserve the ordering. If the definition of Turing self-reducibility were strengthened to mean that every query generated is less than the input string, independent of choice of oracle, then the proof of Theorem 4 would not require the OK ordering to be polynomial time recognizable. In particular, this kind of uniformity holds for $\leq_{tt}^P$-self-reducibility. Thus, if the assertion of Theorem 4 was restricted to $\leq_{tt}^P$-self-reducibility, polynomial time recognizability of the OK ordering would not have been required.

This theorem has interesting corollaries. First we consider the consequences that occur when $L \in P$.

Corollary 7 *If B is self-reducible and B is $\leq_T^P$-reducible to a sparse set, then B is generalized low$_2$. In particular, $B \in \Sigma_2^P$. If $B \in NP$, B is self-reducible, and B is $\leq_T^P$-reducible to a sparse set, then B is low$_2$ [KS85].*

Corollary 8 *If B is self-reducible and B is $\leq_T^P$-reducible to a p-selective set, then B is low$_2$.*

This result is a nice contrast to the result in [Sel82] that a set belongs to P if and only if it is both $\leq_d^P$-self-reducible and p-selective.

Next we consider the consequences of letting B be an NP-complete set.

Corollary 9 *If A is NP-hard (i.e., A is $\leq_T^P$-hard for NP) and $A \in P^L/Poly$, then L is generalized high$_2$.*

Corollaries 10 and 12 to follow are what motivated this development.

Corollary 10 *If A is NP-hard, then every solution of PP-A is generalized high$_2$.*

Corollary 11 *If A is NP-hard, $A \in P^L/Poly$, and L is generalized low$_2$, then the polynomial hierarchy collapses to Σ_2^P.*

Corollary 11 follows immediately from Corollary 9, for a set, L, cannot be both *generalized high$_2$* and *generalized low$_2$* unless the hierarchy collapses to Σ_2^P. Since a set cannot be both *generalized high$_2$* and *generalized low$_i$* unless the hierarchy collapses to Σ_i^P, we have the following corollary.

Corollary 12 *If A is NP-hard, then no solution of PP-A is generalized low$_i$, for any $i \geq 2$, unless the polynomial hierarchy collapses to Σ_i^P.*

The well-known result of Karp and Lipton [KL80] follows immediately by considering the case that $L \in P$.

Corollary 13 ([KL80]) *NP $\subseteq$ P/Poly, then the polynomial hierarchy collapses to Σ_2^P.*

Corollary 11 is even stronger than the following generalization to Corollary 12 that was first proved in [AFK87].

Corollary 14 ([AFK87]) *If NP $\subseteq$ (NP $\cap$ coNP)/Poly, then the polynomial hierarchy collapses to Σ_2^P.*

Noting that NP$\cap$coNP $= low_1$ and that P$^{NP\cap coNP}$ = NP$\cap$coNP, the corollary follows readily.

Next, we state some corollaries that extend these results to arbitrary levels of the polynomial hierarchy.

Corollary 15 *Let $i \geq 1$. If A is a $\leq_T^P$-hard set for Σ_i^P and $A \in P^L/Poly$, then L is generalized high$_{i+1}$.*

Proof. This follows from Theorem 4. Let B be a self-reducible complete set for Σ_i^P. Then, $B\leq_T^P A$ and so $BR_2^P L$. Thus, $\Sigma_{i+2}^P = \Sigma_2^{P,B} \subseteq \Sigma_2^{P,L} \subseteq \Sigma_{1+1}^{P,L}$. So, L is generalized high$_{i+1}$. $\square$

Corollary 16 *Let $i \geq 1$. If A is a $\leq_T^P$-hard set for Σ_i^P, $A \in P^L/Poly$, and L is generalized low$_{i+1}$, then the polynomial hierarchy collapses to Σ_{i+1}^P.*

Corollary 17 *For any L and for $i \geq 1$, if L is generalized low_{i+1} and $\Sigma_i^P \subseteq P^{\Sigma_i^{P,L} \cap \Pi_i^{P,L}}/Poly$, then $\Sigma_{i+2}^P = \Sigma_{i+1}^P$.*

Proof. Assume the hypothesis is true and let A be a self-reducible complete set for Σ_i^P. Then, $A \in P^{\Sigma_i^{P,L} \cap \Pi_i^{P,L}}/Poly$. So, there exists a set $L_1 \in \Sigma_i^{P,L} \cap \Pi_i^{P,L}$ such that $A \in P^{L_1}/Poly$. By Theorem 4, $AR_2^P L_1$. Thus, $\Sigma_{i+2}^P = \Sigma_2^{P,A} \subseteq \Sigma_2^{P,L_1} \subseteq \Sigma_{i+1}^{P,L}$. Thus, L is generalized $high_{i+1}$, so the result follows from the hypothesis that L is generalized low_{i+1}. □

In [BBS86a] the authors show that the polynomial hierarchy does not collapse if and only if for every sparse set S the polynomial hierarchy relative to S does not collapse. Now we show that the prinicpal tool used to obtain this result in [BBS86a] is also obtainable as a corollary to Theorem 4.

Corollary 18 ([BBS86a]) *If A is a self-reducible set and there is a $k \geq 0$ and a sparse set S such that $A \in \Sigma_k^{P,S}$, then $\Sigma_2^{P,A} \subseteq \Sigma_{k+2}^P$.*

Proof. Assume the hypothesis holds and let L be any complete set for Σ_k^P. Then, there is a sparse set S such that $A \leq_T^P L \oplus S$ and so $A \in P^L/Poly$. From Theorem 4 (letting $A = B$) $AR_2^P L$ follows. This means that $\Sigma_2^{P,A} \subseteq \Sigma_2^{P,L} = \Sigma_{k+2}^P$. □

Traditional proofs of results such as Corollaries 13, 14, 16, and 17 are more complicated than the ones given here. For example, consider Corollary 13, a traditional proof (i.e. the one presented in [KL80]) consists of two parts. First, one shows from the hypothesis NP $\subseteq$ P/$Poly$ that every set in the polynomial hierarchy belongs to P/$Poly$. This is proved by mathematical induction. Then, in order to show that the hierarchy collapses, one uses the conclusion that Σ_2^P-complete sets are in P/$Poly$ in order to show that they are also in Π_2^P. This step is comparable to the analysis contained in the proof of Theorem 4 above; our proof and the proof in [KL80] both require efficient representation of the set of "good advice." Since Theorem 4 establishes only a reduction (via the R_2^P reducibility), no induction step is required. Furthermore, since the Corollaries follow so simply from Theorem 4, we see that the techniques used here render the induction step in the original proofs to be unnecessary.

Acknowlegements The authors are grateful to Ron Book for making them aware of similarities between this work and the elegant results in [BBS86a].

References

[AFK87] M. Abadi, J. Feigenbaum, and J. Kilian. On hiding information from an oracle. In *Proc. 19th ACM Symp. Theory of Computing*, pages 195–203, 1987.

[BBS86a] J. Balcázar, R. Book, and U. Schöning. The polynomial-time hierarchy and sparse oracles. *J. Assoc. Comput. Mach.*, 33(3):603–617, 1986.

[BBS86b] J. Balcázar, R. Book, and U. Schöning. Sparse sets, lowness, and highness. *SIAM J. Comput.*, 15:739–747, 1986.

[ESY84]   S. Even, A. Selman, and Y. Yacobi. The complexity of promise problems with applications to public-key cryptography. *Information And Control*, 61(2):159–173, May 1984.

[EY80]   S. Even and Y. Yacobi. Cryptocomplexity and NP-completeness. In *Proc. 8th Colloq. on Automata, Languages, and Programming, Lecture Notes in Computer Science*, pages 195–207, Springer-Verlag, Berlin, 1980.

[KL80]   R. Karp and R. Lipton. Some connections between nonuniform and uniform complexity classes. In *Proc. 12th ACM Symp. on Theory of Computing*, pages 302–309, 1980.

[Ko83]   K. Ko. On self-reducibility and weak P-selectivity. *J. Comput. System Sci.*, 26:209–211, 1983.

[KS85]   K. Ko and U. Schöning. On circuit-size and the low hierarchy in NP. *SIAM J. Comput.*, 14(1):41–51, 1985.

[Lon82]   T. Long. Strong nondeterministic polynomial-time reducibilities. *Theor. Comput. Sci.*, 21:1–25, 1982.

[MP79]   A. Meyer and M. Paterson. *With What Frequency are apparently Intractable Problems Difficult?* Technical Report MIT/LCS/TM-126, M.I.T., 1979.

[Sch83]   U. Schöning. A low and a high hierarchy within NP. *J. Comput. System Sci.*, 27:14–28, 1983.

[Sch84]   U. Schöning. Generalized polynomial reductions, degrees, and NP-completeness. *Fundamenta Informaticae*, 7:77–843, 1984.

[Sel71]   A. Selman. Arithmetical reducibilities I. *Zeitschr. f. math. Logik und Grundlagen d. Math.*, 17:335–350, 1971.

[Sel82]   A. Selman. Reductions on NP and P-selective sets. *Theor. Comput. Sci.*, 19:287–304, 1982.

[Sel88]   A. Selman. Promise problems complete for complexity classes. *Information and Computation*, 78:87–98, 1988.

On the Construction of Abstract Voronoi Diagrams [1]

K. Mehlhorn and St. Meiser
FB Informatik
Universität des Saarlandes
D-6600 Saarbrücken, West Germany

C. Ó'Dúnlaing
Department of Mathematics
Trinity College Dublin
Dublin, Ireland

Abstract: We show that the abstract Voronoi diagram of n sites in the plane can be constructed in time $O(n \log n)$ by a randomized algorithm. This yields an alternative, but simpler, $O(n \log n)$ algorithm in many previously considered cases and the first $O(n \log n)$ algorithm in some cases, e.g., disjoint convex sites with the Euclidean distance function. Abstract Voronoi diagrams are given by a family of bisecting curves and were recently introduced by Klein [Kl88a]. Our algorithm is based on Clarkson and Shor's randomized incremental construction technique [CS].

Key words: Voronoi diagrams, randomized algorithms

I. Introduction

The Voronoi diagram of a set of sites in the plane partitions the plane into regions, called Voronoi regions, one to a site. The Voronoi region of a site s is the set of points in the plane for which s is the closest site among all the sites.

The Voronoi diagram has many applications in diverse fields, cf. Leven/Sharir [LS86] or Aurenhammer [A88b] for a list of applications and a history of Voronoi diagrams. Different types of diagrams result from considering different notions of distance, e.g., Euclidean or L_p-norm or convex distance functions, and different sorts of sites, e.g., points, line segments, or circles; cf. also section IV. For many types of diagrams efficient construction algorithms have been found; these are either based on the divide-and-conquer technique due to Shamos/Hoey [SH], the sweepline technique due to Fortune [F87] or geometric transforms due to Brown [Br] and Edelsbrunner/Seidel [ES].

A unifying approach to Voronoi diagrams was recently proposed by Klein [Kl88a]. He does not use the concept of distance as the basic notion but rather the concept of bisecting curves, i.e., he assumes for each pair $\{p, q\}$ of sites the existence of a bisecting curve $J(p, q)$ which divides the plane into a p-region and a q-region. The intersection of all p-regions for different q's is then the Voronoi-region of site p. He also postulates that Voronoi-regions are simply-connected and partition the

[1] This work was supported by the DFG, Me 620/6, and ESPRIT P3075 ALCOM

plane. He shows that abstract Voronoi diagrams have already many of the properties of concrete Voronoi diagrams, cf. section II. He also shows that the divide-and-conquer technique can be used to construct abstract diagrams efficiently. More precisely, if the basic geometric operations on bisecting curves take time $O(1)$ and if any set S of sites can be split in time $O(|S|)$ into about equal sized subsets L and R such that the bisector between L and R (= the common boundary of regions in L with regions in R) is acyclic then the Voronoi diagrams of L and R can be merged in time $O(|S|)$ and hence the diagram of n sites can be constructed in time $O(n \log n)$. Klein's result subsumes many of the previous results and goes far beyond them. There are, however, situations, e.g., circle sites under Euclidean distance, where it is not known how to determine L and R in the divide-and-conquer algorithm such that their bisector is acyclic; cf. Sharir [S].

The purpose of this paper is to show that there is an $O(n \log n)$ randomized algorithm for constructing (a subset of Klein's) abstract Voronoi diagrams even without the acyclicity assumption. The subset is defined by the following two general position assumptions: We do not allow bisecting curves to touch but require that all intersections are crossings and that no four bisecting curves go through a common point.

The algorithm is given in section III and applications can be found in section IV. In many concrete situations, e.g., point sites with Euclidean distance function, our algorithm is just another $O(n \log n)$ algorithm, albeit simpler. There are however at least two cases where we achieve $O(n \log n)$ for the first time: For disjoint convex sites the best deterministic algorithm runs in time $O(n(\log n)^2)$ [LS86] and for line segments under the Haussdorff metric, i.e., a point x and a line segment $s = \overline{s_1 s_2}$ have distance $max(|x - s_1|, |x - s_2|)$, an $O(n \log n)$ algorithm was only known in the special case of so-called α-disjoint segments [A88b]. We also want to stress that the new algorithm is uniform in the sense that only a small number of primitives, cf. section II, are problem specific.

Our algorithm is based on Clarkson and Shor's randomized incremental construction technique [CS]. The idea is to construct the abstract Voronoi diagram of a set S of sites incrementally by adding site after site in random order. When $R \subseteq S$ is the current set of sites, the Voronoi diagram $V(R)$ and a conflict graph $G(R)$ is maintained. The conflict graph contains all pairs $\{e, t\}$, where e is an edge of $V(R)$ and $t \in S - R$ is a site still to be considered, such that addition of site t causes the edge e to be removed (either completely or partially) from the diagram. In order to make Clarkson and Shor's method applicable one has to show that for a site $s \in S - R$ the diagram $V(R \cup \{s\})$ and the conflict graph $G(R \cup \{s\})$ can be constructed from $V(R)$ and $G(R)$ in time

$$O\left(\sum_{\{e,s\} \in G(R)} deg_{G(R)}(e) \right)$$

where $deg_{G(R)}(e)$ is the degree of e in $G(R)$ and the summation is over all edges e of $V(R)$ which conflict with the new site s. This is the content of Theorem 1 of section III. If the method is applicable the expected running time is

$$O\left(n + m(n) + n \cdot \sum_{1 \leq r \leq n/2} m(r)/r^2\right)$$

where $m(r)$ is the expected number of edges in $V(R)$. For abstract diagrams $m(r) \leq 3r$ and hence the algorithm runs in time $O(n \log n)$.

Throughout we use the following notation:
For a subset $X \subseteq \mathbb{R}^2$ the closure, boundary and interior of X are denoted by $cl\ X$, $bd\ X$ and $int\ X$ respectively.

II. Abstract Voronoi Diagrams

Let $n \in \mathbb{N}$, and for each pair of integers p, q such that $1 \leq p \neq q < n$ let $D(p,q)$ be either empty or an open unbounded subset of $\mathbb{R}^2$ and let $J(p,q)$ be the boundary of $D(p,q)$. We postulate:

1) $J(p,q) = J(q,p)$ and for each p, q such that $p \neq q$ the regions $D(p,q)$, $J(p,q)$ and $D(q,p)$ form a partition of $\mathbb{R}^2$ into three disjoint sets.

2) If $\emptyset \neq D(p,q) \neq \mathbb{R}^2$ then $J(p,q)$ is homeomorphic to the open interval $(0,1)$.

We call $J(p,q)$ the bisecting curve for sites p and q. The abstract Voronoi diagram is now defined as follows:

Definition (R. Klein [Kl88a]):
a) Let $S = \{1, \ldots, n-1\}$ and

$$R(p,q) := \begin{cases} D(p,q) \cup J(p,q) & \text{if } p < q \\ D(p,q) & \text{if } p > q \end{cases}$$

$$\text{VR}(p, S) := \bigcap_{\substack{q \in S \\ q \neq p}} R(p,q)$$

$$V(S) := \bigcup_{p \in S} bd\ \text{VR}(p, S)$$

$\text{VR}(p, S)$ is called the Voronoi region of p w.r.t. S and $V(S)$ is called the Voronoi diagram of S.

b) We postulate that the Voronoi regions and the bisecting curves satisfy the following two conditions:

1) Any two bisecting curves have only a finite number of points in common. Any point in common to two bisecting curves is a proper crossing between the two curves, cf. Figure 1.

2) For any non-empty subset S' of S
   A) if $\text{VR}(p, S')$ is non-empty then $\text{VR}(p, S')$ is path-connected and has non-empty interior for each $p \in S'$,
   B) $\mathbb{R}^2 = \bigcup_{p \in S'} \text{VR}(p, S')$ (disjoint) $\square$

Remark 1: Klein's definition is actually more liberal. He allows that bisecting curves may touch and only requires that their intersection consists of finitely many connected components. In 2A) he postulates that each $\text{VR}(p, S')$ is non-empty. The weaker assumption made here does not harm his theory. $\square$

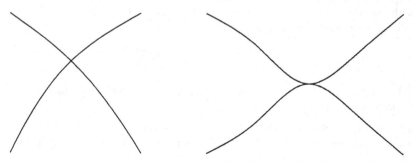

Figure 1. A crossing and touching point

Fact 1 (R. Klein [Kl88c]):

a) Voronoi regions are simply connected.

b) The following holds for each point $v \in V(S)$: There are arbitrarily small neighborhoods U of v that have the following properties. Let $\mathrm{VR}(p_1, S), \mathrm{VR}(p_2, S), \ldots, \mathrm{VR}(p_k, S)$ be the sequence of Voronoi regions traversed on a counterclockwise march around the boundary of U and let $I_1, I_2, \ldots, I_k$ denote the corresponding intervals of ∂U, where $I_j = \langle w_j, w_{j+1} \rangle \subseteq \mathrm{VR}(p_j, S)$ for $1 \leq j \leq k$ (indices must be read mod k). The intervals may be open, half-open or closed. We have $w_j \neq w_{j+1}$ for $1 \leq j \leq k$. The common boundary of $\mathrm{VR}(p_{j-1}, S)$ and $\mathrm{VR}(p_j, S)$ defines a curve segment $\beta_j \subseteq J(p_{j-1}, p_j)$ connecting v and w_j. $V(S) \cap U$ is the union of the curve segments β_j together with the point v. Each β_j is contained in the Voronoi region of $min\{p_{j-1}, p_j\}$. The open "piece of pie" bordered by β_j, β_{j+1} and I_j belongs to $\mathrm{VR}(p_j, S)$. The point v belongs to the region of $min\{p_1, \ldots, p_k\}$. Finally, $p_i \neq p_j$ for $i \neq j$. □

For the sequel, it is helpful to restrict attention to the "finite part" of $V(S)$. Let Γ be a simple closed curve such that all intersections between bisecting curves lie in the inner domain of Γ. We add a site ∞ to S, define $J(p, \infty) = J(\infty, p) = \Gamma$ for all p, $1 \leq p < n$, and $D(\infty, p)$ to be the outer domain of Γ for each p, $1 \leq p < n$.

Fact 2 (R. Klein [Kl88c]):

The boundary of each non-empty Voronoi region is a simple closed curve. Moreover, the closure of each non-empty Voronoi region $\mathrm{VR}(p, S)$, $p \neq \infty$, is homeomorphic to a closed disc. A Voronoi diagram can be represented as a planar graph in a natural way. The vertices of the graph are the points of $V(S)$ which belong to the boundary of three or more Voronoi regions and the edges of the graph correspond to the maximal connected subsets of $V(S)$ belonging to the boundary of exactly two Voronoi regions. The faces of the graph correspond to the non-empty Voronoi regions. We use $V(S)$ to also denote this graph. For the algorithmic treatment of Voronoi diagrams we also need to make a feasibility assumption about the bisecting curves.

Definition (R. Klein):

The following operations on bisecting curves are assumed to take time $O(1)$.

1) Given $J(p, q)$ and a point v, determine if $v \in D(p, q)$ holds.

2) Given a point v in common to three bisecting curves, determine the clockwise order of the curves around v.

3) Given points $v \in J(p, q)$ and $w \in J(p, r)$ and orientations of these curves, determine the first point of $J(p, r)|_{(w, \infty]}$ crossed by $J(p, q)|_{(v, \infty]}$.

4) Given $J(p, q)$ with an orientation, and points v, w, x on $J(p, q)$, determine if v comes before w on $J(p, q)|_{(x, \infty]}$. □

For simplicity we also make the following general position assumption.

General Position Assumption: No four bisecting curves have a point in common. □

The general position assumption and Fact 1 imply that each vertex of the Voronoi diagram has degree three. It lies at the intersection of three bisecting curves as shown in Figure 2.

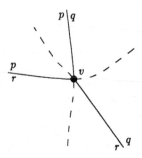

Figure 2. The bisecting curves $J(p,q), J(p,r), J(r,q)$ intersect at v. The domains $D(p,q)$ and $D(q,p)$ are indicated by the letters p and q on the two sides of the bisecting curve $J(p,q)$. The parts of the bisecting curves which define region boundaries are shown solid.

Remark 2: The requirement that the Voronoi regions partition the plane is a severe restriction on the family of bisecting curves. Consider a crossing of $J(r,p)$ and $J(r,q)$ as in Figure 3. Then $J(p,q)$ must also pass through v with $D(q,p)$ on its right.

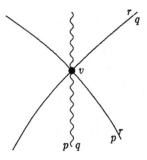

Figure 3.

We close this section with a simple but important property of Voronoi edges:

Lemma 1: Let $R \subseteq S$ and $t \in S - R$. Let e be an edge of $V(R)$ which separates the regions $VR(p, R)$ and $VR(q, R)$ of the two sites $p, q \in R$. Then $e \cap VR(t, R \cup \{t\}) = e \cap VR(t, \{p,q,t\})$.

Proof: $\subseteq$: This follows immediately from $VR(t, R \cup \{t\}) \subseteq VR(t, \{p,q,t\})$.

$\supseteq$: Let $x \in e \cap VR(t, \{p,q,t\})$. From $x \in e$ we conclude $x \in VR(p, R) \cup VR(q, R)$ and hence $x \notin VR(r, R) \supseteq VR(r, R \cup \{t\})$ for any $r \in R - \{p,q\}$. From $x \in VR(t, \{p,q,t\})$ we conclude $x \notin VR(p, \{p,q,t\}) \cup VR(q, \{p,q,t\}) \supseteq VR(p, R \cup \{t\}) \cup VR(q, R \cup \{t\})$. Thus $x \notin VR(r, R \cup \{t\})$ for any $r \in R$ and hence $x \in VR(t, R \cup \{t\})$. □

Informally, Lemma 1 states that the influence of a site on a given edge depends only on the sites defining this particular edge.

III. Incremental Construction of Abstract Voronoi Diagrams

In this section we describe the incremental construction algorithm. We start with three sites ∞, p, q where p and q are chosen at random and then add the remaining sites in random order. At the general step we have to consider a set $R \subseteq S$ of sites with $\infty \in R$ and $|R| \geq 3$. We maintain the following data structures.

1) The Voronoi diagram $V(R)$: It is stored as a planar graph as described in the previous section.

2) The conflict graph $G(R)$: The vertices of the conflict graph $G(R)$ are the edges of $V(R)$ and the sites in $S - R$. There is an edge (read: conflict) between the edge e of $V(R)$ and the site $s \in S - R$ iff $e \cap \text{VR}(s, R \cup \{s\}) \neq \emptyset$.

Remark: Recall that an edge of a Voronoi diagram is an open set and that a Voronoi region may contain part of its boundary. For the definition of conflict graph it is however immaterial whether we intersect open sets or their closures.

Lemma 2: $cl\ e \cap cl\ \text{VR}(s, R \cup \{s\}) \neq \emptyset$ implies $e \cap \text{VR}(s, R \cup \{s\}) \neq \emptyset$.

Proof: Let $x \in cl\ e \cap cl\ \text{VR}(s, R \cup \{s\})$. Assume first that x is an endpoint of e. Then x lies at the intersection of three bisecting curves of sites in R. Hence no bisecting curve $J(s, r)$, $r \in R$, can go through x and therefore an entire neighborhood of x must belong to $\text{VR}(s, R \cup \{s\})$. Thus $e \cap \text{VR}(s, R \cup \{s\}) \neq \emptyset$.
Assume next that $x \in e \cap bd\ \text{VR}(s, R \cup \{s\})$. Then $x \in J(p, q) \cap J(s, r)$ for some sites $p, q, r \in R$. The bisecting curves $J(p, q)$ and $J(s, r)$ cross at point x and hence there is a point $y \in e$ in the neighborhood of x such that $y \in \text{VR}(s, R \cup \{s\})$. $\qquad\square$

We next discuss how to update the data structures after the addition of a site $s \in S - R$ to R. We first concentrate on the construction of the Voronoi diagram $V(R \cup \{s\})$ from $V(R)$ and $G(R)$.

Let $S = \text{VR}(s, R \cup \{s\})$. We proceed in several steps. Lemma 3 deals with the case $S = \emptyset$. The case $S \neq \emptyset$ is dealt with in Lemmas 4 and 5. We show that the intersection of the current diagram $V(R)$ with the region S is a connected set (Lemma 4) and that the intersection $e \cap S$ for an edge e of $V(R)$ consists of at most two components (Lemma 5). From Lemmas 4 and 5 we derive the update algorithm.

Lemma 3: $S = \emptyset$ iff $deg_{G(R)}(s) = 0$.

Proof: If $S = \emptyset$ then clearly $deg_{G(R)}(s) = 0$. So let us assume $S \neq \emptyset$. If $deg_{G(R)}(s) = 0$ then $cl\ S \subseteq int\ \text{VR}(r, R)$ for some $r \in R$. Next observe that $\text{VR}(r, R \cup \{s\}) = \text{VR}(r, R) - S$. Also $r \neq \infty$ since $\text{VR}(\infty, P)$ is the outer domain of the closed curve Γ for all P, $\infty \in P \subseteq S$. Thus $\text{VR}(r, R \cup \{s\})$ is bounded but not simply connected. This contradicts Fact 1a. $\qquad\square$

If $S = \emptyset$ then $V(R \cup \{s\}) = V(R)$. So let us assume $S \neq \emptyset$ and hence $deg_{G(R)}(s) \neq 0$. Let $I = V(R) \cap cl\ S$.

Lemma 4: I is a connected set which intersects $bd\ S$ in at least two points.

Proof: The boundary $bd\ S$ is a simple closed curve which does not go through any vertex of $V(R)$. This follows from Fact 2 and the general position assumption. Also $I \neq \emptyset$ by Lemma 2. Let $I_1, I_2, \ldots, I_k$ be the connected components of I.

Claim: Each I_j, $1 \leq j \leq k$, contains two points of $bd\ S$.

Proof: Assume first that I_j contains no points of $bd\ S$, i.e., $I_j \subseteq int\ S$. Then there is a simple closed curve $C \subseteq int\ S$ such that I_j is contained in the inner domain of C and C does not intersect $V(R)$. Thus $C \subseteq int\ \mathrm{VR}(r, R)$ for some $r \in R$. Since Voronoi regions are simply connected, C and its interior must belong to $\mathrm{VR}(r, R)$ and hence C cannot contain a component I_j in its interior. Assume next that I_j intersects $bd\ S$ in exactly one point, say x. Then there is a simple closed curve C containing I_j in its inner domain such that $x \in C$, $C - \{x\} \subseteq int\ S$ and $C - \{x\}$ does not intersect $V(R)$. Thus $C - \{x\} \subseteq \mathrm{VR}(r, R)$ for some $r \in R$ and hence x is a point on an edge of $V(R)$ such that both sides of the edge belong to the same Voronoi region. This contradicts Fact 1. $\square$

Assume now that $k \geq 2$. Then there is a path $P \subseteq cl\ S - (I_1 \cup \ldots \cup I_k)$ connecting two points on the boundary $bd\ S$ such that one component of $S - P$ contains I_1 and the other component contains I_2. Let x and y be the endpoints of P and let $r \in R$ be such that $P \subseteq \mathrm{VR}(r, R)$. Since $x, y \notin V(R)$ we conclude that $\mathrm{VR}(r, R \cup \{s\}) = \mathrm{VR}(r, R) - S \neq \emptyset$. Thus $x, y \in cl\ \mathrm{VR}(r, R \cup \{s\})$ and hence there is a simple path $Q \subseteq cl\ \mathrm{VR}(r, R \cup \{s\})$ with endpoints x and y. The cycle $P \circ Q$ is then contained in $cl\ \mathrm{VR}(r, R)$ and contains either I_1 or I_2 in its interior. Thus $\mathrm{VR}(r, R)$ is not simply connected, a contradiction to Fact 2. $\square$

Lemma 5: Let e be an edge of $V(R)$. If $e \cap S \neq \emptyset$ then either $e \cap S = V(R) \cap S$ and $e \cap S$ is a single component or $e - S$ is a single component; cf. Figure 4.

Proof: Assume first that $e \cap S = V(R) \cap S$. Since $V(R) \cap S$ is connected by Lemma 4 we conclude that $e \cap S$ is connected. Assume next that $e \cap S \neq V(R) \cap S$. Then with every point $x \in e \cap S$ one of the subpaths of e connecting x to an endpoint of e must be contained in S. Hence $e - S$ is a single component. $\square$

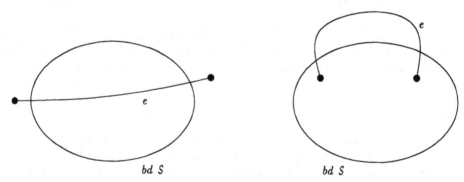

Figure 4. Two cases of Lemma 5

Let $L = \{e$ edge of $V(R)$; $\{e, s\} \in G(R)\}$. For $e \in L$ let $e' = e \cap S$. Note that $e' = e \cap \mathrm{VR}(s, \{p, q, s\})$ by Lemma 1 where e separates the regions of sites p and q; hence e' can be computed from e in time $O(1)$. We have shown above that the set $\bigcup_{e \in L} cl\ e' = V(R) \cap cl\ S$ is connected. Let $B = \{x; x$ is an endpoint of e' which is not an endpoint of e for some $e \in L\} = V(R) \cap bd\ S$. Since $bd\ S$ is a simple closed curve by Fact 2, $bd\ S$ induces a cyclic ordering on the points in B. Since $V(R) \cap S$ is connected this cyclic ordering can be determined by a traversal of the planar graph $V(R) \cap cl\ S$. It is now easy to update the Voronoi diagram as follows:

Step 1: Compute e' for each $e \in L$. Remove e' from $V(R)$ for each $e \in L$.

Step 2: Compute B and the cyclic ordering on B induced by $bd\ S$.

Step 3: Let $x_1, \ldots, x_k$ be the set B in its cyclic ordering and
let $r_i \in R$ be such that $\{x_i, x_{i+1}\} \subseteq bd\ \mathrm{VR}(r_i, R)$.
(1) **for** i **from** 1 **to** k
(2) **do** add the part of $J(r_i, s)$ with endpoints x_i and x_{i+1} to the Voronoi diagram
(3) **od**

For the time bound we only have to observe that steps 1 and 2 take time $O(|L|)$ and that step 3 takes time $O(k) = O(|L|)$. This proves the following

Lemma 6: Let $s \in S - R$. Then $V(R \cup \{s\})$ can be constructed from $V(R)$ and $G(R)$ in time $O(deg_{G(R)}(s) + 1)$.

We now turn to the update of the conflict graph.

Lemma 7: Let $s \in S - R$. Then $G(R \cup \{s\})$ can be constructed from $V(R)$ and $G(R)$ in time

$$O\Big(\sum_{\{e,s\} \in G(R)} deg_{G(R)}(e) \Big).$$

Proof: In this proof we distinguish three cases: edges of $V(R \cap \{s\})$ which already were edges of $V(R)$, edges which are part of edges of $V(R)$, and edges which are completely new. The only difficult case is the third one; it is dealt with in Lemma 8.

As above let $L = \{e; e$ is an edge of $V(R)$ and $e \cap S \neq \emptyset\}$ where $S = \mathrm{VR}(s, R \cup \{s\})$. For $e \notin L$ the conflict information does not change. This follows from $e \cap \mathrm{VR}(t, R \cup \{s,t\}) = e \cap (\mathrm{VR}(t, R \cup \{t\}) - \mathrm{VR}(s, R \cup \{s,t\}))$ and $(e \cap \mathrm{VR}(t, R \cup \{t\})) - (e \cap \mathrm{VR}(s, R \cup \{s,t\})) = e \cap \mathrm{VR}(t, R \cup \{t\})$.

Let us next consider an edge $e \in L$. If $e \subseteq S$ then e has to be deleted from the conflict graph. This certainly takes time $O(deg_{G(R)}(e))$. If $e \not\subseteq S$ then $e - S$ consists of at most two subsegments by Lemma 5. Let e' be one of those subsegments and let $t \in S - R - \{s\}$. Then $e' \cap \mathrm{VR}(t, R \cup \{s\} \cup \{t\}) = e' \cap \bigcap_{r \in R} R(t, r) \cap R(t, s) = e' \cap \mathrm{VR}(t, R \cup \{t\}) \cap R(t, s) \subseteq e \cap \mathrm{VR}(t, R \cup \{t\})$ and hence any site t in conflict with e' must be in conflict with e.

It remains to consider those edges of $V(R \cup \{s\})$ which are not fragments of edges of $V(R)$. Let e_{12} be one of those edges. The endpoints x_1 and x_2 of e_{12} lie in the interior of edges e_1 and e_2 on $bd\ \mathrm{VR}(p, R)$ for some $p \in R$. Also e_{12} is part of the bisecting curve $J(p, s)$. Note that $p \neq \infty$ since $J(\infty, s) = \Gamma \subseteq V(R)$. Let P be that part of $bd\ \mathrm{VR}(p, R)$ which connects x_1 and x_2 and is contained in S in all sufficiently small neighborhoods of x_1 and x_2.

Claim: $P \subseteq S$.

Proof: $bd\ \mathrm{VR}(p, R)$ is a simple closed curve and $int\ \mathrm{VR}(p, R)$ is the bounded domain defined by this curve. Assume now that P crosses $bd\ S$. Then $\mathrm{VR}(p, R \cup \{s\}) = \mathrm{VR}(p, R) - S$ is not connected, a contradiction. $\square$

Lemma 8: Let $t \in S - R - \{s\}$, and let t conflict with e_{12} in $V(R \cup \{s\})$. Then t conflicts in $V(R)$ with either e_1 or e_2 or one of the edges of P.

Proof: Consider $VR(p, R)$.

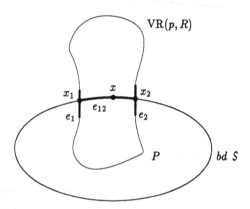

Figure 5.

By the definition of conflict a point $x \in e_{12}$ exists such that $x \in VR(t, R \cup \{s, t\}) \subseteq VR(t, R \cup \{t\})$. Since we claim a contradiction we assume that t is not in conflict with P, e_1 or e_2 in $V(R)$. Thus, $VR(t, R \cup \{s, t\}) \cap U(x_1) \subseteq VR(t, R \cup \{t\}) \cap U(x_1) = \emptyset$ for any sufficiently small neighborhood $U(x_1)$ of x_1. Now consider in any such neighborhood of x_1 the wedge spanned by e_{12} and the part of e_1 outside S. The points in this wedge all belong to $VR(p, R \cup \{s, t\})$. The same is true for any sufficiently small neighborhood of x_2 with e_2 instead of e_1. Since $VR(p, R \cup \{s, t\})$ is connected, there is a path Q from x_1 to x_2 running completely inside $VR(p, R \cup \{s, t\}) \subseteq VR(p, R \cup \{t\})$ except at the endpoints.

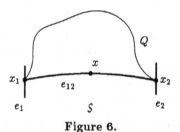

Figure 6.

By definition of P and Q the Voronoi region $VR(t, R \cup \{t\})$ cannot intersect these two paths. Moreover, x lies in the interior of the cycle $x_1 \circ P \circ x_2 \circ Q$; otherwise $VR(p, R)$ would not be simply connected. From $x_1, x_2 \notin VR(t, R \cup \{t\})$ and $x \in VR(t, R \cup \{t\})$ we conclude that $VR(t, R \cup \{t\})$ lies in the interior of the cycle. This is a contradiction to the fact that $VR(p, R \cup \{t\})$ is simply connected. $\square$

Lemmas 8 and 1 together allow us to compute the conflict information for the new edges. Let $e_{12} \subseteq J(p, s)$ be any new edge. A site t in conflict with edge e_{12} must have conflicted in $G(R)$ with either e_1, e_2 or one of the edges on the path P by Lemma 8. Also for any such site t we can compute the conflict information $e_{12} \cap VR(t, R \cup \{s, t\})$ in time $O(1)$ by Lemma 1. Thus the set of neighbors of edge e_{12} in $G(R \cup \{s\})$ can be computed in time

$$O\left(\sum_{e \in P \cup \{e_1, e_2\}} deg_{G(R)}(e) \right)$$

where the sum is over all edges in $P \cup \{e_1, e_2\}$. Next observe that every edge $e \in V(R)$ with $e \cap VR(s, R \cup \{s\}) \neq \emptyset$ can belong at most two times to a path P for some new edge by planarity. Thus $G(R \cup \{s\})$ can be obtained from $G(R)$ in time

$$O\left(\sum_{\{e,s\} \in G(R)} deg_{G(R)}(e) \right).$$

This proves Lemma 7. $\qquad \square$

Theorem 1: a) Let $s \in S - R$. Then the data structures $G(R \cup \{s\})$ and $V(R \cup \{s\})$ can be obtained from $G(R)$ and $V(R)$ in time

$$O\left(\sum_{\{e,s\} \in G(R)} deg_{G(R)}(e) \right).$$

b) For $R \subseteq S$, $|R| = 3$ and $\infty \in R$ the data structures $V(R)$ and $G(R)$ can be set up in time $O(n)$ where $n = |S|$.

Proof: a) This point summarizes Lemma 6 and 7.

b) The Voronoi diagram $V(R)$ for three sites ∞, p and q has the structure shown in Figure 7 and can certainly be set up in time $O(1)$. Also for each of the edges e of $V(R)$ and each of the $n-3$ sites in $S - R$ one can test $e \cap VR(t, R \cup \{t\}) \neq \emptyset$ in $O(1)$ by Lemma 1. This proves b). $\qquad \square$

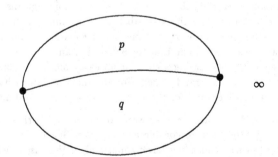

Figure 7. The Voronoi diagram for sites ∞, p and q.

Lemma 9: The number of edges of $V(R)$ is at most $3|R|$.

Proof: $V(R)$ is a planar graph with at most $|R|$ regions. Also, each vertex has degree three. The number of edges is therefore at most $3|R|$ by Euler's Formula. $\qquad \square$

Theorem 2: The abstract Voronoi diagram $V(S)$ of n sites can be constructed by a randomized algorithm in time $O(n \log n)$.

Proof: In [CS], Clarkson and Shor show that randomized incremental construction has expected running time

$$O\Big(m(n) + n \cdot \sum_{1 \le r \le n/2} m(r)/r^2 + n\Big)$$

provided that initialization takes time $O(n)$ and addition of an object (here site) s to the set R takes time proportional to

$$\sum_{\{e,s\} \in G(R)} deg_{G(R)}(e),$$

where the summation is over all regions (here edges) of the current structure (here Voronoi diagram $V(R)$) which conflict with site s. Also $m(r)$ is the expected size of the structure for a random subset $R \subseteq S$ of r elements. In our case we have $m(r) \le 3r$ by Lemma 9. Finally, the assumptions of Clarkson's theorem are satisfied by Theorem 1. The time bound follows. □

Remark: In our algorithm $\infty \in R$ always. An inspection of Clarkson's argument shows that this minor deviation from randomness does not change the time bound.

IV. Applications

Many previously considered types of Voronoi diagrams fall under the framework described above.

1. Point Sites: In their pioneering paper Shamos/Hoey [SH] showed how to construct the Voronoi diagram for point sites under the Euclidean metric in time $O(n \log n)$. This was later extended to arbitrary L_p-metrics, $1 \le p \le \infty$, by Lee [L], to the L_2-metric with additive weights by Sharir [S] and Fortune [F87], to the so-called Moscow-metric by Klein [Kl88b], to convex distance functions by Chew/Drysdale [CD] and Fortune [F85] and to abstract Voronoi diagrams by Klein/Wood [KW] and Klein [Kl88a]. The previous algorithms for abstract diagrams had to assume, as they were based on the divide-and-conquer approach, that the set of sites S can be partitioned into about equal sized subsets L and R such that the bisector between L and R is acyclic. This assumption is crucial for the efficiency of the merging step. For all cases mentioned our algorithm gives an alternative $O(n \log n)$ solution, albeit randomized. For abstract diagrams ([Kl88a]) we do not need the acyclicity assumption, however, and for the L_p-norm we may also add additive weights.

2. Beyond Point Sites: Point and line sites were considered by Kirkpatrick [Ki] and Fortune [F87], and disjoint convex objects were considered by Leven/Sharir [LS86]. In the latter case, the running time is $O\big(n(\log n)^2\big)$ since the Leven/Sharir algorithm uses divide-and-conquer and the bisector between the subsets L and R of S mentioned above is not necessarily acyclic. Our algorithm runs in time $O(n \log n)$. Other applications are the Voronoi diagrams for circles under the Laguerre distance (Imai/Iri/Murota [IIM], Aurenhammer [A87], [A88a]) and for disjoint convex polygons under a convex distance function (Leven/Sharir [LS87]).

Of course, there are also types of Voronoi diagrams which do *not* fall under the framework, e.g., the diagram for points sites under the Euclidean metric with multiplicative weight (Aurenhammer/Edelsbrunner [AE]), the diagram for points and circular arcs, and the diagram for points under metrics which arise from weighted partitions of the plane (Mitchell/Papadimitriou [MP]). In all three cases the bisector $J(p,q)$ of two sites may be a closed curve, cf. Figure 8.

Figure 8. The bisector for a point and a circular arc.

V. Conclusions and Open Problems

We showed that Clarkson and Shor's randomized incremental construction method works for (a subset of) Klein's abstract Voronoi diagrams. Many previously considered types of Voronoi diagrams can thus be handled by the same simple algorithm. In [KMM] the results of this paper are extended in two ways. We show that the algorithm can be programmed on a schema level such that specific Voronoi diagram algorithms can be derived in a simple way; we also drop the general position assumption and the assumption that bisecting curves may not touch. Nevertheless, many open problems remain:

1) Can the concept of abstract Voronoi diagram be generalized to higher dimensions?

2) What can be done in two dimensions without the assumption that bisectors are non-closed curves?

3) Can the algorithm be modified in order to handle higher-order Voronoi diagrams?

VI. References

[A87]   Aurenhammer, F.: *Power diagrams: properties, algorithms and applications*, SIAM J. of Computing 16 (1987), pp. 78–96.

[A88a] Aurenhammer, F.: *Improved algorithms for discs and balls using power diagrams*, J. Algorithms 9 (1988), pp. 151–161.

[A88b] Aurenhammer, F.: *Voronoi Diagrams — A survey*, Tech. Report 263, Institutes for Information Processing, Graz Technical University, Austria (1988)

[AE]   Aurenhammer, F., and Edelsbrunner, H.: *An optimal algorithm for constructing the weighted Voronoi diagram in the plane*, Pattern Recognition 17 (2) (1984), pp. 251–257.

[Br]   Brown, K.Q.: *Voronoi diagrams from convex hulls*, IPL 9 (1979), pp. 223–228.

[CD]   Chew, L.P., and Drysdale III, R.L.: *Voronoi diagrams based on convex distance functions*, Proc. 1st ACM Symp. on Computational Geometry (1985), pp. 235–244.

[CS]   Clarkson, K.L., and Shor, P.W.: *Algorithms for diametral pairs and convex hulls that are optimal, randomized and incremental*, Proc. 4th ACM Symp. on Computational Geometry (1988), pp. 12–17.

[ES]   Edelsbrunner, H. and Seidel, R.: *Voronoi diagrams and arrangements*, Discrete & Computational Geometrie 1 (1986), pp. 25–44.

[F85]   Fortune, S.: *A fast algorithm for polygon containment by translation (extended abstract)*, Proc. 12th Int. Colloq. Automata, Languages and Programming (1985), LNCS 194, Springer-Verlag, New York, pp. 189–198.

[F87]   Fortune, S.: *A sweepline algorithm for Voronoi diagrams*, Algorithmica 2 (1987), pp. 153–174.

[IIM]   Imai, H., Iri, M., and Murota, K.: *Voronoi diagram in the Laguerre geometry and its applications*, SIAM J. of Computing 14 (1985), pp. 93–105.

[Ki]   Kirkpatrick, D.G.: *Efficient computation of continuos skeletons*, Proc. 20th Symp. on Foundations of Computer Science (1979), pp. 18–27.

[Kl88a] Klein, R.: *Abstract Voronoi diagrams and their applications (extended abstract)*, in: H. Noltemeier (ed.), Computational Geometry and its Applications (CG '88), Würzburg (1988), LNCS 333, pp. 148–157.

[Kl88b] Klein, R.: *Voronoi diagrams in the Moscow metric (extended abstract)*, in: Graphtheoretic Concepts in Computer Science (WG '88), Amsterdam (1988), to appear in LNCS.

[Kl88c] Klein, R.: *On a generalization of planar Voronoi diagrams (Habilitationsschrift)*, Mathematische Fakultät der Universität Freiburg i. Br. (1988)

[KMM]   Klein, R., Mehlhorn, K., and Meiser, S.: *On the Construction of Abstract Voronoi Diagrams, II*, Tech. Report, FB Informatik, Universität des Saarlandes (1989)

[KW]   Klein, R., and Wood, D.: *Voronoi diagrams based on general metrics in the plane*, in: R. Cori and M. Wirsing (eds.), Proc. 5th Annual Symp. on Theoretical Aspects of Computer Science (STACS), Bordeaux (1988), LNCS 294, pp. 281–291.

[L]   Lee, D.T.: *Two-dimensional Voronoi diagrams in the L_p-metric*, J. ACM 27 (1980), pp. 604–618.

[LS86]   Leven, D., and Sharir, M.: *Intersection and proximity problems and Voronoi diagrams*, in: J. Schwartz and C.K. Yap (eds.), Advances in Robotics, Vol. 1 (1986), Lawrence Erlbaum.

[LS87]   Leven, D., and Sharir, M.: *Planning a purely translational motion for a convex object in two-dimensional space using generalized Voronoi diagrams*, Discrete & Computational Geometry 2 (1987), pp. 9–31.

[MP]   Mitchell, J.S.B., and Papadimitriou, C.H.: *The weighted region problem*, in: Proc. 3rd ACM Symp. on Computational Geometry, Waterloo (1987), pp. 30–38.

[S]   Sharir, M.: *Intersection and closest-pair problems for a set of planar discs*, SIAM J. of Computing 14 (1985), pp. 448–468.

[SH]   Shamos, M.I., and Hoey, D.: *Closest point problems*, Proc. 16th IEEE Symp. on Foundations of Computer Science (1975), pp. 151–162.

Approximation of Convex Figures
by Pairs of Rectangles*

Otfried Schwarzkopf

Ulrich Fuchs

Günter Rote[†]

Emo Welzl

Institut für Informatik, FB Mathematik, Freie Universität Berlin
Arnimallee 2–6, D-1000 Berlin 33
West Germany

Abstract

We consider the problem of approximating a convex figure in the plane by a pair (r, R) of homothetic (i.e. similar and parallel) rectangles with $r \subset C \subset R$. We show the existence of such pairs where the sides of the outer rectangle have length at most double the length of the inner rectangle, thereby solving a problem posed by Pólya and Szegő.

If the n vertices of a convex polygon C are given as a sorted array, such an approximating pair of rectangles can be computed in time $\mathcal{O}(\log^3 n)$.

1   Introduction

Let C be a convex figure in the plane. A pair (r, R) of rectangles is called an approximating pair for C, if $r \subset C \subset R$ and if r and R are homothetic, i.e. they are parallel and have the same aspect ratio. Note that this is equivalent to the existence of an expansion $x \mapsto \lambda(x - x_0) + x_0$ (with center x_0 and expansion factor λ) which maps r into R.

We measure the quality $\lambda(r, R)$ of our approximating pair (r, R) as the quotient of the length of a side of R divided by the length of the corresponding side of r. This is exactly the expansion factor λ used in the expansion mapping defined above.

The motivation for our investigation is the use of r and R as simple certificates for the impossibility (possibility) of translational obstacle-avoiding motions of C. Note first that if R can be moved along a path, then this is also possible for C. Moreover, let us say that a motion planning problem for C is *simple* if a motion is still possible for C expanded by a factor of 2. Now, if (r, R) has quality 2, then every simple motion planning problem for C has also a solution for R. More details can be found in [AFM*].

Pólya and Szegő showed in [PS51] that for every convex figure C there is an approximating pair (r, R) with $\lambda(r, R) \leq 3$, and raised the question whether that upper bound could be improved. In fact, an improvement to $2\sqrt{2}$ follows from work done by

---

*This research was supported by the Deutsche Forschungsgemeinschaft under Grant Al 253/1-1, Schwerpunktprogramm "Datenstrukturen und effiziente Algorithmen"

[†]Current address: Institut für Mathematik, Technische Universität Graz, Kopernikusgasse 24, A-8010 Graz, Austria

John [Joh48] and Leichtweiß [Lei59]. They prove that for every convex figure C in the plane there is an approximating pair of homothetic ellipses with quality 2. Since it can be easily shown that for any ellipse there is an approximating pair of rectangles with quality $\sqrt{2}$, the claimed bound of $2\sqrt{2}$ follows. A related problem has been considered by Lassak [Las89], who shows that for every centrally symmetric convex body M there are affine images a and A of M with $a \subseteq C \subseteq A$, where A can be obtained from a by an expansion with expansion factor λ and center in the center of a. He proves that λ can always be chosen to be $\sqrt{2} + 1$, which is optimal.

The question of further improvement in our problem has remained open. In the present paper we settle the problem by demonstrating that for every convex figure there exists an approximating pair (r, R) with a factor $\lambda(r, R) \leq 2$. This bound is optimal, since for a triangle there is no approximating pair with a factor less than 2 (this can be seen by comparing the areas of a minimum circumscribed and a maximum inscribed rectangle for a triangle).

In Section 2 we consider approximations by rectangles with a given fixed orientation. On the one hand, this prepares the basics for the upper bound, on the other hand we show that an optimal approximating pair with a fixed orientation can be computed in time $\mathcal{O}(\log^2 n)$ if C is a convex n-gon whose vertices are stored in a sorted array. In Section 3 we show the existence of approximating pairs of quality 2 and in Section 4 we present an algorithm which computes such a pair in time $\mathcal{O}(\log^3 n)$.

2 Approximation with a Fixed Orientation

Let r be a rectangle with a counterclockwise numbering $v_1(r)$, $v_2(r)$, $v_3(r)$, $v_4(r)$ of its vertices. Then the *orientation* $\alpha(r)$ is the angle of the vector from $v_1(r)$ to $v_2(r)$, and the *aspect ratio* $\sigma(r)$ is

$$\overline{|v_3(r)v_2(r)|} \,/\, \overline{|v_1(r)v_2(r)|};$$

($\overline{|pq|}$ denotes the length of the segment connecting p and q). By $\mathcal{R}(\alpha, \sigma)$ we denote the set of all rectangles with orientation α and aspect ratio σ, see Figure 1.

Note that, depending on the choice of the vertex v_1, a rectangle belongs to the classes $\mathcal{R}(\alpha, \sigma)$, $\mathcal{R}(\alpha + \frac{\pi}{2}, \frac{1}{\sigma})$, $\mathcal{R}(\alpha + \pi, \sigma)$, or $\mathcal{R}(\alpha + \frac{3\pi}{2}, \frac{1}{\sigma})$. For the time being, whenever we talk about a rectangle, we assume that we have a fixed counterclockwise numbering of the vertices.

Let C denote a convex figure in the plane. For every α there is a unique minimum area rectangle $R(\alpha)$ with orientation α enclosing C. Let $\sigma(\alpha)$ denote the aspect ratio of $R(\alpha)$; so $R(\alpha) \in \mathcal{R}(\alpha, \sigma(\alpha))$. $\sigma(\alpha)$ is the quotient of the "width" of C when seen from directions $\alpha + \pi/2$ and α. Since the width is a continuous function of α and it is bounded away from 0, σ is also continuous.

Now consider an approximating pair (r, R) for C with orientation α. R contains the minimum area enclosing rectangle $R(\alpha)$. Since we can shrink r and R appropriately, we may as well assume that $R = R(\alpha)$, so $r \in \mathcal{R}(\alpha, \sigma(\alpha))$. The problem of finding the best approximating pair with orientation α thus reduces to the problem of finding the largest rectangle with orientation α and aspect ratio $\sigma(\alpha)$ contained in C. If we define

$$\mathcal{F}(\alpha) := \{r \in \mathcal{R}(\alpha, \sigma(\alpha)) \mid r \subseteq C\}$$

the problem becomes: Find the largest rectangle in $\mathcal{F}(\alpha)$.

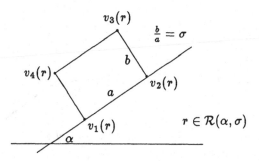

Figure 1

We have

Lemma 1 *Let r be a largest rectangle in $\mathcal{F}(\alpha)$. Then two diagonal vertices of r lie on the boundary ∂C of C.*

Proof: If at most one vertex of r lies on ∂C, r is clearly not maximal. So assume vertices $v_1(r)$ and $v_4(r)$ lie on ∂C, while $v_2(r)$ and $v_3(r)$ don't, i.e. there is some $\epsilon > 0$ such that the ϵ-disks U_2, U_3 around $v_2(r)$ and $v_3(r)$ are contained in C. By convexity of C, the convex hull C' of $v_1(r)$, $v_4(r)$, U_2, and U_3 is contained in C. But here is a larger copy of r contained in C', contradicting the maximality of r. $\qquad\square$

We give an algorithm that computes the largest rectangle with fixed orientation and shape contained in a polygon with n vertices in time $\mathcal{O}(\log^2 n)$. Since $\sigma(\alpha)$ can be computed in time $\mathcal{O}(\log n)$ using standard search techniques, the best approximating pair with fixed orientation α can be computed in the same time.

The algorithm assumes that $v_1(r)$ and $v_3(r)$ lie on ∂C. If it fails to find a rectangle, we use the analogous algorithm assuming that $v_2(r)$ and $v_4(r)$ lie on ∂C. Due to the previous lemma this is sufficient.

Since we know orientation α and aspect ratio $\sigma(\alpha)$ of r, we also know the orientation β of the first diagonal of r. Since C is convex, it has two supporting lines ℓ_1 and ℓ_2 with orientation β. Between ℓ_1 and ℓ_2, C can be decomposed into a lower and an upper chain as sketched in Fig. 2. $v_1(r)$ must lie on the lower chain, $v_3(r)$ on the upper chain.

Any point p on the lower chain determines a unique rectangle $r(p) \in \mathcal{R}(\alpha, \sigma(\alpha))$ with $v_1(r(p)) = p$ and $v_3(r(p))$ on the upper chain. Given p, $r(p)$ can be computed in time $\mathcal{O}(\log n)$ by checking the intersection of the line with orientation β through p with ∂C (Using binary search, the intersection of a line with ∂C can be found in time $\mathcal{O}(\log n)$).

Now consider the function f : lower chain $\longrightarrow \mathbb{R}^+$, where $f(p)$ is defined as the length of the intersection of C with a line through p with orientation β. Since C is convex, f is bitonic, i.e. there is some p_0 on the lower chain with $f(p_0)$ maximal, and f increases between ℓ_1 and p_0 and decreases between p_0 and ℓ_2.

This point p_0 can be found in time $\mathcal{O}(\log^2 n)$ by binary search on the vertices of both chains (For every vertex v the value $f(v)$ can be determined in time $\mathcal{O}(\log n)$ by the above argument).

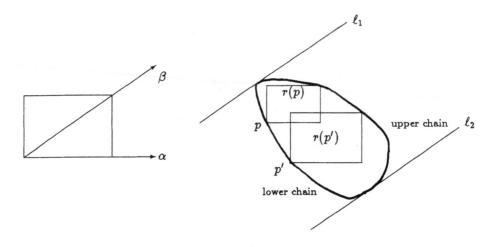

Figure 2

We now have the following

Lemma 2 *Let p, p' be points on the lower chain with p' closer to ℓ_2 than p, see Fig. 2. Then*

(i) *If $v_4(r(p)) \in C$, then $v_4(r(p')) \in C$*

(ii) *If $v_2(r(p')) \in C$, then $v_2(r(p)) \in C$*

Proof: Since statements are symmetric, we prove only *(i)*. Consider the convex hull C' of $v_1(r(p)) = p$, $v_1(r(p')) = p'$, $v_3(r(p'))$, $v_3(r(p))$, and $v_4(r(p))$, which is contained in C. It is easy to verify that $v_4(r(p'))$ lies in C', so $v_4(r(p')) \in C$. $\square$

This lemma shows that the set

$$I := \{p \in \text{lower chain} \mid r(p) \subseteq C\}$$

is a connected subchain of the lower chain.

For which $p \in I$ is $r(p)$ largest? The size of $r(p)$ is determined by $|\overline{v_1(r(p))v_3(r(p))}|$, i.e. by $f(p)$. Since f is bitonic, there are two cases: Either $p_0 \in I$, which implies that $\max_{p \in I} f(p)$ is attained in p_0, or $p_0 \notin I$ and the maximum is attained in one of the two endpoints of I. It therefore suffices to find the endpoints of I. We consider the left endpoint p_1 of I. It is determined as the unique point where $v_4(r(p_1))$ lies on ∂C, and it can be found as follows:

1. Perform binary search on the vertices of the lower chain. For each vertex p, determine whether $v_4(r(p))$ lies in C. If so, p_1 lies closer to ℓ_1, otherwise closer to ℓ_2. As demonstrated above, every test takes time $\mathcal{O}(\log n)$.

2. We now have an edge of the lower chain that contains p_1. When a point p moves on this edge, $v_3(r(p))$ moves along a subchain of the upper chain. We continue the binary search on the vertices of this subchain.

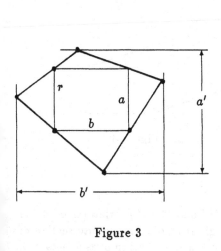

Figure 3

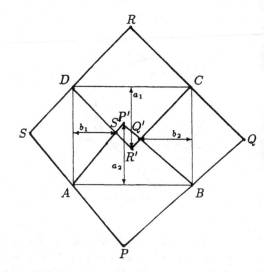

Figure 4

3. Now we have a line segment a on the lower chain that contains p_1, and when a point p moves on a, $v_3(r(p))$ moves on a line segment on the upper chain, so $v_4(r(p))$ moves on a line. We compute this line and find the intersection with ∂C. As mentioned above, this takes time $\mathcal{O}(\log n)$.

There are $\mathcal{O}(\log n)$ steps in the binary search, so we have

Theorem 3 *Given a polygon with n vertices in the plane, the optimal approximating pair with a fixed orientation α can be computed in time $\mathcal{O}(\log^2 n)$.*

3   The Upper Bound Result

We now solve the problem posed by Pólya and Szegő.

Theorem 4 *For every convex figure there exists an approximating pair (r, R) with $\lambda(r, R) \leq 2$.*

In a first step we show that if we consider an approximating pair $(r, R(\alpha))$ where all four vertices of r touch the boundary of C, we have $\lambda(r, R) \leq 2$. Using a continuity argument we then show that such a pair always exists.

Lemma 5 *Let q be a quadrilateral with inscribed rectangle r. If every vertex of r touches q like in Fig. 3, then one of the following holds:*

$$a' \leq 2a \qquad or \qquad b' \leq 2b.$$

Proof: Let q and r as in Fig. 4. We reflect P at AB to obtain P', Q at BC etc. In other words, we "wrap" a sheet with the shape of q around the rectangle r. (We may think of r as being a piece of chocolate!) We have to show that either $a_1 + a_2 \leq a$ or $b_1 + b_2 \leq b$.
   There are two cases: If the triangles ABP', BCQ', CDR', DAS' do not overlap, their area is less than the area of $ABCD$, so we have $\frac{1}{2}(a_2 b + b_2 a + a_1 b + b_1 a) = \frac{1}{2}((a_1 + a_2)b + a(b_1 + b_2)) \leq ab$. This is impossible for $a_1 + a_2 > a$ and $b_1 + b_2 > b$.

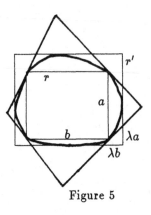

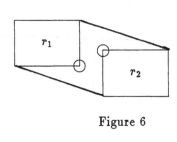

Figure 6

Figure 5

So assume – without loss of generality – that ABP' and CDR' overlap (as depicted in Fig. 4). Then we can cut $ABCD$ vertically through any point in the intersection of ABP' and CDR'. S' lies to the left, Q' to the right of this cut. This implies $b_1 + b_2 \leq b$. $\square$

Lemma 6 *Let C be a convex figure with an approximating pair (r, R) such that*

(i) every vertex of r touches the boundary ∂C of C, and

(ii) every edge of R touches C.

Then $\lambda(r, R) \leq 2$.

Proof: Introduce supporting lines for C in every vertex of r. They form a quadrilateral q which contains C like in Fig. 5. Denote the lengths of the sides of r by a and b, and the lengths of the corresponding ones of R by λa and λb. Since $C \subseteq q$ and because of (i) and (ii) $\lambda a \leq 2a$ or $\lambda b \leq 2b$ holds due to Lemma 5. But in any case this implies $\lambda(r, R) = \lambda \leq 2$. $\square$

Thus, in order to prove Theorem 4 we have to find a direction α and an approximating pair of rectangles fulfilling the conditions of Lemma 6. The idea of the proof is to consider, for each direction α, the unique smallest rectangle $R(\alpha)$ enclosing C, and the largest inscribed homothetic copy $r(\alpha)$ of $R(\alpha)$, as in Section 2. By Lemma 1 $r(\alpha)$ must touch ∂C at two diagonal vertices, either v_1 and v_3 (case 1) or at v_2 and v_4 (case 2). If we rotate α from 0 to $\pi/2$, cases 1 and 2 exchange roles. Intuitively, there must be an intermediate direction where the situation changes and all four vertices touch ∂C.

To make these ideas and the underlying continuity arguments precise requires a little more formal work, mainly to cope with possible degeneracies, e.g., (the placement of) $r(\alpha)$ need not be unique.

Lemma 7 *For some α let $r_1, r_2 \in \mathcal{F}(\alpha)$ such that $\{v_1(r_1), v_3(r_1)\} \subset \partial C$, $\{v_2(r_2), v_4(r_2)\} \subset \partial C$. Then there is some $r \in \mathcal{F}(\alpha)$ such that $\{v_1(r), v_2(r), v_3(r), v_4(r)\} \subset \partial C$.*

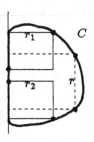

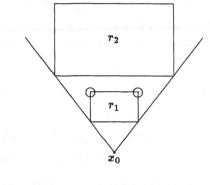

Figure 7

Figure 8

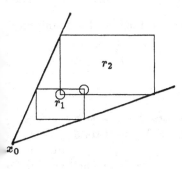

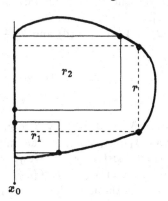

Figure 9

Figure 10

Proof: If $r_1 = r_2$, we are done. So assume $r_1 \neq r_2$. There are several cases:

Case 1 The rectangles r_1, r_2 are congruent. This implies the existence of a translation $\tau : x \mapsto x + t_0$ such that r_1 is mapped into r_2. There are two cases:

  Case 1.1 t_0 is not parallel to any edge of r_1, r_2 (Fig. 6). But then the two encircled vertices in Fig. 6 lie in the interior of the convex hull of r_1 and r_2, hence in the interior of C. This contradicts the assumption of the lemma.

  Case 1.2 t_0 is parallel to an edge of r_1. We have a situation as shown in Fig. 7. Note that the left sides of r_1 and r_2 lie on a supporting line of C. Using continuity arguments the reader can show the existence of a rectangle $r \in \mathcal{F}(\alpha)$ which touches in all four vertices, as indicated by the dashed lines in the figure.

Case 2 The rectangles r_1, r_2 have different size. Assume that r_1 is the smaller one. There is an expansion $\zeta : x \mapsto \lambda(x - x_0) + x_0$, $\lambda > 1$, which maps r_1 into r_2. There are three cases (depending on how many edges of r_1 are visible from x_0):

  Case 2.1 Only one edge of r_1 is visible from x_0, see Fig. 8. Then two adjacent vertices of r_1 lie in the interior of C, which is impossible.

  Case 2.2 Two edges of r_1 are visible from x_0, see Fig. 9. This is impossible for the same reason as Case 1.1.

Case 2.3 x_0 lies on the line through an edge of r_1. This situation is shown in Fig. 10. Again an edge of both r_1, r_2 lies on a supporting line of C. By the same argument as in Case 1.2 there is a suitable rectangle r.

$\square$

Proof: (of Theorem 4) It is easy to see that the mapping $\alpha \mapsto \sigma(\alpha)$ is continuous. Now define

$$A_1 := \{\alpha \in [0, \tfrac{\pi}{2}] \mid \exists r \in \mathcal{F}(\alpha) \text{ with } \{v_1(r), v_3(r)\} \subset \partial C\} \text{ and}$$
$$A_2 := \{\alpha \in [0, \tfrac{\pi}{2}] \mid \exists r \in \mathcal{F}(\alpha) \text{ with } \{v_2(r), v_4(r)\} \subset \partial C\}.$$

Note that this definition requires only the *existence* of rectangles with the specified touching vertices; it says nothing about largest rectangles. From Lemma 1 it follows that $A_1 \cup A_2 = [0, \tfrac{\pi}{2}]$.

Since $\sigma(\pi/2) = 1/\sigma(0)$, $\mathcal{F}(0)$ and $\mathcal{F}(\tfrac{\pi}{2})$ contain the same rectangles. By definition we have

$$0 \in A_1 \implies \tfrac{\pi}{2} \in A_2$$
$$0 \in A_2 \implies \tfrac{\pi}{2} \in A_1$$

This implies $A_1 \neq \emptyset$, $A_2 \neq \emptyset$. We will soon show that A_1, A_2 are closed sets. Since $[0, \tfrac{\pi}{2}]$ is connected and $A_1 \cup A_2 = [0, \tfrac{\pi}{2}]$, this implies that $A_1 \cap A_2 \neq \emptyset$. So let $\alpha_0 \in A_1 \cap A_2$. By definition there exist $r_1, r_2 \in \mathcal{F}(\alpha_0)$ with $\{v_1(r_1), v_3(r_1), v_2(r_2), v_4(r_2)\} \subset \partial C$. By Lemma 7 there is a rectangle $r \in \mathcal{F}(\alpha_0)$ such that all vertices of r lie on the boundary of C. Since r is homothetic to the unique minimum area rectangle r' with orientation α circumscribed to C, (r, R) forms an approximating pair. By Lemma 6 we have $\lambda(r, R) \leq 2$, and we are done.

It remains to be shown that A_1 and A_2 are closed sets. Because of symmetry we consider A_1 only. Let $(\alpha_i)_{i \in \mathbb{N}}$, $\alpha_i \in A_1$ be a sequence with $\lim_{i \to \infty} \alpha_i = \alpha_0$. We want to show that $\alpha_0 \in A_1$. For every i, choose a rectangle $r_i \in \mathcal{F}(\alpha_i)$ with $\{v_1(r_i), v_3(r_i)\} \subset \partial C$. By the theorem of Bolzano and Weierstraß we can select a subsequence of rectangles, such that their lower left vertices v_1 converges. Repeating this, we can select a subsequence in which the vertices v_3 converge, too. By change of notation we denote this subsequence again by (α_i). It is easy to see that $v_2(r_i)$ and $v_4(r_i)$ also converge.

Let us denote

$$\lim \alpha_i =: \alpha \quad \text{and}$$
$$\lim v_j(r_i) =: v_j \quad \text{for} \quad j = 1, 2, 3, 4.$$

We claim that the quadrilateral with vertices v_j, $j = 1, 2, 3, 4$, is a rectangle r with orientation α and aspect ratio $\sigma(\alpha)$. That is, $r \in \mathcal{F}(\alpha)$. If it were not, we could find neighborhoods U_j, $j = 1, 2, 3, 4$, of the four vertices of r and neighborhoods U_α of α and U_σ of $\sigma(\alpha)$, such that any quadrilateral with its vertices in the U_j's would either be no rectangle at all or have orientation not in U_α or aspect ratio not in U_σ. This contradicts the definitions of the vertices v_j as limits. (Recall here that σ is continous.)

Since ∂C is closed, $\{v_1, v_2, v_3, v_4\} \subset \partial C$.

$\square$

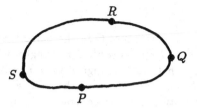

Figure 11:

4 Computing an Approximating Pair

Theorem 8 *An approximating pair (r, R) with $\lambda(r, R) \leq 2$ for a convex polygon C (with n vertices in sorted order) can be computed in time $\mathcal{O}(\log^3 n)$.*

Proof: From the last section we know that for every convex polygon C there is at least one orientation α_0 such that the largest rectangle in $\mathcal{F}(\alpha_0)$ touches ∂C with all four vertices. We search for α_0 by binary search on the interval $[0, \frac{\pi}{2}[$. First we find the best approximation for orientation 0 using the algorithm of Section 2. We check whether $0 \in A_1$ and whether $0 \in A_2$. If $0 \in A_1 \cap A_2$ we are done as in Theorem 4. So we assume that $0 \in A_1 \setminus A_2$. Now we test another orientation $\alpha \in [0, \frac{\pi}{2}[$. If $\alpha \in A_1$, we continue the search in the interval $[\alpha, \frac{\pi}{2}[$, otherwise in $[0, \alpha[$.

Since we want to compute an approximating pair with factor at most two, we have to use a discrete set of search orientations: Let P, Q, R, S be the downmost, rightmost, upmost, and leftmost point of C, see Fig. 11. Consider the orientations of the edges between P and Q. Since C is convex, the sequence of orientations of these edges is strictly increasing, so we can perform binary search on them. After $\mathcal{O}(\log n)$ tests we have found two adjacent edges with orientations α', α'' and we know that $\alpha_0 \in [\alpha', \alpha''[$. Now consider the edges between Q and R. We continue the binary search on the set

$$\{\alpha - \frac{\pi}{2} \mid \alpha \text{ is the orientation of an edge between } Q \text{ and } R\} \cap [\alpha', \alpha''[$$

In the same manner we proceed with the orientations of the edges between R and S and between S and P.

Every test takes time $\mathcal{O}(\log^2 n)$ by Theorem 3. Since there are $\mathcal{O}(\log n)$ tests, after time $\mathcal{O}(\log^3 n)$ we have found orientations α_1, α_2. There are no edges of the polygon with orientation between α_1 and α_2, so the enclosing rectangles $R(\alpha_1)$ and $R(\alpha_2)$ touch C in the same four vertices V_1, V_2, V_3, V_4. Let r_1, r_2 be the largest rectangle in $\mathcal{F}(\alpha_1)$, $\mathcal{F}(\alpha_2)$ resp. By assumption, $\alpha_1 \in A_1$, $\alpha_2 \in A_2$, so $\{v_1(r_1), v_3(r_1), v_2(r_2), v_4(r_2)\} \subset \partial C$. Let C' be the convex hull of r_1, r_2, and $V_1, \ldots, V_4$. Clearly we have $C' \subseteq C$ and $\{v_1(r_1), v_3(r_1), v_2(r_2), v_4(r_2)\} \subset \partial C'$ (since $\partial C \cap C' \subseteq \partial C'$). But now we have reduced the problem to one of constant size! C' is an at most 12-gon, $R(\alpha_1)$ and $R(\alpha_2)$ are the minimum circumscribed rectangles with orientations α_1, α_2, resp., and we still have $\alpha_1 \in A_1$, $\alpha_2 \in A_2$, where A_1, A_2 are defined *with respect to* C'. As before there is some $\alpha_0 \in [\alpha_1, \alpha_2[$ such that there exists an approximating pair (r, R) for C' with $\lambda(r, R) \leq 2$.

Since $C' \subseteq C$, we have $r \subseteq C' \subseteq C$. Since $\alpha_0 \in [\alpha_1, \alpha_2[$, R is determined by the four vertices $V_1, \ldots, V_4$, so we also have $R \supseteq C$. This implies that (r, R) is also an approximating pair for C. $\qquad \Box$

5 Conclusion

We have shown that for any convex figure C in the plane there exists an approximating pair of homothetic inscribed and circumscribed rectangles with quality (ratio) at most 2. Moreover, we have given an $\mathcal{O}(\log^3 n)$ algorithm for constructing such a pair for a convex n-gon. Note that we do not construct the pair with the *optimal* quality for a given convex n-gon. This question and the generalization to higher dimensions remains still open at this point.

References

[AFM*] Helmut Alt, Rudolf Fleischmer, Kurt Mehlhorn, Günter Rote, Emo Welzl, and Chee Yap. On certificates for polygon containment and shape approximation. (manuscript).

[Joh48] F. John. Extremum problems with inequalities as subsidiary conditions. In *Courant Anniversary Volume*, pages 187–204, New York, 1948.

[Las89] Marek Lassak. Approximation of plane convex bodies by centrally symmetric bodies. 1989. To appear in *J. London Math. Soc.*

[Lei59] K. Leichtweiß. Über die affine Exzentrizität konvexer Körper. *Arch. Math.*, 10:187–199, 1959.

[PS51] G. Pólya and G. Szegő. Isoperimetric inequalities in mathematical physics. *Ann. Math. Stud. Princeton*, 27, 1951.

Nonblocking Graphs:
Greedy Algorithms to Compute Disjoint Paths

Andreas Schwill

Fachbereich Informatik, Universität Oldenburg,

Postfach 2503, D-2900 Oldenburg, West Germany

e-mail: schwill@uniol.UUCP

Abstract. We define and characterize a class of graphs, called nonblocking graphs of order n, in which one can *incrementally* compute n vertex-/edge-disjoint paths for any n pairs of vertices such that each path connects one pair of vertices. We then investigate a subclass of these graphs, called geodetically nonblocking graphs of order n, in which all paths incrementally constructed are required to be *minimal*, i.e., to have a length equal to the distance of the resp. pair of vertices. The results may be of practical relevance when considering processor networks in the model of open-line communication in which communication requests arise at random times and have to be satisfied by communication paths which are node-/line-disjoint to the paths already established for previous requests.

1 Introduction

One essential element in parallel or distributed computation models, which extremely influences the execution speed of the entire system, is information exchange between individual processors. The standard solution for performing data transmission between processors is a sparse communication network, in which each processor is connected by a bidirectional line to few other processors. One distinguishes two basic methods for performing communications between processors: *packet routing*, not considered here, and *open-line communication*, which we adopt in this paper. Open-line communication is a suitable method when data of variable length have to be transfered in bidirectional way. If a pair of processors (call such a pair a *communication request* or *request*, for short) wants to communicate, the network satisfies the request by establishing a path between this pair. The nodes/lines on such a path are exclusively assigned for this purpose and will not be released until the communication finishes. If several pairs of processors wish to communicate simultaneously, the network reserves paths that are *node-* or *line-disjoint* to the paths already established for previous requests in order to ensure that messages between different pairs do not interfere.

Now consider a single communication path between two processors. Each line on that path as well as each intermediate processor may cause a time delay and transmission faults when forwarding an incoming message. Hence, the total delay resp. number of transmission faults increases with the length, i.e. the number of lines and processors, of a communication path. So, in order to maximize the communication performance the network should always establish paths of *minimal* length.

If we model processor networks by undirected graphs, in which vertices and edges represent processors and bidirectional communication lines, respectively, we are facing the following problem:

(Π) Given a sequence $\{(s_i,t_i,T_i)\}_{i \in \mathbb{N}}$ of communication requests arising at times $T_1 \leq T_2 \leq T_3 \leq ...$ between processors s_i and t_i. At time T_i a path connecting s_i and t_i (if any) has to be computed that is vertex-/edge-disjoint to the paths already established at times $T_1,...,T_{i-1}$ between $s_1,t_1,...,s_{i-1},t_{i-1}$.

In Section 3 we define and characterize a class of graphs, called *nonblocking graphs of order n*, in which any such sequence $\{(s_i,t_i,T_i)\}_{1 \leq i \leq n}$ of at most n requests can be satisfied by vertex-/edge-disjoint paths. We show that every (2n-1)-vertex-connected (2-edge-connected) chordal graph is nonblocking of order n (order 2) with respect to vertex-(edge-)disjointness of paths.

We then extend this notion and require the paths incrementally constructed to be *minimal*, i.e., to have a length equal to the distance of the pair of vertices to be connected. This leads to a class of graphs, called *geodetically nonblocking graphs of order n*, which we define and characterize in Section 4. While we do not know how to efficiently decide whether a graph is a nonblocking graph of order n, there is a simple algorithm to decide whether a graph is *geodetically* nonblocking of order n.

The class of geodetically nonblocking graphs of order n is also interesting from another point of view. Since problem Π does not take into account intermediate terminations of communications, we cannot be sure that a request $(s_{n+1}, t_{n+1}, T_{n+1})$ is satisfiable in a nonblocking graph of order n, even if all pairs $(s_1, t_1), ..., (s_{n-1}, t_{n-1})$ have released their paths. This leads to the following stronger problem:

(Π')   Given a sequence $\{(s_i, t_i, T_i, b_i)\}_{i \in IN}$ of requests ($b_i=1$) and releases of paths ($b_i=0$) arising at times $T_1 \leq T_2 \leq T_3 \leq ...$ between processors s_i and t_i. At time T_i, if $b_i=1$, a path connecting s_i and t_i (if any) has to be computed that is vertex-/edge-disjoint to the paths currently in use. Otherwise, if $b_i=0$, the path connecting s_i and t_i has to be released.

In the class of geodetically nonblocking graphs of order n any such (infinite) sequence $\{(s_i, t_i, T_i, b_i)\}_{i \in IN}$ of requests and releases (with minor exclusions) can be satisfied by minimal vertex-/edge-disjoint paths provided that less than n paths are established whenever a request arises.

So far, the concept of nonblocking graphs has been investigated for switching networks mainly, i.e., for directed acyclic graphs where a fixed set of "input vertices" and a fixed set of "output vertices" is specified. A switching network is nonblocking if any pair of inputs and outputs can be connected by a path that is vertex-disjoint to the paths already established (see e.g. [B65] for a comprehensive study or [FFP88] for recent results).

Mader [M85] has shown that for every pair of vertices there is a path so that the edge-connectivity of the graph decreases by at most two when deleting the edge-set of the path. Consequently, (2n-1)-edge-connected graphs are nonblocking graphs of order n with respect to edge-disjointness. However, it is not clear whether such a path can be computed efficiently.

A related problem has been studied by Dirac and Thomassen [DT73] for *two* paths connecting a *single* pair of vertices: What is the structure of graphs in which every path has a detour, i.e., a path internally vertex-disjoint to the first path? This class of graphs is very small: A graph G with $p \geq 3$ vertices belongs to the class iff it is complete or a cycle or p is even and G is the complete bipartite graph $K_{p/2, p/2}$.

A completely different approach has been taken by Shamir and Upfal [SU83]. They developed a distributed algorithm which incrementally computes in random graphs with p vertices $O(p^{1/2})$ vertex-disjoint paths connecting random pairs of vertices with high probability.

There are quite a lot of papers concerning problem Π when all requests arise at the same time, i.e. $T_1=T_2=T_3=...$. A few of these results are reviewed in the following.

Karp [K75] has shown that it is NP-complete to decide, given a graph and n pairs of vertices, whether the graph contains n pairwise vertex-disjoint paths each one connecting a single pair of vertices.

However, the problem is solvable in polynomial time if n is *fixed*, that is, for each $n \in IN$ there is a polynomial algorithm that, given a graph and n pairs of vertices, computes n pairwise vertex-disjoint paths so that each path connects one pair of vertices. This result has recently been obtained by Robertson and Seymour [RS86] in a sequence of fundamental papers. Their algorithm runs in $O(|V|^2 \cdot |E|)$ steps where V and E are the sets of vertices and edges of the graph, respectively. The algorithm is, however, unpractical due to a leading constant (hidden by the "big O") of horrible size.

Several practical algorithms to connect *two* pairs of vertices by vertex-disjoint paths have been developed in [S80], [O80], [KPS88] and [SP89]. These algorithms can also be employed to determine *edge*-disjoint paths using a polynomial reduction of LaPaugh and Rivest [LR78].

Moreover, the following results on the edge-disjoint version of the problem are known.

Cypher [C80] has proposed polynomial algorithms that determine n edge-disjoint paths ($n \leq 5$) connecting n pairs of vertices in (n+2)-edge-connected graphs.

Frank [F85] developed an $O(|V|^3 \cdot \log|V|)$ algorithm to compute n edge-disjoint paths between n pairs of vertices if the graph is planar and the 2n vertices lie on the outer face of a planar embedding of the graph and all vertices not on the outer face have even degree.

Peleg and Upfal [PU87] designed an $O(n \cdot |V|^2)$ algorithm to construct n edge-disjoint paths connecting n given pairs of vertices in the class of d-regular expander graphs, where $n \leq |V|^\sigma$ and $\sigma = \sigma(\alpha, \beta, \gamma, d)$ is a constant depending on the expansion constants α, β, γ and the degree of the vertices d.

The author [S89] has characterized the class of graphs, in which any n requests can be satisfied by *minimal* edge-disjoint paths, and given efficient algorithms. The vertex-disjoint version thereof (without algorithms) has been treated by Enomoto and Saito [ES84].

Characterizations of those graphs in terms of their connectivity that contain n vertex-/edge-disjoint paths for any n requests are given in [LM70], [J70], [O88] and [HKS88].

2 Preliminaries

We only consider finite undirected graphs without loops and multiple edges. All notions not defined in the following are taken from [H72].

Let G=(V,E) be a graph. Let $S \subseteq V$ and $T \subseteq E$. G\S is the graph obtained from G by deleting the vertex set S and all edges having a vertex in S. G\T is defined to be the graph (V,E\T). $N_G(v) := \{u \in V | \{u,v\} \in E\}$ (or N(v) for short) denotes the set of **neighbours** of $v \in V$.

Let $P=(v_0, v_1, ..., v_{n-1}, v_n)$ be an (n+1)-tuple of vertices of G. P is a **path of length** $|P| := n$ between v_0 and v_n if $\{v_{i-1}, v_i\} \in E$ for $1 \leq i \leq n$. P is called **minimal** if there is no path between v_0 and v_n of length less than n. We usually denote P or subpaths of P by adding their terminal vertices, i.e. $P=P[v_0, v_n]$ or $P[v_i, v_{i+k}]$ for the subpath $(v_i, v_{i+1}, ..., v_{i+k})$ of P, $0 \leq i \leq i+k \leq n$. V(P) and E(P) are the sets of vertices and edges of P, respectively. P is called **simple** if $v_i \neq v_j$ for $0 \leq i < j \leq n$. An edge $\{v_i, v_j\} \in E \backslash E(P)$ is called a **chord**. A **chordless** path has no chords. The operation • **concatenates** two paths, i.e., if $P=(v_0, ..., v_n)$ and $Q=(u_0, ..., u_m)$ are two paths and $v_n = u_0$, then P•Q denotes the path $(v_0, ..., v_n = u_0, ..., u_m)$. A path $P=(v_0, v_1, ..., v_n)$ is a **cycle of length** n if $n \geq 3$, $v_n = v_0$ and $P[v_0, v_{n-1}]$ is a simple path.

Two paths P and Q are called **vertex-disjoint** resp. **edge-disjoint** if $V(P) \cap V(Q) = \emptyset$ resp. $E(P) \cap E(Q) = \emptyset$. Two paths P[u,v] and Q[u,v] are **internally vertex-disjoint** if $V(P) \cap V(Q) = \{u,v\}$.

$\delta_G(x,y)$ (or $\delta(x,y)$ for short) is defined to be the **distance**, i.e. the length of a minimal path (if any), between two vertices $x, y \in V$. We set $\delta_G(x,y) = \infty$ if there is no path connecting x and y. $\Delta(G) = \max\{\delta_G(x,y) | x, y \in V\}$ is the **diameter** of G.

A **vertex separator** $S \subseteq V$ (**edge separator** $S \subseteq E$) is a set of vertices (edges) such that for two vertices $x, y \in V \backslash S$ ($x, y \in V$) it holds $\delta_G(x,y) < \delta_{G \backslash S}(x,y) = \infty$. S is a **minimal** vertex (edge) separator if no proper subset of S is a vertex (edge) separator.

A graph G is called **chordal** if every cycle $C=(v_0, v_1, ..., v_{n-1}, v_0)$ of length $n \geq 4$ has a chord.

Theorem A [e.g. G80].

Let G=(V,E) be a graph, $|V| \geq 2$. If G is chordal, then G\{x} is chordal for every $x \in V$.

Theorem B [D61].
Let G=(V,E) be a graph. G is chordal iff every minimal vertex separator induces a complete graph.

Theorem C [M27].
Let G=(V,E) be a graph. The maximal number of internally vertex-disjoint paths connecting two non-adjacent vertices $s,t \in V$ equals the minimal number of vertices in a vertex separator for s and t.

3 Nonblocking Graphs

We begin with a very general (recursively defined) framework that formalizes our notion of nonblocking graphs. For the entire section $\pi = \pi(P,G)$ denotes an arbitrary predicate defined for paths P in a graph G, i.e., $\quad \pi: \{(P,G) \mid P \text{ is a path within the graph } G\} \rightarrow \{\underline{\text{true}}, \underline{\text{false}}\}$.

A graph G=(V,E) is called π-**connected**, if for every two vertices $x,y \in V$ there is a simple path P[x,y] satisfying π in G.

Roughly speaking, a nonblocking graph of order n is a π-connected graph for which the deletion of any simple path satisfying π leaves a nonblocking graph of order n-1.

Definition A.
Let G=(V,E) be a graph and π be a predicate.
(1) G is a **vertex-nonblocking (edge-nonblocking)** graph **of order 1 with respect to** π if G is π-connected.
(2) G is a **vertex-nonblocking** graph **of order n>1 with respect to** π if G is π-connected and for every simple path P in G satisfying π G\V(P) is a vertex-nonblocking graph of order n-1 with respect to π.
(3) G is an **edge-nonblocking** graph **of order n>1 with respect to** π if G is π-connected and for every simple path P in G satisfying π the graph G\E(P) is an edge-nonblocking graph of order n-1 with respect to π.

It is easy to see that the class of vertex-/edge-nonblocking graphs of order n covers our problem Π mentioned in the Introduction, i.e., any sequence of requests $(s_1,t_1,T_1),....,(s_n,t_n,T_n)$ can be satisfied by vertex-/edge-disjoint paths each one satisfying π.

Some remarks shall illustrate the usefulness of predicate π. When considering processor networks one may not simply be interested in satisfying a request by *any* communication path, but the paths often have to satisfy further conditions, e.g.:
- Paths should avoid processors which are already heavily loaded handling communication paths.
- Paths have to pass through at least one of several distinguished processors being suited for accounting purposes.
Such and other constraints may be covered by a suitable choice of π.

Examples.
1. Let $\pi_{arb}(P,G):=$"P is an arbitrary path in G". The complete graph K_5 is an edge-nonblocking graph of order 2 with respect to π_{arb}.
2. Let $\pi_r(P,G):=$"P is a path of length $\leq r$ in G", $r \geq 1$. Every cycle with r+2 vertices is a vertex-nonblocking graph of order 2 with respect to π_r.

3. Let $\pi_{min}(P,G):=$"P is a minimal path in G". Fig. 1 shows a vertex-nonblocking graph of order 3 with respect to π_{min} (to verify use Theorem D).

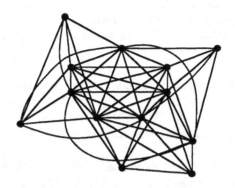

Fig. 1.

For employing this definition in practice paths satisfying the predicate π should be efficiently computable. The most suitable predicate seems to be π_{min} mentioned above. Paths satisfying π_{min} can be computed in linear time, and, since the resp. minimal paths block as few vertices and edges as possible, one can expect high orders of non-blockage of the underlying graphs. In the sequel we characterize the nonblocking order of graphs with respect to π_{min} in more detail. Obviously, a graph is π_{min}-connected iff it is connected. For convenience, we omit the "with respect to π_{min}" henceforth.

At first glance one may try to relate the connectivity of a graph and its order of nonblockage. But, while a graph, in order to be vertex-nonblocking of order n, has to be at least n-vertex-connected, there are graphs of arbitrarily large vertex-connectivity that are *not* vertex-nonblocking of order 2. For it take two copies G' and G" of a graph G with vertex-connectivity $n{\geq}1$ and diameter $\Delta(G)>n$. Let $P'=(v_0,v_1,...,v_{\Delta(G)})$ and $P"=(u_0,u_1,...,u_{\Delta(G)})$ be two minimal paths in G' and G", respectively. Construct H from G' and G" by identifying, as single vertices, v_i with u_i, $0{\leq}i{\leq}\Delta(G)$. H is n-vertex-connected and P'=P" is minimal in H. But H is not vertex-nonblocking of order 2, since the deletion of P' leaves the "empty graph" or a graph that is not connected. A similar result may be obtained for the edge-case.

The opposite direction of this observation gives a simple characterization of nonblocking graphs of order 2.

Proposition B.
Let G be a graph.
(1) If G is n-vertex-connected, $n{\geq}3$, and $\Delta(G)<n-1$, then G is a vertex-nonblocking graph of order 2.
(2) If G is n-edge-connected, $n{\geq}2$, and $\Delta(G)<n$, then G is an edge-nonblocking graph of order 2.

The first theorem gives a sufficient condition for a graph being vertex-nonblocking of order n. It is based on the following lemma.

Lemma C.
Let G be an (n+2)-vertex-connected graph. Then $|V(G)\backslash V(P)|>n$ for every minimal path P in G.
Proof.
If $\Delta(G)=1$, i.e., G is complete, the assertion is obvious. So suppose $\Delta(G){\geq}2$.

Let $x,y \in V$ satisfy $\delta(x,y)=\Delta(G)$. By Menger's Theorem C [2] there are n+2 internally vertex-disjoint paths $P_1[x,y],...,P_{n+2}[x,y]$ of length at least $\Delta(G)$ each. Counting the vertices on $P_1,...,P_{n+2}$ gives a lower bound for $|V|$: $\qquad |V| \geq (n+2)(\Delta(G)-1)+2=(n+2)\Delta(G)-n$.

Now let P be a minimal path in G. Since $|P| \leq \Delta(G)$ it holds:

$$|V(G) \backslash V(P)| \geq |V|-(\Delta(G)+1) \geq (n+2)\Delta(G)-n-\Delta(G)-1=(n+1)\Delta(G)-n-1 > n, \text{ if, as supposed, } \Delta(G) \geq 2. \quad \blacklozenge$$

Theorem D.

Let $n \geq 1$. Every (2n-1)-vertex-connected chordal graph is a vertex-nonblocking graph of order n.

Proof. (By induction on n).

n=1. Obvious.

n-1→n. Let G=(V,E) be a (2n-1)-vertex-connected chordal graph and P be a minimal path in G. G\V(P) is chordal by Theorem A [2].

In order to apply the induction hypothesis we only have to show that G\V(P) is (2n-3)-vertex-connected. Suppose the contrary. Then by Lemma C it holds $|V \backslash V(P)|>2n-3$. So, let $S \subseteq V \backslash V(P)$ be a vertex separator for $x,y \in V \backslash (V(P) \cup S)$ with $|S|<2n-3$. Then $S \cup V(P)$ is a vertex separator for x and y in G. Let $S' \subseteq S \cup V(P)$ be a minimal vertex separator. Since, by assumption, G is (2n-1)-vertex connected, it holds $|S'| \geq 2n-1$. On the other hand, we have $|V(P) \cap S'| \leq 2$ for the following reason: S' induces a complete graph (Theorem B [2]) and P is chordless. Then it holds $|S'| \leq |S \cap S'|+|V(P) \cap S'| \leq |S|+2<2n-1$. A contradiction. So G\V(P) is (2n-3)-vertex-connected and, by induction hypothesis, a vertex-nonblocking graph of order n-1. Thus, G is a vertex-nonblocking graph of order n. $\quad \blacklozenge$

One easily verifies that the connectivity bound of 2n-1 is optimal. As a consequence of Theorem D we obtain a simple greedy algorithm to compute n vertex-disjoint paths connecting n *distinct* pairs of vertices in (2n-1)-vertex-connected chordal graphs. This extends a result obtained by Perl and Shiloach [PS78] for n=2. (Let bfs(G,s,t) be a procedure that returns a minimal path between vertices s and t in graph G.)

Theorem E.

Let G=(V,E) be a (2n-1)-vertex-connected chordal graph. The following algorithm computes in $O(n \cdot |E|)$ steps n vertex-disjoint paths $P_1[s_1,t_1],...,P_n[s_n,t_n]$ for any 2n *pairwise distinct* vertices $s_1,t_1,...,s_n,t_n \in V$:

```
read(G,n,s1,t1,...,sn,tn);
for i:=1 to n do
    P:=bfs(G\{si+1,ti+1,...,sn,tn},si,ti);
    write(P); G:=G\V(P)
od.
```

Proof. (By induction on n).

n=1. Obvious.

n-1→n. Let G=(V,E) be a (2n-1)-vertex-connected chordal graph and $s_1,t_1,...,s_n,t_n \in V$ be pairwise distinct. $G \backslash \{s_n,t_n\}$ is (2n-3)-vertex-connected and chordal. Hence, by induction hypothesis, there are n-1 vertex-disjoint paths $P_1[s_1,t_1],...,P_{n-1}[s_{n-1},t_{n-1}]$ in $G \backslash \{s_n,t_n\}$. We may assume that each P_i is chordless. Suppose there is no path $P_n[s_n,t_n]$ in G being vertex-disjoint to $P_1,...,P_{n-1}$. Then $V(P_1) \cup ... \cup V(P_{n-1})$ is a vertex separator for s_n and t_n. Let $S \subseteq V(P_1) \cup ... \cup V(P_{n-1})$ be a minimal vertex separator. Then $|S| \geq 2n-1$, since G is (2n-1)-vertex-connected. On the other hand, since S induces a complete graph by Theorem B [2], it holds $|V(P_i) \cap S| \leq 2$, $1 \leq i \leq n-1$, otherwise P_i is not chordless. So $|S| \leq |V(P_1) \cap S|+...+|V(P_{n-1}) \cap S| \leq 2n-2$. A contradiction. Thus, there is a path $P_n[s_n,t_n]$ in $G \backslash (V(P_1) \cup ... \cup V(P_{n-1}))$.

Correctness and complexity of the algorithm is an easy consequence. $\quad \blacklozenge$

Next, we turn to the edge-disjoint case which seems more complicated. Since we are not aware of any reasonable characterization of *edge* separators in chordal graphs (along the lines of Theorem B [2]), Theorem D does not carry over. We only have a weak result for n=2 and a lower bound for the connectivity of 2n-3.

Theorem F.
Every 2-edge-connected chordal graph is an edge-nonblocking graph of order 2.
Proof.
Let $G=(V,E)$ be a 2-edge-connected chordal graph. Let P_1 be a minimal path in G.
In order to obtain a contradiction, suppose that there are two vertices s,t such that there is no path P[s,t] in $G\backslash E(P_1)$. Then $E(P_1)$ separates s and t. Let $T\subseteq E(P_1)$ be a minimal edge separator for s and t.
Let $e=\{u,v\}\in T$. As G is 2-edge-connected, $G\backslash\{e\}$ is connected. Let Q[u,v] be a minimal path in $G\backslash\{e\}$. Due to G's chordality |Q|=2, Q=(u,w,v) say. Obviously, either the edge {u,w} or {w,v} lies in T, otherwise T is not an edge-separator. Now, (u,w,v,u) is a cycle of length 3 in G and $u,v,w\in V(P_1)$. A contradiction to the minimality of P_1. ◆

Corollary G.
In 2-edge-connected chordal graphs $G=(V,E)$ two edge-disjoint paths $P_1[s_1,t_1]$, $P_2[s_2,t_2]$ can be computed in linear time for any four vertices $s_1,t_1,s_2,t_2\in V$.

Proposition H.
Every chordal edge-nonblocking graph of order $n\geq2$ is (2n-3)-edge-connected.
Proof.
If n=2 the assertion is obvious. The graph depicted in Fig. 2 constructed from two copies of the complete graph K_{2n} is (2n-4)-edge-connected and chordal. Choose $P_1=(s_1,t_1)$ and $P_i=(s_i,z_{i-1},t_i)$, $2\leq i\leq n-1$, each of which being minimal in $G\backslash\bigcup_{j=1,...,i-1}E(P_j)$. Then, there is no edge-disjoint path between s_n and t_n. Thus, G is not edge-nonblocking of order n. ◆

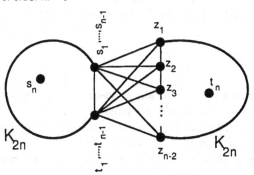

Fig. 2.

A major problem in this context is still unsolved. What is the complexity of computing the order of nonblockage of a graph? We conjecture that it is co-NP-complete to decide whether a graph is a vertex-nonblocking (edge-nonblocking) graph of order n even if n=2.

4 Geodetically Nonblocking Graphs

In the remainder of this paper we focus on the geodetic version of nonblocking graphs. Whereas in Definition A [3] with $\pi=\pi_{min}$ the paths successively constructed are merely minimal within the resp. intermediate graphs, in geodetically nonblocking graphs the paths are required to be minimal with respect to the graph started with. This additional condition helps to cover our problem Π' mentioned in the Introduction, i.e., in a geodetically nonblocking graph of order n (almost) any sequence of requests and releases of paths $\{(s_i,t_i,T_i,b_i)\}_{i\in IN}$ is satisfiable by vertex-/edge-disjoint paths provided that at every time T_i with $b_i=1$ less than n paths are established.

As above we distinguish between the vertex- and the edge-disjoint case, the latter excluding requests of adjacent vertices. We cannot avoid this lack for the following reason: Suppose a minimal path P=(s,x,y,t) has already been established. If now x and y wish to communicate, they cannot be connected by a minimal edge-disjoint path, because edge {x,y} is busy, yet.

Definition A.
Let G=(V,E) be a connected graph and A={{u,v}| {u,v}∉ E, u,v∈ V, u≠v} be its set of non-adjacent vertices.
(1) G is a **geodetically vertex-nonblocking (edge-nonblocking)** graph **of order** 1.
(2) G is a **geodetically vertex-nonblocking** graph **of order** n>1 if for every minimal path P in G G\V(P) is a geodetically vertex-nonblocking graph of order n-1 and for every two vertices x,y∈ V it holds $\delta_G(x,y)=\delta_{G\backslash V(P)}(x,y)$.
(3) G is a **geodetically edge-nonblocking** graph **of order** n>1 if for every minimal path P[u,v] in G with {u,v}∈ A the graph G\E(P) is a geodetically edge-nonblocking graph of order n-1 and for every {x,y}∈ A it holds $\delta_G(x,y)=\delta_{G\backslash E(P)}(x,y)$.

The characterizations of geodetically nonblocking graphs are based on the notion of geodetic connectivity first introduced by Entringer, Jackson and Slater [EJS77]. Roughly speaking, a graph is called n-geodetically vertex-connected if at least n vertices have to be removed from the graph to destroy all minimal paths between any pair of the remaining vertices. An analogous definition exists for geodetic edge-connectivity.

Definition B.
Let n∈ IN.
(1) A graph G=(V,E) is called **n-geodetically edge-connected** if $\delta_G(x,y)=\delta_{G\backslash T}(x,y)<\infty$ for any set T⊆E with |T|≤n-1 and for every pair of non-adjacent vertices x,y∈ V.
(2) A graph G=(V,E) is called **n-geodetically vertex-connected** if $\delta_G(x,y)=\delta_{G\backslash S}(x,y)<\infty$ for any set S⊆V with |S|≤n-1 and for every pair of vertices x,y∈ V\S.
(3) The **geodetic vertex-/edge-connectivity** of a graph G is the largest integer n such that G is n-geodetically vertex-/edge-connected.

Note that (1) and (2) differ in that the vertices x and y are required to be non-adjacent in (1). Otherwise, since multiple edges are not allowed, no n-geodetically edge-connected graphs would exist.

Examples.
1. Fig. 3 shows a 2-geodetically vertex-connected graph.
2. Note that a complete graph is n-geodetically vertex-connected (resp. edge-connected) for every n∈ IN. The geodetic vertex- resp. edge-connectivity of a complete graph is undefined.

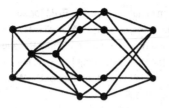

Fig. 3.

Entringer, Jackson and Slater gave a nice characterization of geodetically connected graphs.

Theorem C [EJS77].
Let $G=(V,E)$ be a graph and $n\in$ IN. The following statements are equivalent:
(1) G is n-geodetically edge-connected.
(2) G is connected and for every pair of vertices $x,y\in V$ satisfying $\delta(x,y)=2$ it holds that $|N(x)\cap N(y)|\geq n$.
(3) G is n-geodetically vertex-connected. ♦

Since the notions of geodetic edge-connectivity and geodetic vertex-connectivity of a graph coincide, we use the terms "geodetically connected" or "geodetic connectivity" henceforth.
The most interesting characterization, which will be intensively exploited in this section, gives statement (2) of Theorem B: To determine whether or not a graph is n-geodetically connected, it suffices to explore the neighbourhood of all pairs of vertices having distance 2. This easily gives Theorem D.

Theorem D [S89].
The geodetic connectivity of a graph $G=(V,E)$ can be computed in time $O(\min\{|V|\cdot|E|,\mu(|V|)\})$, where $\mu(k)$ is the time necessary to multiply two $k\times k$ integer matrices (by now $\mu(k)=O(k^{2.376})$ [CW87]).

The following result completely characterizes geodetically edge-nonblocking graphs of order n.

Theorem E.
Let $n\geq 1$. A non-complete graph is geodetically edge-nonblocking of order n iff it is (2n-1)-geodetically connected.
Proof.
"=>": The complete bipartite graph $K_{2n-2,2n-2}=(V,E)$ is (2n-2)-geodetically connected, where $V=V'\cup V''$ and $V'=\{s_1,t_1,...,s_{n-1},t_{n-1}\}$, $V''=\{s_n,t_n,x_1,...,x_{2n-4}\}$. The deletion of the edges of the paths (s_i,s_1,t_i), $1\leq i\leq n-1$, leaves a graph that is not connected. Thus, $K_{2n-2,2n-2}$ is not geodetically edge-nonblocking of order n.
"<=": (By induction on n).
n=1. Obvious.
n-1→n. Let $G=(V,E)$ be a non-complete (2n-1)-geodetically connected graph and $A=\{\{u,v\}|\ \{u,v\}\notin E,$ $u,v\in V, u\neq v\}$ be the set of non-adjacent vertices of G. By induction hypothesis, G is geodetically edge-nonblocking of order n-1. So, we can incrementally construct n-1 minimal edge-disjoint paths $P_1[s_1,t_1],...,P_{n-1}[s_{n-1},t_{n-1}]$ in G for any n-1 pairs of vertices $\{s_1,t_1\},...,\{s_{n-1},t_{n-1}\}\in A$.
We have to show that $\delta_G(u,v)=\delta_{G\setminus T}(u,v)$ for every $\{u,v\}\in A$ where $T:=E(P_1)\cup...\cup E(P_{n-1})$.
Suppose the contrary. Then there are two vertices $\{s,t\}\in A$ such that every minimal path connecting s and t in G is *not* edge-disjoint to $P_1,...,P_{n-1}$. Now define

M:={(P,x,y) | P[s,t] is minimal, {x,y}∈ E(P)∩E(P$_j$) for some j∈{1,...,n-1}

and E(P[s,x])∩E(P$_i$)=∅ for all i∈{1,...,n-1}},

i.e., if (P,x,y)∈ M then {x,y} is the first edge of P that P and any P$_j$ have in common.

Choose (P*,x*,y*)∈ M such that |P*[s,x*]|=max{|P[s,x]| | (P,x,y)∈ M}, i.e., there is no minimal path from s to t whose "initial edge-disjoint fragment" is longer than that of P*. We distinguish two similar cases:

(i) s≠x*. Then P*=(s,...,a,x*,y*,...,t) (possibly s=a).

(ii) s=x*. Then t≠y* and P*=(s,y*,a,...,t) (possibly t=a).

W.l.o.g. we may assume the first case. The other one may be treated analogously.

Since G has geodetic connectivity 2n-1 and δ(a,y*)=2, Theorem C(2) implies that there exist 2n-1 vertices v$_1$,...,v$_{2n-1}$∈ N(a)∩N(y*). Define Q$_i$=(a,v$_i$,y*) and Q={Q$_1$,...,Q$_{2n-1}$}. By construction of P* for every Q∈ Q there is some P$_j$, 1≤j≤n-1, so that E(Q)∩E(P$_j$)≠∅. Hence, by the pigeon-hole principle, there is some path P$_j$ and three paths Q$_p$,Q$_q$,Q$_r$∈ Q such that E(P$_j$)∩E(Q$_p$)≠∅≠E(P$_j$)∩E(Q$_q$)≠∅≠E(P$_j$)∩E(Q$_r$). Then v$_p$,v$_q$,v$_r$∈ V(P$_j$) and, up to symmetry, {a,v$_p$},{a,v$_q$}∈ E(P$_j$) and {a,v$_r$} or {y*,v$_r$}∈ E(P$_j$). It is easy to verify that this contradicts the minimality of P$_j$. Thus, there is a path Q∈ Q such that E(Q)∩E(P$_i$)=∅ for all i∈{1,...,n-1}. Then P*[s,a]•Q is minimal and edge-disjoint to each P$_i$, 1≤i≤n-1, and longer than |P*[s,x*]|. A contradiction to the construction of P*.

Hence, there is a minimal path P[s,t] in G\(E(P$_1$)∪...∪E(P$_{n-1}$)) which is also minimal with respect to G and edge-disjoint to P$_1$,...,P$_{n-1}$. So G is a geodetically edge-nonblocking graph of order n. ◆

Corollary F.

In (2n-1)-geodetically connected graphs G=(V,E) n minimal pairwise edge-disjoint paths P$_1$[s$_1$,t$_1$],...,P$_n$[s$_n$,t$_n$] can be computed in O(n·|E|) steps for any 2n vertices s$_1$,t$_1$,...,s$_n$,t$_n$∈ V such that s$_i$,t$_i$ are non-adjacent, 1≤i≤n.

Next we tackle the vertex-disjoint case. We approximately proceed as in statements C and D of Section 3. As a by-product of Theorem H we obtain an essential simplification of the complicated proof of Enomoto's and Saito's theorem [ES84] stating that (3n-2)-geodetic connectivity is sufficient to ensure the existence of n minimal vertex-disjoint paths connecting n arbitrary distinct pairs of vertices. Moreover, our proof yields a simple algorithm to compute the paths.

To this end, we need a lemma which may be of independent interest. The lemma characterizes like Theorem B [2], yet weaker, a *geodetic* vertex separator, i.e. a set of vertices whose deletion destroys all minimal paths between two vertices x and y. It reads as follows: Let G be an n-geodetically connected graph. For every geodetic vertex separator S there is a vertex z adjacent to at least n vertices of S. Precisely:

Lemma G.

Let G=(V,E) be an n-geodetically connected graph and S⊆V such that δ$_G$(x,y)<δ$_{G\S}$(x,y) for two vertices x,y∈ V\S. There are a set S'⊆S, |S'|≥n, and a vertex z∈ V such that {z,s}∈ E for all s∈ S'.

Proof.

Let G=(V,E), S⊆V and x,y∈ V according to the assumption. Define

M:={P[x,v] | P is minimal, v∈ V, δ$_G$(x,v)+δ$_G$(v,y)=δ$_G$(x,y) and V(P)∩S=∅}.

It holds M≠∅, since x∉ S and the path P=(x) of length 0 is in M. Choose P*[x,z]∈ M such that |P*|=max{|P| | P∈ M}. Let w∈ V such that δ$_G$(z,w)=2 and δ$_G$(z,w)+δ$_G$(w,y)=δ$_G$(z,y). w exists (possibly w=y), otherwise δ$_G$(z,y)=1 and the path P*•(z,y) is minimal and connects x and y within G\S. A contradiction.

Since G is n-geodetically connected, by Theorem B(2) we have |N(z)∩N(w)|≥n, and N(z)∩N(w)⊆S by construction of z. Define S':=N(z)∩N(w). z (and also w) satisfies the assertion. ◆

Theorem H.

Let $n \geq 1$. A non-complete graph is a geodetically vertex-nonblocking graph of order n iff it is (3n-2)-geodetically connected.

Proof.

"=>": Consequence of Theorem 3 in [ES84], where a (3n-3)-geodetically connected graph and 2n distinct vertices $s_1, t_1, \ldots, s_n, t_n$ are specified that cannot be connected by n minimal vertex-disjoint paths.

"<=": (By induction on n).

$\underline{n=1}$. Obvious.

$\underline{n-1 \rightarrow n}$. Let $G=(V,E)$ be a non-complete (3n-2)-geodetically connected graph and P be a minimal path in G. In order to apply the induction hypothesis it suffices to show that $G':=G \setminus V(P)$ is (3n-5)-geodetically connected. Note that $|V(G')| > 3n-4$ by Lemma C [3].

Suppose G' is not (3n-5)-geodetically connected and let $S \subseteq V(G')$, $|S| < 3n-5$, be a set such that $\delta_{G'}(x,y) < \delta_{G' \setminus S}(x,y)$ for two vertices $x, y \in V \setminus S$. Then the deletion of $V(P) \cup S$ destroys all minimal paths between x and y in G, i.e., it holds $|V(P) \cup S| \geq 3n-2$ and $\delta_G(x,y) < \delta_{G \setminus (V(P) \cup S)}(x,y)$. By Lemma G there is a subset $S' \subseteq V(P) \cup S$, $|S'| \geq 3n-2$, and a vertex $z \in V$ such that $\{z,s\} \in E$ for all $s \in S'$. Obviously, $|V(P) \cap S'| \leq 3$, otherwise P is not minimal, since there is a shorter path through z. Hence, it follows

$$3n-2 \leq |S'| \leq |S \cap S'| + |V(P) \cap S'| \leq |S| + 3, \text{ i.e. } |S| \geq 3n-5.$$

A contradiction. Now, G' is (3n-5)-geodetically connected and, by induction hypothesis, geodetically vertex-nonblocking of order n-1. Thus, G is a geodetically vertex-nonblocking graph of order n. ♦

Theorem I.

Let $G=(V,E)$ be a non-complete (3n-2)-geodetically connected graph. The algorithm of Theorem E [3] computes in $O(n \cdot |E|)$ steps n *minimal* vertex-disjoint paths $P_1[s_1,t_1], \ldots, P_n[s_n,t_n]$ for any 2n pairwise distinct vertices $s_1, t_1, \ldots, s_n, t_n \in V$.

Proof. (By induction on n).

$\underline{n=1}$. Obvious.

$\underline{n-1 \rightarrow n}$. Let $G=(V,E)$ be a non-complete (3n-2)-geodetically connected graph and $s_1, t_1, \ldots, s_n, t_n \in V$ be pairwise distinct. $G \setminus \{s_n, t_n\}$ is (3n-4)-geodetically connected. Hence, by induction hypothesis, there are n-1 minimal vertex-disjoint paths $P_1[s_1,t_1], \ldots, P_{n-1}[s_{n-1}, t_{n-1}]$ in $G \setminus \{s_n, t_n\}$, which are also minimal with respect to G.

Suppose there is no minimal path $P_n[s_n, t_n]$ in G being vertex-disjoint to $P_1[s_1,t_1], \ldots, P_{n-1}[s_{n-1}, t_{n-1}]$. Then the deletion of $S := V(P_1) \cup \ldots \cup V(P_{n-1})$ from G increases the distance between s_n and t_n, i.e., $\delta_{G \setminus S}(s_n, t_n) > \delta_G(s_n, t_n)$. Due to Lemma G there exists a vertex $z \in V$ and a subset $S' \subseteq S$ such that $|S'| \geq 3n-2$ and $\{z,s\} \in E$ for all $s \in S'$. By the pigeon-hole principle there is a path $P_i \in \{P_1, \ldots, P_{n-1}\}$ and four vertices $u, v, w, x \in V(P_i) \cap S'$. Hence, two of these vertices, u and v say, satisfy $\delta_G(u,v) > 2$. But on the other hand, since $\{z,u\}, \{z,v\} \in E$, we have $\delta_G(u,v) \leq 2$. A contradiction. Thus, there is a minimal path $P_n[s_n, t_n]$ in $G \setminus (V(P_1) \cup \ldots \cup V(P_{n-1}))$, which is also minimal with respect to G.

Correctness and complexity of the algorithm is an easy consequence. ♦

As a consequence of Theorems E and H using Theorem D we obtain an efficient algorithm to compute the geodetic nonblocking order of a graph.

Corollary J.

It can be computed in $O(\min\{|V| \cdot |E|, \mu(|V|)\})$ steps whether a graph $G=(V,E)$ is a geodetically vertex-nonblocking (edge-nonblocking) graph of order n.

5 Conclusions

In this paper we have investigated the problem of incrementally establishing disjoint communication paths connecting pairs of processors in networks.

Transfered to graphtheoretical notions we have defined two classes of graphs. Within graphs of the first class, called nonblocking graphs of order n, it is possible to construct incrementally n vertex-/edge-disjoint paths satisfying any n requests (problem Π in the Introduction). We have given necessary and sufficient conditions for a graph to be nonblocking of order n.

While the paths constructed in the first class of graphs do not satisfy any reasonable length constraints, we have defined a second class, called geodetically nonblocking graphs of order n, in which each path satisfying some request has to be minimal. For technical reasons, however, we had to exclude requests of adjacent vertices. We have given a complete characterization of geodetically nonblocking graphs in terms of their geodetic connectivity. There is an efficient algorithm to check whether a graph is a geodetically nonblocking graph of order n.
Graphs of the second class are, in particular, interesting from the practical point of view, since they solve problem Π' mentioned in the Introduction.

Finally we mention some open problems for future research:
1) Find a necessary *and* sufficient condition for a graph to be nonblocking of order n.
2) Find other classes of graphs that are nonblocking. (Using the techniques developed in this paper one may easily show that (3n-2)-vertex-connected *weakly triangulated* graphs (defined in [H85]) are nonblocking of order n)
3) Prove or disprove that every (2n-1)-edge connected chordal graph is edge-nonblocking of order n with respect to π_{min}.
4) What is the complexity of deciding whether a graph is nonblocking of order n? Is the problem co-NP-complete even if n=2?
5) Characterize the class of nonblocking graphs for predicates π other than π_{min} the paths have to fulfill.
6) Find larger classes of graphs that solve problem Π' mentioned in the Introduction.

References

[B65]   V.E. Benes: "Mathematical theory of connecting networks and telephone traffic", Academic Press 1965
[C80]   A. Cypher: "An approach to the k paths problem", Proc. of the 12th STOC (1980) 211-217
[CW87]   D. Coppersmith, S. Winograd, "Matrix multiplication via arithmetic progression", Proc. of the 19th STOC (1987) 1-6
[D61]   G.A. Dirac: "On rigid circuit graphs", Abh. Math. Sem. Univ. Hamburg 25 (1961) 71-76
[DT73]   G.A. Dirac, C. Thomassen: "Graphs in which every finite path is contained in a circuit", Math. Ann. 203 (1973) 65-75
[EJS77] R.C. Entringer, D.E. Jackson, P.J. Slater: "Geodetic connectivity of graphs", IEEE Trans. on Circuits and Systems 24 (1977) 460-463
[ES84]   H. Enomoto, A. Saito: "Disjoint shortest paths in graphs", Combinatorica 4 (1984) 275-279
[F85]   A. Frank: "Edge-disjoint paths in planar graphs", J. Combin. Th. 39B (1985) 164-178
[FFP88] P. Feldman, J. Friedman, N. Pippenger: "Wide-sense nonblocking networks", SIAM J. Discr. Math. 1 (1988) 158-173
[G80]   M.C. Golumbic: "Algorithmic graph theory and perfect graphs", Academic Press 1980

[H72]   F. Harary: "Graph theory", Addison-Wesley Publishing Company 1972

[H85]   R.B. Hayward: "Weakly triangulated graphs", J. Combin. Th. 39B (1985) 200-209

[HKS84] T. Hirata, K. Kubota, O. Saito: "A sufficient condition for a graph to be weakly k-linked", J. Combin. Th. 36B (1984) 85-94

[K75]   R.M. Karp: "On the computational complexity of combinatorial problems", Networks 5 (1975) 45-68

[KPS88] S.V. Krishnan, C. Pandu Rangan, S. Seshradi: "A new linear time algorithm for the two path problem on chordal graphs", Proc. of the 8th FST&TCS (1988) 49-66

[LM70]   D.G. Larman, P. Mani: "On the existence of certain configurations within graphs and the 1-skeleton of polytopes", Proc. London Math. Soc. 20 (1970) 144-160

[LR78]   A. LaPaugh, R.L. Rivest: "The subgraph homeomorphism problem", Proc. of the 10th STOC (1978) 40-50

[M85]   W. Mader: "Paths in graphs, reducing the edge-connectivity only by two", Graphs and Comb. 1 (1985) 81-89

[M27]   K. Menger: "Zur allgemeinen Kurventheorie", Fund. Math. 10 (1927) 96-115

[O80]   T. Ohtsuki: "The two disjoint path problem and wire routing design", Proc. of the 17th Symp. of Res. Inst. of Electrical Comm. (1980) 257-267

[O88]   H. Okamura: "Paths in k-edge-connected graphs", J. Combin. Th. 45 (1988) 345-355

[PS78]   Y. Perl, Y. Shiloach: "Finding two disjoint paths between two pairs of vertices in a graph", J. of the ACM 25 (1978) 1-9

[PU87]   D. Peleg, E. Upfal: "Constructing disjoint paths on expander graphs", Report RJ 5568 (56687), IBM Almaden Research 1987

[RS86]   N. Robertson, P.D. Seymour: "Graph minors XIII. The disjoint paths problem", Manuscript 1986

[S89]   A. Schwill: "Shortest edge-disjoint paths in graphs", Proc. of the STACS (1989) 505-516

[S80]   Y. Shiloach: "A polynomial solution to the undirected two paths problem" J. of the ACM 27 (1980) 445-456

[SP89]   A. Srinivasa Rao, C. Pandu Rangan: "Linear algorithms for parity path and two path problems on circular-arc graphs", Preprint 1989

[SU83]   E. Shamir, E. Upfal: "A fast construction of disjoint paths in communication networks", Proc. of the FCT (1983) 428-438

Infinite trees and automaton definable relations over ω-words

Wolfgang Thomas

Institut für Informatik und Praktische Mathematik
Universität Kiel, Olshausenstr. 40, D 2300 Kiel

Abstract.   We study sets of infinite trees that are equipped with a valuation which codes a tuple of paths. Via the identification of paths with ω-words, such tree sets correspond to relations over ω-words ("ω-relations"). Call an ω-relation "Rabin definable" if its associated tree set is recognized by a Rabin tree automaton. We characterize these relations by a restricted second-order logic over trees, "weak chain logic", thus answering a question of Rabin. We also characterize the strictly larger class of "Büchi definable" ω-relations (defined in terms of Büchi automata) by an extension of chain logic, where the "equal level predicate" over trees is adjoined. The theory of the k-ary tree in this logic is shown to be decidable; it covers tree properties which are not expressible in the monadic second-order logic SkS. We give an application of this decidability result to the verification of finite-state programs.

1.   Introduction

In this paper we consider sets of valued infinite trees where the valuation codes a tuple of infinite paths. Such "path valued" trees are useful in two respects: First, they can be considered as coding tuples of ω-words (via the correspondence between ω-words over an alphabet with k letters and paths through the k-ary tree). Thus sets of such trees correspond to relations over ω-words, or ω-relations for short, and tree automata can be applied in the investigation of these relations. Secondly, the "path valued" trees arise in the study of those logics over infinite trees, where quantifiers over paths are used, for instance in branching time logics. The purpose of the paper is to connect these aspects and to obtain results in both directions: We characterize the ω-relations which are recognized by Rabin tree automata (when considered as sets of trees) in terms of several logics, compare these relations with other ones which are defined using sequential automata, and obtain new decidability results for logics with path quantifiers.

We give the basic definitions and a more detailed summary, assuming that the reader is familiar with automaton models over infinite words (nondeterministic Büchi automaton, deterministic Muller automaton) and over infinite trees (Rabin tree automaton). A B-valued k-ary tree is a map $t:\{0,...,k-1\}^* \rightarrow B$; the node represented by $w \in \{0,...,k-1\}^*$ carries value $t(w)$. Denote the set of B-valued k-ary trees by $T_k(B)$. Let A be an alphabet with k letters, without loss of generality $A = \{0,...,k-1\}$. We associate with any tuple $\alpha = (\alpha_1,...,\alpha_n) \in (A^{\omega})^n$ a $\{0,1\}^n$-valued tree t_α. Define $t_\alpha:\{0,...,k-1\}^* \rightarrow \{0,1\}^n$ by setting the i-th component $(t_\alpha(w))_i$ of $t_\alpha(w)$ to be 1 iff w is a finite prefix of α_i. For an ω-relation $R \subseteq (A^{\omega})^n$ let

$$T_R = \{t_\alpha \in T_k(\{0,1\}^n) \,|\, \alpha = (\alpha_1,...,\alpha_n) \in R\}.$$

Definition. An ω-relation $R \subseteq (A^{\omega})^n$ is <u>Rabin definable</u> iff the set T_R is recognized by a Rabin tree automaton (in the sense of [Ra69]). Let ω-RBN be the class of Rabin definable ω-relations.

As shown in [Ra69], a set of k-ary trees is recognized by a Rabin tree automaton iff it is defined by a formula of the monadic second-order theory SkS. SkS has function constants for the k successor functions in the k-ary tree, and variables and quantifiers for nodes and for sets of nodes.

Läuchli and Savioz [LS87] have investigated the Rabin definable (or SkS definable) relations over <u>finite</u> words (over A*). The main result of [LS87] states that a set $R \subseteq (A^*)^n$ (consisting of n-tuples of nodes of the k-ary tree) is definable in SkS iff it is definable in the <u>weak</u> monadic theory WSkS (where all set quantifiers are restricted to range only over finite sets). [LS87] attribute to Rabin the question whether a corresponding result holds for ω-relations.

A positive answer is given in Section 2 of this paper. Moreover, it is shown that for the description of a Rabin definable ω-relation it suffices to use quantifiers over special finite sets, namely finite <u>chains</u>, i.e. finite subsets of paths through the infinite k-ary tree. The proof combines a consideration of Rabin tree automata on trees t_α with a reduction of the one successor theory S1S to the weak theory WS1S. So for definability of tree sets T_R (coding ω-relations R) the full monadic second-order theory SkS is equivalent to a small fragment, <u>weak chain logic</u>, where set quantification is restricted to finite sets which are totally ordered by the partial tree ordering. It follows that the "intermediate" system which allows quantification over arbitrary chains, called <u>chain logic</u>, is also equivalent to SkS for definition of sets T_R.

In Section 3 the Rabin definable ω-relations are located in a taxonomy of ω-relations defined by variants of sequential Büchi automata. We consider the "componentwise recognizable", the "Büchi definable", the "deterministic rational" and the "rational" ω-relations. All these classes are different, forming a strictly increasing hierarchy, and the class of Rabin recognizable ω-relations is located properly between the first two levels. The unary relations in each of these classes yield precisely the class of regular ω-languages.

In the remainder of the paper we focus on the "Büchi definable" ω-relations, obtained by the most natural representation of ω-relations in terms of ω-languages: We use the identification of $R \subseteq (A^{\omega})^n$ with a sequence set $L_R \subseteq (A^n)^{\omega}$, defined by

$$L_R = \{\beta \in (A^n)^{\omega} \mid \exists(\alpha_1,...,\alpha_n) \in R \text{ s.t. } \beta = (\alpha_1(0),...,\alpha_n(0))(\alpha_1(1),...,\alpha_n(1)) ... \}.$$

Definition. An ω-relation $R \subseteq (A^{\omega})^n$ is <u>Büchi definable</u> iff $L_R \subseteq (A^n)^{\omega}$ is regular (i.e., recognized by a Büchi automaton over the alphabet A^n). The class of Büchi definable ω-relations is denoted by ω-BÜC.

For a quick orientation on these definability notions, the reader may consult Proposition 3.1 below, where typical examples are listed. (In [Th89] the Büchi definable ω-relations were called "sequential", reminding of the "sequential calculus" of [Bü62]. We use a different term here in order to avoid confusion with the sequential functions and transducers in the sense of [Be79].)

In Section 4 the Büchi definable ω-relations are characterized by an extension of (weak or strong) chain logic. It is obtained by adjoining the <u>equal level predicate</u> E over A*, with $(u,v) \in E$ iff $|u| = |v|$. We call this system <u>chain logic + E</u>. By a reduction to Büchi's theory S1S it is also shown that the theory of the k-ary tree in the language of chain logic + E is decidable. In contrast, it is known that from the decidable theory SkS or even the weak theory WSkS one obtains (for $k \geq 2$) an undecidable theory when the predicate E is added. Thus chain logic + E is a "manageable" formalism which allows to treat tree properties that are not expressible in SkS.

Quantification "along paths" in trees, as provided by chain logic, suffices for many applications of monadic second-order logic over trees; in particular, most systems of temporal and modal logic can be embedded in chain logic. The predicate E adds a feature which allows to treat certain "uniformity conditions". We discuss this aspect in Section 5, where an application to the model checking problem for finite-state programs is given.

At the end of the paper some directions for further work are indicated.

2. Rabin definable ω-relations and chain logic

If $t: \{0,...k-1\}^* \to B$ is an B-valued k-ary tree, a <u>chain</u> through t is a subset of the domain $\{0,...,k-1\}^*$ which is totally ordered by the prefix relation $<$. A <u>path</u> is a chain which is maximal w.r.t. set inclusion. If π is a path, $t|\pi$ denotes the restriction of the map t to π. Given a set $X \subseteq \{0,...,k-1\}^*$, define its <u>hull</u> by

$$\text{hull}(X) = X \cup \{u \in \{0,...,k-1\}^* \mid u \notin X, \text{ and } u = wi \text{ for some } w \in X, i < k\}.$$

A <u>Rabin tree automaton</u> over B-valued k-ary trees is of the form $\mathcal{A} = (Q,q_o,\Delta,\mathcal{F})$ with finite state set Q, initial state $q_o \in Q$, transition set $\Delta \subseteq Q \times B \times Q^k$ and a system $\mathcal{F} \subseteq 2^Q$ of final state sets. A <u>run</u> of $\mathcal{A}$ on $t \in T_k(B)$ is a tree $r:\{0,...,k-1\}^* \rightarrow Q$ such that $r(\varepsilon) = q_o$, $(r(w),t(w),r(w0),...,r(w(k-1))) \in \Delta$ for $w \in \{0,...,k-1\}^*$. The run r is <u>successful</u> if for all paths π the set $In(r|\pi)$ of states which occur infinitely often in $r|\pi$ belongs to $\mathcal{F}$. A set $T \subseteq T_k(B)$ is <u>Rabin recognizable</u> if for some Rabin automaton $\mathcal{A}$ the set T consists of the trees on which there is a successful run of $\mathcal{A}$. Recall that an ω-relation R is Rabin definable iff T_R is Rabin recognizable.

We introduce the necessary logical terminology. A $\{0,1\}^n$-valued k-ary tree t will be identified with the model theoretic structure

$$\underline{t} = (t_k, P_1,...,P_n)$$

where

$$t_k = (\{0,...,k-1\}^*, \varepsilon, \cdot 0,...,\cdot(k-1), <)$$

is the unvalued k-ary tree with with root ε (empty word), with $\cdot 0,...,\cdot(k-1)$ as the k successor functions on $\{0,...,k-1\}^*$ and < as the prefix relation, and where

$$P_i = \{w \in \{0,...,k-1\}^* \mid (t(w))_i = 1\}.$$

The corresponding monadic second-order formalism <u>SkS</u> ("second-order theory of k successors") has variables x,y,... and X,Y,... for elements ("nodes"), resp. subsets of $\{0,...,k-1\}^*$. The atomic formulas are written $\tau = \tau'$, $\tau < \tau'$, $\tau \in X$ where τ, τ' stand for terms built up from ε and variables x,y,... by means of the k successor functions. Formulas are built up from the atomic formulas using boolean connectives and the quantifiers $\exists$, $\forall$ applied to either kind of variables. If $\varphi(X_1,...,X_n)$ is a formula of this language with the free set variables $X_1,...,X_n$ we write $(t_k,P_1,...,P_n) \models \varphi(X_1,...,X_n)$ to indicate that the k-ary tree satisfies φ with P_i as interpretation for X_i. Let for $\varphi = \varphi(X_1,...,X_n)$

$$T(\varphi) = \{t \in T_k(\{0,1\}^n) \mid \underline{t} \models \varphi(X_1,...,X_n)\}.$$

T is called <u>SkS-definable</u> if $T = T(\varphi)$ for some SkS-formula φ. Rabin showed in [Ra69] that a set T of k-ary trees is SkS-definable iff it is Rabin recognizable. The system <u>WSkS</u> (weak second-order theory of k successors) is obtained by restricting the range of the set quantifiers to finite sets only.

The corresponding notions for the case of <u>one</u> successor (Büchi and Muller automata on ω-words which characterize the <u>regular ω-languages,</u> and the theories S1S and WS1S) will be used without introducing the technical details (see e.g. [Th88]).

We call <u>chain logic</u> (resp. <u>weak chain logic</u>) the formalism which results from SkS by restricting the set quantifiers to chains (resp. finite chains). If $T = T(\varphi)$ for a formula φ with this restricted interpretation, we say that T is <u>definable in chain logic,</u> resp. <u>definable in weak chain logic</u>. Since the property of being a chain is definable in SkS, and being a finite chain is definable in chain logic, we have for $T \subseteq T_k(\{0,1\}^n)$:

- If T is definable in weak chain logic, then T is definable in chain logic,
- If T is definable in chain logic, then T is definable in SkS.

We now show the converse for tree sets T_R which code ω-relations R.

2.1 Theorem. An ω-relation R is Rabin definable iff T_R is definable in weak chain logic.

<u>Proof.</u> It suffices to show the direction from left to right. Let $A = \{0,...,k-1\}$ and $R \subseteq (A^\omega)^n$. Suppose $\mathcal{A} = (Q,q_0,\Delta,\mathcal{F})$ is a Rabin tree automaton which recognizes T_R. The desired formula $\varphi(X_1,...,X_n)$ defining T_R will be a conjunction of the (first-order expressible) formula

(0) "for i = 1,...,n: X_i forms a path"

with a formula which expresses in weak chain logic that

(1) "there is a successful run of $\mathcal{A}$ on the $\{0,1\}^n$-valued tree given by $X_1,...,X_n$".

Call a state q of $\mathcal{A}$ <u>zero-accepting</u> if the automaton $(Q,q,\Delta,\mathcal{F})$ accepts the trivial k-ary tree t_0 with $t_0(w) = (0,...,0)$ for all $w \in \{0,...,k-1\}^*$. Condition (1) is equivalent to

(2) "there is a partial run r: $\text{hull}(X_1 \cup...\cup X_n) \to Q$ of $\mathcal{A}$ which is successful on the paths $X_1,...,X_n$ and which reaches zero-accepting states on the difference set $\text{hull}(X_1 \cup...\cup X_n) - (X_1 \cup...\cup X_n)$."

A partial run as specified in (2) can be described by an assignment $\underline{r}$ from $X_1 \cup...\cup X_n$ to the set Δ of transitions of $\mathcal{A}$. Since Δ is finite, the transitions can be coded by 0-1-vectors of an appropriate length m, and the existence of the assignment $\underline{r}$ can be expressed by claiming the existence of corresponding subsets $Y_1,...,Y_m$ of $X_1 \cup...\cup X_n$. We obtain a condition of the form

(3) "there are subsets $Y_1,...,Y_m$ of $X_1 \cup...\cup X_n$ which code a partial run as in (2)".

We have to reduce the Y_i to finite chains. Call $w \in X_1 \cup...\cup X_n$ a <u>branching point</u> of $X_1 \cup...\cup X_n$ if w is the empty word ε or not all paths X_i which pass through w also pass through a single successor of w. By a <u>last branching point</u> of $X_1 \cup...\cup X_n$ we mean a branching point which is maximal w.r.t. <. The property of being a branching point (resp. last branching point) is first-order definable in terms of $X_1 \cup...\cup X_n$. The branching points define a decomposition of $X_1 \cup...\cup X_n$ into the segments given by the pairs of <-consecutive branching points (which are finite chains) and into infinite chains starting at the last branching points. Assuming that there are p such finite and infinite segments, each of the sets Y_i can be split into subsets $Z_{i1},...,Z_{ip}$ that that the Z_{ij} code partial runs delimited by (and including) branching points. Since the Z_{ij} are finite chains when contained in segments between consecutive branching points, it suffices to treat the case of sets $X_i[w] := X_i \cap \{u \mid w \leq u\}$ for last branching points w. So it remains to reduce to weak chain

logic a condition of the form

(4) "there are subsets $Z_1,...,Z_m$ of $X_i[w]$ which code a partial run of $\mathcal{A}$ on $X_i[w]$ as in (2)".

This condition is expressible in monadic second-order logic S1S as a statement on ω-words over the alphabet $\{0,...,k-1\}$ (representing $X_i[w]$). By [Th80] (see also [Th88]), an S1S-formula is equivalent to a formula of the weak monadic theory WS1S. The retranslation into chain logic over the k-ary tree is a formula of weak chain logic which expresses (4). ❏

We note two consequences of Theorem 2.1 and its proof: The first presents a normal form for Rabin definable ω-relations in terms of regular languages and ω-languages, which is a natural extension of the "special relations" over A* as introduced by [LS87]. The second shows that deterministic Rabin tree automata suffice for recognizing tree sets T_R.

The description of Rabin definable ω-relations in terms of languages is based on the above mentioned decomposition of a tuple of paths into the segments delimited by the branching points. The representation is technically cumbersome due to the necessary distinction of the possibilities by which the individual paths may diverge. Given an n-tuple $(\alpha_1,...,\alpha_n)$, the segments between consecutive branching points, respectively starting at last branching points (as introduced in the above proof), form a finite tree, where each node represents a segment. Label each node by those indices i such that the corresponding segment is a segment of α_i. Call the resulting finite tree labelled by nonempty subsets of $\{1,...,n\}$ the <u>branching pattern</u> of $(\alpha_1,...,\alpha_n)$. (Its root is labelled $\{1,...,n\}$, and the labels of the sons of a node x form a proper partition of the label of x.)

Example.

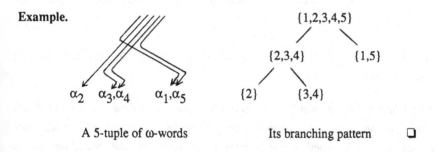

A 5-tuple of ω-words   Its branching pattern   ❏

Now suppose that to each inner node of a branching pattern p a language $W \subseteq A^*$ and to each leaf an ω-language $L \subseteq A^\omega$ is associated. Let these languages and ω-languages be indexed as $W_1,...,W_r,L_{r+1},...,L_{r+s}$. Given an n-tuple $(\alpha_1,...,\alpha_n)$ with branching pattern p, the <u>index sequence</u> of the i-th component α_i is the finite sequence of indices of the W_j,L_j which are associated with the path through p whose nodes contain i.

Example (continued).   Given $(\alpha_1,...,\alpha_5)$ as above and $(\omega$-)languages associated to its branching pattern in the form

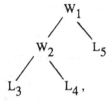

the index sequence of α_1 is $(1,5)$, and the index sequence of α_2 is $(1,2,3)$. ❑

Assume that to the nodes of a branching pattern p the languages $W_1,...,W_r,L_{r+1},...,L_{r+s}$ are associated. An ω-relation $R \subseteq (A^\omega)^n$ is <u>generated by</u> $W_1,...,W_r,L_{r+1},...,L_{r+s}$ <u>via the branching pattern</u> p if R contains those n-tuples $(\alpha_1,...,\alpha_n)$ having branching pattern p, such that there are words $w_1 \in W_1,..., w_r \in W_r$ and ω-words $\beta_{r+1} \in L_{r+1},..., \beta_{r+s} \in L_{r+s}$ with

$$\alpha_i = w_{i(1)} \cdots w_{i(m-1)} \beta_{i(m)}$$

where $(i(1),...,i(m))$ is the index sequence for α_i.

2.2 Definition.

An ω-relation $R \subseteq (A^\omega)^n$ is <u>special</u> if there are a branching pattern p, regular languages $W_1,...,W_r \subseteq A^*$, and regular ω-languages $L_{r+1},...,L_{r+s} \subseteq A^\omega$ such that R is generated by $W_1,...,W_r,L_{r+1},...,L_{r+s}$ via p.

From the proof of 2.1 we obtain

2.3 Corollary.   An ω-relation is Rabin definable iff it is a finite union of special ω-relations. ❑

Applied to "finitary" relations $R \subseteq (A^*)^n$, the argument of 2.1 and 2.3 reproves (in simplified form) the main result of [LS87].

Let R be a special ω-relation. A Rabin tree automaton that recognizes T_R has to check the designated paths of an input tree against a certain branching pattern, and along each designated path has to check whether the segments delimited by the branching points belong to given regular (ω-)languages. Both tests can be performed deterministically (in the second case due to McNaughton's Theorem on determinizing ω-automata). So any special ω-relation is defined by a deterministic Rabin tree automaton. Since each input tree t_α determines a unique branching pattern, unions of special ω-relations can be defined by products of deterministic Rabin automata. Hence we obtain

2.4 Corollary.   An ω-relation is Rabin definable iff T_R is recognized by a deterministic Rabin tree automaton. ❑

3. Classes of automaton definable ω-relations

In this section we describe some possibilities to specify ω-relations in terms of finite automata. The different versions of acceptance for tuples of ω-words are obtained by allowing different kinds of dependency between the (one-way) scanning processes on the components of a tuple. The scanning may proceed completely independently on the components, or "strictly in parallel", or by means of reading heads which may move at different speeds on the components and communicate via the finite control. These three possibilities lead to the classes of "componentwise recognizable", "Büchi definable", and "rational" ω-relations, respectively.

We call an ω-relation $R \subseteq (A^{\omega})^n$ <u>componentwise recognizable</u> iff it is a finite union of sets $L_1 \times ... \times L_n$ where each ω-language L_i is regular (i.e., recognized by a Büchi automaton over A). Thus membership of tuples $(\alpha_1,...,\alpha_n)$ of ω-words in R is determined by membership of the components α_i in given regular ω-languages. Let ω-RCG be the class of componentwise recognizable ω-relations.

If one uses Büchi automata over A^n, which scan the components of an n-tuple $(\alpha_1,...,\alpha_n)$ letter by letter "strictly in parallel" from left to right, one views an n-tuple from $(A^{\omega})^n$ as an ω-word from $(A^n)^{\omega}$. The ω-relations recognized in this way by Büchi automata are the <u>Büchi definable</u> ω-relations as defined in the introduction.

It is straightforward (but again technically cumbersome) to define "special Büchi automata" over A^n which characterize the special n-ary ω-relations as introduced in Section 2. Since these automata are nondeterministic and thus are closed under union, this yields a description of the <u>Rabin definable</u> ω-relations. The idea is to specialize the model of Büchi automaton on A^n (as used for the Büchi definable relations) in the following way: The automaton reads any components α_i and α_j of $(\alpha_1,...,\alpha_n)$ in parallel <u>as long as they coincide,</u> and afterwards proceeds on the individual components α_i, α_j without further dependencies between them. The model is thus located between the automaton characterization of ω-RCG, where the components are scanned individually from the start, and that for ω-BÜC, where the parallel scanning of the components continues through the whole ω-computation. This gives the idea for a proof that we have ω-RCG $\subsetneq \omega$-RBN $\subsetneq \omega$-BÜC.

The last automaton model, considered by Gire and Nivat in [GN84], employs n reading heads which are moved forward independently on the n components of an n-tuple $(\alpha_1,...,\alpha_n)$ (given to the automaton on n right infinite input tapes). The nondeterministic transition table specifies for any state and any n-tuple of scanned letters which possibilities are admitted to move one or more reading heads forward by one tape cell and to reach a new state. An ω-relation $R \subseteq (A^{\omega})^n$ is called <u>rational</u> iff it is recognized by an acceptor of this type (where an n-tuple $(\alpha_1,...,\alpha_n)$ is accepted if it admits an infinite run such that each component α_i is scanned completely and some final state is reached infinitely often). Gire and Nivat [GN84] characterize these ω-relations by a calculus of rational expressions. The ω-relations recognized by deterministic multihead acceptors of this kind will be called <u>deterministic rational.</u> By ω-DRAT (resp. ω-RAT) we denote the classes of the deterministic rational (resp. the rational) ω-relations.

3.1 Proposition. We have

$$\omega\text{-RCG} \subset \omega\text{-RBN} \subset \omega\text{-BÜC} \subset \omega\text{-DRAT} \subset \omega\text{-RAT},$$

and all inclusions in this chain are strict.

<u>Proof</u> (Outline). The inclusions $\omega\text{-RCG} \subseteq \omega\text{-RBN} \subseteq \omega\text{-BÜC} \subseteq \omega\text{-DRAT} \subseteq \omega\text{-RAT}$ are easy.

Let $A = \{a,b\}$. The following relations $R_1,...,R_4$ can serve as examples showing the strictness of the inclusions (from left to right). Proofs are omitted here.

$(\alpha,\beta) \in R_1$ iff for some i, $\alpha \in a^i b A^\omega$ and $\beta \in a^i b A^\omega$ (i.e. α and β start with the same number of letters a before the first b),

$(\alpha,\beta) \in R_2$ iff for some i, $\alpha(i) = b$ and $\beta(i) = b$ (i.e. α and β have some letter b on the same position),

$(\alpha,\beta) \in R_3$ iff for some i, $\alpha \in b^*a^i b A^\omega$ and $\beta \in b^*a^i b A^\omega$ (i.e. the first segments of letters a in α and β are finite and have the same length),

$(\alpha,\beta) \in R_4$ iff for some i, $\alpha \in A^*ba^i b A^\omega$ and $\beta \in A^*ba^i b A^\omega$ (i.e. some segment of α formed by letter a and some segment of β formed by letter a have the same length). ❑

3.2 Remark.

(a)   From the definitions it is immediate that the <u>unary</u> ω-relations in any of the classes of 3.1 coincide with the regular ω-languages.

(b)   The statement of 3.1 is true also for the corresponding classes of relations over A*. (In the definition of the example relations R_i, replace A^ω everywhere by A*.) ❑

4.   Büchi definable ω-relations and chain logic with the equal level predicate

Elgot and Rabin studied in [ER66] the "theory of generalized successor", denoted GS, the first-order theory of the structure $(\{0,1\}^*, \varepsilon, \cdot 0, \cdot 1, E)$ with the empty word ε, the two successor functions and the equal length predicate E on $\{0,1\}^*$. Since we view $\{0,1\}^*$ as the full binary tree, we refer to E as the "equal level predicate". Elgot and Rabin [ER66] showed that GS is decidable, and they raised the question of decidable extensions of GS. They proved that many predicates and functions cause undecidability when added to GS. While GS with predicates like $P = \{0^i | i \text{ is a factorial}\}$ remains decidable, no "interesting" binary predicate P on $\{0,1\}^*$ is known such that the extension of GS by P is decidable.

In this paper we introduce a different proper extension of GS which is decidable, by allowing quantifiers ranging over chains in the tree of finite words. It will be shown that this theory, called <u>chain logic + E</u>, and the monadic theory S1S of one successor can be interpreted in each other. This yields a characterization of Büchi definable ω-relations in terms of chain logic + E, as well as decidability of the theory of the infinite k-ary tree in the language of chain logic + E. For simplicity of exposition we treat only binary trees; the generalization to k-ary trees needs additional coding.

S1S-formulas $\varphi(X_1,...,X_n)$ are satisfied by n-tuples of subsets of 0^*, or equivalently of the set ω of natural numbers. Each subset of ω can be represented by its characteristic function (an ω-word over $\{0,1\}$). Hence the possible models for S1S-formulas $\varphi(X_1,...,X_n)$ may be considered as n-tuples $\alpha = (\alpha_1,...,\alpha_n) \in (\{0,1\}^\omega)^n$.

Let us represent "chain valued" tree models for formulas $\psi(X_1,...,X_n)$ of chain logic + E in a similar way. To describe such a tree model, it suffices to specify the n chains which serve as interpretation of the X_i. One chain C can be represented as a pair (δ,β) of 0-1-sequences, where δ (the "direction sequence") codes the leftmost path through the binary tree of which C is a subset, and β indicates which nodes on this path belong to C and which do not. Given a binary tree model $\underline{t} = (t_2,P_1,...,P_n)$, where the P_i are chains, we say that the sequence tuple $(\delta_1,\beta_1,...,\delta_n,\beta_n)$ codes $\underline{t}$ if for $i = 1,...,n$ the pair (δ_i,β_i) represents chain P_i in this way.

4.1 Theorem.

(a) Chain logic + E over the binary tree can be interpreted in S1S in the following sense: For any formula $\varphi(X_1,...,X_n)$ of chain logic + E there is by effective construction an S1S-formula $\psi(Y_1,Z_1,...,Y_n,Z_n)$ such that for all tree models $\underline{t} = (t_2,P_1,...,P_n)$ with chains P_i we have

$$\underline{t} \models \varphi(X_1,...,X_n) \quad \text{iff} \quad \psi(Y_1,Z_1,...,Y_n,Z_n) \text{ is satisfied by the sequence tuple}$$
which codes $\underline{t}$.

(b) S1S can be interpreted in chain logic + E over the binary tree in the following sense: For any S1S-formula $\varphi(X_1,...,X_n)$ there is by effective construction a formula $\psi(X_1,...,X_n)$ of chain logic + E such that

$$\varphi(X_1,...,X_n) \text{ is satisfied by } \alpha = (\alpha_1,...,\alpha_n) \quad \text{iff} \quad \underline{t}_\alpha \models \psi(X_1,...,X_n).$$

Proof.

(a) It is convenient to work with a version of chain logic in which only set variables (but no individual variables) occur. The atomic formulas are of form $X_1 \subseteq X_2$ ("chain X_1 is included in chain X_2"), Sing X ("chain X is a singleton"), $X_1 \text{ succ}_i X_2$ ("chains X_1,X_2 are singletons $\{x_1\},\{x_2\}$ such that x_1 has x_2 as i-th successor"), and $X_1 \text{ E } X_2$ ("chains X_1,X_2 are singletons with elements on the same level of the tree"). It is easy to see that this version of chain logic is expressively equivalent to the original one.

Now the proof is a straightforward induction over the formulas of this modified chain logic. As an example of an atomic formula consider X_1 E X_2: The desired formula $\psi(Y_1,Z_1,Y_2,Z_2)$ reads

$$\exists x(x \in Z_1 \wedge x \in Z_2 \wedge \forall y(\neg x = y \rightarrow (\neg y \in Z_1 \wedge \neg y \in Z_2))).$$

The induction steps (for which the cases $\neg$, $\vee$, $\exists$ suffice) are obvious; here one existential quantifier in chain logic + E is translated into two existential quantifiers in S1S.

(b) By [Bü62], an S1S-formula is equivalent to a Büchi automaton $\mathcal{A}$ over $\{0,1\}^n$. So it suffices to find for any such Büchi automaton $\mathcal{A}$ a formula $\psi(X_1,...,X_n)$ of chain logic + E such that

$$\mathcal{A} \text{ accepts } \alpha = (\alpha_1,...,\alpha_n) \text{ iff } t_\alpha \models \psi(X_1,...,X_n).$$

The formula ψ has to express the existence of a successful run of $\mathcal{A}$ on α. If there are (without loss of generality) 2^m states in $\mathcal{A}$, given as 0-1-vectors of length m, this can be formulated as the existence of an m-tuple $(Y_1,...,Y_m)$ of subsets of the leftmost path of the binary tree. For instance, if the run assumes state $(1,0,1)$ at step $y \in 0^*$, we should have $y \in Y_1$, $y \notin Y_2$, $y \in Y_3$. In expressing that the state sequence is compatible with the input α and the transition table of $\mathcal{A}$ we use the predicate E: If, for example, we deal with the alphabet $\{0,1\}^2$ and state set $\{0,1\}^3$, and the transition $(q,(1,0),q')$ is applied with $q = (0,0,0)$ and $q' = (1,1,1)$ at step $y \in 0^*$, we have

$y \notin Y_1, y \notin Y_2, y \notin Y_3,$
$x_1 1 \in X_1$ for the unique $x_1 \in X_1$ with yEx_1 ,
$x_2 0 \in X_2$ for the unique $x_2 \in X_2$ with yEx_2 ,
and $y0 \in Y_1, y0 \in Y_2, y0 \in Y_3$.

Let $\delta(y,X_1,...,X_n,Y_1,...,Y_m)$ be the disjunction of these formulas over all transitions of $\mathcal{A}$. Then the desired formula ψ can be written in the form

$$\exists Y_1...Y_m(\delta_0(Y_1,...,Y_m) \wedge \forall y(y \in 0^* \rightarrow \delta(y,X_1,...,X_n,Y_1,...,Y_m)) \wedge \delta_1(Y_1,...,Y_m)),$$

where δ_0 expresses the initial state condition and δ_1 the acceptance condition. $\square$

Part (a) of the above proof extends to the case of k-ary trees (say for $k = 2^r$) by replacing the sequences δ_i by r-tuples of 0-1-sequences. The following results are consequences of 4.1 (in the generalization to k-ary trees).

4.2 Corollary. An ω-relation R is Büchi definable iff T_R is definable in chain logic + E.$\square$

For the proof of 4.2 (from right to left) note that formulas of chain logic + E are interpreted only over trees t_α, i.e. with designated paths only (instead of chains). Hence in the coding of trees t_α by tuples of 0-1-sequences the β_i-components can be cancelled, and the S1S-formula obtained by 4.1(a) is of form $\psi(Y_1,...,Y_n)$, defining an n-ary Büchi definable ω-relation as desired.

By decidability of S1S we conclude from 4.1(a)

4.3 Corollary. The theory of the k-ary tree in the language of chain logic + E is decidable. ❑

The predicate E is not definable in full monadic second-order logic SkS, and when adjoined to SkS it yields an undecidable theory (see [LS87] or [Th88] for a proof). So chain logic + E over the k-ary tree gives a decidable theory in which tree properties can be defined which are not expressible in SkS.

Finally, by the reduction of S1S to WS1S as mentioned in Section 2 we obtain

4.4 Corollary. Over tree models t_α, chain logic + E is expressively equivalent to weak chain logic + E. ❑

5. An Application to the Verification of Finite-State Concurrent Programs

In the present paper we do not consider the interpretation of formulas of chain logic + E over arbitrary valued trees (where the free set variables of a formula $\varphi(X_1,...,X_n)$ are interpreted by arbitrary sets but the quantified set variables by chains only). However, the methods of this paper already allow to treat a special case of valued trees which suffices for certain applications: the case of regular trees.

A k-ary B-valued tree t is called <u>regular</u> if t contains only finitely many nonisomorphic subtrees. Equivalently, for each letter $b \in B$ the set

$$V_b = \{w \in \{0,...,k-1\}^* \mid t(w) = b\}$$

is regular. The following lemma is shown using definability in WS1S of regular sets of finite words:

5.1 Lemma. Let t be a regular B-valued k-ary tree. Then for each letter $b \in B$ there is a formula $\varphi_b(x)$ of weak chain logic with one free individual variable x such that the unvalued k-ary tree t_k with designated node w satisfies $\varphi_b(x)$ iff $t(w) = b$.

<u>Proof.</u> Suppose that the set V_b is recognized by the finite automaton $\mathcal{A}$. The formula $\varphi_b(x)$ expresses that $\mathcal{A}$ has a successful run when reading as input the directions taken on the finite path up to node x. This can be expressed in weak chain logic, using auxiliary subsets of the finite path up to x as codes for the states assumed by the automaton. ❑

5.2 Theorem. It is decidable whether an effectively given regular $\{0,1\}^n$-valued k-ary tree (i.e. a model $(t_k,P_1,...,P_n)$) satisfies a given formula $\varphi(X_1,...,X_n)$ of chain logic + E.

<u>Proof.</u> We transform $\varphi(X_1,...,X_n)$ into a <u>sentence</u> in the language of chain logic + E (i.e., a formula without free variables) which is true in the unvalued tree t_k iff $(t_k, P_1,...,P_n)$ satisfies $\varphi(X_1,...,X_n)$. Then the result follows by 4.3. For the transformation, one only has to replace each of the X_i by an explicit definition in chain logic. This explicit definition is provided by 5.1 since the given tree is regular. More precisely, one substitutes each atomic formula $x \in X_i$ in $\varphi(X_1,...,X_n)$ by the disjunction of all formulas $\varphi_b(x)$ such that the i-th component of $b \in \{0,1\}^n$ is 1. $\square$

An effective test as guaranteed by 5.2 is needed in the verification of finite-state programs with respect to specifications in a system of branching time logic ("model checking", cf. [CES86]). For this purpose, several systems of branching time logic have been considered in the literature (such as CTL, CTL*, ECTL*), which can all be considered as fragments of chain logic interpreted over k-ary trees (see e.g. [HT87]). In the sequel we consider the properly more expressive system of chain logic + E as a specification language for finite-state programs.

In this context, a (possibly concurrent) finite-state program P is considered as a finite directed graph G_P whose nodes represent the program's states and whose edges represent the possible transitions in one step. There is a designated initial state s_0. If for the specification the state properties $q_1,...,q_m$ are relevant, each state s is annotated by those q_i which are true in s. Let t_P be the state tree which results from G_P by unravelling it from the initial state, where again the nodes are labelled by the q_i as prescribed by G_P. A specification for P is a formula φ to be interpreted in t_P; in our case φ is a formula of chain logic + E where for each state property q_i the atomic formula $x \in Q_i$ ("in state x the property q_i holds") is available. Program P is correct with respect to the specification φ if t_P satisfies φ.

Note that by finiteness of G_P the tree t_P is at most $|G_P|$-ary and regular; also, given P this tree is effectively presented. Hence we obtain from 5.2:

5.3 Theorem. With respect to specifications in chain logic + E, the correctness of finite-state programs is decidable. $\square$

The predicate E allows to express over infinite trees that node x has equal distance to nodes y and z (in the subtree at x). As mentioned in the previous section, such "uniformity" conditions ([Em87]) transcend the expressive power of SkS and Rabin tree automata. This applies a fortiori to chain logic and the above mentioned systems CTL, CTL*, ECTL* of branching time logic. The additional expressive power provided by the E-predicate may be useful in applications where one wants to express liveness properties combined with time constraints (guaranteeing the "uniform occurrence" of certain events along all computation paths).

The complexity of the algorithm given by 5.3 is nonelementary in the length of the specification in chain logic + E (since the theory S1S, used in the decision procedure, is nonelementary). It remains to be investigated how a better complexity bound can be obtained by rebuilding the syntax of chain logic + E, for example when replacing quantifiers by suitable automaton operators in the sense of [VW88]. Note that S1S is expressively equivalent to such a system with automaton operators ("extended temporal logic" ETL, cf. [VW88]), for which the satisfiability problem is in PSPACE.

6. Concluding Remarks

We have studied several classes of automaton definable ω-relations and their description in terms of tree automata, sequential automata, and systems of monadic second-order logic. For technical convenience only relations over ω-words were considered; one can adjust the characterization results to the more general case of relations $R \subseteq (A^\infty)^n$, where $A^\infty = A^* \cup A^\omega$.

Compared with the extensive research on regular ω-languages, there are only few papers concerned with automaton definable ω-relations (or functions over ω-words). As the above results indicate, this subject is of interest not only by the diversity of definability notions (which collapse to one notion in the case of ω-languages, cf. Remark 3.2.(a) above), but also by its close connection to path-oriented logics over trees, and in view of other applications. For instance in the analysis of concurrent systems it can be useful to extend the study of properties of execution sequences, prevailing in the literature, to the investigation of relations between sequences.

We list some (rather arbitrarily chosen) topics for further investigation. One question concerns a logical characterization of ω-DRAT or ω-RAT. Since neither of these relation classes is closed under the boolean operations, the logic should involve restrictions on the use of negation. A possible approach is to consider logics with quantifiers for transitive closure or the least fixed point operator (cf. [Im87]). An alternative is to investigate the boolean closures of ω-DRAT, resp. ω-RAT.

Between ω-BÜC and ω-DRAT there is a gap in expressiveness. Since the concatenation relation on A^* is deterministic rational, the Post Correspondence Problem can be coded in terms of such relations (cf. [Be79, p. 87 ff.]). So the equivalence problem for deterministic rational and for rational ω-relations is undecidable, while it is decidable for ω-RCG, ω-RBN, and ω-BÜC. Again by the presence of the concatenation relation, the closure of ω-DRAT and of ω-RAT under projections and boolean operations includes all recursive ω-relations and hence is as expressive as first-order arithmetic, whereas ω-BÜC is closed under projections and boolean operations (cf. [Qu46], [Th89]). This suggests a study of relation classes between ω-BÜC and ω-DRAT.

The strictness of the inclusions of Proposition 3.1 raises the question whether there are algorithms which decide membership in ω-RCG, ω-RBN, ω-BÜC, ω-DRAT for a given relation in ω-RAT, similarly for membership in ω-RCG, ω-RBN for a given relation in ω-BÜC. (Within ω-RAT, the property of being a rational function is decidable by [Gi86].)

Finally, concerning the system chain logic + E, it seems interesting to look for other relations R such that chain logic + R (or chain logic + E + R) is decidable. Also the case of arbitrary valued trees as underlying models (not necessarily coding tuples of paths) remains to be investigated. We conjecture that in this general case SkS and chain logic + E are incompatible in expressive power, i.e. that there are SkS-definable tree sets which cannot be defined in chain logic + E. A proposed example is the set of {0,1}-valued trees having finitely many nodes with value 1, such that the number of <-maximal nodes with value 1 is even.

References

[Be79]   J. Berstel, Transductions and Context-Free Languages, B.G. Teubner, Stuttgart 1979.

[Bü62]   J.R. Büchi, On a decision method in restricted second order arithmetic, in: "Logic, Methodology and Philosophy of Science. Proc. 1960 Intern. Congr." (E. Nagel et alt, Eds.), Stanford University Press 1962, pp. 1-11.

[CES86] E.M. Clarke, E.A. Emerson, A.P. Sistla, Automatic verification of finite-state concurrent systems using temporal logic specifications, ACM Trans. on Progr. Lang. and Systems 8 (1986), 244-263.

[ER66]   C.C. Elgot, M.O. Rabin, Decidability and undecidability of second (first) order theory of (generalized) successor, J. of Symbolic Logic 31 (1966), 169-181.

[Em87]   E.A. Emerson, Uniform inevitability is tree automaton ineffable, Inform. Process. Lett. 24 (1987), 77-80.

[HT87]   T. Hafer, W. Thomas, Computation tree logic CTL* and path quantifiers in the monadic theory of the binary tree, Proc. 14th ICALP (T. Ottmann, Ed.), LNCS 267 (1987), 269-279.

[Gi86]   F. Gire, Two decidability problems for infinite words, Inform. Process. Lett. 22 (1986), 135-140.

[GN84]   F. Gire, M. Nivat, Relations rationelles infinitaires, Calcolo 21 (1984), 91-125.

[Im87]   N. Immerman, Languages that capture complexity classes, SIAM J. Comput. 16 (1987), 760-778.

[LS87]   H. Läuchli, C. Savioz, Monadic second order definable relations on the binary tree, J. of Symbolic Logic 52 (1987), 219-226.

[Qu46]   W.V. Quine, Concatenation as a basis for arithmetic, J. of Symbolic Logic 11, (1946), 105-114.

[Ra69]   M.O. Rabin, Decidability of second-order theories and automata on infinite trees, Trans. Amer. Math. Soc. 141 (1969), 1-35.

[Th80]   W. Thomas, On the bounded monadic theory of well-ordered structures, J. of Symbolic Logic 45 (1980), 334-338.

[Th88]   W. Thomas, Automata on infinite objects (preliminary version), Aachener Informatik-Berichte 88-17 (to appear in: Handbook of Theoretical Computer Science, J.v. Leeuwen, Ed., North-Holland).

[Th89]   W. Thomas, Automata and quantifier hierarchies (to appear in: Proc. 16ème Ecole de Printemps d'Inform. Théor. "Propriétés Formelles des Automates Finis et Applications", Springer LNCS 386 (1989)).

[VW88]   M.Y. Vardi, P. Wolper, Reasoning about infinite computation paths, to appear.

Enumerative Combinatorics and Computer Science

(summary)

Xavier Gérard Viennot
LaBRI*
Université de Bordeaux I & CNRS
33405 Talence Cedex France

This short paper is a summary of a survey talk given on the interplay between enumerative Combinatorics and Computer Science.

Introduction

Combinatorics (also called combinatorial analysis) is an old and classical branch of Mathematics. In the last twenty years considerable interest has been given, especially with the fast development of Computer Science. Both domains have enriched each other. Here we concentrate on "enumerative Combinatorics" with particular attention to the appearance of "bijective proofs". These "bijective methods" can be seen as a new "paradigm" in Combinatorics and in some other parts of Mathematics (the word "paradigm" is used here in the sense of the scientific philosopher Thomas Kuhn). This paradigm fits very well within the context of the interplay between Combinatorics and Computer Science.

* Laboratoire Bordelais de Recherche en Informatique
Unité associée au Centre National de la Recherche Scientifique n°726
work partially supported by PRC "Mathématiques et Informatique"

1. Enumerative Combinatorics

Enumeration is a classical and old topic. In secondary schools, every student learn about *"arrangements"*, *"combinations p to p"* or *"permutations"* of n objects. These students have heard about *coloring* maps with four colors, and may be, some curious problems as the *"problème des ménages"* or the *"problème des rencontres"*, which can be found in mathematical recreational books, rather than in classical books of Mathematics.

Although some magistral books appeared in the beginning of this century as Major P.A. MacMahon's monograph, followed by classical books of E.Netto, J.Riordan, and L.Comtet, only recently attention has been given among mathematicians. In the last twenty years the field has exploded, especially under the *"bijective paradigm"*. General tools and standard enumerative technics have been settled, as said by G.C. Rota in the introduction of the book of I.Goulden and D.Jackson:

> *"The progress of mathematics can be viewed as a movement from the infinite to the finite. At the start, the possibilities of a theory, for example, the theory of enumeration, appear to be boundless. Rules for the enumeration of sets subject to various conditions, or combinatorial objects as they are often called, appear to obey an infinite variety of recursions, and seem to lead to a welter of generating functions. We are at first led to suspect that the class of objects with a common property that may be enumerated is indeed infinite and unclassifiable. As cases file upon cases, however, patterns begin to emerge. Freakish instances are quietly discarded; impossible problems are recognized as such, and what is left organizes itself along a few general criteria.".*

But what is enumerative Combinatorics?

Roughly speaking and for short, the first preoccupation in enumerative Combinatorics is to find a "formula for a_n", where a_n is the number of ways to perform a certain construction starting from n *"elementary objects"*, or equivalently the number of certain finite *"combinatorial objects"* having size n. If an explicit formula does not seem possible at first hand, then one may try to give an *asymptotic* estimate for a_n.

A very powerful tool is the *generating function* $f(t) = \Sigma_{n \geq 0} a_n t^n$. A formula for a_n may be very complicated, while an explicit formula for $f(t)$ may be much simpler. At least, one may try to find a system of functional or algebraic equations satisfied by $f(t)$.

2. The bijective paradigm

We start with a simple and classical example. Let C_n be the number of *binary trees* with n (*internal*) vertices (and n+1 *external* vertices). The recurrence definition of binary trees as a triple formed by a root, a left and right *subtree*, leads immediately to a recurrence for C_n that is: $C_{n+1} = \Sigma_{i+j=n} C_i C_j$ with initial condition $C_0 = 1$. This recurrence is equivalent to the equation $y = 1 + ty^2$ satisfied by the generating function $y = \Sigma_{n \geq 0} C_n t^n$. Solving this algebraic equation and expanding into power serie leads to the familiar formula for the Catalan numbers $C_n = (2n)!/[(n!)(n+1)!]$. In this analytic calculus, the original combinatorial object is completely lost. It is much more natural to prove the formula for C_n by giving a *bijection* between subsets of n elements among 2n elements (enumerated by the binomial coefficient $(2n)!/(n!)^2$) and the set of binary trees with n internal vertices where one of its (n+1) external vertices is pointed (this set is enumerated by $(n+1)C_n$).

Such proof is constructive. Is is called a *bijective proof.*

bijective proof of identities

This way of proving enumeration formulae has been systematically investigated, especially in the last twenty years. Bijective methods are applied to all kind of identities, not only those directly connected to enumeration, but also those coming from other part of Mathematics (Algebra and Analysis).

The art of bijection

Thousands of bijections have been constructed and published by combinatorists. A whole "science" of bijections and correspondences has emerged. Some of them have become classical and are used many times, some present an aesthetic beauty and give very elegant proof, while others are very complicated. At the beginning very classical identities have been proved again. Recently open problems have been solved, as for example G.Andrew's q-Dyson conjecture, proved by D.Bressoud and D.Zeilberger using bijective technics. These technics put some order in the jungle of enumeration formulae. The garden of bijections is itself under organization. Bijective tools are appearing, leading to what I would call *combinatorial models.* These models can interpret facts or operations in Algebra or Analysis: model for handling operations on generating functions, for matrices calculus, special functions, orthogonal polynomials and continued fractions, etc...

3. Analysis of algorithms

Since the pioneer work of D.Knuth, the relationship between enumerative Combinatorics and analysis of algorithm in Computer science is well known. The time or space analysis of many algorithms, especially those related to *representation of data structures*, is equivalent to the analysis of certain parameters among families of combinatorial objects. Particularly, the analysis of the *average cost* is equivalent to the problem of finding the mean of a parameter over a set of combinatorial objects, each of these objects is supposed to appear with the same probability. Usually these objects are *words, permutations* or various families of *trees*.

Modern combinatorics gives standard tools to go straight from combinatorial objects to equations satisfied by generating functions. An example is Joyal's theory of *species* developed by the québecoise school of combinatorics at UQAM, Montréal. Such tools can also be used to derive, in a systematic way from the definition of the algorithm, equations satisfied by the cost generating function. A kind of *symbolic calculus* going from algorithms to generating functions is thus developed, especially by the french school around P.Flajolet. The underlying combinatorial structures are in a certain sense *"decomposable"*.

In this survey talk, I put some emphasis on less classical ideas: the use of bijections in the analysis and conception of algorithms. The bijective "paradigm" fits very well in this domain. One interest of bijective analysis can be to underline certain similarities between different parameters appearing in completely different algorithms. This unification may leads to a better understanding of the combinatorics behind the algorithms, and sometimes to an improvement of the algorithms themselves. We show that the same combinatorics is underlying the following three different problems: algorithms related to the classical *binary search trees*, algorithms related to the data structure *pagoda* representing *priority queues* (J.Françon, X.G.Viennot, J.Vuillemin) and the Naïmi-Trehel *exclusion algorithm* (A.Arnold, M.Delest, S.Dulucq, C.Lavrault, M.Naïmi, M.Trehel, X.G.Viennot).

4. Analysis of parallelism

This section is much less classical than section 3. Enumerative combinatorics can also be used in the analysis of some problems related to *parallelism* and *concurrency* in data structures. The comparison of algorithms controlling concurrent access to a database has been studied qualitatively, as for example by C.H.Papadimitriou. For a quantitative study, certain quantities need to be introduced, such as the *parallelism ratio*, *average delay* imposed by a concurrency control to an arbitrary execution, frequency of *deadlocked executions*. The analysis of these quantities has been done for the *timestamp* ordering and the *two phases locking* concurrency control algorithms (D.Arquès, J.Françon, M.T.Guichet, P.Guichet).

The underlying combinatorial problems are enumerative problems on words, *shuffle* of words, and equivalence classes of words in *commutation monoids* (more classically called partially commutative free monoids). These monoids and their subsets (called *trace* languages) have been used as an algebraic model for parallelism and concurrency problems in Computer Science. Many works have been done recently in this setting. Curiously, as shown by the author, certain enumerative problems about words classes in these monoids are also equivalent to problems in statistical mechanics (model for *phase transitions* and *critical phenomena*).

5. Coding planar "figures" with words of algebraic languages

This section is mainly concerned with the interaction between enumeration and *algebraic languages* and *automata* theory. Many combinatorial objects which can be drawn in a plane have an algebraic generating function. In particular this is the case for the classical *planar maps* (planar graphs embedded in a plane). M.P.Schützenberger has invented a powerful method for explaining the algebricity. The method is in three steps: first find a bijection between the combinatorial objects of "size" n and certain words of length n of an algebraic language described by a *non-ambiguous algebraic grammar*, second introduce the *non-commutative generating function* of this language and the corresponding algebraic system of equations. The third step is going back to commutative variables and classical analytic calculus on ordinary generating functions.

Such methods has been studied by R.Cori and B.Vauquelin for planar maps. Since, it has been intensively applied for the so-called animals and polyominoes. Many open enumerative problems on these objects have been solved, in deep connection with statistical mechanics motivations from Physics (M.Delest, S.Dulucq, J.M.Fedou, D.Gouyou-Beauchamps, J.G.Penaud, X.G.Viennot). Such studies need the construction of "algebraic" codings of these planar combinatorial objects. Here bijections give a very powerful tool, since the combiatorial structures such as animal and polyominoes are not easily "decomposable" in the sense of section 3.

From this study, a certain *discrete geometry* is emerging: the geometry of objects embedded in a *planar lattice*. This geometry and codings which were introduced for enumeration purpose, are related to (and sometimes can be used in) different other contexts coming from practical considerations in Computer science. We mention *discretization* problems in Computer Graphics, *compactification* of *binary images*, algorithmic problems related to *integrated circuit manufacture* and *binary search networks*.

Remark that the interaction between enumerative Combinatorics and Computer Science works in both directions. Some other concepts from theoretical Computer Science have been introduced in enumerative Combinatorics. Mention the use of *attribute grammars* in solving certain open problems on *"q-enumeration"* of polyominoes (M.Delest, J.M.Fedou). In return, this lead to the introduction of *q-analogs* of algebraic grammars.

6. Formal calculus

In the context of our discussion, formal calculus is concerned at two different levels.

The first level is the use of symbolic systems such as MAPLE, MACSYMA, REDUCE, MATHEMATICA or SCRATCHPAD for research purposes in the discovery (resp. proof) of enumeration formulae. Mention here works on *q-identities* (Andrews), *special functions* (Zeilberger), *polyominoes* (Delest, Fedou). Symbolic calculus is mainly used for the manipulation of formal power series.

The second level is the development of specific tools and symbolic systems related to combinatorics or algorithms. I mention LUO, for the automatic analysis of algorithms (P.Flajolet, B.Salvy, Zimmerman) and DARWIN (G.Cartier, F.Bergeron) for the manipulation of combinatorial objects and generating functions based on Joyal's *species* theory. This two systems introduce a certain symbolic calculus on combinatorial objects, analog to the symbolic calculus on polynomials and formal power series. As we have seen above, the introduction of symbolic operations on combinatorial objects is at the very heart of the "bijective paradigm" in modern enumerative Combinatorics.

7. Computer Graphics

This survey talk ends with some examples of the application of enumerative Combinatorics in Computer Graphics.

Geometric modeling of 3D objects is a very active field of Computer Graphics, particularly for *image synthesis*. Many modelizations have been proposed and studied, depending upon the type of applications. Recently, modelings based on the combinatorial notion of *planar maps*, begin to appear (D.Arquès, I.Jacques, Dobkin, Laszlo, P.Lienhardt, J.C.Spehner). The coding (i.e.bijection) of combinatorial planar maps by a pair of two permutations plays a crucial role. The interest is to separate the different levels: *combinatorial, topological* and *geometric*. This separation can be very useful for practical consideration. These various modelings extend to 3D objects the combinatorial and algorithmic tools related to planar maps. The notion of *pavements* introduced by D.Arquès and P.Koch, allows to modelize in a very convenient way every kind of solid.

At the 2D level, practical applications have been shown by M.Gangnet in 2D *drawing application* with *incremental insertion* of curves in a planar map.

Another possible application of concepts and methods of bijective Combinatorics to Computer Graphics is in image synthesis of *organic structures*.

Operators defined on combinatorial maps have been used by J.Françon and P.Lienhardt for image synthesis of *leaves* and *flowers*.

A very rich topic in the combinatorics of binary trees is the so-called *Horton-Strahler analysis*. This was initiated in Hydrogeology by R.E.Horton and A.N.Strahler in the morphological study of *river networks*. The parameters involved have a very rich combinatorial background, also appearing in Molecular Biology (*prediction* and *homologies* of *secondary structures* of *single stranded nucleic acids*) and in Theoretical Computer Science (minimum number of *registers* needed to compute an arithmetical expression). The Horton-Strahler analysis have been refined with the introduction of the notion of *ramification matrix* associated to any binary tree or *ramified pattern*, and applied to give synthesic images of trees (D.Arquès, G.Eyrolles, N.Janey, X.G.Viennot). This matrix contains some very sensitive information about the *"shape"* of the binary tree. The *geometry* of the tree is completely determined from the combinatorial parameters defining the ramification matrix. Images of leaves are obtained from a combinatorial model based on the underlying *planar trees*. An interactive software, called DUNE, can produce very quickly on a microcomputer various images of trees, leaves and landscapes, with a powerful control of the final shape.

Failures Semantics Based on Interval Semiwords

is a Congruence for Refinement

Walter Vogler

Institut für Informatik, Technische Universität

Arcisstr. 21, D-8000 München 2

Abstract

In this paper concurrent systems are modelled with safe Petri nets. The coarsest equivalence contained in failures equivalence is determined that is a congruence with respect to refinement. It is shown that in this context partial orders are necessary for the description of system runs: What is needed here are so-called interval orders.

1. Introduction

Concurrent systems can be modelled by process algebras like CCS, $TCSP$ or ACP or by Petri nets. Process algebras have the advantage of being modular by definition and having well-developed equivalence notions like bisimulation, failures or testing equivalence, algebraic laws and complete proof systems. Petri nets on the other hand offer a clear description of concurrency, a long tradition in the study of 'true' concurrency, and a graphical representation. Also a lot of effort has been put into the study of modular construction of Petri nets, especially by refining transitions.

Recently there has been some new interest in the question of refinement, since the refinement issue might shed some light on the old dispute of interleaving vs. true concurrency. In [Pr1] and [CDP] it is argued that partial order semantics is useful when dealing with refinements, see also [NEL] and [De].

In this paper we study refinements of actions using safe Petri nets as a model for concurrent systems. Process algebras usually do not offer a refinement operator, but see [AH] and [NEL] for two first studies. In the light of recent papers connecting Petri nets and process algebras ([GV], [DDM], [Go], [Ta]) it is hoped that our results also have some impact on the study of refinement in process algebras. So far in the Petri net literature mostly transition refinements were studied which preserve behaviour ([Mü], [SM], [Va], [Vo1]). The refinements in this paper (and also the split-operator in [GV]) are different: Here we want to replace an action a for example by a sequence $a_1 a_2$ of actions. We cannot expect that the refined net has the same behaviour as the original net, since totally different actions are possible in the two nets. Instead we expect that if two nets with equivalent behaviour are refined in the same way then the resulting nets have equivalent behaviour again. In other words, we should have a behaviour notion which is a congruence with respect to refinement.

The starting point of our considerations is a failures semantics [BHR] without divergence. It is purely an interleaving semantics and has been shown to be useful, if one constructs nets with a parallel composition operator with synchronization and is mainly

interested in the deadlocking behaviour of systems [Vo2]. We study how this failures semantics has to be modified to become a congruence for refinements, i.e. we determine the
coarsest equivalence contained in failures equivalence which is a congruence with respect
to refinement. It turns out that we must not describe system runs by sequences of actions,
but have to use some partial order semantics. Here we mean by 'partial order semantics'
any semantics that assigns to each net a set of labelled partial orders. The term does
not refer to any fixed intuition, especially it does not necessarily refer to anything like
'causality'. But usually the idea behind such a labelled partial order is that unordered
elements correspond to actions that are concurrent or in some sense independent. Thus
the more action occurrences are ordered the less concurrency is 'contained' in the labelled
partial order.

In the literature there exists a variety of partial order semantics for nets. We find
processes, see e.g. [GR] or [BD], and traces, see e.g. [Ma], partial words of nets are
studied in [Gra] – also called partial order computations [Re] or pomsets [Pr2] –, and we
also find a slight restriction of partial words, namely semiwords [St], which for safe nets
coincide with partial words. Here we work with safe nets, and we will introduce a special
class of semiwords, so called interval semiwords, specified by the requirement that the
partial order involved is an interval order. (A partial order $(A, <)$ is an interval order if
for each $x \in A$ we find a closed interval in $\mathbf{R}$ such that $x < y$ if and only if the interval
of x is totally to the left of the interval of y.) The idea is that when observing a system
run we see actions starting and finishing, i.e. the execution of an action corresponds to
some interval, and we order these action occurrences such that one is less than the other
if it finishes before the other starts. Hence unordered action occurrences correspond to
overlapping intervals, i.e. we observe that they happen concurrently. This idea is closely
related to the idea behind ST-bisimulation [GV] which is for event structures a congruence
with respect to refinement [Gl].

The coarsest congruence we are looking for can be defined similarly to the (linear)
failures semantics, but based upon interval semiwords instead of sequences. Thus we
can prove what has been suspected for long: Partial order semantics is needed when
dealing with refinements. But we also show that we do not need the full strength of
the usual partial order semantics of Petri nets, i.e. we distinguish fewer nets than some
other partial order semantics for the following reason: Interval semiwords are semiwords,
but in general semiwords might 'contain more concurrency' than interval semiwords.
On the other hand, interval semiwords are more distinctive than step sequences, i.e.
step sequences are interval semiwords, but in general interval semiwords might 'contain
more concurrency' than step sequences. One could say that the issue of this paper is
to determine the right 'amount of concurrency' needed to deal with refinement. We also
shortly discuss how semiwords and the so called event structures of processes behave with
respect to refinement.

In a recent paper [GG] conflict-free refinements of event structures in the sense
of [NPW] are studied (more precisely, of prime event structures with binary conflict,
which form a special class of infinite, acyclic safe nets). Congruences for refinements
are exhibited, but the authors do not consider the problem of finding some coarsest
congruence — also their congruences are not based on failures semantics, but mostly on
bisimulation.

In Section 2 some preliminaries are presented including the linear failures semantics
of nets we start from. In Section 3 the refinement we use here is defined. Section 4

deals with semiwords and interval semiwords; more precisely, we introduce semiwords with termination set: A (part of a) system run is not only described by a partial order of transition firings, but it is also noted which transition firings have terminated and which have started but have not terminated yet. Section 5 shows how to calculate semiwords of a refined net from semiwords of the original net and of the inserted nets, while finally in Section 6 the new failures semantics based on interval semiwords is presented and shown to induce the coarsest congruence with respect to refinement contained in the linear failures equivalence.

Due to lack of space the proof can only be sketched by presenting the intermediate results, but the reader can find most of the full proofs in [Vo3].

2. Preliminaries

Let Σ be an infinite set of actions. A labelled Petri net (short: a net) is a tuple $N = (S_N, T_N, W_N, M_N, l_N)$ consisting of the (not necessarily finite) disjoint sets S_N of places and T_N of transitions, the weight function $W_N : S_N \times T_N \cup T_N \times S_N \to \mathbf{N}_0$, the initial marking $M_N : S_N \to \mathbf{N}_0$ and the labelling function $l_N : T_N \to \Sigma \cup \{\lambda\}$, where λ is the empty word. If a transition is λ-labelled, then it represents an internal action, not visible for an external observer; two equally labelled transitions represent the same action, occurring in different internal situations. We are mainly interested in so-called safe nets (see below), hence we assume that W_N is in fact a function into $\{0, 1\}$.

The preset of a transition t is ${}^{\bullet}t = \{s \in S_N \mid W(s, t) \neq 0\}$, the postset is $t^{\bullet} = \{s \in S_N \mid W(t, s) \neq 0\}$. For all nets considered here we assume that every transition has a nonempty preset. A marking of N is a function $S_N \to \mathbf{N}_0$. Some $T \subseteq T_N$ is enabled under a marking M, $M[T\rangle$, if for all $s \in S_N$ $\Sigma_{t \in T} W(s, t) \leq M(s)$. We say that M_1, defined by $M_1(s) = M(s) + \Sigma_{t \in T}(W(t, s) - W(s, t))$, is the follower marking of M under T, $M[T\rangle M_1$. We write $M[t\rangle$, $M[t\rangle M_1$ instead of $M[\{t\}\rangle$, $M[\{t\}\rangle M_1$.

These notions are generalized to sequences of transitions as usual: For $w = w_1 \ldots w_n \in T_N^*$ write $M[w\rangle$, $M[w\rangle M_n$ if $w = \lambda$ and $M_0 = M$ or $n \geq 1$ and there are markings M_i, $i = 1, \ldots, n-1$ with $M[w_1\rangle M_1[w_2\rangle \ldots [w_n\rangle M_n$. We write $[M\rangle = \{M_1 : S \to \mathbf{N}_0 \mid \exists w \in T_N^* : M[w\rangle M_1\}$. We call M a reachable marking if there is $w \in T_N^*$ such that $M_N[w\rangle M$. Then w is called a firing sequence.

We may only be interested in the labels of enabled transitions or firing sequences. For this we extend l_N to T_N^* as usual. Then $v \in \Sigma^*$ is image enabled under M, $M[v\rangle\rangle$, yielding the follower marking M', $M[v\rangle\rangle M'$, if there is $w \in T_N^*$ with $M[w\rangle$, $M[w\rangle M'$, and $l_N(w) = v$. We call w a firing sequence underlying the image firing sequence v.

A net N is safe if for all reachable markings M and $s \in S_N$ $M(s) \leq 1$. A loop in a net or as a net consists of a place s and a transition t such that $W(s, t) = W(t, s) = 1$.

Let $(A, \leq)$ be a partial order, i.e. $\leq$ is a reflexive, transitive, antisymmetric relation on A. As usual $x < y$ means $x \leq y$ and $x \neq y$. Define $max\ A = \{x \in A \mid \forall y \in A : x \leq y \Rightarrow x = y\}$, $min\ A = \{x \in A \mid \forall y \in A : y \leq x \Rightarrow x = y\}$. A set $B \subseteq A$ is left-closed if $x \leq y \in B$ implies $x \in B$, B is a co-set if for all $x, y \in B$ neither $x < y$ nor $y < x$, B is a cut if B is a maximal co-set with respect to set inclusion.

In general we do not distinguish isomorphic nets, isomorphic partial orders etc., i.e. we really work with isomophism classes.

(Linear) failures semantics has been developed for the process algebra $TCSP$ [BHR] and translated to safe nets in [Po] as follows (ignoring divergence, i.e. infinite internal loops): Let N be a safe net. Then $\mathcal{F}(N) = \{(v, X) \mid X \subseteq \Sigma$ and $\exists M : M_N[v\rangle M \wedge \forall a \in X : \neg M[a\rangle)\}$.

The elements of $\mathcal{F}(N)$, the so-called failures pairs, consist of a history v, which describes a possible system run as seen by an external observer, and a refusal set consisting of some actions that are not possible after this system run.

Safe nets N_1, N_2 are failures equivalent ($\mathcal{F}$-equivalent) if $\mathcal{F}(N_1) = \mathcal{F}(N_2)$. In [Vo2] it is shown that failures equivalence is just the right equivalence notion if one wants to construct nets by a parallel composition operator with synchronization, corresponding to merging of some transitions, and is mainly interested in the deadlocking behaviour of systems. For details see [Vo2]. Failures semantics and $\mathcal{F}$-equivalence form the starting point of our considerations.

3. Refinements

First we will define the kind of nets we use to refine transitions. Such a refinement net should be able to simulate the firing of a transition as far as the movement of tokens is concerned. It will contain a special place $start$ representing the environment of the transition that should be replaced.

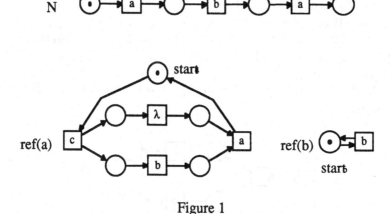

Figure 1

Definition 3.1: A <u>refinement net</u> is a pair $(N, start)$ such that N is a safe net, $start$ is a place of N and the following hold:

i) For all transitions t of N enabled under M_N we have $start \in {}^\bullet t$ and there is some $t \in T_N$ enabled under M_N.

ii) For all reachable markings M of N there is some $M' \in [M\rangle$ with $M'(start) = 1$.

iii) For all reachable markings M of N $M(start) = 1$ implies $M = M_N$.

A transition t with $start \in {}^\bullet t$ is called a <u>start transition</u>, a transition t with $start \in t^\bullet$ is called an <u>end transition</u> of $(N, start)$. Let $init(N, start) = \{a \in \Sigma \mid M_N[a\rangle\}$.

A <u>refinement function</u> ref associates with each $a \in \Sigma$ a refinement net $ref(a)$ such that for any end transition t of $ref(a)$ $l_{ref(a)}(t) \neq \lambda$. Additionally we define $ref(\lambda)$ as the refinement net consisting of one λ-labelled transition which is on a loop with the marked place $start$. If ref is understood we will denote $ref(a)$ simply as $(N_a, start_a)$ with $N_a = (S_a, T_a, W_a, M_a, l_a)$.

Condition i) ensures that any firing of transitions of N starts a simulation of the replaced transition, ii) says that any simulation of a firing can be brought to an end, while iii) says that the refinement net does not 'remember anything' of past simulations.

We have made the above requirement for the labels of end transitions of $ref(a)$, since without this requirement refining a net could mean turning a visible transition into an internal one, which may lead to difficulties later on.

We have more or less adopted the refinement nets used in [Va]; the only difference is that in [Va] there is only one start and one end transition, while we allow several of them. Other possibilities of refining a transition are discussed in the full version of this paper.

The next definition explains how the refinement of transitions works: We replace each transition by a refinement net (without the start place) and connect every place in the preset of the deleted transition to every start transition, and every place in the postset to every end transition of the inserted net.

Definition 3.2: Let ref be a refinement function and N a safe net. We define the refined net $der(N, ref) = (S, T, W, M, l)$, where der stands for derivation, as:
$S = S_N \cup \{(t, s) \mid t \in T_N, s \in S_{l_N(t)} - \{start_{l_N(t)}\}\}$
$T = \{(t, t') \mid t \in T_N, t' \in T_{l_N(t)}\}$
$W(s, (t, t')) = 1$ if $W_N(s, t) = 1$ and t' is a start transition of $ref(l_N(t))$
$W((t, t'), s) = 1$ if $W_N(t, s) = 1$ and t' is an end transition of $ref(l_N(t))$
$W((t, s), (t, t')) = 1$ if $W_{l_N(t)}(s, t') = 1$, $W((t, t'), (t, s)) = 1$ if $W_{l_N(t)}(t', s) = 1$
W is 0 in all other cases.
$M(s) = 1$ if $M_N(s) = 1$, $M((t, s)) = 1$ if $M_{l_N(t)}(s) = 1$, M is 0 in all other cases
$l((t, t')) = l_{l_N(t)}(t')$.

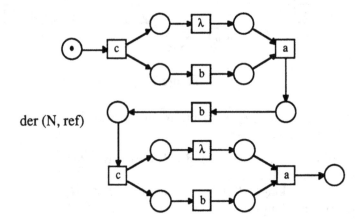

der (N, ref)

Figure 2

Example: Figure 1 shows a net N and two refinement nets $ref(a)$ and $ref(b)$. Refining N means replacing each a-labelled transition t by a copy of $ref(a)$ without the place $start_a$ and connecting the transitions of this copy to the pre- and postset of t as they were connected to $start_a$. The same is done for b, but due to the special form of $ref(b)$ the b-labelled transition is simply preserved. The result is shown in Figure 2. Note that due to our assumption on $ref(\lambda)$ internal actions cannot really be refined.

4. Semiwords with termination

Partial words were introduced in [Gra] to describe the behaviour of Petri nets. They were discussed e.g. in [Ki2], also under the name of partial order computations in [Re] and under the name of pomsets in [Pr2]. Semiwords [St] are special partial words. For unlabelled safe nets semiwords and partial words coincide, since safe nets do not allow the self-concurrent firing of a transition. In the following we are interested in safe nets and thus could use the notion partial word as well, but we will prefer the notion semiword since our refinement nets only allow the refinement of transitions which cannot fire self-concurrently.

The idea behind these notions is to describe one system run not by a sequence, i.e. a total order of transition firings, but by a partial order, since Petri nets model distributed systems, where events may occur independently of each other.

We give here a slight variation, namely semiwords with termination. The idea behind this notion is similar to that for ST-bisimulation [GV]: Since we want to refine transitions we do not regard the firings of transitions as instantaneous, but they have a beginning and an end. Consequently the description of a system run is not simply a semiword, but it contains also the information which transition firings have already terminated. Naturally a transition firing has terminated if some other has started after it, i.e. non-terminated transition firings must be maximal elements of the involved partial orders.

Definition 4.1: Let N be a net. A <u>labelled partial order with termination set</u> (*lpot*) is a tuple $p = (A_p, \leq_p, l_p, ter_p)$ where $(A_p, \leq_p)$ is a finite partial order, l_p is some labelling of A_p and $ter_p \subseteq A_p$ is a set containing at least all non-maximal elements of A_p (but possibly more). The tuple is a <u>semiword with termination set</u> (*swt*) of N if l_p is a function from A_p to T_N and the following holds:

For all co-sets C of $(A_p, \leq_p)$ and $B \subseteq A_p$ such that B and $B \cup C$ are left-closed and $B \cap C = \emptyset$ we have

i) l_p is injective on C
ii) $l_p(C)$ is enabled under

$$M_N + \sum_{x \in B} W_N(l_p(x), .) - \sum_{x \in B} W_N(. , l_p(x)).$$

The marking reached after p is

$$M_N + \sum_{x \in ter_p} W_N(l_p(x), .) - \sum_{x \in A_p} W_N(. , l_p(x)).$$

Note that any $x \in A_p - ter_p$ represents a still active transition, i.e. $l_p(x)$ has already removed the tokens from its preset but has not returned the tokens to its postset. The *lpot p* is called <u>terminated</u> if $ter_p = A_p$. A <u>semiword</u> of a net N is an *swt* of N restricted to its first three components.

We have defined *swt*'s for all nets N, not only for safe nets, since we will construct nets and work with their *swt*'s before we know that they are safe. 4.1 i) ensures that equally labelled elements of an *swt* are ordered, which is not necessary for partial words in the sense of [Gra].

We define a partial order $\preceq$ on *lpot*'s, which stands for less sequential:

Definition 4.2: Let p, q be *lpot*'s. Then p is <u>less sequential than</u> q, $p \preceq q$, if $A_p = A_q$, $l_p = l_q$, $ter_p = ter_q$ and $\leq_p \subseteq \leq_q$. As usual $p \prec q$ means $p \preceq q$ and $p \neq q$.
An *swt* of a safe net which is minimal with respect to $\preceq$ is called a <u>process structure with termination set</u>. If we take the first three components of such an *swt* (i.e. delete the termination set) we get a <u>process structure</u>.

Processes give a well-established partial order semantics of nets, which is intended to model causality and takes markings into account explicitly. If we restrict a process to its partial order of transition occurrences, we get the so-called event structure of the process. In [Ki1] it is shown that for safe nets these event structures of processes are just what we call process structures here, compare also [Ki2], Proposition 5.3(3).

Example: Figure 3 shows a net N and three *swt*'s p_1, p_2, p_3 of N, such that $p_2 \preceq p_3$. The *swt*'s p_1 and p_2 are process structures with termination set.

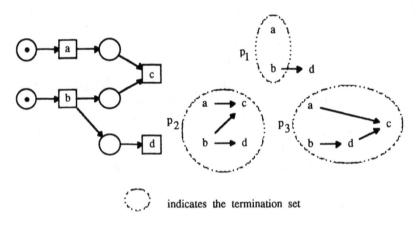

.·⌣. indicates the termination set

Figure 3

Proposition 4.3: Let p, q be *lpot*'s and N a net. If p is an *swt* of N and $p \preceq q$, then q is an *swt* of N. The marking reached after p is the same as the marking reached after q.

An *swt* p of a refinement net (N, start) is an *swt* of N with the additional requirement that for at most one $x \in A_p$ $l_p(x)$ is a start transition. We call p <u>complete</u> if it is terminated and for some $x \in A_p$ $l_p(x)$ is an end transition.

The following lemma gives information on the form of *swt*'s of refinement nets.

Lemma 4.4: Let p be an *swt* of a refinement net $(N, start)$. If A_p is non-empty, then it has a single minimal element x and $l_p(x)$ is a start transition. There is at most one $y \in A_p$ such that $l_p(y)$ is an end transition, and in this case y is the single maximal element of A_p.

We will be interested in a special type of *swt* which we define next. The name interval order is explained by the result afterwards.

Definition 4.5: A partial order $(A, \le)$ is an <u>interval order</u> if for all $w, x, y, z \in A$ with $w < x$ and $y < z$ we have $w \le z$ or $y \le x$. If p is an *lpot*, an *swt* of some net N resp., such that $(A_p, \le_p)$ is an interval order, then p is an <u>interval *lpot*</u>, an <u>interval semiword with termination set</u> (*iswt*) of N resp. If we restrict an *iswt* to its first three components we get an <u>interval semiword</u> (*isw*).

Theorem 4.6 [Fi]: A partial order $(A, \le)$ with finite or countably infinite A is an interval order if and only if there are closed intervals $I(x)$, $x \in A$, of the real line such that $x < y$ if and only if for all $r \in I(x)$, $s \in I(y)$ we have $r < s$.

Thus the intuition behind an interval *swt* is an observation of a system run where each firing took some time and we order the transition firings such that one is less than the other if it ended before the other began. We study these *swt*'s because they allow to describe the coarsest equivalence we are looking for.

Definition 4.7: An *lpot* p is an <u>image *swt* with ready set</u> R of some net N if there is some *swt* q of N such that

i) For all $x \in A_q$: $l_N \circ l_q(x) = \lambda$ implies $x \in ter_q$.
ii) $A_p = \{x \in A_q \mid l_p(x) \ne \lambda\}$ and $\le_p$, l_p and ter_p are the restrictions of $\le_q$, $l_N \circ l_q$ and ter_q to A_p.
iii) For the marking M reached after q we have $R = \{a \in \Sigma \mid M[a\rangle\}$.

We call q an *swt* <u>underlying</u> p. If q is an interval *lpot* then p is called an <u>image *iswt*</u>. If q is a process structure with termination set, then p is called an <u>image process structure with termination set</u>, and p projected to its first three components is an <u>image process structure</u>. Analogously <u>image semiwords</u> and <u>image interval semiwords</u> are defined.

If q is terminated and $\le_q$ is total, then we identify p with the image firing sequence $a_1 \ldots a_n$, where the a_i are the labels of the elements of A_p ordered according to $\le_p$.

An image *swt* p of a refinement net is called <u>complete</u>, <u>nonempty</u> resp., if the corresponding q is complete, nonempty resp.

Note the following: The idea behind semiwords is to disallow autoconcurrent transition firings, but on the image level we may nevertheless have autoconcurrent labels.

Lemma 4.8: If p is an image *swt* with ready set R of some net N and q is an *lpot* with $q \succeq p$, then q is an image *swt* with ready set R of N, too.

Note that an image *swt* p is an image *iswt* if the underlying *swt* is an interval order. Alternatively one could require p to be an interval order. This would coincide with our definition as the next proposition, which is based on 4.3, shows.

Proposition 4.9: Let p be an image *swt* of some net, q its underlying *swt*. Then p is an image *iswt* if and only if p is an interval *lpot*.

5. Semiwords of refined nets

In this section we will obtain results that show how we can construct the swt's of a refined net from the swt's of the original net and the refinement nets. The next definition describes the following: If p is a semiword with termination set of a safe net N and we are given a refinement function, then we can construct a labelled partial order with termination set by replacing each occurrence of a transition t in p by an swt of the refinement net corresponding to t. When doing this we have to replace a terminated occurrence of a transition by a complete swt. Theorem 5.2 shows that this $lpot$ is indeed an swt of the refined net obtained from N.

Definition 5.1: Let p be an swt of a safe net N, ref a refinement function. A <u>semiword</u> (sw) <u>refinement function</u> $refsw$ for p and ref associates to each $x \in A_p$ a nonempty swt of $ref(l_N(l_p(x)))$ such that $refsw(x)$ is complete iff $x \in ter_p$.
We define the $lpot$ $q = der(p, refsw)$ by putting
$A_q = \{(x, y) \mid x \in A_p, y \in A_{refsw(x)}\}$,
$(x, y) \leq_q (x', y')$ if $x <_p x'$ or $(x = x'$ and $y \leq_{refsw(x)} y')$,
$l_q(x, y) = l_{refsw(x)}(y)$,
$(x, y) \in ter_q$ if $y \in ter_{refsw(x)}$.
Analogously, let p be an image swt of a safe net N, ref a refinement function. An <u>image sw refinement function</u> $refsw$ for p and ref associates to each $x \in A_p$ an image swt of $ref(l_p(x))$ which is nonempty, and which is complete iff $x \in ter_p$. Now $der(p, refsw)$ is defined analogously as above.
If for all $x \in A_p$ $refsw(x)$ is an $iswt$, an image $iswt$ resp., we speak of an <u>isw refinement function</u>, an <u>image isw refinement function</u> resp.

Theorem 5.2: If p is an swt of some safe net N, ref a refinement function and $refsw$ an sw refinement function for p and ref, then $q = der(p, refsw)$ is an swt of $der(N, ref)$. If M is the marking reached after p and M_x is the marking of $ref(l_N \circ l_p(x))$ reached after $refsw(x)$, then the marking M_1 reached after q is given by:

$$M_1(s) = M(s) \qquad \text{for all } s \in S_N$$
$$M_1(t, s) = \begin{cases} M_x(s) & \text{if } x \in A_p - ter_p, \, l_p(x) = t \\ M_{l_N(t)}(s) & \text{otherwise} \end{cases}$$

Theorem 5.2 gives a result on semiwords of refined nets, i.e. a result on the level of transitions. Next we lift this to a corresponding result on the image level, i.e. for image semiwords.

Theorem 5.3: Let p be an image swt of some safe net N with ready set R, ref a refinement function and $refsw$ an image sw refinement function for p and ref. For $x \in A_p - ter_p$ let $ready(x)$ be a ready set of $refsw(x)$ for the net $ref(l_p(x))$. Then $q = der(p, refsw)$ is an image swt of $der(N, ref)$ with ready set $\{a \mid \exists b \in R : a \in init (ref(b))\} \cup \bigcup_{x \in A_p - ter_p} ready(x)$.

So far we have shown how semiwords or image semiwords of a refined net can be obtained from semiwords or image semiwords of the original net and the refinement nets. Next we study the reverse problem: Given a semiword or an image semiword of a refined net, can we construct it in the fashion described above? This is not completely true, but true enough for our purpose. Theorem 5.6 states that applying the above construction and making the result more sequential if necessary we can obtain every semiword of a refined net.

Two lemmas are needed. The first states that in an *swt* of a refined net we may reduce some of the partial order and still have an *swt*. What we can reduce is related to the special form of *swt*'s of refinement nets noted in 4.4. In the second lemma we show that an *swt* of a refined net for which the partial order has been reduced can indeed be obtained by refining an *swt* of the unrefined net.

Lemma 5.4: Let N be a safe net, ref a refinement function, q an *swt* of $der(N, ref)$. Let $q' = (A_q, \leq_{q'}, l_q, ter_q)$, where $z_1 \leq_{q'} z_2$ if $l_q(z_1) = (t_1, t_1')$, $l_q(z_2) = (t_2, t_2')$ and either $t_1 = t_2$ and $z_1 \leq_q z_2$ or $t_1 \neq t_2$ and there are z_1', z_2' such that $z_1 \leq_q z_1' \leq_q z_2' \leq_q z_2$ and $l_q(z_1') = (t_1, t_1'')$, $l_q(z_2') = (t_2, t_2'')$ and t_1'' is an end transition and t_2'' is a start transition. Then q' is an *swt* of $der(N, ref)$.

Lemma 5.5: Let N be a safe net, ref a refinement function, q an *swt* of $der(N, ref)$ such that for all $z_1 \leq_q z_2$ with $l_q(z_1) = (t_1, t_1')$ and $l_q(z_2) = (t_2, t_2')$ either $t_1 = t_2$ or $t_1 \neq t_2$ and there are z_1', z_2' such that $l_q(z_1') = (t_1, t_1''), l_q(z_2') = (t_2, t_2''), t_1''$ is an end transition and t_2'' a start transition and $z_1 \leq_q z_1' \leq_q z_2' \leq_q z_2$. Then there is an *swt* p of N and an *sw* refinement function $refsw$ such that $q = der(p, refsw)$.

Theorem 5.6: Let N be a safe net, ref a refinement function, q an *swt* of $der(N, ref)$. Then there are an *swt* p of N and an *sw* refinement function $refsw$ for p and ref such that:

i) $q \succeq der(p, refsw)$,

ii) for $x_1, x_2 \in A_p$ $x_1 <_p x_2$ if and only if there are y_1, y_2 such that $l_{refsw(x_1)}(y_1)$ is an end transition, $l_{refsw(x_2)}(y_2)$ is a start transition and $(x_1, y_1) <_q (x_2, y_2)$,

iii) for $(x, y_1), (x, y_2) \in A_q$ $(x, y_1) \leq_q (x, y_2)$ if and only if $y_1 \leq_{refsw(x)} y_2$.

Corollary 5.7: Let N be a safe net and ref a refinement function. Then $der(N, ref)$ is safe.

Due to the extra properties we have stated in 5.6 ii) and iii) we can transfer the result of 5.6 to interval semiwords:

Corollary 5.8: Let N be a safe net, ref a refinement function, q an *iswt* of $der(N, ref)$. Then there are an *iswt* p of N and an *isw* refinement function $refsw$ for p and ref such that $q \succeq der(p, refsw)$.

We close this section by exhibiting three semantics which induce congruences with respect to refinement. Let the <u>process structure semantics</u>/<u>semiword semantics</u>/<u>interval semiword semantics</u> of a safe net be the set of all its image process structures/image semiwords/image interval semiwords. Safe nets with the same semantics are called <u>process structure equivalent</u>/<u>semiword equivalent</u>/<u>interval semiword equivalent</u>. Note that process structure equivalence is finer than semiword equivalence, which in turn is finer than interval semiword equivalence.

Theorem 5.9: For safe nets process structure equivalence, semiword equivalence and interval semiword equivalence are congruences with respect to refinement.

This result on process structures has been argued for in [CDP]. It is shown in [GG], but for a different systems model and for a different sort of refinement.

6. A new failures semantics

In this section we will define a new failures semantics such that the corresponding equivalence is the coarsest equivalence which is contained in the linear failures equivalence and is a congruence with respect to refinement. This way we do not only show that a non-interleaved semantics is useful when considering refinements, but also that it is necessary.

Definition 6.1: Let N be a safe net. Then $ref\mathcal{F}(N) = \{(p, X) \mid X \subseteq \Sigma,\ p$ is an image $iswt$ of N with ready set R and $X \cap R = \emptyset\}$. Safe nets N_1, N_2 are <u>$ref\mathcal{F}$-equivalent</u>, if $ref\mathcal{F}(N_1) = ref\mathcal{F}(N_2)$.

Proposition 6.2: Let N be a safe net, $(p, X) \in ref\mathcal{F}(N)$, $p' \succeq p$ and $Y \subseteq X$, then $(p', Y) \in ref\mathcal{F}(N)$.

Proposition 6.3: If safe nets N_1, N_2 are $ref\mathcal{F}$-equivalent, then they are $\mathcal{F}$-equivalent.

The following theorem, phrased in technical terms, is the first part of our main result. It shows how one can determine the $ref\mathcal{F}$-semantics of a refined net from the $ref\mathcal{F}$-semantics of the unrefined net and the refinement function. Special care has to be taken to calculate the refusal sets.

Theorem 6.4: Let N be a safe net, ref a refinement function. Then

$$ref\mathcal{F}(der(N, ref)) = \{(q, X) \mid \text{ there is an image } iswt\ p \text{ of } N \text{ and a set } Y$$

$$\text{with } (p, Y) \in ref\mathcal{F}(N),$$
$$\text{an image } isw \text{ refinement function } refsw \text{ for } p \text{ and } ref,$$
$$\text{sets } Y(x) \text{ with } (refsw(x), Y(x)) \in ref\mathcal{F}(ref(l_p(x)))$$
$$\text{for } x \in A_p - ter_p,$$
$$\text{such that } q \text{ is an interval } lpot \text{ with } q \succeq der(p, refsw) \text{ and}$$
$$X \cap \{a \mid \exists b \in \Sigma - Y : a \in init(ref(b))\} = \emptyset \text{ and}$$
$$X \subseteq \bigcap\nolimits_{x \in A_p - ter_p} Y(x)\}.$$

This theorem shows that we can calculate $ref\mathcal{F}(der(N, ref))$ from $ref\mathcal{F}(N)$ and knowledge about the refinement nets $ref(a)$, $a \in \Sigma$. Thus for safe nets $ref\mathcal{F}$-equivalence is a congruence with respect to refinements, i.e. for safe nets N_1, N_2 and a refinement function ref $ref\mathcal{F}(N_1) = ref\mathcal{F}(N_2)$ implies $ref\mathcal{F}(der(N_1, ref)) = ref\mathcal{F}(der(N_2(ref))$.

It would be equally possible to give equivalences which are based on image semiwords with termination set or image process structures with termination set, such that these equivalences are contained in the linear failures equivalence and are congruences with respect to refinement. But neither of these would be the coarsest such equivalence.

The following theorem is the main result of this paper, collecting the results of the above efforts: Partial order semantics is not only useful when dealing with refinements, it is also necessary to a certain degree. This degree is exactly described by interval semiwords.

Theorem 6.5: For safe nets $ref\mathcal{F}$-equivalence is the coarsest equivalence contained in $\mathcal{F}$-equivalence which is a congruence with respect to refinement. This also holds if for refinements only finite refinement nets are considered.

Probably $ref\mathcal{F}$-equivalence is not the coarsest equivalence in the sense of Theorem 6.5 if we only consider splitting, i.e. refining transitions by sequences of transitions. For the moment it remains an open problem to determine the coarsest equivalence in this case.

One can show that $ref\mathcal{F}$-equivalence is a congruence with respect to $\|_A$, the operator for parallel composition with synchronization used in [Vo2]. Furthermore it is possible to give a variation of $ref\mathcal{F}$-equivalence that takes divergence into account and is a congruence for refinement and parallel composition with synchronization as well.

References

[AH]   Aceto, L., Hennessy, M.: Towards action-refinement in process algebras. University of Sussex, Computer Science Report 3/88, 1988

[BD]   Best, E., Devillers, R.: Sequential and concurrent behaviour in Petri net theory. Theor. Comp. Sci. 55 (1987) 87-136

[BHR]   Brookes, S.D., Hoare, C.A.R., Roscoe, A.W.: A theory of communicating sequential processes. J. ACM 31 (1984) 560-599

[CDP]   Castellano, L., De Michelis, G., Pomello, L.: Concurrency vs. interleaving: an instructive example. Bull. EATCS 31 (1987) 12-15

[DDM]   Degano, P., De Nicola, R., Montanari, U.: CCS is an (augmented) contact free C/E system. In: M.V.Zilli(ed.): Mathematical Models for the Semantics of Parallelism. Springer LNCS 280 (1987) 144-165

[De]   Devillers, R.: On the definition of a bisimulation notion based on partial words. Petri Net Newsletter 29 (1988) 16-19

[Fi]   Fishburn, P.C.: Intransitive indifference with unequal indifference intervals. J. Math. Psych. 7 (1970) 144-149

[Gl]   van Glabbeek, R.: The refinement theorem for ST-bisimulation semantics. Unpublished manuscript

[GG]   van Glabbeek, R., Goltz, U.: Equivalence notions for concurrent systems and refinement of actions. Arbeitspapiere der GMD 366, 1989

[GV]   van Glabbeek, R., Vaandrager, F.: Petri net models for algebraic theories of concurrency. In: J.W. de Bakker et al.(eds.): PARLE Vol. II, Springer, LNCS 259 (1987) 224-242

[Go]   Goltz, U.: On representing CCS programs by finite Petri nets. In: M.P.Chytil et al.(eds.): Proc. MFCS 1988, Carlsbad. Springer, LNCS 324 (1988) 339-350

[GR]   Goltz, U., Reisig, W.: The non-sequential behaviour of Petri nets. Information and Control 57 (1983) 125-147

[Gra]   Grabowski, J.: On Partial Languages. Ann. Soc. Math. Pol., Fundamenta Informaticae IV.2 (1981) 428-498

[Kil]   Kiehn, A.: On the concurrent behaviour of Petri nets. Techn. Rep. FBI-HH-B 120/86, Univ. Hamburg, Fachber. Informatik, 1986

[Ki2]   Kiehn, A.: On the interrelationship between synchronized and non-synchronized behaviour of Petri nets. J. Inf. Process. Cybern. EIK 24 (1988) 3-18

[Ma]   Mazurkiewicz, A.: Trace theory. In: W. Brauer, W.Reisig, G. Rozenberg (eds.): Petri Nets: Applications and Relationships to Other Models of Concurrency. Sprin- ger, LNCS 255 (1987) 279-324

[Mü]   Müller, K.: Constructable Petri nets. EIK 21 (1985) 171-199

[NEL]   Nielsen, M., Engberg, U., Larsen, K.: Partial order semantics for concurrency. In: Course material of the REX School/ Workshop on Linear Time Branching Time and Partial Orders in Logics and Models of Concurrency Nordwijkerhout, 1988

[NPW]   Nielsen, M., Plotkin, G.D., Winskel, G.: Petri nets, event structures and domains, part I. Theoret. Comp. Sci. 13 (1981) 85-108

[Po]   Pomello, L.: Some equivalence notions for concurrent systems - an overview In: G. Rozenberg(ed.): Advances in Petri Nets 1985. Springer, LNCS 222 381-400

[Pr1]   Pratt, V.R.: On the composition of processes. In: Proc. 9th ACM Symp. on Principles of Programming Languages 1982, 213-223

[Pr2]   Pratt, V.: Modelling concurrency with partial orders. Int. J. of Parallel Programming 15, 1986

[Re]   Reisig, W.: On the semantics of Petri nets. In: E.J.Neuhold, G.Chroust(eds.) Formal Models in Programming, Proc. IFIP TC2 Working Conf. on the Role of Abstract Models in Inf. Processing, Wien, 1985. North-Holland 1985 347-372

[SM]   Suzuki, I.,Murata, T.: A method for stepwise refinement and abstraction of Petri nets. J. Comp. Syst. Sciences 27 (1983) 51-76

[St]   Starke, P.H.: Processes in Petri nets. EIK 17 (1981) 389-416

[Ta]   Taubner, D.: The finite representation of abstract programs by automata and Petri nets. Dissertation, Techn. Univ. München, 1988

[Va]   Valette, R.: Analysis of Petri nets by stepwise refinements. J. Comp. Syst. Sciences 18 (1979) 35-46

[Vo1]   Vogler, W.: Behaviour preserving refinements of Petri nets. Proc. 12th Int. Workshop on Graph Theoretic Concepts in Computer Science, Bernried/München, 1986. Springer, LNCS 246 (1987) 82-93

[Vo2]   Vogler, W.: Failures semantics and deadlocking of modular Petri nets. Acta Informatica 26 (1989) 333-348. An extended abstract has appeared in: M. P Chytil et al.(eds.): Proc. MFCS 1988, Carlsbad; Springer, LNCS 324 (1988 542-551

[Vo3]   Vogler, W.: Failures semantics based on interval semiwords is a congruence for refinement. Techn. Rep. TUM-I8905, Techn. Univ. München, 1989

THE ANALYSIS OF LOCAL SEARCH PROBLEMS
AND THEIR HEURISTICS

Mihalis Yannakakis

AT&T Bell Laboratories
Murray Hill, NJ 07974
U.S.A.

1. Introduction

Local search is a widely used, general approach to solving hard optimization problems. An optimization problem has a set of *solutions* and a *cost function* that assigns a numerical value to every solution. The goal is to find an *optimal* solution, one that has the minimum (or maximum) cost. To obtain a local search heuristic for an optimization problem, one superimposes a *neighborhood structure* on the solutions, that is, one specifies for each solutions a set of "neighboring" solutions. The heuristic starts from some initial solution that is constructed by some other algorithm, or just generated randomly, and from then on it keeps moving to a better neighboring solution, as long as there is one, until finally it terminates at a *locally optimal* solution, one that does not have a better neighbor.

This scheme has been used successfully for several problems. The two important issues concerning a local search heuristic are: (1) the quality of the obtained solutions, that is, how good are the local optima for the chosen neighborhood structure and how do they relate to the global optima; and (2) the complexity of the local search heuristic, how fast can we find local optima. There is a clear trade-off in the choice of the neighborhood structure: the larger the neighborhoods, the better will be the local optima, but it may be harder to compute them. Designing a good local search heuristic involves choosing a neighborhood that strikes the right balance. Although a few principles and techniques have been identified, the design and analysis of good local search heuristic has remained up to now mainly an experimental art.

Over the last few years there has been renewed activity on local search: both on the experimental front with the design of faster algorithms that find reasonable solutions in reasonable amounts of time for very large instances of classical optimization problems such as the Traveling Salesman Problem, and on the theoretical front with the development of a complexity theory of local search. In this paper we will survey some of the theoretical work on local search.

Local optimization has been applied both in the context of continuous and discrete optimization problems. In Section 2 we will discuss very briefly the case of continuous problems. In the rest of the paper we will be concerned only with discrete, combinatorial problems. In Section 3 we describe some of the classical combinatorial optimization problems, and the neighborhood structures that are associated with them in local search heuristics. There is a number of other search problems, which do not arise directly from optimization, but which can be expressed naturally as instances of local search. One example is the problem of finding stable configurations in neural networks. We describe this and other search problems of this type, where the goal is to find a local optimum for an appropriately defined cost function.

Given an optimization problem, the number and quality of the locally optimal solutions, and their relationship to the global optima depends on the complexity of the optimization problem. There are several results formalizing this dependence, which are summarized in Section 4.

In Section 5 we discuss the complexity of local search problems and their associated heuristics. Empirically, local search heuristics appear to converge rather quikly, within low-order polynomial time. There is not much analytical work supporting these experimental observations, and even analyzing the worst-case complexity of the heuristics is often a nontrivial task. Even if the local search heuristic has exponential (worst-case) complexity, this does not preclude the possibility of finding local optima faster by other, possibly non-iterative, methods. Linear Programming is an interesting example in this regard: this problem can be viewed as a local search problem, where the "solutions" are the vertices of a polytope, and the neighborhood structure is given by the edges of the polytope. In this case local optimality coincides with global optimality, and the standard local search algorithm is Simplex, which has been shown to require an exponential number of iterations in the worst case (for most pivoting rules). However, Linear Programming can be solved in polynomial time by other direct methods such as the Ellipsoid or Karmakar's algorithms that do not even work with the vertices of the polytope [Kh, Ka].

The complexity of finding locally optimal solutions for many interesting problems remains open. A complexity class was introduced for this reason in [JPY] to capture these problems. This class, called PLS (standing for *Polynomial-time Local Search*), lies somewhere between P and NP. Recent results show that many important local search problems are complete for PLS (under an appropriately defined reduction), and that therefore PLS characterises the complexity of local search problems in the same sense that NP characterises the complexity of (hard) combinatorial optimization problems. We discuss this work in Section 5, and we summarize in Section 6.

2. Continuous Problems

When one hears of "local optimality", the first image is of an optimization problem in a Euclidean space R^n of some finite dimension, with the natural Euclidean neighborhood. In a continuous optimization problem, minimize $c(x)$ subject to $x \in S$, the set $S \subseteq R^n$ of solutions is usually specified by a set of inequality constraints $g_1(x) \leq 0$, ..., $g_m(x) \leq 0$, where the g_i's are (in general, arbitrary) real-valued functions of the variable vector $x \in R^n$. A solution $x \in S$ is called *locally optimal* if there is no better solution within some open ball centered at x, that is, if there is an $\varepsilon > 0$ such that $c(x) \leq c(y)$ for all solutions $y \in S$ that are within distance ε of x.

The simplest type of a continuous optimization problem is *Linear Programming*, where both the cost function $c(x)$ and the functions $g_i(x)$ defining the feasible space of solutions are linear. In this case, local optimality coincides with global; i.e., every locally optimal solution is also globally optimal. The same property is true more generally for *Convex Programming*, where both the cost function is a convex function, and the feasible space S is a convex set (if S is specified by the functions g_i as above, then these functions are convex). Linear Programming can be solved in polynomial time by the Ellipsoid algorithm of Khachian or by Karmakar's algorithm [Kh, K]. Furthermore,, Convex Programming can be solved also in polynomial time by the Ellipsoid algorithm, provided that we have an algorithm for the "separation" problem: given a point $x \in R^n$, decide whether $x \in S$, and if this is not the case, output a hyperplane that separates x from S (see [GLS] for more information).

If the cost function is not convex, then the optimization problem is considerably harder, even if the feasible space S is polyhedral (the g_i's are linear). First, it is not any more true that local optimality implies global. Further, it is quite easy to encode NP-hard problems into a quadratic cost function. For example, consider the Knapsack (or Subset-Sum) problem: Given integers $a_1, ..., a_n$ and an integer b, decide whether b is equal to the sum of some of the a_i's, i.e., for some $I \subseteq \{1,...,n\}$, we have $\sum_{i \in I} a_i = b$. This problem can be reduced to the problem of minimizing the cost function $\sum_{i=1}^{n} x_i (1 - x_i)$ subject to the constraints $\sum_{i=1}^{n} a_i x_i = b$, and $0 \leq x_i \leq 1$ for all $i = 1,...,n$. A solution has cost equal to 0 (the smallest possible) if and only if every variable x_i has value 0 or 1, and the variables with value 1 form a solution to the knapsack problem. Thus, the (global) optimization problem is NP-hard.

In general, algorithms for nonconvex programs are usually of an iterative nature, choosing in each iteration a "good" direction to move from the current point (solution) to the next one. In most cases, these algorithms cannot hope for global optimality, and can only aim really at finding a local optimum. Results of Murty and Kabadi, Pardalos and Schnitger and Vergis, Steiglitz and Dickinson [MK, PS, VSD] indicate that even this modest goal is in general difficult. In particular, they show that even testing whether a given solution is locally optimal is NP-hard, and furthermore this is true in rather simple types of nonconvex programs.

An interesting case where one can find local optima in polynomial time is that of Concave Knapsack problems [MV]: minimize $\sum_{i=1}^{n} q_i(x_i)$ subject to the constraints $\sum_{i=1}^{n} a_i x_i = b$, and $l_i \leq x_i \leq u_i$ for all $i = 1,..,n$, where each q_i is a strictly concave differentiable function. Observe that this problem includes the above formulation of the Knapsack problem and thus finding a global optimum is NP-hard. Note also that in minimizing a concave function over a convex set S we may restrict attention to the extreme points of S [MV], and thus if S is a polytope as above, then we may regard the problem either as a continuous or as a discrete optimization problem, where the solutions are the vertices of the polytope.

3. Discrete Problems

Here the set S of solutions is a discrete, finite set. As we noted above, the distinction between continuous and discrete problems is not always clear, and many times we may regard the same problem as either a discrete one or a continuous. For example, we may view Linear Programming as a discrete problem; assumming for simplicity that the feasible space is a (bounded) polytope, the solutions are the vertices of the polytope, and the neighbors of a vertex are its adjacent vertices on the polytope. Under this formulation also, Linear Programming has the important property that local optimality implies global optimality.

We will describe first local search heuristics associated with some basic problems in combinatorial optimization. Then we will discuss some problems that can be formulated in terms of local search.

Optimization Problems

Unlike the case of continuous problems, here there is not a "natural" neighborhood, but we may associate any number of different neighborhood structures with the same optimization problem. In fact, finding a good neighborhood structure is the central part in designing a good local search heuristic. We define below few problems and possible neighborhoods.

Max Cut. Given a graph with weights on the edges, find a partition of the nodes into two parts that maximizes the weight of the cut, i.e., the sum of the weights of the edges connecting the two parts. The simplest neighborhood for this problem is to have two partitions be neighbors if one partition can be obtained from the other by moving a single node from one side of the partition to the other side.

Graph Partitioning. We are given again a graph with weights on the edges and want to find a partition of the nodes into two parts V_1, V_2 of *equal size* to minimize (or maximize) the weight of the cut. (The minimization and maximization versions of the problem are equivalent.) The simplest neighborhood here is the *swap* neighborhood: swap a vertex of the one side V_1 with a vertex from the other side V_2. A much larger and more powerful neighborhood is explored by the Kernighan-Lin heuristic [KL]. This neighborhood is not symmetric and depends on the edge weights. The Kernighan-Lin heuristic moves from one partition to a neighboring partition by performing a sequence of greedy swaps; in each step of the sequence, we choose to swap the best possible pair of nodes among those that have not been moved in the previous steps of the sequence, where "best" means that the swap results in the minimum cost differential, i.e., the weight of the cut decreases the most or increases the least. The neighbors of a partition are the partitions obtained after the first, second, ..., nth swap of the above sequence. This basic idea of allowing a move from one solution to a neighbor consist of an arbitrary number of changes, and using a greedy criterion to control the potentially exponential search of unbounded depth, appears to be a fundamental, very succesfull technique in local search. Several variations of the basic algorithm are possible. A modification proposed by Fiduccia and Matheyses [FM] breaks each swap of the sequence into two steps, where first one chooses the best (unmoved) node and moves from one side to the other, and then balances the partition by moving the best node from the opposite side. These heuristics have been used successfully in several applications, for example to lay out circuits [DK]. They converge reasonably fast to locally optimal solutions of good quality. Extensive experimental results and comparison with simulated annealing are reported in [JAMS1].

The Kernighan-Lin heuristic can be generalized to partitions into more than two parts [GZ]. Another heuristic for this problem with a nontrivial neighborhood is proposed in [BVW]; this heuristic solves a transportation problem in each iteration to decide which nodes to redistribute in going from one partition to a neighboring partition.

Traveling Salesman Problem (TSP). We are given weights on the edges of the complete graph on n nodes (the "cities"), and we want to find the least weight tour that passes exactly once through each city. A special case is when the cities are points on the plane, and the weights of the edges are the Euclidean distances between the points. The simplest neighborhood is *2-opt*: replace two edges (a,b), (c,d) by two other edges (a,c) and (b,d) to form another tour (see Figure 1). For example, in the planar Euclidean case, if the two edges (a,b) and (c,d) cross each other, then this replacement always yields a better tour because of the triangle inequality. Note however, that on the plane, even a tour that does not self-intersect may have a cost improving 2-opt move. This neighborhood can be extended to 3-opt, and more generally, k-opt, where we replace at most k edges of the current tour by k new edges.

The Lin-Kernighan heuristic allows the replacement of an arbitrary number of edges in moving from a tour to a neighboring tour, where again complex greedy criterion is used in order to permit the search to go to an unbounded depth without an exponential blow-up [LK]. We can sketch the basic idea as follows. Given a tour, we can remove an edge (a,b) to obtain a Hamilton path with endpoints a and b. Regard one of the endpoints, say a as fixed, and the other, b, as variable. If we add an edge (b,c) from the variable endpoint, a cycle is formed; there is a unique edge (c,d)

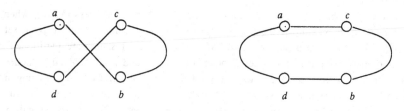

Figure 1

incident to c whose removal breaks the cycle resulting in a new Hamilton path with a new variable endpoint d (see Figure 2). This operation is called a *rotation*. We can always close a tour by adding the edge connecting the fixed endpoint a with the current variable endpoint d. A move of the Lin-Kernighan heuristic from one tour to a neighbor consists of first removing an edge to form a Hamilton path, then performing a sequence of rotations, and finally reconnecting the two endpoints to form a tour. The rotations of the sequence are chosen greedily subject to the condition that one cannot reintroduce a previously deleted edge.

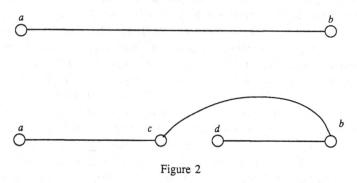

Figure 2

Experiments by Bentley and Johnson with 2-opt, 3-opt and Lin-Kernighan applied to very large instances are reported in [B, BJMR, JAMS3]. For instances consisting of randomly distributed points on the plane, 2-opt comes within 5.5% of optimal, 3-opt comes within 3.5%, and Lin-Kernighan within 1.5% of optimal.

Search Problems

In general, a search problem is specified by a relation that associates with every input a set of one or more acceptable outputs. The goal is, given an input to produce one of this outputs. There is a number of search problems, where one can define an appropriate cost function and formulate the problem as that of fining any local optimum for this function. For example, consider the following problem proposed by Knuth: Given an $m \times n$ matrix A with $m < n$, find a (nonsingular) $m \times m$ sumatrix B of A such that all entries of $B^{-1}A$ have absolute value at most one. Using Cramer's rule, it is not hard to see that this problem is equivalent to the following local search problem. The solutions are the $m \times m$ (nonsingular) submatrices of A, the cost of a submatrix is the absolute value of its determinant, and two matrices are neighbors if one can be obtained from the other by exchanging a column.

The following problem arises in a finite-state Markov Decision Process (MDP), when we want to find a policy which maximizes the probability that the process hits one of a given set of target states [C, H]. We are given a directed graph M whose nodes (or states) are partitioned into three sets: a set R of randomizing nodes, a set C of control nodes, and a set T of target nodes. We are also given a transition probability p_{ij} for every edge $i \to j$ out of each randomizing node i. A (Markov) policy τ chooses one transition out of each control node. The problem is to find a policy which maximizes the probability that starting from a given initial state, the process will hit a target state. Assuming for simplicity that every node can reach some node in T, this problem is equivalent to finding a set of values $v(i)$ for all the nodes i of M satisfying the following constraints:

$$(1) \quad v(i) = 1 \quad \text{if} \quad i \in T;$$

$$(2) \quad v(i) = \sum_j p_{ij} v(j) \quad \text{if} \quad i \in R;$$

$$(3) \quad v(i) = \max_{i \to j} v(j) \quad \text{if} \quad i \in C.$$

The values $v(i)$ are the maximum probabilities that the process starting from node i will hit a target state under an optimal policy. These values can be computed by an iterative algorithm: given a policy τ, compute the probabilities $v_\tau(i)$ that the MDP with policy τ will hit the set T starting from state i. Clearly, the values $v_\tau(i)$ satisfy the constraints (1) and (2). If they also satisfy constraints (3), then τ is an optimal policy; otherwise, let $i \in C$ be a control node for which (3) is violated, that is, for some immediate succesor j of i we have $v_\tau(i) < v_\tau(j)$. Define a new policy τ' which is identical to τ, except that the control node i chooses the edge going to j. This iterative algorithm converges in finite time, and the reason is basically that every iteration increases the function $\sum v_\tau(i)$; that is, the iterative algorithm can be viewed as a local search heuristic for this cost function. This algorithm may require an exponential number of iterations, but the solution can be computed in polynomial time by solving the Linear Program: minimize $\sum v(i)$ subject to constraints (1), (2) above, and (3') $v(i) \geq v(j)$ for all nodes $i \in C$ and edges $i \to j$. A very similar problem arises in the evaluation of logical rules [UvG]. One wants to find a solution to a set of constraints (1)-(3) as above, but there the numbers p_{ij} are nonnegative integers. Ullman and van Gelder show that in this case one does not have to resort to Linear Programming because an iterative algorithm converges after at most n iterations.

A more complex problem arises when the Markov Decision Process is extended to a two-person game with randomization [C]. We have again a directed graph M whose states are partitioned into a set R of randomizing states, a set T of target states, a set $C1$ of states controlled by player 1, and a set $C2$ of states controlled by player 2. We are also given transition probabilities for the edges out of the randomizing states. Player 1 is trying to maximize the probability of hitting a target state, whereas Player 2 is trying to minimize it. The problem is to compute optimal strategies for the two players. Assume for simplicity that all the nodes can reach a state of T regardless of the policy of Player 2 (the graph can be preprocessed to reduce the problem to this case). Then, the problem is equivalent to finding a solution to the following set of constraints: (1) $v(i) = 1$ if $i \in T$; (2) $v(i) = \sum_j p_{ij} v(j)$ if $v \in R$; (3) $v(i) = \max_{i \to j} v(j)$ if $v \in C1$; (4) $v(i) = \min_{i \to j} v(j)$ if $v \in C2$. We can find again a solution by an iterative algorithm. Given a policy τ for $C2$, i.e., a choice for each node $i \in C2$ of an immediate successor $\tau(i)$, we can compute as above in polynomial time (by Linear Programming) a solution to the constraints (1)-(3) and $v(i) = v(\tau(i))$ for $i \in C2$. If the solution satisfies the constraints (4), then τ is the optimal policy of $C2$, and the solution gives also the optimal policy for $C1$; if (4) is not satisfied, then we can modify τ by changing the choice for a node $i \in C2$ for which (4) is violated. Again, the iterative algorithm converges because it decreases a certain cost function, and as above, the problem can be viewed as one of computing a locally optimal solution for this cost function [C]. In this case we do not know whether the problem can be solved in polynomial time.

Finally, another important example, where local optimization is used only as a proof tool, is finding stable configurations in neural networks in the Hopfield model [Ho]. We are given an undirected graph with a (positive or negative) weight w_e on each edge e and a threshold t_v for each node v. A *configuration* assigns to each node v a state s_v which is either 1 ("on") or -1 ("off"). (Some authors use the values 1 and 0 instead of 1 and -1; the two versions are equivalent.) A node v is *happy* if $s_v = 1$ and $\sum_{(u,v) \in E} w_{u,v} s_u + t_v \geq 0$, or $s_v = -1$ and $\sum_{(u,v) \in E} w_{u,v} s_u + t_v \leq 0$. A configuration is *stable* if all the nodes are happy. The problem is to find a stable configuration for a given network. It is not obvious a priori that such a configuration exists; in fact, in the case of directed networks it may not exist [Go, Li]. Hopfield showed that in the undirected case there is always a stable configuration [Ho] (see also [GFP]). To prove this he introduced a cost function $\sum_{(u,v) \in E} s_u s_v + \sum_{v \in V} t_v$ and argued that if a node is unhappy, then changing its state will increase the cost; that is, the stable configurations coincide with the locally optimal solutions for this function with respect to the neighborhood that flips the state of a single node. Hopfield proposed to use this model in [Ho] as a content adressable memory with error correction, where the stored words correspond to the stable configurations. Later papers consider using such networks for combinatorial optimization (either in its original discrete, or in a continuous analog version) [HT, BG]. There is now an extensive literature on this model, see [Go, Li, P] for more information.

4. Local Versus Global Optima

We say that a neighborhood structure is *exact* for a given optimization problem if every local optimum is also a global optimum. For example, an exact neighborhood for the minimum spanning tree problem is the one where we can go from one solution (spanning tree) to a neighbor by adding an edge to the tree and then removing another edge of the (unique) cycle that is thus formed. In any optimization problem, one can always make local and global optima coincide by choosing a large enough neighborhood structure. The problem is that it may be hard then to search the neighborhood, i.e., determine whether a solution is locally optimal, and find a better neighbor if it is not. In fact, in many classical, well-solved optimization problems, an important step in the solution was to characterize the exact neighborhood, that is, prove a theorem stating that a solution is not optimal if and only if it can be improved by a certain kind of perturbation, and then find an efficient algorithm to search for such a perturbation. For example, in the maximum flow problem (and the cardinality matching problem), a flow (or matching) is not maximum iff it has an augmenting path; in the minimum cost flow problem (and in the weighted perfect matching problem), a flow (or perfect matching) is not optimal if there is a cycle in a "residual" network of negative cost (respectively, a negative cost alternating cycle) [PS2]. It is clear that one would not expect to find such good characterizations for NP-hard optimization problems. In order to use a neighborhood structure as part of a reasonable local search heuristic, at the very least, we must be able to search the neighborhood.

There are various results pointing out limitations for NP-hard problems. Several authors have shown that in the Traveling Salesman Problem, neighborhoods that are exact must be exponentially large (assumming that they are data-independent, i.e., do not depend on the distances) [WSB, V]; this fact is true even if one is concerned only with instances where all distances are 1 or 2 (and thus, satisfy the triangle inequality). Papadimitriou and Steiglitz have shown that, assuming that P ≠ NP, if we can search the neighborhood in polynomial time, then it cannot be exact, and furthermore, in the absence of the triangly inequality there must be local optima that are arbitrarily worse than the global optimum [PS2]. Also, they have constructed bad examples for the k-opt heuristics: in their examples, there is only one optimal tour, but there are exponentially many second best tours that (i) cannot be improved by changing less than 3/8 of the edges, and (ii) have very large cost, arbitrarily worse than the optimal (in the absence of triangle inequality). Thus, for k-opt with fixed k (actually, for $k < 3n/8$), all these exponentially many tours are local optima of bad quality [PS1]. Rodl and Tovey consider the maximum independent set problem, and construct a graph G which has the property that for any neighborhood structure of polynomial size, the graph G (possibly after a renaming) has exponentially many independent sets that are locally optimal solutions, but not globally [RT].

Empirically, local search heuristics seem to produce very good approximate solutions. For example, as we mentioned, TSP heuristics come within a few percentage points of the optimum for "typical" instances on the plane, and outperform other algorithms with better worst-case approximation properties (for example, Christofides' algorithm). We do not know of any analytical results supporting this behaviour. In terms of worst-case quality of approximation, most of the heuristics have bad examples and cannot guarrantee any bounded ratio to the optimum. In the case of max cut, any locally optimum cut with respect to the simple-minded neighborhood, has weight at least half of the total weight of all the edges, and thus is trivially within a factor of 2 of the optimum. This factor of 2 can be achieved also by various other methods, but we do not know of any approximation algorithm that can guarrantee a better ratio.

5. Complexity

Consider a local search problem Π. The problem has a set of instances, every instance has a set of solutions, and there is a cost function and a neighborhood structure associated with the solutions. In studying the complexity of Π and its corresponding local search heuristics, there are various interesting issues that arise. First, note that some solutions may have more than one better neighbors, and a heuristic has the freedom to choose any one of these neighbors to move to. We call a rule for choosing a better neighbor out of each solution that is not locally optimal, a *pivoting rule*. The choice of a pivoting rule may affect drastically the complexity of a local search heuristic. For example, consider the max flow problem with the neighborhood structure corresponding to augmentation along a path: It is well known that if we choose arbitrarily the augmenting paths, then an exponential number of augmentations may be required, but if we always augment along shortest paths, then the optimum will be found after a polynomial number of iterations (see for example [PS2]). Thus, in examining a local search heuristic, we want to analyze its complexity for different pivoting rule, and also try to characterize the best possible rule.

Second, note that even if a local search heuristic has exponential complexity, this does not mean that we cannot find local optima easier by other, completely different methods. For instance, the best way to solve the minimum spanning tree problem is not by a local search heuristic, but by the standard greedy algorithm. Thus, when we talk about the complexity of the search problem itself (i.e., find some local optimum), we must allow any type of algorithms.

Analyzing the complexity of particular local search problems and heuristics is not an easy task.

Consider for example the case of Linear Programming, with the Simplex algorithm as its corresponding local search algorithm. Several papers have examined the complexity of Simplex and have constructed bad examples for many common pivoting rules, showing that they lead to an exponential number of iterations [KM, J]. However, it is still not known whether there is a rule that turns Simplex into a polynomial-time algorithm. The related Hirsch conjecture asserts that every (bounded) polytope has always small diameter, at most $m - d$ for a polytope in dimension d with m facets [KW]; this claim has been shown for some polytopes, but in general it remains open. It is known that the *monotone* version of the Hirsch conjecture (i.e., if the cost has to improve in each step) is not true: Todd presents an example where, regardless of the pivoting rule, the number of iterations must exceed $m - d$, although the lower bound in this example is still only linear [T]. Finally, note that determining the complexity of the Linear Programming problem itself was an open problem for quite a long time, until the discovery of the Ellipsoid algorithm [Kh], a completely different algorithm that does not employ local search.

Characterizing the complexity of many other local search problems presents similar challenges. For this reason, a complexity class, called *PLS*, was introduced in [JPY] to capture these problems. A local search problem Π is in the class PLS essentially if its neighborhood can be searched in polynomial time. More formally, Π is in PLS if there are three polynomial time algorithms A, B, C as follows.

1. Given an instance I of Π, algorithm A produces some feasible solution for I.
2. Algorithm B, given an instance I and a string s determines whether s is a solution for I, and if so computes its cost.
3. Algorithm C, given an instance I and a solution s, determines whether s is a local optimum, and if it is not, C outputs a neighbor with better cost.

All the common local search problems (for example, those described in Section 3) are in PLS. This class lies somewhere between P_S and NP_S, the search problem analogs of P and NP. It is conceivable that it may coincide with one of these two classes, but the most plausible conjecture is that it lies properly in-between. One the one hand, it is shown in [JPY] that no problem in PLS can be NP-hard unless NP=co-NP, which is widely believed to be false, and thus it is unlikely that PLS is equal to NP_S. On the other hand, showing that all PLS problems can be solved in polynomial time would require a general approach to finding local optima, at least as clever as the Ellipsoid algorithm, since Linear Programming is in PLS, and in fact is one of its better behaved members (for example, local and global optimality coincide, the global optimization problem is in P and not NP-hard as is the case with other problems in PLS).

A reduction among local search problems was defined in [JPY], called PLS-reduction: A problem A reduces to a problem B if there is a polynomial time algorithm f that transforms an instance I of A to an instance $f(I)$ of B, and another polynomial time algorithm that constructs a locally optimal solution for the instance I of A from any locally optimal solution of the instance $f(I)$ of problem B. Showing that a problem A is PLS-complete under this reduction means that we can find local optima for A in polynomial time if and only if we can for all problems in PLS. Two problems were shown PLS-complete in [JPY]. One was a generic problem called FLIP, and the other one was the Graph Paritioning problem under the Kernighan-Lin neighborhood. Recall from Section 3, that this is a rather complicated neighborhood, and from a given partition we may have to perform an unbounded number of swaps until we obtain a better neighboring partition. It was observed in [JPY] that determining whether a solution is locally optimal with respect to this neighborhood is a P-complete problem, and that the same is true of FLIP. They conjectured that this is necessary for a problem to be

PLS-complete, the rationale being that if the algorithm C in the above definition of a PLS problem Π works, say, in LOGSPACE, then it does not use the full power of polynomial time that is allowed for PLS problems, and thus, one should not expect Π to be able to simulate all problems in PLS (of course, assumming that $P \neq$ LOGSPACE).

Susprisingly, this conjecture was disproved recently by Krentel [K1] who showed that the following Maximum Satisfiability problem is PLS-complete: given a weighted set of clauses, find a truth assignment such that the total weight of the satisfied clauses cannot be increased by flipping the truth value of any single variable. Checking local optimality for this problem is in LOGSPACE. This result raised the possibility that other such problems could be also complete.

Several interesting local search problems with simple neighborhoods have been shown recently to be PLS-complete: in particular, the Max Cut problem, the Graph Partitioning problem under the swap neighborhood, the Maximum Satisfiability problem with length 2 clauses, and the problem of finding stable configurations in neural nets [SY]. A way to interpret the last result is that neural nets have a universality property, in the sense that any local search problem in PLS can be encoded into a neural net by adjusting properly its weights. For the TSP problem, Papadimitriou has proved recently that it is PLS-complete under the Lin-Kernighan neighborhood [P]. Krentel has shown PLS-completeness for k-opt for some fixed (though impractically large) value of k [K2]. What all these results indicate is that PLS-completeness is a widespread phenomenon like NP-completeness (though it is usually several orders of magnitude harder to prove). Just as the class NP characterizes the complexity of combinatorial optimization (many natural, important problems are NP-complete), the class PLS provides the right characterization for local search.

Although PLS was introduced to study the complexity of the search problems themselves, the completeness results help also in analyzing the local search heuristics. There had been very few results on the complexity of the heuristics, and these are usually based on ad hoc constructions and concern individual pivoting rules. For the problem of finding stable configurations in neural networks, Goles and Olivos show in [GO] that it takes exponential time to converge if all nodes update their states synchronously in parallel. Haken and Luby show in [HL] that the local search heuristic with the steepest-descent rule has exponential complexity.

In all of the PLS-completeness proofs mentioned above, the reductions can be made "tight" in a technical sense (see [SY] for a definition), so that there is a correspondence between local optima of the two problems, and the behaviour of the local search heuristic for the first problem A simulates the behaviour of the heuristic for the second problem B. It is quite easy to construct artificial problems in PLS for which the local search heuristic takes exponential time. It follows then that, for all the PLS-complete problems mentioned above, their associated local search heuristics have exponential complexity, and this holds regardless of the pivoting rule that they use.

Another question for a given local search problem is the following: Given an instance and a solution s, find a local optimum that can be reached by the local search heuristic starting from s. This question is much harder: it is PSPACE-complete for all of the above problems. The related question of finding a local optimum that is at least as good as s (though, not necessarily reachable by the heuristic) is an easier problem: it is itself a local search problem, and thus is "only" PLS-complete.

An interesting problem that is not resolved is 2-opt for the TSP. Lueker has constructed examples, where the 2-opt heuristic may take an exponential number of iterations under a particular pivoting rule [Lu]; it is not known whether this is unavoidable, or whether 2-opt is polynomially bounded under some other rule. In the case of the TSP on the plane, van Leeuwen and Shoone prove that one can eliminate all edge crossings after at most $O(n^3)$ edge swaps [vLS]; note that eliminating all edge crossing is not sufficient in general for a tour on the plane to be 2-opt.

In practice, local search heuristics have been observed to converge very quickly. This situation is similar to the case of the Simplex algorithm. Several papers considered probabilistic models for Linear Programming, and analysed the expected performance of Simplex proving that the average complexity is bounded by a low order polynomial. The probabilistic analysis of sophisticated local search heuristics (for example Lin-Kernighan) appears to be a very difficult problem. Kern examines in [Ke] the 2-opt heuristic for randomly distributed points in the unit square and proves a polynomial upper bound on the expected complexity of 2-opt (although the polynomial is n^{18}). Tovey [T1, T2] analyzes an abstract model for local search problems, where the neighborhood structure is an n-dimensional hypercube, whose vertices correspond to the solutions. The cost function induces an orientation of the hypercube from worse to better solutions. Tovey considers various natural probability distributions on the possible orientations, for example, one such distribution has all possible orderings of the vertices according to cost be equally likely. He proves then that the expected complexity of the local search heuristic under these distributions is bounded by a low order polynomial.

Parallel Complexity

Local search heuristics require exponential time only if the numbers (weights, distances etc.) are large and are encoded in binary. When the numbers are small (polynomially bounded) or if the problems are not weighted, the heuristics terminate in polynomial time because every iteration decreases the cost function, and there are only polynomially many possible different costs. In this case, we would like to find algorithms that work faster in parallel. An interesting paradigm for parallel computation is the *maximal independent set* problem. This problem can be viewed as a local search problem (we go from one independnet set to a neighbor by adding a node), the local search heuristic takes linear time, but the problem can be solved in NC by more sophisticated parallel methods [KWi, Lu]. Luby showed that the maximal independent set problem can be formulated as a special case of the stable configuration problem by choosing appropriate (small) weights, and raised the question of the parallel complexity of the latter problem. It turns out that the stable configuration problem with all edge weights -1, as well as the unweighted versions of several other problems (for example, max cut, graph partitioning under the swap neighborhood) are P-complete [SY].

6. Conclusions

We reviewed some of the theoretical work that has been done on local search problems. There are related topics that we did not discuss. For example, *simulated annealing*, a randomized extension of local search that permits occasional uphill moves [KGV]. Specifically, in each iteration, this heuristic generates a random neighbor of the current solution; if the neighbor has better cost, then the heuristic moves to it, otherwise it moves to the neighbor with a probability $p(\Delta, T)$ that depends on the cost differential Δ and on an adjustable parameter T (the so-called "temperature"). During the course of the algorithm, the parameter T is adjusted starting from a high value (which yields higher probability p of an uphill move) and tending towards 0. (A similar extension applied to the neural net framework leads to so-called "Boltzman machines", see eg [KA].) There is extensive literature on simulated annealing, both experimental and theoretical (see [vLA, JAMS] and the references therein).

There are many remaining open theoretical problems in local search. The most important and difficult question is the relationship of PLS to P and NP. Besides this, there are many interesting local search problems that we do not know to be in P or to be PLS-complete. For example, TSP under the 2-opt neighborhood, the subdeterminant problem, and the problem of randomized 2-person game from Section 3. Finally, there has been very little work on analysing the average performance of local search heuristics, both in terms of complexity and quality of approximation.

REFERENCES

[BVW]   E. R. Barnes, A. Vanelli and J. Q. Walker, A New Heuristic for Partitioning the Nodes of a Graph, *SIAM J. Disc. Math.* 1(1988), pp. 299-305.

[B]   J. L. Bentley, Experiments on Traveling Salesman Heuristics, Proc. First ACM-SIAM Symposium on Discrete Algorithms, 1990.

[BJMR] J. L. Bentley, D. S. Johnson, L. A. McGeosh and E. E. Rothberg, Near Optimal Solutions to Very Large Traveling Salesman Problems, in preparation, 1990.

[BG]   J. Bruck and J. W. Goodman, A Generalized Convergence Theorem for Neural Networks, *IEEE Trans. Inf. Theory* 34(1988), pp. 1089--1092.

[C]   A. Condon, *Computational Models of Games*, MIT Press, 1989.

[DK]   A. E. Dunlop and B. W. Kernighan, A Procedure for Placement of Standard-Cell VLSI Circuits *IEEE Trans. CAD* 4(1985), pp. 92-98.

[FM]   C. M. Fiduccia and R. M. Mattheyses, A Linear-Time Heuristic for Improving Network Partitions, Proc. 19th Annual Design Automation Conference, 1982, pp. 175--181.

[GJ]   M. R. Garey and D. S. Johnson, *Computers and Intractability: A Guide to the Theory of NP-Completeness*, W. H. Freeman, 1979.

[GZ]   J. R. Gilbert and E. Zmijewski, A Parallel Graph Partitioning Algorithm for a Message-Passing Multiprocessor, *Intl. J. Paral. Prog.* 16(1987), pp. 427-449.

[G]   G. Godbeer, On the Computational Complexity of the Stable Configuration Problem for Connectionist Models, Master's Thesis, Dept. of Comp. Sci., U. of Toronto, September, 1987.

[GFP]   E. Goles-Chacc, F. Fogelman-Soulie and D. Pellegrin, Decreasing Energy Functions as a Tool for Studying Threshold Networks, *Discrete Appl. Math.* 12(1985), pp. 261-277.

[GO]   E. Goles and J. Olivos, The Convergence of Symmetric Threshold Automata, *Information and Control* 51(1981), pp. 98-104.

[GLS]   M. Grotschel, L. Lovasz and A. Schrijver, *Geometric Algorithms and Combinatorial Optimization*, Springer Verlag, 1988.

[HL]   A. Haken and M. Luby, Steepest Descent Can Take Exponential Time for Symmetric Connection Networks, *Complex Systems* 2(1988), pp. 191--196.

[Ho]   J. J. Hopfield, Neural Networks and Physical Systems with Emergent Collective Computational Abilities, *Proc. Nat. Acad. Sci.* 79(1982), pp. 2554--2558.

[HT]   J. J. Hopfield and D. W. Tank, Neural Computation of Decisions in Optimization Problems, *Biol. Cyber.* 52(1985), pp. 141--152.

[H]   D. Howard, *Dynamic Programming and Markov Processes*, MIT Press, 1960.

[J]   R. J. Jeroslow, The Simplex Algorithm with the Pivot Rule of Maximizing Criterion Improvement, *Disc. Math.* 4(1973), pp. 367-378.

[JAMS1] D. S. Johnson, C. R. Aragon, L. A McGeoch, and C. Schevon, Optimization By Simulated Annealing: An Experimental Evaluation, Part I (Graph Partitioning), *Operations Research*, to appear.

[JAMS2]   D. S. Johnson, C. R. Aragon, L. A McGeoch, and C. Schevon, Optimization By Simulated Annealing: An Experimental Evaluation, Part II (Graph Coloring and Number Partitioning), manuscript, 1989.

[JAMS3]   D. S. Johnson, C. R. Aragon, L. A McGeoch, and C. Schevon, Optimization By Simulated Annealing: An Experimental Evaluation, Part III (The Traveling Salesman Problem), in preparation, 1990.

[JPY]   D. S. Johnson, C. H. Papadimitriou, M. Yannakakis, How Easy Is Local Search?, *J. Comp. Syst. Sci.* 37(1988), pp. 79--100.

[K]   N. Karmarkar, A New Polynomial Time Algorithm for Linear Programming, *Combinatorica* 4(1984), pp. 373-395.

[KWi]   R. M. Karp and A. Wigderson, A Fast Parallel Algorithm for the Maximal Independent Set Problem, *J. Assoc. Comput. Mach.* 32(1985), pp. 762-773.

[Ke]   W. Kern, A Probabilistic Analysis of the Switching Algorithm for the Euclidean TSP, *Mathematical Programming* 44(1989), pp. 213-219.

[KL]   B. Kernighan and S. Lin, An Efficient Heuristic Procedure for Partitioning Graphs, *Bell Syst. Tech. J.* 49(1970), pp. 291--307.

[Kh]   L. G. Khachian, A Polynomial Algorithm for Linear Programming, *Soviet Math. Doklady* 20(1979), pp. 191-194.

[KGV]   S. Kirkpatrick, C. Gelat, and M. Vecchi, Optimization by Simulated Annealing, *Science* 220(1983), pp. 671-680.

[KM]   V. Klee and G. J. Minty, How Good is the Simplex Algorithm?, in *Inequalities III*, O. Shisha, ed., Academic Press, 1971.

[KW]   V. Klee and D. W. Walkup, The d-step Conjecture for Polyhedra of Dimension $d < 6$, *Acta Math.* 117(1967), pp. 53-78.

[KA]   J. H. M. Korst and E. H. L. Aarts, Combinatorial Optimization on a Boltzman Machine, *J. Parallel and Distr. Comp.* 6(1989), pp. 331-357.

[K1]   M. W. Krentel, On Finding Locally Optimal Solutions, Proc. 4th Annual Structure in Complexity Conference, 1989, pp. 132--137; also to appear in *SIAM J. Comp.*

[K2]   M. W. Krentel, Structure in Locally Optimal Solutions, Proc. 30th Annual Symposium on Foundations of Computer Science, 1989, pp. 216-221.

[L]   S. Lin, Computer Solutions of the Traveling Salesman Problem, *Bell Syst. Tech. J.* 44(1965), pp. 2245-2269.

[LK]   S. Lin and B. Kernighan, An Effective Heuristic for the Traveling Salesman problem, *Oper. Res.* 21(1973), pp. 498--516.

[Li]   J. Lipscomb, On the Computational Complexity of Finding a Connectionist Model's Stable State of Vectors, Master's Thesis, Dept. of Comp. Sci., U. of Toronto, October, 1987.

[LTT]   D. C. Llewellyn, C. Tovey and M. Trick, Local Optimization on Graphs, *Discrete Appl. Math.* (1989).

[Lub]   M. Luby, A Simple Parallel Algorithm for the Maximal Independent Set Problem, *SIAM J. Comp.* 15(1986), pp. 1036--1053.

[Lue]   G. Lueker, manuscript, Princeton University (1976).

[MV]   J. J. More and S. A. Vavasis, On the Solution of Concave Knapsack Problems, Preprint, Argonne National Laboratory, (1988).

[MK]   K. G. Murty and S. N. Kabadi, Some NP-complete Problems in Quadratic and Nonlinear Programming, *Mathematical Programming* 39(1987), pp. 117-129.

[P]   C. H. Papadimitriou, The Complexity of the Lin-Kernighan Heuristic for the Traveling Salesman Problem, manuscript, (1989).

[PS1]   C. H. Papadimitriou and K. Steiglitz, Some Examples of Difficult Traveling Salesman Problems, *Oper. Res.* 26(1978), pp. 434-443.

[PS2]   C. H. Papadimitriou and K. Steiglitz, *Combinatorial Optimization: Algorithms and Complexity*, Prentice-Hall, 1982.

[Pa]   I. Parberry, A Primer on the Complexity Theory of Neural Networks, to appear in *A Sourcebook on Formal Techniques in Artificial Intelligence*, R. B. Banerji, ed., Elsevier, 1989.

[PSc]   P. M. Pardalos and G. Schnitger, Checking Local Optimality in Constrained Quadratic Programming is NP-hard, *Oper. Res. Let.* 7(1988), pp. 33-35.

[RT]   V. Rodl and C. Tovey, Multiple Optima in Local Search, *J. of Algorithms* 8(1987), pp. 250-259.

[SH]   G. H. Sasaki and B. Hajek, The Time Complexity of Maximum Matching by Simulated Annealing, *J. Assoc. Comput. Mach.* 35(1988), pp. 387-403.

[SY]   A. A. Schaffer and M. Yannakakis, Simple Local Search Problems That Are Hard to Solve, manuscript, (1989).

[T]   M. J. Todd, The Monotonic Bounded Hirsch Conjecture is False for Dimension At Least 4, *Math. Oper. Res.* 5(1980), pp. 599-601.

[T1]   C. A. Tovey, Hill Climbing with Multiple Local Optima, *SIAM J. Alg. Disc. Meth.* 6(1985), pp. 384-393.

[T2]   C. A. Tovey, Low Order Polynomial Bounds on the Expected Performance of Local Improvemnet Algorithms, *Mathematical Programming* 35(1986), pp. 193-224.

[UvG]   J. D. Ullman and A. Van Gelder, Efficient Tests for Top-Down Termination of Logical Rules, *J. Assoc. Comp. Mach.* 35(1988), pp. 345-373.

[vLA]   P. J. M. van Laarhoven and E. H. L. Aarts, *Simulated Annealing: Theory and Practice*, Kluwer Academic Publishers, 1987.

[vLS]   J. van Leeuwen and A. A. Schoone, Untangling a Traveling Salesman Tour in the Plane, Technical Report RUU-CS-80-11, University of Utrecht (1980).

[VSD]   A. Vergis, K. Steiglitz and B. Dickinson, The Complexity of Analog Computation, *Math. and Comp. in Simulation* 28(1986), pp. 91-113.

[V]   V. G. Vizing, Complexity of the Traveling Salesman Problem in the Class of Monotonic Improvement Algorithms, *Eng. Cyb.* 4(1978), pp. 623-626.

[WSB]   P. Weiner, S. L. Savage and A. Bagchi, Neighborhood Search Algorithms for Guaranteeing Optimal Traveling Salesman Tours Must be Inefficient, *J. Comp. Sys. Sci.* 12(1976), pp. 25-35.

Index of Authors

Vol. 379: A. Kreczmar, G. Mirkowska (Eds.), Mathematical Foundations of Computer Science 1989. Proceedings, 1989. VIII, 605 pages. 1989.

Vol. 380: J. Csirik, J. Demetrovics, F. Gécseg (Eds.), Fundamentals of Computation Theory. Proceedings, 1989. XI, 493 pages. 1989.

Vol. 381: J. Dassow, J. Kelemen (Eds.), Machines, Languages, and Complexity. Proceedings, 1988. VI, 244 pages. 1989.

Vol. 382: F. Dehne, J.-R. Sack, N. Santoro (Eds.), Algorithms and Data Structures. WADS '89. Proceedings, 1989. IX, 592 pages. 1989.

Vol. 383: K. Furukawa, H. Tanaka, T. Fujisaki (Eds.), Logic Programming '88. Proceedings, 1988. VII, 251 pages. 1989 (Subseries LNAI).

Vol. 384: G. A. van Zee, J. G. G. van de Vorst (Eds.), Parallel Computing 1988. Proceedings, 1988. V, 135 pages. 1989.

Vol. 385: E. Börger, H. Kleine Büning, M. M. Richter (Eds.), CSL '88. Proceedings, 1988. VI, 399 pages. 1989.

Vol. 386: J.E. Pin (Ed.), Formal Properties of Finite Automata and Applications. Proceedings, 1988. VIII, 260 pages. 1989.

Vol. 387: C. Ghezzi, J. A. McDermid (Eds.), ESEC '89. 2nd European Software Engineering Conference. Proceedings, 1989. VI, 496 pages. 1989.

Vol. 388: G. Cohen, J. Wolfmann (Eds.), Coding Theory and Applications. Proceedings, 1988. IX, 329 pages. 1989.

Vol. 389: D.H. Pitt, D.E. Rydeheard, P. Dybjer, A.M. Pitts, A. Poigné (Eds.), Category Theory and Computer Science. Proceedings, 1989. VI, 365 pages. 1989.

Vol. 390: J.P. Martins, E.M. Morgado (Eds.), EPIA 89. Proceedings, 1989. XII, 400 pages. 1989 (Subseries LNAI).

Vol. 391: J.-D. Boissonnat, J.-P. Laumond (Eds.), Geometry and Robotics. Proceedings, 1988. VI, 413 pages. 1989.

Vol. 392: J.-C. Bermond, M. Raynal (Eds.), Distributed Algorithms. Proceedings, 1989. VI, 315 pages. 1989.

Vol. 393: H. Ehrig, H. Herrlich, H.-J. Kreowski, G. Preuß (Eds.), Categorical Methods in Computer Science. VI, 350 pages. 1989.

Vol. 394: M. Wirsing, J.A. Bergstra (Eds.), Algebraic Methods: Theory, Tools and Applications. VI, 558 pages. 1989.

Vol. 395: M. Schmidt-Schauß, Computational Aspects of an Order-Sorted Logic with Term Declarations. VIII, 171 pages. 1989. (Subseries LNAI).

Vol. 396: T.A. Berson, T. Beth (Eds.), Local Area Network Security. Proceedings, 1989. IX, 152 pages. 1989.

Vol. 397: K.P. Jantke (Ed.), Analogical and Inductive Inference. IX, 338 pages. 1989. (Subseries LNAI).

Vol. 398: B. Banieqbal, H. Barringer, A. Pnueli (Eds.), Temporal Logic in Specification. Proceedings, 1987. VI, 448 pages. 1989.

Vol. 399: V. Cantoni, R. Creutzburg, S. Levialdi, G. Wolf (Eds.), Recent Issues in Pattern Analysis and Recognition. VII, 400 pages. 1989.

Vol. 400: R. Klein, Concrete and Abstract Voronoi Diagrams. IV, 167 pages. 1989.

Vol. 401: H. Djidjev (Ed.), Optimal Algorithms. Proceedings, 1989. VI, 308 pages. 1989.

Vol. 402: T.P. Bagchi, V.K. Chaudhri, Interactive Relational Database Design. XI, 186 pages. 1989.

Vol. 403: S. Goldwasser (Ed.), Advances in Cryptology – CRYPTO '88. Proceedings, 1988. XI, 591 pages. 1990.

Vol. 404: J. Beer, Concepts, Design, and Performance Analysis of a Parallel Prolog Machine. VI, 128 pages. 1989.

Vol. 405: C. E. Veni Madhavan (Ed.), Foundations of Software Technology and Theoretical Computer Science. Proceedings, 1989. VIII, 339 pages. 1989.

Vol. 407: J. Sifakis (Ed.), Automatic Verification Methods for Finite State Systems. Proceedings, 1989. VII, 382 pages. 1990.

Vol. 408: M. Leeser, G. Brown (Eds.) Hardware Specification, Verification and Synthesis: Mathematical Aspects. Proceedings, 1989. VI, 402 pages. 1990.

Vol. 409: A. Buchmann, O. Günther, T. R. Smith, Y.-F. Wang (Eds.), Design and Implementation of Large Spatial Databases. Proceedings, 1989. IX, 364 pages. 1990.

Vol. 410: F. Pichler, R. Moreno-Diaz (Eds.), Computer Aided Systems Theory – EUROCAST '89. Proceedings, 1989. VII, 427 pages. 1990.

Vol. 411: M. Nagl (Ed.), Graph-Theoretic Concepts in Computer Science. Proceedings, 1989. VII, 374 pages. 1990.

Vol. 412: L. B. Almeida, C. J. Wellekens (Eds.), Neural Networks. Proceedings, 1990. IX, 276 pages. 1990.

Vol. 413: R. Lenz, Group Theoretical Methods in Image Processing. VIII, 139 pages. 1990.

Vol. 414: A. Kreczmar, A. Salwicki, LOGLAN '88 – Report on the Programming Language. X, 133 pages. 1990.

Vol. 415: C. Choffrut, T. Lengauer (Eds.), STACS 90. Proceedings, 1990. VI, 312 pages. 1990.